Islam and Politics
in Indonesia

Islam and Politics in Indonesia

The Masyumi Party between Democracy and Integralism

Rémy Madinier

Translated by Jeremy Desmond

NUS PRESS
SINGAPORE

© 2015 Rémy Madinier

Published by:

NUS Press
National University of Singapore
AS3-01-02, 3 Arts Link
Singapore 117569

Fax: (65) 6774-0652
E-mail: nusbooks@nus.edu.sg
Website: http://www.nus.edu.sg/nuspress

ISBN 978-9971-69-843-0 (Paper)

National Library Board, Singapore Cataloguing-in-Publication Data

Madinier, Rémy.
    Islam and politics in Indonesia: the Masyumi Party between democracy and integralism / Rémy Madinier; translator, Jeremy Desmond. – Singapore: NUS Press, [2015]
    pages cm.
    ISBN: 978-9971-69-843-0 (paperback)

    1. Masyumi (Organization) – History. 2. Political parties – Indonesia – History – 20th century. 3. Muslims – Political activity – Indonesia – 20th century. 4. Islam and politics – Indonesia – History – 20th century. 5. Indonesia – Politics and government – 1942–1949. 6. Indonesia – Politics and government – 1950–1966. I. Title.

JQ779.A553
324.2598 — dc23   OCN900183544

First published by Karthala as *L'Indonésie entre démocratie musulmane et Islam intégral: Histoire du parti Masjumi* in 2011.

Cover: Artwork based on the flag of Masyumi.

Printed by: Markono Print Media Pte Ltd

Contents

List of Illustrations

Acknowledgements

The author and translator are deeply indebted to Dr. Kevin Fogg for his very valuable advice on specific terms and references in English. We would also like to extend our warm thanks to all those who helped with both the comprehension of the French text and the proofreading of the English version, namely Bénédicte Desmond, Jessica Lichy, Eoin Campbell, Neil Carmody, Alan Geary, David Lewis and Kieran Woods. Their help is greatly appreciated.

The translation of this book was made possible thanks to the support of the Centre National du Livre, the Institut d'Études de l'Islam et des Sociétés du Monde Musulman (EHESS) and the Centre Asie du Sud-Est (CNRS-EHESS).

Author's Note

Since the 1970s, the term "Islamist" has taken on a pejorative connotation, as it has come to encompass all radicals, including those who are ready to use violence to impose their vision of Islam's role in society. This was not, however, the original acceptation of this term, which merely referred to Muslims who wished to see their religion play a role in public life, thus meaning that it could quite readily be applied in relation to Masyumi's leaders.

I have used, for convenience' sake, the term "modernist" and "reformist" interchangeably with relation to Islam, except in cases where it might lead to confusion. The two movements are very similar, although reformism, unlike its modernist counterpart, includes the proponents of Wahhabi fundamentalism.

I have often referred to the secular nationalists simply as "nationalists", in contrast to the representatives of political Islam. It should not be forgotten however that the latter were also nationalists insofar as they also supported the struggle for national independence.

Since independence, Indonesian spelling has undergone two reforms. The first one, in 1947, replaced "oe" by "u", while the second, in 1972, changed "dj" into "j", "tj" into "c", "sj" into "sy" and "ch" into "kh". I have respected these new rules when using terms in Indonesian, except for quotations. For proper nouns, I have used the most common spelling; there is no general rule concerning people's names: certain Indonesians have adapted their names, others have not (Sukarno, for example, is still often written Soekarno). Arabic terms are written here according to their Indonesian transcription, which is sometimes slightly different to that used in English.

All quotations from the Koran come from the Saheeh International version published in 1997 by Abul-Qasim Publishing House.

Rémy Madinier
Lyon, 2015

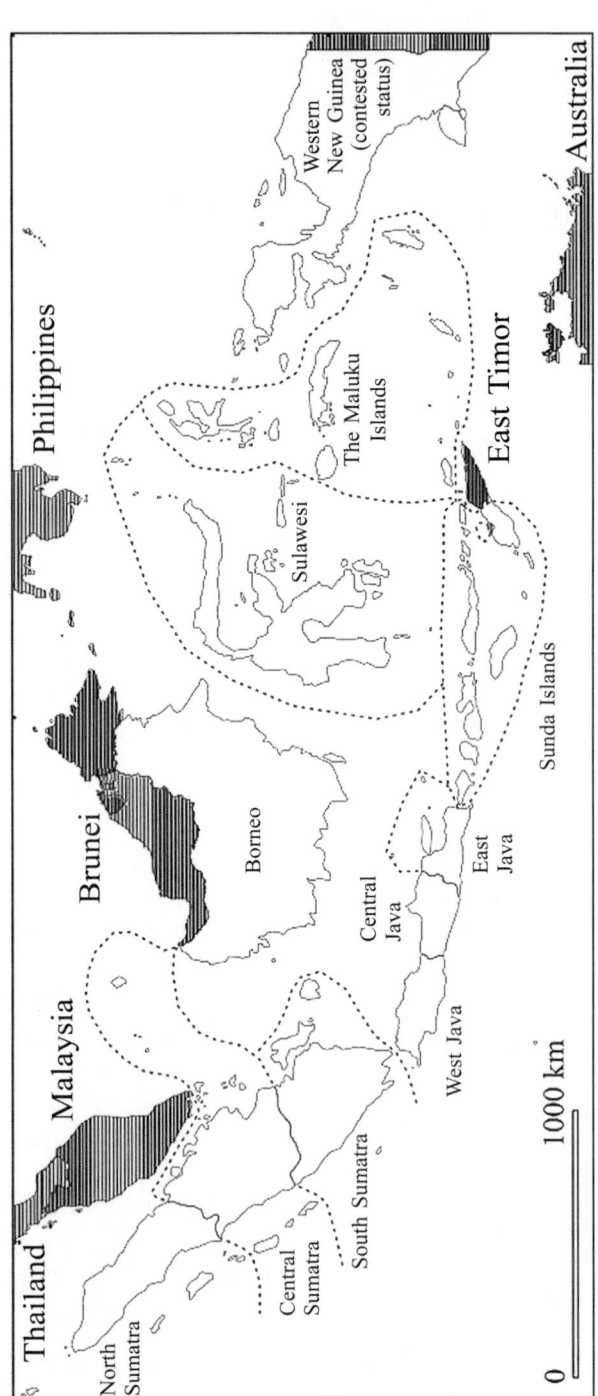

Map 0.1 The Ten Provinces of the Unitary Republic of Indonesia, August 1950.[1]

---

[1] The maps used in this book were drawn up by Frederic Durand, to whom I am most grateful.

Introduction

At its height, the Masyumi Party, with a membership of tens of millions, was without doubt the largest Islamic party in the world. It represented the most comprehensive attempt to reconcile Islam and democracy, for a movement of this size at least, yet its history is not without a certain number of inconsistencies and contradictions. It was founded in 1945 with the intention of rapidly establishing an Islamic state in Indonesia, but was eventually banned in 1960 for having resolutely defended a universal model of parliamentary democracy.

A Contextualised Approach to the Relation between Islam and Politics

Although the leaders of Masyumi were the champions of a humanist tradition within the Muslim reform movement which came to prominence during the first decades of the 20th century, they also contributed, from the late 1960s onwards, to the radicalisation which led to the party's original message being lost. What is initially most striking about these party leaders is the unexpected compromises they made, but also their constant wavering between an ambitious programme of secularisation and an overcautious tendency to emphasise the importance of religion. These apparent contradictions require one to examine the movement closely through a contextualised study of the links between Islam and politics.

The history of Masyumi contradicts the short-sighted essentialist perception of the relationship between Islam and politics which is based on the premise that Islam knows no separation between the temporal and the spiritual, and which, as a result, "reduces the study of Muslim societies to a study of their theology."[1] Indeed, it is surprising to notice to what extent the Western perspective on Islam today is willing to let itself be limited to a narrow vision of a militant and insular Islam, despite many repeated warnings from specialists in the field.[2] This seems to be leading to the formation of a strange "holy alliance which unites the most outspoken form of Islam to the most stereotypical form of Orientalism resulting in a version of Islam being posited that is historically inaccurate, ideologically loaded and intellectually dubious."[3] Contrary to what is claimed by a whole body of work which is both imprecise and deliberately polemical, the concept of Islam as *din wa dawl* (religion and state) is neither a monolithic programme nor a historically incontrovertible fact.[4] Going beyond these facile generalisations and understanding the link between Islam and politics from a genuinely historical perspective involves painstaking work. It requires original research examining a specific place and time, based on an exhaustive study of local sources. Such research must go beyond a literal and lazy interpretation of koranic norms and be founded upon a critical analysis of the concrete experience of those who invoked those norms within a political context. Various studies have already adopted this approach to show that the compromises which were reached in different parts of the Muslim world between divine commands and human realities were clearly both historically determined and transient.[5] An eminently

---

[1] Burhan Ghalioun, *Islam et politique. La modernité trahie* (Paris: La Découverte, "Textes à l'appui/islam et société", 1997), p. 9.

[2] Robert Hefner contends that Islamism is too often seen through the prism of the transformation it underwent in the 1970s, influenced by a new generation of activists. These activists sometimes received their religious instruction outside of traditional educational circuits, and they based their authority not on any exhaustive knowledge of sacred texts, but rather on their ability to propose simple and accessible interpretations justifying their political activity. See Robert W. Hefner and Patricia Horvatich, eds., *Islam in an Era of Nation-States: Politics and Religious Renewal in Muslim Southeast Asia* (Honolulu, HI: University of Hawai'i Press, 1997), Introduction.

[3] Ghassan Salamé, *Maghreb-Machreq-Monde arabe*, September 1990, quoted by François Burgat, *L'islamisme en face*, 2002 (1st ed., 1995), p. 17. A good example of this interpretation can be found in Anne-Marie Delcambre, *L'Islam des interdits* (Paris: Desclée de Brouwer, 2003).

[4] See, for example, the pamphlet written by Jean-Claude Barreau, *De l'islam en général et de la modernité en particulier* (Paris: Pré aux Clercs, 1991).

[5] Concerning works written in French on this topic, the reader can refer in particular to those written by Olivier Carré, François Burgat, Marc Gaborieau, Olivier Roy, Gilles Kepel, Jean-Louis Triaud and Malika Zeghal, cited in the bibliography.

useful distinction has also been established between the religion of Islam, founded by Mohammad, and Islam as it manifests itself in various societies or civilisations.[6]

A Complex and Little-Known History with a Disputed Heritage

The Indonesian case presents a particular interest in the greater historical scheme of things for two main reasons. The first is the speed and diversity of the changes proposed by Masyumi. These transformations were, in equal measure, contradictory and essential, and they took place over the course of almost a single generation (those who came to power after independence). They thus allow one to grasp within the space of a lifetime the important issues which have dominated the Muslim world since the middle of the 19th century. Such a historical study allows an analysis of the political, religious, cultural and social mechanisms at play in Indonesia at a time when it was faced with an essential choice between, on the one hand, a Western-inspired Muslim democracy, and on the other, a form of Islam integralism which is partially responsible for the renewed growth in fundamentalism witnessed by the country over the past 20 years. The surprising discovery that there could coexist within a single group, and sometimes even within a single leader, two apparently contradictory positions leads one to the conclusion that, as far as Indonesia is concerned at least, the idea of a clear and unambiguous border between secularism and religion needs to be revised.

The history of Masyumi reveals the scope of its secularisation project. It extended to the very heart of activist Islam, and mirrored the first of the five principles of Indonesia's national ideology (*Pancasila*) which asserted the belief in a single God, thus establishing a link rather than an opposition between secularism and religion. It also suggests that if one is prepared to examine how the norms of Islam were actually implemented in public life, the simple juxtaposition between secular modernism on the one hand, and activist Islam on the other, simply disappears. In other words, contrary to what has sometimes been

---

[6] Translator's note: This distinction is rendered more concisely in French by using "*islam*" to refer to the former and "*Islams*" to refer to the latter. Such uses of the word are not possible in English, however.

affirmed, a whole range of positions exists on the spectrum of ideas which goes from Mustapha Kemal to Rachid Rida.[7]

The second reason why this historical study of Masyumi is important lies in the fact that it concerns a form of Islam which is not only peripheral and Asian, but also atypical. Avoiding the Arabo-Muslim paradigm which dominates the field of Islamic studies enables us to bring to the analysis of political Islam a perspective which can no longer be avoided today, given the demographic reality of the Muslim world. More than half of the global Muslim population lives today in Asia, and the Indonesian archipelago—which has the largest Muslim population in the world—contains almost as many Muslims as the whole of the Arab world.[8] The importance of this so-called peripheral Islam, far from its original homeland, offers one a broader perspective on the Muslim religion.[9] In addition, links can be established here with the vast question of Westernisation dealt with by Denys Lombard, who rightly points out the extent of Islam's role in that process.[10] In short then, since the first decade of the 20th century, Indonesia has been the backdrop to a delicately balanced conjunction of two value systems with universal pretensions—Islam and European-inspired political modernism—both of which came from outside Indonesia and have so often found their legitimacy challenged in the archipelago.

---

[7] An example of this binary opposition can be found in Martine Gozlan, *Pour Comprendre l'intégrisme islamiste* (Paris: Albin Michel, 1995). On the other hand, Shamsil A.B. should be commended for his attempt to classify political Islam into different categories, going from the "global mindset" of the Muslim Brotherhood or Mawdudi to the "rooted practice" inspired by the mode of government used in the Malay kingdoms where a ruler does not base his Islamic legitimacy on his own expertise but rather on a circle of "bhramic" *ulamas*. Shamsul A.B., "Islam Embedded: 'Moderate' Political Islam and Governance in the Malay World", in *Islam in Southeast Asia, Political, Social and Strategic Challenges for the 21st Century*, ed. K.S. Nathan and Mohammad Hashim Kamali (Singapore: Institute of Southeast Asian Studies, 2008), pp. 103–20.

[8] Anne-Laure Dupont, *Atlas de l'islam dans le monde. Lieux, pratiques et idéologie* (Paris: Éditions Autrement, 2005).

[9] As the valuable collection of texts on Islam edited by Greg Fealy and Virginia Hooker demonstrates, *Voices of Islam in Southeast Asia: A Contemporary Sourcebook* (Singapore: Institute of Southeast Asian Studies, 2006).

[10] Denys Lombard, *Le carrefour javanais*, vol. 3 (Paris: Éditions de l'EHESS, 1990).

This sometimes complicated balance between modernism and Islam has remained at the heart of divisive moments in recent Indonesian history[11] and the importance of Masyumi's role in the debates on this question during the 1950s and 60s means that the party has occupied an important place in the country's historical narrative.[12] The first of these divisive periods occurred at the beginning of the 1970s and centred on the figure of Nurcholish Madjid; a second one took place in the 1990s focussed on the actions of the minister for justice of the day, Yusril Ihza Mahendra, who was president of a party claiming its heritage from Masyumi.[13]

These disputes thrived on a fairly widespread ignorance within the country of the historical details of the Masyumi party. Few scholarly works have examined this topic, which no doubt partly explains why the field of Islamic studies has for so long lacked a comparative study exploring the relations between religion and politics in Indonesia. Outside the classic studies dealing with the history of Indonesia since independence—notably the three scholarly tomes written by George Kahin, Benedict Anderson and Herbert Feith[14]—a good number of authors have touched on the history of Masyumi. However, only six authors have made a genuine contribution to establishing the modernist party's history. Four of those were either party members or sympathisers. Harun Nasution, in 1965, devoted his MA thesis at McGill University to examining the question of an Islamic state in Masyumi's ideology; Muhammad Asyari in his thesis at the same university in 1976 looked at the role of the *ulama* within Masyumi in the period 1945–52; Deliar Noer initially wrote an MA thesis in 1960 at Cornell University

---

[11] For further analysis of these issues, see Rémy Madinier and Andrée Feillard, *The End of Innocence: Indonesian Islam and the Temptations of Radicalism* (Singapore: NUS Press, 2011).

[12] This issue was analysed by Greg Fealy and Bernard Platzdasch, "The Masyumi Legacy: Between Islamist Idealism and Political Exigency", *Studia Islamika* 12, 1 (2005): 73–99.

[13] See infra. Epilogue.

[14] George MacTurnan Kahin, *Nationalism and Revolution in Indonesia* (Ithaca, NY: Cornell University Press, 1952); Benedict R.O'G Anderson, *Java in a Time of Revolution, Occupation and Resistance, 1944–1946* (Ithaca, NY: Cornell University Press, 1961); Herbert Feith, *The Decline of the Constitutional Democracy in Indonesia* (Ithaca, NY: Cornell University Press, 1962).

on the history of Masyumi up to 1957, before developing his work further in 1987 in a book entitled *Islam on the National Stage*; finally, Yusril Ihza Mahendra, mentioned above, attempted in his 1993 doctoral thesis to establish a comparison between Masyumi and Jamaat-i-Islami in Pakistan.[15]

All of this research was carried out conscientiously, in particular Deliar Noer's, and unlike the hagiographies written about certain Masuyumi leaders, these studies were factually accurate. Nonetheless, their authors' involvement in the historical events they were writing about made it difficult for them to possess a sufficiently critical perspective on their subject matter. There were two consequences to this, which at first sight appear to be contradictory. The first of these no doubt owes to the authors' concern not to be accused of writing an account justifying the party and its policies. This preoccupation was exacerbated by the very dim view taken of Masyumi by the New Order authorities, which too often led the authors to focus on a minute description of the facts and thus fail entirely to develop any analysis. The embarrassing question of Darul Islam—a dissident fundamentalist movement which emerged from circles close to Masyumi—was thus only dealt with summarily, as were the internal party conflicts. The second consequence stems from the first and concerns the false impression of ideological and political coherence that one gets from the writings of Masyumi's leaders, and which shroud, it seems to me, a major aspect of the party's history. They lead one to believe that the party's aspiration to found an Islamic state made perfect sense to its leaders and so does not need to be expounded upon. On the contrary, however, this aspiration corresponds to an ill-defined, multi-faceted project which abounded with contradictions.

The diversity of the various branches within Masyumi have been examined by B.J. Boland, Allan A. Samson and Luthfi Assyaukanie in their respective books on the question of political Islam in Indonesia, but as they study the entire spectrum of Islamic movements, they do not look in depth at the modernist party. Boland studies the period from 1945 to the 1970s and only devotes a few dozen pages to

---

[15] Yusril Ihza Mahendra, "Modernisme dan Fundamentalisme dalam Politik Islam: satu Kajian Perbandingan kes Parti Masyumi di Indonesia dan Jama'at-i-Islami di Pakistan (1940–1960)", PhD diss., Kuala Lumpur University, 1993. [Translator's note: translations of all titles in Indonesian can be found in the bibliography.]

Masyumi. Samson writes on the New Order era and proposes a useful distinction between "constitutionalist Islamists" and "Sharia-minded Islamists" within the party, though he does not detect how these two opposing points of view were in fact intertwined. Assyaukanie's work astutely identifies Masyumi as the model of a "democratic Islamic state", which he distinguishes both from a "democratic religious state" and a "democratic liberal state". However, his book only contains about a dozen pages on the history of the party.[16] Finally, we should mention the work of Robert Hefner, Greg Fealy, Bernard Platzdasch and Masdar Hilmy, who have undoubtedly contributed to a better understanding of the movements which emerged from Masyumi; their research, however is mainly focussed on the party's contemporary legacy rather than an analysis of its doctrine and its activity in the 1950s.[17]

A Religious, Political, Social and Cultural History

The history of Indonesia's Muslim intellectuals and of the political doctrines they elaborated is a field of research which has been progressively expanded both by native scholars and by foreign academics. Masyumi, through its leading figures, contributed to the construction of an Islamic political doctrine, but it was above all a political party constantly confronted with events. It is for this reason that the chapters which follow will be founded upon the party's political history, which has up until now been poorly understood. An exhaustive analysis of the party's main press organs (notably the daily newspaper, *Abadi*, and magazines such as *Hikmah*, *Suara* and *Partai Masyumi*), its archives and the writings of its leaders will allow us to better follow in Chapter 2 the party's establishment in the throes of the country's revolution. Chapter 3 will then look at its gradual identification with Indonesia's fragile

---

[16] B.J. Boland, *The Struggle of Islam in Modern Indonesia* (The Hague: Martinus Nijhoff, 1982); Allan Arnold Samson, "Islam and Politics in Indonesia", PhD diss., University of California, Berkeley, 1972; Luthfi Assyaukanie, *Islam and the Secular State in Indonesia* (Singapore: Institute of Southeast Asian Studies, 2009).
[17] Robert W. Hefner, *Civil Islam: Muslims and Democratization in Indonesia* (Princeton, NJ: Princeton University Press, 2000); Fealy and Platzdasch, "The Masyumi Legacy"; Bernard Platzdasch, *Islamism in Indonesia: Politics in the Emerging Democracy* (Singapore: Institute of Southeast Asian Studies, 2009); Masdar Hilmy, *Islamism and Democracy in Indonesia, Piety and Pragmatism* (Singapore: Institute of Southeast Asian Studies, 2010).

parliamentary democracy, which, as we shall see in Chapter 4, ultimately led to its prohibition and decline. Although our study of the party's history accords considerable importance to this political aspect, it is essential to explore other approaches also, notably those looking at the intellectual and social backgrounds of its leaders, which will be examined in Chapter 1. These leaders were the scions of a vast reformist movement which reached Indonesia at the beginning of the last century, but also the products of a new education system set up by the Dutch colonial administration a few years later. This multi-layered approach is a necessary prerequisite to examining Masyumi's dual goal of not only founding an Islamic state, which will be looked at in Chapter 5, but also of establishing an Islamic society, which we shall examine in Chapter 6.

Masyumi's programme was indeed a two-pronged one, but while its political aspect was largely documented and elaborated through party programmes and the political writings of its leaders, its social facet was never comprehensively formulated and thus needs to be inferred from its political activity. By adopting an approach towards primary sources that goes beyond the mere study of official documents and looks also at Masyumi's reaction to events, I wish to show to what extent the latter was constitutive of the party's identity and hence of its political and social programme for Indonesia. This detailed analysis has allowed me to highlight certain inconsistencies in the party's doctrine. Some of these are an inherent part of a classical phenomenon in politics whereby a party's programme is at a certain remove from the events which gave birth to it;[18] other inconsistencies can be found in the disparity between what Masyumi actually achieved and what its programme aspired to accomplish. To go beyond these inevitable contradictions, one has to apprehend the social make-up of the "Masyumi family"; the dearth of relevant primary material in this area makes it necessary to contrive other means which will allow us to shed light on the question indirectly. Although it is far from giving us the whole picture, this approach does enable us at least to appreciate the gap between the ideal of a society based on a rigorist interpretation of Islam and a reality which was more fallible, more Indonesian and, in short, more human.

---

[18] Cf. Serge Berstein, "Les partis", in *Pour une histoire politique*, ed. René Rémond (Paris: Seuil, 1996 [1st ed. 1988]), pp. 49–84.

CHAPTER ONE

The Party's Infancy: Its Political Genesis and Historical Lineage

The history of the men and organisations behind the creation of Masyumi in November 1945 is clearly marked by a dialectical movement inherent in Indonesian Islam. This dynamic oscillated for four decades between a tendency to assert the different sensibilities which existed within it and a necessity for these different strands to unify. From the opening years of the 20th century, the desire amongst Indonesia's Islamic modernists to establish organisational structures which would enable them to exist on the political landscape contained the seeds of their split from the country's traditionalist Muslims. These "pioneers of traditionalism",[1] in response to the initiatives undertaken by modernists and in an attempt to defend the values which they considered to be under threat from the reformist zeal of Muhammadiyah and Sakerat Islam, set up their own movement in 1926: Nahdlatul Ulama. The two branches of Islam also experienced periods of unity, however, between 1937 and 1943 with the Supreme Islamic Council of Indonesia (Madjelis Islam A'la Indonesia, MIAI) and later from 1945 to 1952 with Masyumi.

The extent of the Muslim community's contribution to Indonesian politics and society cannot be reduced, however, to the polar opposites of traditionalism and modernism. In the 1920s, for example,

---

[1] To use the expression employed by Andrée Feillard in *Islam et armée dans l'Indonésie contemporaine: Les pionniers de la tradition* (Paris: L'Harmattan, 1995).

1

a movement began to emerge which, while not rejecting Islam, wished to limit it to the sphere of people's private lives. This nationalist secular current entered the political scene in 1927 with the creation of Sukarno's Partai Nasional Indonesia (PNI). The grassroots of this new party were sociologically very close to the supporters of modernism—they had often attended the same Dutch schools and knew each other from their participation in certain organisations together—and indeed the PNI provided serious competition to Muslim parties and organisations for public support. Finally, it should be noted that within the modernist movement certain cracks had begun to appear which resulted as much from the clash of ambitious personalities as from differences of opinion concerning political strategy (there was a constant debate in particular concerning the attitude to be adopted towards the Dutch colonists). These cracks led to several schisms within the movement, and this break-up of the Muslim body politic during the interwar years was the most significant political legacy inherited by Masyumi. In order to understand such a legacy, it is necessary to examine both the main stages in the formation of this Islamic political movement and the way in which its leaders, in their writings, turned their interpretation of history into a political tool.

Perspectives on the History of Indonesian Islam— References to the Founding Fathers

The advent of Islam in Indonesia remains today a very controversial historical topic. There is no clear historical evidence which allows one to point to the existence of Muslim states in the country before the emergence in the 13th century of Samudra-Pasai, a small principality in the region of North Sumatra.[2] Indian Muslims who used the ancient

---

[2] The first tombstone revealing the presence of a Muslim dynasty in the Malay region dates back to 1297 and belonged to Sultan Malik as-Salih from Samudera Pasai. Marco Polo signalled the existence of the trading kingdoms of Perlak and Samudera Pasai on his way to Sumatra in 1292. For a comprehensive overview of the different studies on the arrival of Islam in Indonesia, see G.W.J. Drewes, "New Light on the Coming of Islam to Indonesia", *B.K.I.* 124 (1968): 433–59. Drewes contests in particular the hypothesis of an earlier Islamisation based on the discovery of the Leran Tombstone, an Islamic Tombstone in Java carrying the date 1082. The work carried out by Ludvik Kalus and Claude Guillot has confirmed Drewe's doubts, showing that the Leran Tombstone was no doubt removed from its original cemetery somewhere in the Middle East to be used as ballast on a boat; "La stèle de Leran (Java) datée de 475/1082", *Archipel* 67 (2004). On the

maritime network running from the Indian Ocean to the China Seas appear to have played an important role in the spread of Islam.[3] Their part in the Islamisation of the region was made easier by the influence of Indian culture in the Indianised kingdoms of Java and Sumatra, but they were not the only ones to contribute to this process. Chinese Muslims, in particular during the great Ming maritime expeditions in the first half of the 15th century, clearly had a role to play as well, though it is somewhat more difficult to know the exact nature of this influence.[4]

It seems certain in any case that after Islam was embedded in the north of Sumatra, there was, from the second half of the 14th century onwards, a tolerant attitude towards the Muslim religion within the Hindu-Buddhist royal court in Majapahit, in East Java. Later in the 15th century, the sultanate of Malacca on the Malay peninsula emerged as the main commercial hub in the region, and Islam spread along the trade routes leading to and from it, notably those concerning the trade of spices, to the northeast towards Brunei, to the southeast in the direction of the northern Javanese coast and further east to the Maluku Islands. When Malacca was seized in 1511 by the Portuguese, this gave a considerable boost to the sultanate of Aceh, located to the north of Pasai, which, along with other sultanates, became the new focal point for Muslim trade in the region.

On the island of Java during the 15th century, the development of sultanates on its north coast, in the area known as Pasisir, meant that it progressively removed itself from the dominion of the Indianised

---

Islamisation of the region, see also Ahmad Ibrahim et al., eds., *Readings on Islam in Southeast Asia* (Singapore: Institute of Southeast Asia Studies, 1985), p. 407 and Alijah Gordon, ed., *The Propagation of Islam in the Malay Archipelago* (Kuala Lumpur: Malaysian Sociological Institute, 2001), p. xxv.

[3] Indian influences have been highlighted by several studies in Javanese literature: P.J. Zoetmulder, *Pantheism and Monism in Javanese Suluk Literature: Islamic and Indian Mysticism in an Indonesian Setting* (Leiden: KITLV Press, 1995) has shown how certain Javanese texts (*suluk*) show Islamic influences which have come through India and Hindu-Javanese. The study of *Serat Centhini* led Soebardi to the same conclusion in "Santri-Religious Elements as Reflected in the Book of Tjentini", *B.K.I.* 127 (1971): 331–49. On the way in which *Serat Centhini* is part of the process of Islamisation, see Marcel Bonneff, "Centhini, servante du Javanisme", *Archipel* 56 (1998): 483–511.

[4] Concerning these expeditions and the other aspects of the Chinese influence on Indonesian Islam, see Denys Lombard, *Le Carrefour javanais*, vol. 2 (Paris: L'EHESS, 1990), Chapter 1.

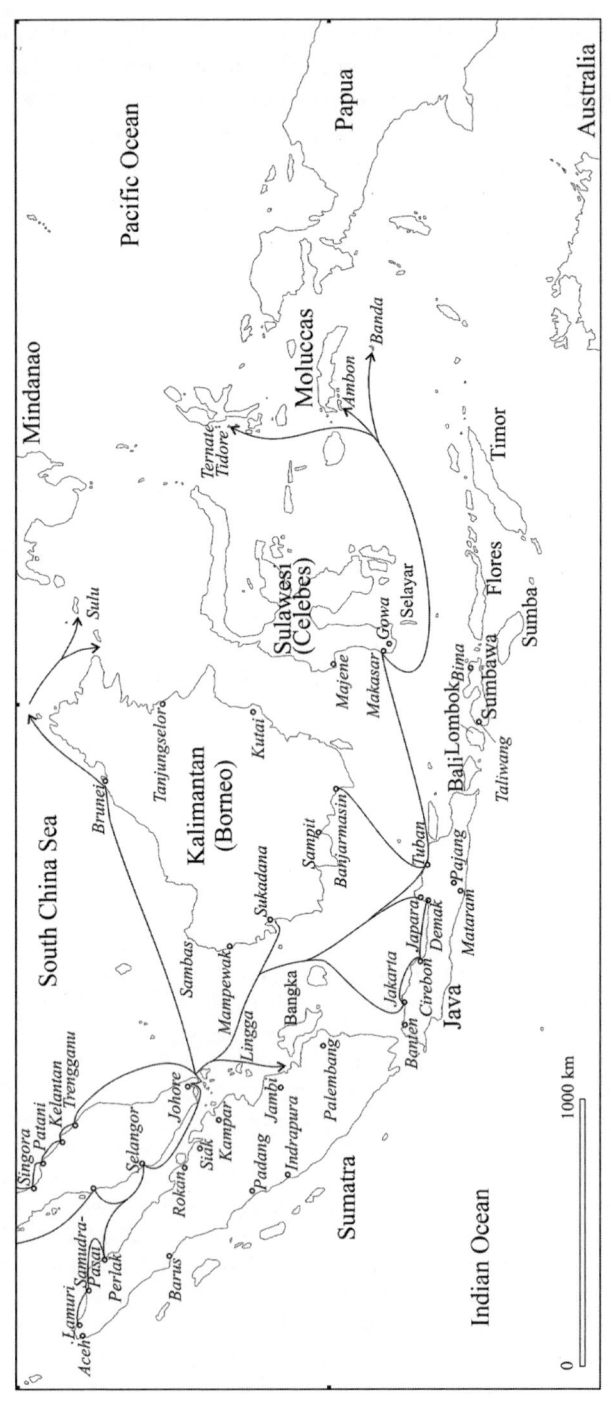

Map 1.1 The Spread of Islam across the Indonesian Archipelago.

kingdom of Majapahit, enabling Islam to spread further along the trade routes established by Muslims. The expansion of Islam on the island can be partly explained by the role of Sufism, which seems to have contributed to the acceptance of Islam in certain Hindu-Buddhist royal courts. After the shift in power from the Majapahit kingdom to the sultans of Pasisir in the 16th century, the Islamisation of Java, which up until then had been largely peaceful, became more belligerent. In 1527, the small Muslim coastal kingdom of Demak precipitated the collapse of the last Hindu-Buddhist kingdom in Daya, and by the middle of the 16th century, the entire north coast of Java was governed by Muslims, namely the sultans of Cirebon and Banten. At the end of the 16th century, a successor to the Majapahit kingdom appeared with the rise of the kingdom of Mataram, which had by then been Islamised and whose emergence constituted a significant step in the Islamisation of the inner regions of the island. This expansion of Islam was in large part due to the educational and missionary work of the Koranic schools and the Sufi orders who took on the mantle of the age-old pioneering tradition and combined proselytising with the clearing and cultivation of forestlands.[5]

After three centuries of gradual Islamisation between the 13th and 16th centuries, Islam had become the lodestar which all governments needed to use as their reference point. Is it possible, though, to regard this period as a sort of golden age in Indonesia when a true Islamic state existed? In other words, are the partisans of an Islamic state (Negara Islam) in Indonesia justified in using the pre-colonial period as a sort of model to aspire to? The answer is undoubtedly no, for the simple reason that Islamic law was never used as the exclusive source of law—and this is true also for other parts of Southeast Asia—but had to give way also to local customary law, known as *adat*, particularly in Java and in the Minangkabau region in Central Sumatra. A majority of the Malay legal codes contained references to *sharia* law but these references were mainly confined to the domains of commercial and marriage law. In the area of criminal law, for example, the sentence of

---

[5] According to Martin van Bruinessen, however, most of the orders still present today in the country had not appeared before the second half of the 18th century. "L'Asie du Sud-Est", in *Les Voies d'Allah. Les Ordres mystiques dans l'islam des origines à aujourd'hui*, ed. Alexandre Popovic and Gilles Veinstein (Paris: Fayard, 1986), pp. 274–84. On the same topic, see also his book, *Kitab Kuning, Pesantren dan tarekat. Tradisi-Tradisi Islam di Indonesia* (Bandung: Mizan, 1995).

corporal punishment provided for by Koranic penal law (*hudud*) was generally commuted to a fine.[6]

The expansion of Islam began to slow when European colonists arrived in the region. The Portuguese arrived in the Maluku Islands in 1521 and were later replaced by the Dutch, whose influence, though initially confined to the east of the country, gradually expanded over the course of the 17th and 18th centuries. While it is true that the VOC[7] never really supported either of the two main Christian religions —indeed the Protestant Dutch saw Catholicism as their biggest threat —the monopoly which the Dutch company held over the traditional trade routes from the town of Batavia (founded in 1619) and from Melacca (captured from the Portugese in 1641), weakened the position of the sultanates on the Indonesian archipelago considerably. In the 19th century, after the VOC went bankrupt, the Dutch crown took over their operations and Christianity prospered in the non-Islamic parts of the country thanks to the loosening of restrictions which had been imposed on missionaries by the previous colonial authorities.[8] This period also saw the weakening of the sultanate "model of government": in 1825, the Sultanate of Palembang, which had replaced the kingdom of Srivijaya, disappeared, followed in 1860 by the Sultanate of Banjarmasin and in 1903 by the Sultanate of Aceh.

A close examination of the place which this glorious period of Indonesian Islam held in Masyumi's collective consciousness, through the analysis of the speeches and writings by its main leaders, brings a number of discoveries to light. The first of these is that references to that golden age were, in fact, rare. In the 15 or so treatises written by the party's main theorists on the political role of Islam, reference to Indonesia's Islamic past was, at best, minimal and more often than not non-existent. In the case of speeches made by party leaders, the choice to omit references to Indonesia's Islamic past was not a rhetorical one;

---

[6] A.C. Milner, "Islam and the Muslim State", in *Islam in Southeast Asia*, ed. M.B. Hooker (Leiden: E.J. Brill, 1983), pp. 27–8.

[7] Abbreviation of *Vereenigde Oostindische Compagnie*, the Dutch East India Company. On the VOC's religious policy, see Karel Steenbrink, *Dutch Colonialism and Indonesian Islam: Contacts and Conflicts, 1596–1950* (Amsterdam and Atlanta, GA: Rodopi, 1993).

[8] See Remy Madinier, "Les chrétiens d'Indonésie à l'époque contemporaine: heurs et malheurs du statu quo religieux dans l'Archipel", in *Christianisme, modernité et démocratie en Asie*, ed. Paul Jobin (Paris: Les Indes Savantes, 2008), pp. 145–58.

they were often abundantly illustrated with other historical examples. Isa Anshary, for example, in his book, *The Philosophy of the Combat of Islam*, refers to Roosevelt, Ernst Renan and Mohammad 'Abduh; he also mentions Hitler and Mussolini, but he says nothing about the history of his own country.[9] The same can be said about most of the books written by a whole range of Masyumi theorists—Zainal Abidin Ahmad, Moenawar Chalil, HAMKA, Prawoto Mangkusasmito, Mohammad Natsir, Jusuf Wibisono and Sjafruddin Prawiranegara—all of whom wrote abundantly over the years on the political philosophy of their party.[10]

The second important discovery concerning references by Masyumi leaders to Indonesia's Muslim past is that where they did exist they were often brief in nature and rarely developed to any great extent.[11] The sultanates that existed in Indonesia, for example, were

---

[9] Isa Anshary, *Falsafah Perdjuangan Islam* (Medan: Saiful, 1949 [2nd edition, 1951]), p. 287. We shall return later to the references to Western history and to the founders of Islamic modernism.

[10] See Zainal Abidin Ahmad, *Islam dan Parlementarisme* (Bandung: Aliran Islam, 1950), p. 80 and *Dasar-dasar Ekonomi dalam Islam* (Jakarta: Sinar Ilmu, 1950), p. 140; Isa Anshary, *Revolusi Islam* (Surabaya: Hasan Aidid, 1953), p. 59; *Aqidah jama'ah dan imamah* (CV Publicita, 1969 [2nd edition, 1975]), p. 23; *Mujahid Da'wah*, Pembimbing Muballigh Islam (Bandung: Diponegoro, 1968 [4th edition, 1991]), p. 318; Chalil Moenawar, *Ulil-Amri*, Solo, AB Sitti Sjamsijah, 1958; HAMKA, *Islam dan Demokrasi*, Bukit Tinggi, Tjerdas (undated); Kasman Singodimejo, *Renungan dari Tahanan* (Jakarta: Permata, 1967 [4th edition, 1974]); *Pancasila dan sedjarahnja* (Jakarta: Lembaga Riset dan Perpustakaan, 1961), p. 26; Mohammad Natsir, *Capita Selecta*, vol. 1 (Bandung: IW. Van Hoeve, 1946; vol. 2, Jakarta: Pustaka Pendis, [undated]); Sjafruddin Prawiranegara, *Islam sebagai pedoman hidup, Kumpulan karangan terpilih disunting oleh Ajip Rosidi*, vol. 1 (Jakarta: Idayu, 1986); *Ekonomi dan Keuangan: makna ekonomi Islam, Kumpulan karangan terpilih disunting oleh Ajip Rosidi*, vol. 2 (Jakarta: Idayu, 1988); Mohammad Roem, *Semangatnya tak kunjung padam* (Jakarta: Yayasan Idayu, 1977), p. 40, Soekiman Wirjosandjojo, *Wawasan Politik Seorang Muslim Patriot. Kumpulan Karangan* (Jakarta: YP2LPM, 1984).

[11] One of the few exceptions to this general rule is a book by HAMKA, *Antara fakta dan Khayal, "Tuanku Rao"* (Jakarta: Bulan Bintang, 1974), p. 364, in which the former Masyumi deputy refutes in great detail the claims made by one of his friends, Mangaradja Onggang Parlindungan, in a book entitled *Tuanku Rao* (80 per cent of which he alleges to be false), devoted to Haji Piobang, one of the instigators of the Padri movement at the beginning of the 19th century (see infra). Beyond HAMKA's desire to restore the historical truth on Haji Piobang's life, it is difficult to see what motivated him to undertake such a project, as he never draws any conclusions about Piobang himself.

never presented as a model for political government, and no mention was made either of the Wali Songo, the nine saints who are traditionally thought to have converted Java to Islam. When explaining the development of their religion or elaborating their theories on a Muslim state, Masyumi's writers systematically preferred to turn to examples taken from the life of the Prophet or from the accounts of the great Arab dynasties.[12]

The few references to Indonesia's past which did exist were there to prove that Islam's part in the Indonesian struggle for independence was a long-established one. The historical figures referred to had often won their place in history thanks to their resistance to colonial rule between 1825 and 1830, as opposed to their part in the spread of Islam. Those most frequently mentioned were Diponegoro, a Javanese prince and hero of the Java War between 1825 and 1830; Sultan Agung, sovereign of Mataram who held out in Batavia when it was besieged by the Dutch in 1825 and again in 1830; and finally Tuanku Imam Bonjol, the spiritual mentor of the resistance movement against the Dutch in Minangkabau. There were also occasional references made to Sultan Hasanuddin of Makassar, who in 1667 repelled a prolonged assault by the VOC before finally surrendering, and also to Cik di Tiro, one of the instigators of the holy war in Aceh against Dutch troops between 1880 and 1903.[13]

---

[12] See, for example, Mohammad Natsir's 1936 article, "Islam and Culture" ("Islam dan Kebudayan"), dealing with the former grandeur of Muslim civilisation in which he makes no reference to Indonesia. Natsir, *Capita Selecta*, pp. 3–6. However, the major states in Islamic history were not considered as models. Cf. infra Chapter 5.

[13] See, for example, Isa Anshary's speech in Magelang, *Abadi*, 8 September 1954. See also Soekiman Wirjosandjojo, "Perlu wajah baru di Indonesia", a text written in 1958 and published in *Wawasan Politik Seorang Muslim Patriot. Kumpulan Karangan* (Jakarta: YP2LPM, 1984), pp. 246 ff. Of the 132 articles contained in the two volumes of Mohammad Natsir's *Capita Selecta*, only two allude to the history of Indonesian Islam. The first, "Perspectives on Fictional Works" ("Pemandangan tentang buku2 roman", vol. 1, p. 41) looks at the novel's cultural role. Natsir explained that he decided to write the article after receiving a copy of the book devoted to Tuanku Imam Bonjol. His article avails of references to Western literature—Cyrano de Bergerac, Voltaire, Zola, Locke and Montesquieu—but no mention is made of the heroes of Indonesian Islam. In the "Indonesian Revolution" ("Revolusi Islam", vol. 2, p. 124), he merely recalls the spirit of sacrifice (*semangat pengurbanan*) of heroes such as Sultan Hasanuddin, Cik di Tiro, Tuanku Imam Bonjol, Diponegoro and Sultan Hidayat, devoting most of his article to the Muslim organisations of the opening decades of the century.

When referring to these figures, historical details concerning them were never really developed or analysed. As they were national heroes, a simple reference to their name sufficed. Mayumi's pantheon, then, was also the nation's pantheon and it was made up entirely of individuals who would later become national heroes in the Republic of Indonesia.[14] By doing this, Masyumi's theorists wished to draw attention to the prominent role played by religion in motivating those whom the entire nation recognised as being its founding fathers, rather than focussing on figures whose importance was limited only to the Muslim community. This choice was clearly a political one and it gave the party the ammunition it needed to fend off attacks from secular nationalists.

> Although it has been clearly established that Diponegoro was a Muslim who was devoted to his religion and that within his nationalist spirit, which was set alight by his opposition to the Dutch colonization, lay in fact the soul of a true Muslim, this has been forgotten intentionally by half of our national leaders. Even though this omission may be understandable, as it is in accordance with a desire to conceal the multiple factors which remind us of the merits of Islam and its combat and a preference for emphasizing other nationalist factors, such an attitude constitutes a sort of betrayal of history.[15]

This determination by Masyumi's leaders to depict Islam as an integral part of the nationalist project was not limited to their historical portrayal of the colonial period but extended also to the revolutionary period. Isa Anshary, for example, mentioned, amongst the heroes of Islam, General Sudirman, the first commander-in-chief of the Indonesian armed forces who was also a devout Muslim and a supporter of Masyumi.[16] Mohammad Natsir even added Bung Tomo (Sutomo), a hero of the war of independence, to this list, claiming that in November 1945, he had launched the rebellion against English troops in

---

[14] See Jacques Leclerc, "Iconologie politique du timbre poste indonésien", *Archipel* 6 (1973).

[15] Concerning the celebration by the Republic of the centenary of Diponegoro, see *Hikmah*, 15 January 1955.

[16] Speech by Isa Anshary in Magelang, *Abadi*, 8 September 1954.

Surabaya to the cry of "Allah is great."[17] This claim made by Masyumi's president was designed to include Sutomo's military feat in a long Muslim tradition embodying an Indonesian nation which pre-existed colonisation and which had struggled "for [the previous] 350 years not using mortars and canons (*mortar dan meriam*) but using faith and devotion (*iman dan takwa*)."[18]

By paying homage to the important figures of Indonesia's past in this way, Masyumi's leaders were glorifying a more intense vision of Islam rather than one which saw it as a "state institution". This more intense form of Islam would be able to instil in every believer the revolutionary spirit necessary to transform the world, and it gave a strong pedagogical dimension to the party's message. A Muslim hero and, by extension, a national hero was somebody who, in the name of religion, never gave up the fight and thus showed the way for the entire *umma* to follow. Isa Anshary, in one section of his booklet, *The Revolution of Islam*, entitled "the hero of Islam" illustrated clearly how becoming a hero was accessible to all.[19] It was a section of the book which glorified the religious dimension of the struggle carried out by those Indonesian Muslim patriots (*putera-patriot Muslimin Indonesia*) who, despite their involvement in the fight for independence, had remained in the background of history.

Even during Masyumi's darkest hours, the notion of a Muslim as somebody who, like his illustrious forebears, would be able to use his faith to find the resources of courage and self-sacrifice necessary for his cause remained a constant theme in the rhetoric used by the party's theorists. This vision is borne out in the following lines written by Kasman Singodimedjo from the confines of his cell shortly after Masyumi was banned:

> A Muslim must continue the struggle. Muslim law obliges him to do so. He must struggle throughout his whole life. Life is a struggle. A Muslim today must not be fearful. He must not consider that his previous struggles have failed, merely that they have not

---

[17] Bun Tomo was one of the most emblematic figures of the passionate youth groups (the *pemuda*) who played an important role in the Indonesian Revolution. See Benedict O.G. Anderson, *Java in a Time of Revolution: Occupation and Resistance, 1944–1946* (Ithaca, NY: Cornell University Press, 1961), pp. 155–8.

[18] Speech by Natsir in Makassar, *Abadi*, 24 June 1955.

[19] "Pahlawan Islam", in Isa Anshary, *Revolusi Islam* (Surabaya: Hasan Aidid, 1953).

attained their goals. The struggle led by Tengku Umar, Tuanku Imam Bonjol, Diponegoro, H.O.S. Cokroaminto, H.A. Salim and others has not failed; it has not yet reached its goals. We who are still alive have to continue their struggle.[20]

In the eyes of Masyumi, then, the history of Indonesian Islam never attained the status of a golden age which the contemporary period could draw upon for solutions to its problems. Their historical vision of pre-colonial Indonesia contained no trace of the "fabled past" which Denys Lombard has identified amongst certain groups of Indonesian Muslims.[21] None of the Islamic states which had existed in Indonesia constituted for Masyumi a model to be followed. The reason for this was not so much because of the imperfect nature of their institutions and their application of Islamic law—something which people were largely ignorant of in the 1950s—and more due to a certain interpretation of history which was characteristic of the modernist Islamic movement.

The Legacy of Muslim Reformism

This brief description of the Islamisation of Indonesia does not do justice to the sociological complexity that arose from the haphazard nature of the region's conversion. The varying degrees of acculturation on Java have long been reflected in the distinction established between two groups of Muslims: the *abangan* and the *santri*. The former refers to those village communities who practised a popular religion consisting of "a balanced integration of animist, Hinduistic and Islamic elements, a basic Javanese syncretism which is the island's true folk tradition, the basic substratum of its civilisation."[22] The second group, the *santri*,

---

[20] Kasman Singodimejo, *Renungan dari Tahanan*, p. 33.

[21] He employs Jacques Goff's expression. Lombard, *Le carrefour javanais*, p. 26.

[22] I am using the terms employed by the American anthropologist, Clifford Geertz in *The Religion of Java* (London: The Free Press of Glencoe, Collier-MacMillan Ltd, 1960), p. 5. Geertz added a third group to the traditional distinction made between *santri* and *abangan*: the *priyayi*, made up of aristocrats and descendants of the Javanese aristocracy. This classification has been contested by numerous Islamicists, as it is based more on social than religious divisions. Other criticisms of Geertz's classifications as well as the debates it has provoked can be found summarised in Koentjaraningrat, *Javanese Culture* (Singapore: Oxford University Press, 1985).

takes its name from the pupils of Koranic schools, known as *pesantren*. The *santri* are sometimes referred to as *kaum putihan*, meaning the "white group", a term which takes its meaning from the colour of the garment they wore. The use of the term gradually evolved to refer to the most pious Muslims, often from trading backgrounds, who were partisans of a religious tradition which consisted "not only of a careful and regular execution of the basic rituals of Islam—the prayers, the Fast, the Pilgrimage—but also of a whole complex of social, charitable and political Islamic organizations."[23]

This distinction is operative so long as one does not assume that it marks out a rigid frontier between the two groups but rather designates two polar extremes which allow for a whole range of variations in-between.[24] It will be an important distinction for our study insofar as it overlaps with the division between Muslims who wished to limit Islam to the private sphere (the "religiously neutral" nationalists, to use the Indonesian expression *netra agama*) and those who, on the other hand, actively campaigned for its involvement in politics (the Islamists, in the strict sense of the term). Up until the 19th century, then, Islam for a large number of the Muslim faithful in Indonesia amounted to an orthodox Sunnite veil—of the Shafi'i school—discreetly covering a considerable variety of syncretic and heterodox practices. These multiple variations of Islam in the country provided a fertile terrain for the demands made by reformist organisations calling for more orthodox religious practices. In Java and particularly in the heart of the former domains of the kingdom of Mataram—the Islamic successor to the Hindu-Buddhist empire of Majapahit—Muslim belief adopted syncretic religious practices which presented Islam as a simple receptacle (*wadah*) allowing the believer to cultivate the essential values of Javanese culture, namely spiritual purification and the ultimate experience of unity between the human and the divine.[25] In these regions,

---

[23] Ibid., p. 6.

[24] Concerning Geertz's tripartite categorisation, Denys Lombard has rightly pointed out that "such a tripartism is not at all like the Indo-European version, and it is only by twisting words that one can discern a 'structure'." Lombard, *Le Carrefour javanais*, p. 78.

[25] For a description of these synthetic practices and spiritual compromises, see James Peacock, *Indonesia: An Anthropological Perspective* (Pacific Palisades, CA: Goodyear, 1973). For a more historical analysis of the process, see MC. Ricklefs, *Mystic Synthesis in Java: A History of Islamization from the Fourteenth to the Early Nineteenth Centuries* (Norwalk: EastBridge, 2006).

Muslims worshipped the *keramat* (holy places and saints' tombs), gave offerings to the spirits, held *slametan* or *kenduri* (ceremonial meals for the spirits), and used *azimat* (amulets) to protect themselves from evil spirits. The condemnation of these practices, which was part of the reformist struggle against heresy, superstition and innovation (*bid'ah*), gave rise to a fundamental shift within the *santri* community which, over time, left its mark on the political destiny of Indonesian Islam.[26] It led to the emergence of a split between the supporters of a complete reform of these practices, composed mainly of modernists, and the traditionalists who defended a certain religious status quo. Reformism, then, encouraged its members to let their religious faith inspire an active participation in the nationalist movement, but at the same time, it sowed the seeds within the Muslim community of a division which would, to a large extent, be responsible for the failure of political Islam.

During the first decade of the 20th century, the Muslim community in Indonesia was affected by the vast reform movement pervading the entire Muslim world at that time. By the end of the 18th century, in India and in several Middle Eastern countries, voices were speaking out to denounce the paralysis of the Muslim world's institutions and social structures. As a result of their experience of colonisation, which constantly demonstrated to them the indisputable technical superiority of the West, Muslim thinkers increasingly denounced the excessive rigidity of Islam's interpretation of the divine message. Its vitality, they felt, had gradually been smothered by the codification attempted by the founders of the four Sunni schools of jurisprudence between the eighth and ninth centuries. Following the tradition of such illustrious theologians as al-Ghazali in the 12th century and Ibn Taimiyya in the 14th century, the reformist movement wanted to reclaim the legacy of the first generation of Muslims, those "devout pioneers" (*Salaf*) who gave their name to the Salafi movement (*Salafiyya*).[27] This evolution

---

[26] Among the traditions which reformists were most critical of included the celebration of the Prophet's birth (*mawlid al-nabi*), recitations of odes to the Prophet such as *Barzanji, Qasidat al-Burdah, Diba'i*. For a complete account these debates, see Fauzan Saleh, *Modern Trends in Islamic Theological Discourses in 20th Century Indonesia: A Critical Survey* (Leiden: Brill, 2001), pp. 86–91.

[27] See Article "Islah", EI2 online, 2008. For a clear overview of the different generations of the reformist movement, see Sabrina Mervin, *Histoire de l'Islam. Fondements et doctrines* (Paris: Flammarion editions, Champs Université, 2000), pp. 152–68.

took place almost simultaneously in India and the Middle East. In India, the movement began with Shah Walli Ullah (d. 1762), was carried on by Sayyid Ahmad Khan (d. 1898), founder of the Aligarh Muslim University, and was finally led by Muhammad Iqbal (d. 1938), the spiritual father of the Pakistani nation. In the Middle East, Jamal al-Din al-Afghani, having travelled throughout India, Central Asia and Europe, returned home to denounce the region's European imperialism and the conservatism of feudal Muslim leaders who were opposed to any modernisation in their countries. This reformist movement advocated a return to the Koran, stripped of all the commentaries which had skewed its message, the adoption of European technical progress, the struggle against fatalism and the recognition of freedom and reason. Al-Afghani, the father of modern Pan-Islamism, exercised a considerable influence over the entire Muslim world. His main disciple, the Egyptian Mohammad 'Abduh (d. 1905), campaigned throughout his life for the reform of the curriculum in Al-Azhar, the Islamic university in Cairo. He maintained that true Islam was not in contradiction with modern science and he campaigned for the introduction of mathematics, history and geography courses. 'Abduh is considered by a number of writers to be the father of modernism, a branch of the reformist movement which emphasised the need to open up to the West in order to incorporate its model of democratic institutions.

However, within the reformist movement, a fundamentalist wing developed which was much more intransigent towards the West. Following in the footsteps of Mohammad Ibn 'Abd al-Wahhab (d. 1791), this branch wished to restore Islamic belief and dogma to their original purity. It idealised primitive Muslim society and its goal was not to elaborate new interpretations of the holy books, but simply to return to the letter of the Koran. Wahhabism was supported by the Ibn Saud dynasty which has come to power twice in Saudi Arabia (once from 1804 to 1818 and again from 1926 to the present day) and its message attracted many followers throughout the Muslim world. In India, it inspired two movements: the Faraizi from Bengal and the Tariqa-i Muhammadiyah led by Syed Ahmad Barelwi.[28] It should be noted that

---

[28] See article "Hind", E12 online, 2008. Two recent studies of Indian Islam are also worth consulting: Marc Gaborieau, *Un autre islam. Inde, Pakistan, Bangladesh* (Paris: Albin Michel 2007); and Denis Matringe, *Un islam non arabe, Horizons indiens et pakistanais* (Paris: Téraèdre, 2005).

some of Mohammad 'Abduh's followers were attracted by Wahhabi fundamentalism. Led by the Syrian Rashid Rida, they developed 'Abduh's analysis of Islam along much narrower lines. Their journal, *Al-Manar* ("the Lighthouse") often became the mouthpiece for the Hanbali School's rigid interpretations, and was more influenced by the fundamentalism of Ibn Taimiya, the most radical opponent of both the officials in charge of medieval schools of jurisprudence and of Sufi innovations, than by the conciliatory theologian al-Ghazali who inspired 'Abduh. This neo-fundamentalism gained some success between the two world wars through the foundation of two important groups: the Association of Algerian Muslim Ulema founded by Ben Badis and the Muslim Brotherhood founded by Hassan al-Banna in Egypt. These were followed later in the 1940s with the foundation in India of Jama'at-i Islami, a branch of neo-fundamentalism which paralleled somewhat the Persatuan Islam movement in Indonesia led by Ahmad Hassan. These thinkers distinguished themselves from the modernism of 'Abduh by their more intransigent attitude towards the West, and this inflexibility no doubt explains their success amongst radical Muslims whose movement began to develop from the 1970s onwards, built on the ruins of a more conciliatory form of modernism.

The revival which took place at the end of the 19th century was not limited to the emergence of reformist ideas. In Indonesia, as elsewhere, some supporters of the schools of Islamic jurisprudence (*madhhab*), who had also noticed the development of practices considered to be heterodox, began to mobilise themselves. Under pressure from the reformists who tarnished with the same brush the rites originating from the principal schools of jurisprudence and certain forms of polytheism (*shirk*), they set out to restore Islam to what they considered to be its purest form: medieval Islam.[29] Like the modernists, they adopted Western methods of teaching and developed a vast missionary activity. In Indonesia, some *ulama* but also certain important Sufi orders, such as the *Sammaniyah*, the *Qadiriyah wa Naqshbandiyah* and the *Naqshabandiyah Khaliddiyah*, attempted to persuade their fellow Muslims who were influenced by customary practices (*adat*) or

---

[29] The same phenomenon took place in India with the Deobandi movement founded in 1867 which assembled the moderate disciples of Sayyid Ahmad Barelwi wishing to remain loyal to the Hanafi School.

by Javanese spirituality movements (*aliran kebatinan* or *kejawen*) to adopt a more orthodox form of Islam, which generally meant the form taught by the Shafi'i school. In reality, numerous religious dignitaries often departed from the teachings preached by the founders of the schools of jurisprudence but preferred instead to adhere to the subsequent teachings of an *imam* who regularly strayed from the original message.[30] As a result, in a number of regions in the country, Islam had taken on a local flavour and while the partisans of a strict Shafi'i tradition remained sensitive to some of these religious rites, they endeavoured to correct what they considered to be their most obscurantist aspects.

The traditionalists' mobilisation can be seen as a combination of their desire for modernity and their need to invoke religious orthodoxy. It was an approach which was not altogether different in nature from that of the reformists, and indeed some traditionalists were active for a time within modernist organisations. However, their historical eras of reference, which were the yardsticks for their respective orthodoxies, differed. While the traditionalists founded their practice on texts largely taken from the speculations on Islam during the medieval period, the reformists set out to use resources taken exclusively from the earliest days of Islam. These resources could be used either as the basis for a new interpretation considered more appropriate for contemporary times—in the case of modernists—or they could be used as a model for contemporary behaviour if one simply took refuge in the craven imitation of the customs and practices of the first Muslims—as was the case with the fundamentalists.

Middle-Eastern reformism first manifested itself in Indonesia at the beginning of the 19th century with the Padri movement.[31] This branch of Islam, inspired by Wahhabism, was introduced to West Sumatra by pilgrims who had been very taken by the new rigorist movement they had observed during their stay in Mecca. The reforms which they attempted to impose ran up against a reluctant population who

---

[30] Deliar Noer, *The Modernist Muslim Movement in Indonesia* (Kuala Lumpur: Oxford University Press, 1973 [2nd edition, 1978]), p. 300.

[31] It was long thought that the term "Padri" came from the port of Pedir from which Muslims set out on their pilgrimage to Mecca. It is now considered more likely to have come from the Portuguese word "padre", given by the Portuguese explorers to religious figures, including Muslim ones.

were very attached to the syncretism embodied in their customary practices (*adat*). The leaders of the Padri movement, namely Haji Miskin
and Tuanku Nan Rinceh, launched a civil war which ended with their
new moral order being imposed across most of the Minangkabau region. It was hereafter forbidden to organise cock-fighting, betting or to
consume tobacco, alcohol and opium; in addition, it became obligatory
for men to wear beards, for women to wear a veil and for everyone to
wear white clothes and pray five times a day. It was finally the intervention of Dutch troops in 1838 that ended this campaign carried out
by the Padri, and with it came to a close the first Wahhabi experiment
in Indonesia.[32] The influence of Wahhabism, which symbolised intransigence and fanaticism, remained limited to this region, and Masyumi
never considered it to be an exemplar. By focussing on the resistance
of the Tuanku Imam Bonjol during the Padri War, mentioned earlier,
they chose to see in it the embodiment of stubborn defiance towards
the colonist rather than the symbol of civil strife.[33]

The influence of the modernist branch of Muslim reformism in
Indonesia was of an altogether different nature. It spread mainly by
means of periodicals controlled by two groups: those of Arab descent
and the Minangkabu diaspora in Indonesia. Masyumi's future leaders,
who were to participate in this proliferation of intellectual and religious
activity from the 1920s onwards, drew many of their beliefs from it.
The growth of the reformist movement in the Middle East at the end
of the 19th century had coincided with a marked increase in the number of Indonesian pilgrims travelling to the Holy Land, due in no
small part to the opening of the Suez Canal in 1869, which made the
journey easier and cheaper. Between 1850 and 1910, the number of
pilgrims soared from 2,000 to 20,000 per year;[34] their journey did not

---

[32] For further reading on this intervention, see Christine Dobbin, *Islamic Revivalism in a Changing Peasant Economy: Central Sumatra, 1784–1847* (London and
Malmö: Curzon Press, 1983), XII: 300. Though they did not openly claim to
be part of the Wahhabi movement, two other puritan movements were also
present in Java. At the end of the 17th century, in the Banten region, religious
leaders, dressed in Arab clothing, outlawed tobacco and opium. At the beginning
of the 19th century, the Badiah movement in the north of Java showed similar
characteristics.

[33] With the exception of the book, mentioned above, written by HAMKA on
Haju Piobang.

[34] Lombard, *Le carrefour javanais*, p. 66.

always come to an end at Mecca either, and some who were attracted by Mohammad 'Abduh's ideas travelled on to Cairo to continue their studies at Al-Azhar University.[35] This was the case for Syeikh Muhammad Alkalali, who came from the Minangkabau region and who, after his stay in the Middle East, settled in Singapore.[36] There, in the company of some of his fellow students, he edited, starting from 1905, the periodical *Al-Imam* which disseminated in Malay the ideas of Rida's journal *Al-Manar*. Their example was soon to be followed in Minangkabau, where in 1911 the periodical magazine *Al-Munir* (in Malay, but written using the Jawi script) was published in Padang under the editorship of H. Abdullah Ahmad, H. Abdul Karim Amrullah and Sutan Muhammad Salim.[37] Two more periodical magazines were to follow: *Al-Mizan*, published in Maninjau, and in Padang Panjang, *Al-Munir al-Manar*, the successor to *Al-Munir*, which had stopped publication in 1915. The religious figures of the Minangkabau region clearly played a significant role in the diffusion of reformist ideas,[38] and at the beginning of the 1930s, another generation, which included future Masyumi figures, continued this tradition of publishing. In Medan, one of the

---

[35] Mona Abaza, *Indonesian Students in Cairo: Islamic Education, Perceptions and Exchanges*, Cahier d'Archipel (Paris: EHESS, 1994).

[36] The Minangkabau region was at that time in the throes of a debate arising from the dispute over *adat*. It opposed the traditional leaders, who defended the matrilineal system which was deeply rooted in the region, and the radical *ulamas* who wished to put an end to it. A movement inspired by the "Young Turks" and led by Datuk Sutan Maharadja even attempted to modernise *adat* by focussing on, amongst other things, its feminist dimension. Cf. Taufiq Abdullah, *Schools and Politics: The Kaum Muda Movement in West Sumatra (1927–1933)* (Ithaca, NY: Cornell University Press, 1971), pp. 8–13. Several Minangkabau religious figures, such as Sjech Ahmad Chatib, who became *imam* of the Al Haram mosque in Mecca, refused to return to their native region in protest at this modernisation of *adat*. Noer, *The Modernist Muslim Movement in Indonesia*, p. 19.

[37] H. Abdul Karim Amrullah—sometimes known as HAKA or Hadji Rasil—had a son called Hadji Abdul Malik Karim Amrullah (HAMKA) who became president of Muhammadiyah and was also a Masyumi deputy in Parliament. Sutan Muhammad Salim was K.H. Agus Salim's father, one of the most eminent figures in the Partai Sarekat Islam Indonesia and one of Masyumi's founders.

[38] Another group, the Hadrami community—composed of Arabs from Hadramont and their descendants—also played an important role. One of their representatives, Hamid Algadri, explained that during the colonial period, most of his friends read periodicals from Egypt which propagated modernist ideas, in particular those belonging to Al-Afghani.

most active publishing centres in the country, Zainal Abidin Ahmad published *Pandji Islam*, while HAMKA and Yunan Nasution published *Pedoman Masjarakat*. These two weekly periodicals were amongst the most prestigious publications in the country and attracted contributions from prominent figures in the nationalist movement, such as Sukarno and Mohammad Hatta. They allowed the Minangkabau who had settled in Java to stay in contact with their home region. Mohammad Natsir, who was living at the time in Bandung, published his first articles in these periodicals under the pseudonym A. Moechlis.[39]

With the growth of the first reformist organisations, there was quite an unprecedented development in publishing activity, which spread across most of Indonesia. To name but a few examples of these publications, Muhammadiyah published no fewer than six periodicals (*Penyiar Islam, Pancaran Amal, Suara Muhammadiyah, Almanak Muhammadiyah* and *Suara Aisyah*) and Persatuan Islam published four (*Al Lisan, Al Fatwaa, Pembela* and *Al Taqwa*).[40] Generally, a few thousand copies of each periodical were printed and they constituted the main outlet for relaying reformist ideas in Indonesia. The religious and political ideas of Masyumi's future leaders were forged through reading these publications, and for many of them also through participating in them. As in the Middle East, few books were in circulation, with the exception of collections of articles. These periodicals, then, in their sections containing letters to the editor, allowed a prompt and precise response to be given to the questions which intrigued readers, and their pages were often full of heated debates.[41] By getting around the control which the colonial authorities exercised over public life, and by allowing people to exchange ideas across the country, these publications constituted a veritable sounding board for the future Masyumi leaders' political ideas.

---

[39] Further details on Natsir's childhood and education can be found in Audrey R. Kahin, *Islam Nationalism and Democracy: A Political Biography of Mohammad Natsi* (Singapore: NUS Press, 2012), pp. 1–9.

[40] "Media Massa Islam", *Ensiklopedi Islam* (Jakarta: Pt Ichtiar Baru van Hoeve, 1993).

[41] For an analysis of the debates published in *Pembela Islam* which opposed the modernists belonging to Persis on the one hand, and the traditionalists and nationalists on the other, see Howard M. Federspiel, *Persatuan Islam: Islamic Reform in Twentieth Century Indonesia* (Ithaca, NY: Modern Indonesia Project, Cornell University Press, 1970), Chapters 4 and 6.

From their earliest writings, the party's future leaders identified themselves clearly with the ideas of this reformist movement. References to the movement's principal theorists crop up regularly throughout their articles, speeches and lectures. Al-Ghazali, for example, who is considered a forerunner of the movement, was referred to in glowing terms by Mohammad Natsir in an article published in 1937 in *Pedoman Masjarakat*. Natsir, who compared his work to that of Thomas à Kempis, the author of *The Imitation of Christ*, explained that "700 years before David Hume", al-Ghazali had managed to solve the thorny question of causality.[42]

The theorists most often mentioned were the founders of modern reformism, Al-Afghani and Mohammad 'Abduh. For Masyumi members, Al-Afghani was generally considered to be the father of Pan-Islamism who made it possible for the Muslim world, downtrodden by colonialism, to rediscover its dignity.[43] Mohammad 'Abduh, on the other hand, embodied a spirit of tolerance and opposition to all forms of religious extremism, and his memory was evoked in a speech given in Medan by Mohammad Natsir in December 1953, during which he warned his fellow Muslims against the dangers of the radical solutions proposed by the separatist movement Darul Islam.[44]

It is in Masyumi's adherence to the central points of the reformist doctrine, however, rather than in mere references to the movement's founding fathers, that the party's reformist identity is most clearly visible. Direct references by Masyumi leaders to *ijtihad*, the right to interpret holy texts, were nonetheless relatively few and initially, in fact, references to it only appeared implicitly. These could be found in the arguments condemning the passivity of *taqlid*, which was considered to be the practice of faith without any personal discernment.

> Islam clearly forbids any blind belief in the theories and criticisms which are not founded on divine revelation, that is to say, which only carry over the old interpretations from generation to generation without verifying their sacred nature.

---

[42] "Abu Hamid Bin Muhammad Bin Muhammad Al-Ghazali", reproduced in Natsir, *Capita Selecta*, vol. 1, pp. 19–23.

[43] See, for example, the short analysis provided by Anshary, *Falsafah Perdjuangan Islam*, p. 62 and by Jusuf Wibisono, *Hikmah*, 3 April 1954.

[44] *Abadi*, 2 December 1953. See. infra, Chapter 3.

'And do not pursue that of which you have no knowledge. Indeed, the hearing, the sight and the heart—about all those [one] will be questioned' (Koran, 17:39)[45]

After the split from Masyumi by the traditionalist Nahdlatul Ulama branch in 1952, the importance of *itjihad* was asserted more clearly. A few months after this split, which undermined Masyumi considerably, Isa Anshary took advantage of some time he had to spend in hospital to launch an appeal to the Muslim community which, according to him, needed to accomplish a genuine internal revolution, the cornerstone of which would be *ijtihad*. It would of course be carried out according to strict guidelines and could only be performed by the religious authorities who were qualified to do so. It should also go hand in hand with a critical mindset and spirit of contradiction (*ruh intikad*) on the part of the entire *umma*. Only if these two conditions were fulfilled could the "struggle in the way of God" (*jihad*) progress:

> How can we fulfil the commandments of the Koran if our minds and our thoughts are bound by the chains of *taqlid*?... How can we turn fanaticism into conviction if we do not free our minds from this archaic submission to the domination of *taqlid*? The door leading to *ijtihad* is open to *ulama* and jurists who possess the ability to perform it. *Ijtihad* purifies our thoughts and our interpretations which are still erroneous and fallacious, and it confirms those thoughts and convictions which are in keeping with the principles of the true religion.... The struggle will not achieve its goal if we are satisfied with an audience which is great in number but which is composed of corpses who obey orders without question and are devoted but lacking in conviction. It is the 'discipline of corpses' like that seen in fascist and communist countries.... Blessed is the Muslim community which has *ulamas* capable of carrying out *ijtihad*, the basis of any *jihad*. Blessed is the Islamic struggle which possesses an *umma* endowed with critical faculties. The revolution of Islam will be quick and fresh if it is carried out by *ulama* who are able to carry out *ijtihad* and by an *umma* that possesses critical faculties.[46]

---

[45] Mohammad Natsir, "Sikap Islam terhadap kemerdekaan-berfikir", Pandji Islam, April–June 1940, in *Capita Selecta*, vol. 1, pp. 206–29.
[46] Isa Anshary, "Ruh Intikad dan Idjtihad", in *Revolusi Islam* (Surabaya: Hasan Aidid, 1953), pp. 31–4.

It is nonetheless quite difficult to discern in any precise way what the leaders of Masyumi meant by *ijtihad*.[47] The exercise of this right to interpret sacred texts was never accompanied by any preliminary declaration. As we will examine later, Masyumi's unique position on the political landscape—in particular its almost visceral attachment to the principles of democracy—did not stem from their exegesis of religious texts. Whenever religious texts were referred to, it was invariably in order to settle a contentious debate which was at the centre of a dispute with other branches of Islam. To take an example from 1958, Moenwar Chalil, one of the most influential *ulamas* within Masyumi, published a booklet devoted to the notion of *Ulil-Amri*. This title, meaning "those who hold the command", had been at the centre of a bitter controversy a few years earlier in 1954 when at a meeting of *ulamas* belonging to Nahdlatul Ulama, the term had been used to refer to President Sukarno, thus making him a sort of religious leader whom all Muslims had to obey. In response, Moenwar Chalil, along with the rest of Masyumi, raised objections to this interpretation and he outlined them in his short 60-page book where he engaged in an in-depth analysis of verse 59 of *Sura An-Nisa* (The Women) which is the basis for the notion of *Ulil-Amri*.[48] Basing his ideas on the analysis of Mohammad 'Abduh and Rashid Rida, he showed how, in his opinion, the use of the term to refer to Sukarno constituted a corruption of the sacred text.[49] Did Moenwar Chalil consider, when writing this disquisition, that he was exercising his right to perform *ijtihad*? It is difficult to say with any certainty that he did, not only because we have no clear indication on his part,[50] but also because it was not particularly unusual to engage in this sort of analysis—as the *ulamas* of Nahdlatul Ulama had just demonstrated in their controversial interpretation of the Koran.

Although the references by Masyumi to the thinkers and doctrine of the reformist movement show that the party clearly identified itself

---

[47] Before the 1960s, the theological debates within Indonesian Islam, though they were often virulent, were not generally very detailed. The main reasons for this can be found in Saleh, *Modern Trends in Islamic Theological Discourses in 20th Century Indonesia*, pp. 6 ff.

[48] Koran (IV, 59).

[49] Moenawar Chalil, *Ulil-Amri*, Solo, AB Sitti Sjamsijah, 1958.

[50] Thoha Hamim, "Moenawar Chalil's Reformist Thought: A Study of an Indonesian Religious Scholar (1908–1961)", PhD thesis, McGill University, 1996.

with this movement, it was never completely comfortable with this identification. Masyumi leaders seemed loath to define themselves as representatives of a modernist movement—*kaum muda*—in opposition to a traditionalist movement—*kaum tua*. This was not a sign of hypocrisy or a rejection of the modernist movement but rather a consequence of one of the fundamental contradictions of the party. Although Masyumi was founded mainly on modernist principles and was dominated by representatives of modernism from its outset in 1945, and even more so after Nahdlatul Ulama broke away from the party in 1952, it always saw itself as the mouthpiece for all Indonesian Muslims. Indeed it should be noted that after the breakaway of NU, a few small traditionalist organisations remained within the party's ranks. If Masyumi were to display too close an adherence to the modernist movement, it would risk cutting itself off from millions of Muslims who were attached to the Shafi'i tradition. During the general election campaign of 1955, the leaders of the party did their utmost to adopt a very broad-minded approach to questions of religion, so, for example, the religious council of the party (*Madjelis Sjuro*) adopted a *fatwa* at the time recognising the validity of schools of jurisprudence (*madhhab*).

Given this desire for inclusiveness which pervaded the party, the article written by Jusuf Wibisono, one of the party's leaders, in April 1954, in which he outlined his personal convictions concerning the role of Islam, stands out as something of an anomaly. In this article, he was responding to three criticisms commonly made of the party's ideology, one of which consisted in claiming that religion could not be the basis on which to build a state. In his response to this point, Wibisono clearly aligned himself with modernist organisations:

> The public probably knows that there are today in the Muslim world two branches: the orthodox one and the modernist one. The difference between these two branches hangs on the fact that the orthodox branch maintains that contemporary generations are not entitled to carry out new interpretations of the Koran. Traditionalists think, in fact, that we have become too removed from the great *ulama* who lived in the first three centuries following the Hijra, that is to say about ten centuries ago. They consider that contemporary generations can only obey the principles defined by those great *ulama*.
>
> If the Muslim world is led by a group of Muslims like the traditionalists, I do not think it will be possible to establish a modern

state based on the principles of Islam. Obliging Muslims to submit to the teachings of *ulama* from the past, no matter how great those *ulama* were, amounts to denying their freedom and closing their minds. However, a few years ago, there appeared an important thinker, Jamal al-Din Al-Afghani, who founded a reform movement (a renaissance movement) in Islam. He held that in order to move forward one had to return to the Koran. This reformist branch gradually spread, moving on to India and eventually to Indonesia. In my opinion, it is this modernist branch that allows us to hope that Islam will be capable of becoming the cornerstone of a state which is not opposed to but rather in tune with the progress of our times. Masyumi is a part of this movement which the West has named 'modernist', and it unites Muslim leaders who consider that each generation is entitled to interpret the Koran directly according to the needs of the day. If this approach is not followed, then it will undoubtedly be impossible for Islam to be the basis on which a modern state can be established.[51]

Although this article summarises many of the arguments familiar to the leaders of the party, it constitutes nonetheless a singular exception. For reasons mentioned earlier, no official party document or, to the best of our knowledge, no speech given by a high-ranking party official stated so explicitly the importance of the modernist legacy to Masyumi. The reluctance to recognise this obvious link adds no doubt to the originality of the Masyumi position within Muslim reformism and, as we will see later, allows us to shed light on some of the political stances it adopted.

Learning from the West

As with other parts of the world, the emergence of Indonesian reformism was largely a reaction to the challenges which arose from Western colonisation. The responsibility of the Dutch in this emergence of a desire for change was quite complex, however, and they were far more than simply an anti-model which jolted national pride awake. By participating in what Robert Van Nie called "the general tendency of the development of an Indonesian elite", that is to say the transformation "from a traditional, cosmologically oriented hereditary

---

[51] Jusuf Wibisono, "Ideologi Politik Masjumi", *Hikmah*, 3 and 10 April 1954.

elite to a modern welfare-state oriented education-based elite", the colonial authorities contributed significantly to the formation of an ideal breeding ground for the inception of Islamic nationalism.[52]

This contradiction, which is inherent in all forms of modern colonisation and which contrasts with the Colbertist mercantilism practised by the French East-India Company, was of course not specific to Indonesia. By promoting progress throughout the colonised world, Westerners willingly sowed the seeds for the destruction of a system which they had hoped to perpetuate. Masyumi was indebted to the West in two significant respects which are intimately linked, namely for the education received by its leaders and the importance of references to the West in their writings.

The Ethical Policy Generation

The senior members of Masyumi, those who developed and defended the party's policies within the party's executive committee and in parliament, were for the most part the products of an educational system which had been put in place by the Dutch colonial power as part of its "ethical policy". After the abuses of power carried out during the "system of forced cultivation", which were denounced by Multatuli in his novel, *Max Havelaar*, the government of the Netherlands recognised that its duty as a colonial power was not only to promote the infrastructural improvement and economic development of their territories, but also to better indigenous people's lives socially and culturally.

Between the beginning of the century and the 1930s, the colonial government progressively put in place a complete educational programme, going from primary school to third-level education, which was open to the indigenous population. However, Indonesians only progressively entered this educational system. In the early years of the century, a little less than 3,000 of them were attending primary schools (Holland Inlander School, HIS) and only 25 were attending secondary school (Meer Uitgebreid Lager Onderwijs, MULO, the lower half of secondary school; and Algemene Middelbare School, AMS, the upper half). In 1928, there were 75,000 indigenous children enrolled in the primary system and 6,500 in the secondary; on the eve of the Japanese

---

[52] Robert Van Niel, *The Emergence of the Modern Indonesian Elite* (The Hague and Bandung: W. Van Hoeve Ltd, 1960), pp. 1–2.

invasion, nearly 90,000 were attending a HIS, 8,000 were enrolled in a MULO and 1,800 were going to an AMS, as against 5,700 Europeans.[53] Access to Dutch higher education in Indonesia, which consisted mainly of law schools, medical schools and institutes of technology, was even more restrictive for Indonesians. In 1920, only 20 managed to obtain a university diploma, and in 1930 there were barely 160; by the beginning of the Second World War, their number had risen to 200.[54]

The future leaders of Masyumi made up a fair proportion of the happy few who benefitted from a Western education. Of the 57 party representatives elected to parliament in 1955, which is the largest statistical sample available to us, 32, that is to say more than half, had received at the very least their primary education in the Dutch system (HIS). Of these 32, 26 had continued their studies in the Dutch system up until secondary school (MULO and AMS) and 12 of them had received third-level diplomas from Dutch institutions. Six of them had pursued legal studies, three had been to medical school, two had obtained diplomas from the School of Public Administration and one had graduated from veterinary school. Of these 12 third-level graduates, only one, Soekiman, had pursued his studies in the Netherlands.[55]

The Dutch curriculum was in fact not the only one in Indonesia which allowed students access to a "Western-style" education. Most of the 25 deputies who had not been educated in the Dutch system had attended schools run by reformist associations (Al Irshad, Muhammadiyah and Persatuan Islam), whose programmes were not entirely dedicated to religion but devoted a significant amount of time to the teaching of classical subjects. This openness to the Western system of education was, of course, typical of modernist organisations. Modernist schools did not have a monopoly over the education received by Masyumi leaders, however. When Anwar Haryono, for example, after having attended both Dutch schools and an institution run by Muhammadiyah, decided to become a *santri*, he chose to prepare himself

---

[53] George McTurnan Kahin, *Nationalism and Revolution in Indonesia* (Ithaca, NY: Cornell University Press, 1952), p. 31. In 1939, the Indonesian population represented 60 million inhabitants of which 240,000 were Europeans.
[54] Ibid., p. 32.
[55] Parlaugan (Press-Officer Parlement), *Hasil Rakjat Memilih, Tokoh-Tokoh Parlemen di Republik Indonesia* (Jakarta: C.V. GITA, 1956).

for this in the famous *pesantren* of Tebuireng, birthplace of the traditionalist movement, Nahdlatul Ulama. At that time, the school had a reputation even in modernist circles, for being intellectually open-minded. Wahid Hasjim, son of the school's founder, had even carried out some reforms which meant that 70% of teaching time was devoted to general (i.e. non-religious) subjects.[56] It can safely be said, then, that the 22 Masyumist deputies who were trained in the Islamic secondary level educational institutions also received their fair share of Western ideas and values (the three others make no mention of any schooling). Indeed, it should be pointed out that the two curriculums were by no means mutually exclusive, as almost half of the deputies who had come out of the Dutch education system had at one stage or another in their schooling attended a religious institution. The other deputies owed their knowledge of Islam to evening classes which they were given from an *ulama*, although, generally, only those who had attended the most prestigious *kiyai* mentioned it in their official biography.[57]

If we move on to look at the upper echelons of the party, we see that the imprint of the Dutch education system is even more significant on them. Of the 15 members of the party's executive committee elected in 1954, only two (Taufiqurrahman and Fakih Usman) had received their education exclusively from religious schools. Five of them had received secondary school diplomas from Dutch schools (Mohammad Natsir, Prawoto Mangkusasmito, Mohammad Sardjan, Nj. Sunarjo Mangunpuspito and Nj. Zahra Hafni Abuhanifah), while the remaining eight had received third-level education. Of the latter, five had graduated from the Rechts-Hogeschool, where as well as courses in law it was also possible to study economics and sociology (Kasman Singodimedjo, Mohamad Roem, Sjafruddin Prawiranegara, Jusuf Wibisono and Boerhanoeddin Harahap), two had been to medical school, known as STOVIA (Soekiman and Abu Hanifah) while Isa Anshary indicated in his biography that he had studied economics and political science in Bandung though he never really specified which institution he had attended.

---

[56] Lukman Hakiem, *Perjalan mencari keadilan dan persatuan. Biografi Dr Anwar Harjono, S.H.* (Jakarta: Media Da'wah, 1993), p. 34 ff.

[57] A deputy from Central Sumatra, Dr. H. Ali Akbar, indicated, for example, that he had followed the teachings of Sjech Muhammad Djamil Djambek, one of the most renowned reformist *ulamas* of the Minang region.

As public opinion regarded this type of education as very prestigious, the leaders of Masyumi often drew attention to it, sometimes to the detriment of the religious education they may have received, either from schools run by Islamic organisations or informally from *ulamas*. In the biographies of Masyumi leaders published by *Abadi* in the months running up to the 1955 general election, only four of them (Isa Anshary, Nj Sunarjo Mangunpuspito, K.H. Taufiqurrahman and Fakih Usman) mentioned it, despite the fact that all of them had received a religious education of some description. For their generation, an Islamic education had become less important, not just because less time was devoted to it in schools, but also because it held less weight in public perception. It seemed to the party's candidates that it was more beneficial in the eyes of the voter to be a past-pupil of a Dutch secondary school or university than to have followed courses in a Muhammadiyah school or in a *pesantren* in the Minangkabau region.

In order to understand the importance of a Western-style education for those who took over the leadership of the party at the end of the 1940s, it needs to be examined in the context of the broader transformation of a social category which was the crucible of Indonesian nationalism: the middle class. George McTurnan Kahin has shown how the business community became a minority within the middle class in the last decades of Dutch colonialism, compared with civil servants, private sector employees and teachers. The latter two categories owed their success to a Western-style education, whereas Islamic education still figured prominently for those amongst the business community.[58] The men who came to occupy the highest echelons of the party during the 1950s were typical, then, of the sociological transformation which the Muslim reformist movement had undergone. Where the reformist leaders of Sarekat Islam and Muhammadiyah in the previous generation had come mainly from the business community and had received, for the most part, an exclusively religious education, Masyumi's leaders, thanks to their education in the Dutch system, worked in the intellectual professions until their election to parliament at least. Looking at the 57 Masyumi parliamentarians, we can see that 21 of them were civil servants, 17 were teachers, five of them were journalists and four were members of one of the liberal professions. Only nine of them were members of the business community, i.e. slightly more than 15

---

[58] Kahin, *Nationalism and Revolution in Indonesia*, p. 29.

per cent (one of the deputies, a woman, did not give a profession).[59] Amongst the leadership of the party, only Jusuf Wibisono and Kasman Singodimedjo had experience in the business world as employees of Dutch firms.

The Western culture with which the future Masyumi leadership were imbued, left a profound influence on them, and this is evidenced in the system of references that they gradually established in their writings.

References to the West

The intellectual influence of Western culture appears in various forms in the Masyumi leaders' ideas. First of all, they were intellectually drawn to the issues raised by European history and American history and often referred to them in their writings. Second, and perhaps most strikingly, Western thinkers, in the eyes of Masyumi writers, were seen to lend more credibility to their arguments. References to the West were not, then, simply negative ones used to score political points by attacking the representatives of western culture. Although it should be said that there were occurrences of this during the formative years of the nationalist movement, such as when Mohammad Natsir crossed swords in the 1930s with a Dutch pastor in the AIT newspaper. In this heated exchange, Natsir, naturally, adopted a position contrary to his opponent's system of references;[60] but after the struggle for independence, we begin to see in these references the signs of the intellectual debt owed to the West by Masyumi's theorists.

The political considerations elaborated by Masyumi's theorists belonged, for the most part, to the tradition of Western thought. Indeed, their writings and speeches leave a European historian with the uncanny feeling of being on very familiar ground. Allusions to the West, whether to its culture or to its important historical figures, are far more frequent than references to Islam or Indonesia's past. If we look at classical antiquity to begin with, little mention is made of Ancient Greece and Rome, and although the early Greek philosophers were highly

---

[59] Parlaungan, *Hasil Rakjat Memilih, Tokoh-Tokoh Parlemen di republik Indonesia* (Jakarta: C.V. GITA, 1956).

[60] Ajip Rosidi, *Mohammad Natsir, sebuah biografi* (Jakarta: PT Girimukti Pusaka, 1990), pp. 42–3.

respected—Kasman said that "Socrates, even for Muslim philosophers, will remain famous until the end of time"—their writings were only rarely analysed.[61] Moving on to the Christian era, two periods were seen by the party's thinkers as examples to be avoided when establishing an Islamic state: first, the Middle Ages which were seen as a period of total political domination by the Catholic church but also the 17th and 18th centuries, described as a period of absolute monarchy in Europe. Isa Anshary, for example, did not want "a state led by a supreme leader who embodied both political and religious authority, like what we saw in the Middle Ages when the Catholic Church commanded and oppressed mankind (both physically and morally) with a philosophy known as Universalism."[62]

Logically enough, Enlightenment ideas were celebrated by Masyumi writers, such as Soedjino Hardjosoediro, who offered readers of the *Hikmah* newspaper a detailed analysis of the *"trias politica"* theory. In it, he underlined the importance of contributions made to this theory by Montesquieu and John Locke, and explained why a strict separation of powers was vital in a democracy.[63] However, if the party's theorists joined with the philosophers of the 18th century in condemning absolutism and the concentration of power in one branch of government, part of the Enlightenment legacy was nonetheless rejected. This is where the difference between Masyumi and nationalists, who were religiously neutral, became apparent:

> We need to understand that as the colonial mindset shaped and left its mark on half of our intellectuals, there has appeared in the struggle for independence a principle which holds that religion and politics must be separated. [This doctrine can be explained by] the spirit of individualism which was advocated enthusiastically by some seventeenth and eighteenth century experts in social sciences, the most famous of whom is J.J. Rousseau.[64]

The West's political theories and historical experiences at that time inspired and illustrated most of the Masyumi leadership's political ideas. Isa Anshary's analysis of the French revolutionary experience led

---

[61] Kasman Singodimejo, *Renungan dari Tahanan*, p. 142.
[62] Anshary, *Falsafah Perdjuangan Islam*, p. 216.
[63] *Hikmah*, 27 March, 3 and 10 April 1954.
[64] Anshary, *Falsafah Perdjuangan Islam*, p. 91.

him to conclude that a political revolution without a social revolution would necessarily be vain.[65] Such considerations clearly showed the proximity between Masyumi's theoretical framework. Indeed, one of Masyumi's dilemmas was how to distance itself from Marxism, an ideology which of course the party had to spurn because of its impiety. Marxism and its Leninist and Stalinist offshoots held a real fascination for the Masyumi leadership, and they undoubtedly knew those political theories better than any other. Jusuf Wibisono, quoting Jules Monnerot, stated that communism was similar to a religion;[66] Isa Anshary devoted long sections of his book, *Philosophy of Islamic Struggle*, to considerations on *Marxistiche Historische materialische Weltanschauung* and *Marxistische Staatsfilisofie*, which he often supplemented with long quotations in German.[67] Communism was condemned, alongside fascism and Nazism, in a long list of models which were the antithesis of an Islamic state. Anshary denounced regimes

> in which all authority is held by one man, who is of a superior race, a supreme leader, before whom the people are answerable instead of the contrary, like the fascism of Mussolini and Hitler who both idolized the Führerprinzip, or a totalitarian government led by one man, a proletariat dictator from the Bolshevik movement, which is founded upon the philosophy of dialectical materialism and implemented through communism or Leninism.[68]

However, Masyumi's leaders observed various Marxist movements closely, and also identified more positive models there. At the beginning of the 1960s, Kasman Singidimedjo made an appeal to his supporters from his prison cell to adopt a "progressivist-revolutionary" attitude in line with that exemplified by Rosa Luxemburg:

---

[65] "Katja suram dari Revolusi Perantjis", ibid., pp. 137 ff.

[66] *Hikmah*, 3 April 1954.

[67] Anshary, *Falsafah Perdjuangan Islam*, pp. 90, 198–200. It is legitimate to wonder to what extent Indonesian readers understood these long quotations, whose origin, moreover, was rarely specified. One of the longest of these was an extract from "a book by Marx and Engels", no further details being given. It was taken from the magazine *Ilmu Masyjarakjat* and illustrates the importance of the role played by periodicals in allowing access to original works which were otherwise difficult to come by.

[68] Anshary, *Falsafah Perdjuangan Islam*, p. 216.

In the final analysis, we must accomplish the duty which Islam imposes on us to struggle until we manage, in accordance with Rosa Luxemburg's theory of spontaneous organisation (which is consistent with being a progressivist revolutionary), to overcome more rapidly the previous dispensation which was willingly organized and then purposely neglected by Dutch colonisation and imperialism in Indonesia. We should read the Koran, verse 70 of the Sura Al Baqarah, which forbids us from being conservative.[69]

The recent history of North America and Western bloc countries also gave Masyumi thinkers examples to follow in their policies. The question of the nation-state when it was addressed was almost always preceded by a reminder of Renan's definition. The author of "What is a nation?" offered a tailor-made conceptual framework for contemporary Indonesia where the interests and aspirations of different ethnic groups posed a potential threat to its stability. The American and European experiences in establishing constitutions were often used to provide a legal framework for the party's considerations on Indonesia's future constitution.[70] Moreover, Western states were often used as examples when trying to avoid any demonisation of the question of an Islamic state; those who had founded their institutions on religion were also shown to be paragons of democratic values. Mohammad Natsir, for instance, in a famous speech made in Karachi in April 1952 declared that:

> We should be careful to pay attention to a misinterpretation by the West which leads to Islamic states like Pakistan, who are founded on religious principles and recognize Islam as the state religion, being suspected of wanting to become theocratic states. Unfortunately, we do not really know what exactly this term 'theocracy' signifies, beyond the fact that it must be rejected.
>
> Many Americans, and by that I mean North Americans, consider their people and their country to be Christian. The late president,

---

[69] Kasman Singodimejo, *Renungan dari Tahanan*, p. 55. *Koran* (II, 87).

[70] See, for example, Soekiman Wirjosandjojo, "Indonesia Berparlement", a series of articles which appeared in the weekly magazine *Adil* and reproduced in *Wawasan Politik Seorang Muslim Patriot. Kumpulan Karangan* (Jakarta: YP2LPM, 1984), p. 40. The edition of *Hikmah* which appeared on 19 November 1955, just before the elections for the Constituent Assembly, also proposed a special report on the history of the American and French constitutions.

Franklin Delano Roosevelt, was clearly Christian and rarely forgot to mention the Christian religion in his appeals to the nations of the world during the Second World War. The English too are unmistakably a Christian people with a state religion. They have a king who is the head and the defender of the Anglican faith and numerous national events include religious ceremonies. Likewise, the Dutch are a Christian people whose constitution stipulates that the sovereign has to be a Protestant. All these states, as well as the other Christian countries of Europe, including even France, although it does not clearly recognize the place of religion in the state, have always given their support to Christian missionary activities outside of Europe, whether in Asia, Africa or Australia, particularly in colonised or semi-colonised countries.[71]

Another striking feature of the West's influence on the ideas of Masyumi's leaders is the role played by American and European authors in lending credibility to the party's message. In this regard, references to the West revealed a mindset which was eager to convince its public but also no doubt somewhat prone to an inferiority complex. Statements about the benefits of Islam for public life, the greatness of Muslim civilisation or the importance of a revered expounder of Islam only seemed to have currency insofar as they had been recognised by a member of the Western intellectual community. Mohammad Natsir, when praising al-Ghazali, referred to the English scholar, Dr. Zwene who, curiously enough, ranked the Muslim philosopher as the "fourth most important person in the history of Islam".[72] Jusuf Wibisono, who was keen to rid Islam of its image as a misogynistic religion, quoted Gustave Le Bon, a sociologist and psychologist who had said in a book entitled *The Civilisation of the Arabs* that Islam was the first religion to recognise the status of women.[73] Finally, the writings of the important Islamicists of the day, H.A.R. Gibb, Nothrop Sterling and Lothrop Stoddard, who all taught in prestigious universities in England and America, were often quoted to support an observation or an interpretation.

---

[71] Mohammad Natsir, "Sumbangan Islam bagi perdamaian dunia" (Islam's Contribution to the Pacification of the World), in *Capita Selecta*, vol. 2, pp. 61–80.
[72] "Behind Mohammad, Al Buchari and Al Asj'ari" Natsir, *Capita Selecta*, vol. 1, p. 23.
[73] *Hikmah*, 3 April 1954.

If we were to look, then, only at the education and writings of the party leaders, Masyumi's Western heritage would seem to be essential. The same could no doubt be said to be true of the intermediary echelons of the party, the local party heads, members of the *petite bourgeoisie* working in administrative jobs or owners of small businesses. These were the main readers of the periodicals and books published by the national leaders. The same does not hold, however, if we go further down the pyramid and look at the grassroots activists and particularly at the party's electorate. What resonance could the references which we have just mentioned have for people who were illiterate or had no access to a Western-style education? They no doubt provoked conflicting reactions of fascination and aversion: fascination on the one hand for the technical superiority observed during the colonial period and which continued after decolonisation with the importation of certain consumer goods, but aversion also to a civilisation judged to be corruptive and domineering. Such contradictory sentiments could be reconciled effortlessly by the theorists of the party, but from the beginning of the 1950s, they undoubtedly contributed to the disenchantment with Masyumi amongst the broader Muslim electorate when the promised benefits of a western-style system of government failed to materialise.

A Lasting Tradition of Unity and Discord

When it was founded in 1945, Masyumi saw itself as a political focal point for various strands within the *umma*. It was also the heir to an age-old dialectical tension between unity and division which had heretofore shaped the troubled history of Indonesian Islam. All those who played a role of any importance in the foundation of the party brought with them, in some way or other, the legacy of existing or defunct organisations which they had been or still were members of.

The birth of an Islamic political movement within Indonesia was intimately linked to the propagation of reformist ideas across the country. The theme of renewal and the adoption of Western methods of organisation, both of which typified modernism, provided the groups which formed at the beginning of the 20th century with the motivation, the critical framework and the organisational structures necessary for their fledgling struggle. For these groups, however, the original impetus of the reformist movement, which had led to an awakening within part of the Muslim community, arose initially from the desire to protect a certain number of established interests. The reformist movement was limited initially to a few specific social groups—members of the Arab community and *batik* traders—before gradually developing its support base to encompass the whole of Indonesian society. It thus grew from defending the interests of a community to participating in the nationalist struggle. Its first political activity was motivated by its observations of the West's political and economic hegemony but also by the increasing domination of Western religions. Since the beginning of the 20th century, Christian missionaries had begun to reach out to the *abangan* population on Java with a certain degree of success, and this success was attributed, by some, to the paralysis within Islam and to the subverting of its practices.

The first signs of the reformist movement appeared in the Hadhrami community which was composed of Arabs or descendants of Arabs from Hadramout living in Indonesia. This community, which was well-structured and relatively affluent, had maintained close links with its native region and kept itself informed of the various movements which were developing in the Middle East. In 1901, some members of the community founded the Djamiat Chair ("Charitable Society"), which was a conservative association whose goal was to educate the children of the Arab community. The movement remained relatively small-scale until a split in 1915 leading to the emergence of a more progressivist organisation, Al-Irsyad, which played a significant role in the diffusion of modernist ideas throughout Indonesia.[74]

The second Muslim organisation to be established took the form of a trade association set up by *batik* traders. At the beginning of the second decade of the 20th century, the Dutch administration progressively loosened the strict control it had maintained up until then over

---

[74] For more on the birth of Al-Irsyad, as well as the religious education in Mecca received by its founder, the Soudanese Ahmad Surkati and the dispute over the *sayyid* which was behind the creation of the new organisation, see Ahmed Ibrahim Abu Shouk, "An Arabic Manuscript on the Life and Career of Ahmad Luhammad Sûrkatî and His Irshâdî Disciples in Java", in *Transcending Borders: Arabs, Politics, Trade and Islam in Southeast Asia*, ed. Huub de Jonge and Nico Kaptein (Leiden: KITLV Press, 2002), pp. 203–17. For an overall view of how the political mobilisation within the Hadrami community was transformed, see Natalie Mobini-Kesheh, *The Hadrami Awakening: Community and Identity in the Netherlands East Indies, 1900–1942* (Ithaca, NY: Southeast Asia Program, Cornell University, 1999).

Chinese activity in Indonesia. As a result, Peranakan traders, who were of Chinese origin, were entitled to travel, trade and invest much more freely than they had been able to previously. This led to much stiffer competition for the indigenous bourgeoisie around Surakata and Yogyakarta, notably in the *batik* trade.[75] In 1911, Muslim traders, in an attempt to defend their interests, founded a mutual assistance association in Solo known as the Rekso Roemekso. This organisation, which had no legal status and had been threatened with a ban by the authorities after its implication in anti-Chinese riots, changed dramatically in 1912 when, upon the initiative of its leader, Hadji Samanhoedi, it registered itself officially as an organisation and changed its name to Sarekat Islam (Muslim Union).[76] The reasons for the founding of this new association were more sociological in nature than religious. Sarekat Islam was much more concerned with defending and protecting the interests of Muslims as a social group than with working to restore Islam's place in Indonesian society, and indeed Oemar Said Tjokroaminoto, who was in charge of running the association for more than 20 years, was not himself a religious figure. For a time, Tjokroaminoto was likened to the *Ratu Adil*, the just king of Javanese folklore, and he was never presented as a particularly pious Muslim. In fact, he drew his political inspiration more from socialism than from Islam.[77] The spectacular development of Sarekat Islam during the first 10 years of its existence relied largely on the Marxist networks which sought to involve the movement in radical and revolutionary activities. At the same time, however, the growing influence of Muhammadiyah within the organisation led to the emergence of a powerful anti-communist branch.

The third important pillar of Indonesian reformism, Muhammadiyah, was created in 1912. Its founder, Ahmad Dahlan, was a licensed member of the Islamic clergy who had spent years in Mecca

---

[75] Takashi Siraishi, *An Age in Motion: Popular Radicalism in Java, 1912–1926* (Ithaca and London: Cornell University Press, 1990), pp. 37–9.

[76] It is commonly known as the Sarekat Dagang Islam (Union of Muslim Traders), however, as it appeared, initially, as the local branch of an organisation with the same name founded in Bogor in 1909. Ibid., pp. 42–3.

[77] The place occupied by Islam in the SI's political programme, defined at its 1917 congress, was very limited. It stipulated that "the state and the government should not be influenced by the interference of one religion, but should place itself above all religions." Noer, *The Modernist Muslim Movement in Indonesia*, p. 127.

and whose father was a religious official of the Yogyakarta *Kauman*.[78] He adopted the reformist philosophy and participated actively in the organisations which were the precursors to the nationalist movement of the 1930s and 40s, namely Djamiat Chair, Boedi Oetomo and Sarekat Islam. Muhammadiyah's objectives were above all educational and social; it considerably extended the reach of reformism amongst the Indonesian public through its networks of mosques and schools but also thanks to the work of a charitable committee, a women's organisation and scout groups.[79] It was not involved directly in politics, but many of its members were active within Sarekat Islam (SI) and, in 1920, the link between the two organisations was made official. At that point, Muhammadiyah became the religious arm of SI and strengthened the anti-communist branch within it.

The driving force behind this merger was Agus Salim. He had formerly been a translator in the Dutch East Indies consulate in Jeddah and upon his return to Indonesia, he was charged by the Dutch authorities with the surveillance of Sarekat Islam. He had been a confirmed member of the reformist movement since 1915 and so he quickly abandoned his mission and was soon made second-in-command to Tjokroaminoto.[80] He was respected for his religious knowledge and was opposed to any attempt at organising a revolution. At the 1921 congress, he contributed to SI's definitive break with its Marxist wing, which meant that the former "red" sections of SI (SI Merah) were left with no other option but to join the newly-created Communist Party.[81]

It is important to mention also the foundation at this time of another organisation which was to play an important role in the history of Indonesian Islam: Persatuan Islam (Unity of Islam, also known

---

[78] The *Kauman* was originally the district inhabited by the religious officials of the sultanate. For further examination of Dahlan's role in the transformation of the *Kauman*, see Marcel Bonneff, "Le *kauman* de Yogyakarta. Des fonctionnaires religieux convertis au réformisme et à l'esprit d'entreprise", *Archipel* 30 (1985).

[79] For concrete examples of the activities organised by this reformist organisation, see Mitsu Nakaruma, *The Crescent Arises over the Banyan Tree: A Study of the Muhammadiyah Movement in a Central Javanese Town* (Yogyakarta: Gadjah Mada University Press, 1983).

[80] Noer, *The Modernist Muslim Movement in Indonesia*, p. 124.

[81] The work of reference on the birth and development of Indonesian communism remains. Ruth McVey, *The Rise of Indonesian Communism* (Ithaca, NY: Cornell University Press, 1965), p. 510.

as Persis), which was created in Bandung in 1923. This organisation was founded in West Java by the descendants of families who had originated from Sumatra—mainly from the Minangkabau region—and had emigrated in search of new trading opportunities. One of the main figures of the movement, Hadji Zamzam, had studied for three years in Mecca and was close to Ahmad Surkati, the founder of the Al Irshad movement, the forerunner of radical reformism in Indonesia. The most prominent member of Persis, however, was Ahmad Hassan (often called Hassan Bandung) who was born in Singapore to a Tamil father and a Javanese mother. He joined the movement in 1924 and rapidly rose to become its leader. Under his leadership, Persis enjoyed a considerable degree of influence within the Indonesian public. The organisation was only composed of a few hundred members, which meant that it did not experience any of the organisational problems and internal crises which hampered Sarekat Islam, Muhammadiyah and Al Irshad (the latter, for example, was involved in a long drawn-out dispute with Djamiat Chair concerning the status of Indonesians of Arab origin). It was therefore able to devote all its time and energy to religious questions. Through the work it carried out in the fields of translation and education, but above all through the influence of its periodical, *Pembela Islam*, Persis played a central role in the religious debates of the 1920s and 1930s.[82]

The beginning of the 1920s marked the apogee of the Muslim reformist movement. It was freed from its bonds with communism and had set down firm roots throughout the country, both through a religious and social care organisation (Muhammadiyah) and through a political organisation (Sarekat Islam). It had a clear identity and counted hundreds of thousands of Muslims amongst its ranks. The creation in 1925, on the joint initiative of Sarekat Islam and Muhammadiyah, of an organisation of young Muslims, the Jong Islamieten Bond (JIB), confirmed the bright prospects which lay ahead for the reformist movement.[83] On this point at least, the collaboration between the two big reformist movements proved to be fruitful. The JIB constituted a veritable breeding ground for the future leadership of Masyumi,

---

[82] See Federspiel, *Persatuan Islam: Islamic Reform in Twentieth Century Indonesia*, Chapters 4 to 7.

[83] On the birth of this organisation which emerged from the split within Jong Java, see Van Niel, *The Emergence of the Modern Indonesian Elite*, p. 168.

but as we will see later, the golden age of cooperation between Muhammadiyah and SI was short-lived. This was partly due to the fact that the Dutch, through a series of skilful political manoeuvres, eventually forced Islamic organisations into making painful choices.

The Netherlands' policy with regard to Islam was, for almost 40 years, heavily influenced by the analysis of Snouck Hurgronje. Snouck, who was a professor at the University of Leiden and also a consultant for the Office of Indigenous Affairs in the Ministry of the Colonies, managed to ease the fears of his fellow-Dutchmen towards Indonesian Muslims and initiate a new policy towards Islam. On his advice, the colonial administration authorised and even encouraged Muslim initiatives as long as they were limited to social and religious fields. Any political manifestations of Islam, however, were kept on a tight rein.[84] This subtle distinction established by the Dutch colonial authorities helped drive a wedge between Muhammadiyah and SI and put an end to their collaboration. In 1923, Sarekat Islam, which had just changed its name to Partai Sarekat Islam, adopted a policy known as Hijira (*Hijra*), which Agus Salim compared to Gandhi's policy of non-cooperation.[85] It involved each of the party members refusing any collaboration with the Dutch. Despite the fact that Muhammadiyah disapproved of this policy of opposition to the colonial administration, from whom it received a significant amount of subsidies for its schools, Tjokroaminoto refused to compromise on this issue. Muhammadiyah's position convinced him of the necessity to persuade his party to adopt a measure forbidding joint membership of the two organisations, which he succeeded in doing in 1927. At the same time as this split began to appear within the reformist movement, the appearance of two formidable rival organisations succeeded in putting an end to the hegemonic position held by Sarekat Islam as the main political representative of Indonesian Muslims.

The first of these two opponents emerged from a desire amongst the representatives of a traditionalist Islam (*kuam tua*) to form their

---

[84] Certain movements were invited to participate in the Volksraad—the consultative assembly set up by the Dutch—but the most active members were exiled, in particular Muhammadiyah members from the Minangkabau region. Noer, *The Modernist Muslim Movement in Indonesia*, p. 108.

[85] To be understood here in its original meaning of a rupture with the colonial government. Ibid., p. 159.

own movement. Since the beginning of the century, two major points of discord had appeared between reformists and traditionalists. First of all, the reformists, by advocating *ijtihad*, refused to recognise any particular value in the interpretations proposed by the Shafi'i school of jurisprudence; secondly, two religious rites which traditionalists were particularly attached to attracted the ire of reformists, namely prayers for the dead (*tahlilan*) and the cult of saints (*ziarah*). Despite these differences, in the first two decades of the century, there existed a certain amount of collaboration between the two branches of Islam. As we saw earlier, traditionalists who were part of the Shafi'i schools of jurisprudence in Indonesia had not been spared by the winds of reformism which had swept through Indonesian Islam. The traditionalists who advocated a return to the orthodoxy of the *madhhab* were in reality adopting a similar approach to their reformist opponents, and some traditionalists even joined reformist groups. Several representatives of the traditionalist *kaum tua* branch, for example, participated in the foundation of Persatuan Islam. This, of course, was several years before Persatuan Islam became the defender of *kaum muda*, the modernist branch of Islam.[86] Another example is that of Kyai Abdul Wahab Hasbullah, who was one of the linchpins of the traditionalist movement but also participated in the Sarekat Islam group.[87] His work in the traditionalist movement drew him closer to Kyai Hasjim As'j'ari, the heir of a prestigious family of *ulamas* and the founder of the Tebuireng Pesantren in the East Javanese region of Jombang which became a focal point for the traditionalist revival.

These "pioneers of tradition" agreed with modernists on the necessity to reform the curriculum of Koranic schools in order to introduce western subjects.[88] They often read the same newspapers and had the same opinion on the necessity to open up to the modern world.[89]

---

[86] It was not until 1926 that the traditionalist representatives left Persis to found their own organisation, which was later to be integrated into NU. Federspiel, *Persatuan Islam: Islamic Reform in Twentieth Century Indonesia*, p. 14.

[87] On the role played by Kyai Wahab, see Feillard, *Islam et armée dans l'Indonésie contemporaine*, pp. 24 ff.

[88] The efforts made in this regard by Kyai Hasjim Asjari, who introduced the teaching of general subjects into his pesantren in 1929 can be likened to Mohammad Natsir's endeavours at the time within Persatuan Islam.

[89] Aboebakar, *Sejarah Hidup K.H.A. Wahid Hasjim*, Panitya Buku Peringatan alm. K.H.A. Wahid Hasjim (Jakarta, 1957), pp. 152 ff.

However, as the years went by and the number of reformist organisations grew, the traditionalists began to feel less and less at home in them. The malaise, which had remained in the background for a long time but finally came to the fore with the question of the Caliphate, was fuelled by two factors: the ongoing transformation of Sarekat Islam into the political branch of Muhammadiyah and the questioning of the authority of traditionalist *ulamas* by the modernists, who judged them to be too out of date (*kolot*). The first Al-Islam congress, held in 1922 in Cirebon, was the scene of violent confrontations on this issue between representatives of *kaum tua* and *kaum muda*.[90] At the second congress held in Garut in 1924, only the modernist movement was represented,[91] and in January 1926 when it was decided to send two Indonesian representatives to the World Pan-Islamic Congress to be held in Mecca in June of that year, it was again two modernists, Tjokroaminoto and K.H. Mansur, who were chosen.[92] For the traditionalist branch, it was essential to be able to defend its religious practices which had been called into question by the Wahhabi purists. They therefore decided to create a Committee for the Reconquering of Hijaz (Komite Merembuk Hijaz) which was to represent the traditionalist branch before King Ibn Saud. To help in this task, an organisation was set up a few days later, called "the Revival of the Ulama" (Nahdlatul Ulama), which officialised the split between the two branches of Islam.

At the same time as Islam's political unity fell apart, the identification of nationalism with Islam, which Sarekat Islam had managed to embody, also ended, with the establishment of a powerful secular nationalist branch. With the exception of the Marxist movement which had fallen into disarray since the attempted insurrection in 1926, several organisations contributed to the emergence of a political movement no longer bound by references to Islam. The Taman Siswa organisation, for example, founded in Yogyakarta in 1921 by Ki Hadjar

---

[90] Greg Fealy, "Ulama dan Politics in Indonesia: A History of Nahdlatul Ulama, 1952–1967", PhD thesis, Monash University, 1998, p. 29.

[91] Van Niel, *The Emergence of the Modern Indonesian Elite*, p. 209.

[92] The Indonesian Al-Islam Kongres joined the World Islamic Congress and became its East Indies section (MAIHS). A permanent secretariat was established in Surabaya under Agus Salim. Alexandre Von Arx, "L'évolution politique en Indonésie de 1900 à 1942", PhD thesis, Fribourg University, Artigianelli-Monza, Fribourg, 1949, p. 182.

Dewantoro, developed a network of schools which promoted an education system blending aspects of Javanese and Western culture. These schools became the crucible for many of the Indonesian nationalist leaders. But the organisation which played the biggest part in the birth of this secular movement was Perhimpunan Indonesia (Indonesian Union).

Initially merely a students' organisation (known as the Indies Association) composed of Indonesians studying in the Netherlands, Perhimpunan Indonesia's development as a nationalist movement was the unintentional outcome of the colonial government's ethical policy. The colonial authorities had created a system of scholarships which allowed the brightest Indonesian pupils to pursue their studies in the metropolis; the aim of this project was to create an indigenous elite, which they naturally hoped would be favourable to Dutch interests. However, this generous policy however quickly backfired. Perhimpunan Indonesia, as it became known after its transformation into a nationalist organisation in 1922, was an anti-colonial organisation, and it fully exploited its network of former scholarship pupils, who had now returned to their home country, in an attempt to build a pro-independence party for the Dutch East Indies.[93] These efforts came to fruition in 1927 with the birth of the National Indonesian Party (Partai Nasional Indonesia, PNI). The new party came rapidly under the control of the charismatic personality of a young engineer educated in Bandung: Sukarno. The first version of the PNI had a short and turbulent exitence. By 1930, it was outlawed and saw its members disperse into several small parties (Partai Rakyat Indonesia, Partindo and Klub Pendidikan, for example). Despite the break-up of the party, Sukarno already exercised at this time considerable influence over Indonesian political life. In the hope of bringing about a future independent Indonesia made up of non-Muslims as well as Muslims, he wished to limit Islam to the private sphere and so became the mouthpiece for a secular conception of the state and the champion of an Indonesian form of Kemalism, though in a less anti-religious form than the original version. Through the epic debates he held with Ahmad Hassan and Mohammad Natsir (at that time Hassan's brilliant right-hand man within Persis), he obliged the supporters of a political role

---

[93] Van Niel, *The Emergence of the Modern Indonesian Elite*, pp. 119–22.

for Islam to clarify their vision for the future.[94] Though he was not able to shake Ahmad Hassan's belief in his own radicalism, he undoubtedly contributed to Natsir's conversion to a certain form of realism, the extent of which could be seen later in the 1950s when Natsir became prime minister.

The emergence of new organisations onto the Indonesian political landscape was not the only reason for the reformist movement's decline in power. During the 1930s, while a new generation of nationalist leaders was forming in the organisations which had sprouted from the PNI after it was banned, political Islam was continuing to splinter, riven by conflicting egos and disagreements on which strategy to follow.[95] In 1933, Soekiman was expelled from Sarekat Islam following a dispute with Tjokroaminto, one of its leaders.[96] Those within SI who disapproved of this decision created a committee called the Persatuan Islam Indonesia and, along with the PSII Merdeka from Yogyakarta, created a new party: the Partai Islam Indonesia (PARTII). Although this new party received a favourable reception in many parts of Java, it eventually waned and disappeared in the years following its foundation. Its leaders, who were close to important figures in Muhammadiyah, notably its president, K.H. Mas Mansur, had suggested that Sarekat Islam should consider changing their *hijra* policy and no longer view it as an immutable principle which could not be adapted to particular events and circumstances. They also asked SI to limit themselves to politics and to leave social care and educational projects under the responsibility of the organisations which had been created for this purpose. It was as a result of SI's refusal of these requests that Partai Islam Indonesia (PII) was founded in 1937. While all this was going on, the dispute within SI concerning what attitude to adopt towards

---

[94] See, in particular, his "Surat-surat Islam dari Endeh" in *Dibawah Bendera Revolusi*, vol. 1 (Jakarta, 1964), pp. 325–47.

[95] In the following years, it was the PNI rather than SI which led Indonesian rural unrest. This consolidated its role in the struggle against colonial domination. Harry J. Benda, *The Crescent and the Rising Sun: Indonesian Islam under the Japanese Occupation 1942–1945* (The Hague and Bandung: W. Van Hoeve Ltd, 1958), p. 55.

[96] Soekiman publicly denounced the embezzlement carried out by SI leaders within Persatuan Pegawai Pegadaian Hindia (the East Indies Union of Employees of the Pious Mounts). Noer, *The Modernist Muslim Movement in Indonesia*, p. 155. Accusations of financial misdealings had already been made against Tjokroaminoto during the first decade of the century.

the colonial authorities had become even more rancorous after Tjokro-aminoto's death, with the new leadership's opposition to any form of cooperation leading Agus Salim to found a rival organisation, Barisan Penjadar PSII (Awareness Front of the PSII).[97]

As the 1930s came to a close, the Islamic political movement, led by the reformists, now had to reconcile itself to the fact that it was no longer the only component of the nationalist movement. They were now forced to come to a consensus with traditionalists before being able to speak on behalf of Indonesian Muslims, and so in 1937 they joined with the traditionalists in a Supreme Council of the Muslims of Indonesia (Madjlis Islam A'la Indonesia, MIAI). They also participated alongside nationalists in two organisations created in 1939: the Political Federation of Indonesia (Gabungan Politik Indonesia, GAPI) and the Council of the Indonesian People (Madjlis Rakjat Indonesia, MRI) which was composed of the GAPI, the MIAI and the Federation of Government Workers (the PVPN).

This historic alliance between the different strands of Indonesian nationalism in which the Islamic branch had managed—with some difficulty—to find its place did not survive the debates provoked by the question of how to react to the Japanese threat, however. The fragile alliance fell apart at the beginning of 1942 when the Indonesian nationalists, without consulting the representatives of the Islamic movements, spoke out on behalf of the MRI to support the Dutch in the war against Japan.

Masyumi, which brought together in 1945 all the Islamic organisations in Indonesia, inherited the complex history of these movements which we have just sketched. The party carried with it the *umma's* hopes for unity, and it often made reference to the 12 Islamic Congresses (Al-Islam first, and then Konggres Muslimin Indonesia) which had been held in Indonesia between 1921 and 1941. The commemorations of these congresses during the 1950s provided Masyumi's newspapers and magazines with opportunities to make stirring appeals for unity.[98] However, the legacy of the interwar years for the party also included an extraordinary propensity for in-fighting amongst the representatives of the Muslim community. This characteristic of Indonesian Islamic identity was less celebrated, but it was no doubt the one which

---

[97] Ibid., p. 163.
[98] See, for example, *Suara Partai Masjumi*, February 1951.

left the greatest mark on Masyumi. The end of the 1920s saw the appearance within the Muslim community of a culture in which power tended to split into little baronies. This could be the result either of the ambition of a charismatic leader, geographic or social differences within the Muslim community, or sometimes because of differences in worship practices. Masyumi bore the scars of this culture of divisiveness which was responsible for the schisms of 1947 (the revival of the Partai Sarekat Islam Indonesia) and 1952 (the departure of Nahdlatul Ulama).

Another legacy of the 1920s and 30s for the party was the organisational networks which had been established at that time. The future Masyumi leaders had, for the most part, earned their political spurs in the 1920s and 30s in the organisations which we have just mentioned. Within the Masyumi party, wings formed which reflected the organisations they had previously belonged to and which they generally remained faithful to. The changes in the composition of the party leadership over the years were an accurate reflection of the evolution in the balance of power between these different groups.[99] At its foundation in 1945, the party executive reflected Masyumi's aspiration to bring together the different Muslim organisations but also revealed their respective political influences. Composed of a Party Leadership Council (Dewan Pimpian) and of a Religious Council (Madjelis Sjuro, which literally means Consultative Council), the partly leadership was mainly composed of former members of PSII (Abikusno Tjokrosujoso, Harsono Tjokroaminoto and Anwar Tjokroaminoto); and also of those who had joined it after breaking away from both PII (Soekiman, Wali al-Fatah, Mr A. Kasmat and M. Natsir) and from Gerakan Penjadar (H.A. Salim and Mohamad Roem). Behind PSII came Muhammadiyah, which had eight representatives on the committee (Prawoto Mangku-sasmito, Mawardi, Faried Ma'ruf, Junus Anis, Faqih Usman, Dr. Sjam-suddin, Ki Bagus Hadikusumo, Kasman Singodimedjo and K.H.A. Wahab), twice as many as Nahdlatul Ulama which only had four seats (K.H.A. Dahlan, K.H. Fathurrahman, Hasjim As'jari and K.H.A. Wahid Hasjim). Three small local organisations accounted for the remaining seats: the Perikatan Umat Islam (PUI) from Majalengka, a small traditionalist organisation represented by K.H. Abdul Halim; the Persatuan Umat Islam Indonesia from Sukabumi, represented by

---

[99] Although the members of the Party's executive committee were elected by the congress, they were not considered as representatives of their original organisations.

K.H. Sanusi; and the Madjedis Islam Tinggi (MIT) from Sumatra, represented by Sjech M. Djamil Djambek.

10 years later, the political diversity of Masyumi had noticeably diminished. It had become the descendant of a much more coherent political movement made up of activists from Jong Islamieten Bond (JIB), Muhammadiyah and Sarekat Islam's splinter groups. Of the 57 Masyumi deputies elected to Parliament, only one of them said that he had been a member of Sarekat Islam. However, 15 deputies had come from its splinter groups, namely Gerakan Penjadar and Partai Islam Indonesia, and they were often members of Muhammadiyah as well. 12 deputies stated that they had been members of JIB. The break with PSII in 1947 was essentially along the lines of the divisions which affected PSII's illustrious forerunner Sarekat Islam in the 1930s. In other words, those who had been loyal during the war to H.O.S. Tjokroaminoto and to his brother, Abikusno Tjokrosujoso, transferred their loyalty to Harsono Tjokroaminoto, the son of Sarekat Islam's founder. Conversely, those activists who had split from SI and joined breakaway groups such as Gerakan Penjadar (PII) refused to join PSII in 1947 and remained members of Masyumi. The same loyalty could be seen amongst the traditionalists in the party, as only two Masyumi deputies declared that they were members of Nahdlatul Ulama. As for the other organisations mentioned in deputies' biographies, they attest to the party's implantation on a local level (Persuatan Islam Cirebon, Persatuan Ulama Seluruh Aceh and Al-Jamiyatul Wasilyah from North Sumatra, for example).[100]

If we move on to look at the executive committee of the party in the early 1950s, we can identify a small coterie of leaders, united by links that had been created in the 1930s. Jong Islamieten Bond, especially its Bandung branch, had a significant role to play in creating the bonds that existed between this little group of individuals. All of them were born between 1904 and 1910, and took their first steps in the political arena under the benevolent eyes of the elder members of Sarekat Islam and Muhammadiyah.

Mohammad Natsir, who was the most prominent member of the party leadership from 1949 onwards, was born in Alahan Panjang in West Sumatra in 1908. Having completed his first year of studies in Padang in his home province, he settled in Bandung in 1927 to attend

---

[100] Parlaungan, *Hasil Rakjat Memilih, Tokoh-Tokoh Parlemen di republik Indonesia.*

classes given in a Dutch secondary school (AMS). At that time, he joined JIB, and in 1929, became head of its local branch. Thanks to his position in JIB, he came in contact with Haji Agus Salim, who is often considered to be the spiritual mentor to the young generation of modernists which Natsir was part of.[101] More importantly, he also became close, at that time, to other activists within JIB who, 20 years later, were to become his right-hand men within the Masyumi leadership, namely Kasman Singodimedjo, Mohamad Roem and Jusuf Wibisono. These early days earned the future leader of Masyumi a solid reputation as something of an expert on religion. Disconcerted by the lack of interest shown by other students in Islam, he organised a series of classes and lectures to remedy this situation.[102]

Jusuf Wibisono, who was one year younger than Natsir, attended the same school, and he soon joined the Bandung branch of JIB. He subsequently moved to Batavia in order to pursue third-level studies at the Higher School of Law (Rechts Hooge School) and became the leader of JIB's branch there. In Batavia, he met Mohamad Roem (born in 1908) and Kasman Singodimedjo, who at that time was the national president of JIB.[103] Following a disagreement concerning the best strategy for the organisation to follow, Wibisono and Roem decided in 1934 to create a new organisation, the Studenten Islam Studie-club, whose

---

[101] On this period, see in particular, Yusril Ihza, "Combining Activism and Intellectualism: The Biography of Mohammad Natsir", *Studia Islamika* 2, 1 (1995) and Aboebakar, *Sejarah Hidup K.H.A. Wahid Hasjim*, pp. 217–20. The dates used by the latter are sometimes far-fetched, however.

[102] Ajip Rosidi, *Moh. Natsir sebuah biografi* (Jakarta: Pt Girimukti Pasaka, 1990), pp. 51–4.

[103] Kasman, according to his father, was born in 1904, but most documents relating to him mention 1908 as his date of birth. The explanation for this is rather comical: given the lack of a reliable civil register, it was common at the time to allow a child to register for school when he was able to pass his right hand over his head and touch his left ear. When Kasman was a boy, his younger brother was already at school while he himself was still unable to register. When he was finally accepted, he decided to move his date of birth back four years, so embarrassed was he to be behind his brother. Panitia peringatan 75 tahun, *Kasman, Hidup itu berjuang, Kasman Singodimedjo 75 tahun* (Jakarta: Bulan Bintang, 1982), p. 4. Mohammed Roem, Kasman Singodimedjo and Jusuf Wibisono had already become friends a few years previously when attending medical school (STOVIA) together. Wibisono was later obliged to abandon his studies after a medical visit declared him unfit.

objectives were close to JIB's but who only admitted students, unlike JIB which also admitted secondary school pupils. The new organisation's newspaper, which was first called *Orgaan van de Studenten Islam Studie-Club* before changing its name to *Moslims Reveil*—though it continued to be written in Dutch—was an efficient means of disseminating the Muslim nationalist movement's ideas amongst students.[104] The organisation was joined in 1938 by Boerhanoeddin Harahap— born in 1917 and appointed to the Masyumi executive committee in 1952—who became its secretary during his studies in the Rechts Hooge School after having been a JIB activist while studying in Yogyakarta.[105] One of the few Masyumi leaders to have been a member neither of JIB, the *Studie-Club* nor PII was Sjafruddin Prawiranegara. Born in 1911 in the region of Banten, his education followed a very classical path—he attended an AMS in Bandung before entering the BHS in Batavia in 1939—which brought him rapidly into contact with his future political allies. However, the first organisation he joined, the Unitas Studiosorum Indonesiensis (USI), was non-political. It had been set up with the help of the Dutch authorities with the aim of thwarting the influence of student nationalist movements.[106]

At the same time, in Medan a second group of modernist intellectuals emerged which, unlike Natsir and Isa Anshary, had not moved to Java. They were led mainly by Z.A. Ahmad, Yunan Nasution and Abu Hanifah, who all later became members of Masyumi's leadership council in the 1950s, as well as by HAMKA, who was part of the Muhammadiyah leadership and later a Masyumi deputy in 1955. Although this small group of intellectuals came to prominence in particular for their considerable publishing output, which we mentioned earlier, they were also active politically. They were initially members

---

[104] Soebagio I.N., *Jusuf Wibisono. Karang di Tengah Gelombang* (Jakarta: Gunung Agung, 1980), pp. 27–8.
[105] Busjairi Badruzzaman, *Boerhanoeddin Harahap Pilar Demokrasi* (Jakarta: Bulan Bintang, 1982), pp. 12–3.
[106] See Benedict R. O'G Anderson, *Java in a Time of Revolution: Occupation and Resistance, 1944–1946* (Ithaca, NY: Cornell University Press, 1961), p. 439. Sjafruddin's biography published by *Abadi* a few weeks before the 1955 elections says nothing about his involvement in this organisation, while the one published by Ajip Rosidi, *Sjafruddin Prawiranegara, Islam sebagai pedoman hidup. Kumpulan karangan terpilih disunting oleh Ajip Rosidi*, vol. 1 (Jakarta: Idayu, 1986), p. 8, mentions nothing of the links between USI and the colonial administration.

of Permi, and when it was outlawed in 1933, most of them joined Soekiman and Natsir in PII,[107] and indeed Z.A. Ahmad became head of PII in Sumatra.[108]

The contacts made before the outbreak of the war by the future Masyumi leadership were not exclusively in Muslim modernist circles. The enthusiasm typical of many young people's political activism added to the very wide range of organisations that sprang up during the 1920s and 30s, and meant that the wide-ranging nationalist movement contained many different and sometimes tortuous political itineraries. Soekiman Wirjosandjojo, who was president of Masyumi between 1945 and 1951, started out in politics as a secular nationalist. Born in 1898 in Sewu, near Sukarta in Central Java, he came from a family that worked in the retail business and was close to organisations which were the forerunners of the Javanese nationalist movement. His brother Satiman Wirjosandjojo was one of the founding members of Tri Koro Dharmo (Three Noble Goals), the youth organisation within Budi Utomo, which, three years after its foundation, changed its name to Jong Java in 1915.[109] As a young man, Soekiman, who graduated from medical school (STOVIA) in 1922, went on to study in the Netherlands where he became actively involved in Perhimpunan Indonesia. He became president of the organisation in 1925 thanks to the support of Mohammad Hatta, the future vice president of the Republic of Indonesia.[110] Shortly after that, he returned to Indonesia and continued his political activity there in the ranks of PSII. As we do not have a detailed biography of Soekiman, it is unfortunately difficult to explain this change in political orientation, but it shows that there was a certain amount of interplay between the different strands within Indonesian nationalism.[111] Indeed, Soekiman maintained excellent relations

---

[107] In 1930, the modernist organisation, Sumatra Thawalib, founded by HAMKA's father, broadened its activities beyond its traditional field of education and became involved in the political domain. It later became Persatuan Muslimin Indonesia (Indonesian Muslim Union, PMI), and in 1932 took the name of Permi.

[108] Soebagijo I.N., *Riwayat Hidup dan Perjuangan H. Zainal Abidin Ahmad* (Jakarta: Pustaka Antara, 1985).

[109] Van Niel, *The Emergence of the Modern Indonesian Elite*, p. 169.

[110] C.L.M. Penders, ed., *Mohammad Hatta, Indonesian Patriot: Memoirs* (Singapore: Gunung Agung, 1991), p. 95.

[111] The only book to be published on Soekiman that we are aware of is a collection of his political writings, which contains no biographical details.

with secular nationalists, and in 1932, it was to Mohammad Hatta that he gave the job of editor-in-chief of the daily newspaper which he had just launched, *Utusan Indonesia* ("the Indonesian Messenger").[112]

Another political career illustrating the ties that were forged outside of Islamic circles is that of Isa Anshary. Isa was head of Masyumi in West Java before becoming a member of the executive committee of the party in 1954. He was considered a radical, and was very hostile to the nationalist secularist movement. From 1953, he repeatedly launched stinging attacks on Sukarno, despite the fact that the president had in fact been Isa's first political mentor.[113] Isa came from Sungai Batang in Central Sumatra and arrived in Bandung in 1932 at the age of 16. It was at this time that he became fascinated with the ideas put forward by Sukarno and he even went so far as to spend a whole night in a conference hall so as to be able to listen to one of Sukarno's speeches.[114] This revelation convinced Isa to abandon his initial project, which was to pursue his studies in Yogyakarta, and to take up a political career instead. He signed up for Partindo, lying about his age to do so, and threw himself into political activism. At the same time, he became one of the leaders of the Bandung branch of the Persatuan Pemuda Rakjat Indonesia (Popular Union of Indonesian Youth), a radical revolutionary organisation. Unlike Soekiman, the circumstances of Anshary's conversion to Islamic nationalism are well-documented. It was a conversion which further demonstrated the links that existed between the different strands within nationalism, although those very strands were later to fall out over various issues. Alongside his involvement in Partindo, Anshary was also taking part in religion classes organised by Perstuan Islam. He gradually became more involved in the Muslim movement and took over the leadership of the Preparatory Committee of Permi's Bandung Branch (Panitia Persiapan Permi Tjabang Bandung). The Sumatran party at that time considered establishing itself in Java, but it eventually abandoned the idea following an agreement with Partindo's leadership. The two parties realised that they had common goals and decided not to compete against each other. After the break-up of Partindo in 1934, Anshary restricted his political activity to Islamic

---

[112] Penders, ed., *Mohammad Hatta, Indonesian Patriot: Memoirs*, pp. 139–40.

[113] See *infra*, chapter 4.

[114] He did so in order to avoid the police stopping him from getting into the conference hall; at that time, political rallies were forbidden for those under 18. Aboebakar, *Sejarah Hidup K.H.A. Wahid Hasjim*, p. 220.

organisations, becoming a member first of Muhammadiyah and then of Perstuan Islam. It was at this time that his political career became linked to Natsir's, whom he was very close to, and when Natsir later became chairman of the Bandung branch of the Partai Islam Indonesia, Isa became its secretary.[115]

The creation of a multi-party system at the end of 1945 as well as subsequent political events meant that political careers, which had up until then evolved in a relatively erratic fashion, became a lot more predictable. After independence, it became a lot rarer for political figures or activists to move from secular nationalism to Islamic nationalism. The pursuit of power and the prospect of elections led the two sides to develop opposing policies despite the fact that their electoral bases often came from more or less the same sociological class. The paths followed over the years by Mohammad Hatta and Soekiman Wirjosandjojo show how fine the boundary was between the two movements. Although the two men were very close and shared the same opinions at university, by 1945 they symbolised two very different visions for society. Their policies were not as far apart as their spirited clashes might lead one to believe however, and indeed, during the 1950s and the first years of the New Order, their paths were to join again.[116]

Masyumi—A Japanese Invention?

Although the Japanese occupation of Indonesia only lasted three years, from March 1942 to August 1945, it constitutes an essential stage in the emergence of Masyumi. During this period, the Japanese military government tried to harness Islam to serve their war policy. This policy was known as "the Asian Co-prosperity Sphere", but it was not implemented consistently, sometimes carried out in earnest and other times half-heartedly. It gave birth in November 1943 to a first version of Masyumi: the Consultative Counsel of Indonesian Muslims (Madjlis Sjuro Muslimin Indonesia). It is not as easy as it might appear to determine the extent of this organisation's influence on the Muslim party of the same name founded in November 1945. The composition of the Japanese version of Masyumi can probably explain the way positions

---

[115] Ibid., p. 221.
[116] Cf. infra, Epilogue, and Deliar Noer, *Mohammad Hatta, biografi politik* (Jakarta: LP3ES, 1990), pp. 463–4.

of responsibility in the new Masyumi were distributed between, on the one hand, *ulamas* who were at the head of important Muslim organisations (such as Muhammadiyah and Nahdlatul Ulama) and on the other, politicians who had come from Sarekat Islam. The former had been in charge of the Japanese Masyumi and so remained somewhat in the background when the party was founded, whereas the latter had been less involved in collaboration with the Japanese and so took over most of the party's executive positions.

It was in the middle of the 1920s that the Japanese came into contact with Islam, and soon afterwards they chose it to be one of the main pillars of their regional policy. They sent students to Egypt to become trained in the art of Muslim propaganda, and in 1939, Tokyo hosted a pan-Islamic conference in which MIAI participated. In the months leading up to the Japanese invasion, clandestine networks were established in Indonesia, which contributed to the success of the landing of troops in at least two regions of Sumatra.[117] Once these troops had a foothold in the country, they attempted to harness the support of Muslim organisations in order to curry favour with the local population.

The initial measures taken by the occupier, however, indicated a refusal to allow Islam any form of political expression. Only two organisations—PSII and PII—were officially abolished, in March 1942,[118] but the Japanese military authorities also set up at this time their own system for controlling Islam. This was composed essentially of two organisations: a Preparatory Committee for the Unity of the Muslim Community (Persiapan Persatuan Ummat Islam), led by Abikusno Tjokrosujoso, a former president of PSII and a brother of H.O.S. Tjokroaminoto; and an Office of Religious Affairs (Shumubu), which was first of all led by a Japanese official until August 1944, when a traditionalist leader, K. Hasjim Asj'ari, took over. As the Japanese occupier wanted to be able to avail of a mass movement which would reach all Muslims, they allowed MIAI to be revived in September 1942. The organisation was given an important role to play in the "Triple A Movement"—"Japan leader of Asia, Japan protector of Asia and Japan light of Asia."

---

[117] Benda, *The Crescent and the Rising Sun*, pp. 103–7.
[118] The other political parties were not directly banned, but as all political activity was now outlawed, they were effectively muzzled.

This recognition of Islam's prominence in the country did not, however, fulfil the hopes which had initially been raised on both sides. The Indonesians quickly realised that the occupiers' goodwill was nothing more than a carefully planned attempt to use Muslim organisations for their own ends, that is to say the enhancement of Japan's military operation. The *ulamas* cooperated tentatively at first, but this cooperation was rapidly jeopardised by a series of Japanese blunders. The ceremony of *sakeirei* imposed by the Japanese was particularly hard for religious dignitaries to accept. This ceremony was a reverence for the emperor performed facing the direction of Tokyo and so was offensive to Muslims because of its similarity with *rukun salat*, the Muslim prayer performed facing Mecca. Indeed, two members of Nahdlatul Ulama's leadership, Hasjim Asj'ari and Kiai Mahfudz, spent several months in prison for refusing to perform this reverence. In addition to this problem, it seemed that the Japanese authorities were beginning to lose control of MIAI, which was dominated by former members of PSII. The organisation had put in place, since January 1943, a vast programme to help people in need, which was financed by a centralised system of almsgiving (*zakat*). The system, known as Bait al-Mal, quickly became successful. It soon extended to 35 regencies in Java and was in danger of competing with the Office of Religious Affairs that had been set up by the Japanese to control Islam at a local level. It was for this reason that the military authorities intervened to shut down the operation only a few months after the project had been launched.[119]

Realising the failure of their "Muslim operation", the Japanese authorities then turned their hopes and attention to the nationalist camp which they had, up until then, been marginalised. In March 1943, they created the Putera (Pusat Tenaga Rakjat, meaning Organisation for the People's Power), which gathered under one umbrella all the political and social care associations of Java and Madura and was charged with the task of preparing Indonesia for independence. The new organisation had a collegial leadership, known as the *empat seangkai* (four-in-one-bundle), reflecting the new balance of power which the Japanese wanted to impose. Of the four members of the new organisation's leadership, there was only one representative of political Islam, K.H. Mansur, who was one of Muhammadiyah's leaders, compared to three

---

[119] Benda, *The Crescent and the Rising Sun*, pp. 145–7.

nationalist leaders, Sukarno, Mohammad Hatta and Ki Hadjar Dewantoro. A few months later, the Putera was allowed to set up its own
militia, the Volunteer Army for the Defence of the Nation (Soekarela
Tentara Pembela Tanah Air, PETA).

However, by the end of 1943, the shortcomings of this new dispensation were already beginning to show. Realising that the Putera
was achieving more for the nationalist movement than for the Japanese
war effort, the military authorities decided to close it down.[120] At the
same time, they once again turned to the Muslim community, though
this time they looked to the rural Muslim dignitaries to help them
thwart the ambitions of both the urban Islamists and the secular
nationalists who had let them down in the past. In November 1943,
the Japanese founded the Consultative Council of Indonesian Muslims
(Madjelis Sjuro Muslimin Indonesia, Masyumi) and by so doing rid
themselves of MIAI which was dominated by former members of PSII,
who had by this time started to adopt an anti-Japanese tone. For the
Japanese, then, Masyumi was a fresh attempt to manipulate the Indonesian Muslim community to their own advantage. Two types of
members could join the new organisation: firstly, Muslim associations
who had been accorded a legal status by the military government, and
secondly, authorised *kiais* and *ulamas* whose authorisation, naturally
enough, had been given by the Office of Religious Affairs. The issue of
the voting rights which these religious figures would receive was not
clearly dealt with in the organisation's statutes, however.[121] Two organisations were to dominate Masyumi: Muhammadiyah and Nahdlatul
Ulama, which were the only two organisations to obtain the necessary
legal status when Masyumi was founded. They were joined later by two
smaller traditionalist organisations, Persatoean Oemmat Islam Indonesia
(the Union of the Indonesian Ummah) led by K. Ahmad Sanusi, and
Perikatan Oemmat Islam (the Association of the Ummah) led by K.H.
Abdul Halim in Cirebon.[122] By favouring relations with non-political
associations and prominent local figures, the Japanese wanted to defuse

---

[120] It was replaced in March 1944 by Perhimpunan Kebaktian Rakyat (the
People's Loyalty Association), better known under its Japanese name of Djawa
Hokokai.

[121] Benda, *The Crescent and the Rising Sun*, p. 151.

[122] Two associations which included in their statutes the goals of the Asian Co-
Prosperity Sphere.

any potential local rebellions which Islamic movements could become a focal point for. This unofficial role given to Masyumi became apparent in the early months of 1944 when the occupying authorities increased their requisition of rice from peasants. In February, a rebellion broke out against this decision in the village of Singaparna, near Tasikmalaya in the Priangan regency. It was led by Kiai Zainal Mustapha, a prominent religious leader in the region and a member of Nahdlatul Ulama. Following repression of the uprising by the police force, several Masyumi emissaries were sent to the region to explain to the local population that their former *kiai* had lost his senses and had strayed from the true path of Islam.[123]

Up until February 1945, Masyumi benefitted from the Japanese authorities' urgent desire to limit the influence of nationalists by promoting a countervailing force within the Islamic community. In January 1944, for example, a new organisation, Djawa Hokokai, was created to replace Putera, which meant that the nationalist organisation was no longer the exclusive representative of the Indonesian people. Djawa Hokokai was a vast movement which included nationalists as well as numerous organisations controlled by the occupier. At the same time, Masyumi was given every means necessary to extend its influence throughout the country. While MIAI had never been able to spread its organisational network beyond its headquarters in Jakarta, the new Muslim organisation received the authorisation to create branches at every administrative level, from regency to village. It was even allowed to establish itself in the neighbourhood associations (*tonari gumi*) which had been created two years earlier by the Japanese. This enabled local Islamic brigades (*barisan pekerja*) close to Masyumi to infiltrate these structures, and meant that at least one person in each *tonari gumi* was a member of these brigades. Finally, in December 1944, in reaction to the creation in September of that year of the *Barisan Pelopor* (the Pioneer Corps), which was run entirely by nationalist members of the civilian population, the Japanese announced the creation of an army of Muslim volunteers: Hizboellah (the Army of Allah). They were intended to be the reserve army of the PETA but in fact became Masyumi's army. The organisation was charged with setting up Hizboellah's central command and regional delegations as well as the provision of equipment for its troops. The militia's recruits, after three months of

---

[123] Ibid., p. 160.

training, were then supposed to train the students of Koranic schools themselves.[124]

The promise of Indonesian independence in "the near future", made during a speech given by the Japanese prime minister, Koiso, on 7 September 1944, marked the end of this subtle policy of manipulating the balance of power between Muslims and nationalists, and also announced a swing in favour of the latter. Six months later in March 1945, the composition of the Investigation Committee for the Independence of Indonesia (Badan Penjelidik Kemerdekaan Indonesia, BPKI), nominated by the Japanese, confirmed this new balance of power. Of the 63 members initially nominated, only 10 could be considered part of the Islamist movement, and most of these lacked the political and administrative skills necessary to be able to contribute meaningfully to the debates.[125]

Although Masyumi was not in principle supposed to have a political dimension, the role given by the Japanese to some important Muslim figures within the country's institutions in the months leading up to September 1944, and most importantly the role it played in villages, meant that it had become a highly political organisation. In the space of a little over a year, Masyumi had achieved what no other Muslim organisation had before. It had built a network throughout the country, recruited a militia of considerable size and, above all, it now benefitted from a notoriety which could rival that of the nationalist leaders, Sukarno and Hatta.[126] This was the part of the Japanese organisation's legacy which the founding members of the party wished to keep when they decided in November 1945, after a difficult and protracted debate, to retain the name Masyumi.[127] They took some time to decide the matter at their inaugural congress as they knew that the Japanese legacy was also associated with collaboration with the enemy which, during the first months of the country's independence, recalled some embarrassing memories for the party. Apart from a few rare

---

[124] Ibid., p. 280n27.

[125] Benedict R. O'G Anderson, *Some Aspects of Indonesian Politics under the Japanese Occupation: 1944–1945*, Interim Reports Series (Ithaca, NY: Cornell University Press, 1961), p. 21.

[126] In order to obtain the authorisations necessary to organise any gathering, almost all religious meetings from the end of 1943 took place under the aegis of Masyumi. Aboebakar, *Sejarah Hidup K.H.A. Wahid Hasjim*, p. 334.

[127] See infra Chapter 2.

hostile actions towards the occupier, Mayumi otherwise scrupulously performed the role of propagandist for Japanese imperialism. In October 1944, for example, Masyumi adopted a series of resolutions on the future of Indonesia, the first of which concerned the "recognition of the role played by the commander of the Japanese army in the future independence of Indonesia." The party called on people, in their resolution, to "mobilise further still the combined forces of the Indonesian *umma* so as to precipitate final victory and to combat the manoeuvres and offensives carried out by the enemy who wishes to prevent the independence of Indonesia and the liberation of Islam." It also invited all Muslims to "fight nobly together side by side with the Japanese, in the path ordained by Allah, to destroy the cruel enemy."[128] In the same vein, the party's official newspaper, *Suara Muslimin Indonesia*, up until the spring of 1945, published the death count of the "enemy soldiers" (*serdadu musuh*) killed in battle in the Pacific Islands.[129]

Did this collaboration with the Japanese weigh on the party members' minds when they came to make their choice for party leadership in November 1945? The answer appears to be no, as there were no real purges within the party after the Japanese occupation. In fact, four of the five most important leaders of Japanese Masyumi—K.H. Hasjim Asj'ari, Ki Bagus Hadikusumo, K.H.A. Wahid Hasjim and K.H. Abdul Wahab—were given positions in the upper echelons of the party. The only one not to appear in the party's new leadership structure was K.H. Mas Mansur, one of the most collaborationist of the religious dignitaries. He was arrested by the allies at the end of the war and was initially in danger of facing trial before finally being released. His health deteriorated considerably during his time in prison and he died in April 1946, only a few months after his release.[130] Mas Mansur's absence from the party's leadership can no doubt be attributed to his poor health, however, and not to his collaborationist activity. It should be noted, though, that the four party leaders mentioned all sat on the religious council (Majelis Syuro) and not on the executive committee of the party. This may have been a choice on their part: it is possible that as religious dignitaries, they preferred to contribute

---

[128] Aboebakar, *Sejarah Hidup K.H.A. Wahid Hasjim*, pp. 340–1.
[129] See, for example, *Suara Muslimin Indonesia*, 21 March 1945.
[130] Soebagijo I.N., *K.H. Mas Mansur. Pembaharu Islam di Indonesia* (Jakarta: Gunung Agung, 1982), pp. 123–4.

to the party through their religious knowledge. However, it can legitimately be argued that their place in the new composition of the party leadership was due in part to their involvement with the Japanese. Those who were elected to the executive committee had managed to distance themselves from the occupier, and so were a more suitable choice to represent the party on the political battlefield of the new Republic.[131] It is true to say that none of them had rebelled openly against the occupier and indeed most of them had been given positions of responsibility by the Japanese authorities. Soekiman, for example, represented Yogyakarta within the Putera, Jusuf Wibisono was a prosecutor for cases concerning commercial law and Natsir was in charge of an education programme in Bandung. However, these positions of responsibility were less important and did not greatly compromise their integrity; in fact, they even allowed them, at times, to disseminate ideas which were hostile to the Japanese. The courses organised by Natsir, for instance, gave him the opportunity to organise, along with Sjafruddin Prawiranegara, a chain of spiritual resistance to Japanese propaganda.[132] In the case of Isa Anshary, who had been appointed secretary of MIAI for the residency of Priangan, he actually spent a month in prison, no doubt because of his action within Angkatan Muda Indonesia, an organisation which promoted the independence of Indonesia.[133]

Most members of Masyumi's new executive committee came from the group of urban Muslims who had headed MIAI and who, as a consequence, had been courted by the Japanese as part of their policy regarding Islam.[134] However, as we have already seen, the creation of

---

[131] It should not be forgotten that the Americans, encouraged by the Dutch government, were wary of Sukarno and Hatta, who were accused of collaborating with the Japanese. This led Sukarno and Hatta to appoint Sjahrir, the main opponent of the Japanese occupation, as prime minister.

[132] Kahin, *Nationalism and Revolution in Indonesia*, p. 113. Kahin, however, does not cite any source to substantiate this affirmation. Deliar Noer, "Masjumi: Its Organization, Ideology, and Political Role in Indonesia", Master thesis, Cornell University, 1960, p. 28, uses testimony from Persatuan Islam's leaders in 1956 to explain that the education programmes organised by the *ulama* in Bandung "may have been directed against the Japanese occupation policy, prompted by Mohammad Natsir, who was in charge of the local education programmes."

[133] Aboebakar, *Sejarah Hidup K.H.A. Wahid Hasjim*, pp. 221–3.

[134] Soekiman, Harsono Tjokroaminoto and Wondoamiseno were members of the MIAI leadership put in place by the Japanese in September 1942. Benda, *The Crescent and the Rising Sun*, p. 113 ff.

Masyumi in November 1943 was precisely what marked the end of Japanese collaboration with MIAI and the beginning of a new policy oriented more towards rural Muslim leaders. With the advent of Indonesian independence, these rural *ulamas*, took a back seat—perhaps because they were obliged to do so—and it was thus the group linked to MIAI who came to the fore again. Abu Hanifah's career is a perfect illustration of this reversal of fortune. As a member of MIAI who was also involved in the Bait al-Mal project, he was given no official position within the Japanese Masyumi.[135] In May 1945, he launched an appeal in *Soeara Muslimin Indonesia* inviting the Masyumi leadership to free itself from Japanese control and to create a new organisation which would bring the Muslim community together.[136] In November 1945, his fortunes changed radically when he became a member of the executive committee of the new Masyumi party.

The period of Japanese occupation had, on the whole, two major consequences on the place occupied by Islam in Indonesian society. As a result of the successive policy U-turns by the Japanese occupying force, both the supporters and the opponents of political Islam benefitted from a significant increase in their potential scope for political action. They now had at their disposal nationwide vehicles for their propaganda and, as result, the notoriety of Islamic and nationalist organisations spread throughout the country. However, at the same time, the Japanese manipulation of the balance of power within political Islam, through its control over both Masyumi and the BPKI, benefitted religious dignitaries without much experience of political battle. This was done at the expense of the pre-war leaders of modernist organisations (Sarekat Islam, PII, Permi, Barisan Penjadar and Jong Islamieten Bond) and it led, as a result, to a favourable balance of power for secular nationalists in their post-war struggle with political Islam.

Although Masyumi originated at a time of a radical break with the past—the "Physical Revolution" of the Indonesian people against the return of the Dutch—it nonetheless bore the marks of the colonial period. Its future leaders identified strongly with the vast movement of renewal which, from the end of the 19th century, had spread to

---

[135] Ibid., p. 259n76.
[136] *Soeara Muslimin Indonesia*, 10 May 1945, quoted in Benda, *The Crescent and the Rising Sun*, p. 287n68.

all corners of the Muslim world, and they looked to Western culture for solutions to their questionings about Muslim identity. Within the Masyumi leadership, a small group of individuals stood out who shared certain common traits. They were products of the education system put in place by the Dutch, often came from Sumatra, and they crossed swords with the previous generation of leaders within Sarekat Islam who were markedly Javanese in origin. They were also part of a tradition which favoured an attitude of openness to the rest of the world, and forged for themselves a political culture which was a mixture of Western references and Muslim values. As members of the Masyumi leadership in the early 1950s, they were the inspiration behind some of the most original pages of its history.

CHAPTER TWO

The Early Signs of Political Schizophrenia: Caught between Stability and Revolution

It took Masyumi almost four years to build a coherent political position, between its foundation in November 1945 and the party congress in December 1949, which saw the young generation, led by Mohammad Natsir, take over the party leadership. It was caught between two opposing forces: a tendency towards unity, which had arisen both from the struggle against the Dutch colonial power and from the party's goal of unifying the whole Muslim community, but also a propensity for division which came from Masyumi's need to carve out a place for itself on the country's fraught political landscape. It appeared during this period to be Janus-faced. On the one hand, a revolutionary organisation built on a sometimes intransigent spirit of nationalism, whose leaders flirted at times with the limits of the law; on the other, a party of government that produced some of the architects of the new Republic whose painstaking work led to the country's recognition by the international community.

The Summer of 1945—From an Islamic State to an "Islamisable" State

The refusal by the Japanese authorities to support the creation of an Islamic state in Indonesia meant that the representatives of the Muslim community had to try to convince their fellow countrymen of its necessity. Over the course of a number of successive forums held between April and August 1945, representatives of various political forces drew up the institutional framework for an independent Indonesia. The Committee for Preparatory Work for Indonesian Independence (Badan Penjelidik Usaha-Usaha Kemerdekaan Indonesia, BPUKI) was at the forefront of these endeavours, holding two sessions: one from 29 May to 2 June, and another from 10 July to 17 July. It was made up of 62 Indonesian members as well as eight special members who were Japanese, one of whom was a committee vice-chairman, and it was overwhelmingly dominated by the supporters of a secular state led by Sukarno and Mohammad Hatta.[1] Although there were few representatives of political Islam—only 16 members in all[2]—they nonetheless succeeded in putting the question of an Islamic state at the top of the agenda. The choice between an Islamic state and a secular state was at the forefront of the committee's debates. However, the tenor of these debates is known to us only through the accounts given in later years by some of its participants, the most comprehensive of which was provided by Muhammad Yamin, one of the main nationalist ideologists.[3]

Pancasila—Sukarno's Challenge to Political Islam

On the eve of independence, the leaders of the Muslim community were in a peculiar situation. The vast majority of them considered

---

[1] The chairman of this committee was Dr. Radjiman Wediodiningrat, one of the founders of the Javanese nationalist movement Budi Utomo in 1908.

[2] Taking into account not only those who had been appointed by the Japanese to represent the Muslim community, but also the members on the committee who systematically supported their proposals. The latter group was composed of Abikusno (PSII), K.H. Ahmad Sanoesi (POII Sukabumi), K.H.A. Halim (POI Madjalengka), Ki Bagoes Hadikoesomo (Muhammadijah), K.H. Masjkoer (N.O), K.H.M. Mansoer (Muhammadijah), R. Rooslan Wongsokoesoemo (ancien Parindra puis Masjumi), R. Sjamsoeddin (Parindra puis Masjumi), Soekiman (Masjumi), K. Wahid Hasjim (NU), Mme Sunarjo Mangunpuspito (Masjumi), A.R. Baswedan (Partai Arab Indonesia), Abdul Rahim Pratalykrama and Kijahi Abdoel Fattah. These last two figures supported the demands made by the Islamic movement despite the fact that they were not recognised figures within it. H. Agus Salim, on the other hand, who was a respected figure within Sarekat Islam, more often than not distanced himself from Islamic demands. Deliar Noer, "Masjumi: Its Organization, Ideology, and Political Role in Indonesia", Master thesis, Cornell University, 1960, p. 31.

[3] Muhammad Yamin, *Naskah Persiapan Undang-Undang Dasar 1945*, 3 vols. (Jakarta, 1959–60).

Islam and nationalism to be inseparable. Islam had been the source of their involvement in the struggle for an independent Indonesia, and so they considered that the new state they were about to build should serve their religion. The question of the new state's constitution did not appear to them to be open to political debate; they saw instead a preordained answer dictated by their faith. The rhetoric used by the nationalist secularists during the summer of 1945 was particularly skilful, then, for the way in which it gradually centred the debate around the question of what type of institutions should be established in the new Indonesian state, while at the same time preserving their own credentials as good Muslims. In the absence of any official records of the committee meetings, it is difficult to assess with any precision the respective roles played by Muhammad Yamin and Sukarno in these delicate political manoeuvres.[4] Both of them stated their desire that

---

[4] Assuming that Muhammad Yamin's transcription in 1959 of the speech he gave on 29 May 1945 was exact (*Naskah*, I: 83–107), it could be considered as laying the foundations of what was to become the ideology of the Indonesian state, making him the true founder of *Pancasila*. This was confirmed, moreover, by several former Masyumi figures in 1967. B.J. Boland, *The Struggle of Islam in Modern Indonesia* (The Hague: Martinus Nijhoff, 1982), p. 17. Boland, however, seems convinced that Yamin gives himself credit which he is not due. Four of the five principles of *Pancasila* had already been formulated by Sukarno in July 1933 during a conference organised by Partindo. H. Endang Saifuddin Anshary, *Piagam Jakarta 22 juni 1945 dan sejarah konsensus nasional antara nasionalis islami dan nasionalis "secular" tentang dasar negara republik indonesia, 1945–1959* (Bandung: Pustaka, 1983), p. 17.

Another tendentious account of the birth of *Pancasila* is that given by Kyai Masykur, one of NU's leaders. He described how in May 1945 when he was a captain in the Sabilillah militia, a meeting took place between Sukarno, Yamin, Wahid Hasjim, Kahar Muzakkir and himself in order to determine the principal components of the national ideology. This account was recorded by the Indonesia National Archive Services in an interview which took place on 1 October 1988 and is transcribed by Andrée Feillard in his study of NU, *Islam et armée dans l'Indonésie contemporaine: Les pionniers de la tradition*, Cahier d'Archipel 28 (Paris: L'Harmattan, 1995), pp. 39–40. It tries to show how Islam's representatives, and notably those belonging to NU, contributed equally, along with Sukarno and Yamin, to the emergence of the state ideology. This account by Kyai Masykur has never been corroborated by another source, however, and so needs to be treated with circumspection. It seems above all to reflect the Muslim community's change in attitude towards *Pancasila* which was now considered to be a permanent cornerstone of national identity.

It could be added that the desire of former Masyumi figures to attribute the conception of *Pancasila* to Yamin can be readily explained by their hope, in the

the future state be built upon religious foundations, but at the same time they proposed an institutional framework for this which would absolve them from having to make any practical commitments to back up these statements. The most developed presentation of this nationalist vision was delivered in a famous speech, later known as "the Birth of *Pancasila*", given by Sukarno on 1 June.[5] This long speech, made the day before the end of the first committee session, contained a vast array of references from Jaurès and Sun Yat-sen to Marhaen (a modest peasant who was not afraid to be enterprising, despite his poor background). In the course of his speech, Sukarno laid out "five principles" —*Pancasila* in Sanskrit—as the cornerstones of the new Indonesian state. They were: nationalism (*Kebangsaan*); internationalism or humanism (*Perikemanusiaan*); democracy by consensus (*Permyusawaratan*); social prosperity (*Kesejahteraan sosial*); and belief in one God (*Ketuhanan yang Maha Esa*). Two sections of the speech in particular, setting out the secularists' ideas on the place that Islam would occupy in an independent Indonesia, were intended for the Muslim group in the committee.

The announcement of the fifth principle, "belief in one God", was greeted with a sigh of relief by the Muslim representatives, as it ruled out the prospect of a completely secular state.[6] Independent Indonesia would, then, as Muhammad Yamin had proposed a few days earlier, be religious (*akan berketuhanan*). However, Sukarno, explaining the nature of religion in the new state, said:

> ...every Indonesian wants to be able to worship his faith in his own way. Christians according to the commands of Jesus, Muslims according to the Prophet Mohammad's, the Buddhists according to their Holy Books...It is within this fifth principle, my friends,

---

early days of the New Order, for an ideological reassessment of the regime. Given that President Sukarno still benefitted at that time from a considerable amount of prestige, the fact that they were not attacking his legacy could only make it easier for this aspiration to be fulfilled.

[5] For a complete French translation and analysis of this speech as well as an examination of the extraordinary political destiny of what still remains today the official ideology of the Republic of Indonesia, see Marcel Bonneff et al., *Pancasila, trente années de débats politiques en Indonésie* (Paris: Editions de la Maison des Sciences de l'Homme, 1980).

[6] A few weeks later, "belief in one God" became the first of *Pancasila*'s principles.

that all religions which exist in Indonesia at the moment will be able to find their place.[7]

Islam, then, was simply referred to in the same vein as the country's other religions. No recognition was given to a particular status which Muslims considered themselves entitled to, given their numerical superiority in the country. In the Sukarnist worldview, Islam was not a source of law, but rather a source of inspiration, a personal matter to be left to each individual's conscience.

> All of us, myself included, are Muslims. My practice of Islam, God forgive me, is far from being perfect, but, my friends, if you were to look into my heart and read my mind, you would find nothing other than the heart of a Muslim. Bung Karno wishes to defend Islam through consensus and consultation...If we are truly a Muslim people, let us do our best to ensure that the majority of the seats we are about to create will be filled by representatives of Islam. If the Indonesian population genuinely contains a majority of Muslims, and if Islam is to be a religion that is alive and well in our country, then we, its leaders, must capture the people's imagination so that it sends the greatest number of Muslim representatives possible to Parliament. Let us say that there are one hundred seats in Parliament, well then we must strive to ensure that sixty, seventy, eighty, ninety seats are occupied by Muslim figures. It will go without saying, then, that the laws voted by this assembly will be Muslim laws.[8]

Muslims still had a duty, an special duty even, to assist in the triumph of their religion's values, but these values would be expressed in Parliament. Islamic values were not a given, they had to be fought for. Sukarno put his finger on one of the major contradictions in the Muslim community's claim to be democratic. Rather than promising the unilateral creation of a state which recognised Islam as its cornerstone, he preferred to guarantee the Muslim community the prospect of a fair chance of seeing their values prevail in Parliament, values which, as a wily political animal, he claimed to defend. Instead of an Islamic

---

[7] Bonneff et al., *Pancasila, trente années de débats politiques en Indonésie*, p. 73.
[8] Principles which were expounded as an explanation for the third tenet: consensus (*mufakat*) and deliberations amongst representatives (*permusyawaratan*). Bonneff et al., p. 70.

state, Sukarno proposed an "Islamisable" state. His proposals, though, ran into the stubborn opposition of Islam's representatives who, from the outset, refused to abandon the possibility of a special position for Islam in the new state. However, behind the twists and turns of this debate and the respective stances adopted during June 1945, one could detect at work the forces which led, in November, to the formation of Masyumi. Some members of the Muslim group, who were not only keenly aware of the balance of power within the country and the general mood in the international community but who also no doubt sincerely believed the secularist argument was sound, were already busy responding, on behalf of Islam, to the challenge laid down to them in Sukarno's speech.

The Jakarta Charter—A Blueprint for Islamic Demands

The 62-member Committee adjourned on 2 June, with the question of the country's future institutions still unresolved. Discussions continued, however, both within the sub-committee which had been charged with elaborating a programme for a constitution and within the Tyuo Sangi In (the Central Consultative Committee). The Tyuo Sangi In was created in 1943 by the Japanese to allow Indonesians to become involved in government and some of its members also participated in the work of the BPUKI. In response to the significant and persistent disagreements between nationalists and Islam's representatives, all the members of the BPUKI who were still present in Jakarta met again to nominate a special committee of nine members who were given the task of drawing up a compromise solution to this thorny problem. The committee comprised four representatives from the Islamic movement (Haji Agus Salim, Kiai Wahid Hasjim, Abikusno and Abdul Kahar Muzzakir) and five from the nationalist group (Sukarno, Mohammad Hatta, A.A. Maramis, Achmad Subardjo[9] and Muhammad Yamin), and it came up with a compromise on 22 June which Yamin subsequently

---

[9] Although he later became a member of Masyumi and represented the party at the cabinet table during Soekiman's time as prime minister, Subardjo, who was close to Sukarno during the 1920s and 1930s, was unknown within the Muslim community in 1945 and could not be considered a representative of political Islam. Cf. Benedict O.G.M, *Java in a Time of Revolution: Occupation and Resistance, 1944–1946* (Ithaca, NY: Cornell University Press, 1961), pp. 91–3.

called "the Jakarta Charter" (*Piagram Jakarta*). This document was supposed to be the preamble to the future constitution of an

> Indonesian state which is a republic resting upon the people's sovereignty and founded on the belief in God, with the obligation for adherents of the Islamic faith to abide by Islamic laws, in accordance with the principle of righteous and just humanity, the unity of Indonesia, and a democracy led by wise guidance through consultations, ensuring social justice for the whole Indonesian people.[10]

The importance of this text which borrowed heavily from the principles announced by Sukarno on 1 June, lies in the assertion of a particular religious obligation for Indonesian citizens of the Muslim faith. These "seven words"[11] were the result of a compromise which had been reached by two of the Muslim representatives, Abikusno and Kahar Muzakkir, and the Christian nationalist, Maramis.[12] In the absence of any specific detail on the nature of the duty owed by Muslims —was it to be a legal duty or simply a moral one?—and given the vagueness surrounding the notion of Islamic laws, the practical implications of this principle for the country's new institutions were entirely predicated on its interpretation and concrete application by those in power. Nonetheless, as soon as the second session of the BPUKI opened on 10 July,[13] some nationalist representatives expressed their concerns, considering the charter to be a serious attack on the principle of a secular state by allowing a sort of "Islamic state within the state" to exist for an overwhelming majority of the population. These concerns were exacerbated by the attitude among some of the Muslim representatives, who seemed to indicate that they now considered the Jakarta Charter as the starting point for a new series of negotiations.[14] Wahid

---

[10] The complete text of the charter can be found in Boland, *The Struggle of Islam in Modern Indonesia*, p. 243.

[11] In Indonesian, "dengan kewadjiban menjalankan sjari'at Islam bagi pemeluk-pemeluknja" ("with the obligation for Muslims to follow Islamic law").

[12] Noer, "Masjumi: Its Organization, Ideology, and Political Role in Indonesia", p. 33.

[13] Now composed of 68 members.

[14] Agus Salim, however, refused to follow his fellow Muslims into this dangerous territory.

Hasjim, supported by Soekiman, demanded that Islam be declared the state religion, and that there be an obligation for both the president and the vice president to be Muslim.[15] Ki Bagus Hadikusumo, leader of Muhammadiyah, highlighted the potential difficulties for the country if two legal systems coexisted, and declared that it would be simpler if the duty to respect Islamic law was extended to the entire population.

In response to the refusal by nationalists to make any new concessions, the Muslim representatives adopted an unusual stance. In a motion tabled by Kahar Muzakkir, they declared that if the new state were not to be Islamic, then its institutions should contain no reference to religion at all. Sukarno considered that the disillusionment contained in this proposal clearly showed that the situation between Muslims and nationalists had become critical. Thus, on 16 July, at the opening of the day's proceedings, he asked the nationalist group to agree to make a major sacrifice by accepting to include in the future Constitution not just the seven words of the Jakarta Charter, but also the obligation for the president to be Muslim. That evening, as the Committee for Preparatory Work finished what was to be their last day of discussions, it seemed to the Muslim representatives that they had got the upper hand. This impression, however, was short-lived. With defeat imminent, the Japanese high command in Saigon decided, on 7 August, to form an Indonesian Council which was supposed to take over the government of the country from the Japanese armed forces. Chaired by Sukarno (Mohammad Hatta was vice-chairman) and composed of members from all of the country's regions, the Preparatory Committee for the Independence of Indonesia (Panita Persiapan Kemerdekaan, PPKI) was named on 14 August. It comprised 21 members, but, much to the disappointment of the Muslim community, included only two of their representatives: Ki Bagus Hadikusumo and Wahid Hasjim, the leaders of the two main Islamic organisations, Muhammadiyah and Nahdlatul Ulama.

On 17 August 1945, Sukarno and Hatta, under pressure from revolutionary youth groups, declared independence. The following day, the Preparatory Committee met again, now acting as a provisional constituent assembly and containing five extra members. These new

---

[15] Hasjim's official biographer, H. Aboebakar (a civil servant in the Ministry of Religions) made no mention of his role in this debate. *Sejarah hidup K.H.A. Wahid Hasjim dan karangan tersiar* (Jakarta: Panitia buku peringatan, 1957).

members had been nominated by Sukarno, with only one of them belonging to the Islamic movement: Kasman Singodimedjo. He was commander of the PETA garrison in Jakarta, and his nomination to the provisional constituent assembly was above all to ensure the support of the militia group he headed. The Preparatory Committee constituent assembly's first session finally got underway late, after two hours of frenzied chatter amongst the members, and an agreement was quickly reached on certain modifications to be made to the wording of the Constitution. Indonesia was to be founded on a belief in God, but the "seven words" which defined an obligation specific to Muslims were replaced[16] by a much more neutral expression concerning the single nature of the divine being, one of the elements of *Pancasila*—Yang Maha Esa. In addition, the obligation for the president to be Muslim was removed from Article 6, paragraph 1. Thus, in the space of a few hours and with the consent of its representatives, the Muslim community saw all its political gains disappear.

This sudden abandonment of a compromise that had been hard won by political Islam seems difficult to fathom. To understand it, one needs to appreciate the feverish atmosphere that pervaded the Committee on that morning of 18 June. The previous day's proclamation of independence had dealt a blow to the Japanese occupier, who had promised on 24 June to give Indonesians their independence. With the imminent arrival of the Allied troops, it was obvious that Dutch soldiers would soon return to the country with the intention of restoring the Netherlands' colonial authority there. The definition of Indonesia's religious status was therefore no longer the theoretical question it had been during the discussions in the Preparatory Committee in June. It was now an issue that had to be resolved quickly and that could have far-reaching consequences for Indonesia's aspirations for independence. The day before, on 17 August, Mohammad Hatta had, at the request of Admiral Mayeda, received a visit from a Japanese naval officer who alerted him to the violent opposition of the Christian community on the edges of the archipelago to the "seven words" of the Jakarta Charter:

> They recognise that this part of the sentence is not binding on them and concerns only Muslims. Nonetheless, the inclusion of such a

---

[16] In the preamble and in Article 29 concerning religion.

statement as part of the foundation of the Constitution amounts to organising discrimination towards minority groups. If this 'discrimination' is confirmed, they would prefer to remain outside the Republic of Indonesia.[17]

This threat of secession was raised by Sukarno and Hatta during their meeting with the representatives of Islam in the provisional constituent assembly in the early hours of the morning of the 18th. It was, therefore, to ensure national unity that Wahid Hasjim,[18] Ki Bagus Hadikusumo, Kasman Singodimedjo and Teuku Mohamad Hassan (a representative from Aceh)[19] agreed to sacrifice the demands of their political group.[20]

The history of the Jakarta Charter and of its "loss" (*kehilangan*) was a crucial moment for the Muslim cause in Indonesia and, in the years that followed, became a central theme of Masyumi's political identity. The party made several calls for the Charter to be included in the Constitution, in particular during the debates which preceded the adoption of the Provisional Constitution in 1950 and also during the proceedings of the Constituent Assembly in Bandung between 1956 and 1959. In addition, a number of party members or sympathisers

---

[17] Mohammad Hatta, *Sekitar Proklamasi 17 août 1945* (Jakarta: Tintamas, 1970), p. 66, quoted by Anshary, *Piagam Jakarta 22 juni 1945 dan sejarah konsensus nasional antara nasionalis islami dan nasionalis "secular" tentang dasar negara republik indonesia, 1945–1959*, pp. 10–1.

[18] Hasjim's presence has been challenged by H. Endang Saifuddin Anshari (p. 48) who explains that he was in West Java at the time. Hatta (Boland, *The Struggle of Islam in Modern Indonesia*, p. 35), Kasman Singodimedjo and others confirmed that he was indeed there. As Andrée Feillard has highlighted (*Islam et armée dans l'Indonésie contemporaine*, p. 42), had Wahid Hasjim been absent, none of the Islamist signatories of the Jakarta Charter would have approved its abandonment, as it would have discredited the legitimacy of the meeting on 18 August.

[19] The region of Aceh is one of the cradles of Indonesian Islam and enjoyed a considerable amount of prestige within the Muslim community in Indonesia. Mohammad Hassan, then, was very ideally situated, despite his proximitiy to the secular nationalists, to convince the Muslim representatives to accept the withdrawal of their demands. Indeed, Sukarno and Hatta are said to have charged him with this task. Anderson, *Java in a Time of Revolution*, p. 87.

[20] A few days later, when speaking at a conference organised by his organisation, Muhammadiyah, Ki Bagus Hadikusumo expressed his discontent concerning the outcome of the Preparatory Committee and pointed out that political Islam's struggle was still in its infancy. Noer, "Masjumi: Its Organizazion, Ideology, and Political Role in Indonesia", p. 37.

wrote studies on the Charter.[21] These studies focussed on two themes in particular: first, they looked at the sacrifice made by the Muslim community as a foundational element of the Indonesian nation, with the insinuation that the latter owed a debt to the former. The second theme, linked to the first, was the notion of Islamic patriotism which compared favourably with the patriotism of secular nationalists, who had allowed their actions to be dictated by the Japanese naval high command.

Once the thorny question of Islam's place in the new Indonesia had been dealt with, the promulgation of the Constitution was able to go ahead the same day without further ado. Sukarno and Hatta were elected president and vice president of the new Republic of Indonesia, and the country's political landscape began to take shape amid its budding institutions.

The Foundation of Masyumi

On 29 August, the BPUKI was dissolved and replaced by a Central Indonesian National Committee (Komite Nasional Indonesia Pusat, KNIP). In accordance with the presidential system then in place, a cabinet was formed on 4 September under Sukarno's leadership. Political Islam was relatively poorly represented in the new provisional institutions with the government comprising only two of its representatives. These were the former president of PSII, Abikusno Tjokrosujoso, who was named minister for public works, and K.H.A. Wahid Hasjim, who did not have a ministerial portfolio as such, but was in charge of religious affairs. Of the 136 members of the KNIP, who were chosen by the president, only 15 could be considered to belong to political Islam.[22] One of these, Kasman Singomdimedjo, was elected to chair

---

[21] Prawoto Mangkusasmito, *Pertumbuhan Historis Rumus Dasar Negara dan Sebuah Proyeksi* (Surabaya: Facta Documenta, 1966); *Pancasila dan Sejarahnya* (Jakarta: Lembaga Riset dan Perpustakaan, 1972); H. Endang Saifuddin Anshari, author of *Piagam Jakarta 22 juin 1945*, is himself a former official of Peladjar Islam Indonesia and the son of Isa Anshary, the very energetic "boss" of Masyumi in West Java.

[22] These were Abikusno Tjokrosujoso, Kasman Singodimedjo, Jusuf Wibisono, Dahlan Abdullah, Mohamad Roem, A.R. Baswedan, A. Bajasut, Harsono Tjokroaminoto, Mrs. Sunarjo Mangunpuspito, Wahid Hasjim, Ki Bagus Hadikusumo, Zainul Arifin, Hadji Agus Salim, Hadji Ahmad Sanusi and Anwar Tjokroaminoto.

the assembly during its second session, which took place between 15 and 17 October 1945. However, he was taken to task violently by one of the assembly members who accused him of authorising his troops to be disarmed by the Japanese when he was head of PETA in Jakarta, and had to resign. He was replaced by Sjahrir, president of the small Indonesian Socialist Party (PSI) who was one of the few nationalist leaders not to have collaborated with the Japanese. For the representatives of political Islam, such as Anwar Haryono who witnessed the ousting of Kasman, the election of Sjahrir confirmed the victory of the "secular group".[23] During the same session, the KNIP was given real legislative power and decided to establish a Working Committee (Badan Pekerdja) composed of 15 members in order to help it with this task.[24] Two prominent figures of the resistance to the Japanese occupation, Sjahrir and Amir Sjarrifuddin, were elected chairman and vice-chairman respectively of this committee, and subsequently chose the 13 other committee members. Of these, there were only two representatives of political Islam (Wahid Hasjim and Sjafruddin Prawiranegara) but this figure increased to three (Sjafruddin Prawiranegara, Mohammad Natsir and Jusuf Wibisono) when the committee was expanded to 17 members, and their number increased to four when they were joined by Mohammad Zein Djambek in December 1945.

Although political Islam was poorly represented within the country's new institutions and its moral authority within the country had not been constitutionally recognised, it took its time before organising itself into a political force. Indeed, it did so reluctantly, due to its opposition to the creation of a party political system which it feared would bring an end to the spirit of national unity. Although their primary demand—recognition of Indonesia's Islamic identity—had not been satisfied, the country's Muslims hoped that they could still be considered as the religious conscience of the nation. The single-party presidential system established in the summer of 1945 was better suited to fulfilling this aspiration, and indeed in the lead-up to the vote which

---

[23] *"Kelompok Sekular"* Lukman Hakiem, *Perjalan mencari keadilan dan persatuan. Biografi Dr Anwar Harjono, S.H.* (Jakarta: Media Da'wah, 1993), p. 79.
[24] Inspired by the example of Indian National Congress (George McTurnan Kahin, *Nationalism and Revolution in Indonesia* [Ithaca, NY: Cornell University Press, 1952], p. 152), this committee was to meet at least every 10 days and the KNIP was to assemble at least once a year.

was to give to the KNIP a legislative function and set up a multi-party political system, none of the Islamic members campaigned for these changes. They could no doubt sense the danger, inherent in political battles with their relativist logic, that Islam would be reduced to being just another political doctrine, and so they only entered the political ring when events forced them to do so. Although the mutation of the Islamist movement into a political party was not desired by its members, the groundwork for this transformation had nonetheless already been laid. It was the work of a small group of figures who, for the most part, belonged to the pre-war modernist Muslim organisations and to the Japanese Masyumi: Agus Salim, Abdul Kahar Muzakkir, Abdul Wahid Hasjim, Mohammad Natsir, Mohammad Roem, Prawoto Mangkusasmito, Soekiman Wirjosandjojo, Ki Bagus Hadikusumo, Mohammad Mawardi and Abu Hanifah.

This generation of Muslim leaders remained uncertain for a long time, however, as to how and when they should enter the political fray, and so they initially focussed on creating a Muslim youth movement. Using the Islamic Higher School (Sekolah Islam Tinggi) as a platform for their ideas, they encouraged a group of students there to found the Movement of Young Muslims (Gerakan Pemuda Islam Indonesia, GPII) on 2 October 1945.[25] Bringing together young Muslims who had attended both religious establishments (*pesantren*) and non-religious schools, the GPII's goals were to defend the Indonesian Republic and to spread Islam.[26] The debate within the Islamist movement as to which type of organisation would be the most suitable vehicle (*wadah*) for their political message quickly led its leaders to the conclusion that the best solution was to transform the powerful Muslim organisation created by the Japanese, which still had most of its organisational infrastructure intact.[27] It was with this in mind that they summoned the Congress of the Indonesian Umma (*Kongres Umat Islam Indonesia*) to Yogyakarta on 7 and 8 November.

---

[25] See Chapter 6 for the description of this organisation and its role in the emergence of Masyumi.

[26] "*Mempertankan Negara Republik Indonesia*". "*Menyiarkan Agama Islam*".

[27] Mohammad Roem confided to Deliar Noer that in early September 1945, he pledged, along with Wahid Hasjim and Kahar Muzakkir, to revive the Japanese-created Masyumi. Noer, "Masjumi: Its Organization, Ideology, and Political Role in Indonesia", p. 39.

Despite the great disorder that reigned in Java at that time, almost 500 delegates from the principal Muslim organisations managed to make it to one of the last remaining cities in the hands of the republican government. After two days of debate, the Congress "representing the entire Indonesian Muslim community, which accounts for 65 million souls" considered "that all forms of colonisation are cruel, violate human rights and are clearly forbidden (*diharamkan*) by Islam"; it further stated that "in order to eliminate successive imperialist measures in Indonesia, all Muslims must, without fail, fight body and soul for the liberation of their country and of their religion" and decided "to adapt the organisation and the position of Masyumi, the Heart of the Unity of the Indonesian Umma, in order to mobilise and lead the struggle of the entire Indonesian *umma*".[28]

The unity which the Congress called for was to be the unity of the entire nation. The gathering was opened by President Sukarno and closed by the Sultan of Yogyakarta. In the minds of the organisers, it was less about organising the creation of a new political organisation and more about making it known that there was a religious duty towards the nation. The fact that this mobilisation of the Muslim community took on the shape of a political party was merely the consequence of the "regrettable" decision by the government to create a multi-party system. Soekiman, the first president of Masyumi, reminded people of that when he presented the decisions of the Congress:

> In such a critical moment, which required the people to unite body and soul, we regret the announcement by the government of its proposal to found parties, a move which will only lead to division amongst the people.[29]

By sacrificing their demands for the sake of the struggle to maintain independence, the representatives of the Muslim community had hoped that they were inaugurating a new period of political consensus and leaving party politics behind, an aspiration which still prevailed at the

---

[28] Resolutions from the Party Congress in November 1945. Pengoeroes Besar Partai Masjoemi, *Masjoemi, Partai Politik Oemmat Islam Indonesia* (Yogyakarta, 1945), pp. 15–6.

[29] Soekiman, "Kewadjiban Oemat Islam dewasa ini"; Pengoeroes Besar Partai Masjoemi, *Masjoemi, Partai Politik Oemmat Islam Indonesia*, p. 7.

foundation of Masyumi. By a small majority, the Congress representatives preferred a transformation (*penjelmaan*, literally meaning "reincarnation"), of Madjelis Sjoero Moeslimin Indonesia over the proposal to found a Partai Rakjat Islam (Muslim People's Party) made by a group of representatives who were firmly resolved to bring about the Muslim community's entry into the political arena.[30] The new organisation only adopted the acronym, Masjoemi,[31] rather than the Japanese organisation's full name, and it also added the subtitle, Partai Politik Oemmat Islam Indonesia (the Political Party of the Indonesian Muslim Community), to its name. Their choice may have been guided mainly by obvious strategic reasons, not least Masyumi's organisational network which the new party would later avail of. Nonetheless, the path chosen by Islam's representatives, one which left them open to accusations of collaboration which had also been aimed at certain members of the Muslim elite, revealed a certain circumspection towards the new political dispensation. There were other examples of this reticence towards entering the political arena, namely the fact that the Congress not only created a political party but also spawned a vast and complex web of social care organisations which revealed a vision of politics that was still very community-based.[32]

The other theme, which was developed substantially in the documents produced by the Congress, was that of a holy war which was supposed to ensure Indonesia's independence. Of the final resolutions, the first two dealt with this issue, while the creation of Masyumi was not mentioned until the third resolution. These two resolutions called on Muslims to:

1. Reinforce the Muslim community's preparation for the struggle in the path of Allah
2. Reinforce, by all the efforts that Islam imposes, the troops for the defence of Indonesia.[33]

---

[30] The debate between the two sides was a lively one and the winning margin was only one vote (52 to 51).

[31] This was the original spelling of the party at its foundation in 1945. See "Author's Note", this volume.

[32] Cf. infra, Chapter 6.

[33] Pengoeroes Besar Partai Masjoemi, *Masjoemi, Partai Politik Oemmat Islam Indonesia*.

Shortly afterwards, these decisions gave birth to an organisation charged with mobilising all Muslims, Barisan Sabilillah, which was placed under the authority of Masyumi.[34] The members of this militia integrated the army as Extraordinary Forces and, in theory, this group was a sort of civil defence force supposed to provide support for Hizboellah, the military organisation inherited from the original Masyumi and which became part of the overall structure created by the Congress. The resolutions stated that "Hizboellah would be the only military organisation" and that "Gerakan Pemoeda Islam Indonesia [Indonesia's Muslim Youth Movement] constituted the only avenue open to young Muslims' political struggle".[35]

The birth of the second Masyumi did not arise, then, from a specific political programme but rather emerged from a defensive community-based attitude which assimilated Islam's followers and the new Republic's citizens. It was only once the party entered the Indonesian political fray that it began to evolve slowly towards becoming a party of government.

Political and Military Divisions within Indonesia

The day of Masyumi's foundation, 7 November, was also the day when most of Indonesia's other political organisations were created. These organisations had three distinct sources of inspiration: nationalism, socialism and Islam, whose sole national representative until 1947 would be Masyumi. The Partai Nasional Indonesia (PNI) at its creation benefitted from the prestige associated with the pre-war nationalist movement and the notoriety of its illustrious predecessors with the same name. Even though it had no direct link with either the organisation founded by Sukarno in 1927 or with the state party, born just after independence, which controlled the single-party system (before being replaced by the KNIP), the PNI remained for the vast majority of the population the president's party. Likewise, on the left of the political spectrum, the Partai Komunis Indonesia (PKI), led by Mohammed Yussuf, had no close affiliation with its predecessors from the colonial

---

[34] "Barisan Sabilillah" literally means "forces in the path of God".
[35] "Gerakan Pemoeda Islam Indonesia, Anggaran Dasar". Pengoeroes Besar Partai Masjoemi, *Masjoemi, Partai Politik Oemmat Islam Indonesia*, p. 23.

period. These included the Indonesian Communist Party founded in 1920, an illegal PKI, created in 1935 after the almost complete disappearance of its predecessor following the failed rebellion of 1927, and finally, the clandestine PKI created during the Japanese occupation. Most of the country's Stalinists did not join the new PKI and instead became members of the Socialist Party, the Labour Party (Partai Buruh Indonesia) or the Pesindo militia.[36] Finally, in December 1945, the merger of Amir Sjarrifuddin's Partai Sosialis Indonesia and Sutan Sjahrir's Partai Rakjat Sosialis gave birth to the Partai Sosialis. Although its electoral base was a lot smaller than its predecessors, it managed nonetheless to punch far above its weight politically thanks to its excellent organisational capacity and the competence of its leaders. Apart from these four main political parties, a number of other smaller political groups shared the often rather chaotic political landscape. These included the Socialist People's Party (Paras); a Protestant party, Parkindo, led by Leimena; and a Catholic party.

There gravitated around these organisations an array of armed forces, either left over from the Japanese era or newly created, which had not yet been integrated into the fledgling national army. Most of these groups of young combatants, like Hizboellah and Barisan Sabilillah which were controlled by Masyumi, supported a political party or movement. Barisan Pelonor, which had become Barisan Banteng (the Buffalo Legion), was close to the left wing of the PNI. It was based in Surakarta and gradually became exclusively controlled by Tan Malaka.[37] Laskar Rakjat (the People's Militia), which was close to the Sultan of Yogyakarta, represented the right wing of the PNI, while the Pesindo militia (Indonesian Socialist Youth Movement) grouped together young Indonesians who supported Sjahrir. These militia groups embodied the courage of the *pemuda* in their struggle against foreign armed forces and provided vital assistance to the political parties they were associated with. However, because they were often poorly armed and lacking in

---

[36] Kahin, *Nationalism and Revolution in Indonesia*, p. 159.
[37] Tan Malaka was one of the most prominent figures in Indonesian communism. He was a PKI official in the 1920s before becoming a Comintern representative for Southeast Asia. As a result of the 1926–27 revolts and the subsesquent crackdown on communism, he had to flee his country. He returned in 1942 and lived through the war in complete anonymity, only returning to politics after independence. See Anderson, *Java in a Time of Revolution*, pp. 269–95.

discipline, they had, during the first years of the new Republic, a destabilising effect on politics. They were gradually, but with some difficulty, integrated into the Indonesian army, bringing with them their partisan differences.[38]

The struggle for Indonesian independence took place in such a heady atmosphere of extreme confusion that it is not easy to tease out the different political identities it contained. Most of the country's regions were isolated from one another and the fighting accentuated the administrative division established by the Japanese authorities.[39]

This administrative chaos made it difficult for information to be communicated, even within the regions controlled by the new Indonesian government, making the political parties' task all the more difficult. In the case of Masyumi, these difficulties had a knock-on effect on the content of its official newspaper, *Al-Djihad*. As a result of the unreliability of the postal service, the newspaper abounded with practical information, such as notifications for meetings (sometimes concerning only a few people). In these circumstances, proper political strategy was often replaced by one-upmanship, the exaggeration of minor events and occasional political bluster. Throughout 1946, for example, *Al-Djihad* helped maintain an atmosphere of anxiety in the country to such an extent that one could have been forgiven for thinking that the Third World War was about to break out. The number of armed forces within the country was colossal, according to Abiksuno Tjokrosujoso, one of Masyumi's vice presidents—no fewer than three million members of Hizboellah and two million members of Barisan Sabilillah—which seemed to presage a confrontation of apocalyptic proportions.[40]

---

[38] The period of sacred union enjoyed by Indonesian youth groups during the struggle for and defence of independence did not last. The Youth Congress, which took place in Yogyakarta on 10 and 11 November 1945, led to the creation of the Pesindo which supported Amir and Sjahrir, thus officialising the politicisation of the *pemuda* movement.

[39] During this period, Sumatra came under the control of the Headquarters of the Seventh Area Army in Singapore which also controlled Malaysia. A special command was created for Java and Madura while Borneo and the East were placed under the authority of the Navy Headquarters for the Southern Seas in Makassar in Sulawesi.

[40] *Al-Djihad*, 16 February 1946. According to Kahin, Hizboellah only made up between 20,000 and 25,000 combatants. Kahin, *Nationalism and Revolution in Indonesia*, p. 162.

The exact nature of the transformation that took place in the Indonesian population in the midst of such turmoil has been the source of much debate. For Benedict Anderson, the Indonesian National Revolution was never anything more than a political revolution, and "what it might have been can only be glimpsed in the short-lived, isolated social revolutions in the provinces and in the memories of some of the survivors."[41] This vision has been shared by Indonesian historians who focus mainly on the struggle for independence, but it has been qualified, and in some cases contested, by Western writers. Peter Carey, for example, claims that "without a doubt, more Indonesians were killed or tortured at the hands of their fellow countrymen during these tragic months than were killed in the whole guerrilla struggle against the Dutch".[42]

The transformation of Masyumi from an inward-looking organisation into a political party did not happen uniformly across the country. The war of independence, which was beginning at that time, divided the country politically as well as militarily. In August 1945, the entire country became the theatre of operations for British and Australian forces, having previously played host to the Americans. The English landed in Jakarta at the end of September, and first of all entered into dialogue with the new Republic's authorities, thus awarding them de facto recognition. In response to the total refusal of the Dutch to enter into any discussions with the Sukarno government, which they considered to be a Japanese creation, the British facilitated the appointment of Sjahrir as prime minister on 13 November. Negotiations were then opened between the new prime minister and a Dutch representative, Van Mook. However, these discussions were rapidly broken off because of the Netherlands' refusal to stop landing their troops in Indonesia. As a result, the confrontations between militia groups and Dutch and British forces, which had been intensifying up until that point, escalated further. In the following months, despite the fact that

---

[41] Anderson, *Java in a Time of Revolution*, p. 409.

[42] In the most recent official version of Indonesian history, only a tiny footnote is devoted to the elimination from the country's regions of both administrative structures and the elite groups who supported the Dutch. Marwati Djoened Poesponegoro and Nugroho Notosusanto, eds., *Sejarah Nasional Indonesia*, vol. 6 (Jakarta: Balai Pustaka, 2008). See Colin Wild and Peter Carey, eds., *Born in Fire: The Indonesian Struggle for Independence*, BBC Publications (Athens, OH: Ohio University Press, 1988), pp. xxii–xxiv.

Dutch and English diplomats, under pressure from the United States, were attempting to find a peaceful solution to the crisis, Dutch troops reoccupied Borneo, Sulawesi, the Maluku Islands and the Lesser Sunda Islands. They renewed contacts with the traditional leaders of these regions, confirmed the agreements made with them before the war and gradually swept aside the supporters of the new Republic. Faced with this *fait accompli*, the British finally agreed, on 15 July 1946, to hand over the entire Indonesian territory, apart from Java and Sumatra, to the Dutch military command. The former colonial power thus reclaimed complete control over a significant part of the country.

The circumstances of the Masyumi leaders' experience of the Revolution greatly influenced their political leanings. Three towns were particularly important in the history of the laborious emergence of Masyumi's political identity. In Jakarta, which was occupied by the Allies from the end of September 1945, there were few opportunities for the pemuda to cause political wrangling or disorder. It was here that diplomacy was carried out, even after the departure of the government in January 1946. For the political officials who lived there, Jakarta was at the centre of international diplomatic proceedings, a place where *realpolitik* prevailed. Yogyakarta, on the other hand, was a bustling hub of militia activity where impending combat loomed, and it had been the spiritual home of the Indonesian National Revolution since August 1945. It was militarily more secure than Jakarta and became the headquarters for the new Republic's administration in January 1946. Surakarta, also known as Solo, which harboured an old rivalry with Yogyakarta, was the natural headquarters for the opponents to the Sjahrir government.[43] It hosted meetings between some of Masyumi's leaders and the leaders of Persatuan Perjuangan, the Struggle Union, which brought together the prime minister's opponents. Between November 1945 and July 1947, the Muslim party, like many other political parties, hesitated—or rather, was divided—as to which path to follow between participation in government and opposition, between revolutionary idealism and diplomatic pragmatism. The causes of this "schizophrenia" have already been touched on earlier: it can be attributed to the different geographic origins of the party's leaders but also

---

[43] In 1755, the Kingdom of Mataram split into two principalities: Yogyakarta and Surakarta.

to their different social milieus. The different elective affinities between political figures also played a role, as can be seen in the friendship between Sukarno, Soekiman and Tan Malaka, on the one hand, and the close ties between Sjahrir, Natsir and Agus Salim, on the other. These first two years of the Revolution saw, then, the slow emergence of Masyumi as a party of government, which we will come back to later. It was, however, a mutation brought about by a small group within the party who had no means of communicating their message through propaganda or through spectacular accomplishments. The vast majority of the party faithful only gradually and reluctantly abandoned their revolutionary identity, under the guidance of Masyumi's most senior leaders.

A Revolutionary Party in Opposition

Sjahrir's First Cabinet: The Definition of Masyumi's Political Line

The transformation of the political system into a multi-party one led rapidly to the formation of a parliamentary cabinet. The obvious choice to head the cabinet was Sutan Sjahrir, a vanguard member of the intransigent Indonesian resistance to the Japanese. He represented a more favourable alternative to the presidential cabinet, which had been criticised for containing ministers who had collaborated with the Japanese. The first Sjahrir government, which was formed on 14 November 1945, was composed mainly of members of his own political party, the PSI. Sjahrir himself occupied the position of minister for foreign affairs and also minister for home affairs, as well as that of prime minister. Amir Sjarifuddin, the other powerful political figure in the cabinet and also a member of the PSI, was given two portfolios: the Ministry of Security and the Ministry of Information. All those who had collaborated with the Japanese occupier were excluded from power, and only one Masyumi member, Rasjidi, was included in the cabinet.[44] Although he did not initially have a portfolio, he was later put in charge of the new Ministry of Religions which was created when the government

---

[44] Rasjidi explained to me in March 1992 in Jakarta that he had never actually formally joined Masyumi but was widely considered to be one of its representatives.

moved to Yogyakarta in January 1946. The transfer of the government to Yogyakarta coincided with the nomination to cabinet of a second Masyumi member, Mohammad Natsir, who replaced Amir Sjarifuddin as minister for information. However, Rasjidi and Natsir's decision to participate in government was a personal one rather than a party one. The Masyumi leadership, influenced by the revolutionary atmosphere that reigned in Yogyakarta, adopted a policy of systematic opposition to the new government. This position was illustrated in a document entitled *The Masyumi Manifesto concerning the Change of the Cabinet of Ministers*, outlining the party's grievances with the new government, which was published shortly after the nomination of Sjahrir as prime minister.[45] The manifesto drew attention to the fact that the Indonesian constitution was only a few months old ("a brief instant in relation to historical time which is measured in years and centuries"), stating that it had not been "created precipitously, particularly concerning its principles" and that it had availed of "the past experiences of several famous countries across the world in relation to systems of government". It went on to denounce the formation of a parliamentary cabinet as contrary to the provisions of the recently adopted constitution which provided for a presidential system that was much better adapted to the demands of the moment.[46] The manifesto also hinted at a certain bitterness amongst the party leadership. Two of its members, Abikusno Tjokrosujoso and Wahid Hasjim, had been passed over for cabinet positions because of implied accusations of collaboration. The manifesto called this a "spurious pretext" given that "a large portion of the cabinet" was composed of "people who collaborated with both the Japanese and the Dutch." Finally, it put forward another argument that was to be a recurring element of Masyumi's opposition to Sjahrir, namely that it "was neither the place nor the time for the government to organise negotiations, particularly with the Dutch".

By the end of November 1945, then, the main points of Masyumi's political stance had been defined, and its leaders were to defend

---

[45] *Manifest Masjoemi berhoeboeng dengan pergantian Dewan Kementerian*, published by the party leadership alongside the congress resolutions voted on 7 and 8 November 1945.

[46] "The only general obligation is unity and the rallying together of the forces of the Indonesian people, young and old of all groups, around a government for whom support is as widespread as possible, including all the revolutionary groups and movements (who are not opposed to the way of God)". Ibid.

them over the following two years. The party called for the reinstitu-
tion of a system of national government led by the president, an absolute refusal to enter into negotiations with the Dutch unless they first
recognised Indonesian independence, and the removal of the tandem
formed by Sjahrir and Amir Sjarifuddin. This policy led Masyumi early
in 1946 to join a coalition of opposition set up by Tan Malaka, one
of the main figures of the Indonesian Marxist movement. Malaka had
already approached Sjahrir in an attempt to convince him to make a
move against Sukarno and Hatta, but during a tour of Java, Sjahrir had
been able to gauge the level of support enjoyed by the president, and
he declined this offer. This refusal, however, did not lead Tan Malaka
to rally behind Sukarno. Having abandoned the idea of entering into
direct confrontation with Sukarno and Hatta, he asked them to write
a sort of "political testament" wherein he would be their successor in
the event of their deaths. The two leaders agreed to his proposal but
modified its terms when they drafted the document, proposing instead
a quadrumvirate representing the new Republic's main political currents.
Power was to be divided between Tan Malaka, representing the left's
Marxist wing; the socialist Sjahrir; Wongsonegoro who defended the
interests of the aristocracy and the old line of state functionaries; and
Iwa Kusumasumantri, political Islam's representative.[47] However, Tan
Malaka, with the complicity of Subardjo, whom he had grown close
to since the latter's removal from government, fabricated a fake will
in which Sukarno and Hatta designated him as the sole beneficiary of
their powers. He then travelled across Java brandishing this document
and claiming that as Sukarno and Hatta had been imprisoned by the
British, he was to inherit all their powers. This manoeuvre, which
obliged Sukarno to leave the capital and go on a tour of the republican
territories to deny the rumour, was, according to Kahin, one of the
reasons for the government's transfer to Yogyakarta.[48]

A few weeks after the failure of his ruse, Tan Malaka created, on
15 January 1946, Persatuan Perjuangan (Struggle Union), a coalition
which was soon to contain 137 organisations and which received the
support of General Sudirman, chief of staff of the armed forces. Masyumi, through its representative Wali al-Fatah, occupied a prominent

---

[47] Kusumasumantri was Subardjo's candidate and was preferred over Soekiman,
who was, at the time, in Central Java.
[48] Kahin, *Nationalism and Revolution in Indonesia*, p. 152.

place in the new organisation's governing body. Persatuan Perjuangan united the country's opposition and it quickly adopted a programme entitled "the Seven Pillars of the Indonesian Revolution." It called for negotiations on the basis of total independence, popular government, a citizen army, disarmament of the Japanese, confiscation of property held by Europeans and, finally, the requisition and management of plantations and factories. This programme was approved by the Working Committee in the KNIP, which called upon the people to adopt its objectives. During its first party congress in Solo from 10 to 13 February 1946, Masyumi adopted the main aspects of these demands, though no direct mention was made of Persatuan Perjuangan. It added a particular demand of its own concerning regions inhabited by a majority of Muslims, declaring its wish to see Muslims appointed as heads of local government there.[49]

The conference in Solo established Masyumi as a party directly opposed to the cabinet. Most of the conference speeches developed the themes laid out a few months earlier in the Manifesto. They also demonstrated a certain conviction that the leaders of political Islam had a greater natural legitimacy to lead the nation's struggle for independence than the government, which they judged to be unrepresentative of the people. Although the party never went as far as to call for open rebellion against Sjahrir's cabinet, nor indeed for the withdrawal of the two Masyumi members from government, it constantly highlighted the legitimacy and reasonableness of their demands as those of the Muslim community, the overwhelmingly largest community in the country. Nonetheless, the insistence with which these demands were made did lead one to think that in the minds of at least a section of the Masyumi leadership, failure to meet these demands could open the door to much more radical means of political expression.[50]

The Second Sjahrir Cabinet—The Political Realignment of Masyumi towards the Centre Ground

Faced with such strong opposition to his cabinet, Sjahrir resigned on 28 February 1946. Sukarno subsequently invited Persatuan Perjuangan

---

[49] *Al-Djihad*, 15 February 1946.

[50] Abikoesno Tjokrosudjoso, for example, declared that "although Masyumi had five million armed men behind it, it did not wish to abuse this power and so had called for a coalition cabinet in Parliament." *Al-Djihad*, 16 February 1946.

to form a new government, but when it proved unable to do so, he offered the position of prime minister once again to Sjahrir. Shortly after his reappointment, a new cabinet was announced. It was a bit more diverse this time round and included Masyumi members. Mohammad Natsir kept his position as minister for information, Rasjidi officially became minister for religions, while Arudji Kartawinata was named deputy minister for defence and Sjafruddin Prawiranegara became deputy minister for finance. Like in Sjahrir's first cabinet, these ministers' participation in the government was an individual decision rather than a party one. After 10 days of indecisiveness, the party leadership finally decided to adopt the same position as the Persatuan Perjuangan not to support the new government. However, no measures were taken to demand the Masyumi ministers to act in accordance with the party's decision.

On 17 March 1946, the government took firm action to provisionally put an end to the machinations of Persatuan Perjuangan. During a rally organised in protest at the formation of the new Sjahrir cabinet, Tan Malaka and six members of the organisation's leadership were arrested. Of these, two were members of Masyumi: Abikusno Tjokrosujoso and Wondoamiseno.[51] The setback that this inflicted on the Persatuan Perjuangan leadership, particularly the arrest of Abikusno, led Masyumi to tone down its demands towards the government and realign itself politically towards the middle ground. On 11 May 1946, the Muslim party took part in the birth of a new organisation, named Konsentrasi Nasional (National Concentration), which for the most part took on board the policies of Persatuan Perjuangan, but did away with its systematic opposition to the government in favour of a more constructive form of criticism.[52] It consisted of 31 political organisations, some of which were favourable towards Sjahrir, and was presided over by Sardjono, the new leader of the PKI.

Masyumi's participation in this new organisation did not signify, however, that it had now aligned itself politically with Sjahrir's new cabinet. The Muslim party maintained close links with its former partners in Pesatuan Perjuangan, and at the end of May, shortly after the

---

[51] They were sent to the rally as observers, according to Kahin, *Nationalism and Revolution in Indonesia*, p. 178.

[52] The somewhat ambiguous attitude of this new coalition has led George McTurnan Kahin (Kahin, *Nationalism and Revolution in Indonesia*, p. 183) to conclude that it was initiated by the government. This seems unlikely to me.

foundation of National Concentration, it signed a "Joint Proclamation" (*Maklumat Bersama*) with the Indonesian Labour Party (Partai Buruh Indonesia) and the Indonesian Labour Front (Barisan Buruh Indonesia). This proclamation declared that the government's diplomatic efforts were at an impasse (*jalan buntu*) because of the obvious desire on the part of the Dutch to restore their control over the country. It also called for the formation of a "government composed of representatives of all political parties, which is the only way to obtain the consensus necessary for the nation's fighting power."[53]

The bleak outlook described in the proclamation concerning the future prospects of negotiations with the Netherlands was to be confirmed in the following weeks. The Dutch elections of 17 May brought to power a coalition, led by the Catholic right wing, which was against making any concessions to the Republic's government and who walked back on some of its predecessor's promises. By the beginning of June 1946, the negotiations had, unsurprisingly, reached an impasse, and towards the end of the month the political situation also worsened. On the 27th, a commando group led by General Sudarsono freed Tan Malaka and the other leaders of Persatuan Peerjuangan from their prison in Surakarta. The same evening, Prime Minister Sjahrir and several members of his inner circle were taken hostage. The goal of the operation was to force President Sukarno to replace the government with a supreme political council made up of 10 members and led by Tan Malaka, and also to hand over military power to General Sudirman (under the Constitution, the president was the commander-in-chief of the armed forces). The president reacted quickly to this attempt to destabilise him by declaring a state of siege. On 3 July, General Sudarsono and Muhammad Yamin went to meet Sukarno at the presidential palace, but the president refused point blank to give in to their demands and had the two men arrested. Meanwhile, although senior military staff, in particular Sudirman, had refused to intervene in the situation, the Siliwangi Division, assisted by members of the Pesindo, occupied Madiun and Surakarta and marched on Yogyakarta to demand the liberation of the prime minister. Faced with the risk of a civil war, Sudirman finally allowed Sukarno to convince him to do something

---

[53] *Al-Djihad*, 28 May 1946.

about the situation: he declared his support for Sjahrir and ordered the arrest of those responsible for the operation.[54]

The ambivalence of Mayumi's political stance was manifest in its attitude towards this attempted coup d'état. One of the vice-chairmen of its religious council was a member of the political council chaired by Tan Malaka,[55] but conflicting testimony has been given concerning the position adopted by Masyumi's president, Soekiman. He was among the political representatives who turned up at the presidential palace to demand the dissolution of Sjahrir's cabinet, and he allegedly declared, according to one of the organisers of the operation, Muhammad Yamin, that by making these demands they were merely exercising their right to petition (*implementasi hak petisi*).[56] However, according to Hatta, who was also present at the meeting on 3 July, Soekiman had been duped into going to the presidential palace. General Sudarsono allegedly asked him to come along to listen to a presidential announcement of great importance, and then presented his attendance there as a sign of his support for the group's demands. Soekiman, who had been waiting in an adjoining room, is said to have left the palace immediately once he had been informed by Hatta of Sudarsono's real intentions.[57]

Masyumi's official reaction to these events was adopted on 7 July. The party's communiqué reaffirmed their loyalty towards President Sukarno, but it nonetheless stopped short of formally denouncing the rebels' actions. Condemning Sjahrir's policies, it reiterated the party's demands: the formation of a coalition government and the breaking off of all negotiations with the Dutch. Above all, the party denounced the tendentious account of the events given by the government, which presented the operation as a plot designed to undermine the authority of the state, and called for all political prisoners, with the exception of spies, to be either released or given a speedy trial in accordance with the laws of the Republic.[58]

---

[54] Kahin, *Nationalism and Revolution in Indonesia*, pp. 188–92. Curiously enough, Kahin gives the date of the attempted coup d'état as 2 July, when in fact it took place the following day.

[55] Deliar Noer, *Partai Islam di Pentas Nasional* (Jakarta: Pustaka Utama Grafiti, 1987), p. 162.

[56] Ibid., p. 161.

[57] Mohammad Hatta, *Indonesian Patriot: Memoirs* (Singapore: Gunung Agung, 1981), pp. 259–62.

[58] *Al-Djihad*, 9 July 1946.

The Third Sjahrir Cabinet: Masyumi's Opposition to the Linggadjati Agreement

On 2 October 1946, the Republic's institutions were back in proper functioning order with a presidential decree entrusting executive power to Sjahrir's recently formed third cabinet. The new government was more diverse than its predecessors, and among it were eight Masyumi members or sympathisers. Mohamad Roem was named as minister for home affairs, Sjafruddin Prawiranegara was appointed minister for finance, Faturrachman was in charge of the Ministry of Religion, Natsir was deputy minister to A.R. Baswedan in the Ministry of Information, Jusuf Wibisono became deputy minister for prosperity, H. Agus Salim deputy minister for foreign affairs,[59] Harsono Tjokroaminoto deputy minister for defence, and finally K.H. Wahid Hasjim became a minister without portfolio.

Although the Muslim party was very well-represented in cabinet, this did not prevent Masyumi from having another falling out with the government. On 24 November, having consulted with the representatives of GPII, Muslimaat, the Hizboellah and Sabilillah militias as well as its main constituent organisations, the party leadership refused to support the agreement reached between the Republic of Indonesia and the Netherlands which had been signed on 17 October in the mountain health resort of Linggadjati, near Cirebon.[60] The agreement provided for the immediate recognition by the Dutch of the de facto power of the Republic in Java and Sumatra, the creation by 1 January 1949 of a federal democratic state, the United States of Indonesia, and finally the establishment of a Netherlands-Indonesian Union. Masyumi's main reservation with the agreement was that it did not formally recognise Indonesian independence. Given that the Republic was considered to be legitimate only in Java and Sumatra, this implied that the resistance struggle on the other islands had to be abandoned. It was difficult for them to accept that, especially since the Dutch, only a few weeks beforehand, had established, unilaterally and in violation

---

[59] Hadji Agus Salim was often named either as a Masyumi member or as a member of PSII. He had been one of PSII's leaders before the war and was very close to the modernists in Masyumi, but in actual fact he was a member of neither party after the war.
[60] *Al-Djihad*, 27 October 1946.

of previous agreements, the State of East Indonesia. On 12 December 1946, on the initiative of Masyumi, a federation of all the organisations and militias opposed to the agreement was formed. It was symbolically christened Benteng Republik (Republican Fortress) and it adopted precise organisational rules,[61] and a four-point programme which aimed at:

> ...making the entire population aware of the necessity to refuse the Dutch-Indonesian agreement; demanding the formation of an assembly which had the confidence of all the people; preparing for the aftermath of the agreement's rejection; demanding the immediate commencement of trials for political prisoners with a view to the immediate release of those who were innocent.[62]

It was in this context of violent opposition to the diplomatic policy of Sjahrir's third cabinet that Sukarno decided to adjust the balance of power in favour of his prime minister. A presidential decree issued on 29 December 1946 increased the number of seats in the KNIP from 200 to 514. Of the 314 new members, only 93 held seats as representatives of a political party, the other 221 had been chosen as representatives either of the various interest groups such as peasants or industrial workers, or of regions outside Java. This new composition was at first refused by the KNIP's Working Committee who saw in it a manoeuvre by Sukarno in favour of Sajap Kiri, a left-wing coalition which supported the prime minister.[63] It was finally accepted on 5 March 1947 after a forceful speech by Vice President Mohammad Hatta, who warned that both he and the president would resign if the new composition was not approved. Masyumi and the PNI left the plenary session in protest.[64] The Muslim party, despite its number of representatives going from 35 to 65, suffered an overall loss of power.[65]

---

[61] It contained an executive council, a political council and a defence council, and motions were to be carried by a qualified majority.

[62] *Al-Djihad*, 13 December 1946.

[63] Sajap Kiri, meaning "left wing", was composed of the Socialist Party, the PKI, the Pesindo, the Partai Buruh and the Christian parties.

[64] Noer, *Partai Islam di Pentas Nasional*, p. 167.

[65] This loss of power was somewhat attenuated by the fact that the new Working Committee comprised five Masyumi members (S.M. Kartosuwirjo, Mahmud L. Latjuba, Prawoto Mangkusasmito, Mr Samsuddin and Mohammad Sardjan) as well as a representative of *Sarekat Tani Islam Indonesia*, Abu Umar.

During a plenary conference held by the party between 19 and 20 March in Yogyakarta, Masyumi set out in a document entitled "Urgency Programme", all its grievances and demands concerning the Sjahrir government. This relatively short text containing the resolutions made by the party was published shortly afterwards by the leadership, accompanied by a 40-page commentary, which mainly attempted to impugn the government's legitimacy to rule. The principal demand made was for a democratic government, which was a direct response to the president's new nominations. Masyumi called for the repeal of the government's decree that applied the president's decision and demanded the election, within four months, of an assembly based on genuine popular sovereignty.[66] The commentary concerning the first point implicitly developed the notion, which we have already seen, that Indonesia's institutions lacked legitimacy.[67] It affirmed that in a country under the control either of a single man—a *raja*, a king or a dictator —or of a "little group of feudal aristocrats", "the people were given no other choice but to follow the law without being able to participate in the elaboration of those laws or without being entitled to either control or oversee how the country was being run, and thus [they could] not feel responsible for the destiny of their country."[68] The leadership sent out a warning to the government:

> For this reason, when this government, which is not supported by the people, suffers at some stage or other some ill fate, it will be overturned and destroyed by its own people because it is not a government in accordance with the wishes of the people, who for their part are convinced that all their misfortunes are due to the fact that it is governed arbitrarily.[69]

While the nomination of deputies to the KNIP was justified at the outset of the new Republic, in the eyes of the senior members of

---

[66] Pengoeroes Besar Masjoemi, *Tafsir Urgentie Program. Kepoetoesan Konferensi kilat, tg. 19–20 mrt. 1947 di Djogjakarta*, Articles Ia and Ib.

[67] It is interesting to note that most of the party's direct criticisms of and threats towards the government were contained in this official commentary (published with the approval of the party's executive committee) and not in the Urgency Programme. It reveals the internal debates which were going on within the party on which opposition strategy to adopt towards the government.

[68] Pengoeroes Besar Masjoemi, *Tafsir Urgentie Program*, pp. 4–5.

[69] Ibid., p. 5.

the Muslim party, they considered that the absence of elections and the expansion of the Assembly through nominations were "in persistent opposition to democratic principles".[70] According to them, the two arguments advanced by the "undemocratic" side, which were the illiteracy and the political immaturity of the people as well as the impossibility of organising elections, did not stand up to analysis: "you cannot raise the spectre of the people's lack of political intelligence, for there exists no country in the world where the entire population has this political intelligence".[71] The party recognised the logistical difficulties surrounding the organisation of an election, and pointed out that although it should in principle be a general election, it could, for the moment at least, be an indirect election. However, Masyumi demanded the establishment of an electoral college (one elector for every 250 citizens) and objected to allowing parliamentary deputies to be appointed by the existing local and regional assemblies who, "for the most part, had not been democratically elected".[72]

The second point developed by the programme was a plea for the army to remain revolutionary. The resolutions concerning questions of national defence and the commentaries that accompanied them revealed the party's apprehension about the government's plan to professionalise the army. This plan was termed "rationalisation" and aimed at progressively integrating militia groups into the regular army. The Masyumi position on this plan was based on two somewhat contradictory concerns. The first of these was a suspicion that the army would be politicised, and that this would be to the advantage of one of the factions within the army which supported the government. The party leadership demanded the dissolution of the "Inspection Offices for the Armed Struggle" (*Inspektorat-inspektorat Bureau Perdjoeangan*), which they opposed as organisations that were "clearly acting as the zealots of a political party's ideology".[73] The target of this attack was the PSI and particularly those members of it who were close to Amir Sjarifuddin, the minister for defence. These inspection offices were accused of having set up parallel military organisations that were controlled by the minister's henchmen. All of Masyumi's constituent organisations were

---

[70] Ibid., p. 6.
[71] Ibid.
[72] Ibid., p. 9.
[73] Ibid., p. 3.

therefore asked not to participate in any of these bodies' activities. This boycott had already been voted by the Barisan Sabilillah during its conference on 13 and 14 April 1947, and the GPII refused to allow the Barisan Republik Muda and the Asrama Republik, both of which had been created by the Inspection Office, to join their organisation.[74]

Masyumi was also opposed, however, to the creation of a professional army cut off from its roots among the people. It laid heavy emphasis on the importance of the mobilisation of the people after the proclamation of independence, contrasting the heroic struggle of the masses "unparalleled in the entire history of Indonesia" with "the partisan politicians who arrived on the scene late in the day with the sole aim of leading and showing the way".[75] The mobilisation of the people had taken place from a very early stage, guaranteeing the army a place of precedence in revolutionary mythology. The armed struggle had revealed the people's worth; they had

> ...found in it a new spirit, a heroic spirit which allowed them to defeat the Japanese army easily, to confront, with ease also, the English army...to contain and resist against the Dutch colonial military force, which is the size of an international army. [...] It was neither diplomatic skill nor political perseverance nor the intellectual experts nor the crafty politicians who won independence, but rather the heroes covered in blood.[76]

Maintaining popular militia groups also served the interests of national security, of course, which it would have been "reactionary and dangerous" to weaken, given that a threat still existed: "the enemy of independence [...] has perhaps laid down his arms" but he "has not yet been destroyed". Above all, the existence of this revolutionary army had a political justification:

> The militia groups constituted a guarantee of the people's aspirations, so that the government would maintain the confidence of the Revolution; a guarantee which an official army, which would be completely under the control of the government and would thus become its instrument, could not provide.[77]

---

[74] Ibid., p. 14.
[75] Ibid., p. 12.
[76] Ibid., p. 13.
[77] Ibid., p. 20.

The same analysis of the Revolution can be found in the criticisms which were outlined in the third resolution of the plenary congress, entitled "In Response to the Linggadjati Document". Masyumi challenged the government's outlook for the future, which considered that the armed conflict was finished and that a new stage of the Revolution was about to begin. It criticized the Ministry of Information, despite the fact that it was run by Natsir, for having co-authored with the Dutch authorities a joint communiqué which expressed the hope "that between the Indonesian nation and the Dutch nation, a spirit of real comprehension would appear, and that feelings of bitterness and vengeance would be rejected".[78] The joint reduction in arms provided for in the Linggadjati Agreement left the Netherlands with a significant strategic advantage, due to the superiority of their equipment, and, more importantly, sanctioned the Dutch occupation of part of the Republic's territory. These were all concessions that the Muslim party refused to endorse. The resolution referred to the fact that during the parliamentary session which ratified the agreement, the party had clearly indicated that it would not consider itself bound by the agreement if it came to be signed.[79] Naturally, the party called for the struggle to be continued and also to be broadened to include all areas of society:

> The battlefields, which today contain more traps and dangers due to the coming into force of the agreement, have become more and more vast. There is a military struggle, a political struggle, a social struggle, an economic struggle, a spiritual struggle (in the areas of religion, upbringing, education and science) and many others.[80]

The need to continue the struggle in all areas gave the authors of the commentaries on the Urgency Programme the opportunity to call to order party members participating in the government. The document also reveals certain disagreements within the party, which we will come back to later: "Masyumi has supported its leadership and called for greater respect for party discipline from some of its representatives who are part of the government, the KNIP and the parliamentary committees."[81]

---

[78] Ibid., p. 23.
[79] Ibid., p. 25.
[80] Ibid., p. 27.
[81] Ibid.

The last section of the Urgency Programme stipulated that the struggle against the occupied forces should not be confined to Java. The party leadership called on its members to "intensify their spiritual and material efforts which will strengthen the union and the unity of all the regions of Indonesia which some today would like to like to see broken up".[82] These efforts, the commentary specified, should notably take the form of infiltration operations on Kalimantan, Sulawesi, the Maluku Islands and the Lesser Sunda Islands. In these regions, "small groups with money and a plan must provide, by peaceful means or otherwise, anything which could help those regional Muslim communities in their struggle."

Masyumi's firm commitment to the continuation of an armed struggle against Holland heightened tensions further in the country. Under pressure from some sections of the Catholic party, as well as the conservative right, to be more intransigent towards the republicans, the Dutch government finalised, on 27 May 1947, the terms of an ultimatum which amounted to placing the Republic under Dutch federal control.[83] The Sjahrir government was caught between a desire to resist Dutch pressure and an urge to nonetheless maintain dialogue with the former colonial power. Sjahrir was abandoned by his own majority coalition, Sajap Kiri, and resigned on 27 June.

The End of the Myth of Unity

Since the end of 1946, there had been increasing tensions within the Masyumi leadership. Although the party was somewhat compromised by the increasing number of "individual" participants in the government, it continued to criticise the pursuance of negotiations with Holland, one of the main planks of the government's policy. However, the prospect of entering government began to whet people's appetites for power. The different wings within the party, which up until now had been united around a clear policy and the simple watchwords dictated by the Revolution, began to assert themselves. Former leaders of Partai Sarekat Islam Indonesia had for some time been convinced

---

[82] Resolution 4a of the Urgency Programme.

[83] For further reading on these proposals and on the Dutch manœuvres in the spring of 1947, see Françoise Cayrac-Blanchard and Philippe Devillers, *L'Asie du Sud-Est*, coll. "L'Histoire du XXe Siècle", vol. 1 (Paris: Sirey, 1970), pp. 330–1.

that they had not been given the position they deserved within the party and they seized the opportunity offered by the formation of a new government.

Amir Sjarifuddin, who was appointed prime minister by the president, was far more hostile towards Masyumi than Sjahrir had been. The former defence minister had not forgotten the virulent attacks on his defence policy made by the Muslim party. Politically, however, he could not do without the approval of the representatives of Islam, and so he looked favourably on the proposal made by Wondoamiseno and Arudji Kartawinata to reform PSII in exchange for seats at the cabinet table.[84] The newly re-formed party received six seats in the cabinet, which was formed on 3 July 1947. Wondoamiseno was named minister for home affairs, Sjahbudin Latif deputy minister for information, Arudji Kartawinata deputy minister of defence, Sukoso Wirjosaputro deputy minister for social affairs, and H. Anwaruddin minister for religions.[85] Feelings ran high in Masyumi after this. The re-emergence of the PSII had destroyed what, until then, was the almost sacred principle of the Muslim community's political unity. With Soekiman's party no longer the sole representative of the *umma*, its position was clearly weakened. In the medium term, this no doubt encouraged the party to adopt a more realistic and less intransigent stance, but in the short term, it meant that Masyumi, for the first time since the proclamation of independence, was simply another opposition party without any real leverage over the government.

This latest discord between the Muslim party and the government was short-lived, however. The Indonesian government's refusal to give in to Dutch demands led the Netherlands to launch their first "police action"[86] against the Republic's territories on the 21 July 1947. In less

---

[84] According to George McTurnan Kahin, the revival of PSII took place against the wishes of its former president Abikusno Tjokrosujoso who, at the time, was in prison for his involvement in the events which took place during the summer of 1946. Kahin, *Nationalism and Revolution in Indonesia*, p. 210. Moreover, two other PSII leaders, Kartosuwirjo and Anwar Tjokroaminoto, also disapproved of this initiative. Kartosuwirjo refused the position of deputy minister for defence and both of them remained part of Masyumi's executive committee. Susan Finch and Daniel Lev, *Republic of Indonesia Cabinets, 1945–1965* (Ithaca, NY: Cornell University Press, 1965), p. 11; Noer, *Partai Islam di Pentas Nasional*, p. 170.

[85] It was K. Achmad Asj'ari, also a member of PSII, who had initially been nominated to this position but he was not able to leave Sumatra to take up office.

[86] To use the term employed by the Dutch authorities.

than two weeks, Dutch armoured columns, backed up by strong aerial support, made deep inroads into republican territory. Most of the towns and ports of East Java and West Java, as well as the richest areas of Sumatra, were occupied. For the most part, the Indonesian armed forces did not engage directly with the advancing forces, preferring instead to take refuge, according to a pre-established plan, in remote areas which were difficult to access. However, the speed of the Dutch advancement prevented their adversaries from stowing away the planned amount of food and military equipment. The Dutch troops had managed to get their hands on most of the means of food production in republican territory and since the beginning of the blockade had cut off production.

This "first Dutch aggression", to employ the term used in Indonesian historiography, can be considered a turning point in the constitution of Masyumi's political identity. The increased republican unity that it provoked helped the Muslim party to take a decisive step towards committing itself to taking part in running the country's affairs. This gradual mutation from being a revolutionary party and an intransigent advocate of total independence to becoming a party of government had been prepared, as we will see, by a small group of men. It did not come about smoothly, however, and the party's period in opposition left a permanent mark on the burgeoning political consciousness of the Muslim community.

The theme of the arithmetic legitimacy of an Islamic majority which trumped the government's illegitimacy was a recurrent one in Masyumi's propaganda. It no doubt contributed to the emergence of some of the arguments used to justify the rebellions carried out by Darul Islam and, to a certain extent, by the PRRI, the revolutionary government in Sumatra that certain Masyumi leaders were associated with from 1958 onwards. In short, at the same time as the conditions for Masyumi's political success were appearing, the seeds of contestation which would lead to its downfall were being sown.

The Emergence of a Party of Government

Between autumn 1945 and summer 1947, Masyumi was more than just the revolutionary party and standard-bearer for unconditional independence which we have just described. A few men, who were not yet very influential within the party, were already preparing it for government. On the occasion of the transferral of the Republic's capital from

Jakarta to Yogyakarta on 3 January 1946, Mohammad Natsir was appointed minister for information. He became a focal point for the political forces within Masyumi which were prepared to support Sjahrir's policies. A few weeks after Natsir's appointment, one of his close allies, Sjafruddin Prawiranegara, secretary of the KNIP's Working Committee, formulated their political credo:

> Japanese flattery has exaggerated the importance of *semangat* [enthusiasm] beyond all limits and has derided and aroused hatred for *akal* [reason] as though *akal* were simply a Western invention—an invention of the imperialists and capitalists, which has had an evil influence upon our people.[87]

According to Sjafruddin, this revolutionary spirit had led to the formulation of unrealistic demands by otherwise well-intentioned young people. He recalled the examples provided by Lenin and Stalin (examples which no doubt were not chosen randomly), whom he described as "great realists, often attacked by their own less clear-sighted juniors",[88] and denounced Indonesian socialists' incomprehension of their own ideology. The popular enthusiasm that sent out young people armed only with bamboo spears to fight the allied forces with their firearms was, according to him, "stupid if not criminal".[89] He denounced the ignorance of a large part of the population concerning Indonesia's military and diplomatic weakness, and encouraged his fellow countrymen to support Sjahrir's *realpolitik*. The influence of this small group of men grew rapidly in the months that followed. At the next cabinet reshuffle in March 1946, Natsir was joined in government by Sjafruddin Prawiranegara, Arudji Kartawinata and Agus Salim. Agus Salim, who was on the fringes of the Muslim party due to his falling out with Soekiman, was something of a spiritual mentor to the other two.[90] Shortly after the creation of the new government, Natsir was sent to Sumatra, which was in the throes of a social revolution, in order to

---

[87] *Berita Indonesia*, 5 February 1946. Quoted in Anderson, *Java in a Time of Revolution*, p. 310n1.
[88] According to Anderson's reformulation of Sjafruddin's terms. Anderson, *Java in a Time of Revolution*, p. 311.
[89] Ibid.
[90] Noer, *Partai Islam di Pentas Nasional*, p. 59.

re-establish the central government's authority.[91] His skill in managing this difficult task led him to acquire, in the corridors of power, a new stature and allowed him to work at bringing his party and the government closer together.

The relationship between the Masyumi leadership and the government was not devoid of ambiguity. Although the party was officially in opposition, it tolerated, as we have already seen, the individual decisions of some of its members to join Sjahrir's cabinet. During the summer of 1946, however, there were increasing signs that the government and the party were finding more and more common ground. At the end of June, the Muslim party used its propaganda machine to help promote the sale of government bonds which the government had just launched.[92] The abduction of the prime minister and the fallout from this event, which became known as "the Affair of 3 July", only gave rise to a minor disagreement between Masyumi and the government; later that year in the autumn, during discussions concerning the formation of a new cabinet, the Masyumi leadership submitted to Sjahrir a list of party figures likely to accept a seat in his cabinet, eight of whom ended up joining the government. Two of those eight members were close to Soekiman: Jusuf Wibisono and Wahid Hasjim, the leader of Nahdlatul Islam and president of Masyumi's *Majelis Sjuro*.

The signing of the Linggadjati Agreement put an end to this rapprochement and led to a direct clash between the party leadership and those party members who were part of the cabinet. Up until that point, in the various resolutions condemning Sjahrir's policies, Masyumi had always limited itself to calling for the formation of a coalition government. Before the Surakarta Conference on 4 and 5 December 1946, the resignation of Masyumi's ministers had never been called for. On 24 November, Mohamad Roem had made a speech on the radio in defence of the draft agreement that had just been signed. He asked the Masyumi leadership to defer any vote on the issue in order to give him the time to return to Yogyakarta and defend the government's position before the party's governing body. However, on his arrival in the Republic's capital, he discovered that Masyumi had just announced its rejection of the Linggadjati compromise. In a letter to the leadership, he denounced this decision which was taken without giving the

---

[91] Kahin, *Nationalism and Revolution in Indonesia*, pp. 180–2.
[92] *Al-Djihad*, 21 June 1946.

party members sitting in cabinet an opportunity to express themselves, and which was thus in complete contradiction with the principles of democracy and consultation (*musjawarah*) defended by the party.[93] On 4 and 5 December 1946, a joint congress organised by Masyumi and GPII in Surakarta confirmed the rejection of the agreement. In a joint statement made by the two organisations, they declared that they "counted on the members of Masyumi sitting in the current cabinet to abide loyally by their party's decision to reject the Dutch-Indonesian agreement".[94] On 28 December 1946, in response to this warning, the Masyumi ministers meeting in Purwokerto signed the following clarification:

1. The current cabinet is a national cabinet and not a coalition cabinet. Consequently, in accordance with parliamentary rules and political custom, it is not necessary for a party to decide what political position should be adopted by ministers who are its members.
2. For this reason, the Masyumi ministers will settle directly with its leadership problems concerning the decisions taken in the Masyumi congress in Solo.[95]

This dismissal of the party's injunction was signed by all of the ministers concerned, and it is interesting in more than one respect. Firstly, it demonstrates the signatories' capacity for independent thought; they were convinced of the legitimacy of their position even when faced with the opposition of their own party. Furthermore, and most significantly, it reveals something very important about the political culture of those concerned. Although they had only been ministers for a few months and despite the fact that the Republic was less than two years old, they referred nonetheless to "parliamentary rules" and to "political custom". They replied to the religiously inspired dictates of the party leadership by using references to what, in their eyes, was

---

[93] Noer, "Masjumi: Its Organization, Ideology, and Political Role in Indonesia", p. 99, Hakiem claims that Mohammad Roem was indeed present at the conference: Hakiem, *Perjalan mencari keadilan dan persatuan. Biografi Dr Anwar Harjono*, p. 100.

[94] Kementerian Penerangan Republik Indonesia, *Daerah Istimewa Jogjakarta*, n.d., p. 166. Hakiem, *Perjalan mencari keadilan dan persatuan. Biografi Dr Anwar Harjono*, p. 101.

[95] Kementerian Penerangan Republik Indonesia, *Daerah Istimewa Jogjakarta*, p. 173.

another norm, namely that of a parliamentary regime inspired by the West. It is here that we can see the first signs of what was to characterise Masyumi under Natsir's leadership.

The Dutch attack, in July 1947, against the Republic's territories initially boosted political unity within the fledgling state. Masyumi, which had up until that point been opposed to Amir Sjarifuddin's government, agreed to join it and on 11 November 1947, a new cabinet was formed. The Muslim party was given a prominent place at the cabinet table, to the detriment mainly of PSII. Masyumi received five cabinet seats on top of Agus Salim's portfolio as minister for foreign affairs. Samsuddin became the first deputy prime minister, Kasman Singodimedjo was named deputy justice minister, Mohammed Roem became minister for home affairs, K.H. Masjkur was appointed minister for religions, while Anwar Tjokroaminoto became a minister without portfolio. This participation in government, the first to be really organised and assumed by the party, did not last long, however. Masyumi was opposed to the diplomatic concessions made by Amir Sjarifuddin, and withdrew its support for the government. On 16 January, on the eve of the signing of the Renville Agreement, its ministers resigned.[96] On 23 January 1948, in Yogyakarta, a demonstration led by Anwar Haryono of the GPII called for the resignation of the entire cabinet, which was duly announced that evening.[97] This created a problematic situation, however, as any new cabinet would have to ensure the execution of an agreement that most political parties rejected.[98] The solution to this problem came in the form of a presidential cabinet led by Mohammad Hatta and made up mainly of a PNI-Masyumi coalition. Masyumi members were given the Ministry of Home Affairs (Soekiman Wirjosandjojo), the Ministry of Information (Mohammad Natsir), the Ministry of Prosperity (Sjafruddin Prawiranegara) and the Ministry of Religion (K.H. Masjkur), while H. Agus Salim remained minister for foreign affairs. It was to this government that the arduous task of dealing with the crisis fell, one which would eventually lead the country towards internationally recognised independence.

---

[96] H. Agus Salim, however, remained a cabinet member.

[97] Hakiem, *Perjalanan mencari keadilan dan persatuan. Biografi Dr Anwar Haryono*, p. 105.

[98] Shortly beforehand, the PNI had also denounced the agreement and withdrawn its support from Amir Sjarifuddin's government.

On 30 July 1947, India and Australia referred the Indonesian conflict to the UN Security Council. After a period of shuttle diplomacy, the Council decided to form a Good Offices Committee which was to arrive in Indonesia at the end of October. Its members managed to convince the Republic that it had everything to win by transferring their struggle into the political field. Their army's military capacity was limited to guerrilla warfare, and economically the population could not put up with the hardships caused by the Dutch blockade for very much longer. In addition, it became easy for the former colonial authorities, in the areas where they had regained control, to present themselves as the solution to the problems they had created. On 17 and 19 January 1948, the Renville Agreement was signed, which required both sides to respect a border known as the "Van Mook Line",[99] and which provided for the Republic to become one of the states of a future federal Indonesia. This agreement was more than favourable towards the Dutch and it triggered further machinations by them: in violation of the spirit, if not the letter, of the agreement, they encouraged the creation of new political entities, thus further weakening the influence of the Republic in the future federation. In January, the State of Madura was created, followed at the end of February by Pasundan, also known as the State of West Java. Finally, on 9 March 1948, Van Mook announced the establishment of an interim federal government which, in the absence of republican representatives, was entirely composed of Dutch members, and which was to remain in place until the creation of the United States of Indonesia. As George Kahin wrote, it was "merely the old Netherlands Indies regime in new dress and was run by the personnel of the colonial regime with a few anti-Republican Indonesians included to present a better façade."[100]

In the summer of 1948, the operation, launched almost a year before by the Netherlands, seemed to be on course for success, while the future prospects of the Republic were looking increasingly bleak. The Dutch exploited the emerging Cold War climate in Europe and managed to obtain a certain amount of leniency from the United States. The Americans' objections remained moderate, and much to the

---

[99] Named after the Lieutenant Governor General of the time. This line, drawn a few months earlier by the Dutch, gave them control over certain zones into which their troops had not yet entered.

[100] Kahin, *Nationalism and Revolution in Indonesia*, p. 245.

republicans' despair, they seemed ready to believe in the Dutch fiction of a federal Indonesia. In the spring of 1948, the Netherlands received 506 million dollars as part of the Marshall Plan, 84 million of which were to be used for the Dutch administration in Indonesia.[101] The Republic was isolated on the international scene, economically stifled and hampered by a domestic situation that was worsening by the day. It only remained for the Dutch, then, to wait until it crumbled, and the last major obstacle to their return to the colony they had abandoned six years earlier would be removed.

Towards Political Coherence

Retrospectively, 1948 appears as the year when things became somewhat clearer, not just for Masyumi but for Indonesian political life in general. Up until that point, public debate was dominated by questions of diplomacy, creating a division in Indonesian politics between pragmatists, who were convinced of the necessity to negotiate with the former colonial power, and idealists, who were opposed to any concession made concerning absolute independence. This division was itself mirrored within Masyumi. Three events, however, contributed to a profound transformation of the Indonesian political landscape: the communist rebellion in Madiun, the emergence of Darul Islam and the second Dutch "police action". The extent of the threat which the combination of these three crises posed to the young Republic favoured the appearance of a lasting consensus between the main Indonesian political parties by allowing the Republic's opponents to be clearly identified and subsequently marginalised. This consensus concerned not only the strategy to be adopted in countering the Dutch political manoeuvres, but also the rules necessary for the efficient running of political life.

Madiun or the Emergence of Anti-Communism

As a member of the Indonesian delegation, Sjafruddin Prawiranegara participated in the discussions in the Economic Council for Asia and the Far East (ECAFE) which were held in Manila in 1947. His discussions with other delegates led him to understand that he and his Indonesian colleagues were perceived by many to be communist. He was bothered by this association and on his return to Indonesia, he

---

[101] Ibid., p. 254.

started writing a booklet entitled *Politik dan Demokrasi Kita* (*Our Politics and Democracy*), which was published in mid-1948 and which clarified the relationship between communism and Islam. In it, he recognised the disorderly nature of Indonesian politics, which had led Masyumi, for example, to collaborate with the Communist Party within Persatuan Perjuangan. He also argued for some party discipline to be imposed within political parties so that every party member might be completely in agreement with the party line. He acknowledged, moreover, the necessity for a social doctrine:

> Our National Revolution needs an ideology which can guarantee the realisation of social justice. However, I believe that Marxism cannot fulfil that need; in addition, Marxism is contrary to the Constitution. The ideology which is suitable to our society is Religious Socialism, an ideology which is in harmony with the Constitution. Religious Socialism does not abolish individualism, individual initiative and individual responsibility.[102]

The desire on the part of Masyumi's leaders to distinguish themselves clearly from communism appeared during the course of 1947.[103] Up until that point, the actions of the PKI, which did not have any significant political influence, had attracted very little of the party's attention. In its accounts of communist meetings, *Al-Djihad*, one of Masyumi's mouthpieces, never risked making negative comments.[104] However, in the spring of 1947, relations turned sour between GPII and the Marxist youth movements, testifying yet again to the vanguard role of the *pemuda*. In May, at the Second Council of the Youth Congress of the Republic of Indonesia (Badan Kongres Pemuda Republik Indonesia, BKPRI), GPII denounced the domination of the Pesindo in the council, and announced that it was withdrawing from the organisation. In August, it—along with other youth organisations, namely Pemuda Demokrat and Pemuda Kristen—formed a Front Nasional Pemuda (FNP) that elected as its president Anwar Haryono, a party

---

[102] Quoted by Kahin, *Nationalism and Revolution in Indonesia*, p. 310. We will look at this notion of religious socialism later in Chapter 6.

[103] The political divisions which existed during the first months of the revolution can nonetheless be analysed from a religious perspective. Further reading on this topic can be found in Merle C. Ricklefs, *Islamisation and Its Opponents in Java, c. 1930 to the Present* (Singapore: NUS Press, 2012), pp. 69–79.

[104] See, for example, *Al-Djihad*, 12 February 1946.

official in GPII.[105] This radicalisation of the opposition between communists and non-communists was, naturally, not specific to Indonesia and was due, in large part, to the evolution of the international situation. The emergence of two blocs, encapsulated in the words of the Zhdanov Doctrine in autumn 1947, led to a number of schisms on the fringes of the communist bloc, which were similar to those taking place in Indonesia. Before the year was out, a powerful wing favourable to Moscow had formed within the Indonesian left, and within the Socialist Party differences of opinion were deepening. Amir Sjarifuddin aligned his position increasingly with Moscow's, and he persuaded Sajap Kiri to adopt a position of systematic opposition to Hatta's government. This led Sjahrir's supporters to withdraw from the Partai Sosialis and Sajap Kiri and to found, on 13 February 1948, their own party, the Partai Sosialis Indonesia, which supported Hatta's cabinet. Shortly after 26 February, Sajap Kiri became the Front Demokrasi Rakjat (FDR), whose main bastions of support were the army (especially the auxiliary forces of the TNI-Masjarakat), and the large trade union federation, SOBSI. Benefitting from the Dutch blockade, which prevented the exchange of books and newspapers with the outside world, communist publications, no doubt heavily subsidised by Moscow, were able to spread their ideas and allow them take a foothold in the towns within the narrow area of republican territory.[106] To counter the growing influence of these political forces close to Moscow, the government released the leaders of Persatuan Perjuangan, who immediately created the Gerakan Revolusi Rakjat (GRR) under the leadership of Tan Malaka. This new organisation was hostile to the FDR, and Hatta backed its programme, declaring it to be "a national programme of resistance and union". In addition, the cabinet initiated a rationalisation programme for the army which gradually removed its auxiliary units, thus depriving the FDR of its armed wing.

In one sense, this policy served the interests of Masyumi, who had for several months denounced the systematic infiltration of the armed forces carried out by Amir Sjarifuddin's supporters. At the same time, however, the Muslim party feared that its own militia would come under threat. At its third party congress held in the Javanese town

---

[105] Hakiem, *Perjalan mencari keadilan dan persatuan. Biografi Dr Anwar Harjono*, pp. 109–10.
[106] Kahin, *Nationalism and Revolution in Indonesia*, p. 253.

of Madiun from 27 to 31 March, it adopted a resolution asking the government to recognise the legality of the Hizboellah and Sabilillah militia groups.[107] In August 1948, Musso, one of communism's prestigious leaders, returned from Prague and took over the leadership of the PKI. Under his leadership, the Proletarian Party, Murba, and Amir Sjarifuddin's Socialist Party decided to join with the Communist Party, thus ensuring it the control of the FDR, which subsequently became known as the PKI-Musso.[108] During the summer of 1948, there was an increasing number of clashes between the military wings of different factions, and then at the beginning of September, large-scale confrontations took place between, on the one hand, FDR troops—namely the Pesindo and AMRI[109]—and on the other, pro-government armed forces—in particular the Barisan Banteng militia controlled by Tan Malaka and the Siliwangi Division. In Surakarta, the pro-government forces began to gain the upper hand, and the communist troops were ejected from the town on 17 September. This setback, according to Kahin, was no doubt what encouraged certain militia commanders to take action without deferring to the PKI's leaders, and to undertake on 18 December the military phase of a plan which had already been hatched within the FDR in June, consisting in taking control of Madiun.[110]

On 20 September, a revolutionary government with Amir Sjarifuddin at its head was formed in Madiun. However, the rebellion was ill-prepared and did not win over the popular support it had hoped for. By 30 September, forces loyal to the government, notably the Siliwangi Division which distinguished itself during the fighting, had regained control of the city. Abandoning Madiun, the rebel forces hoped to find refuge in the surrounding mountains where they would be able to wait for the next Dutch attack which, they felt, was imminent. As they were fleeing Madiun, pursued by government forces, they executed numerous government officials, symbols of the administration they despised, and Masyumi members in particular were victims of these attacks.[111] On

---

[107] Madiun Congress Resolutions in Aboebakar, *Sejarah hidup K.H.A. Wahid Hasjim dan karangan tersiar*, pp. 364–5.

[108] Kahin, *Nationalism and Revolution in Indonesia*, p. 281.

[109] *Angkatan Muda Republik Indonesia*, Young Generation of the Republic of Indonesia.

[110] Kahin, *Nationalism and Revolution in Indonesia*, p. 290.

[111] Ibid., p. 300.

MENGENANG PERISTIWA MADIUN

Plate 2.1   "Remember Madiun" (*Hikmah*, 17 September 1955).

7 December 1948, the military staff of the TNI announced the end of the rebellion; the death of its leaders, in particular Musso and Amir Sjarifuddin, meant that the Indonesian communist movement was to remain rudderless for the foreseeable future.

The Madiun uprising was a traumatic episode in the Republic's history which gave rise to a virulent form of anti-communism amongst the leaders of political Islam. Throughout the period of liberal democracy, it was referred to constantly in their speeches and was an essential element in the party's pro-coalition policy.[112]

Darul Islam—The Temptation of Radicalism

While the communist groups' growing opposition to the government contributed to Masyumi's rapprochement with the coalition in power,

---

[112] Even if some sections of the communist movement did not take part in the uprising, the FDR branches in Sumatra and Bantam, for example, remained loyal to the government. Ibid., p. 300.

the emergence of a radical Islamic movement in West Java also obliged it to break with the populist intransigence which had heretofore inspired much of its policy. In accordance with the Renville Agreement signed in January 1948, republican forces, including militia groups, were to withdraw from the territory controlled by the Dutch, situated to the west of the "Van Mook Line". Close to 4,000 men refused to comply with this directive, most of whom were members of Hizboellah and Sabilillah hailing from villages in the region. These combatants had taken up arms to defend their land and their religion, and at each break in hostilities, they returned to their homes. It was thus very difficult for them to leave their families and to abandon a struggle for the sake of political considerations, when up until that point, their struggle had been successful. One of Masyumi's founders, Kartosuwirjo, held a certain sway over the youth organisations in West Java.[113] In the years leading up to the war, he used the "Suffa Institute" in Garut to instil dozens of young people with an anti-Dutch, and indeed an anti-West, attitude.[114] Within Masyumi, Kartosuwirjo had been one of those who adopted a hard-line stance towards the Dutch. His disappointment with what he saw as his party's lack of firmness towards the Sjahrir government led him to distance himself from it somewhat and give up his seat on the party's executive committee. He remained, however, its representative in West Java, and in 1947, he had refused to participate in the reconstruction of PSII, explaining that he "still felt a sense of duty towards Masyumi".[115] It was on behalf of Masyumi that he founded, in November 1947, two new organisations: the Defence Council of the Islamic Community (Dewan Pertahanan Ummat Islam) in Garut, and the Council of the Indonesian Islamic Community (Majelis Ummat Islam Indonesia) in Tasikmalaya.

After the signing of the Renville Agreement, however, a split with Masyumi became inevitable. Although the Muslim party was opposed

---

[113] Sekarmaji Marjan Kartosuwiryo was born in 1905 in East Java. His family belonged to what in the early 20th century was called the "low-*priyayi*" class and he was himself educated in the Dutch school system, at least until his expulsion from Surabaya medical school in 1927. On his life and political activity before the outbreak of the rebellion, see Chiara Formichi, *Islam and the Making of the Nation: Kartosuwiryo and Political Islam in 20th Century Indonesia* (Leiden: KITLV Press, 2012), pp. 15–77.

[114] Noer, *The Modernist Muslim Movement in Indonesia, 1900–1942*, pp. 148–9.

[115] Cees Van Dijk, *Rebellion under the Banner of Islam* (The Hague: Martinus Nijhoff, 1981), p. 83.

to the solution envisaged by the agreement, it had gradually become one of the parties of government and, as such, it had to bear responsibility for the agreement's execution. In March 1948, Kartosuwirjo organised a gathering of all the Hizboellah militia regiments in the region of Priangan in West Java during which the participants denounced the "suicidal" policy of the republican government and, disregarding the orders they had received from their military command, decided to continue their combat against Dutch troops. An organisation was created under the leadership of Kartosuwirjo called Darul Islam (the Abode of Islam). It did not initially assert itself as an opponent to the republican government, but in December 1948, following the "second police action", when the Siliwanggi Division was forced to retreat to West Java, the republican armed forces were not very well received and clashed with Darul Islam troops. After the signing of the Roem-Van Royen Agreement, the situation rapidly worsened, and on 7 August 1949, having deemed that the Republic had capitulated to the former colonial power, Kartosuwirjo declared an Indonesian Islamic State (Negara Islam Indonesia).

Although Darul Islam did not have any official ties with Masyumi, it did make use of the Muslim party's local organisational structures, and also adopted many of the themes the Muslim party had developed up until 1948, namely the question of a holy war and the ruling elite's illegitimacy to govern.[116] The new organisation's rebellion against the government's legitimacy forced the party to distance itself more and more from Darul Islam's radical policies and simplistic rallying cries and thus contributed to the political realignment of the party towards the centre ground.

The Emergence of a Generation of Statesmen and the Advent of Independence

The failure of the communist rebellion in Madiun put paid to Dutch speculation about the republican government's collapse, and also removed their trump card for maintaining the support, or at least the goodwill, of the Americans. The Dutch were keen to put an end to the republican government rapidly, and so they issued a new set of demands. On 19 December 1948, following the refusal of the Republic,

---

[116] On the question of the links between Darul Islam and Masyumi, see infra, Chapter 3.

which comprised 40% of Indonesia's population, to enter into the federation on the same basis as the 15 states controlled by the Netherlands, Dutch troops initiated their second "police action" and took over Yogyakarta. The majority of the cabinet were captured and deported to Bangka. The Dutch took control of the entire Javanese part of the republican territory and also launched an offensive against the Sumatran regions controlled by the government. Despite the resounding success of these initial military operations, this manoeuvre was to be the swansong of the Dutch colonial presence in Indonesia. Firstly, the Dutch troops encountered much stronger military resistance from the Indonesians than expected. Although they had taken the republican leaders by surprise, their offensives did not succeed in disorganising the Republic's army completely. The Siliwangi Division, for example, in its retreat from Central Java to West Java, inflicted heavy losses on Dutch troops. In January 1949, the 145,000 Dutch soldiers stationed in the country were on the defensive in Java and Sumatra; in March, republican troops regained control of a large part of Yogyakarta. In addition, Dutch machinations had attracted a considerable amount of disapproval from the international community. At the end of January 1949, Amsterdam was forced to consent to reopen negotiations with republican representatives, having come under pressure both from the United Nations Security Council, which passed a resolution calling for such a course of action, and the United States, which threatened to suspend Marshall Aid. Above all, the political and military brutality of the Netherlands had the effect of awakening a deep nationalist sentiment throughout Indonesia, and in particular in the areas where the former colonial power felt sure it was in control. Some of the governments which controlled the "*negara*", such as Adil Puradiredja's government in Pasundan and Anak Agung's in East Indonesia, resigned in protest, sensing that their fellow countrymen's sympathies lay very much with the Republic. This "about-turn in the federalists' mindset"[117] destroyed the influence which the Dutch, through a system combining a subtle mix of genuine paternalism and a much more prosaic form of imperialism, had managed to regain in the country. The Netherlands' new colonial policy, which was summed up in Kahin's words as: "(1) a new and elaborate formula of indirect rule wherein the ultimate Dutch control was much more skilfully camouflaged than previously; (2) more

---

[117] Cayrac-Blanchard and Devillers, *L'Asie du Sud-Est*, p. 338.

Indonesians holding middle and upper administrative posts and having in a few of the constituent states a small measure of governmental initiative subject to supervision and control from Batavia; (3) more Dutch military and police power standing in the back of this structure; and (4) more Indonesian nationalists in jail"[118] began to show its limitations.

This dramatic final phase of the struggle for independence confirmed the stature of a small group of leaders within Masyumi (particularly Natsir, Roem and Sjafruddin) as statesmen, and placed them in the inside track for future promotion to positions of government responsibility. A few weeks before the "second police action", Sjafruddin Prawiranegara, minister for finance in Hatta's government, left for Bukittinggi, the republican capital of Sumatra. When he learned of the fall of Yogyakarta and the arrest of the government, he formed and led an Emergency Government of the Republic of Indonesia (Pemerintah Darurat Republik Indonesia, PDRI), which for seven months ensured the continuous existence of the Indonesian state.[119] This preservation of a republican government through a provisional cabinet based in West Sumatra and pursued by Dutch troops left a lasting impression on the public consciousness.[120] Bolstered by the prestige it had gained from having avoided capture by the Dutch, thanks to the loyal support of the local population, it was with a certain reluctance that the PDRI handed back its power to the newly released government on 13 July 1949. Although Sjafruddin denied contesting the legitimacy of the reinstalled government, he publicly expressed his disappointment with the Roem-Van Royen Agreement. According to him, "its contents were

---

[118] Kahin, *Nationalism and Revolution in Indonesia*, p. 351.

[119] According to Kahin in *Nationalism and Revolution in Indonesia*, p. 394, Hatta was worried about possible Dutch manœuvres, and so before leaving for Sumatra he handed over to Sjafruddin an authorisation to take control of the government if ever he or Sukarno were prevented from exercising their office. In his different writings about this period, Sjafruddin does not mention this authorisation and, according to Noer (*Partai Islam di Pentas Nasional*, p. 188), he never even received the message which the government sent him after the capture of Yogyakarta enjoining him to continue the struggle. Mohammad Roem, in his memoirs, gives the same version of events. *Diplomasi ujung tombak perjuangan RI* (Jakarta: Pt Gramedia, 1989), p. 60.

[120] This memory was reawakened a little over 10 years later when the same Sjafruddin Prawiranegara led the Revolutionary Government of the Republic of Indonesia (Pemerintah Revolusioner Republik Indonesia, PRRI) in the same region against the government in Jakarta. See infra, Chapter 4.

too weak and didn't reflect the strength of the PDRI struggle, because we really were far stronger than people on Bangka (where Sukarno and Hatta were held by the Dutch) suspected."[121]

In response to Sjafruddin's misgivings and in order to convince the leaders of the PDRI to return to Yogyakarta, Mohammad Hatta sent Mohammad Natsir to Sumatra at the beginning of July 1949. Natsir's delegation met the PDRI in the village of Padang Japang where they had taken refuge. Following "marathon negotiations" (*secara marathon*), Natsir managed to convince his friend to hand executive power back to the government in Yogyakarta. Although Natsir himself was opposed to the agreement with the Dutch, he defended it in a speech made to the local population. He said that the compromise, though unsatisfactory, was merely a necessary step towards a united and sovereign Indonesia, explaining to his fellow countrymen that they should not "feel ashamed when looking at the map" (*"jangan kita berkecil hati melihat kaart"*). Responding to Natsir's speech, Sjafruddin Prawiranegara echoed the disappointment of the local population but agreed, however, in the name of national unity, to respect the commitments that had already been made:

> We are convinced, and we repeat here that the president and the vice president are our leaders, that they are sure that we will obey them like a child obeys his parents. However, what surprises us is why the president and the vice president made such a decision [to sign this agreement with the Dutch]? Earlier, Bung Natsir explained that the government of the Republic had returned to Yogyakarta, but who then actually fought the battle? Was it the men who remained inactive in Yogya, or was it us, who were pursued over hill and vale? What is to happen now to the leaders who are happily enjoying cheese and butter and other pleasant foods in Bangka? That is the question that comes to mind. I am not opposed to the whole world knowing about Roem, but what is important is to know if all the aspects of the agreement were really considered, before it was signed. The agreement has not yet been ratified by the government, the cabinet and the Parliament, and yet the president and vice president have already given guarantees to the Dutch. In such cases, we must remember the necessity to obey our leaders.

---

[121] "Emergency Government, an interview with Syafruddin Prawiranegara", in *Born in Fire*, ed. Wild and Carey, p. 195.

> Let us not create a split because we are unhappy with the agreement, but let us rather make sure that we remain united both internally and externally... If we are to be destroyed, better it were together, if we sink, we will do so together, though I am convinced that if we remain united, we will not founder.[122]

Mohammad Natsir's role in this affair no doubt contributed to his star rising both on the national political scene and within his own party. Even though the minister for information had himself resigned from the delegation led by Roem in protest over the concessions made in the agreement, the fact that he managed to convince one of his close allies to accept it illustrated the discipline and the legalism which typified the future head of Masyumi.

The third party figure to distinguish himself during this critical period, Minister for Home Affairs Mohamad Roem, did so as the head of the delegation that entered into negotiations with representatives of the Dutch government on 14 April 1949, under the aegis of the United Nations Commission for Indonesia. The talks concluded on 7 May 1949 with the signing of what was called the Roem-Van Royen Agreement. It provided, as a pre-condition for the Republic's entry into the United States of Indonesia, that the republican government would be released and reinstated in Yogyakarta with a view to preparing roundtable talks in the Hague, which would prepare the transfer of sovereignty. Despite open hostility to the agreement amongst certain senior Masyumi party figures, the fact that it was one of its own members who had led this final round of shuttle diplomacy convinced the party that the compromise obtained was the best possible one available, and this contributed to their acceptance of it, after a long and arduous debate.[123]

The prominence of the roles played by this triumvirate of Masyumi leaders—one of them saved the Republic, one led the diplomatic

---

[122] Quoted by Lukman Harun, "Hari-Hari Terakhir PDRI. Beberapa Catatan", in *Pak Natsir 80 Tahun. Buku Pertama. Pandangan dan Penilaian Generasi Muda*, ed. H. Endang Sajifuddin Anshari and Amin Rais (Jakarta: Media Da'wah, 1988), pp. 10–1.

[123] Deliar Noer draws this conclusion from the numerous interviews he was able to carry out with Masyumi leaders in Java and Sumatra between 1955 and 1958. Noer, "Masjumi: Its Organization, Ideology, and Political Role in Indonesia", p. 125.

battle, while the third enabled the first two to get on—had two major consequences on the Muslim party. The first of these was to allow this trio to enhance their stature within the party. Up until that point, they had been the low-key advocates of a policy that was more in tune with certain political realities. They now, however, became for the general Muslim populace the prestigious representatives of a generation who had just demonstrated in spectacular fashion their ability, in the face of adversity, to take charge of the country's destiny, and so naturally the party's destiny also. Secondly, the deeds of these three senior party figures gave Masyumi a clear advantage in the race for power that had just begun, now that a sovereign state had become a very real prospect.

On 23 August, a conference opened in the Hague under the auspices of the United Nations Commission for Indonesia, which brought together delegations from the Netherlands, the Republic and the Federal Consultative Assembly (Bijeenkomst voor Federal Overleg, BFO). At the end of two months of negotiations, an agreement was signed on 2 November 1949 providing for a complete transfer of sovereignty to the Republic of the United States of Indonesia, which would be composed of the Republic and the 15 political entities created by the Dutch. Two major concessions by the republican delegates had allowed the agreement to be concluded. First, the new Republic would assume most of the debts incurred by the former Dutch East Indies, and furthermore, Dutch New Guinea was to remain under the control of the Netherlands pending new negotiations. In accordance with the agreement, Dutch sovereignty was transferred to the Republic of the United States of Indonesia on 27 December 1949. The two legislative chambers of the new federal state had just elected Sukarno as president and approved the formation of a new cabinet led by Mohammad Hatta. The new government, which was composed in total of five federalists and 11 republicans, included four members of Masyumi, making it the main government party.[124]

The new cabinet was not answerable to the parliament, and so, in theory, it was destined to last until the election of a new assembly. Masyumi had full confidence in Mohammad Hatta, and so was prepared to accept this temporary state of affairs. However, it intended to

---

[124] Sjafruddin Prawiranegara was minister for finance, Abu Hanifah minister for education, Wahid Hasjim minister for religions and Mohammad Roem minister of state.

tackle without delay the task of transforming Indonesian political life. The party's fourth congress, which took place in Yogyakarta between 15 and 19 December, was to pave the way for its undertakings in the newly independent country. The decisions of the congress covered three aspects of the country's future reorganisation, namely its institutional, political and social reconstruction. Apart from those decisions, an outline programme was drawn up dealing with economic and social issues, and an appeal was made to hold discussions with the Darul Islam movement, both of which will be examined later on.

The first part of the "Urgency Programme" adopted by the party insisted on the necessity to establish a new consensus on what form the new Indonesian state would take. Masyumi set out

> ...to examine the content of the Constitution of the RUSI and to prepare a new constitution, in accordance with the people's aspirations which will be made clear by the Constituent Assembly...due to be established over the course of 1950.[125]

Thus, without rejecting the current Constitution outright or coming out in favour of a unitary or federal model for the new state, Masyumi indicated that it considered the institutional situation merely as an intermediary stage at that point. In addition to calling for immediate general elections, it also demanded the "organisation, as soon as possible, of referendums that would determine the status of the member states and of the regions" of the Republic of the United States of Indonesia.

The second theme which the delegates at the congress focussed on was the rebuilding of a society that had been deeply affected by four years of conflict. They were particularly concerned about the fate of members of the militia groups controlled by Masyumi. Masyumi decided to dissolve its armed groups in accordance with Presidential Decree Number 3 of 1947, which banned any armed forces besides the National Army (Tentara Nasional Indonesia, TNI). In reality, a part of the Hizboellah and Sabilillah had already been integrated into the TNI. In his commentary on the resolutions made at the congress, Mohammad Natsir drew attention to the necessity to strive for the social "rehabilitation" of those who now found themselves unemployed. For the new chairman of the executive board of Masyumi, all the

---

[125] *Urgency Programme* 1949, Section I, article B1.

party's efforts should be focussed on making every individual responsible as part of the democratisation of Indonesia's unstable society (*masyarakat yang goyang*):

> If we were to content ourselves with waiting for government measures, if we were merely spectators…it would be proof that we were not aware of our status as citizens of an independent country. I have high hopes, then, my brothers, that we, members of Masyumi and leaders of the most important group in Indonesian society, will be able to focus the people's attention and lead their efforts in the areas mentioned above.[126]

The ambition was a lofty one but on a par with the influence which the party's leaders considered they held in Indonesian society. In short, it consisted of anticipating government plans, such as the reconstruction of housing or the regeneration of the country's agricultural sector, which would require long periods before being implemented. Such an undertaking required a reorganisation of Masyumi, which was the third objective established by the congress. The second police action carried out by the Dutch authorities had severely weakened the party's organisational network. With the Revolution now finished, it was necessary also to adapt its organisational structure and to regain control over the party machinery, which in many regions was operating completely independently. In order to allow the new leadership to concentrate entirely on this task, it was decided that the party head could not participate in government.[127] Finally, the congress decided to transfer the party headquarters from Yogyakarta to the new capital of the Republic of the United States of Indonesia, Jakarta.

Masyumi's demands concerning the holding of referendums in the different federal states, was soon to become a moot issue. Scarcely six weeks after the transfer of sovereignty, the Republic of the United States of Indonesia began to disintegrate. In less than eight months, the entire edifice which the Dutch had patiently constructed in order to maintain their influence in the country had collapsed. The process was hastened by the prestige which the Republic benefitted from among

---

[126] *Berita Partai Masjumi*, February 1950.

[127] Noer, "Masjumi: Its Organization, Ideology, and Political Role in Indonesia", p. 213. This decision is contained, however, neither in the congress resolutions nor in the reports on the congress which I was able to consult.

the population of the other states in the federation as well as the manoeuvres attempted by certain federalist leaders, such as the attempted coup d'état by Captain Westerling in which Sultan Hamid II of West Borneo was involved. By 10 February, the State of South Sumatra had dissolved itself, and it was soon to be followed by others. The Christian community in the Maluku Islands, who had long provided significant numbers of soldiers to the Dutch army, created the Republic of South Maluku, which was also swept aside. In the east of the country, however, it took longer to overcome the resistance of former federalists, now turned separatists. The final stage came on 19 May 1950, with the signing of an agreement between the Republic of Indonesia and the State of East Indonesia, designed to create a unitary state.[128] For two months, delegates from the RUSI's representative chamber and from the KNIP gathered to draw up the provisional constitution of the unitary state, pending elections to be held at a later date. After ratification by the chambers of both states, it was promulgated on 15 August 1950, and two days later on 17 August, the anniversary of the proclamation of independence, the Republic of Indonesia was officially born.

At its foundation in November 1945, Masyumi had a simple programme that appealed to a large audience. It was easy to recognise its followers; they included those who did not differentiate their identity as citizens from their identity as Muslims and who thus saw the struggle for independence as a religious duty. However, between the ideal of Masyumi's objectives and the reality of its actions, a contradiction was soon to appear which would plague the party in the early years of its existence.

The supporters of the Marxist wing had at their disposal a clearly identified ideological corpus, and those who aligned themselves with

---

[128] Masyumi activists like to highlight the role played by Mohammad Natsir in the finalisation of this agreement. At the end of April, he presented a proposal entitled *Mosi Integral*, which would allow a resolution of the thorny issue of whether East Indonesia should be incorporated into the Republic or whether both states should disappear and be replaced by the RIS. This simple issue, which touched on both sides' sensitivities, has received very little attention from English-speaking historians—notably George McTurnan Kahin—but is nonetheless sometimes presented as one of the major episodes in the history of the Indonesian state. See in particular Anwar Harjono, ed., *Pemikiran dan perjuangan Mohammad Natsir* (Jakarta: Pustaka Firdaus, 1996), p. 160, notably Yusril Ihrza Mahendra's prologue.

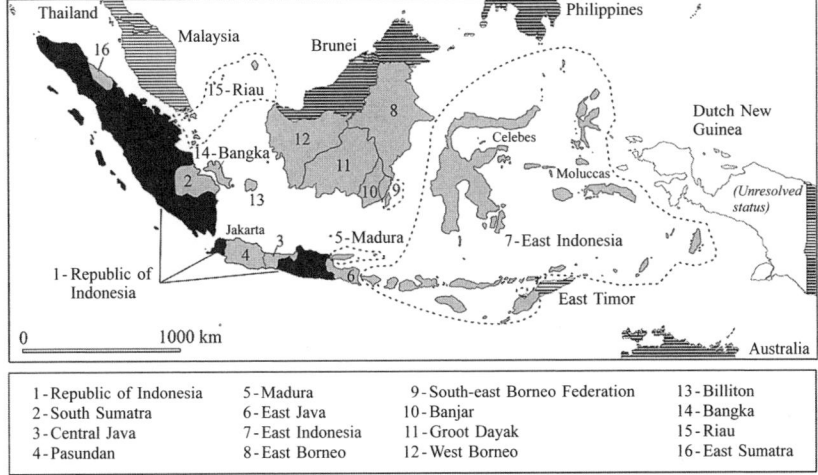

1 - Republic of Indonesia	5 - Madura	9 - South-east Borneo Federation	13 - Billiton
2 - South Sumatra	6 - East Java	10 - Banjar	14 - Bangka
3 - Central Java	7 - East Indonesia	11 - Groot Dayak	15 - Riau
4 - Pasundan	8 - East Borneo	12 - West Borneo	16 - East Sumatra

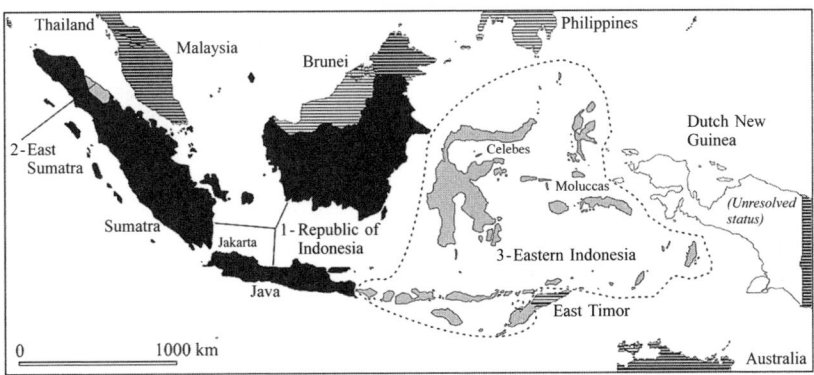

Map 2.1 The Disintegration of the United States of Indonesia, January and April 1950.

Moscow also received clear guidelines. The supporters of secular nationalism had their guide in the person of Sukarno. The Muslims, on the other hand, had neither a clearly defined doctrine nor an uncontested leader. Some found both of these by rowing in behind Kartosuwirjo, but others were aware of the gap between the simplicity of a demand for an Islamic state and the complexity of actually accomplishing it. In the second half of the 1940s, this dilemma resulted in the participation of the Masyumi leadership in motley coalitions assembling momentarily over the course of the negotiations with forces opposed to the former colonial power.

It was only in reaction to events that Masyumi eventually decided to choose the tortuous path which would lead it from a religious ideal to a political programme. Darul Islam and Kartosuwirjo showed that a radical political message would lead to an impasse ending in secession, thus converting most party members to a more moderate position, while the events of 1948 in Madiun helped to forge their aversion to communism.

CHAPTER THREE

Confronting Reality: Masyumi and the Exercise of Power

The period from September 1950 to April 1957 was Indonesia's only experience of parliamentary democracy in its history prior to the fall of the Suharto regime in 1998. During this period, six different governments held power, but despite the remarkable similarity between the different parties' programmes (with the exception of the communists and the dissident Muslims), none of them enjoyed the time and stability necessary to implement meaningful reforms.[1] All were in favour of promoting a mixed economy based on cooperatives which were partially exposed to market forces as well as a Western-style republican model of government. However, as they had never really been schooled by their colonial masters in the art of democracy, the elite group placed at the head of their country following the Revolution put in place a parliamentary system which was not really suited to Indonesian realities. The notion of a majority and an opposition inherent in Western institutions were transferred en bloc to an Indonesian system where authority and social harmony were traditionally the prevailing values, illustrated by a system of long consultations (*musjawarah*) designed to arrive at a consensus (*mufakat*) which would be acceptable to all.[2]

---

[1] Detailed information on the composition of Indonesian governments from 1945 to 1965 can be found in Susan Finch and Daniel Lev, *Republic of Indonesia Cabinets, 1945–1965* (Ithaca, NY: Cornell University Press, 1965).

[2] Françoise Cayrac-Blanchard and Philippe Devillers, *L'Asie du Sud-est*, coll. L'Histoire du XXe Siècle, vol. 1 (Paris: Sirey, 1970), p. 342.

Plate 3.1 The "oriental" transferring the contents of the "problem container" into a "synthesising machine" turned to "Western speed", which transforms them into laws, ordinances and motions (*Abadi*, 20 December 1952).

During this period, Masyumi was the main party of government. Of the five governments formed in the Provisional Assembly between September 1950 and March 1956, three were led by Masyumi members —Natsir, Seokiman and Harahap, with a fourth one also jointly led by a party member, Wilopo. The chronic instability of the coalition governments and the fragmentation of Indonesian party politics forced the party to take sides for or against various political forces, thus obliging it to clarify further its political identity.

Masyumi—A Participant in and a Fierce Opponent of "Partocracy"

Although it was hastily drafted and supposed to be replaced within a few months, the Provisional Constitution of August 1950 remained in force until 1959, when the 1945 text was restored. The centrepiece of the institutions established by the 1950 Constitution was the unicameral parliament which, pending elections, was to be composed of representatives from the assemblies of the two states which had just merged: the Republic of Indonesia and the Republic of the United States of Indonesia.[3] The cabinet, which was accountable before the Provisional Assembly, had at its disposal a wide range of powers, notably the power to issue emergency decrees which would be valid as long as Parliament did not expressly voice its opposition to them. The president, on the other hand, held relatively limited powers: all his decrees had to be countersigned by the relevant minister.

From the outset, the 1950 document had two key flaws: it provided no solutions in the event of repeated ministerial crises and it established a form of presidential office which was ill-fitted for its incumbent, Sukarno, who held a considerable degree of political power. The only mechanism provided by the Constitution for breaking institutional gridlock was Article 84, which authorised the president to dissolve the Assembly on condition that new elections would be organised within 30 days. This clause was interpreted such that a dissolution of Parliament would only be possible if an election could be held in the month that followed. In a country whose first general election took five years to organise, such a provision remained a dead letter. The authors of the Constitution, including a number of Masyumi members, showed, not for the last time, their penchant for being excessively optimistic.[4]

The other source of the new state's institutional imbalance was the lack of presidential power provided for by the 1950 Constitution. A whole section of the political class, led within Masyumi by Mohammad Natsir, intended to limit Sukarno to a narrow interpretation of his constitutional authority.[5] During his time as prime minister between

---

[3] The Republic was to have 46 deputies in the KNIP and 13 in the High Council, while the Republic of the United States of Indonesia obtained 147 members in the People's Representative Council (Bijeenkomst voor Federal Overleg, BFO) and 31 in the Senate. The entire Provisional Assembly therefore had a total of 237 seats.

[4] Burhanuddin Harahap made a similar observation in 1954 when he was head of the Masyumi group in Parliament: "at that time [in 1950] we tackled [those problems] with a sense of optimism, perhaps excessively so." "Parlemen dan Kabinet," in *Muktamar Masjumi ke VII di Surabaja, 23–27 desember 1954*, Panitya Mukatamar Masjumi VII, 1954.

[5] Pending the establishment of a real presidential regime in which the head of state would be accountable to Parliament. Masyumi had been calling for such a regime since 1949.

September 1950 and April 1951, the president of the Muslim party reminded Sukarno on several occasions that it was the government, accountable before the Parliament, that was responsible for making policy decisions for the country; this attitude earned Natsir longstanding resentment from the head of state. Soekiman, who succeeded Natsir as prime minister but was his predecessor as head of the party, adopted a much more compliant attitude, however. He maintained that the president should not limit himself to his constitutional role, thus allowing Sukarno the political room to manoeuvre in accordance with his ambitions. This difference in interpretation by two important party figures was due in large part to their respective personal relationships with Sukarno before the outbreak of the Second World War.[6] It was a difference which, during the 1950s, was to weigh considerably on the division between their respective factions within Masyumi.

The Splintering of Political Forces and Governmental Instability

The Indonesian political landscape was made up of almost 40 political parties. In August 1950, 16 of them were able to constitute parliamentary groups within the Assembly appointed by the president.[7] The parties were organised along three different lines: religion, nationalism and Marxism.

The revival of the Partai Sarekat Islam Indonesia in April 1947 seemed to have put an end to Masyumi's hegemony over political Islam. However, the newly re-established party became discredited after the support provided by its president, Wondoamiseno, for Amir Sjarifuddin during the Madiun rebellion, never managed to regain a prominent position on the political landscape. The PSII held eight seats in Parliament while Masyumi, on the strength of their significant contribution during the closing stages of the Revolution, established itself as the strongest political party in the new regime with 50 deputies. The Christian parties in the Assembly—Partai Katolik with nine seats and the Protestant Parkindo (the Christian Indonesian Party) with five seats—enjoyed a disproportionate amount of political influence given the number of Indonesian Christians they represented: in total, only

---

[6] Cf. Supra, Chapter 1.
[7] In 1954, the number rose to 17.

three million Protestants and one million Catholics. This was due in part to the presence of a Christian majority in some of the country's outlying regions, which gave their representatives an essential role in the preservation of Indonesian unity, but also to the over-representation of Catholics and Protestants in the army and civil service.[8]

Political nationalism was mainly represented by the Partai Nasional Indonesia (PNI) with 41 seats. Heir to the great pre-war nationalist tradition and to the state party created after the proclamation of independence, it benefitted from a misconception in public opinion which led it to be considered as President Sukarno's party. Its members were mainly recruited from national and regional civil servants, and it advocated a sort of proletarian nationalism called Marhaenism, claiming to defend the interests of the ordinary man. The party was very badly organised, and several wings had developed within it because of personality clashes between individuals. These divisions had given rise to several dissident organisations, including the Greater Indonesia Unity Party (Partai Persatuan Indonesia Raja, PIR) with 18 seats in the Assembly, and the National People's Party (Partai Rakjat Nasional, PRN) with six seats.

On the Marxist side of the political spectrum, the events in Madiun had led to a reorganisation marked by the marginalisation of those who were close to Moscow. The Democratic People's Front (Front Demokrasi Rakjat, FDR) was dissolved and the PKI, although it was not dissolved, went through a protracted slump and was never allowed to participate in government. In the months following the Madiun rebellion, it faced competition with the arrival of a new movement also claiming to be Marxist-Leninist, the Proletarian Party (Partai Murba). The announcement of this new party's foundation was made on 3 October 1949 by the main constituent organisations of the People's Revolutionary Movement, the organisation founded by Tan Malaka, who had died in February 1949. This new organisation based on "religion, nationalism and socialism" differentiated itself from the PKI by declaring that the interests of Indonesia should come before the interests of the Soviet Union, and it accused the PKI of being infiltrated by Dutch agents. The Partai Murba only counted four seats in Parliament, but had numerous sympathisers amongst the PNI and

---

[8] Herbert Feith, *The Decline of Constitutional Democracy in Indonesia* (Ithaca, NY: Cornell University Press, 1962), p. 145.

the PSI. The Partai Sosialis Indonesia (PSI), which held 15 seats in the Assembly, also claimed to be a Marxist party. However, its president, Sjahrir, was convinced that the Marxist doctrine of class struggle could not be applied to Indonesia given the social conditions present in the country, and so he did not try to turn his party into a mass movement by attracting those who were disenchanted with the PKI. He busied himself with building a party of well-trained individuals who were convinced of the dangers of communist totalitarianism and were capable of fostering in the general public political critical faculties and an ability to think independently. The calibre of the PSI's leaders allowed the party to play a prominent role on the Indonesian political scene; meanwhile, its political rival, Amir Sjarifuddin's Partai Sosialis, with only two seats, now merely constituted a grouplet in Parliament.

The dispersal of parliamentary seats across the Indonesian political landscape was a legacy of the revolutionary period. In the absence of elections since 1945, successive Indonesian governments had followed a certain principle which consisted in allowing a political movement deemed to be any way significant a place at the cabinet table. The formation in 1950 of the new Provisional Assembly which included representatives from both the Republic and the federal state inherited from the Dutch added to this confusion, with the addition of two new parliamentary groups, SKI and Fraksi Demokrat, and the almost twofold increase of independent representatives from 13 to 25. This multiplication of the number of parties was not only recognised but even encouraged—the composition of parliamentary committees and various government bodies, as well as the legislative councils formed in the provinces, regencies and municipalities, was to be established on the basis of one representative per party. The unstable political coalitions which marked the beginnings of the unitary state increased the influence of the party executive committees over the government's actions. Consequently, the decisions taken during cabinet meetings were often limited to those which had already been approved in the meetings of party leaders beforehand.[9] All five governments formed according to the balance of power in the Provisional Assembly reflected this fragmentation of political power, and this can be seen clearly when comparing the distribution of seats in the Assembly with the number

---

[9] Herbert Feith, *The Wilopo Cabinet, 1952–1953: A Turning Point in Post-Revolutionary Indonesia* (Ithaca, NY: Cornell University Press, 1958), p. 202.

of places at the cabinet table. Of the 16 parliamentary groups formed in 1950 (including the independent deputies), 13 obtained positions in government.[10] The two largest parties in the Assembly, and so the two parties most able to bring a certain amount of institutional stability, were slightly under-represented, which benefitted the smaller groupings who were thus able to bring all their political influence to bear on the government of the country.

Masyumi was, naturally, strongly critical of this state of affairs as they were convinced that they were one of the few political groups in the country to have a broad electoral base. In February 1952, an editorial in *Abadi* highlighted the limits of the debate which opposed the supporters of a "business cabinet" (*zaken kabinet*), on the one hand composed of experts supposed to be independent of their political parties, and the advocates of a "coalition government" (*kabinet koalisi*), on the other.[11] The Muslim daily newspaper explained that these notions corresponded to political realities in European democracies, but could not be applied to Indonesia where the party structure was still "unclear" (*katjau balau*) and where the Parliament was far from being representative. In November 1954, Boerhanoeddin Harahap developed this thesis further in an article which was included in the preparatory documents for the seventh Masyumi congress. In it, he lamented the splintering of the parliamentary groupings, which weakened the executive, and he denounced the presence in Parliament of groups whose existence was based on "neither a party nor any other mass organisation".[12] However, apart from proposing the rapid organisation of elections, Masyumi never put forward a concrete solution to the problems it lamented. It rejected, for example, an original proposal made by Mukarto, one of the *formateurs* named after the fall of Wilopo's cabinet, which consisted of obliging the government to take decisions based on a majority, with minority factions forbidden from withdrawing their ministers from government.[13]

---

[10] Nahdlatul Ulama's parliamentary group was only created in April 1952, following the formation of the party.

[11] *"Kabinet Apa?"* (Which Cabinet?), *Abadi*, 27 February 1952.

[12] He no doubt had in mind Parindra and Fraksi Demokrat. Burhanuddin Harahap, "Parlemen dan Kabinet", *Muktamar Masjumi ke VII di Surabaja, 23–27 desember 1954*, 1 December 1954.

[13] *Abadi*, 29 June 1953.

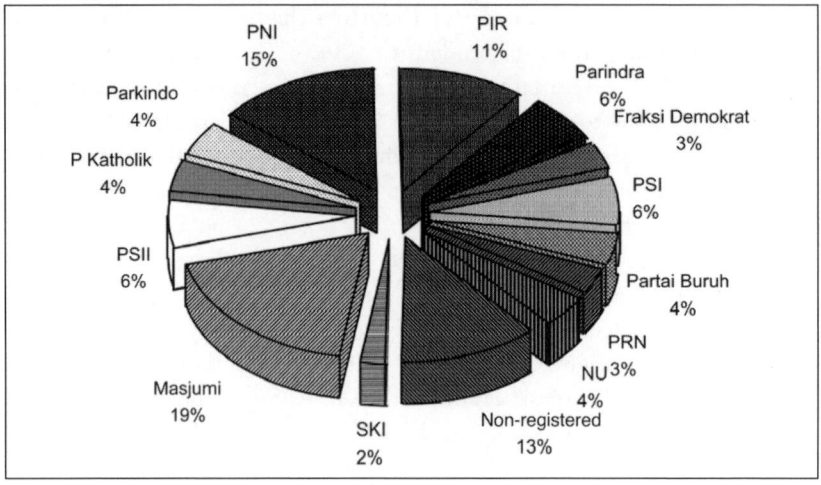

Plate 3.2 The Government Parties in Indonesia 1950–56 (by percentage of ministerial positions).

The Weakness of Indonesian Democracy's Cultural and Social Foundations

To understand the chronic ministerial instability of the day, one needs to look beyond the country's political and institutional system and examine Indonesian political culture in its entirety. First of all, the fact that political leaders came from a relatively select milieu posed a problem. Unlike the West or Japan, there did not exist in 1950s Indonesia a bourgeoisie, i.e., a class involved in business who had the means to exert influence on government policy. Only a tiny minority of those who held a seat in cabinet (three in total, between 1945 and 1955) had a background in trade. Most public representatives had been government employees in the Dutch East Indies, but had generally worked as engineers in technical departments, or as doctors or teachers rather than in general administration departments. The remaining politicians were journalists, teachers in private schools or members of the liberal professions.[14] This governing elite was a very uniform category:

---

[14] Malcom R. Willison, "Leaders of Revolution: The Social Origins of the Republican Cabinets Members in Indonesia 1945–55", MA Thesis, Cornell University, 1958. Quoted in Feith, *The Decline of Constitutional Democracy in Indonesia*, p. 101.

its members had received the same type of education and had been involved in similar political causes in their youth during the colonial period; they lived in the same neighbourhoods, met one another very often and often married within their closed circle. Certain relationships, as we shall see later in the case of Masyumi, transcended political divides in a most surprising fashion.

Beyond this little core of Indonesia's elite, which all too often operated in a vacuum, a politically aware audience began to appear, which we could define as the newspaper-reading public. Given that each copy of a daily newspaper was read by three people on average, this politically literate audience was estimated to stand at around 1.5 million, making up three per cent of the country's adult population.[15] However, this educated social group which had direct access to information remained too modest in size to be able to set up the kind of representative bodies which its Western counterparts could. Most people's understanding of politics, therefore, came through charismatic leaders whose sphere of political influence was generally confined to a regional level. This situation was encapsulated in the dichotomy established by Herbert Feith between, on the one hand, a qualified and uniform elite without any real support in society ("administrators"), and on the other, popular political figures who had no governmental responsibility ("solidarity makers").[16] It contributed to a large extent to the frailty of successive governments and to the discrediting of the young parliamentary democracy in the eyes of the Indonesian population.

Their ability to provide access to positions of power meant that the political parties had an essential role to play in social mobility. Ministerial positions were of course enormously prestigious, and the system also extended to civil service positions and even to the world of

---

[15] At the end of 1950, the diffusion of daily newspapers stood at 499,150. 338,300 of these were made up of publications written in Indonesian (167 different newspapers in total), 87,200 were published in Dutch (totalling 11 publications) and 73,600 were in Chinese (with 15 different daily newspapers). Their content was largely given over to political issues. Jayasan Lembaga Pres dan Pendapat Umum, *Almanak Pers Indonesia 1954–1955* (Djakarta: JLPPU, 1955), p. 36.

[16] Feith, *The Decline of Constitutional Democracy in Indonesia*, pp. 113 ff. Feith highlights the fact that unlike in India, the members of the Indonesian executive at the beginning of the 1950s—almost all of whom were "administrators"—only represented a small section of the political elite. Most of the "solidarity makers" were to be found outside the government.

business. At the highest levels of government and in the civil service, belonging to a political party could enable you to obtain houses, holidays and business opportunities, and at lower levels in society it was the best way to guarantee you a job. Almost all civil servants were members of a party and even when they were not formally registered with any particular organisation, they were almost always attached to a powerful clique who helped them to guarantee a future career.[17] Masyumi was no exception to this rule. The nominations handed out to party members were of course never published in the pro-Masyumi press, but the extent of this "partocratic" system could be seen in the articles written during the Ali government protesting at the removal of its members from important positions.[18]

In this context, it is easy to see how political parties found it difficult to explain to their supporters what role they played during their time in opposition. After 1950, once independence had been achieved and the exercise of governmental power had completely regained its prestige, opponents to this power now went from being intransigent revolutionaries to becoming obstacles to the national unity necessary for the reconstruction of the country. The parties outside of government now had to justify their existence in a political system where legitimacy was traditionally considered to lie only with those who held power. It was to this task that the Masyumi leadership turned its efforts between August 1953 and August 1955 when the government led by Ali Sastroamidjojo kept them out of office for the first time since 1945.[19] A few days after the formation of the Sastroamidjojo cabinet,

---

[17] The first three governments of the unitary republic benefitted nonetheless from a small core of senior civil servants. Of the 18 departmental secretaries (or their equivalents), all but three of them had already occupied their positions before August 1950. This changed with the arrival of the Ali government in August 1953, however, when six of the secretaries were replaced in favour of government party candidates. Feith, *The Decline of Constitutional Democracy in Indonesia*, p. 367.

[18] When Masyumi found itself in opposition, its head of the West Java branch, Isa Anshary, complained that "democracy has changed, it has become partocracy" (*Abadi*, 30 December 1953). The Masyumi newspaper listed on 2 February 1954 all of the civil servants close to Masyumi "who were being evicted".

[19] For an analysis of the Muslim perspective on being in the opposition, the reader should refer to Luthfi Assyaukanie, *Islam and the Secular State in Indonesia* (Singapore: Institute of Southeast Asian Studies, 2009), pp. 74–6, which offers, in particular, an interesting study of the writings of Zainal Abidin Ahmad.

Natsir launched an appeal to the entire "Masyumi family" which affirmed that being in opposition was an integral part of both democracy and Islam.[20] His message was a simple one: Masyumi's situation was a normal one, as being in opposition was "a role and a duty whose foundations can be located in the teachings of Islam";[21] an opposition party was not a *"quantie negligeable* [*sic*] which you can ignore because it does not sit in government."[22] In the weeks following this declaration, the party organised visits by its leaders to different provinces in the country in an attempt to spell out this message.[23] Despite their best efforts, the public at large still misunderstood the status of an opposition party, as if, as a despondent Sjafruddin Prawiranegara noted in November 1953, "the goal of being in opposition was to bring down the government or to hinder it and so prevent it from achieving its goals."[24]

This misapprehension of an opposition party's role was also common in the corridors of power, and Masyumi's press did not hesitate to let it be known when the party was a victim of this attitude. In September 1953, for example, four daily newspapers deemed hostile to the government—*Abadi, Sumber, Pedoman* and *Indonesia Raya*—were banned from prisons.[25] Even more surprising was the decision by the public prosecutor in January 1954 to question Jusuf Wibisono for two hours after he had declared that certain members of the government did not possess the abilities necessary to overcome the difficulties which the country was going through.[26] These violations of the freedom of expression, which the party's newspapers created a huge furore

---

[20] *Keluarga Masyumi* was the expression used to refer to the entire collection of the party's satellite organisations.

[21] Speech by Mohammad Natsir, 6 August 1953, Dewan Pimpinan Masyumi Wilayah Sumatera Utara, *Dasar-Dasar Perdjuangan Partai Politik Islam Indonesia Masjumi* (Medan, 1954), pp. 100–3.

[22] *Masjumi bukan "quantie negligeable" jang dapat disampingkan Perdjuangan Partai Politik Islam Indonesia Masjumi* (Medan, 1954), pp. 100–3.

[22] "Masjumi bukan begitu sadja jika ia tidak duduk dalam pemerintah", Abadi, 15 August 1953.

[23] See, for example, the account of the trip made by Mohamad Roem and Zainal Abidin Ahmad to Western Sumatra, *Abadi*, 14 and 27 August, 1953.

[24] "Seolah-olah tudjuan opposisi ialah menggulingkan pemerintah atau merintangi dan menghalangi keberhasilan pemerintahan", *Abadi*, 16 November 1953.

[25] The SOB camps (*Staats van Oorlog Beleg*, meaning state of emergency and war).

[26] *Abadi*, 6 January 1954.

over, did not stop the party from providing firm opposition to the Ali government, using means such as the boycotting of parliamentary sessions[27] and the moving of no-confidence motions.[28] It was nonetheless with great relief that Masyumi returned to government in August 1955. With the general election approaching (it was set to take place in September), it became vitally important to regain once again the political legitimacy mentioned above.[29]

Masyumi: Its "Friends and Enemies"[30]

The Highs and Lows of the Party's Cooperation with the Nationalists

As the two largest political parties in Parliament, the PNI and Masyumi appeared to be the two natural pillars upon which the unstable institutional edifice established by the 1950 Constitution could repose. However, the distribution of political power between the various parties in the Provisional Assembly meant that not only would their alliance not permit them to obtain the majority required to govern, but in addition, as the Natsir and Sastroamidjojo cabinets demonstrated, an agreement between the two parties was not a *sine qua non* for the formation of a government. The two parties agreed to temporarily put to one side their main bone of contention, pending the election of a Constituent Assembly which, in theory, would settle definitively the

---

[27] In particular, in July 1955, during the debates on the ratification of the protocol to dissolve the Netherlands-Indonesian Union, despite the fact that the Round Table Conference Agreement establishing this union had been signed by the previous government, which Masyumi had participated in. *Abadi*, 6 July 1955, cf. infra, Chapter 3 "Foreign Policy".

[28] In April 1955 against the minister for justice, Djody Gondokusomo, accused of having received money from a Chinese person in exchange for a naturalisation certificate. A motion of no confidence in the government had already been moved in December 1954.

[29] To such an extent that during the election campaign, several of the PNI's regional figures, now in opposition, declared that their party was still in power. Herbert Feith, *The Indonesian Elections of 1955* (Ithaca, NY: Cornell University, 1957), p. 14.

[30] From the Indonesian "*Lawan den kawan*", the title of a section in the weekly publication, *Hikmah*, devoted to different political movements in Indonesia and throughout the world.

question of what sort of state, secular or Muslim, the new Republic should have. A certain number of disagreements remained between the two parties, however, which could be observed at the formation of each new government, when the possibility of a coalition between Masyumi and the PNI inevitably arose.[31] More often than not, the two sides came to the conclusion that these differences of opinion, whether they were on the date of future elections, the question of the Netherlands-Indonesian Union, or the opening of an embassy in Moscow, concerned questions of form as opposed to questions of principle. There was no single issue which constituted, in itself, an insurmountable obstacle to cooperation between the two sides.[32]

However, the distribution of ministerial portfolios, which was both a cause and a consequence of ministerial instability, seemed to be a constant source of discord between the parties. Following a procedure which gradually became an established ritual, the formation of a government began with a consultation between the leaders of the various political parties. An overview of the problems of the day was chaired by President Sukarno or, in his absence, by Vice President Hatta. At the end of this first stage, the president designated a *formateur* charged with submitting a proposal for a new government to him. It was only at this point that negotiations between the parties really began. The talks which preceded the formation of the five governments linked to the Provisional Assembly always examined first of all the possibility of a coalition between Masyumi and the PNI. Once the items on the programme for government were finalised, the focus then turned to the thorny issue of ministerial portfolios. There was generally a broad consensus on the number of government positions to be given to the two largest parties in the Assembly, with each party generally receiving four or five cabinet seats. The main stumbling blocks were, first of all, the allocation of the more prestigious ministries, and second, the specific candidates put forward for each position. The most sought-after positions, apart from that of prime minister of course, were minister for home affairs (it was he who nominated the regions' governors and most senior civil servants—positions of great importance in light of the

---

[31] See, for example, *Abadi*, 25 February 1952, two days after the break-up of the Soekiman government.
[32] See the editorial in *Abadi* published on 4 March 1953, "The Co-operation between Masyumi and the PNI".

upcoming general election) minister for defence; minister for economics (who was in charge of the country's lucrative import licences); and the minister for education (which Masyumi wanted so as to promote its religious policy, a move which the PNI attempted to prevent).

An examination of the prolonged negotiations which preceded the formation of the Soekiman government reveals another element which is important in the understanding of the relations between the two parties, namely the existence within each party of factions with differing opinions about entering into coalition with their main rival. On 26 March 1951, the day after the resignation of the Natsir government, Sukarno designated a member of the PNI, Sartono, as *formateur*. Sartono spent 18 days trying to find an agreement with the Masyumi leadership, but contrary to a parliamentary convention which they were themselves to invoke at a later date, they demanded to be given the position of prime minister and proposed Natsir as a candidate to succeed himself.[33] A compromise was finally reached, but only after Sukarno had named two new *formateurs*, the president of the PNI, Sidik Djojosukarto, and the president of Masyumi's leadership council, Soekiman. They managed to strike an agreement, and the PNI agreed to allow Masyumi to occupy the role of prime minister, on condition that Natsir should not be reappointed to the position. Within Masyumi, there existed two groups, which we will examine further at a later stage, opposing the "young generation" led by Natsir and the "old generation" who supported Soekiman and who, like him, had maintained a certain proximity with the secular nationalist group which had developed during the pre-war years as a result of their common struggle for independence.[34] The PNI, on the other hand, had been dominated since its party congress in May 1950 by a group led by Sidik Djojosukarto composed of revolutionary leaders who were fiercely opposed to the pragmatic policies which Hatta had proposed. Their

---

[33] There was an unwritten rule that the prime minister should come from the same party as the *formateur*. In the negotiations which finally led to the formation of the Ali cabinet, for example, Burhanuddin Harahap occupied, for a time, the role of *formateur*. When the PNI called for the position of prime minister to be given to one of its members, objections were raised in *Abadi* (18 July 1953).

[34] This generation gap was not only a question of age. Jusuf Wibisono, who was a loyal supporter of Soekiman's, was born in the same year as Natsir. The difference between the two was more a question of sensibilities: the "older generation" continued to be guided by the principle of national unity irrespective of religious differences.

form of nationalism was intransigent and it was impossible for them to get along with Natsir. They did manage to cooperate, however, with Soekiman. The other important group within the PNI was led by Sartono and Surwirjo, who recognised the capabilities of those in Natsir's inner circle.[35]

The existence of these different groups within the two main parties could facilitate the creation of coalitions by allowing their differences to be put to one side, but at the same time they could also weaken those very same governments. On 26 April 1951, on the eve of the announcement of Soekiman's new cabinet, the tensions within Masyumi were clear to see: the executive committee, at a meeting chaired by Natsir, refused to approve Soekiman's nomination as prime minister.[36] The official reason for this decision was that Soekiman had only been invested by the party to be *formateur*, but this should not let us be distracted from the real issue. What Natsir wanted to punish Soekiman's supporters for was a recently signed agreement with the PNI and, more importantly, their lack of support when he was prime minister. Despite statements to the contrary by the different protagonists, this was a serious crisis for the party.[37] It was only after three weeks of prevarication that Masyumi decided, on 19 May, "to give a chance to the Soekiman cabinet to implement its programme".[38] Naturally, this crisis did not augur well for the new government, and throughout its time in office support from Masyumi was never forthright with the party's executive committee threatening to withdraw its support on several occasions. In the end, it was their refusal to sanction Subardjo's risky foreign policy, coupled with a similar refusal shortly afterwards by the PNI, which finally led to the resignation of the government on 23 February 1952.[39]

---

[35] For more on these, and other factions within the PNI, see Feith, *The Decline of Constitutional Democracy in Indonesia*, pp. 139–42. Feith includes the first group in his group of "solidarity makers" and the second one in his group of "administrators" (supra. p. 127).

[36] Muhammad Asyari, "The Rise of Masjumi Party in Indonesia and the Role of the Ulama in Its Early Development, 1945–1952", MA Thesis, McGill University, 1976, pp. 114–5.

[37] In *Abadi* on 28 April 1951, Natsir wrote that he was convinced of the stability of Masyumi's unity.

[38] "Kesempatan kepada Kabinet Soekiman untuk melaksanakan programnya", *Abadi*, 21 May 1951.

[39] Cf. infra pp. 186–8.

Having successfully toppled the Natsir and Soekiman governments, the rival wings within the Muslim party handed the job of taking down the Wilopo cabinet over to their nationalist allies. After Soekiman's resignation, the president entrusted the task of drawing up a new government to two *formateurs*: Sidik Djojosukarto from the PNI and Prawoto Mangkusasmito from Masyumi. It was an undertaking, however, which was doomed to failure given the open hostility between the PNI's president and the Natsir wing of Masyumi to which Prawoto belonged. The two men managed to draw up a programme for government, but they could not agree on the distribution of ministerial portfolios. Sidik notably refused to accept the army's preferred candidate for the position of minster for defence: the Sultan of Yogyakarta, who was backed by Prawoto.[40] On 19 March 1952, they handed in their resignation letters to the president, who subsequently designated Prawoto once again as a *formateur*, but this time Wilopo, representing the PNI, was named as the other half of the tandem. Wilopo, who was close to Natsir, was a lot more flexible in his dealings with Masyumi, and on 3 April a government was formed. Wilopo was named the head of the executive, while Prawoto was appointed deputy prime minister. However, the PNI now took up the mantle worn previously by Masyumi, and its attitude towards the government was one of barely concealed opposition, despite the fact that it was led by one of its own members. At the beginning of June 1953, after an announcement by the leadership of the nationalist party that it would vote in favour of a motion of no confidence tabled by a member of Sarekat Tani Indonesia, a party close to the PKI, the Wilopo government resigned before the vote even took place.

Three factors led to the instability of governments built on an alliance between the PNI and Masyumi: policy differences, disagreements over ministerial appointments and the role played by party factions, with the latter being the most preponderant. Certain analysts have laid great emphasis on the PNI's alleged fear of Masyumi's Islamic ideology based on a belief that Darul Islam was an illegal branch of the party.[41] This reading of the situation has been largely confounded by the examination of the different phases of negotiation between the

---

[40] Deliar Noer, *Partai Islam di pentas nasional* (Jakarta: Pustaka Utama Grafiti, 1987), pp. 260–1.
[41] Feith, *The Decline of Constitutional Democracy in Indonesia*, p. 97.

two parties, which shows that such considerations never constituted for the PNI an obstacle to collaboration with Masyumi. The two sides always managed to come to an agreement on a programme for government, and there was a general consensus within both parties that the important question of Islam's role in the state could only be resolved by an elected assembly. However, during the transition period which we are concerned with here, however, cracks began to appear in Indonesian politics, which had up until that point been papered over by the need for unity imposed by the revolutionary period. As a result, a large amount of political energy was taken up with the necessary reorganisation of the country's parties. It is in this context that one needs to look at the skilful manoeuvring involved in the distribution of ministerial portfolios, with every political movement wanting to use them to gain some political advantage over their rivals.

Although the clashes between Natsir's wing and Soekiman's group weakened the party's position as well as the governments it headed, these disagreements, which the party's leadership always made a point of minimising, were invariably patched up. However, another storm was brewing within Masyumi in the shape of Nahdlatul Ulama, a large traditionalist Muslim organisation which was one of Masyumi's constituent groups and whose leaders had already been complaining for a number of years about its position within the party. The formation of the Wilopo cabinet brought about NU's break from the party, and the Ali government led to its entry onto the Indonesian political landscape.

Masyumi and Its "Muslim Brothers"[42]

Before the revival of Nahdlatul Ulama as a political party in 1952, Masyumi held, to all intents and purposes, a monopoly over the representation of Indonesian Muslims. The two other existing Muslim parties were not able to provide a credible alternative to the role it played on the political scene. Perti possessed no representative in Parliament and the PSII had never managed to regain its prestige and recover its pre-war organisational network. The Masyumi leadership's conviction that they were the only ones to possess the ability, and perhaps also

---

[42] We will only look here at the circumstances of the schism which took place in 1952. Analysis of the deeper reasons for this split can be found in Chapter 6.

the legitimacy to govern meant that they received the news of NU's decision with a certain amount of insouciance. The revival of Nahdlatul Ulama was announced at the beginning of April 1952, the day after the formation of the Wilopo government. It was confirmed by the organisation of the party's first congress, which opened a few weeks later in Palembang. By a very large majority (61 votes to 11), Nahdlatul Ulama decided to establish itself as an independent party and invited Masyumi to form an alliance with it within a federation.[43] The Masyumi leadership did not seem to measure the significance of this event, treating the traditionalists' decision with disdain and scepticism. In the eyes of Masyumi's leaders, NU had painted itself into a corner over the previous few months by laying down a set of demands during the protracted negotiations which had preceded the formation of the new government. Early in the negotiations, on 15 March, K.H. Abdul Wahb Hasbullah, the *Rais Am* of NU,[44] had informed the PNI's *formateur*, Wilopo, that he wished to see Soekiman reappointed as prime minister, with, by his side in cabinet, Abu Hanifah as minister for foreign affairs, Zainal Arifin as minister for defence and Wahid Hasjim as minister for religions.[45] The request concerning the Ministry of Religions became, on 20 March, a demand: if it was not given to NU, the organisation would leave Masyumi. Muhammadiyah, through one of its senior leaders, HAMKA, protested vociferously against this manoeuvre, which he judged to be contrary to party procedure.[46] He also referred to the fact that questions concerning the composition of a new government came within the remit of Masyumi's central executive and not of its constituent organisations. The reformist organisation wanted its own candidate, Faqih Usman, to get the position, which it had only ever occupied once,[47] and it was eventually he who was appointed, following an internal vote organised to choose which party member would get the portfolio.

---

[43] *Hikmah*, 10 May 1952.

[44] The *Rais Am*, also known as the *Rois Aam*, is the title of the highest office within Nahdlatul Ulama. He is the president of the Supreme Council, also known as *Syuriah*, which runs the organisation and lays out its general policy.

[45] These last two were members of NU.

[46] Membership of Masyumi was made of individuals, known as ordinary members, but also religious organisations. The traditionalist Nadhlatul Ulama and the modernist Muhammadiyah were by far the biggest religious groups in the party.

[47] By H. Rasjadi in the second Sjahrir government in 1946.

Although the position of minister for religions was a relatively minor one, ranked 16th overall in the cabinet hierarchy, it was of capital importance to the large Muslim organisations. Occupying this position not only meant that an organisation could weigh upon government policy, but also, more importantly, it allowed them to assign people to a significant number of positions. They could appoint teachers, administrative officers for mosques, as well as religious judges, which enabled whatever organisation that occupied the ministry to reward part of its support base and also to spread its doctrine, be it traditionalist or modernist, throughout Indonesia. In the eyes of the modernist members of the Masyumi leadership, NU, by addressing its demands directly to the *formateur*, had violated the procedures in place and furthermore, its decision to found its own party had broken the unity of the *umma*, and had done so for base political motives.[48] They reacted scornfully to the traditionalists' decision and refused to even debate NU's invitation to Masyumi to become a federation.[49] One of the few reactions by the Masyumi leadership to the foundation of NU came from Prawoto Mangkusasmito, who described, in a declaration to the press, what he considered would be the sombre political destiny which now awaited NU following its departure from Masyumi:

> If one accepts the point of view which maintains that Masyumi is a right-wing party, then all the objective evidence which we have at our disposal today indicates that NU will be an extreme right-wing party. History has taught us a lesson, however, which is that it is the nature of extremist parties, on the left or on the right, to always be in opposition, and so if ever they take over the reins of power, the government will gradually adopt a dictatorial system.[50]

These comments are worthy of our attention not only for the fact that they contain an unprecedented admission that Masyumi was a right-wing party, but also because they reveal the bitterness of modernist leaders as well as their scornful attitude towards the *ulama* whenever these religious legal scholars became involved in secular issues.

---

[48] See Mohammad Natsir's editorial in *Hikmak*, 16 April 1952.
[49] "Riwajat singkat partai Nahdlatul-Ulama", in Kementerian Penerangan, *Kepartaian dan Parlementaria Indonesia* (Jakarta, 1954), p. 413.
[50] *Hikmah*, 10 May 1952.

However, this appraisal of the threat posed by NU was soon shown to be flawed and the modernists were shortly to pay the political price for it. The other Muslim parties, who had up until that point been marginalised, could now join with Nahdlatul Ulama and constitute a fairly significant political force.[51] This is what they duly did, creating the League of Muslims a few months after the foundation of the traditionalist party.[52] This structure was loose enough to be able to preserve each of the three parties' desire to remain independent, but owing to a lack of unity, it never managed to become a serious long-term rival to Masyumi. However, it did rapidly present itself to the PNI leadership who were tired of having to find an agreement with Masyumi in an effort to guarantee to the public its Muslim credentials. After the fall of the Wilopo cabinet, on 3 June 1953, the usual long-drawn-out negotiations between the PNI and Masyumi started once again. Having received assurances from NU that it would not take part in any government which excluded the Muslim party from the cabinet table, Masyumi's leaders refused to back down from certain positions they had adopted,[53] notably refusing to accept certain candidates for ministerial positions whom they suspected of having Marxist leanings.[54] On 1 August, when the Ali cabinet was formed, it contained no Masyumi member and five members of the League of Muslims.[55]

The modernist party was, in equal measure, surprised and disappointed by this move. NU's split had heretofore not worried it unduly, but it now revealed its devastating effects as Masyumi was no longer the vital Muslim pillar of political stability, and found itself relegated to the opposition benches. A few days later, *Abadi* devoted its editorial to the new coalition, and behind the high-flown rhetoric of its declarations, which were somewhat contemptuous of its new political

---

[51] NU had seven deputies in Parliament: Zainul Arifin, A.A. Achsien, K.H.A. Wahab, K.H. Ilyas, A.S. Bachmid, Idham Chalid and K.H. Adnan.

[52] Liga Muslimin Indonesia.

[53] Deliar Noer, "Masjumi: Its Organization, Ideology, and Political Role in Indonesia", Master thesis, Cornell University, 1960, pp. 299–300.

[54] In particular, Ong Eng Die, the PNI's candidate for finance minister, and Arudji Kartawinatat, the PSII's candidate for defence minister.

[55] For NU: Zainul Arifin (second deputy prime minister), K.H. Masjkur (minister for religions) and Mohammad Hanafiah (minister for agriculture); for the PSII: Abikusno Tjokrosujoso (minister for communications) and Subidjo (social affairs). Perti only entered government in November, when Sirjajuddin Abbas replaced Subidjo.

opponent, Masyumi's justified concern was plain to see.[56] Its status was changing from being the political incarnation of Islam within the state's institutions to becoming a simple Muslim party amongst others.

> Masyumi is not a political party in the common sense of the term, it is a political movement supported by a large majority of the Indonesian people. Ninety percent of the population is Muslim, and so the Ali government will be faced with an opposition which includes not only Masyumi but also the Indonesian people, who hold the Muslim religion in very high regard. In exchange for giving NU and PSII five cabinet seats (of which only two are important), the Ali government has received in Parliament only seven votes from NU and four from PSII. This support does not hold much weight in society. Without wishing to denigrate the influence of NU and PSII, we think that Wongsonegoro [the *formateur*] has not only pulled the wool over his own eyes, but has also pulled the wool over the eyes of the country's Islamic community as well. It will not be long before the Islamic community asks NU and PSII why they preferred, for the sake of secondary seats in cabinet, to cooperate with non-Muslim parties rather than with Masyumi. We hope that they will get a sincere and appropriate answer to this question. If not, they [NU] will have to face not only the opposition of Masyumi, but also the opposition of the entire Muslim community.

The surprising longevity of the Ali government, in power for almost two years, condemned Masyumi to a long period of exile in opposition. They responded to the legitimacy of their Islamic rivals by portraying themselves as the champions of Islamic unity. A few weeks before the formation of the Ali cabinet, the modernist party had already tried to gain the upper hand over its rivals. In the first months of 1953, *ulamas* close to Masyumi attempted to set up a new body grouping together all Muslim organisations. A gathering of all the *ulamas* of Indonesia was held at the beginning of March 1953 on the initiative of an organisation known as the Front of Muslim Preachers of Medan (Front Muballigh Islam di Medan). Its goal was to try to

---

[56] Published on 7 August 1953, almost one week after the formation of the government, it was clearly not an ill-tempered reaction, but rather an interpretation of events which had no doubt been discussed at length by the newspaper's management.

solve the thorny issue of the unity of the *umma*. To this end, it was proposed to unite the two existing federations: the Committee of the Indonesian Muslim Congress (Badan Kongres Muslimin Indonesia BKMI) and the League of Muslims, in a vast organisation called the Front for the Combat and Defence of Islam (Front Perdjoangan dan Pertahanan Islam). This initiative, which was strongly supported by Masyumi,[57] failed when the League of Muslims refused to participate in it, fearing, with some justification, that their voice would be drowned out in an organisation dominated by Masyumi.[58]

After the formation of Ali's cabinet, calls for unity became increasingly insistent, though they generally came from Masyumi's constituent organisations, or even from its readership, rather than its leadership.[59] These appeals were relayed by the party's press, and indeed hardly a week went by without *Abadi* or *Hikmah* devoting an article to it or publishing a letter about it. This abundance of pleas gave the impression that there was a strong degree of pressure coming from the party's grassroots. Most declarations called on NU and the PSII to withdraw from Ali's cabinet, for the all-important sake of unity amongst Islam's political representatives. They were advised not to content themselves with listing the advantages which their participation in government bestowed upon them, such as "important positions" or "special [import] licences", but to take stock also of the "losses" and "affronts" suffered by the Muslim community.[60] Based on the notion that unity was a divine command, these pleas sometimes used methods which were slightly unorthodox but capable of capturing the public imagination. On 22 August 1954, for example, Little Aisyah, a nine-year-old mystic who toured Java for several months delivering inspired sermons

---

[57] See Mohammad Saleh Suaidy's declaration of support for the new organisation in *Abadi*, 28 February 1953.

[58] *Abadi*, 25 February 1953.

[59] In an article published in *Hikmah* on 26 September 1953, HAMKA explained that in numerous towns across the country, organisations calling for the Muslim community to unite were springing up. In Medan, the Islamic Preachers Front (Front Mubaligh Islam), in Jakarta the Contact Committee for Muslim Organisations (Badan Kontak Organisasi Islam) and in Yogyakarta the Union of Action of the Umma (Kesatuan Aksi Ummat Islam). See also the call for unity made by the leadership of Badan Serun Islam, *Abadi*, 12 November 1953.

[60] See, for example, the editorial published in *Abadi* on 8 September 1954, about the NU congress which was just about to open.

to enthralled audiences, devoted part of her address to the issue, encouraging harmony and cooperation between the three Muslim parties.[61]

The deleterious atmosphere which marked the final months of the Ali government finally put an end to the collaboration between the PNI and the parties of the League of Muslims. Already weakened by the increasing number of hostile declarations by the nationalist camp,[62] government cohesion did not survive the rebellion of a part of the army chiefs of staff which took place during the months of May and June in protest against new nominations to the army which the cabinet had tried to impose. On 20 July, Nahdlatul Ulama declared that it wished to see the cabinet resign, and a mere three days later the government fell. The approaching elections had precipitated its collapse; the different leaders of the various Muslim parties could no longer turn a deaf ear to the calls for unity coming from their electoral base. On 15 June, a declaration of unity was signed by Mohammad Natsir for Masyumi, Arudji Kartawinata for the PSII, K.H. Dahlan for NU and H. Rusli Abdulwahid for Perti.[63] Formed on 11 August 1955, the Boerhanoeddin government marked a moment of reconciliation between the different Muslim parties. Masyumi held three ministries in the new government while Nahdlatul Ulama and the PSII obtained two portfolios each. The greatest task facing the new government was the organisation of elections for the Constituent Assembly and the Parliament which were to take place in September and December 1955. In the run-up to the elections, no serious attempt was made to agree on an electoral alliance between the Muslim parties, and indeed Masyumi itself, despite the lip service it paid to the necessity for unity between

---

[61] *Abadi*, 23 August 1954. The importance which Masyumi's press placed on such accounts seems quite surprising, given that the modernists, who at that point comprised a significant majority of the party, were generally quite sceptical towards any reports of paranormal phenomena.

[62] In September 1953, Kartawinata, the president of a small nationalist organisation PERMAI, allegedly said that the Prophet was a liar and the Koran empty of meaning. These reports caused outrage in the Muslim community. The head of Masyumi's branch in West Java, Isa Anshary, asked for an enquiry to be opened (*Abadi*, 18 November 1953). In January 1954, a huge demonstration was organised in Makassar by PSII (*Abadi*, 5 January 1954). There were other similar controversies, one of which involved the leader of a local PNI branch, a certain Hardi (*Abadi*, 2 February 1954).

[63] *Abadi*, 16 June 1955.

the parties, was not particularly keen on the idea, convinced that it would win single-handedly. The election campaign did not really threaten the government's cohesion, but once the campaign had ended, however, the first signs of tension between the parties soon appeared. In early December, NU and the PSII aired their misgivings in relation to the government's policy on negotiations with the Netherlands. Unwilling to share the responsibility for these talks, they refused to participate in the delegation sent to Geneva.[64] Following Boerhanoeddin Harahap's decision to continue the negotiations, they withdrew their ministers from cabinet and called on the government to resign.[65]

The inability of the Muslim parties to unite their efforts within the same government was a good illustration of the volatile nature of the young Republic's provisional institutions. Differences in approach to the various challenges the successive governments had to face unquestionably existed, on questions such as diplomatic or domestic policy, for example. Nevertheless, these differences, much like the disagreements between Masyumi and the PNI, were ones of form rather than of substance. NU and Masyumi's respective programmes show no fundamental difference between the two parties at this stage in their history. The prospect of an Islamic state was at this point too remote to create a clash over what exact Muslim doctrine it would be founded on. The dispute between NU and Masyumi was above all a question of power and personalities, much like the older quarrel between the PSII and Masyumi, which opposed the two parties despite the fact that they were both part of the modernist movement. If the PSII and NU left Masyumi in 1947 and 1952 respectively, it was because their leaders felt hampered by the party and poorly represented in its ruling body, but, above all, because the period lent itself to launching new political ventures. The successive ministerial crises constituted for every political party, irrespective of size, an opportunity to be grasped,[66] and in the absence of a reliable means for accurately predicting the outcome of a nationwide vote, the prospect of a general election allowed all

---

[64] *Abadi*, 7 December 1955.
[65] The PSII on 18 January and NU on 19 January (*Abadi*, 19 and 20 January 1956). The Harahap government finally resigned on 3 March.
[66] It is significant that the two major splits within Masyumi (the PSII in 1947 and NU in 1952) took place during negotiations for the formation of a new government.

parties to nurture wild dreams of electoral success. To achieve this, it was essential for parties, first of all, to make themselves known to the general public; following that, the next step was to differentiate themselves from rivals who had turned down coalition alliances, thus opening the door to ministerial office for a few months, which would pave the way for electoral success. It was precisely because Masyumi was unable to fulfil this role for the different branches of Islam and provide them with positions of power that PSII and NU broke away. The same interpretation of events was voiced by HAMKA, a member of the party's executive committee, who formulated it in the shape of a self-assessment of the party in September 1953.[67]

Once it had regained its independence, NU's great strength was to be able to collaborate with left-wing parties on the Indonesian political landscape and more importantly with the president. By doing this, they were able to outflank Masyumi, whose certainty about their own policies meant that they were less inclined to make concessions. Sukarno, who desired to go beyond the bounds of the limited institutional role given to him by the 1950 Constitution, benefitted from the support of the traditionalist party. In April 1954, a congress of *ulamas* close to NU gathered in Ciapanas in West Java, on the initiative of the minister for religions, K.H. Masjkur. It awarded the president the title of *Ulil-Amri* (meaning "those who are in command"), which gave Sukarno legitimacy as the Muslim leader of a country which did not fulfil all the criteria of an Islamic state. Although this move was no doubt motivated by considerations concerning Islamic law,[68] in the context of the time it took on an important political dimension. It provoked reactions of indignation from Masyumi leaders as well as from the *ulamas* who had refused to participate in the congress.[69] In

---

[67] "One of the points of contention within Masyumi which explains the departure of NU, the PSII and Perti (H. Siradjuddin Abbas [leader of Perti] was one of the founding members of Masyumi) was the fact that there was not yet any concrete guarantee of power-sharing." *Hikmah*, 26 September 1953.

[68] According to Islamic law, *sharia* courts needed to be designated officially by the authorities who had replaced the Dutch. Andrée Feillard, *Islam et armée dans l'Indonésie contemporaine: Les pionniers de la tradition*, Cahier d'Archipel 28 (Paris: L'Harmattan, 1995), p. 47.

[69] An editorial published in *Abadi* on 13 March 1954 contested the legitimacy of the conference, citing the names of several *ulamas* who had refused to attend it.

response to these objections, a senior civil servant in the Ministry of Religions explained that the decision concerned not only the president but also the Republic's institutions, and that it would have no consequence on the president's power, which was in any case very limited by the Constitution.[70] The alliances between NU and left-wing parties, on the other hand, were a different issue. The modernist party could not really speak out against these as long as they only involved the PNI, but when the spectre arose of an unacceptably indulgent attitude on the part of NU towards the PKI, relations between the two Muslim parties became much more rancorous.

During the Ali government, NU leaders had made declarations concerning the attitude to adopt towards communism, which were, to say the least, contradictory. Part of the leadership adopted an attitude identical to that of Masyumi, consistently denouncing the danger which communism represented for Indonesia in general and for Islam in particular. K.H. Abdul Wahab Hasbullah, the *rais am* of Nahdlatul Ulama, was amongst those opposed to communism, and in a declaration made on 16 December 1954, he argued that there was a great danger that the communists would come to power in Indonesia, which would lead to a severe restriction of Muslims' room for manoeuvre. He added that his organisation had "for some time" (*semenjak dulu*) been favourable towards banning the PKI.[71] A few weeks later, the vice-president of NU's leadership, K.H. Dahlan, declared in *Abadi*, that his party considered communism as "infidel" (*kafir*) and that during the Palembang congress, a resolution was voted banning party members who were not versed (*awam*) in communism's doctrines from reading books on the subject.[72] Another anti-communist crusader was Imron Rosjadi, the president of NU's youth movement, Anshor, who regularly denounced the threats made by the PKI towards Masyumi. In an interview given to the daily newspaper *Keng Po* in June 1955, he promised that the members of his organisation would not for a moment hesitate to come to Masyumi's help if the PKI carried out these threats.[73] Later in 1960 when Masyumi was outlawed, Imron Rosjadi was one of the few NU figures to come to its defence.

---

[70] *Abadi*, 10 March 1954.
[71] *Abadi*, 17 December 1954.
[72] *Abadi*, 17 December 1954.
[73] A declaration which *Abadi* lost no time in publishing on 21 June 1955.

However, much to Masyumi's concern, Nahdlatul Ulama's call for toughness towards the PKI was not unanimous. NU's participation in Ali's cabinet, which was supported by the PKI, was severely criticised.[74] What was more worrying still for the Masyumi leadership was the fact that certain figures within NU went as far as to evoke the possibility of cooperating with the communists. On 24 October 1954, the leader of the NU parliamentary group, A.S. Bachmid, declared that the importance which the PKI had acquired under the Ali government was greatly exaggerated, adding that the PKI was perfectly entitled to support the government if it wished to do so. For him, the cooperation between NU and the PKI was founded on a "common understanding of desired goals".[75] In January 1955, Nahdlatul Ulama's leader in East Java, Murtadji Bisri, adopted a similar stance, declaring in *Keng Po* that he did not agree with the dichotomy generally put forward between Islamic law and communism. According to him, such an attitude was in danger of leading to a clash which would be damaging for the unity of the country. Here again, much ado was made of this declaration and it provoked horrified reactions in the Masyumi press.[76]

NU was not the only Islamic party Masyumi clashed with over the issue of cooperation with the communists. During the Ali government, the PSII also revealed an attitude of openness towards the PKI— in December 1954, PSII's president, Arudji Kartawinata even went so far as to affirm that the alliance of nationalists, communists and Islam in Indonesia "was based on obvious reasons".[77] This stance earned him a sharp rebuke from Isa Anshary who, in a speech given in Palembang, regretted that PSII had abandoned the founding values of its pre-war predecessor.[78]

---

[74] See, for example, *Hikmah*'s editorial of 10 April 1954, criticising the Ali government, and by extension NU, for having "given to the PKI an opportunity to spread propaganda in favour of its campaign for the creation of a 'Popular Republic of Indonesia', akin to Moscow and Bejing."

[75] *Abadi*, 25 October 1954.

[76] See *Abadi*, 10 January 1955. Masyumi's press also echoed concerns voiced by NU figures worried about the rapprochement with the communists. *Hikmah*, 29 January 1955.

[77] "…berdasarkan kenjataan2", *Abadi*, 6 December 1954.

[78] Ibid. In 1923, Sarekat Islam suddenly split from the Marxist movements which it had previously been quite close to.

Masyumi's intransigent anti-communism constituted one of the party's essential traits in the political battle that pitted it against its Muslim rivals. In their desire to be seen as the representatives of the entire Muslim community, its leaders avoided engaging in debates with their opponents in the PSII, NU and Perti on the topic of religious doctrine. By exploiting the ambivalent attitude of these three rivals towards the PKI, however, it became easy for them to claim to be the only party capable of building a solid rampart against communism.

Plate 3.3 Prime Minister Ali Sastroamidjojo torn between his two wives, the PKI and Nahdlatul Ulama (*Abadi*, 21 January 1955).

Intimate Enemies

Up until 1950, the Indonesian Communist Party, which had very nearly been banned following the Madiun rebellion, existed both clandestinely and officially. An illegal PKI pulled the strings of the legal version of the party and also secretly controlled two puppet political parties: the Indonesian Labour Party (Partai Buruh Indonesia) and what was left of Amir Sjarifuddin's party, the Socialist Party (Partai Soisalis). In January 1951, a group within the PKI led by three young party figures, D.N. Aidit, M.H. Lukman and Njoto, took over the party's politburo. These three men remained at the head of the party until 1965 and they changed party policy to promote the development of both mass membership of the party and strategic alliances with other anti-imperialist political movements.[79] From 1951, the party, whose membership until that point had only amounted to a couple of thousand, grew rapidly, and this became a real source of concern for Masyumi. Despite the fact that strikes were illegal, a significant number of them took place between January and August 1951, bringing the country to a halt. There were reports of the existence of pro-communist armed groups in the mountainous areas of Central Java.[80] Following an armed attack in the port of Tandjung Priok in Jakarta, the Soekiman government, claiming that there was a plot to undermine national security, suddenly ordered the arrest of several thousand communist activists. The inability to produce sufficient evidence meant that the majority of those arrested were soon released, but the PKI remained a semi-clandestine party for several months afterwards and the incident embittered the rivalry between the Communist Party and Masyumi. During this forced exile from the political landscape, the communist leadership came to an awareness of the necessity to create an alliance with the country's progressivist forces, which would be able to protect them against the attacks of their main enemies, Masyumi and the PSI.[81] The PNI, President Sukarno and, to a lesser extent NU, soon appeared to them as possible allies in this enterprise. In order to counter the accusations of atheism that were aimed at the party, and which could

---

[79] Françoise Cayrac-Blanchard, *Le parti communiste indonésien* (Paris: Armand Colin, 1973), pp. 59–62.

[80] Cayrac-Blanchard and Devillers, *L'Asie du Sud-est*, p. 345.

[81] Cayrac-Blanchard, *Le parti communiste indonésien*, p. 104.

constitute a stumbling block for the creation of such an alliance, the PKI strived to present the image of a party which was tolerant towards religions. D.N. Aidit, for example, declared that Indonesia should be "a garden where all religions and all political convictions would live in harmony and struggle together to crush imperialism."[82]

Masyumi's anti-communist propaganda consisted in presenting what it considered to be the real face of communism. The party leaders unrelentingly called on people to return to the very sources of their political enemies' doctrine. Natsir recalled Lenin's teachings concerning the elimination of the Revolution's opponents.[83] In a speech made in Tandjung Priok in March 1954, Jusuf Wibisono referred to what he had experienced in a trip to Moscow to "the centre of communism", which led him to the conclusion that a compromise between religion and communism was impossible.[84] Masyumi's leaders also warned their fellow countrymen about the PKI's proposal to replace the reference to a single God in *Pancasila* with a simple affirmation of a principle of religious freedom, which would be the first step in a programme aimed at establishing a "freedom of anti-religious propaganda".[85]

The Masyumi leaders' attacks on the PKI were not confined to the question of religion, however. At a rally in Yogyakarta in July 1954, Jusuf Wibisono was also eager to convince his audience of the "dicta-torial character" of the Soviet regime. He denounced the repression of any opposition to the regime and the lack of a free press, which was reflected in the fact that *Isvestia* and *Pravda* were the only newspapers.[86] Having convinced the Indonesian public of the dangers of the Soviet system, Masyumi went on to explain why it appealed to the PKI. The Muslim party needed to show that behind the old tune which the Indonesian communists banged out about offering an original path for

---

[82] Ibid., p. 121. As a sign of his sincerity, Aidit explained that for the Muslim feast day *Lebaran*, which marks the end of Ramadan, communist leaders would visit Muslim authorities, adding that he personally spent Christmas in the company of Protestants.

[83] *Abadi*, 1 March 1952.

[84] *Abadi*, 30 March 1954.

[85] See the declarations made by the Co-ordination Committee for Muslim Orga-nisations (Badan Koordinasi Organisasi Islam, BKOI), close to Masyumi. *Abadi*, 18 January 1955.

[86] *Abadi*, 6 July 1954.

Plate 3.4 The PKI separating the principle of a unique God from the rest of *Pancasila* (*Hikmah*, 26 June 1954).

their country to follow, the face of totalitarianism lurked menacingly.[87] One of the most commonly used arguments was to refer to the portraits of international communist figures which could be seen at PKI rallies. During a Masyumi rally in Jember on 21 July 1954, for example, Muchtar Chazaly, addressing the audience directly, asked them:

---

[87] On 10 November 1955, *Abadi* published the declarations made by D.N. Aidit, stating that the PKI did not want the Republic of the Proclamation (*Republik Proklomasi*) to be transformed into an Islamic state or a state of Darul Islam (*Negara Islam atau Negara Darul Islam*), and that he had no intention either of declaring a communist state (*Negara kommunis*). The newspaper added: "it is the same old tune played by communist leaders, but the people know exactly what the PKI wants in reality."

"Is there anybody here who has a portrait of Eisenhower?" to which the "tens of thousands of people present" all replied in the negative. Chazaly logically concluded that Masyumi was not an American agent "as the communists claim". The PKI, on the other hand, who often installed "portraits of foreign communist leaders, such as Malenkov, Mao Tse Tsung and others" was in the pocket of "foreign countries".[88]

The confrontations between the two parties sometimes went further than the usual polemics. From 1954, the Masyumi press regularly reported on violent clashes, and one of the most enlightening of these happened on 28 April 1954, at a PKI rally held in Malang which was also attended by Masyumi supporters.[89] In front of the rostrum from which the PKI's first secretary made his speech, a banner was unrolled which read: "Woe upon the terrorist-bandits of the BKOOI and Masyumi."[90] According to the account given of D.N. Aidit's speech in *Abadi*, he explained that the PKI was anti-capitalist and anti-imperialist, and also refuted any accusations presenting him as anti-religious. He declared, on the contrary, that it was Masyumi who was harming religion:

> The Prophet was not a man whose ideas were like Masyumi's, his Islam was better than Masyumi's Islam. To vote for Masyumi is to wish for the world to go to hell. To join Masyumi is *haram*, whereas to join the PKI is *halal*.

This was a direct provocation and all hell broke loose in the audience. Neither the organisers of the rally nor the police force were able to restore order. One part of the audience shouted: "Lies! Not true! Remember Madiun!" The rostrum which Aidit was standing on was surrounded, but "representatives of Islam" intervened at this point, notably Hasan Aidid, the PKI president's namesake who was in charge of the Surabaya branch of Masyumi. They attempted to calm everybody down, but the crowd demanded that D.N. Aidit withdraw his statement, which he finally did, returning to the rostrum to say:

---

[88] *Abadi*, 22 July 1954.
[89] *Abadi*, 30 April 1954. An account of this incident was also included in an opuscule published by the Organisation for the Defenders of Islam. Organisasi Pembela Islam, *Peristiwa rapat P.K.I. di Malang, 28 maret 1954* (Malang, 1954).
[90] "Kutuk teroor-perampok Masjumi-BKOI." A photo of the banner was published by *Abadi* on 17 May 1954.

Plate 3.5 Homage given to Malenkov and Mao (*Hikmah*, 10 April 1954).

> If there are people among you who feel offended by what I said,
> I apologize to them, but I want to say that the PKI is not anti-
> religious.

Tempers in the room flared again, with cries of "Lies! It's not true!" Aidit apologised a second time and a third, but the audience then demanded that the portraits of Marx, Engels and Aidit which were hanging proudly over the rostrum be replaced by those of Sukarno and Hatta. The hammer and sickle emblem was also taken off the wall, and it was only thanks to a police escort that Aidit was finally able to leave the venue.

This was Masyumi's version of events, and naturally enough the PKI's version was much different. In a statement made on 30 May 1954, D.N. Aidit declared that he had been the victim of an attempted assassination during the rally "the first time [this had happened] in Indonesian politics." The first secretary of the Communist Party accused "a group of agitators led by Hasan Aidid of the Surabaya branch of Masyumi".[91] Far from being isolated cases, these clashes between

---

[91] A declaration published in Organisasi Pembela Islam, *Peristiwa rapat P.K.I. di Malang.*

communists and Masyumi during political rallies maintained a climate of violence which was exacerbated by the regular publication of two types of rumours: one concerning blasphemous acts and another about communist threats towards Muslim figures.[92] The cases deemed to be the most serious were the insults to religious symbols. On 22 April 1955, for example, *Abadi* reported that on 27 March of that year a group of Muslim scouts from the village of Sutomujo, in the district of Tuban, were given a page of the Koran by an ice-cream street vendor bearing the emblem of the PKI and the inscription "Masyumi is a dog".[93] The Muslim daily was a bit sceptical about the veracity of these events and so remained prudent in its treatment of them, merely echoing the emotional reactions the affair provoked in the Muslim circles in the region. Concerning threats made against Masyumi, the party's press often incriminated the communists whenever its members were beaten up by unknown individuals.[94] On 11 April 1954, *Abadi* even drew attention to a report by the leadership of the Union of Indonesian Muslim War Veterans (Persatuan Bekas Pedjuang Islam Indonesia) confirming the existence of a secret instruction by the PKI ordering its members to "keep an eye on and eliminate" (*mengawasi dan membasmi*) the leaders of Masyumi.

Nonetheless, numerous figures of the Mulim party, both locally and nationally, endeavoured to minimise the risk of direct confrontations between their supporters and those of the PKI. They made a clear distinction between an ideological battle and their struggle against communists, and often maintained cordial relations with their counterparts in the PKI. In Bandung, one of the local party figures, Umar Suriatmadja, regularly invited members of the local branch of the PKI

---

[92] On 22 July 1954, *Abadi* reported on a meeting held by the PKI in the village of Balung Kidul in Jember, which was "overrun by crowds". A member of the audience asked one of the speakers why the portrait of the president but not of the vice president appeared behind the stage and was told by the communist officials that Sukarno was a friend of the PKI, whereas Mohammad Hatta was not "because his character is not good" ("karena pribadinya tidak baik"). As had happened many times before, the crowd flared up, shouted, "Lies! Lies!", and attempted to climb onto the rostrum. Once again, the PKI officials owed their safety to the intervention of a group of young Muslims and, according to the newspaper, "no incident took place."

[93] "Masjumi seperti Asu".

[94] This was the case, for example, when Udin Sjamsuddin, the president of the Masyumi branch in North Sumatra, was assaulted. *Abadi*, 1 March 1955.

to family events and religious events, and indeed he was often invited to their houses in return.[95] Multiple testimonies have also shown that it was not unusual for Natsir himself to have tea at the Assembly's cafeteria in the company of D.N. Aidit.[96] On several occasions, these leaders intervened to avoid clashes between their supporters spilling over into violence. In June 1955, for example, a Masyumi member in Badung was found dead in suspicious circumstances, and the rumour quickly spread that he had died following an assault by communist sympathisers. In response to the seriousness of the accusations, the PKI sent a delegation to meet with Rusjad Nurdin and Umar Suriatmadja, the Masyumi leaders in West Java and Bandung, respectively. The preliminary enquiries, and particularly the autopsy report, established that the victim's death was not due to an assault, which led Umar Suriatmadja to express his astonishment that such a rumour had appeared in the press. He reminded *Abadi*'s readers that in Islam it was a very serious offence to falsely accuse somebody without foundation.[97]

This desire for a more moderate approach can no doubt explain the lukewarm reception given to Isa Anshary's Anti-communist Front. Founded in September 1954 by the turbulent president of the West Java branch of Masyumi, this group aimed, according to its proponents, at thwarting the PKI's efforts to create a Democratic Popular Front (Front Demokrasi Rakjat).[98] However, during the national tour which he undertook to develop his organisation, Isa Anshary met with wariness from Masyumi leaders. In Palembang on 4 December, he announced his intention to form a local branch of the Anti-communist Front, but the president of the South Sumatra section of Masyumi, Djadil Abdullah, politely refused his invitation to join. He explained that the local leadership had not yet discussed the question and that Isa Anshary's initiative was primarily a regional one.[99] Similar misgivings were advanced by the national leadership of the party. In November, the *ulamas* of Persis[100] announced their support for the Anti-communist

---

[95] Interview with Umar Suriatmadja, Bandung, September 1955.

[96] A. Lukman's interview with Mohammad Natsir in 1988, in Moch. Lukman Fatahullah Rais, ed., *Mohammad Natsir Pemandu Ummat* (Jakarta: Bulan Bintang, 1989).

[97] *Abadi*, 21 June 1955.

[98] *Abadi*, 14 September 1954.

[99] *Abadi*, 6 December 1954.

[100] Persatuan Islam was a radical reformist organisation which was very influential in West Java. Isa Anshary was its spiritual guide.

Front and adopted an intransigent position towards the wayward Muslims "in a party in opposition to the laws of Islam", who, if they persisted would have to be considered as apostates (*murtad*) and could not be buried or honoured religiously.[101] In response, Masyumi's religious council (the *Madjelis Sjuro*) adopted a more moderate stance, merely remarking that communism was, according to Islam, an atheist (*kufur*) doctrine and that those who adhered to it knowingly were infidels (*kafir*). Mohammad Natsir, for his part, declared that although many Masyumi members had joined the Anti-communist Front, the party had no links with it.[102]

Between 1950 and 1956, Masyumi's political influence progressively waned. In 1949, it was considered to be the largest political organisation in the country and was an essential pillar of all coalition governments, but clouds began to appear on the horizon after Natsir and his inner circle took over the reins of the party in 1950. In response to the new leadership's policies, the PNI, NU, PSII and the PKI gradually sketched the outlines of an informal alliance which united around the figure of Sukarno. Natsir and his allies at the head of Masyumi could now only count on the support of three political parties—Sjahrir's PSI and the two Christian parties, Parkindo and Partai Katholik—which, though prestigious, were modest in size. This position was shown to be a very fragile one, given the serious crises which successive Indonesian governments had to overcome during this period.

Islamic Rebellions—Masyumi and Its Wayward Brothers

Between 1950 and 1956, five of the country's regions were the scenes of major rebellions inspired by Islam. These uprisings were the aftershocks of the period known as the Physical Revolution and constituted the main concern of the five successive governments in power during the period. Before 1957, national political leaders were united in a common cause to fight against these rebellions, and even if they did not always agree on the methods to be adopted, they managed to prevent the insurrections from posing any real threat to the Republic's

---

[101] *Abadi*, 12 November 1954. The *ulamas* were quoting verse 11 of the Koran to support their decision.
[102] *Abadi*, 30 December 1954.

territorial integrity. Subsequently, however, movements which associated themselves with Darul Islam rediscovered a regionalist dimension which had previously been toned down for the benefit of the ideal of an Islamic state, and began to participate in a motley coalition opposed to President Sukarno's Guided Democracy. With support now coming from part of the political classes, including certain Masyumi leaders, this coalition planned to extend its political struggle beyond the capital to the whole of Indonesia. Masyumi was involved in the rebellions which took place between 1950 and 1956 in two different respects. On the one hand, some of its local branches which identified with the party's revolutionary heritage took part in the rebellions, and so left the party as a whole open to criticism and also to clampdowns by the government. However, at the same time, as one of the main parties of government, Masyumi also attempted—both through negotiation and repression—to guide their wayward brothers back to the right path, and away from the "shortcut" they had taken which turned out in fact to be a dead end.[103]

Revolutionary Movements Hostile to Any Diplomatic Concession

Throughout the 1950s, West Java, which was the cradle of the Darul Islam movement in Indonesia, remained the epicentre of the struggle between republican troops and supporters of an Islamic state. The split between the movement led by Kartosuwirjo and the Republic was a progressive one. Each diplomatic agreement with the Dutch gave those in favour of an insurrection against the Republic a new pretext to lay another stepping stone towards that goal, and finally, on 7 August 1949 in the village of Cisampang, an Islamic State of Indonesia (Negara Islam Indonesia) was proclaimed.[104] Despite the efforts of the republican

---

[103] "We see some of our own members, who fought in the Revolution choosing a shortcut (*jalan pendek*) in the desire to reach the summit quickly." Speech by Mohammad Natsir made in Medan on 2 September 1953, and published the next day in *Abadi*.

[104] Kartosuwirjo had been forced to leave his headquarters in Mont Sawal, which he considered to be his Mecca, and fled to Cisampang, which he rechristened Medina. A visit to Mont Sawal for Darul Islam's combatants was the equivalent of the Hijra, the pilgrimage to Mecca. Cees Van Dijk, *Rebellion under the Banner of Islam* (The Hague: Martinus Nijhoff, 1981), p. 92.

army, Darul Islam managed throughout the first half of the fifties to reinforce its influence and its military capacity. At its height, around 1957, the rebellion was able to mobilise almost 13,000 men and had at its disposal 3,000 firearms, including machine guns and mortars.[105] At this point, its troops controlled large zones in the counties of Tasik-malaya, Ciamis and Garut, as well as the region around Cianjur, and from their hiding places in the mountains they frequently launched attacks on the nearby villages.

In the region of Central Java, three guerrilla movements claiming to belong to Darul Islam were active during the 1950s. Although they maintained some contact with the rebels in West Java, they neither managed to join forces with them nor to develop their military capa-bility. As a result, republican army operations rapidly reduced their number to a few groups of armed pillagers who were more concerned about their own survival than about the creation of an Islamic state.[106]

In South Sulawesi, the militia groups who had fought against the Dutch, assisted by former soldiers of the KNIL (the Royal Army of the Dutch East Indies), had grouped together and joined the Union of South Sulawesi Guerrillas (Kesatuan Gerilya Sulawesi Selatan, KGSS). In 1950, after talks with the government, their demand to be integrated *en masse* into the republican army was refused by the government.[107] The officer in charge of the negotiations, the former guerrilla coordi-nator for all of East Indonesia, Abdul Kahar Muzakkar, was outraged by the government's attitude and resigned. Although he was at the head of the KGSS, an organisation containing 15,000 men which was now banned, he continued to help the republican troops in their battle against the KNIL's last remaining revolutionary units. However, at the beginning of August, a republican unit killed two leading guerrilla

---

[105] Van Dijk, *Rebellion under the Banner of Islam*, p. 102.

[106] Amir Fatah's mujahideen, K.H. Machfudz's Army of Umma (Angkatan Umat Islam) and the Hizbullah troops battalion 426. See Van Dijk, *Rebellion under the Banner of Islam*, p. 127–56. Some of these insurgents had rebelled because of the social revolution which had affected the regions of Brebes, Tegal and Permalang during the first months of independence. Anton Lucas, "The Tiga Daerah Affair: Social Revolution or Rebellion?", in *Regional Dynamics of the Indonesian Revolu-tion, Unity from Diversity*, ed. Audrey Kahin (Honolulu, HI: University of Hawai'i Press, 1985).

[107] The combatants wished to create a brigade within the army in memory of Hasanuddin, the Sultan of Goa, who in the 17th century had briefly succeeded in resisting the Dutch invasion. Ibid., p. 169.

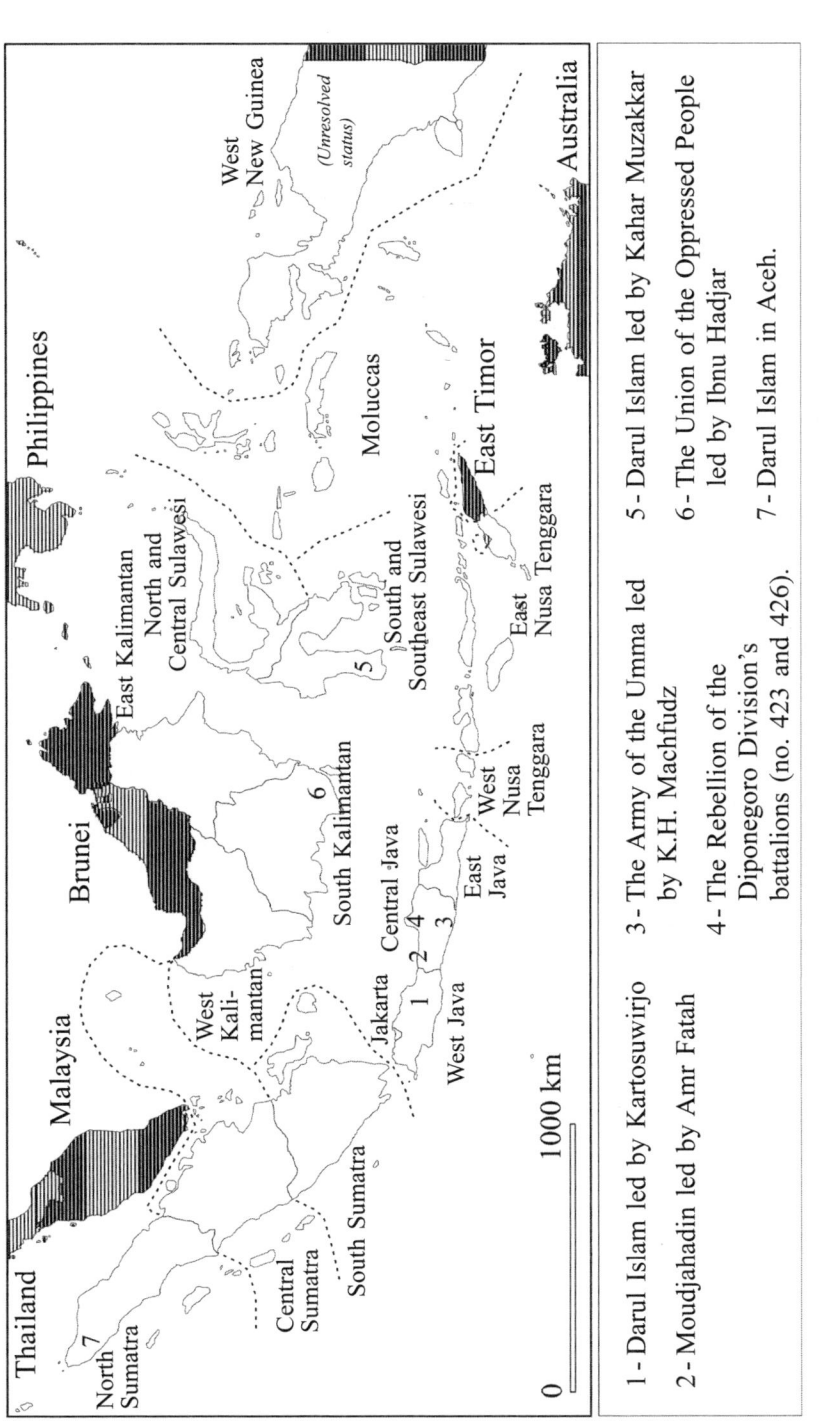

Map 3.1 Movements linked to Darul Islam between 1949 and 1960.

1 - Darul Islam led by Kartosuwirjo

2 - Moudjahadin led by Amr Fatah

3 - The Army of the Umma led by K.H. Machfudz

4 - The Rebellion of the Diponegoro Division's battalions (no. 423 and 426).

5 - Darul Islam led by Kahar Muzakkar

6 - The Union of the Oppressed People led by Ibnu Hadjar

7 - Darul Islam in Aceh.

figures during a meeting which had been planned in advance, and this military blunder marked the beginning of a real rebellion against the Republic. The incident reinforced the population's sympathy towards the rebels, and the conflict rapidly took on an ethnic dimension.[108] Despite efforts by the army and attempts to reconcile the two sides, the Indonesian authorities were not able to stamp out to the rebellion.[109] Meanwhile, Kahar Muzakkar had made contact with Kartosuwirjo, and on 20 January 1952, he officially accepted command of the Indonesian Islamic Army (Tentara Islam Indonesia) for South Sulawesi. In August 1953, Muzzakar proclaimed Sulawesi a part of the Indonesian Islamic Republican State (Negara Republik Islam Indonesia), and on 1 January 1955, Kartosuwirjo named him deputy minister of defence.[110]

In Kalimantan, located in the Indonesian part of Borneo, the rebellion against the republican government broke out, like in Sulawesi, when the creation of the unitary state was announced in 1950. However, it never had the same scope as the uprisings organised by the other organisations affiliated to Darul Islam, and although it certainly mobilised several thousand men, they never had more than a few dozen firearms between them. The main zone affected by this rebellion was the county of Hulusungai; the provincial capital, Banjarmasin, on the other hand, was only occasionally threatened by rebel attacks.[111] The rebellion was led by Ibnu Hadjar, a former officer of the Marine Fourth Division (the Angkatan Laut Republik Indonesia Divisi IV, otherwise

---

[108] Barbara Harvey, "Tradition, Islam and Rebellion: South Sulawesi 1950–1965", PhD Thesis, Cornell University, 1974, p. 227.

[109] As the authorities were aware that the South Sulawesi guerrillas, who requested to be given an important role in the military organisation of the region, were a lot better organised than those in West Java, they finally agreed to create a Hasanuddin Brigade. However, on the morning of 17 August 1951, the date planned for the official inauguration of the brigade, the government officials found the camp deserted. The former guerrillas had retreated to the jungle, bringing with them the money and the 5,000 uniforms they had just been given. Kahar Muzakkar justified this decision by explaining that the army had not respected the unwritten clauses of the agreement, namely the release of their men from prison and the transferral of the officers involved in the Udjung Pandang incident. *Hikmah*, 22 September 1951.

[110] Kahar Muzakkar did not use the official name given to the state founded by Kartosuwirjo, which was called Negara Islam Indonesia. *Abadi*, 8 August 1953.

[111] Van Dijk, *Rebellion under the Banner of Islam*, p. 218.

known as ALRI Div IV), which for four years had successfully tormented the Dutch troops and which often received support from those amongst the population who were unhappy with the new republican order. After re-establishing their control in the region, the Jakartan authorities had undoubtedly upset the fragile social and economic equilibrium established by ALRI Div IV under which the local population had prospered for four years. During that time, the local farmers were cut off from the country's cities, and as a result, organised themselves into cooperatives. They managed to completely control the means of production and channels of distribution of rubber, but when communication with the rest of the country was re-established, retailers from the cities were able to regain control over the rubber trade.[112]

Ibnu Hadjar did not rally behind Darul Islam until the end of 1954, when Kartosuwirjo offered him a seat in the government of the Islamic State of Indonesia. Given the modest size of the Kalimantan guerrilla, Ibnu Hadjar only received a secondary position in cabinet, that of *menteri Negara*, which literally means minister of state, but which in reality meant that he was a minister without a portfolio. However, he was named commander of the Islamic Indonesian Army in Kalimantan. This integration into the Darul Islam movement, however, amounted to nothing more than an Islamisation of Ibnu Hadjar's political rhetoric. He took on the title of *Ulil Amri*, the "Authority" of the Islamic kingdom, and he had a new Indonesian national anthem composed, but he carried out no substantial reforms in the territory he controlled.

The rebellion in Aceh, a region in the very north of Sumatra, broke out in 1953. It was the result of a complex mix of social, religious and political demands, and it came to an end in 1959 once the rebels' main demand—the creation of an autonomous province—was satisfied. Following the proclamation of independence, the republican government, in Aceh as elsewhere, looked for the most experienced people to be its representatives. It was therefore logical for it to confide most of the young administration's responsibilities to the *uléëbalang*, the traditional elite, just as the Dutch and Japanese had done previously.[113]

---

[112] Ibid., p. 250.
[113] The *uléëbalang* generally held the titles of *Teuku*, while the *ulama* held that of *Teungku*; ibid., p. 270.

Between December 1945 and January 1946, they had to face violent opposition in the shape of a "social revolution" which was led by the region's *ulama* and resulted in many of this elite being killed. The surviving *uléëbalang* had to give up their hereditary rights, and were removed from the positions they had occupied within the republican administration.

This outburst of violence was in fact part of an older conflict between traditional and religious elites. Since 1939, the religious elites had been part of the Union of Ulama of Aceh (Persatuan Ulama-Ulama Seluruh Atjeh), and one of its founders, Teungku Daud Beureu'eh, had established himself as the region's strong man in the five years that followed the proclamation of independence. During that period, Aceh found itself in a situation of de facto autonomy, and after the elimination of the *uléëbalang*, Daud Beureu'eh took the rank of military governor, a position which was officially confirmed in May 1949 by Sjafruddin Prawiranegara's emergency government (PDRI). Prawiranegara, who was named deputy prime minister with authority over the question of Sumatra after the republican government was released, divided North Sumatra into two provinces and established Daud Beureu'eh as governor of Aceh in December 1949.

When the unitary Republic of Indonesia was created, however, this new administrative division was abandoned, much to the disappointment of the local population. Subsequently, tensions continued to grow in the area and in September 1953, Daud Beureu'eh and his allies, faced with the threat of being arrested, took to the nearby mountains. The former governor saw his rebellion as part of a struggle in the name of Islam, but although contacts were made with Kartosuwirjo's government, the Aceh branch of Darul Islam never considered becoming part of the Islamic State of Indonesia.[114] The government's successive clampdowns in response to this rebellion were not really effective. Far from weakening Darul Islam's troops, the army's offensives reinforced the local population's support, something which the chiefs of military staff themselves recognised in 1956. After much hesitation, Ali Sastroamidjojo's second cabinet adopted the measures which had previously been initiated by Boerhanoeddin Harahap, and a law was passed in December 1956 which established Aceh as an autonomous province,

---

[114] On the role of the *uléëbalang*, who were theoretically the officers of the sultan but who in actual fact were local potentates, see James Siegel, *The Rope of God* (Berkeley and Los Angeles, CA: University of California Press, 1969), pp. 10 ff.

with A. Hasjami, one of the senior figures of pre-war PUSA, as its first governor.[115]

The rebellions linked to Darul Islam were principally motivated by regionalist demands. These were often accompanied by a social dimension which can be explained by the proximity between the traditional regional elites and the republican government. With the exception of Aceh, religious considerations appeared as a secondary factor in the outbreak of rebellions. The reference to an Islamic state may have allowed the movement to organise itself on a national level, but it never developed into anything more than a shared opposition to the republican state, and the Negara Islam Indonesia never constituted a serious alternative to the regime in Jakarta.

"Masyumi = DI"? The Responsibility of Masyumi in the Islamic Rebellions

Masyumi's political opponents regularly drew attention to the rebellions organised by Darul Islam, which for many years became a burden for the party and tarnished its reputation. The PKI's propaganda machine constantly harped on about Masyumi's supposed involvement in these Islamic revolutionary movements, and it was popularised by the slogan "Masyumi = DI", which rang out at political rallies. This association was not just confined to communist circles, and indeed General Suharto used it in 1969 as an argument to reject the plea made by Masyumi's former leaders for their party's revival.[116] Between these accusations and the blatant insincerity of certain Masyumi figures concerning their complicity with the insurgents, it is difficult to determine the extent of the party's involvement in these rebellions. There was no doubt a link between certain regional party structures and the rebellions, but at the same time, the party never refused to condemn the insurgents' actions. It should also be remembered that the backdrop to this turbulent period was made up of a poisonous combination of rumours, secret emissaries and arbitrary arrests.

A study of the senior figures and combatants belonging to Darul Islam in Indonesia reveals undeniable links between the insurgent

---

[115] At the same time, a former head of the Islamic guerrilla received the military command of the region of Aceh. Discussions then took place with the political representatives of Darul Islam. They were about to reach an agreement when the PRRI-Permesta revolt broke out.

[116] Cf. Infra, Epilogue.

organisations and Masyumi. Of the seven movements who claimed to belong to DI, four of them drew a significant portion of their supporters from Masyumi or from its militia group, Hizboellah.

Kartosuwirjo, for example, had been one of Masyumi's founders at the congress in November 1945. He was a member of the party leadership and was named as one of the five Masyumi representatives on the KNIP's executive committee during its fifth session held in Malang between February and March 1947.[117] In addition, he showed his attachment to Masyumi in July 1947 when Amir Sjarifuddin's cabinet was formed: as a former leader of the PSII, which had been reformed in order to participate in the government, he was offered the post of second deputy minister for defence, but refused because, as he wrote at the time, given that he was not yet involved in the PSII, he "still [felt] obliged towards Masyumi".[118] It was also in the name of Masyumi that in November 1947 he set up in Garut and in Tasikmalaya, in West Java, two organisations to help the Muslim community.[119] When Kartosuwirjo chose the path of secession in February 1948, it was completely logical for him to suspend, with the agreement of the local leaders of GPII, Hizboellah and Sabilillah, Masyumi's activities in West Java.[120] In this region, the party's organisational infrastructure

---

[117] The records of the congress, however, do not attribute any official position to him within the party, contrary to what Pinardi claimed (*Sekarmadji Maridjan Kartosuwirjo* [Jakarta: Aryaguna, 1964], p. 31). Quoted by Van Dijk, *Rebellion under the Banner of Islam*, p. 81. He presented Kartosuwirjo as the first secretary of the party, a position occupied in fact by Harsono Tjokroaminoto Pinardi (Soesoenan Poetjoek Pimpinan Partai "Masjoemi", in Pengoeroes Besar Partai Masjoemi, *Masjoemi, Partai Politik Oemmat Islam Indonesia* [Jogjakarta, 1945], p. 3).

[118] Quoted in Van Dijk, *Rebellion under the Banner of Islam*, p. 83.

[119] See supra. Chapter 2.

[120] There is a lot of uncertainty surrounding this question. The debates between *ulamas* which took place at the congress in December 1949 shed a different light. It was said that the Masyumi branch and its constituent organisations in West Java decided to break up in order to better fight against the Dutch. During these debates, allusion was also made to an organisation called Darussalam which was said to have fought, with the help of the Dutch, against the Darul Islam movement. Did this organisation have links with Masyumi? The participants in the debate remained silent on that question, and highlighted the deep state of confusion which reigned in the region at that time. Badan Usaha dan Penerbitan Muslimin Indonesia, *Kongres Muslimin Indonesia, 20–29 Desember 1949 di Jogjakarta* (undated), pp. 50–2.

was undoubtedly at the origin of the rebellion and Masyumi's national leadership took many months before finally managing to reorganise a regional branch under the direction of Isa Anshary, one of the leaders of Persis.

In Aceh, a comparable situation existed. PUSA was one of the constituent organisations of Masyumi and the party's regional head was none other than Daud Beureu'eh. In fact, one of the reasons he instigated a rebellion was Masyumi's removal from government. The replacement of the Wilopo cabinet—within which the modernist party exercised considerable influence—by the Ali cabinet, which did not contain a single Masyumi member but enjoyed support from the PKI, was interpreted in Aceh as a sign that the central government had fallen into the hands of Islam's enemies. Despite the undeniable involvement of Masyumi's regional branch in the rebellion, which was exploited by its political opponents, the national leaders of the party strenuously denied any accusation of the party's complicity. Kasman Singodimedjo, for example, in an analysis of the events in Aceh given in October 1953, while recognising the involvement of numerous members of his party in the events, explained that the problem was to know if they did so as members of Masyumi or for other reasons. He was also angered at the fact that, for most commentators, the person in charge of the revolution was Daud Beureu'eh "the member of Masyumi", and not Daud Beureu'eh "the former governor of the province of Aceh." [121]

The involvement of Masyumi appears to be less direct in the three rebellions in Central Java. Two of those rebellions—the one led by Amir Fatah and the one instigated by the Diponegoro division—originated in the former units of the Hizboellah.[122] However, the third —Angkatan Umat Islam—had no direct link with the party. Unlike in Aceh and West Java, the Masyumi leadership managed to protect the party's organisational structure in this region from the contagion of revolutionary Islam, thus depriving the rebels of both the logistical and popular support which they would soon be badly in need of.

---

[121] Kasman forgot to mention, however, that Daud Beureu'eh had been appointed to this position by Sjafruddin Prawiranegara, a member of the Masyumi leadership.

[122] Amir Fatah claimed to be the president of the Central Masyumi Defence Council (*Dewan Pembelaan Masjumi Pusat*); Van Dijk, *Rebellion under the Banner of Islam*, p. 138. This position was in fact occupied by Wahid Hasjim, *Al-Djihad*, 12 October 1946. Amir Fatah's usurpation of this title was interesting insofar as it shows how the party, even when it was under fire, remained an indispensable means of gaining credibility within the Muslim community.

In Sulawesi, as in Kalimantan, the rebels for the most part originated from various guerrilla groups unhappy with the future prospects
offered to them by the government of the unitary state. Although
they had sometimes been part of Islamic movements in their youth,
(Kahar Muzakkar, for example, had been a pre-war member of Muhammadiyah), their demands concerning Islam seemed secondary and they
joined Kartosuwirjo's Darul Islam more out of political opportunism
than because of their Islamic convictions. Masyumi and its constituent
organisations were in fact very thin on the ground in these regions
before August 1950, and the groups which the party was closest to
remained loyal to the Republic. In Kalimantan, for example, Hassan
Basri, the founder and vice president of one of Masyumi's constituent
organisations, the Union of Indonesian Muslims (Serikat Muslimin
Indonesia, SERMI), worked hand in hand with his virtual namesake,
Hasan Basry, to stop the rebellion from spreading. Hassan Basri was
subsequently named as Masyumi's representative for South Kalimantan
in the Parliament of the Republic of the United States of Indonesia,
and afterwards appointed to the unitary state's Provisional Assembly.[123]

It was for their alleged support for the movements of Darul Islam,
as opposed to their actual participation in rebellions, that numerous
members of Masyumi were pursued by the Indonesian army. As the
elections of 1955 later showed, the regions in question were strong
bastions of support for the party. Nonetheless, in most cases, the assistance given locally to the rebels did not signify a complete adherence
to the ideals of Darul Islam. During the fighting, numerous villages
found themselves caught in a quandry, with each side suspecting villagers of supporting their opponents and punishing them accordingly.[124]
An acronym was coined to describe these local populations who were
obliged to keep both sides happy. They became known as *Kongres*
because they used to explain to Darul Islam that they supported it
(*menyokong*), while assuring republican troops that everything was in
order (*beres*).[125]

---

[123] *KH. Hasan Basri 70 Tahun* (Jakarta: Media Da'wah, 1990), pp. 29–55.

[124] In January 1953, for example, the KRYT burned down 50 houses in a village
in South Kalimantan whose inhabitants had gone to see President Sukarno, on a
trip to the region. Later the same day, more houses were burned down in the
same village by the army in response to suspected support by villagers of the
rebels. Van Dijk, *Rebellion under the Banner of Islam*, p. 259.

[125] Ibid., p. 105. Karl D. Jackson talks of *gonta-ganti* villages, meaning villages
which alternated between the two sides. The inhabitants in these villages could

In these villages, the government clamped down particularly on Masyumi members and local party leaders. The party's press gave a faithful account of the considerable number of arrests which were made between 1951 and 1953 at all levels of the party. In June 1951, for example, in Bondosowo, a locality near Surabaya, 600 members of the local Masyumi branch were arrested and put in prison.[126] Most of the time, however, only the party's senior figures were targeted. In August of the same year, during the large wave of repression which followed the breakdown in negotiations in West Java, several members of Masyumi's regional membership were arrested, including Isa Anshary, head of the party in West Java.[127] A few days later, K.A. Hassan, the president of Persis and part of Natsir's inner circle, was also placed in custody.[128]

The region of Sukabumi was particularly affected by the government's campaign of repression. Military police arrested the local head of the party in July 1953; he was arrested again in June 1955, this time along with several other of the local branch's senior figures.[129] In most cases, these arrests took place without any official reason and the people concerned were released again a few days later after questioning.[130] In some cases, however, detention periods could last longer, and the party responded by forming a "Committee for the Defence of

---

attend the rallies organised by Darul Islam as diligently as they attended those organised by the republican authorities. He also explains that the local population's political loyalty was very fickle; they supported Masyumi at the beginning of the 1950s before switching over to the PNI camp after the 1955 election, and then supporting NU in the mid-1960s. *Kewibawaan traditional, Islam dan Pemberontakan, kasus Darul Islam Jawa Barat* (A translation of *Traditional Authority, Islam, and Rebellion* published by the University of California Press in 1980) (Jakarta: Grafiti, 1990), pp. 285–7.

[126] *Suara Partai Masjumi*, 29 June 1951.

[127] *Berita Masjumi*, 28 August 1951. The article recounting this event allows us to see a technique frequently used in the Masyumi press when it came to reporting on rebellions. Before mentioning the most plausible hypothesis—that Isa Anshary had been arrested for supporting Darul Islam—a highly improbable explanation was given of Isa Anshary's alleged involvement in an attempted pro-communist coup d'état. Such an idea is outrageous when you remember how virulently anti-communist he actually was.

[128] *Berita Masjumi*, 31 August 1951.

[129] *Abadi*, 28 July 1953 and 6 June 1955.

[130] At the time, the Masyumi press claimed, disingenuously, not to know the reasons behind these arrests.

Political Prisoners belonging to the Masyumi Family of Central Java"
(Panitya Pembela Tahanan Politik Keluarga Masyumi Djawa Tengah).
In December 1952, the committee thanked the command of the Diponegoro Division in Semarang for releasing party members, and asked
for the same clemency to be extended to the remaining prisoners based
on the somewhat curious basis that with the election on the horizon,
these prisoners, who were being held without trial, had to be given the
opportunity to vote.[131]

Most of those charged were not really complicit in the rebellion
in the sense that they did not support the rebels' struggle against the
republican state. According to H. Marcoesyah, a former local party
leader for the village of Banjarsai in West Java, the members of his
branch did not contest the position of the central party leadership condemning the rebels' machinations. Nonetheless, it was impossible for
these party members to turn down offers of help, in the form of food,
money or medical treatment, to their family members who had joined
the Indonesian Islamic Army.[132]

Masyumi's Policy concerning Darul Islam

As of 1949, the party had to progressively clarify its position with respect to the Darul Islam rebels, as it ran the risk otherwise of becoming
associated with them. Masyumi was swift to issue a condemnation in
principle of the rebels' actions, but its message remained for a long
time quite conciliatory, insisting on Islamic movements' original military goal, namely the fight against the Dutch. Although the party
understood the rebel population's discontent and shared some of their
ideals, it nonetheless did not intend to sanction their methods. It was
concerned about the possibility of a religious war breaking out in Indonesia, and it presented itself as the architect of a "psychological solution", as opposed to the "military solution" which a significant portion
of the Indonesian political class was calling for.

The job of establishing an official party line on the question of
Darul Islam fell to the fourth Masyumi congress, held in December
1949 in Yogyakarta. Thanks to the reports of the meetings between
ulama present at the congress, it is possible to get a fairly clear picture
of the debates which preceded the adoption of the motion on DI.

---

[131] *Berita Masjumi*, 2 December 1952.
[132] Interview with H. Marcoesyah, Banjarsari, September 1996.

Several of those who spoke, notably Munawar Cholil, one of the most influential *ulamas* within Masyumi, emphasised the fact that there existed "several sorts of DI". Some of these movements, it was said, were even "the work of the Dutch, created to achieve their policy aims". For these religious figures, the complexity of the situation required one to avoid any rash condemnation and necessitated, above all, the organisation of an official fact-finding committee.[133] The resolution on DI which was adopted by the congress reflected these hesitations. It urged the government to create a commission of enquiry in order to explore all the available solutions, and also asked the authorities to offer "a real opportunity for the divine ideology and religion to develop in all levels of society", and to avert "any measures which were likely to dishearten the Muslim community and to offend its religious sensibilities".[134] The resolution also condemned, for good measure, all attempts at secession in the country, although it only did so implicitly. It launched a warning, in terms that were as cautious as they were convoluted, about the dangers of the "direct path", reminding the public that:

> Whether in its domestic policy or its foreign policy, Masyumi remains committed to the goals outlined in article two of its statute, namely to preserve the sovereignty of Indonesia which resulted from the Revolution of the Indonesian nation on 17 August 1945, and also to achieve the ideals of Islam on a national scale. [The Congress wishes] Masyumi in particular and the Indonesian *umma* in general to become more aware of the fact that the situation requires this ideal to be accomplished by good deeds which need to be better organised and closer to the real goals [of the party].[135]

In the weeks following this warning, Masyumi's attitude towards Darul Islam in West Java remained conciliatory. In an article entitled "Concerning the Problem of Kartosuwirjo's Darul Islam", for example, Sjarif Usman reminded his readers that the rebel leader had proclaimed his Islamic state in a zone controlled by the Dutch and not in the Republic's territory, and as such, was serving the interests of the nation.[136]

---

[133] Badan Usaha dan Penerbitan Muslimin Indonesia, *Kongres Muslimin Indonesia, 20–29 Desember 1949 di Jogjakarta*, pp. 41–54.
[134] *Berita Partai Masjumi*, February 1950.
[135] Ibid.
[136] "Sekitar soal Darul Islam-Kartosuwirjo", *Suara Partai Masjumi*, April–May 1950.

Two months later, an article by Sjafruddin Prawiranegara, "The Indonesian State as a Darul Islam", clearly showed that the language used had none of the inflammatory rhetoric which it was later to acquire.[137] Without making any reference to the movement in West Java, the author expounded the benefits of this "Darul Islam", but by doing so insinuated that Kartosuwirjo should not deter Muslims from their principal objective of establishing an "Abode of Islam". It was only over the following months that the party's position became clearer, no doubt in response to the growing dangers posed to it by any association with Darul Islam. As the idea of Darul Islam could now no longer be distinguished, in the eyes of the public, from the idea of a rebellion against the Republic, Masyumi thereafter refrained from mentioning it. Following the growing number of arrests made of its members, the party leadership intended to distance itself more clearly from the dissident groups. On 21 January 1951, it published a declaration which, through the rhetorical device of repetition, was intended to appear unequivocal:

1. Although Masyumi has, on several occasions, explained the difference in political opinions between the Masyumi party and the Darul Islam movement, it seems that, for a number of people, this difference of opinion is not clear enough.
2. This difference of opinion is not yet clear enough for, amongst others, the employees of our government, particularly low-ranking officials.
3. Therefore, the party leadership considers it necessary to publish a clarification specifying the differences in political opinion between Masyumi and the Darul Islam movement.
4. Masyumi wishes to achieve its goals by following a path of parliamentary democracy, following a path which is in conformity with the Constitution and with the laws of the Republic of Indonesia.
5. With this declaration, we hope that the difference of opinion between Masyumi and the Darul Islam movement will be clearer in the public mind.[138]

---

[137] "Negara Indonesia sebagai Darul Islam", *Suara Partai Masjumi*, August–September 1950.

[138] This declaration was to be adopted again by the fifth party congress in February 1951, and could also be found in *Berita Masjumi*, 24 January 1952.

A year later, the warning addressed by Mohammad Natsir to the members of his party susceptible to being caught up in the revolutionary wave was even stronger. He alerted his fellow countrymen to the dangers of various forms of "populism which strike in particular young minds and the most desperate among us". He referred specifically to the attempts aimed at creating a "state within the state" undertaken by "extremist movements, both left-wing and right-wing (Darul Islam in the region of Priangan and the Popular Republic of Indonesia [Republik Rakjat Indonesia] near Tjirebon)."[139] For the Masyumi president the discontent of a part of the people was understandable, but the party's duty should be to "preserve the Republic of Indonesia, which is the fruit of our holy war" and to "enshrine the principles of Islam in the Constitution". However, Natsir reminded his audience that this had to be done "by following the usual paths in a democratic country", and that any other attitude would be considered irresponsible ("if the house which we have just built does not satisfy our wishes, are we going to burn it straight away?"), "suicidal" and "contrary to God's design".

The party's position towards Darul Islam remained the same subsequently. At the beginning of February 1952, one of Masyumi's radical members, Isa Anshary, who was head of the party in West Java, joined in the chorus. He reminded *Berita Masyumi*'s readers of Article Four of the party's statutes, forbidding its members from becoming affiliated to any other political organisation whatsoever, adding that "Darul Islam should not be an exception to that rule".[140] Once Masyumi's ideological position had been clarified, its leaders hammered home the message that it was now no longer possible to associate the party with Darul Islam, and endeavoured to provide their supporters with arguments proving this. Mohammad Natsir, for example, pointed out that Masyumi was banned in the regions controlled by Kartosuwirjo, and criticised "those who wonder if the ultimate goals of Masyumi and DI are the same". For him, such a question could "only be the fruit of an immature mind" or else was an instance of pure

---

[139] *Berita Masjumi*, 24 January 1952. The Popular Republic of Indonesia in the region of Cirebon was a small left-leaning movement led by Chaerul Saleh, one of Murba's close allies. The scope of this movement cannot be compared to Darul Islam, however.

[140] *Berita Masjumi*, 1 February 1952.

provocation. He went on to remark that "nobody would dream of putting Stalinism and social democracy on the same level even though these movements are both founded on Marxism."[141]

These positions, which were adopted during the first months of 1952, remained the official party line over the following years. Nonetheless, Masyumi always remained somewhat sympathetic towards Islamic insurgents. Although it denounced their actions, it recognised the cause of these revolts and therefore always pleaded for a political rather than a military solution.

The Solution for a "Military, Political and Sociological" Problem[142]

Two important elements need to be kept in mind when considering Masyumi's commitment to a peaceful solution. The first one is that on several occasions, the party's leaders, on behalf of the government, began attempts at reconciliation which, for the most part, failed. The second is that, as a result of these failures, the Muslim party became involved in a policy of secret negotiations on the fringes of the government's official manoeuvrings. The main consequence of these secret negotiations was to give credence to allegations of complicity between Masyumi and the rebels.

In September 1949, Natsir was appointed to chair a commission designed to advise the Hatta government on the question of Darul Islam. However, he did not manage to establish contact with Kartosuwirjo. In December 1949, as we have already seen, the fourth Masyumi congress adopted a motion demanding the formation of a "Resolution Committee". The government yielded to this demand, and one of the architects of the party's initiative, Wali al-Fatah, was appointed by the Hatta government to head this body. A former senior member of Muhammadiyah and Masyumi, Wali had also been a companion of Kartosuwirjo in the PSII during the pre-war years. He managed to make contact with the rebels in May 1950, but subsequently disappeared

---

[141] *Berita Masjumi*, 6 February 1952.

[142] "Guerrilla warfare is not only a military problem, it is also a political and psychological one." Mohammad Natsir's inaugural address, Kementarian Penerangan R.I., *Membangun diantagra tumpukan puing dan pertumbuhan. Keterangan Pemerintah diutjapkan oleh Perdana Menteri Mohammad Natsir dimuka sidang Dewan Perwakilan Rakjat Sementara, 10 oktober 1950* (Jakarta, 1950), p. 20.

without trace for almost two months. He was not located again until mid-July following an attack by the republican army. According to his declarations, the commander of the Indonesian Islamic Army, Oni, refused to allow any meeting between him and Kartosuwirjo.[143] Other accounts maintain that the leader of Darul Islam in West Java had hoped to meet an emissary who was higher up in government and had refused to meet Wali al-Fatah because he did not have the rank of Bupati.[144] In reality, Kartosuwirjo demanded negotiations between governments, which meant that he wanted, prior to the beginning of talks, recognition for his Islamic State of Indonesia by the Republic. At the end of May 1950, Masyumi sent emissaries to K.H. Machfudz, the leader of Angkatan Umat Islam which was in rebellion in Central Java. However, despite the fact that one of these envoys was the minister for religions, K.H. Wahid Hasjim, Machfudz refused to receive them.

With the nomination of Mohammad Natsir at the head of the first government of the unitary Republic, talks began again.[145] His programme for government planned to reintegrate guerrillas into civil society, but the gestures of appeasement made towards the different rebellions in the Indonesian archipelago only brought limited results. It is true that in Aceh, Natsir managed to defuse the emerging conflict. On 23 January 1951, he announced an agreement with PUSA which stipulated that the recent creation of the province of North Sumatra should not be considered a lasting obstacle to Aceh becoming a province. Two days later, the government named a new governor for North Sumatra, Abdul Hakim, who was a member of Masyumi known for his sympathetic attitude towards Aceh's claims for regional independence. In Sulawesi and Kalimantan, however, the efforts of the new prime minister turned out to be a lot less successful. Hasan Basry's reconciliation mission with his former comrades in arms failed, and we have already seen what happened to the agreement made with Kahar Muzakkar providing for the integration of his troops into the new "Hasanuddin brigade". Finally, concerning West Java, the prime minister announced that the combatants who surrendered between 28 November and 14 December would be able to join the armed forces or the police if they wished, provided they were able to pass the relevant

---

[143] Van Dijk, *Rebellion under the Banner of Islam*, p. 114.
[144] Noer, "Masjumi: Its Organization, Ideology, and Political Role in Indonesia", p. 111.
[145] Natsir's government lasted from September 1950 to April 1951.

aptitude tests.[146] The government furthermore committed to finding all members of the brigade new livelihoods.

In reality, these offers of incorporation were largely illusory. The government had already prepared a rationalisation programme for the armed forces which was supposed to limit their number in the following months to 200,000 men.[147] This implied, as Natsir himself revealed at the end of September 1950, the demobilisation of nearly 80,000 soldiers. Although this policy of appeasement was a fiasco, it nevertheless avoided the government from finding itself in a political impasse. For the entire province of West Java, less than 1,200 people surrendered, carrying only 46 firearms.[148] For the government, and especially for the army, it was only the number of arms surrendered that counted in this operation, and Natsir himself later recognised that his policy had been a failure. Commenting on the intention of the new government to follow a "tougher" line towards Darul Islam, he declared that he was "part of those who prayed and hoped that 'tougher' will mean more successful."[149]

Under pressure from the army and from his allies in the PNI, the new prime minister, Soekiman,[150] was forced to give up his search for the political solution which his party demanded, launching the first military operations in West Java in January 1951. In Java, the government's military operations were supported by militia groups close to left-wing parties such as the PKI, Murba and the PNI.[151] On 29 August 1951, the government gave five weeks to the rebels in Sulawesi to surrender before authorising the army to launch its "Operation Merdeka". At the same time, Hasan Basry took it upon himself to begin the crackdown on the rebellion in South Kalimantan. The decision to launch two simultaneous military operations, however, limited their effectiveness considerably, as the army was obliged to disperse

---

[146] *Berita Masjumi*, 12 January 1951.

[147] Van Dijk, *Rebellion under the Banner of Islam*, p. 110.

[148] Ibid., p. 111.

[149] "Saja masuk orang2 jang turut mendo'akan mudah2an 'lebih tegas' itu akan berarti lebih berhasil", *Berita Masjumi*, 16 May 1951.

[150] The Soekiman cabinet was in power from April 1951 until April 1952.

[151] Masyumi Djawa Barat issued a declaration protesting against the creation of these volunteer groups, "some [of whom] were under the control of communists". The numerous assassinations of *ulamas* and Muslim figures, which had taken place in several parts of West Java (Garut, Tasikmalaya, Ciamis), were also denounced. *Abadi*, 22 September 1953.

its troops. Moreover, the army had underestimated the determination of the rebels, and so failed to gain a clear upper hand on either front. Nonetheless, successive governments continued a largely repressive policy for a further four years,[152] and Masyumi denounced on numerous occasions this "military-centred" (*Tentara-centrische*) approach to the problem.[153] The party's representatives were particularly critical of the lack of respect shown by the army towards places of worship. In February 1952, for example, Prawoto Mangkusasmito handed a letter of protest to the government on behalf of Masyumi. The document stated that certain behaviours by republican soldiers often had the effect of increasing the Muslim community's resentment. He mentioned the case of a village in Central Java, Kartirejo, whose mosque had been set on fire by the army and he also reported an account which indicated that in the region of Surakarta, republican troops had entered the prayer hall accompanied by dogs and without taking their shoes off.[154] In April 1954, Natsir offered a very bleak assessment of the Ali government's security policy. Given the sums of money invested by the government and the amount of rebel activity over the previous year, he came to the conclusion that this policy was both harmful and ineffective.[155]

One of the Masyumi leadership's main worries was the prospect of these conflicts escalating into a religious war. If that were to happen, the party would have great difficulty dissuading its members from taking part in it and would find itself even more exposed to machinations by the army. Their warnings against the escalation of violence were addressed as much to the rebels as to the government. In a speech given by Natsir in Medan in December 1953, he denounced those who wanted to "turn everywhere into a place of holy war".[156] In February 1954, Masyumi vigorously opposed a government plan to have the Acehnese rebels condemned by a *fatwa* issued by *ulamas* in the region.

---

[152] In Sulawesi, however, an offer of amnesty made by the government in March 1952 was relatively successful and caused Kahar Muzakkar to lose some of his troops. Van Dijk, *Rebellion under the Banner of Islam*, p. 195.

[153] The expression was used by Natsir in an article entitled "The Current Impasse Requires a New Way" (Dajlan buntu sekarang memerlukan rintisan baru), *Berita Masjumi*, 28 September 1951.

[154] *Suara Partai Masjumi*, 3 March 1952.

[155] *Hikmah*, 28 August 1954.

[156] *Abadi*, 2 December 1953.

The president of Muhammadiyah, A.R. St. Mansur, set out in *Abadi* the reasons for his opposition to this plan.[157] It was, according to him, vain to look to Islamic law for a solution to a problem whose origins were sociological, psychological and economic. He added that this ploy recalled the methods used by the Dutch and Japanese colonisers, which had caused a significant section of the *ulama* to be held in disregard in the eyes of the people. Finally, he pointed out that such practices were in danger of creating a division in the country along religious lines, which would be a lot more harmful than any other type of division.

The entire political class was concerned about the risk of these conflicts degenerating into a large-scale politico-religious confrontation. At the beginning of 1953, a very heated debate followed President Sukarno's speech in Amuntai, in which he warned that if an Islamic state was proclaimed, the country's Christian regions would also secede.[158] In response to this speech and in the absence of any Masyumi representatives in the Ali government, which had been formed in August 1953, Daud Beureu'eh's supporters became convinced of the necessity to begin their rebellion. At the same time, however, Sukarno's words also gave free rein to the supporters of a more repressive policy.

The formation of the government led by Boerhanoeddin Harahap, which was in office from August 1955 to March 1956, restored hope for those who backed a negotiated settlement. With the agreement of Vice President Hatta and Colonel Zulkifi Lubis, the highly controversial deputy chief of staff, the prime minister entered into low-key talks with the rebels of Aceh and West Java.[159] The government, however, was too uneasy about this reconciliation policy for it to succeed, and as soon as the existence of these talks was uncovered, the authorities strenuously denied that any emissaries had been sent to meet with rebels. The rebels' pre-condition for entering talks, though, was precisely their recognition by the government, if not as a state, then at least as a negotiating party. The second Ali government understood this point and in December 1956, it passed a law which accorded to Aceh the status of autonomous province and named a governor from

---

[157] *Abadi*, 24 February 1954.

[158] See infra, Chapter 4.

[159] Daud Beureu'eh's son, Hasballah Daud, was sent to Aceh, and in February 1952 in West Java, the army intercepted and passed on to the press letters signed by Harahap and Lubis, offering Kartosuwirjo a ceasefire. Van Dijk, *Rebellion under the Banner of Islam*, pp. 329–30.

amongst the ranks of PUSA. This policy opened the way for a peaceful resolution of the conflict in North Sumatra, an outcome which had for a time been delayed by the PRRI rebellion.[160]

In West Java, however, none of the government's attempts at reconciliation were successful. Although the republican army managed, as of 1957, to isolate Darul Islam's troops and contain them to certain mountainous areas, the rebels remained a real threat. The attempted kidnapping of Khrushchev in February 1960, during an official visit to Indonesia, illustrated this in spectacular style. On the road between Bogor and Bandung, the Soviet leader narrowly escaped capture by a Darul Islam commando.[161] On 4 June 1962, Kartosuwirjo was finally caught, and shortly after his arrest, one of his sons "on behalf of the imam-president of the Islamic state" ordered his supporters to surrender. On 16 August, Kartosuwirjo was condemned to death and one month later was executed.

Overall, Masyumi did not gain much political capital from its demand for an "alternative path" (*djalan lain*) to the government's policy towards Darul Islam.[162] Others benefitted politically from the peaceful resolution of the conflict in Aceh and, to a lesser extent, in Kalimantan. In West Java, Kartosuwirjo's intransigence and his submission in 1962 justified in retrospect the hawkish enthusiasm of those who opposed any concession. The party's pacifist manoeuvres, however, remained fruitless and they turned out to be disastrous for the party in the long run. Its efforts to resolve the conflict with Darul Islam were primarily focussed on their action in government or within Parliament; however, they also permitted a number of their party members to act as unofficial negotiators who, though largely ineffectual, gave credence in public opinion to the theory of collusion between Masyumi and the rebels. In 1953, two of those negotiators were prosecuted during a high-profile court case which showed the ambiguity of the relations between Masyumi and Darul Islam.

Afandi Ridhwan, who was leader of GPII and a Masyumi representative in West Java's provincial assembly, as well as having been present at the Masyumi congress in 1949, had been one of the initiators of the security resolution passed by the assembly. This document invited

---

[160] See infra, Chapter 4.

[161] Van Dijk, *Rebellion under the Banner of Islam*, p. 125.

[162] "*Djalan lain*" was the usual expression used in writings by party members to signify a policy of reconciliation, as opposed to a policy of repression.

the government to look for an alternative to a military solution to address the problem with DI. Afandi Ridhwan was also the spokesman of the Committee for the Destiny of the People (Komite Nasib Rakjat), an organisation which in its meetings with civil and military authorities, argued for a more measured approach to the crisis. He was part of Natsir's inner circle, and at the party congress of 1949 he did his utmost to bring about the implementation of the motion calling for a peaceful solution to the conflict.[163]

Having informed the military authorities and his colleagues in the provincial assembly, he took the initiative of making contact with Sanusi Partawidjaja, one of his former fellow party members in GPII who had become Kartosuwirjo's main advisor.[164] In January 1952, he went to the headquarters of Darul Islam in Cigadu near Cianjur where he attempted to convince the rebel movement to abandon their demand for recognition by the Republic, prior to negotiations, of the Islamic State of Indonesia, and advised them instead to look for this recognition from Saudi Arabia or from Pakistan. At his trial, Partawidjaja stated that this proposal had in fact been made in jest, but it was taken seriously both by the military authorities, who saw this as proof that he was an active supporter of Darul Islam, and by Kartosuwirjo, who tried unsuccessfully to make contact with foreign embassies.[165]

Afandi Ridhwan managed, however, to obtain from Sanusi Partawidjaja a letter accepting negotiations in principle, on condition that the government gave a guarantee that the army would not interfere in them. He then went to Jakarta and handed the missive over to Deputy Prime Minister Prawoto Mangkusasmito's assistants.[166] Ridhwan, in his account of the events, was then given authorisation by Prawoto to continue his negotiations, and while waiting for a meeting with Sultan Hamengkubuwono IX, the minister for defence, in order to ensure his support, he was arrested and imprisoned at the end of May 1952.

---

[163] His wife had been one of Natsir's pupils when he was a teacher in Persatuan Islam in Bandung. Interview with Afandi Ridhwan, Bandung, September 1996.

[164] Ibid. The idea that the provincial assembly was aware of his actions seems to be corroborated by the motion of confidence which it voted in favour of Affandi in August 1952. *Hikmah*, 2 August 1952.

[165] According to Feith, Darul Islam authorities also made contact with the American embassy which they hoped would provide them with help in the event of a Third World War breaking out. Feith, *The Wilopo Cabinet*, p. 98.

[166] Prawoto Mangkusasmito, moreover, was a member of Masyumi.

His trial began in Bandung on 26 February 1953 and lasted four months, during which *Abadi* gave a faithful account of the hearings. However, neither the newspaper nor the members of Masyumi's leadership risked commenting on this delicate affair.[167] The only one to speak publicly about the case was Kasman Singodmedjo, the second vice president of the party, who did so as the accused's lawyer.

The case was a very sensitive one. The prosecution's main witness was Ijet Hidajat, a former "prefect" of the Islamic State of Indonesia who had been in custody since October 1952. At the hearing of 15 March 1953, he explained that he had been removed from his position in 1950 for having refused to continue the armed struggle after the proclamation of the unitary state in August 1950. He claimed that Natsir subsequently confided him with a mission to negotiate with Darul Islam in order to "end the struggle between us and us".[168] According to Ijet, in 1952, Afandi Ridhwan allegedly gave information to the rebels about the positions of Colonel Kawilarang and Indonesian army units. This testimony, which Afandi refuted, led to him being sentenced to three and a half years in prison.[169] It seems to me, though, that the evidence in this case was rather flimsy. The witness himself admitted that he was no longer a member of Darul Islam at the time of the events. In that case, how could he have known the nature of the information communicated by Afandi Ridhwan to the rebels? The accused was clearly a victim of the change in strategy effectuated in the corridors of power in response to the rebellion which took place after the collapse of Natsir's cabinet. He was no doubt also targeted by one of the sabotage operations which certain sections of the army were fond of carrying out during negotiations. Afandi Ridhwan's greatest crime in this affair was without doubt his naivety. The accusations brought against another member of the party, who was also put on trial a few weeks beforehand for collusion with DI, seemed a lot more credible.

Achmad Buchari, who was vice president of GPII, was also accused of having facilitated contact between Kartosuwirjo's movement

---

[167] On 2 March 1953, for example, *Abadi* indicated the presence of Isa Anshary, while on 16 March, it reported that Mohammad Natsir and Soekiman had "come expressly from Jakarta" to attend the hearings.

[168] An account of the hearing reported in *Abadi*, 16 March 1953.

[169] *Abadi*, 6 July 1953. On his release in January 1956, Affandi Ridhwan returned to sit in the provincial assembly and became a Maysumi party official in West Java. Interview, September 1996.

and Kahar Muzakkar in 1951.[170] His trial saw all the main figures of the Movement of Young Muslims appear in the witness box and, like during Afandi's trial, the benevolent presence of Mayumi's senior figures could be seen in the courtroom.[171] Without delving into the details of this highly complex case, we should note first of all the strong desire on the part of the presiding judge to implicate Masyumi by highlighting the existing links between the party and GPII. The trial's second hearing, held on 6 September 1953, was given over entirely to this question.[172] The judge asked the accused on several occasions to clarify the nature of the links between the two organisations. Denying the obvious, the accused stated that GPII was an independent movement which cooperated with all political parties. He merely acknowledged "a few special links with Masyumi", but nothing more.[173] Second of all, it should be pointed out that Achmad Buchari, like Afandi Ridhwan, thought himself to be entrusted with a negotiation mission by the Indonesian state. This conviction was based on a meeting the president had accorded the GPII leadership in mid-1951 during which Sukarno is said to have shared with these young people—and this was confirmed by other senior figures in the organisation—his hope to see contacts established with Darul Islam.[174] As the government, for political reasons, was unable to do so, the president considered that it was up to Islamic organisations such as Masyumi and GPII to establish preliminary contacts.

At the end of the court proceedings, however, Achmad Buchari's guilt seemed clearly established. He admitted to having conveyed a letter from Kartosuwirjo to Kahar Muzakkar; he explained that he had gone to Makassar solely on behalf of GPII, but rejected the claim that certain former rebels considered him a representative of Darul Islam. Achmad Buchari's explanations seemed much more coherent and appeared to make his involvement in the rebellion a lot more plausible than Afandi's. How could the fact of having conveyed a message—no

---

[170] *Abadi*, 25 August 1953.

[171] On 2 November 1953, Natsir and Mohamad Roem were present. *Abadi*, 3 November 1953.

[172] *Abadi*, 8 September 1953.

[173] GPII was, however, Masyumi's youth organisation. Cf. infra, Chapter 6.

[174] Dahlan Lukman and Anwar Harjono attested to this. *Abadi*, 22 September 1953.

doubt a proposal made by Kartosuwirjo to Kahar Muzakkar planning to integrate Muzakkar's troops into NII—from one rebel zone to another back his claim to have been in favour of a negotiated solution? At the end of his trial, Achmad Buchari, unsurprisingly, was sentenced to three years in prison.

The involvement of certain Masyumi members in rebellions is certainly indisputable, but it took place in differing degrees, and does not, in my view, enable one to conclude that the party was collectively responsible. The revolutionary mentality of the second half of the 1940s certainly inspired many advocates of this "direct path" towards an Islamic state, but from early 1950, the efforts made by the party leadership to bring them back to the "democratic and parliamentary path" left little doubt that it in no way supported the rebels. The fact still remains, however, that by advocating a more "psychological" rather than a military solution, Masyumi left itself open to accusations of leniency towards Darul Islam. The participation of some of its members in secret negotiations, and also the fact that certain leaders, such as Natsir, had been tempted at the beginning of the 1950s to use the rebellions as an argument for claiming a greater place for Islam, helped to cultivate this association between the two organisations.[175] Finally, we should add that on the side of the army and the justice system, but also on the side of Darul Islam, there were many who had an interest in maintaining this belief in a collaboration.[176]

---

[175] An association which is still maintained today by certain anachronisms such as referring to Masyumi's stance during the debates in the Constituent Assembly (i.e. from 1958 to 1960) to explain certain party positions in the early 1950s. See, for example, Hendra Gunawan, *M. Natsir dan Darul Islam. Studi Kasus Aceh dan Sulawesi Selatan, Tahun 1953–1958* (Jakarta: Media Da'wah, 2000), pp. 23–4.

[176] Concerning Darul Islam's desire to have its struggle recognised by Masyumi, one should cite as an example the letter from the Islamic Army of Indonesia's command in the Cianjur region in West Java (TII Komandemen I Tjuempaka Tjiandjur) to Isa Anshary and Kasman Singodimedjo, thanking them for the speeches they made during a Masyumi rally in Cianjur in November 1954. The letter explained that the two Masyumi members' reading of the situation was interpreted as a sign of support for the Islamic Army who were being pursued by "the army of infidels, otherwise known as the communist Republic of Indonesia" (*Tentara Kafir alias Tentara Republik Indonesia Komunis*). The Masyumi official in Cianjur who received this letter pointed out that the party leadership in Cianjur did not wish for an agreement with or promotion of "external groups", who, moreover, were illegal. *Abadi*, 3 January 1955.

The involvement of Masyumi's local branches was extremely variable, then, depending on the region, but it does appear in retrospect that their participation was a necessary condition in order for the rebellions to achieve some degree of success. It is nonetheless difficult to conclude that the party was directly or in some general way responsible for sparking these insurrections. The fact that certain guerrillas fought in the name of the same Islamic ideal which Masyumi had defined in the early years of the Revolution apportioned upon the party a certain degree of moral responsibility. From the beginning of 1950, however, the message addressed by the central leadership to those party members tempted to join the rebellion seemed sufficiently clear for those who were prepared to listen. Moreover, as Cees Van Dijk has shown, the demand for an Islamic state was only one aspect of a more widespread malaise prevalent in numerous regions of the Indonesian archipelago at the end of the Physical Revolution. This malaise was linked both to a sense of resentment towards the growing influence of the republican army, which relegated the country's irregular troops to a secondary position, and to the increasing control which the central government was exerting over the provinces after several years of considerable regional autonomy.

A Pragmatic Foreign Policy which was Open to the West

Five years after the proclamation of independence, the recognition of Indonesia as an independent state became complete with its admission to the United Nations in September 1950. Apart from the thorny issue of its relations with its former colonial master, which had become deeply embittered due to the West Irian question, foreign policy did not constitute an important topic of public debate. Most parties agreed on the principle of a certain degree of neutrality, although Masyumi and the other parties abandoned this term because of its somewhat passive connotation:

> By calling its policy free, the government wishes to follow a concrete path, so that Indonesia may be able to help humanity, in a positive manner, to achieve its aspirations. If a neutral policy is understood as a negative policy, a refusal to get involved in a conflict on the basis that it will not influence our situation, and affect neither our destiny nor the world's; if it is understood as remaining

in peace without doing anything to find a solution, then it is not a policy of neutrality which we wish to pursue.[177]

Despite this consensus on the principle of neutrality, the country's parties clashed on several occasions over the area of foreign policy. The positions adopted by Masyumi at this time revealed the outlines of an approach to international affairs which was chiefly pragmatic. Apart from an openly expressed concern for the problems of the Third World, its policy was above all very anti-communist, and though moderately pro-nationalist, it was in fact relatively unconcerned with religious considerations.

The first diplomatic problem Masyumi had to confront involved the question of Western New Guinea. This region was the only part of the former Dutch East Indies not to have been integrated into the newly independent Indonesia, and according to the agreements which came out of the Dutch-Indonesian Round Table Conference, its future was to be determined, at the latest, by 27 December 1950. This deadline had passed without any sign of talks beginning between the Republic and the Netherlands. On 3 January 1951, Prime Minister Natsir declared before the Parliament that in light of this new situation, relations between the two countries had to be reconsidered, particularly the status of the Netherlands-Indonesian Union (DIU).[178] This reaction was deemed by many to be too timorous, and in fact a motion put before Parliament by the PNI calling for the DIU to be dissolved and the Round Table Conference Agreement to be revoked almost succeeded in being voted.[179] In response, Sukarno called for drastic measures against the Netherlands and declared his intention to announce them himself in an upcoming speech. Natsir responded to this by reminding the president that it was the constitutional role of the government and not the president to draw up policy. This firm reminder led to a deterioration of relations between the two men.

---

[177] Mohammad Natsir's inaugural address. Kementarian Penerangan R.I., *Membangun diantara tumpukan puing dan pertumbuhan. Keterangan Pemerintah diutjapkan oleh Perdana Menteri Mohammad Natsir dimuka sidang Dewan Perwakilan Rakjat Sementara, 10 oktober 1950* (Jakarta, 1950), p. 28.

[178] Noer, "Masjumi: Its Organization, Ideology, and Political Role in Indonesia", p. 225.

[179] 66 votes to 63, on 10 January 1951.

For the Masyumi leadership, negotiations with the Netherlands had to be part of a diplomatic policy aimed at obtaining widespread international recognition for the Republic's claim over West Irian.[180] To this end, it was important for Indonesia to present to the entire world an image of a responsible country, mindful of maintaining cordial relations with other countries, including its former colonial masters. According to Masyumi, a converse policy, such as the hard line called for by the PNI and supported by Sukarno, was in danger of discrediting Indonesia on the international stage, and thus depriving it of the vital support it required to assert its rights with the United Nations.[181] This point of view was echoed during Ali Sastroamidjo's premiership on the occasion of the signature of a protocol providing for the dissolution of the Netherlands-Indonesian Union.[182] It was then made official in a resolution passed by the party congress in December 1954, which stipulated that the struggle for the control of West Irian could not meet with success unless a policy was put in place which restored the international community's confidence in the Republic. Shortly afterwards, the main architect of Masyumi's diplomatic policy, Mohamad Roem, denounced the radical attitude of the parties who supported Ali's government and who were the reason why the Republic had lost the support of certain countries in the United Nations, notably Australia. He singled out for criticism the PKI's proposal to expel Dutch nationals from Indonesia, and reminded the public that Dutch citizens, as long as they respected the laws of the state, should receive its protection. For Roem, a measure such as the one proposed by the PKI would be in total contradiction with the government's demand for negotiations made before the international community.[183]

It finally fell to Boerhanoeddin Harahap's government to implement the diplomatic policy elaborated by Masyumi. As soon as the

---

[180] This was identified by Masyumi's programme of action as a "national requirement".

[181] For a complete account of each party's doctrines concerning the question of West Irian, see Stéphane Dovert's PhD thesis, "Le rattachement de la Nouvelle-Guinée-Occidentale à l'ensemble politique indonésien; intégration ou colonisation?", Institut d'études politiques de Paris, 1995, pp. 253–69.

[182] The Sunario-Luns Protocol did not, however, solve the question of West Irian. The Dutch refused to broach the issue and the protocol was never ratified by Indonesia. Natsir denounced this agreement as useless posturing which was harmful for Indonesia's image internationally. *Abadi*, 23 August 1954.

[183] *Abadi*, 13 January 1955.

new government had taken office, it endeavoured to regain the confidence of Indonesia's former allies, and to this effect a delegation was sent to Australia, headed by Mohamad Roem. Although Roem did not manage to obtain the complete support of their neighbours, the Australian government did at least agree to no longer support the Dutch position.[184] This diplomatic offensive soon yielded further results: in December, the government managed to get the United Nations General Assembly to pass a resolution on West Irian calling on the two parties to enter negotiations.[185] A similar proposal presented by the Ali government had failed a few months earlier and so this proposal led the government to entertain hopes that an agreement might at last be reached.[186] Negotiations came close to finding such an agreement at the end of December, but eventually failed because of an upsurge in nationalist sentiment in both countries.

Masyumi's anti-communism, which formed an integral part of its political identity, naturally played an important part in the elaboration of its diplomatic policy. In 1949, the party's political programme announced a general principle "of friendship with all nations, and particularly with those nations founded on democracy and a belief in God." As communist countries corresponded to neither of these two criteria, friendly relations would be more difficult to establish, and the party endeavoured to avoid any mutual recognition. In the name of neutrality, it never rejected the principle of establishing diplomatic relations with these countries, but it constantly looked for ways of preventing that from happening. The possibility of Indonesia and the Soviet Union exchanging ambassadors was mooted for the first time in September 1950, and in the inaugural address he gave upon taking office as prime minister, Mohammad Natsir saw no objection to it. However, he immediately added that "negotiations must still be organised between our two countries concerning technical matters."[187]

---

[184] *Abadi*, 23 October 1955.

[185] *Abadi*, 19 December 1955.

[186] The Masyumi leadership also saw the negotiations as a means for them to use their poor electoral results to their advantage. The Dutch government was no doubt aware that any future cabinet would be more hostile towards it, and so to refuse to make concessions now would expose Dutch economic interests in Indonesia to unilateral decisions by a future Indonesian government.

[187] Kementarian Penerangan R.I., *Membangun diantagra tumpukan puing dan pertumbuhan*, p. 30.

His government as well as Soekiman's never managed to resolve these "technical matters". In response to this obvious policy of obstruction, those in favour of establishing diplomatic relations with the Soviet Union decided to act. In April 1953, during the Wilopo premiership, a parliamentary deputy, Rondonuwu, tabled a motion in the Assembly to open an embassy in Moscow "before the year was out". Masyumi, who had members in the Wilopo government, showed great unity of purpose in opposing this motion. Jusuf Wibisono explained, once again, that "it was not a question of principle but a question of time".[188] He added, apparently oblivious to the contradiction in his argument, that establishing diplomatic relations with the USSR "would bring nothing to Indonesia" either economically or politically. He further claimed that the presence in Indonesia of Russian diplomats, "known for often operating outside of their diplomatic missions", could be a source of a lot of trouble for the country. These arguments, however, were not enough to convince a majority of the Parliament and the Rondonuwu motion was carried by 82 votes to 43.[189] In response, Boerhanoeddin Harahap declared that his party would envisage withdrawing its ministers from government if an embassy were to open in Moscow.[190] This threat did not materialise, however, as Wilopo's government resigned in June 1953, and despite the constant opposition of Masyumi's deputies, an Indonesian embassy was finally opened in Moscow by the Ali cabinet in March 1954.[191]

Although Masyumi had had a solid reputation since the revolutionary period as being pro-American,[192] there was never the same consensus in the party regarding the question of relations with the United States as there was concerning its attitude towards communism. It was in fact a question which caused one of the most serious crises the party experienced during the 1950–56 period. In mid-August of 1951, the Soekiman government had sent its minister for foreign affairs, Subardjo, to the San Francisco Conference where a peace treaty with

---

[188] *Abadi*, 9 February 1953. This position dates back to the sixth party congress in fact. *Berita Masjumi*, 8 September 1952.
[189] *Abadi*, 10 April 1953.
[190] Feith, *The Wilopo Cabinet, 1952–1953*, p. 173.
[191] Feith, *The Decline of Constitutional Democracy in Indonesia*, p. 385.
[192] For examples which led to this reputation, see Ann Swift, *The Road to Madiun: The Indonesian Communist Uprising of 1948* (Ithaca, NY: Cornell Modern Indonesia Project, Monograph Series, 1989), pp. 16–7.

Japan was supposed to be concluded. On this date, however, the coalition parties who supported the government—mainly Masyumi and the PNI—could not agree on whether their countries' participation in this agreement would be opportune or not.[193] Within Masyumi, there was a particularly lively debate, and during the final days before the signature of the treaty, from 4 to 6 September, the party leadership held meetings continually.[194]

The supporters of the treaty, who backed Prime Minister Soekiman, contended that it would contribute to stabilising the situation in the Pacific, and thus hinder the advance of communism. Faced with the impossibility of creating a third international power in Asia, they maintained that Indonesia should rally behind the West, whose democratic ideology was much closer to *Pancasila* and Islam than communism was. Soekiman explained that this rapprochement in no way signified that the country was abandoning its independence in matters of foreign policy. The minister for finance, Jusuf Wibisono, added economic motivations to the political arguments just mentioned. He emphasised certain advantages which the treaty gave to Indonesia, namely the payment by Japan of war damages as well as the limitation of both Japanese imports and Japanese fishing in Indonesian territorial waters. Natsir's entourage, who were opposed to the agreement, responded to these arguments point by point. For Mohamad Roem, the proposed document did not constitute a guarantee of stability in the region for the coming years. By prolonging the economic and military supervision of Western powers over Japan, it was in danger of provoking the Japanese into a violent reaction. Instead of this multilateral agreement which placed Indonesia in the Western camp, Roem argued for the signature of a bilateral treaty with Japan. This solution would leave open the possibility of cooperating with India and Burma, two countries who had refused to send delegates to San Francisco. He also noted that the treaty was to give to Japan the clause of the most favoured nation, an advantage which Indonesia had refused to give to India a short time before. Sjafruddin Prawiranegara explained that Indonesia did not have to sign a treaty with the Japanese since it had never been at war with Japan. This did not stop him from claiming damages from Japan,

---

[193] Ibid., p. 193.
[194] The most complete account of these debates can be found in *Berita Masjumi*, 21 September 1951.

however, as he maintained that their payment could be founded on Article 4 of the Round Table Conference Agreement which provided for the transfer of all rights and obligations from the Dutch East Indies to Indonesia.

In the end, it was the prime minister's supporters who prevailed.[195] On 6 September, Masyumi authorised the government to sign the San Francisco Treaty, but the affair did not end there. During his stay in the United States, the minister for foreign affairs, Subardjo—a very controversial figure within Masyumi—began discussions with Secretary of State Acheson, concerning American aid to Indonesia.[196] When he returned to Jakarta, he pursued these negotiations with Ambassador Merle Cochran. Up until that point, the aid given to Indonesia by the United States was based on a simple agreement of economic and technical cooperation. In October 1950, Natsir's government, mindful of containing American pressure on the country, turned down an offer of military help by the United States.[197] The subject of the discussions between Subardjo and Cochran was a continuation of American assistance in the form of financial aid provided for in the Mutual Security Act (MSA) which Congress had just passed. In theory, the countries that benefitted from financial assistance had a choice of two options, provided for in Articles 511(a) and 511(b) of the MSA.[198] The first of these articles, 511(a), was the most restrictive on the beneficiary state; it provided for the alignment of its defence policy with the United States. The second article, 511(b), only mentioned much vaguer obligations, with the beneficiary simply committing to joint efforts at promoting and maintaining peace and to take part in jointly defined actions to limit international tension.

---

[195] 33 of the 61 members of the Leadership Council (Dewan Pimpinan) were present at the debate. 17 voted in favour, 14 voted against and two abstained. Ibid.

[196] Achmad Subarjo was a close friend of Soekiman's. He, like Soekiman, had become an activist in Perhimpunan Indonesia during his studies in the Netherlands. After the declaration of independence, he had become involved in Tan Malaka's attempted coup d'état on 3 July 1946. Subarjo was not known for his strong religious convictions and before his nomination as minister for foreign affairs, he had not occupied any position of importance within Masyumi.

[197] Feith, *The Decline of Constitutional Democracy in Indonesia*, p. 175.

[198] For details on these articles, see Feith, *The Decline of Constitutional Democracy in Indonesia*, pp. 199–200. The text of the MSA was published by *Abadi* on 2 February 1952.

On 5 January 1952, Subardjo signed an agreement based on Article 511(a). The signature of this protocol was initially kept secret, and when it was made public at the beginning of February, it sparked an outcry in political circles. Within Masyumi, Natsir's supporters were extremely angry and their reaction led to the summoning of the party leadership to a meeting which was attended by Jusuf Wibisono and Soekiman, but not Subardjo. Soekiman, who was no doubt surprised by the virulence of this reaction, declared that he had not been kept informed of his foreign minister's manoeuvres. At the end of the meeting, the party decided to "refuse to take any responsibility for this signature", though it did not go so far as to withdraw its members from cabinet."[199] On 21 February, Subardjo resigned, but most of the political parties continued to call for the resignation of the entire government,[200] which duly took place two days later on the 23rd.

Masyumi's policy towards countries belonging to neither of the two international blocs followed two main principles: natural solidarity with other Muslim nations, and a circumspect neutrality towards any attempt at getting drawn into an alliance with one of the Cold War protagonists. Masyumi, who often received messages and delegations from Muslim countries, became the advocate of their causes before the Indonesian people. In May 1953, for example, a telegram from the Indonesian Union in Egypt (Persatuan Indonesia di Mesir) warned the party leadership of the nascent conflict between Egypt and Great Britain concerning the Suez Canal. In response, Masyumi called on the Indonesian *umma* to vigorously support Egypt's claims.[201] When the Suez Crisis broke three years later, the Indonesian government, which Masyumi was a member of and which was being led for the second time by Ali Sastroamidjojo, immediately declared that the Egyptian people were within their rights. Natsir expressed his desire for an Indonesian intervention in the conflict, without actually specifying how this would happen.[202] At the beginning of November 1956, the Union of Indonesian Muslim Workers (Sarekat Buruh Islam Indonesia, SBII) even suggested a worldwide strike to protest against the Anglo-French

---

[199] *Berita Partai Masjumi*, 21 February 1952.
[200] Natsir himself declared that the government's decision to remain in office "was incomprehensible". *Abadi*, 22 February 1952.
[201] *Abadi*, 30 June 1953.
[202] *Abadi*, 9 August 1956.

attack. *Abadi* noted that this was an extremely exceptional measure, as the union "was normally opposed to any political strikes".[203]

Palestinian Muslims also benefitted from Masyumi's support. In May and June 1954, three of their dignitaries went to Indonesia where they were invited to various religious ceremonies by Masyumi leaders who assured them of their support.[204] Curiously enough, however, the Palestinian situation was never a topic which generated much real interest within the party. No proposal for concrete action was ever made and the party congress never passed a resolution in relation to it. Masyumi's press published few articles on the Middle East, however, *Abadi*'s readers were much better informed about the events of French political life, with most government resignations there making the front-page news.

The Algerian question, on the other hand, was closely followed by the party. In December 1954, a resolution by the Seventh Masyumi Congress demanded that the United Nations take strict measures obliging France to recognise the independence of its three colonies in North Africa. In June 1956, Mohammad Natsir, in one of his speeches, drew a series of parallels between the Algerian nation's struggle and the struggle which Indonesia had engaged in a few years previously. He proposed the organisation by Muslim countries of a new Afro-Asian conference entirely devoted to the Algerian question, and also asked the government to intervene in the United Nations in order to get a motion passed which would oblige France to begin negotiations geared at giving its colony independence.[205] A few days later, Masyumi's president participated, as Indonesia's representative, in the World Islamic Congress in Damas, which launched an appeal to break off all relations with France.[206]

References to Islam in Masyumi's foreign policy never went beyond paying particular attention to other Muslim countries, which was essentially a rhetorical ploy on their part. Masyumi's struggle was only a political one, and it never envisaged sending combatants or providing arms to its oppressed Muslim brothers abroad. Indeed, the Masyumi leaders' criticism of contemporary Islamic states weakened the prospect

---

[203] *Abadi*, 5 November 1956.
[204] *Abadi*, 24 May and 7 June 1954.
[205] *Abadi*, 6 June 1956.
[206] *Abadi*, 10 July 1957.

of a "Muslim International" which might play a role on the international stage.[207] The idea of setting up an association uniting countries in favour of a neutral stance towards the two superpowers should in theory have appealed to the party leadership who, on several occasions, had made known their refusal to align themselves with either the USA or the USSR. Nonetheless, they were concerned that any such organisation would become a neutral ally for the communist bloc, and so they greeted the Ali government's decision to organise an Afro-Asian summit in Bandung with circumspection. The idea of such a conference, proposed by the Indonesian prime minister during a conference held in Colombo from the 28 April to 2 May 1954, did not receive a warm welcome from the party's leaders. The party's official reason for its lack of enthusiasm was its fear that China's presence, along with the close relations between the Ali cabinet and the PKI, would lead the conference to merely condemn Western imperialism instead of adopting a more balanced and neutral position.[208] But with the elections only a few months away, the party was also wary of the political capital which the prime minister's party, the PNI, could gain from such an event.

A few incidental remarks were made about the summit by party members, but it was Rusjad Nurdin, the secretary of Masyumi for West Java, who developed the most complete commentary of the conference's resolutions in *Abadi*. Analysing one of the resolutions adopted which condemned colonisation in all its forms, he maintained that it was aimed in particular at communism, through the actions of the Soviet Union. As evidence for this claim, he cited the attendance at the conference of representatives of Muslim Turkestan and Buddhist Kalmuk, two minority groups who had suffered oppression under Soviet rule. Their presence had angered the PKI, who accused Masyumi of collaborating with these representatives with a view to sabotaging the conference.[209]

The conference constituted an overwhelming success for the Ali government, and Masyumi's unease with this could be seen clearly in the way the event was treated in *Abadi*. The Muslim daily devoted relatively few pages to the conference's debates and resolutions,[210] but

---

[207] See infra, Chapter 5.

[208] See, for example, an interview with Mohamad Roem published by *Abadi*, 23 December 1954.

[209] *Abadi*, 28 April 1955.

[210] Less than one ariticle per day and rarely on the front page.

reported in great detail on the controversy which arose concerning the "Hospitality Committee". As soon as the conference ended, the Masyumi deputy Nur el Ibrahimy took the government to task over this body, which was supposed to take care of the conference-goers' "naughty needs" (*kebutuhan jang nakal*).[211] In response to the authorities' vigorous denials, *Abadi*, who gave over a large number of pages to this illustrious affair, published an invitation card issued by the committee. It was a personal invitation—though the name of the lucky beneficiary was hidden—written in English which read: "Give this ticket to the lady of your choice. If not 'used', please return it to the Hospitality Committee."[212] In the following weeks, the pro-Masyumi press abounded with new accounts concerning such practices as well as a significant number of condemnations by Islamic organisations. This allowed the party to detract from the government's considerable success in organising the conference.

Overall, the foreign policy pursued by Masyumi, both in government and in opposition, confirmed the strong influence of Western ideas on the party's identity. Islam never appeared as the direct source of inspiration for specific party policies. Although the party's unanimous condemnation of communism had a basis in religion, Masyumi's evolution throughout the period 1945–49 showed that its anti-communism was above all founded on a certain assessment of both the national and global balance of power; political ideology, and therefore Islam, were only referred to afterwards. What was most important for the Masyumi leadership was to keep this bond with the West which characterised their political culture. It was in the West that these men found the touchstone for their political identity, and although they paid lip-service to the idea of remaining neutral in the Cold War struggle which began at the end of the 1940s, they had clearly chosen their side.

There was nonetheless a subtle distinction between open support towards the Western bloc and total alignment with an American position which sometimes divided the party leadership. A certain number of grey areas surrounded the behaviour of the various protagonists in the MSA affair. It would have been logical, for example, for Soekiman, who was at that time still close to Sukarno and who was more nationalistic than Natsir, to have argued within the party for a certain degree

---

[211] *Abadi*, 2 May 1955.
[212] *Abadi*, 5 May 1955.

of neutrality. Was his desire to tie Indonesia's destiny to that of the United States, and more importantly, were the unusual manoeuvres of his minister for foreign affairs, the result of some obscure American machinations? Shortly after the affair, the possibility of such an intrigue was dealt with by the Indonesian press, but the evidence currently available does not allow us to affirm that it actually existed.[213] Audrey and George Kahin, who studied the involvement of the United States in the revolt led by the PRRI, and who had access to declassified CIA documents, mention the Americans' goodwill towards the Masyumi leadership, but they do not reveal, for this period at least, any financial assistance given by the United States to the modernist party.[214]

Economic Policy

The Challenges of Indonesia's Economic Recovery

In 1950, Indonesia had two major challenges to tackle. First, it had to adapt to its new status as an independent state, which notably involved transforming an economy formerly reliant on the Dutch metropole and worldwide markets. The vast majority of the country's economic wealth was in the hands of oligopolistic companies, most of which were Dutch, in control of plantation farms, the oil industry, maritime trade, the aviation industry, the banking sector, as well as foreign trade (approximately 60% of Indonesia's trade with the Netherlands was carried out by five Dutch companies). Domestic trade, on the other hand, was mainly controlled by companies belonging to the country's Chinese minority.[215] In addition, the country had to deal with the problems linked to the aftermath of almost ten years of conflict. The rice harvest, for example, did not recover its 1938 yield levels until 1952, and in the same year, industrial production only represented 60% of a pre-war level which was already quite poor.[216]

---

[213] See infra, Chapter 4.

[214] Audrey Kahin and George McTurnan Kahin, *Subversion as Foreign Policy: The Secret Eisenhower and Dulles Debacle in Indonesia* (New York: The New Press, 1995).

[215] Estimated to be two per cent of the population.

[216] For a complete picture of the country's economic situation at the beginning of the 1950s, see "L'évolution économique de l'Indonésie", in *Notes et études documentaires*, nos. 2014 and 2015 (Paris: La Documentation Française, May 1955).

The Indonesian parties did not possess the skills necessary to elaborate credible economic planning policies. Masyumi, with two relatively reputable economists, Jusuf Wibisono and Sjaffruddin Prawiranegara, both of whom served as minister for finance, was far from being the least qualified in this area.[217] Indeed, it was one of the few parties to have developed an economic programme which went beyond the assertion of a few general claims. Like most of the other political parties, they advocated a pro-active policy based on a large degree of state intervention. The first principle set out in the party's 1949 programme was that of a "planned economy" (*ekonomi terpimpin*). This principle encapsulated planned economic production, limited and constructive competition between companies under the state's supervision, the controlling of prices and salaries and, finally, incentives for cooperatives aimed at promoting indigenous companies.[218] At the Surabaya congress in 1954, Masyumi adopted an emergency economic and financial programme which, in order to attract foreign investors, was published in English as well as in Indonesian, and which constitutes the most complete economic policy document to have been published by the party. It took up the principles which had already been laid down a few years earlier, and sketched out a path which the party thought would help Indonesia emerge from the economic doldrums which it depicted the country to be in.[219]

The first characteristic of Masyumi's economic policy was the necessity for budgetary and economic rigour. For the party's leaders, the spiralling increases in state spending constituted the principal cause of inflation, Indonesia's main economic woe. To remedy this situation, the party proposed focusing public policy efforts on "the restoration of law and order, education and professional training as well as productive activities in areas of public benefit (irrigation, electricity etc.)".[220]

---

[217] The other Islamic parties were cruelly lacking in expertise in this area. Perti was mainly interested in questions of education, while NU made no effort to recruit economic specialists until after their electoral success in 1955. Amongst those whom NU enlisted to provide economic advice was Boerhanoeddin, minister for finance in Ali's second government. Noer, *Partai Islam di pentas nasional*, p. 287.

[218] Masyumi's Programme for Action (II.1), 1949.

[219] Masyumi had at this time been in opposition for almost a year.

[220] Masjumi Congress at Surabaya in December 1954, *Urgency Programme of the Masjumi, to Safeguard the Nation Economically and Financially* (Jakarta, 1954), p. 37.

This restriction of the state's activities was supposed to allow a significant reduction in the number of civil servants, but although it was advocated by the cabinets led by Hatta, Natsir, Soekiman and Wilopo, it was never really implemented.[221] The army was the only state sector to experience a considerable drop in its numbers, with the ensuing problems mentioned earlier.

Within the party, this policy of budgetary rigour was not always interpreted in the same manner. It provoked debates over the question of civil service pay but also the wider issue of how public money should be spent. Under the Natsir government, the finance minister Sjafruddin Prawiranegara posed as the champion of a policy of financial rigour.[222] Despite the enormous growth in state revenue due to the Korean War and the consequent rise in the price of raw materials, particularly tin and rubber, he distributed this financial windfall with extreme parsimony, refusing both to raise civil servants' salaries and to finance political patronage networks.[223] As a result, Indonesia benefitted from its only budgetary surplus of that period.[224] However, this policy of budgetary rigour did not receive unanimous approval within the party, and the Soekiman government which succeeded Natsir's cabinet had every intention of making use of the budgetary reserves accumulated by their predecessors. The new minister for finance, Jusuf Wibisono, handed out generous pay increases to civil servants, notably through a modification of how the *Lebaran* bonus was awarded.[225] He also instituted an informal system, which other governments also adopted, authorising banks controlled by the state to award generous

---

[221] During the Wilopo government, the number of civil servants was roughly the same as it had been four years previously (571,000). Feith, *The Decline of Constitutional Democracy in Indonesia*, p. 302.

[222] He was notably the architect of a comprehensive monetary reform—the money supply was almost halved—accompanied by a strong devaluation of the rupiah. On the extremely complex modalities of these reforms, see "L'évolution économique de l'Indonésie", in *Notes et études documentaires*.

[223] See *Indonesia Dipersimpangan Djalan*, written shortly afterwards.

[224] 1.2 million rupiah for 1951, despite the largesse of the Soekiman government, which came to power on 27 April 1951.

[225] Previously, the government had merely given civil servants an advance at *Lebaran* (the end of Ramadan), which it recovered over the following months by docking it from their pay. Jusuf Wibisono transformed this advance into a simple bonus which would not have to be refunded. Moreover, the government reduced the tax rate for civil servants. "L'évolution économique de l'Indonésie", *Notes et études documentaires*.

credit conditions to companies run by members of the government parties.[226] This spendthrift policy was sternly denounced in the Masyumi press by Sjafruddin Prawinaegara.[227] Prawinaegara finally managed to impose his vision of monetary policy in the Urgency Programme which stated its desire to combat the "demon of inflation".[228]

In other areas of economic policy, Masyumi did not identify itself with any particular school of thought. Nonetheless, the analysis of both its economic programmes and their implementation shows it to have been a party very much located on the supply-side spectrum of economic theories. Its main objective was to contribute to the improvement of productivity levels rather than to stimulate an increase in domestic demand. Economic growth, brought on largely by the Korean War, led to an improvement in exchange rates which brought about significant salary rises: between 1939 and 1951, salaries (calculated in dollars) increased threefold.[229] However, production per inhabitant remained well below its pre-war levels, and so the benefit of these wage increases was lost in the resultant spiralling of inflation.

The country's production capacity at the time depended mainly on a small industrial sector specialising in the transformation of agricultural products. It consisted mainly of family firms, and successive governments worked towards encouraging it to develop further. In 1949, the Hatta government established a programme incentivising the creation of cooperatives between small agricultural producers, most of whom were also engaged in small-scale industrial activity. These programmes were continued and amplified by Masyumi-led governments. In accordance with the programme set out in 1949 and taken up again in 1952, the Natsir government established the "Sumitro Plan".[230] The

---

[226] Herbert Feith, *The Decline of Constitutional Democracy in Indonesia*, p. 218. However, Feith points out a little later in the book (p. 296) that, unlike Iskaq, the minister for finance in the first Ali government, Jusuf Wibisono did not discriminate against any political party when distributing indirect financial assistance, and even allowed the PKI to benefit from it.

[227] See, for example, *Abadi*, 2 July 1951.

[228] Masjumi Congress at Surabaya in December 1954, *Urgency Programme of the Masjumi, to Safeguard the Nation Economically and Financially*, p. 12.

[229] "L'évolution économique de l'Indonésie", in *Notes et études documentaries*.

[230] The name was taken from the minister for trade and industry, Sumitro Djojohadikusumo. He was a former trade attaché to Washington, a member of the PSI and a close supporter of Natsir and Sjafruddin Prawiranegara. He was later called the "most brilliant economist of his generation". The Suharto regime turned to him when it was in its dying days in April and May 1998.

foundations for this plan were laid in October 1950 with the creation of a government body, the Cooperative Service (Jawatan Kooperasi), responsible for encouraging the creation of cooperatives in rural towns and providing small-scale agricultural producers with both technical advice and financial assistance.

The Sumitro Plan encountered a certain degree of success, helped no doubt by the fact that it was maintained under the Ali government.[231] Along with this policy of stimulating growth, Masyumi simultaneously endeavoured to limit payroll costs for businesses and to diminish the number of industrial disputes. In 1950, the government had to promulgate a law dating back to 1948 which established a 40-hour working week and a seven-hour working day. Meanwhile, however, new laws promoting social justice through the provision of social security, old-age pensions and various other benefits, led to small and medium-sized enterprises incurring significant social charges. The Masyumi leadership regularly declared itself in favour of many of these social gains, and indeed in September 1950, the Natsir government established a minimum wage for workers in the plantation sector. However, Masyumi's position concerning questions of economic policy, as in many other areas, was governed by pragmatism. The seven-hour working day was often called into question,[232] and the Masyumi leadership often called on employees to moderate their demands for wage increases, reminding them that the effect of such increases would be cancelled out by their inflationary impact.[233]

In response to the conflicting demands which weighed upon it, the party managed at times to find creative solutions. In an attempt to reconcile economic competitiveness with the need for social justice, for example, Masyumi proposed to create a system in which on top of a minimum wage paid by employers (*upah kerja*), the state would add a supplement (*upah social*), which would allow employees a decent

---

[231] Between 1952 to 1954, the number of cooperative members rose from 1 million to 1.4 million.

[232] In October 1951, Natsir explained that "Our country will not find a way out of its current difficulties by working only seven hours a day at a leisurely pace". *Berita Majumi*, 3 October 1951. In April 1953, Jusuf Wibisono declared that the working day should be increased from seven to eight hours a day. *Abadi*, 1 April 1953. However, these measures were extremely unpopular and were never implemented.

[233] See, for example, Masyumi Congress at Surabaya in December 1954, *Urgency Programme of the Masjumi, to Safeguard the Nation Economically and Financially*.

standard of living. This proposal, formulated in the 1949 Programme for Action, was never in fact put into action. In the area of industrial disputes, however, another original and pragmatic solution did manage to get implemented. In February 1951, in response to a series of strikes which had paralysed the country, the Natsir government issued a directive banning, on pain of being fined or imprisoned, all work stoppages in sectors which could be considered as essential, including transportation, banking and the oil industry.[234] At the same time though, Natsir established, at both national and regional levels mediation committees tasked with holding negotiations between employers and employees. The government's measures limiting strike action were criticised vehemently by the opposition parties, who considered that they were in violation of the Constitution. They nonetheless led to a significant drop in the number of industrial disputes in 1952, including sectors where strikes were permitted.[235]

A National rather than Nationalistic Economy

The entire Indonesian political class agreed on the necessity for creating a genuinely national economy. This objective entailed both the elimination of the country's dependence on exports and the transferral of foreign-owned companies to Indonesian ownership. There was an overall consensus on the means needed to achieve the first of these targets. Successive governments attempted, by means of taxes or import licences, to limit the importation of non-essential products.[236] However, Masyumi spoke out strongly against the abuse of these measures by the first Ali government. The minister for economic affairs, Iskaq Tjokrohadisurjo (PNI), had established a system of awarding import-export licences which favoured native Indonesians at the expense of foreigners but also Indonesian citizens of foreign extraction (the latter were, for the most part, of Chinese origin). Masyumi did not contest the principle of this policy, nor did it object to the xenophobia which

---

[234] The new directive was published by *Suara Partai Masjumi*, March–April 1951.

[235] "L'évolution économique de l'Indonésie", in *Notes et études documentaires*.

[236] For example, the Wilopo government, in February 1952, imposed taxes as high as 200% on luxury products. Another type of measure used included limiting import companies' working capital by requiring the upfront payment of up to 75% of their imported goods and by forbidding banks from extending credit on the strength of those amounts.

underpinned it. However, it did denounce the partisan favouritism and corruption which the awarding of these licences brought about, as well as the way in which they led to an unnecessary increase in the price of imported goods.[237] The party also accused the government of having "failed to bring about the emergence of middle-class entrepreneurs who would be beneficial to our society", and also "having done little more than give birth to a group of flunkies and Ali-Baba and Ali-William entrepreneurs."[238]

From the late 1940s, another much more radical means was proposed in order to allow native Indonesians to regain control of their country's economy. This involved the nationalisation of large companies owned mainly by foreigners or by Indonesians of foreign extraction. Masyumi, contrary to what its political opponents claimed, was in fact very much in favour of this policy, but the party considered that it should be implemented progressively, and should protect both the country's finances and its future prospects of attracting foreign capital investment. Consequently, the 1949 Programme for Action planned to nationalise, in order of priority, "the Central Bank, companies which played an essential role in the area of communications, public service corporations and mining companies", with the proviso that this be carried out according to the "state of public finances and to general economic conditions". The minister for finance in the Natsir government, Sjafrudding Prawiranegara, for example, did not want to nationalise the *Javasche Bank*, as he believed that the Central Bank's Indonesian personnel did not have sufficient experience to run it properly. Jusuf Wibisono, who succeeded Prawiranegara as finance minister when Soekiman became prime minister, shared his predecessor's point of view, but he considered that for symbolic reasons it was important to act. On 30 April 1951, three days after the new government took up office, the *Javasche Bank* was nationalised and became known as *Bank Indonesia*, with none other than Sjafruddin Prawiranegara as its governor.

---

[237] A parliamentary report delivered one year later by the Finance Inspection Committee (*Dewan Pengawas Keuangan*) observed 633 cases of corruption. Noer, "Masjumi: Its Organization, Ideology, and Political Role in Indonesia", p. 314.

[238] The terms "Ali-Baba" and "Ali-William" referred, respectively, to companies owned by Chinese or Dutch businessmen who used Indonesian figureheads. Masjumi Congress at Surabaya in December 1954, *Urgency Programme of the Masjumi, to Safeguard the Nation Economically and Financially*, p. 20.

During Wilopo's premiership, two affairs sparked off a debate between the two main coalition partners, the PNI and Masyumi, over the issue of nationalisation. These affairs concerned the oilfields of North Sumatra and the restitution of an occupied tobacco plantation to its foreign owners. During the Dutch colonial period, significant deposits of oil had been discovered in the north of the island of Sumatra and the concession to exploit these oilfields had been awarded to Bataafse Petroleum Maatshappij (BPM). Following the war, the exploitation of these reserves had been handed over to the company's Indonesian employees, resulting in a substantial drop in oil yields to the extent that its income no longer even enabled it to pay its employees. Faced with the likelihood of bankruptcy, the Wilopo government decided to hand its management and ownership back to the original concessionary company. However, this move was suspended when the PNI demanded, at its party conference in December 1952, that the oil deposits be nationalised, or at the very least that their exploitation be reserved for the government. Though it was in favour of nationalising the exploitation of all of the country's underground resources in the long term, Masyumi was opposed to these demands, considering it necessary first of all to acquire the necessary technical know-how to make the operation successful. Natsir reiterated this position in December 1953 during a visit to Sumatra; the problem had still not been resolved at this stage and the government of the day, under Prime Minister Ali, despite a number of forceful declarations, had not yet found a solution to the technical problems attendant upon nationalisation. At one stage, the possibility of Japanese participation had even been evoked, drawing an ironic reaction from the president of Masyumi, who explained that his own party had often been criticised for kowtowing to foreign investors, but that in this instance the government was planning to simply replace the Dutch with the Japanese.[239] In this affair, Masyumi warned the government against adopting an overly nationalistic attitude which would run the risk of discrediting the country in the eyes of the international business world.[240]

A few months later, the debate over nationalisation arose again with the Tandjung Morawa affair. In East Sumatra, former tobacco

---

[239] *Abadi*, 7 December 1953.
[240] An attitude described as "cowboyish" (*bersifat cowboy-cowboyan*) by Isa Anshary. *Abadi*, 2 February 1954.

plantations had been illegally occupied since the war by families that had developed small subsistence farms there. The Indonesian authorities wished to hand back at least a portion of these lands to the Dutch companies who still held the concessions for them. As with the affair concerning the oil deposits, it was thought not only that this solution would allow a much more profitable exploitation of the plantations and therefore generate revenue for the government, but also that it would send out a positive message to potential foreign investors interested in Indonesia.

In July 1951, the Soekiman government succeeded in reaching a compromise agreement with the former concessionary company. According to the terms of this agreement, half of the plantation land— 130,000 hectares of the total 255,000—would be returned to its original owners, while the rest would be used to rehouse the 62,000 families occupying the land illegally.[241] Although the agreement was drawn up under Soekiman's premiership, it fell to Wilopo's government to implement it, and when the illegal occupants refused to leave the land, it was decided that they were to be removed by force. Tragedy struck, however, on 16 March 1953, when a group of Chinese and Indonesian peasants who were threatened with expulsion tried during a demonstration to seize the weapons belonging to a police station in Tandjong Morawa, a locality situated ten kilometres north of Medan. The police opened fire on the demonstrators, killing five people; a number of protestors were also arrested. The affair provoked an outcry and soon had political repercussions. A PNI deputy Abdullah Jusuf was sent by his party to investigate the incident and his enquiries led him to conclude that the Masyumi governor of North Sumatra, Abdul Hakim, was responsible for the tragic events. Jusuf even accused him of having received significant sums of money from the former concessionary companies.[242] However, the conclusions reached both by representatives of the Home Affairs Ministry and by a delegation of Masyumi parliamentary deputies were quite different. They emphasised the role played by the local branch of the PKI as well as the presence in the area, at

---

[241] Feith, *The Wilopo Cabinet, 1952–1953*, p. 182. The agreement is examined in its entirety by Karl J. Pelzer, "The Agrarian Conflict in East Sumatra", *Pacific Affairs* (June 1957).

[242] For further reading on these accusations and Masyumi's denial, see *Abadi*, 26 May 1953.

the time of the events, of a representative of the Chinese consulate based in Jakarta. In mid-May, Sidik Kertapati, a parliamentary representative of the Union of Indonesian Peasants, SAKTI (Sarekat Tani Indonesia) tabled a motion of no confidence in the minister for home affairs, Masyumi's Mohamad Roem, whom they held responsible for the crackdown on demonstrators. At this point, the PNI threatened to vote in favour of the motion and demanded, in exchange for their abstention, that Masyumi support the PNI's candidate for the vacant position of minister for information.[243] The Masyumi leadership decided to reject this trade-off,[244] and on 3 June, before the motion had even been voted on, the Wilopo government tendered its resignation to the president.

In its Urgency Programme drawn up in December 1954, Masyumi returned at some length to these questions. The programme denounced the "economic policies inspired by a mis-interpretation of nationalism" espoused by its opponents, and it underlined the disastrous economic effects of foreign capital flight.[245] It explained in particular that numerous plantations were not receiving the level of investment necessary for their survival because of concessionary companies' fears of being expelled from the country. This situation was doubly regrettable as the revenue generated by a hectare of rice (2,000 Rp per year) was far below what could be generated by a hectare of sugar cane (28,000 Rp per year) or tobacco (37,000 Rp a year in East Sumatra). The programme consequently advised the government "to look for technical and financial assistance abroad, regardless of its ancestry, and also to mobilise both the entire work-force and all of the available capital in the country." It also called on the plain common sense of their rural electors in an attempt to encourage them to overcome any reluctance towards such a programme:

> If even a buffalo which we use to cultivate paddy fields needs to receive sufficient care and food for us to be sure of his services, will we abandon a human being whose assistance we require to further our own interests?[246]

---

[243] *Abadi*, 28 May 1953.
[244] *Abadi*, 1 June 1953.
[245] "Economic policy from Misinterpreted Nationalistic Viewpoint", Masyumi Congress at Surabaya in December 1954, *Urgency Programme of the Masyumi, to Safeguard the Nation Economically and Financially*.
[246] Ibid.

These concrete aspects of Masyumi's economic policy, defended by the party both when in opposition and in government, constituted a remarkable example of the hiatus—which we will further examine later —that existed between the pragmatism of the actions proposed and implemented by the party and the idealism of the general theories defended by its central figures.[247]

The necessity of economic recovery and, more importantly, the instability of government coalitions did not allow it to implement the Islamic principles which it claimed to be the representative of. The chronic political instability of the young Republic was, at that time, attributed to the Provisional Assembly regime which had been in place since 1945, and which justified the adoption of temporary solutions. With the organisation of legislative and constituent assembly elections planned for September and December 1955, Masyumi hoped to consolidate its policies in the subsequent years. The programme which it formulated for the election campaign was designed to allow it to appeal to voters who were not advocates of political Islam, and thus to become the uncontested political heavyweight of the future Indonesian Parliament.

---

[247] See infra, Chapter 6.

CHAPTER FOUR

The Fall

The policies pursued by Masyumi in government were based above all on pragmatism, far removed from any form of doctrinal rigidity. They showed no clear signs of the far-reaching programme for society which the 1955 election campaign allowed them to elaborate. The run-up to the elections constituted the culmination of a strategy which Mohammad Natsir and his supporters had patiently elaborated. This strategy possessed two complementary characteristics: a complete devotion to Western-style democracy and a secularisation of the party's programme. Masyumi was convinced that it could draw support from beyond the Muslim electorate, and endeavoured to present a tolerant image so as to avoid giving its nationalist opponents any ammunition to criticise the Islamic party.

Given the party's electoral hopes, their poor performance in the polls was particularly disappointing. It led Masyumi to adopt two contradictory attitudes: it presented itself as the final rampart against the threat posed to the country's democratic institutions by President Sukarno, while at the same time in the Constituent Assembly it made hard-line demands for an Islamic state, which eventually contributed to the downfall of Indonesian democracy.

The 1955 Elections—The Broken Hope of Muslim Democracy

The National Assembly and Constituent Assembly elections which were held in September and December 1955 were the indirect cause of a complete transformation of the Indonesian political system. The results, which were officially announced in March and July 1956, constituted a major setback for parliamentary democracy. Although the elections had been postponed several times, there was widespread hope that they would produce a majority which would be both decisive and stable. Such hopes were dashed, however, and the political divisions which had appeared in November 1945, and which had paralysed public life for the following ten years, remained.

The election results had several effects on Masyumi. Up until the elections, it was considered Indonesia's foremost political party, but in their aftermath it was now simply one of four large political parties which could legitimately aspire to a role in government. As the main government party during the country's parliamentary regime, Masyumi embodied its firm attachment to democratic principles, but also its systemic failings.

The Election Campaign's Illusions and Contradictions

The run-up to the elections changed the *modus operandi* of Indonesian political life profoundly. Firstly, it marked, symbolically, the end of a period, which had in fact concluded in 1949, during which political parties did not merely seek power but fought, above all, for the very survival of the Republic. Secondly, the campaign for votes obliged parties to completely revise both how they were organised and how they operated. Up until that point, parties operated on a national level, and indeed, to be more precise, on a Jakartanese level. They had very little real presence locally and their approach to local politics was generally dictated by considerations which only concerned the small political microcosm in the capital.

Parties concerned themselves with regional questions when the nomination of a governor, resident, or other local authority position had to be decided, leading to intense political battles. It had become customary to consider large areas of the country as spheres of influence belonging to a particular party, and, as a result, little effort was made locally to set up the political machinery capable of canvassing for votes (despite the fact that the majority of the country's voters lived in its villages). Two political parties, the Indonesian Communist Party (PKI) and Masyumi, fell outside this general rule. The latter, unlike its opponents, had inherited from the period of Japanese occupation an organisational structure which extended to village-level in a number of regions.[1] In addition to that, the party was composed not only of individual members but also of Muslim organisations, some of which, such as the Muhammadiyah, were present in a large number of the country's villages.

In order to coordinate its electioneering activities, Masyumi set up, alongside its governing body, an Election Action Committee (Komite Aksi Pemilhan Umum, KAPU). This committee had a hierarchical structure headed in Jakarta by Soekiman Wirjosandjojo, the party's vice president. Most of the party's campaign consisted in organising election rallies. It emphasised this mode of electioneering much more than its opponents, and differentiated itself from other parties by allocating considerable sums of money to the purchase of cinematographic equipment, amplifiers and video players, as well as to the creation of a campaign film.[2]

This may partially explain the gap between the hopes entertained by the party during the campaign and the harsh reality of the election results. The large attendance levels at these large open-air election rallies, during which the party's local figures as well as its leadership took the stage, lulled the party's leaders into overestimating its influence. Even in the smallest localities, the crowds attending these rallies could be counted in thousands, according to press accounts;[3] figures such as Isa Anshary, the head of the West Java branch, attracted very large numbers of people.[4] However, the reasons people had for attending these mass meetings were not at all linked to any adherence to the party's ideology. Villagers often either came out of curiosity, for the rally's entertainment value or quite simply because it was a place to meet other people from their village. It was hardly surprising, then, that Isa Anshary, nicknamed "the little Napoleon of Masyumi", attracted such large numbers. For somebody looking for entertainment, such a

---

[1] In certain villages, however, Masyumi branches became sections of Nahdlatul Ulama following the 1952 split.

[2] Herbert Feith, *The Indonesian Election of 1955* (Ithaca, NY: Cornell University Press, 1962), p. 21. Neither *Abadi* nor *Hikmah* mentioned anything about films being projected during rallies, however.

[3] At the rally organised during Roem's visit to Gunung Kesari, *Abadi* reported that he spoke in front of 10,000 people who had come from the surrounding villages.

[4] Soebagijo I.N., *Jusuf Wibisono. Karang di Tengah Gelombang* (Jakarta: Gunung Agung, 1980), p. 231.

brilliant orator guaranteed them a good night out, even if they happened to be communist.

Another electioneering practice used by Masyumi during the campaign consisted of simply adopting the ideas used by its arch political enemy, the PKI. For example, it copied a technique employed by its communist opponents which involved engraving on a considerable number of metal coins the party's symbol—a crescent moon surmounted by a star—and distributing them to the public. Like other political parties, Masyumi had associated symbols with appealing allegorical interpretations designed to create a subliminal bond between voters and the party, which would have more sway over voters than speeches or reasoned arguments. In certain parts of Java, however, this plan backfired, as throughout the campaign Masyumi's opponents never lost an opportunity to remind people of a long-standing superstition which held that the association of the crescent moon with a star was a bad omen.[5]

Masyumi's campaign never gave rise to a clearly defined electoral strategy, and indeed Jusuf Wibisono criticised his fellow party leaders for this. According to him, the absence of a campaign ploy was due to their conviction that Masyumi was the largest political organisation in the country.[6] One of the leadership's main fears, however, and one which was common to the entire political class, was that certain sections of the electorate, most of whom had never voted before, would be intimidated by the complexity of the election and would therefore abandon the idea of voting. As a result, all the major parties organised simulated elections in the weeks leading up to the actual event, with the aim of showing voters how to recognise and punch the correct symbol on their ballot paper. The Election Action Committee for Jakarta Raya, for example, organised at the end of January a preliminary initiation session "reserved for members of Masyumi, Muslimat and the party's constituent organisations".[7]

Apart from this urgency to encourage people to vote, two other important ploys figured in the election campaign, which allowed us to see Masyumi's political identity more clearly. The first of these was designed to present the party as the natural choice for Muslim voters.

---

[5] Feith, *The Indonesian Election of 1955*, p. 17.
[6] Soebagijo I.N., *Jusuf Wibisono. Karang di Tengah Gelombang*, p. 240.
[7] *Abadi*, 1 February 1955.

The aim was to spread a twofold message within the Muslim community which consisted first of all in convincing balloters that voting in accordance with their faith was a religious obligation, and then persuading them that Masyumi was the party which would allow them to fulfil this religious obligation. The party's task was a complicated one, however, as it had to differentiate itself from its Muslim opponents (NU, PSII and Perti) without drawing attention to divisions within the Muslim community.[8] The founding project of the party was to establish the political unity of the *umma*, and so, mention of the schisms which took place in 1947 and 1952 was to be avoided. The party line on this thorny issue was to adopt a conciliatory approach. Whenever the party's divisions were brought up, they were blamed on the opponents of political Islam, notably the PNI which was implicitly accused of having influenced the breakaway of Nahdlatul Ulama.[9]

Another strategy adopted by Masyumi throughout the campaign was to present itself as the last bastion of Muslim solidarity which should allow "[us] to show [our] strength and thus to win the elections."[10] This provoked virulent attacks from its Muslim opponents: the traditionalists of Nahdlatul Ulama in particular attempted to show that Masyumi did not defend the values of the *ahla Sunnah wal-jamaah* (the people of the tradition of Mohammad). They claimed that Masyumi did not respect the authority of the *ulamas*, and they stigmatised the party's tolerance towards those who wore Western clothing during prayer.[11] Masyumi's leaders did not react to these accusations

---

[8] Certain Masyumi editorialists were extremely prudent concerning this question. For example, in *Hikmah*'s last edition before the elections (no. 39, published 24 September 1955), its religious section naively explained that "the symbol of the crescent moon and the star, for example, is that of a Muslim party presenting candidates who you can vote for." The party's representatives did not always bother with such niceties, however; for example, one of Masyumi's candidates for the parliamentary elections, Basri, explained to members of the Association of Muslim Students (Himpunan Mahasiswa Islam) that three major political families were taking part in the election—communism, nationalism and Islam—and that the latter was "represented by Masyumi (*Hikmah*, no. 38, 17 September 1955).

[9] See, for example, the editorial in *Hikmah*, no. 27, 2 July 1955.

[10] Ibid.

[11] Gregory John Fealy, "Ulama and Politics in Indonesia: A Political History of Nahdlatul Ulama, 1952–1967", PhD diss., Monash University, 1998, Chapter 4, "The Quest for Power, 1953–1955".

and they never publicly criticised the other political parties who identified themselves with Islam. The modernist party clearly wanted to
place itself above any such quarrels and appear as the defender of the
unity it had proclaimed.[12]

Although Masyumi was the natural representative of Muslim
values, its election campaign was practically void of any religious references. Natsir's party wished to reach out beyond the traditional electorate of political Islam, which the party seemed to consider it had
already won over, in order to embody the prospect of a peaceable
Muslim democracy. To do this, it needed to shake off the image of
religious extremism which both its nationalist and communist opponents tried to associate it with. Masyumi had been regularly accused
of threatening the country's unity with radical Islamic demands since
President Sukarno's 1953 speech in Amuntai, but during the election
campaign, it presented an image of openness. There was no sign in the
party's press of "Masyumi's clamorous campaign in favour of an Islamic
State" which Goshal Balads spoke of.[13] This important stage in the
development of the party's ideology will be examined later;[14] we will
limit ourselves here to looking at certain aspects which were directly
linked to the election preparations.

The Masyumi leadership wanted above all to reassure the country's
non-Muslim community, and this preoccupation constituted a real
leitmotiv in the party's rhetoric. In June 1955, for example, when Natsir
dealt with the issue of religion in a speech he gave in Manado, he
emphasised Islam's tolerance and invited Muslims to protect and support not only their religion but also that of other communities such as
Christians.[15] A month later, Mohamad Roem, on a visit to Bali, pointed
out that "a state which is founded on Islam would not be the property
of the Muslim community on the pretext that it made up almost eighty
million people."[16] In conjunction with this more religiously inclusive

[12] See, for example, the editorial in *Hikmah*, no. 27, 25 July 1955.

[13] Goshal Baladas, *Indonesian Politics 1955–1959: The Emergence of Guided Democracy* (Calcutta: K.P. Bagchi, 1982), p. 47. Such a campaign would have been
in total contradiction with the *rapprochement* between the PSI, Masyumi and
the Christian parties which had followed the collapse of the Ali government and
which Baladas himself looks at in detail (p. 30).

[14] See infra. Chapter 5.

[15] *Hikmah*, no. 29, 16 July 1955.

[16] *Hikmah*, no. 32, 6 August 1955.

tone, the party completed the process of removing from its political message any vocabulary which could be interpreted as aggressive, even though it ran the risk of losing a part of its Muslim identity by doing so. The term "Muslim state" (Negara Islam) was carefully avoided and no specific measure was mentioned concerning the Islamisation of the country's institutions. In its edition published on 2 April 1955, *Hikmah* explained what would happen "if Masyumi inspired the government". It maintained that if Masyumi was victorious in the elections for Parliament and the Constituent Assembly, "the legislative assembly would constitute a solid bulwark for a government formed and led by Masyumi" and in the new constitution "every article [would be] in accordance with the wishes of the Indonesian Muslim community." Without clarifying the exact nature of these "wishes", the magazine declared that "the fulfilment of Islam's teachings and Islam's laws will become embodied without difficulty and the ideals of the Islamic Republic of Indonesia will be fulfilled."[17]

On top of the vagueness surrounding the party's proposals concerning religion, an effort was made in the lead-up to the election to secularise the party's political programme. In the only real election programme published by the party, no reference to Islam appeared; it proposed 55 measures, most of which were drawn from motions adopted during previous party congresses. Though it did not contain many new ideas, it does enable us to identify the themes which were thought likely to appeal to Masyumi's electorate as well as the degree of importance which the party accorded them.[18]

The programme began with a declaration of a few general principles which constituted a sort of "*Masyumi Pancasila*", although this term was not actually used.[19] The party's main objective was to establish a "state where the rule of law would guarantee to all Indonesia's inhabitants, citizens as well as foreigners, the safety of their souls and of their goods."[20] Other important goals were "the defence of the principles of deliberation and of democracy", the "guarantee of religious freedom" and "of fundamental human rights", with special emphasis put on "women's rights which must be protected in the political, economic

---

[17] Ibid.
[18] Published by *Hikmah*, no. 39, 24 September 1955.
[19] For more on the attitude of Masyumi's leaders towards the national ideology, see infra, Chapter 5.
[20] *Hikmah*, no. 39, 24 September 1955.

and social domains." A series of socially responsible economic measures were also proposed, including the organisation of the production and distribution of goods according to a "plan" (*rentjana*) "aiming at the happiness of the greatest number", "limited and constructive competition under the control of the state", a ban on private monopolies, the nationalisation of essential economic sectors, but also rapid industrialisation and the setting up of various types of cooperatives in order to strengthen the country's economy. In addition, there were nine proposals concerning the country's peasants.

A number of general principles accompanied by a series of concrete measures were set up to assert the importance of recognising and improving their status in society. The "system of large land ownership" (*sistim tuan-tanah*) was to be abolished along with the agrarian decrees which had been issued under colonial rule; the unfair charges which peasants had to pay were also to be abolished, and they were to be given land and assistance to help them organise themselves into cooperatives. The same social importance was accorded to fishermen, who were promised financial assistance in order to improve their skills and modernise both their equipment and the fishing ports they used. Regarding the middle class (*golongan middenstand*), Masyumi contented itself with promising them "the means to develop and strengthen their position within society", without giving any details on how this would happen. Finally, it proposed to guarantee a decent existence to the country's industrial workers, notably by establishing a "social wage" (*upah social*) alongside a "work wage" (*upah kerdjanja*), as well as through the promise of enabling them to found a family and save for their old age. The party devoted its final proposals to the weakest in society—the disabled, widows and orphans—who were to be given the right to a decent existence.

Overall, then, the party's election programme was prudent and reassuring on the question of the country's institutions, and generous, often innovative even, on economic and social issues. However, very little was mentioned about how this programme would actually be implemented. The election manifesto put forward no plan to grant the state new resources for achieving these aims, and the only proposal made concerning fiscal policy consisted in systematically favouring direct over indirect taxation.

Although the party's electoral strategy was never really clearly defined, it was obviously based on a very risky wager on behalf of its leaders. As they were convinced of having already won over most of the Muslim activists' votes, they contented themselves with reminding those same activists of their religious duty while at the same time proclaiming themselves to be the champions of unity. The party's greatest hope, however, was that its election programme, which contained religious moral values but was devoid of any explicit reference to a specifically Islamic political ideology, would appeal to voters far beyond the reaches of Islam. Such a strategy was riddled with contradictions, notably the fact that it called on people to vote out of a religious obligation for a party whose programme had been emptied of references to Islam; it was to cost Masyumi dearly at the polls.

The Election Results—The Limits of the Modernist Influence on a National Level

On 29 September 1955, 37,875,299 Indonesians went to the polls, which constituted 87.65% of those registered to vote.[21] Despite some voter intimidation in certain volatile parts of the country, the elections ran smoothly and the legitimacy of those elected to represent the people was never called into question.[22] Masyumi's poor showing was one of the election's major surprises. With only 20.9% of the popular vote, the party was beaten into second place by the PNI who obtained 22.3%, though both parties won 57 seats in the new Assembly. It was followed closely behind by its Muslim rival, Nahdlatul Ulama, who with 45 seats, won 18.4% of the popular vote and succeeded in defeating Masyumi comprehensively in East Java and Central Java. The party's longstanding enemy, the PKI, ended up with 39 seats, winning

---

[21] The electoral law passed in November 1952 established for both the legislative and constituent elections a list system (though with the possibility for individual candidates to stand for election also) based on proportional representation and an electoral map carved up into regions. The country was divided into 15 electoral districts, each containing a number of seats proportionate to the size of their population, with a minimum of three seats in Parliament and six in the Constituent Assembly. Any surplus seats for which the electoral threshold had not been obtained were divided within each region by agreement between the different parties concerned; if such an agreement could not be reached, they were to be divided up by the central party authorities.

[22] In certain parts of Aceh and West Java, for example, Darul Islam forces were alleged to have "encouraged" people to vote for Masyumi. Feith, *The Indonesian Election of 1955*, p. 45.

16.4% of the vote. The two other parties claiming to represent Islam—
the PSII and Perti—won 12 seats overall, eight for the former and
four for the latter, while the Christian parties received a total of 14
seats: eight for Parkindo and six for the Partai Katolik. The election's
other big losers were the PSI, who only won five seats, and the IPKI
with four seats. The remaining 25 seats in the Assembly were divided
amongst 15 other political parties.

The election results showed Masyumi to be an "extra-Javanese"
party representing the periphery of the country, in contrast to the
trio of the PNI, NU and the PKI, who dominated the centre of the
country.[23] It also showed Masyumi's overwhelming dominance over its
three traditional bastions of power—Central Sumatra, South Sumatra
and South Sulawesi—where it received more than 40% of the vote.
However, the party could not transform the high concentration of its
voters in certain provinces into Assembly seats due to the system of
proportional representation used in the election. There was a strong
correlation, nonetheless, between Masyumi's election score and the
presence of a majority vote for Muslim parties. In five of the six constituencies where these parties won more than half of the vote, Masyumi topped the poll. However, its poor showing of barely 10% in
the sparsely populated regions of East Java and Central Java, where it
lost heavily to Nahdlatul Ulama, contributed to its mediocre nationwide score.

Within Masyumi, there was bitter disappointment with these results. Both the daily newspaper *Abadi* and the weekly magazine *Hikmah*
tried for some weeks to mask this defeat by presenting the election results in a positive light. On several occasions, they published a map of
Indonesia on which each of the 11 regions—out of a total of 15—in
which the party topped the poll was represented with a flag carrying
the party's symbol; no detailed result was ever published by Masyumi's
press, however.[24]

The party's dismay was palpable in the editorials published, but
it nonetheless held out the hope of seeing this poor performance at

---

[23] More than half of Masyumi's parliamentary representatives were elected outside
Java. For NU, the proportion was 18%, for the PNI 21% and for the PKI 10%.
[24] *Abadi* only gave the number of seats obtained by each party (2 March 1956),
while *Hikmah*, for several weeks, limited itself to explaining that the exact election results were still unknown.

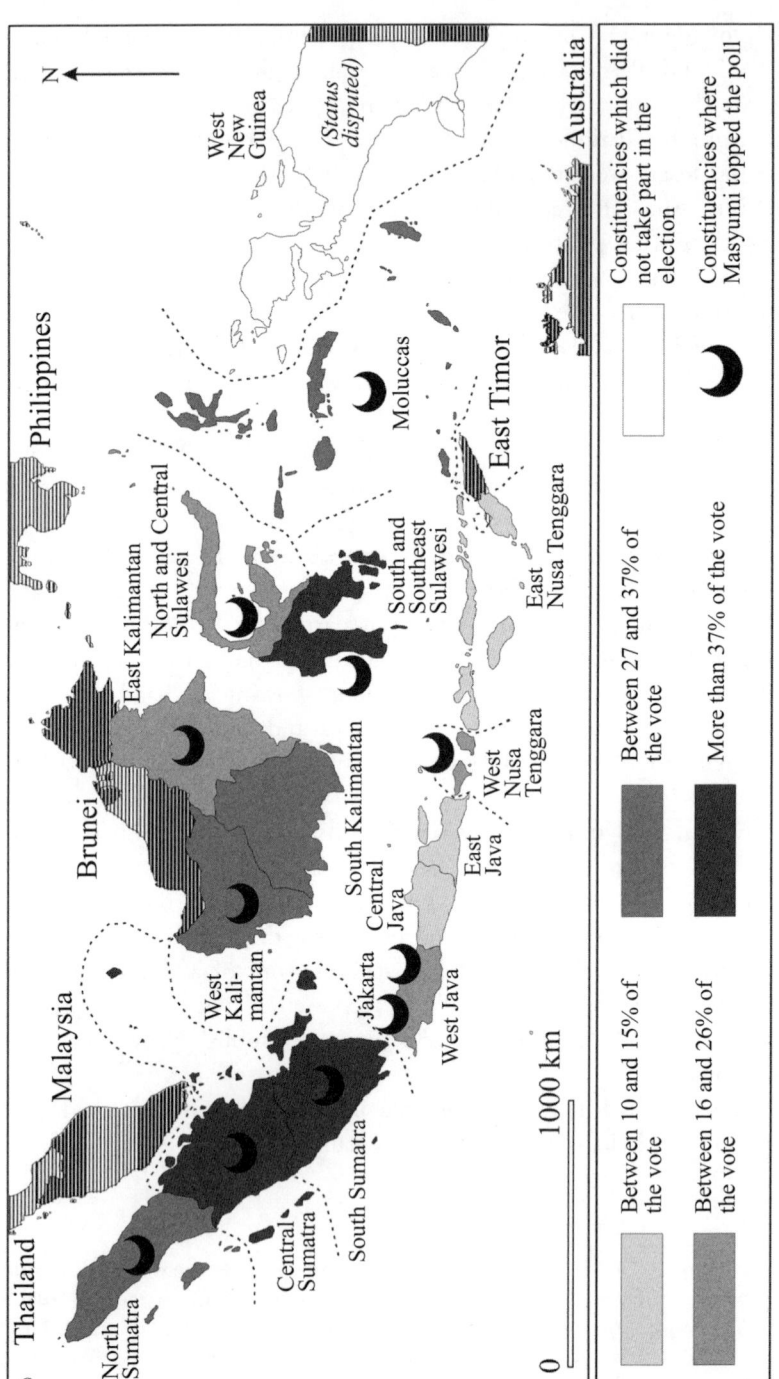

Map 4.1 Masyumi's results in the 1955 elections.

Constituencies which did not take part in the election

Constituencies where Masyumi topped the poll

Between 27 and 37% of the vote

More than 37% of the vote

Between 10 and 15% of the vote

Between 16 and 26% of the vote

1000 km

0

N

Thailand

Malaysia

Philippines

Brunei

West New Guinea

(Status disputed)

Australia

North Sumatra

Central Sumatra

South Sumatra

West Kalimantan

East Kalimantan

North and Central Sulawesi

South and Southeast Sulawesi

Moluccas

East Timor

Jakarta

West Java

Central Java

East Java

South Kalimantan

West Nusa Tenggara

East Nusa Tenggara

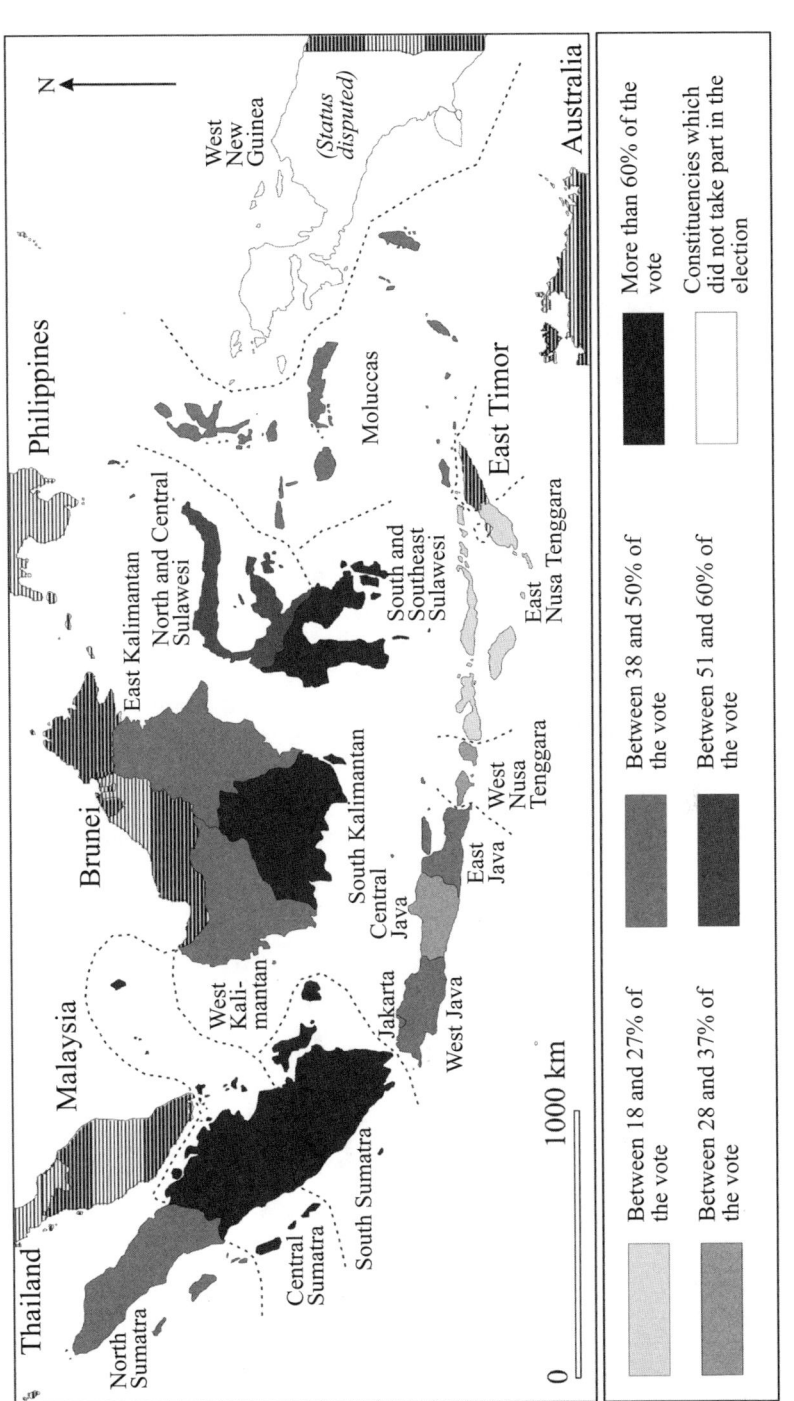

Map 4.2 The combined results of Indonesia's Muslim parties in the 1955 elections.

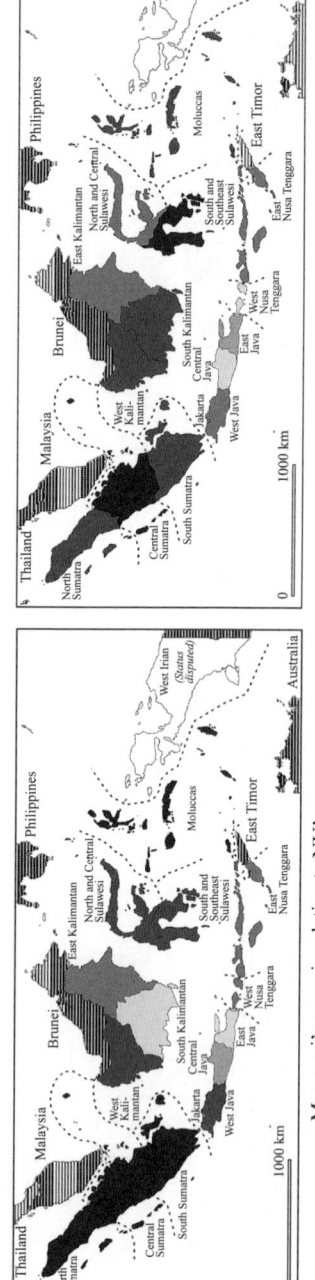

Masyumi's score in relation to NU's

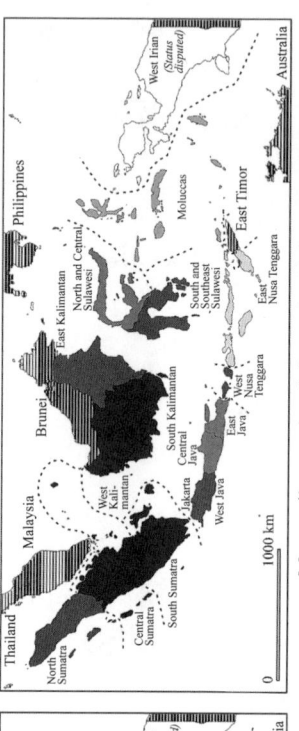

Masyumi's score in relation to the PNI's

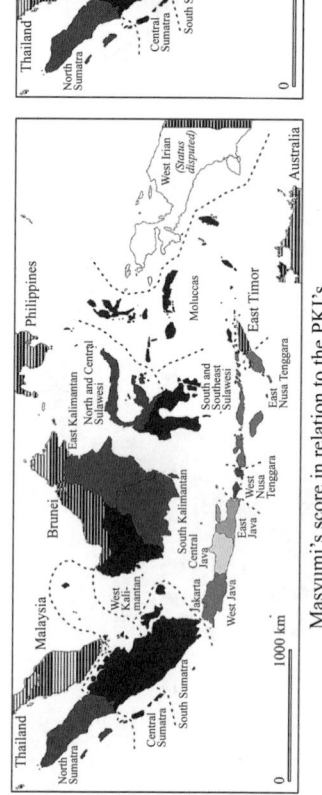

Masyumi's score in relation to the PKI's

Masyumi's score in relation to the Christian parties'

Masyumi's score lower by more than 15%

Masyumi's score lower by less than 15%

Masyumi's score higher by less than 15%

Masyumi's score higher by between 15 and 30%

Masyumi's score higher by more than 30%

Constituencies which did not take part in the election

Map 4.3 Masyumi's results compared with the other main parties in the 1955 elections.

the polls turned around at the election for the Constituent Assembly in mid-December.[25] The voter turnout on 15 December, at 87.77%, was just as high as for the election in September, and the results of the election proved another rude awakening for the party leaders. Masyumi received 100,000 fewer votes than in September. With 112 seats in the Constituent Assembly, the party was this time far behind the PNI who had won 600,000 votes more than in the previous election, leaving it with 119 seats. NU improved slightly on its previous score, winning 91 seats. In total, the parties who identified themselves as Islamic parties counted 228 votes in the Assembly, constituting a little less than half the total number of seats and therefore far short of the two-thirds majority required to vote the adoption of a new constitution. This result was especially disappointing for Masyumi; apart from the PNI,

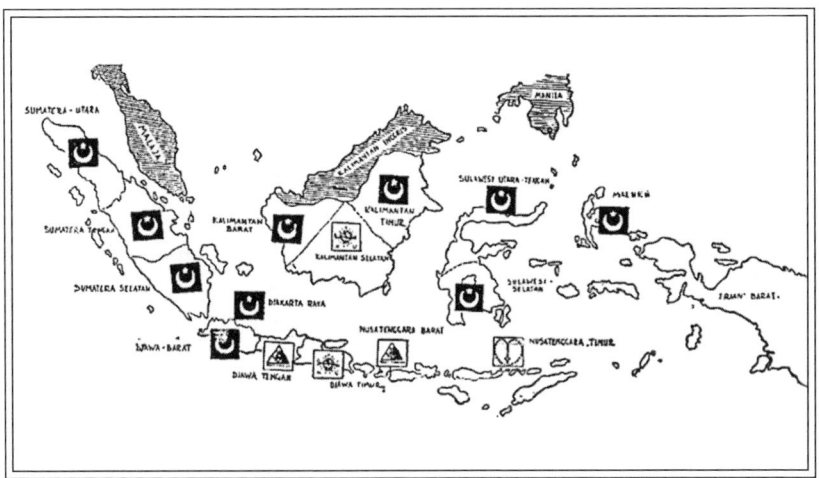

Masjumi Berakar diseluruh Indonesia
Pengaruhnja memperlihatkan kemenangan

Plate 4.1 "Masyumi is implanted throughout Indonesia. Its influence demonstrates its victory" (*Hikmah*, 17 December 1955).

---

[25] An editorial in *Hikmah* (no. 40, 1 October 1955), carrying the headline "The Right Choice", declared: "How we should pity the voter who chose the parties intending to weaken religion!...but those who voted wrongly on 27 September will have a chance to redeem themselves at the next election."

the other parties which progressed the most between the two elections, were the PKI and the Murba Party. Both were extreme left-wing parties whose success sanctioned the failure of Masyumi's campaign against the "enemies of God." The party made no declaration and its press published no editorial in response to this second electoral defeat. It was only a few months later that Mohammad Natsir proposed to draw a certain number of conclusions from the party's performance in the two elections.

> The elections have blown away the smokescreen which previously clouded our vision of things. Up until that point, we, the Muslim community, had always considered ourselves to be largely in the majority. Some spoke of 80%, others of 90%. These certainties led us to think that the elections would without doubt allow us to implement the ideals of Islam. It appears today however, that those who claim to belong to the Muslim community did not uniformly support the ideology of Islam. What this election has proved is that less than 50% of them supported faithfully the ideology of Islam.[26]

Nonetheless Natsir, alongside this clear-sighted analysis, also concluded that the election results could not be "measured in numbers", and that "thanks to hard work based on total sincerity" Masyumi had obtained "a great victory at the elections". He invited his supporters not to "mull over the defeat, but rather to endeavour to view the future in an even more positive light."[27] Coming from a man who was normally a paragon of logic and coherence, the incoherence of his remarks clearly showed the party's disarray in the aftermath of these long-awaited elections.

The party's electoral failure penalised first and foremost the strategy it had adopted over the previous number of years. Its leaders had long convinced themselves that Indonesians' religious faith would carry great weight in their political decisions, and as a result, they mistook their real enemy by focussing most of their campaign on a crusade against the atheism embodied by the PKI. The effects of NU's breakaway were also largely underestimated. It is true that only seven deputies had left the party in 1952 and that, despite these departures, Masyumi remained

---

[26] *Abadi*, 2 March 1956.
[27] Ibid.

the largest party in Parliament. In addition, the split had not brought about a splintering of the different wings within the organisation. However, the emergence of a serious rival on the political scene put a definitive end to the aspirations of uniting political Islam which Masyumi had embodied since 1945. The seven million votes obtained by NU robbed the party of the opportunity to totally dominate the Indonesian political landscape; Masyumi would have held more than 40% of the vote in its pre-1952 configuration. They constituted, above all, the harshest of rejections for the party leadership. These leaders had become obsessed with their internal politicking to such an extent that they became convinced that their importance within Masyumi's governing bodies reflected their influence within the Muslim community. Nahdlatul Ulama's remarkable performance in the elections proved, on the contrary, that the political weight of traditionalist Islam had not been greatly affected by its progressive exclusion from Islam's centres of decision.

The outcome of the elections severely damaged Masyumi's future prospects. After the announcement of the results, the party's sole aim now lay in preparing for the next election; however, the horizon looked fairly bleak. It had managed relatively well up until that point to ride the rocky course of political events; after the election, it became submerged by them. The party became increasingly marginalised as it came to be seen as the perfect embodiment of a parliamentary regime whose influence never actually went beyond the walls of the Assembly and existed only in the minds of a few leaders. It was not surprising, then, that some of its more energetic leaders responded by attempting to relaunch the party in the country's peripheral regions.

The Contradictions of the Party's Struggle for Democracy

With the elections of 1955, the division of the country's democratic representatives into different branches became irreversible, thus throwing the country into political deadlock because of their inability to govern together. Although the electorate were responsible for this situation, many amongst them blamed this situation on the newly weakened political class. Seizing on this ambient mindset, a radical change in the rules of the political game was advocated in some quarters by those who wanted to move political debate away from the parliamentary arena. In the "outer islands"—a term which was taken to refer to the islands outside Java and Madura—a powerful popular movement, encouraged by military officers who had gradually gained control over the local economic networks, had begun to make increasingly vociferous demands for a redistribution of power and wealth between the centre of the country and its periphery. At the same time, President Sukarno, taking advantage of the unrest caused by these demands, endeavoured to gather around him an increasingly divided nation. Although Masyumi was very much opposed to the changes in the political system which the president's aims implied, it nonetheless ended up unintentionally promoting them. By refusing to moderate its stance in its dispute with the PNI, by launching a campaign for an Islamic state in the Constituent Assembly—despite its chances of success being mathematically impossible—and by fanning the flames of regionalist discontent, the party bore its fair share of responsibility for the country's deteriorating situation.

The Resurgence of a Revolutionary Identity

Several weeks before the Harahap government left office, as the results of the legislative elections were gradually being made public, negotiations began between the PNI, Masyumi and NU with a view to forming a coalition government.[28] Because of its fierce opposition to President Sukarno's wish to see the PKI participate in government, Masyumi was not able to negotiate from a position of force.[29] The party received five portfolios in the new government which took office

---

[28] Mohammad Natsir explained at the beginning of February that the collaboration between Masyumi, the PNI and NU was already underway, indicating a new state of mind following the elections. He claimed that instead of dealing with the symptoms of the country's problems, as had previously been done, it would at last treat their causes. "Kerdjasama Masjumi-PNI-NU dapat ditjapai", *Abadi*, 1 February 1956. See also NU's declarations to the same effect, *Abadi*, 22 February 1956.

[29] Certain sections of the PNI at least did not rule out sharing the cabinet table with the PKI. Masyumi's propaganda therefore attempted to put pressure on NU to avoid such a scenario, which would have marginalised Masyumi. On 3 March 1956, the Contact Committee for Islamic Organisations (Badan Kontak Organisasi Islam, BKOI) controlled by Masyumi declared that "it will be possible to achieve a serene political atmosphere only if Masyumi, the PNI and NU form the heart of [the government]." "Suasana politik jg tenang hanja dapat ditjapai, djika Masjumi, PNI, NU sebagai inti." *Abadi*, 5 March 1956.

on 26 March 1956. One of these was an honorary portfolio—that of vice-prime-minister, given to Mohamad Roem—and two others were secondary ministries—the Ministry of Communications was awarded to Suchjar Tedjasukmana and Ministry of Public Works was given to Ir Pangeran Noor—leaving them two important positions: the Ministry of Finance, headed by Jusuf Wibisono, and the Justice Ministry, held by Mr Muljatno.

The second Sastroamidjojo government took office on the same day as the first session of the new legislative assembly; the Constituent Assembly was not inaugurated until November. The new cabinet rapidly demonstrated that the elections had solved none of the country's problems, and the three coalition partners, instead of searching for cooperation, soon began to vie against one another. In an attempt to thwart the influence of the PNI in cabinet, the Masyumi leadership tried to establish an alliance between Muslim parties. After a few meetings, however, the party had to face the fact that such an enterprise would not succeed. By accepting not to speak out against the prime minister's reassuring declarations on foreign policy, NU and the PSII confirmed the new balance of power in place within the government.[30] Faced with a PNI which benefitted both from presidential support and a good relationship with the two other Muslim parties, Masyumi could now only rely on its own political strength.[31]

This marginalisation of Mohammad Natsir's party came at a time when the general political climate was becoming rapidly unstable. The second Ali government's promise to fight against corruption, one of its main objectives, had become a dead letter. The former minister for economic affairs during the first Ali government, Iskaq Tjokrohadisurjo, who had masterminded a vast scheme of abuse of public office, returned with impunity to Indonesia. Masyumi, who had been one of the biggest detractors of Tjokrohadisurjo's methods, now abandoned its role of white knight; it even left the cabinet open to accusations of generalised corruption through the actions of one of its representatives in government, Jusuf Wibisono. In less than ten months, the minister

---

[30] *Abadi*, 24 October 1956.
[31] The election of the speaker of the Constituent Assembly in late November 1956 confirmed this new balance of power. The PNI candidate beat Masyumi's nominee thanks to the votes of NU and the PSII.

for finance allocated some 325 million rupiahs (Rp) in credit to businesses close to the parties in power.[32]

On 29 April, the Assembly had unanimously renewed their confidence in the Ali government, and so in the absence of an opposition
force in Parliament, a group of officers decided to take over the initiative in the fight against corruption. On 13 August, on the orders
of Colonel Kawilarang, commandant of West Java, the minister for
foreign affairs, Roeslan Abdulgani (PNI), was arrested. He was accused
of being complicit in a corruption affair involving the head of the
National Printing Office, but following the intervention of the prime
minister and Army Chief of Staff Nasution, he was released a few
hours later.[33] The "13 August Affair" constituted a turning point in
the army's political role. Up until then, it had contented itself with
preventing civilian intervention in its internal affairs, but faced with a
political class unable to regain the confidence of the people, it now
posed itself as the guardian of the rule of law.

Masyumi's leaders, who could have benefitted from this affair,
soon appeared out of their depth. Wary of poisoning their relations
with the PNI, they initially came to the defence of the minister for
foreign affairs. Mohammad Natsir and the justice minister, Moljatno,
claimed that a minister could not be placed under investigation without the authorisation of the government and the president. They proposed the creation of a ministerial committee charged with deciding
on the appropriateness of pressing charges.[34] This proposal was finally
accepted by the government, and on 29 August, a committee of five
ministers held a meeting chaired by Mohamad Roem. After two days

---

[32] Jusuf Wibisono made no mystery of these practices. When the governor of the
Bank of Indonesia was to be appointed in July 1956, NU was in the position
of arbitrator. In order to avoid it choosing a candidate close to the PNI, Jusuf
busied himself with doing favours for businesses linked to NU, notably the C.V.
Koernia company owned by the Rais Am of NU, Abdul Wahab Hasbullah. He
thus obtained NU's support for the appointment of Sjafruddin Prawiranegara.
Soebagijo I.N., *Jusuf Wibisono. Karang di Tengah Gelombang*, pp. 160–1. One
of the few opponents to the second Ali government, the PSI member Hamid
Algadri, called these practices the "Kuomintang phenomenon". Feith, *The Decline
of Constitutional Democracy in Indonesia* (Ithaca, NY: Cornell University Press,
1962), p. 479.

[33] Baladas, *Indonesian Politics 1955–1959*, pp. 54–5.

[34] *Abadi*, 18 and 22 August 1956.

of hearings, they produced a report clearing Roeslan Abdulgani of the charges brought against him, and so for the government and the Masyumi leadership the case was closed. On 1 September, Mohammad Natsir, presenting the committee's conclusions, explained that justice had been done and that the public should be relieved.[35] This interpretation of the situation was cruelly belied in the following weeks, however, as it became clear that the gap between public opinion and the government was widening. Mochtar Lubris, in his newspaper *Indonesia Raya*, pursued his investigations and published several documents which were damning to the minister for foreign affairs. In response to this press campaign, the government issued an executive order in mid-September banning the publication of "destructive and provocative news stories."[36] The army, which Nasution had regained control over, seized this opportunity to launch a campaign of intimidation against certain journalists. Mochtar Lubis, who was arrested on 13 December 1956, was the main victim of this campaign.

The leadership of the party was bound to the government's failed approach to the scandal, and they now found themselves in an awkward position vis-à-vis the lower echelons of the party. By the end of August, party members were speaking out against the leniency shown to Roeslan Abdulgani.[37] On 13 September, Mohammad Natsir had to respond to a declaration made by the leaders of the Sumatran branch of the party calling for the resignation of the Masyumi members of government. He initially refused to recognise the extent of their outrage, and merely considered it to be the result of local political considerations.[38] However, as the controversy was amplified by new revelations in the press, Natsir resolved on 11 December to ask on behalf of the party for the enquiry to be reopened.[39] The government consequently handed the affair over to the state prosecutor, who deemed a few days later that the case should go to trial. The Masyumi

---

[35] *Abadi*, 1 September 1956.

[36] Baladas, *Indonesian Politics 1955–1959*, p. 55.

[37] The Masyumi deputy, Sjarif Usman, became the spokesperson for those within the party who deplored the fact that the minister for foreign affairs had been shown clemency while ordinary citizens involved in much less serious corruption affairs were being held in jail without trial. *Abadi*, 1 September 1956.

[38] *Abadi*, 13 September 1956.

[39] *Abadi*, 12 December 1956.

leadership then asked for the minister for foreign affairs to resign, a request which was turned down by the PNI.

The "wait and see" tactics used by the leadership in this affair drew harsh criticism during the party's seventh congress which was held in Bandung between 22 and 29 December 1956. Several delegates singled out in particular Mohamad Roem, who had chaired the committee which had cleared Roeslan Abdlugani, criticising him for not having attended the congress. Roem, who had stayed in Jakarta for health reasons, was accused of having shirked his responsibilities and of being "politically ill".[40]

Natsir was obliged to speak out in favour of Roem and he no doubt paid the price for this subsequently. The attitude of the party's grassroots towards its president during the "13 August Affair" crystallised their disapproval of the strategy he had been pursuing over the previous number of years. As a partner in government, Masyumi, in the same respect as the other coalition parties, became discredited in the eyes of the general public; therefore it was not in a position to present itself as a solution to the political quagmire the country found itself in. In addition, its reward for participating in government was a meagre one, as its marginalisation within cabinet meant that it bore little influence on government policy. The party's rank and file, who for years had listened to triumphalist speeches announcing the party's imminent electoral victory, now rediscovered the freedom of tone which they had lost since the years of the "Physical Revolution". The edifice which Natsir had worked to build up—a pragmatic and disciplined party which had abandoned its incendiary revolutionary rhetoric—began to crumble, and the old demons which seemed to have been put to bed resurfaced again in Masyumi's collective consciousness.

In March 1956, during the national convention of Indonesian importers, Assaat, a former minister for home affairs in Natsir's government who did not belong to any political party, called on the government to adopt a policy favouring native Indonesians—known as *pribumi*—over citizens of Chinese origin. He accused the latter of controlling the country's economic system and held them responsible for the difficulties which his fellow countrymen were encountering.

---

[40] According to Deliar Noer, invited by the congress's Organisation Committee to attend the debates. Deliar Noer, "Masjumi: Its Organization, Ideology, and Political Role in Indonesia", Master thesis, Cornell University, 1960, p. 369.

This speech broke a taboo in Indonesian society; the country's political figures had been concerned, since independence, with fostering national unity and had never dared to voice such ideas. A section of the population rallied around Assaat's ideas, and support committees were created in many places around the country. This anti-Chinese fervour was not limited to economic demands, and on several occasions it broke out into riots during which goods and property owned by the *totok* as well as the *peranakan* community were targeted as part of punitive expeditions.[41] Over the following months, the movement's demands extended to areas beyond the economy, and it grew in size to encompass not only the country's trading classes but also certain sections of the army as well as a part of the political class.

Masyumi was not immune to this phenomenon. It was traditionally the party of the Muslim entrepreneurial class, and a number of party figures did not let the calls from the party's grassroots fall on deaf ears. At the beginning of July 1956, for example, Dr. Ali Akbar, a member of the Masyumi leadership and the president of the Parliamentary Commission on Education called for the establishment of quotas for Chinese schools. The reason for such a measure, according to him, was to oblige members of the Chinese community to allow the entire educational system to benefit from their wealth.[42] For the other members of the party leadership, Dr. Akbar's comments were a source of embarrassment.

The demands of the Assaat movement blatantly contradicted the principle of economic non-discrimination which figured in the party's programmes. The popularity of such demands with the party's rank and file underlined a sociological disparity within Masyumi, namely the fact that the party's national figures rarely came from Muslim business circles, which were much better represented in the party's intermediate echelons.[43] The few leadership members who were close to the business world operated at the upper end of that milieu where the Chinese were more often partners rather than competitors. One such party figure was

---

[41] The word "*totok*", meaning "indigenous", refers to foreigners born in their home country who had recently immigrated; the term "*peranakan*", on the other hand, refers to the descendants of those immigrants. Both terms can be used to signify Europeans, Arabs and Indians, but unless otherwise specified, they normally refer to the Chinese in Indonesia.

[42] *Abadi*, 13 and 24 July 1956.

[43] See supra, Chapter 1.

Jusuf Wibisono. Having worked for a Dutch automobile import company from 1953 to 1954, he was approached by a Japanese chemical
company to become the chairman of a bank they had just established.
Despite opposition from Natsir, Jusuf accepted the job offer on condition that his name would not appear on the company's organigram.
At the same time, two other companies had attempted to hire his
services: the bookshop and publishing house Gunung Agung—which
was owned by Tjio Wie Thay, who later changed the company's name
to Mas Agung—and the P.T. Mustika Trading Company, an import-
export business which also had a Chinese chairman.[44] Given his background, it is easy to imagine Jusuf Wibisono's discomfort when, as
minister for finance, he had to offer Mr Assat an audience. In order
to justify his refusal of Assat's proposals, he invoked the Constitution,
explaining that any measure which was liable to distinguish between
different categories of citizens based on their origin was impossible.[45]

Masyumi's press, for its part, had obviously received guidelines
requiring it to treat the Assaat affair with moderation. Neither *Abadi*
nor *Hikmah* joined in the virulent campaign led by *Indonesia Raya*.
Abadi limited itself to reporting the main aspects of the controversy,
without elaborating on them any further, while any references *Hikmah*
made to the case were oblique and always carried a marked pedagogical
tone. In an edition of *Hikmah* published on 2 June, for example, a
copy of an article from a Chinese daily newspaper, *Kuang Po*, was published. The article was preceded by some preliminary words of caution
which reminded the "young generations as well as the older generations who have a short memory" of the prominent role played by certain members of the Chinese community in the nationalist movement.
It consisted in a long letter written, at the request of the owner of
Kuang Po, by A.R. Baswedan, a Masyumi member and a leading figure
in the community of Indonesians of Arab descent. The letter was written in answer to the following question: what were the reasons behind
the success associated with the group of Indonesian citizens of Arab
descent? Theirs was a community which was clearly held in high regard
within the Indonesian Muslim community, and they had plainly been
spared from the discriminatory measures called for at the Importers
Congress. By publishing A.R. Baswedan's letter, *Hikmah* was reminding

---

[44] Soebagijo I.N., *Jusuf Wibisono. Karang di Tengah Gelombang*, pp. 134–41.
[45] Ibid., pp. 157–8.

its readers that the integration of non-native communities within the Republic of Indonesia was not only possible but also profitable, and that the example of the country's Arab descendents should serve as a model for the Chinese community.[46]

Due to the censorship exercised over the Masyumi press, it is difficult to gauge the degree of involvement of the party's grassroots in this anti-Chinese movement. It is nonetheless possible to surmise, given the sociological disparities, mentioned earlier, between the party's leadership and its rank and file, that it was significant and that it constituted a further source of tension within the party. There is no doubt that the small businessmen who were part of the *pribumi* community had at least two good reasons to be unhappy with the policies implemented under the previous two governments by Masyumi and its allies. The first of these was the new ruling adopted by the Harahap cabinet, which had benefitted for the most part foreign importers. The second was the repeal of the Round Table Agreements, which meant that numerous Dutch companies had to sell their business interests in Indonesia. The only Indonesians who possessed the capital necessary to acquire these Dutch businesses were generally members of the Chinese community. This measure meant that the resentment of Indonesian entrepreneurs as well as a part of the rest of the population was also directed towards the Indonesian political establishment.

At the end of 1956, then, Masyumi appeared as a clay-footed giant, weakened by its poor electoral performance and undermined by the revolt of a part of its membership. Paradoxically, it was President Sukarno who, at this point, seemed to give the party the opportunity of a new lease of life. His decision to steadily take apart the final vestiges of Indonesia's parliamentary regime gave Masyumi the chance to take on the role of tragic martyr for democracy.

A New Cause, a New Impetus: Masyumi's Response to the Political, Military and Regional Crisis

On his return from a long overseas trip to China, the USSR and Europe, President Sukarno took advantage of the toxic atmosphere which reigned over Indonesian politics to regain the initiative against his

---

[46] "Apa sebab2nja gerakan bangsa Indonesia turunan Arab berhasil?!", *Hikmah*, 2 June 1956.

rivals. In two separate speeches, made on 28 and 30 October 1956, he invited his fellow countrymen to draw the necessary conclusions from the failure of Indonesia's parliamentary democracy. The country, according to him, had to face up to the fact that the November 1945 decree authorising the creation of political parties had been a grave error. He denounced what he called the "disease of the party system" and stated his wish to "bury" them and set up a "guided democracy" (*demokrasi terpimpin*), better suited to Indonesia's political conditions. Masyumi's condemnation of the president's statements was immediate and unequivocal. On 29 October, Natsir responded to the first of Sukarno's speeches, warning his fellow Indonesians that if the president's proposals were followed, then "democracy would also be buried in the grave."[47] A few days later, on 2 November, the party leadership voted a declaration reminding the public that despite the current difficulties, in no circumstances could "a dictatorship in whatever form constitute a solution."[48]

These responses to the president's proposals marked a new stage in the party's history, as they contained no reference to Islam's values. For Masyumi's leaders, the evocation of democracy—of its spirit, or soul (*djiwa*)—in itself sufficed. It was for its intrinsic values and despite all its imperfections, that it was to be protected, not because of any superior religious norm. Moreover, a significant semantic shift in the language used to refer to democracy could be seen in Natsir's statement, in which he employed expressions such as "way of life" or *dasar hidup* (basis of life) which previously he had normally only used to refer to Islam. This was confirmation of a certain secularisation of the party's political identity. In a speech given on 7 November 1956 on the occasion of the 11th anniversary of the foundation of Masyumi, this was how Natsir defined the party's struggle for democracy. Although Masyumi had certainly not abandoned all references to Islam, its response to President Sukarno's proposals was primarily in the name of a democratic ideal, presented independently of Islam's values. Moreover, this debate on the nature of the country's institutions came at just the right time for the party: through a simple and unifying cause, it allowed Masyumi to regain the momentum it had lost since its electoral defeat.

---

[47] A declaration by Mohammad Natsir to the press, *Abadi*, 30 October 1956.
[48] A declaration by the central executive committee, *Abadi*, 3 October 1956.

The transformation of Masyumi's image, both in the eyes of its members and its opponents, into the defender of a Western-style parliamentary regime, was certainly not immediate; furthermore, initially it was not the only party to condemn Sukarno's proposals. Only the PKI and the much smaller PRI, led by Bung Tomo, gave their unreserved approval; NU spoke of a "desperation policy" which was opposed to the teachings of Islam, while the PNI rejected any measure which affected the system of political parties as a whole.[49] However, these parties gradually accepted in the following months to sign up to the new political framework outlined by Sukarno. Masyumi and the PSI were the only ones who rejected outright any concession, a stance which led eventually to their downfall. The regionalist movement which had started at the same time radicalised the two sides further, and changed the nature of the conflict from political to military.

Since the beginning of the 1950s, the steady decline in government military spending had led certain regional commanders, known as *panglima*, to look for resources elsewhere. In collaboration with local business circles, they put in place parallel channels for the export of raw materials, creating profits which previously went directly to the government in Jakarta. The effect of inflation and the cost of official import-export channels meant that those in the outer islands took home in reality very little of the money generated by their mineral and agricultural raw materials, which constituted 70% of the country's total exports. The parallel economy set up by the military in those regions allowed their inhabitants, therefore, to increase their income significantly. However, in November 1956, the civilian and military authorities in Jakarta started to put an end to these enterprises. The Army Chief of Staff, General Nasution, working closely with the president, drew up a large-scale plan to transfer certain army officers, which was principally designed to regain control over certain regional military commands, but also to sideline the volatile Colonel Zulkifi Lubis, who was Deputy Army Chief of Staff and the main potential threat to Nasution's power within the army.[50]

---

[49] Baladas, *Indonesian Politics 1955–1959*, p. 58.
[50] The rivalry between the two men mirrored the conflict within the army between two traditions, namely one which came from the KNIL (Nasution) and one which came from the PETA (Lubis). In addition to that, there had been, according to Goshal Baladas, a falling out between the two men's parents.

The response of the officers concerned was both quick and forceful. On 16 and 17 November 1956, Colonel Zulkifli Lubis, who had just been given a command in North Sumatra, and Major Djelani, the new commander for West Java, took part in an attempted coup d'état. General Nasution immediately removed their commands and ordered their arrest, but Lubis managed to escape. For the army chief of staff and his deputy, this situation constituted a strange reversal of the roles they had occupied in the 17 October 1952 Affair, during which Sukarno had sided with Lubis against Nasution. During the 1952 crisis, the two opposing factions within the army had finally managed to put their differences aside, but this time the dispute crystallised resentment and discontent well beyond the reaches of the army. The officers facing transfer stood together against Nasution and the government in a united front with the people of the areas they administered. On 26 December 1956, Lieutenant-Colonel Husein, head of the "Banteng Council"—named after the division he commanded—seized power in Central Sumatra. Two days later, Colonel Simbolon, a commander in North Sumatra, announced in turn that he no longer recognised the authority of Ali Sastroamidjojo's government. One of the rebels' demands was the formation of a new government led by Mohammad Hatta; having announced his intention a few months earlier to resign from the position of vice president as soon as the Constituent Assembly was inaugurated, Hatta was now once again in a position to lead the country's affairs.[51]

The regionalist revolt, which came about at the same time as President Sukarno's plan for a "guided democracy", forced the party, under pressure from its grassroots, to adopt a position strongly opposed to the Ali government. The initial stages of the crisis left the party in an uncomfortable position, and its response was overall a prudent one. Wary of stoking up further the tensions which had surfaced in the country, the party's press limited itself to reporting the rebellion's main events without commenting upon them in any way. However, certain members of the party leadership soon found it difficult to hide their sympathy for the rebels' demands.

---

[51] For further reading on the motivations of this movement, which was not a separatist movement but rather one which wished to exercise political influence in the country, see Feith, *The Decline of Constitutional Democracy in Indonesia*, p. 527 ff.

First of all, Masyumi was very much in favour of Mohammad Hatta's return to the centre of the political arena. Since the announcement of his decision to leave the vice presidency, the party's leaders had, on numerous occasions, underlined their high regard for both the person and the calming role he played on the Indonesian political scene. For them, the Dwitunggal, the duumvirate of Sukarno and Hatta which had led Indonesia to independence, was now more than ever the only possible guarantee of stability for the country.[52] Since Sukarno's sensationalist declaration about the necessity to do away with political parties and with an alliance emerging between the president and the army chief of staff, Mohammad Hatta was now the only figure who could counterbalance the power held by the head of state. In addition, the vice president, without opposing Sukarno directly, did hint, on announcing his resignation, at his disagreement with the measures being introduced.

Moreover, the party could no longer ignore the demands of regions which contained the majority of its electorate. Since the failure of the Federal Republic of Indonesia—the last attempt by the Dutch to conserve some degree of influence in the country—a unitary state had become, for Masyumi and for the other parties, Indonesia's only possible form of government. Subsequently, the party's policy concerning the nation's various regions consisted in campaigning for decentralisation with a view to giving them as much autonomy as possible.[53] Now that a regionalist crisis had erupted, calls were made to take this policy a step further and on 2 October 1956, Rusjad Nurdin, a party figure from West Java, declared that his party might advocate a federal state and call for the creation of a senate representing the country's regions.[54] The party leadership refused to confirm this possibility, however, and

[52] See, for example, *Abadi*, 27 April 1956.
[53] See, for example, *Hikmah*, 23 August 1952, in which an editorial proposed a trial period of economic autonomy for the regions in order to examine the viability of the different programmes. An even more revealing indication of Masyumi's official stance on this thorny question was a series of articles by Mohammad Sjafei published in *Hikmah* (23 and 30 April 1955). Sjafei outlined the existing legislation before arguing for the greatest possible autonomy within the existing legal framework for the various administrative divisions, from village level right up to provincial level.
[54] *Abadi*, 3 October 1956.

a week later, Yunan Nasution, on behalf of the party's executive committee (Dewan Pinpinan Partai), contested Rusjad Nurdin's analysis of the situation, quoting the resolutions from the 1952 conference in favour of a "a unitary state with full autonomy." Nasution nonetheless argued in favour of putting in place rapidly a fairer system of redistributing the country's resources between the state and the regions.[55]

With the debate on the most appropriate state model for Indonesia momentarily closed, the party now turned its attention to the question of what attitude to adopt towards the government. On 3 December 1956, the party leadership broke the silence it had observed since the rebellion led by Colonel Zulkifli Lubis in an article published in *Abadi* by Sjarif Usman, president of the Section for the Defence of Parliament, in which he offered his analysis of the uprising. Although he did not go so far as to approve the claims made by the seditious officers in charge of the uprising, he did implicitly criticise the crackdown of the revolt organised by Nasution and also urged the government to revive the Dwitunggal, which, for him, was the only way for the state to restore its credibility in the regions.[56]

Following these comments, other voices in the party spoke out calling for the government to resign. In the midst of a certain amount of confusion, there emerged within the party a debate: should the party demand a change of government, withdraw its ministers from cabinet, or wait until the situation became a little clearer? Mohammad Natsir favoured the latter of these three alternatives. In early December, he declared to the press that his party's withdrawal from government was not on the agenda.[57] As the eighth party congress approached—it was to take place from 22 to 29 December 1956—pressure mounted from the party's grassroots to withdraw from government. Some delegates from Central Sumatra returned home before the debates even opened in order to lend their support to the Dewan Banteng. An editorial in *Abadi*, referring to the discussions underway in the congress, underlined the "particular responsibility" borne by Masyumi and the "sometimes exaggerated" hopes placed in its capacity to find a way out of the country's crisis.[58]

---

[55] *Abadi*, 12 October 1956.
[56] *Abadi*, 4 December 1956.
[57] *Abadi*, 6 December 1956.
[58] *Abadi*, 21 December 1956.

On the opening day of the conference, all of the party's representatives from the outer islands, as well as from West Java, attacked the government's policy violently. They were convinced that the party's stance would determine the government's fate, and they demanded the withdrawal of all Masyumi ministers from government.[59] Mohammad Natsir, whose term in office had come up for renewal, finally went along with the majority opinion.[60] The congress's final resolutions revealed a hardening of positions amongst a certain section of the party's delegates. These delegates demanded that the government modify its first five-year plan (1956–60) so as to redirect government investment and social benefits to those living outside of the major urban centres. More importantly, they revised the economic liberalism contained in the party's 1954 emergency programme. They called on the government to give appropriate economic protection to state companies which were still unable to keep up with foreign competition. They wanted the entire import-export industry to be one of the economic sectors controlled by state companies, and they also called for the use of foreign capital and experts to be limited to a maximum period of 15 years.[61]

The 1956 conference marked the end, then, of the pragmatic line that Natsir had up to that point promoted. Fearing that its abandonment of the coalition formed with the PNI and NU would leave the way open for the PKI to enter government, the party had up until then endeavoured to minimise the differences which arose from the government partnership. With the government's hold over the political situation in rapid decline and part of the army as well as the country's regions in open revolt against its authority, this strategy was leading the party into deadlock. Its participation in government had left it too compromised to hope to benefit from the kind of political renewal that was being called for on all sides. The party's grassroots, whose ideas were relayed by figures such as Sjarif Usman, Anwar Harjono and Isa Anshary, at that point obliged the leadership to change its strategy.

---

[59] *Abadi*, 26 December 1956.

[60] *Abadi*, 28 December 1956. The only ones to oppose this decision were Soekiman's supporters who recommended the continuation of cooperation with the other parties in the Ali government. For them, abandoning governmental responsibilities in the middle of a political crisis amounted to an act of hostility towards Masyumi's former allies.

[61] The same foreign capital and experts which the previous congress had solicited in its resolutions. *Abadi*, 31 December 1956.

These figures were motivated by their sympathy for the regionalist movements, and they were certain that Masyumi's foothold among the electorate meant that it was the only party the country could turn to in the ongoing crisis. In their view, the resignation of Masyumi ministers would automatically bring down the government, and President Sukarno, in order to avoid the rebellion spreading, would then have no choice but to name Hatta at the head of a new government whose core would be made up of Masyumi ministers. Natsir, who was much more *au fait* with politics in Jakarta, reluctantly decided to follow this path.

During the opening days of the party congress, Natsir sent a delegation to speak to Mohammad Hatta, and once he had been re-elected unopposed as head of the party, he duly went about implementing its new strategy. In his closing speech to the conference, however, he pointedly distanced himself from the rebels, explaining "that one didn't have to be a jurist to see that what had been done by Simbolon in North Sumatra, by the Dewan Banteng in Central Sumatra and by Winarno in South Sumatra constituted actions which violated the laws of the land", and that consequently "it was not Masyumi's intention to recognise them." He nonetheless added that the problem went far beyond the fate of the rebel leaders, that "the malaise had profound causes, and so for this reason, one could not just disregard what they had done and act solely using formal legal means and administrative procedures."[62] Calling for national unity in the interests of the country's security, he asked for discussions to be opened between the president "as head of state", Mohammad Hatta "as a national figure" (*sebagai tokoh nasional*) and the leaders of the political parties with a view to forming a government which would symbolise a beacon of hope in the midst of the country's difficulties.

On 9 January 1957, after a final attempt to convince its coalition partners to resign, Masyumi withdrew from government.[63] Subsequent events showed that Natsir's initial forebodings and Soekiman's reservations were both well-founded. Despite the increasingly obvious tensions between the government parties, the Ali government remained

---

[62] *Abadi*, 3 January 1957.
[63] The only organisation to support Masyumi's move was IPKI. Its founder, General Nasution, clearly no longer had complete control over the organisation, which supported certain demands made by Perti as well as by the rebel officers in charge of the regional insurrections. *Abadi*, 8 January 1957.

Plate 4.2 President Sukarno unveils his plan to dismantle the parties (*Hikmah*, 3 November 1956).

in office for a further two months. President Sukarno put this time to good use by setting up a new political order which would marginalise Masyumi definitively.

Towards Guided Democracy

Although it did not cause the rest of the cabinet to leave office, the resignation of the Masyumi ministers did, however, have the result of heightening further the tension between Jakarta and the regions. In the weeks following the party's departure from government, numerous militia groups held rallies to make their positions known, while the

PKI held a series of meetings in order to lend its support to the president and the government. Sukarno, taking full advantage of the growing political chaos, began to sketch out progressively the political alternative which he intended to propose.

Once he had consulted with certain parties, and after a few off-the-record comments made to a group of foreign journalists, the president unveiled his "conception" (*konsepsi*) of democracy in a speech given on 21 February.[64] It was a carefully orchestrated address lasting a few hours, during which the whole nation's attention was focussed on the presidential palace. Siren bells and drums (*lonceng* and *beduk*) sounded; people were allowed to stop their work and the minister for information encouraged those who owned radios to turn the volume up as loud as possible so that everybody, including passersby, might hear the president's voice.[65] Pointing out what he saw as the failure of "Western-style democracy" to meet the needs of the spirit of the Indonesian nation, Sukarno called for the "old style" of government to be abandoned. In its stead, he proposed the formation of a *gotong royong* cabinet, based on the old Javanese principle of mutual assistance between villagers, and the creation of a National Council (Dewan Nasional), whose members would be chosen from the representatives of the "functional groups" (*golongan fungsional*) which Indonesian society was composed of, including industrial workers, peasants, intellectuals, members of the military and the police force, entrepreneurs, Muslims, Catholics and Protestants.

The proposals which the president put forward ruled out any compromise with the regionalist rebels and also excluded the possibility of a revival of the *Dwitunggal*.[66] They did, however, win him two

---

[64] Masyumi was excluded from these discussions and for several weeks it only managed to get rumours of the president's plans. The party leaders denounced these plans, despite not knowing any details about them; they considered these consultations to be manœuvres designed to serve the interests of the PKI. See *Abadi*, 17, 19 and 21 January 1957.

[65] Busjairi Badruzzaman, *Boerhanoeddin Harahap Pilar Demokrasi* (Jakarta: Bulan Bintang, 1982), p. 128.

[66] Sukarno intended to use the political crisis the country was going through to restore the primacy of the president's constitutional role which had been removed by the 1950 Constitution. He therefore had no desire to see his former ally-turned-rival Mohammad Hatta return to prominence. J.D. Legge, *Sukarno: A Political Biography* (Sydney: Allen and Unwin, 1990 [1st edition, 1972]).

powerful allies in the shape of the PKI, which the regional elections of 1956 showed was growing in strength, and the army, who, thanks to the National Council, could at last expect to have the political role it had been calling for. In the days following Sukarno's speech, posters and slogans in favour of the "presidential conception" sprang up on the walls of the capital, and organisations close to the PKI, and to a lesser extent to the PNI, organised a series of marches.[67] Those who opposed the president's plan, foremost amongst whom was Masyumi, came under intense pressure and claimed to have been the victims of harassment and threats.[68]

On 28 February, representatives from the country's political parties went to the palace to give the president their assessments of his proposals. The PNI, the PKI, the Partai Murba and the PRN were the only ones to approve unreservedly of Sukarno's intentions, while NU, the PSII, the Parkindo, the IPKI and the PSI without totally condemning the "conception", did make a significant number of reservations. The Partai Katolik and Masyumi, on the other hand, unequivocally rejected the president's plans. Natsir's party was aware of the crisis facing the country and was not opposed to a greater involvement by the president in political life. A speech made in the Assembly by Boerhanoeddin Harahap, the chairman of the party's parliamentary group, explored several possible ways out of the political deadlock, each of which envisaged Sukarno playing an important role. The last of these potential solutions, and the most innovative of Harahap's proposals, advocated a return to the practices of the Yogyakarta government which allowed the president to attend the most important cabinet meetings in order to put across his opinion.[69]

For Masyumi, however, this increase in the head of state's powers could only be envisaged if it was accompanied by his cooperation with Mohammad Hatta, which would preclude too much power being vested

---

[67] Feith, *The Decline of Constitutional Democracy in Indonesia*, p. 543.

[68] On 2 March 1957, under the headline "Stop Intimidasi dan Terror", *Abadi* reported the complaint lodged with the state prosecutor by representatives of the five parties (Masyumi, NU, Partai Katolik, Parkindo and the PSII) against such intimidation. However, politicians themselves do not appear to have been the victims of direct assaults.

[69] Badruzzaman, *Boerhanoeddin Harahap Pilar Demokrasi*, p. 127.

in one person at the head of the executive.[70] Moreover, the party had two further fundamental objections to the president's proposals. The first of these concerned the nature of democracy itself which, as Mohammad Natsir often repeated, "was oblivious to East and West but constituted a universal value." Masyumi's president gave short shrift to the idea of so-called eastern values referred to by Sukarno; for him, democracy could only be "guided" by the high moral values recognised both by the West and by Islam.[71] The second objection, which was developed by Natsir in a long article published on 8 March, concerned the possibility of the participation in government of the PKI, the "Trojan horse" (*Kuda Troye*) which would smuggle a dictatorship into the country.[72] Masyumi's leaders played on this fear of communism to form a short-lived coalition in defence of parliamentary democracy. On 2 March, Nahdlatul Ulama, the PSII, the Partai Katolik and Masyumi signed a declaration rejecting the president's proposals.[73] The party's success in gathering these signatures allowed it to gain the upper hand politically by showing Sukarno that his proposals had not created the consensus on which he wished to found a new democratic norm.

The continuing spiral of disorder in the regions, however, meant that this victory soon came to appear very empty. On the very day the joint declaration was signed, regionalist unrest spread to East Indonesia which had, until then, been unaffected by the rebellion. On 2 March, in Makassar, Lieutenant-Colonel Sumual announced that he was going to declare a state of siege in the area under his command. Sumual's

---

[70] *Abadi* dedicated a lot of space to Mohammad Hatta's reaction to Sukarno's proposals. Although the former vice president did not condemn the "conceptions of Bung Karno", he did indicate the limitations imposed by the Constitution on the president's plans as well as the difficulties in implementing it. He became an advocate of a presidential cabinet, without stipulating what role he would have in it. Mohammad Hatta, "Menindjau Konsepsi Bung Karno", *Abadi*, 2 March 1957.

[71] Natsir developed the same arguments on many occasions. See the long article published in *Abadi* on 1 March 1951, in which he justifies Masyumi's refusal to approve the president's proposals, using reasons which he had already evoked in October 1947. Natsir opposed Sukarno's "orientalo-centrist" vision, and adopted the prodemocracy arguments used by the Indian deputy prime minister of the day, Radhakrisnan.

[72] *Abadi*, 8 March 1957.

[73] *Abadi*, 4 March 1957.

seizure of power took place at the same time as the diffusion of a "Charter of Common Struggle" which adapted and adopted the regionalist demands already formulated in Sumatra. This document contained a good deal of the ideas put forward by Masyumi, such as a five-year regional development plan, a reform of the distribution of export revenue and the revival of the *Dwitunggal*.[74] It marked, for the insurrectionists, the beginning of a period of "total struggle" (*perjuangan semesta*) from which the movement took its name (Permesta).

These events strengthened the alliance between Sukarno and General Nasution. The army chief of staff advised the president to declare both a state of war and a state of siege (Staat van Oorlog en Beleg, SOB). He argued that this would have the twofold advantage of cloaking the regional commanders' seizure of power with the trappings of legality, while simultaneously giving the president the means to counter these rebellions. Such a measure would also allow Sukarno to take the initiative over the political parties who, in contrast to him, were powerless to act. On Nasution's advice, the head of state seized on the opportunity provided by the resignation of the Ali government to decree a state of war and a state of siege on 14 March. The following day, Sukarno chose the president of the PNI, Suwirjo, to form a new cabinet whose goal would be to implement the first stage of his reform programme by setting up the National Council. However, the *formateur* was not able to reconcile the demands of the various political parties, and two weeks into negotiations he threw in the towel.[75]

Once again, the initiative fell to Sukarno, who on 4 April appointed himself *formateur*. He asked the hundred or so political and military figures who were present at the presidential palace at the time of this announcement to put their reaction to it in writing. Of the five Masyumi members present, two—Mohammad Noor and Muljadi Djojomartono—approved the president's initiative, and they were appointed, respectively, minister for public works and minister for social

---

[74] See Barbara S. Harvey, *Permesta: Half a Rebellion* (Ithaca, NY: Cornell University Press, 1977), pp. 60 ff.

[75] The PKI had threatened to paralyse the country with a general strike if Masyumi took part in a government from which it was excluded. As a result, Masyumi was not invited to sit at the cabinet table. NU considered that Masyumi's participation in government was necessary to solve the regional crisis and so blocked all negotiations aimed at forming a new government. *Abadi*, 20 March and 10 April 1957.

affairs in the new government headed by the politically unaligned Djuanda.

In the confrontation between Sukarno and Masyumi, the formation of the Djuanda government constituted for the president a decisive step towards final victory. The previous weeks had shown the political class's inability to unite around a common programme, and the president's initiative was particularly welcomed as the new government appeared to have a number of trump cards at its disposal. Firstly, Djuanda, apart from the fact that he was not Javanese, also had the advantage of possessing a reputation as honest and reliable. He was a fervent advocate of reconciliation between Java and the regions, and in his first declarations as prime minister he promised to set up a development plan for the outer islands, to grant them greater regional autonomy and to revise the distribution of public money in favour of the regions. In addition to that, the government which he headed was composed of figures recognised for their abilities. None of them had been implicated in any of the various scandals which had rocked the political landscape during the previous years. Moreover, the diversity of the cabinet's political and geographic origins made it one of the most representative governments that Indonesia had seen since independence. Finally, all of the political parties were represented at the cabinet table. Of the larger parties, only the PKI did not officially have a seat, but several independents who had received portfolios were known for their communist sympathies. Moreover, the Communist Party supported the government unreservedly. The response to the new government was positive overall; even the prestigious leader of the PSII, Sjahrir, despite his opposition to Sukarno, approved the composition of the cabinet.[76] The only opposition voices that could be heard against the government came from Mohammad Hatta and Masyumi. The party once again found its views to be in step with those of the former vice president, who had just refused the president's most recent proposal, and it broadcast this convergence of ideas freely.[77]

---

[76] Baladas, *Indonesian Politics 1955–1959*, p. 123.

[77] Hatta, who was very hostile to the *Dewan Nasional*, was offered the presidency of another body, the National Planning Board. *Abadi*, 20 March 1957. The front page of *Abadi* was systematically taken up with Hatta's speeches and political positions, relegating those of the party's leaders to the inside pages. When Hatta did not make any statement, words were put in his mouth: in *Abadi*, a very long

The formation of the Djuanda government signalled Masyumi's move to the margins of the political arena. The party's leadership denounced Sukarno's decision to appoint the new government under the powers given to him by the state of siege, and called for a salutary reaction from "those who loved genuine democracy."[78] A few days later, Mohammad Natsir, hardened the tone of the party's message and in a premonitory speech declared that:

> On this pretext, and on the same legal basis, the head of state, Sukarno, will, tomorrow or the day after, dissolve or suspend Parliament, elected by our people, or maybe break up the parties through emergency legislation.

Faced with such a prospect, it was now no longer possible to satisfy oneself with "polite opposition", as "adopting a tolerant attitude towards such methods, as Prime Minister Djuanda has asked us to do, would amount to ignoring the establishment of a dictatorial power in Indonesia."[79]

This sombre prognosis by Masyumi's president did not, however, succeed in affecting the coalition of support which had grown up around the Djuanda government and given it de facto legitimacy. The PSII and NU adopted a "wait and see" attitude and refused this time to echo Masyumi's denunciation of the president's methods. In a skilful political move, the government avoided requesting a vote of confidence in Parliament, and Masyumi, realising that it was politically isolated, refused to call for one, as a majority vote in favour of the government,

---

account (ten columns in all) was written about an imaginary conversation between the two pillars of the *Dwitunggal*. This strange text often adopted a humorous tone and mocked the president's ideas while depicting Hatta as a man of moderation and conviction; whose ideas were very close to Masyumi's. *Abadi*, 23 to 26 March 1957.

[78] A declaration made by the Masyumi executive committee on 9 April 1957. *Abadi*, 10 April 1957. The executive committee banned its members from taking part in government and announced disciplinary measures which would be taken against those who violated this decision. On 9 May, Pangeran Noor was expelled from the party, while Muljati Djojomartono left the party of his own volition on 24 May, the day he entered cabinet. *Abadi*, 27 May 1957.

[79] A speech given by Mohammad Natsir to Parliament on 15 April 1957. Quoted in Badruzzaman Busjairi, *Catatan Perjuangan H.M. Yunan Nasution* (Jakarta: Pustaka Panjimas, 1985), pp. 243–4.

which was highly likely, would rubberstamp its appointment.[80] Sukarno was the main beneficiary of the legal uncertainty surrounding the government's legitimacy, and in mid-June, he began to implement the second stage of his programme.

On 18 June 1957, the government announced the formation of the National Council which the president had called for. It comprised 42 members and was inaugurated on 12 July. Apart from a few officials—notably the chiefs of staff of the armed forces and the head of police—it was made up mainly of representatives of the "functional groups" reflecting the diversity of Indonesian society[81] as well as the 14 representatives of the country's regions. Despite the absence of representatives from the political parties—these were added to the Assembly in 1959—the council's composition also reflected the political balance sought by Sukarno. Masyumi was the only party to have no sympathisers within the new institution; the PNI and the PKI shared the seats awarded to those representing small farmers, industrial workers, young people and journalists, while NU had a monopoly over the seats belonging to the representatives of the *ulama*. The role attributed to the Council by Sukarno in the inaugural speech he gave was relatively ill-defined. It was to assist the cabinet and lend it greater authority by serving as an intermediary between it and society. In reality, however, the National Council only rarely intervened in the country's political affairs during its first year of existence, and it was only from mid-1958 that it took on the role desired by Sukarno of replacing the party system.

Resolutely faithful to its new role as the staunch defender of parliamentary democracy, Masyumi rejected this new institution as being unconstitutional. It refused to go along with the opinion of eminent specialists in constitutional law who considered that the "groups" (*golongan*) mentioned in the 1950 Constitution allowed a system of "functional" representation of society.[82] The party responded to this legal argument with practical considerations, asking how it could be

---

[80] It was only in February 1958 that Parliament voted confidence in the Djuanda government.

[81] The functional groups represented, amongst others, industrial workers, young people, peasants, women, members of the 1945 generation as well as leaders of the Muslim, Protestant and Hindu communities.

[82] This was the view, in particular, of Professor Djokosartono, a recognised expert in constitutional law. Baladas, *Indonesian Politics 1955–1959*, p. 127.

Plate 4.3 "The cabinet" does not know whether to give its "report" to "the Parliament" or "the National Council".

possible to improve a parliamentary system which functioned poorly despite its clear procedural rules by creating a new institution whose role was ill-defined.

Finally, unlike the other Muslim parties, Masyumi saw the formation of the National Council as part of an ongoing development which would lead to the establishment of the guided democracy sought by Sukarno and thus, sooner or later, to the disappearance of political parties which were held responsible for all of the country's woes. This reading of the situation fell on deaf ears in the Jakartan political class, and so Mohammad Natsir decided to look to the population of Sumatra during a visit there at the beginning of July. During a rally held in Bukittinggi, Masyumi's president vigorously denounced the operation being led from the upper reaches of power aimed at turning the parties into the scapegoat (*kambing hitam*) for the political crisis. His speech received an enthusiastic reception; the reaction of a part of the population to the president's strategy contrasted starkly with the passive policy of consensus and the attitude of resignation which seemed to have taken hold of the capital. In Jakarta, Natsir was marginalised, but here he was on his home ground, leading him no doubt to be tempted by a withdrawal to his native region—hinted at in the speech he gave to close the Central Sumatra Congress:

> It is indeed rather difficult today to find a place where partisan positions can flourish. By the grace of God, the region of Central Sumatra has remained unchanged, which makes it an extraordinary place. I have seen here a people attached to political parties for the delight in being together and not for the sake of creating divisions amongst ourselves, nor for the sake of creating a uniformisation amongst us all.[83]

The resolutions adopted at the congress indicated that the Central Sumatra branch of Masyumi intended henceforth to provide a solution to problems at a regional level. Most of the demands formulated were addressed not to the government in Jakarta but to military authorities who had seized power in the region. The local party leaders wished, in particular, to promote the autonomy of the local customs authority, and to see the revenue generated by exports lodged in the Bank of Indonesia in Padang rather than sent to Jakarta. They also undertook to organise a close cooperation with the region's traditional organisations with a view to promoting justice, security and prosperity "for the people of Central Sumatra in particular and for Indonesia in general."[84]

Natsir's experience in Sumatra, which was corroborated by other Masyumi leaders who visited the region frequently, reinforced the party's conviction that outright opposition to the Djuanda government was the right path to follow. However, by refusing to distinguish the actions of the president from those of the prime minister, who was clearly not pursuing the same aims, the party involuntarily precipitated the reorganisation of political life which Sukarno had been seeking to promote over the previous year. At the beginning of August, the president founded a New Life Movement (Gerakan Hidip Baru), designed

---

[83] *Abadi*, 6 July 1956.
[84] Ibid.

Didaerah sudah lebih dahulu dilaksanakan, New Life Movement

Plate 4.4 While Sukarno gesticulates before a few New Life Movement troops, his objectives are already being accomplished in the regions thanks to the collaboration between the army, the people and the regional administrations (*Abadi*, 5 August 1957).

to promote austerity and revive the national spirit, but with the unstated aim also of marginalising political parties. This organisation, which was inspired by an organisation of the same name created by the Japanese during their occupation of Indonesia, was a total failure. It quickly became the butt of political satire in the capital, and the Masyumi press, naturally, had a field day.[85]

Meanwhile, the government endeavoured to implement the commitments which Djuanda had made to the regions. In June, a new

---

[85] Daniel S. Lev, *The Transition to Guided Democracy: Indonesian Politics, 1957–1959* (Ithaca, NY: Cornell University Press, 1966), p. 30.

system of export licences (*bukti export*) was set up which was fairer towards the sectors producing raw materials. Its benefits were largely offset, however, by the effect of galloping inflation, for which the new system itself was partly responsible. In addition, numerous delegations were sent to the regions in order to document the grievances of the local population and regional authorities. In mid-September, the prime minister organised a National Conference (Mujawarah Nasional) in an attempt to find a long-term solution to the conflict between the capital and the regions. This initiative was relatively successful insofar as certain rebel army officers from Sumatra agreed to attend the conference along-side government representatives. The debates gave rise to the adoption of a number of concrete proposals, most of which aimed at reviving the Dwitunggal and at ensuring, through the transformation of the National Council into a sort of senate, that the country's provinces were better represented.[86] These recommendations went unheeded, however. Neither Sukarno nor Hatta wished to work together again, and the nine-member committee charged with examining the possibility of their collaboration was forced to admit that the gap between the two men was now considerable. Another committee was appointed by the National Conference to solve the army's internal problems. It managed to reach a compromise solution which granted officers involved in rebellions since 1956 an amnesty on condition that they would subse-quently make a clear choice between respecting military discipline and pursuing their political activity.

Masyumi, who was now entrenched in a position of resolute opposition to all government measures, endeavoured to minimise, with a certain lack of sincerity, the progress made by the National Con-ference.[87] Others adopted the same attitude towards the prime minis-ter's efforts. President Sukarno seemed rapidly to lose interest in his prime minister's work, while the army chief of staff, General Nasution, viewed the progress made in the discussions concerning the army in a very unfavourable light, as one of the main demands of most of the regional commanders was his resignation.

---

[86] Baladas, *Indonesian Politics 1955–1959*, p. 129.
[87] Boerhanoeddin Harahap, in a speech he gave in Medan, explained, for exam-ple, that his party, which had long called for such an amnesty, regretted that it had not been given a more official status. *Abadi*, 3 October 1957.

On 30 November 1957, two events of a very different nature sparked off further tension within the country and undid all the efforts made at reconciliation. The first of these incidents was an assassination attempt on Sukarno which took place while he was going to his son's school in the Cikini quarter of Jakarta. Several grenades were thrown in his direction, and although the president escaped narrowly with his life, several people were killed, including children. The tragedy in Cikini, far from weakening Sukarno, strengthened his position further. This was due, first of all, to the emergence, in the aftermath of the incident, of a popular belief, reinforced over time by other failed attacks, that the president was invulnerable.[88] Furthermore, the attempt on his life allowed him, with the help of General Nasution, to compromise and undermine a little further those who were opposed to his programme for guided democracy. Shortly after the attack and before the results of the preliminary investigation were made known, news spread that the perpetrators had acted on the orders of Colonel Zulkifli for religious motives and were carried out in collaboration with certain members of Masyumi. Both Lubis and the Masyumi leadership vigorously denied any participation in the affair. On 8 December, the party published a long declaration denouncing the aspersions cast by certain newspapers close to the parties and organisations supporting the president—*Harian Rakjat Berita Minggu* and *Bintang Timur*, amongst others —and called on the military authorities to respect the principle of investigatory confidentiality.[89] During their trial, the accusations made against Lubis were confirmed by the defendants; those concerning Masyumi's involvement, however, remained based on hearsay.[90] These rumours nonetheless convinced Sukarno that a relentless struggle was now underway between himself and Masyumi. The Cikini attack also provided Nasution with the opportunity he was waiting for to put an end to the talks with rebel officers. A month after the incident, he declared that it was now impossible for the government to negotiate with

---

[88] Legge, *Sukarno*, p. 293.

[89] *Abadi*, 9 December 1957.

[90] Lieutenant-Colonel Sukendro in charge of the investigation declared that members of Masyumi and GPII had indeed taken part in the attack but that it was impossible to affirm that those organisations themselves were directly involved in the affair. *Hikmah*, 11 January 1958.

murderers, and the committee appointed by the National Conference to restore order to the army soon ceased all activity.[91]

At the very same time as a new period of tension was being opened in the capital by the attack against the president, the Western New Guinea question triggered a new crisis between Indonesia and its former colonial masters. The recovery of this part of the Indonesian archipelago, which had remained under Dutch sovereignty, was thought by Sukarno to be one of the few causes likely to allow him to mobilise the nation's support. The question was scheduled to be examined once again by the United Nations General Assembly, with the session due to take place at the end of November. In the month leading up to this crucial debate, the president had launched a series of stinging attacks against the Netherlands. Although Masyumi was fully in favour of Irian Barat becoming a part of Indonesia, it denounced on several occasions the president's approach, which consisted in insulting and threatening the Dutch.[92] Here, the party once again shared the position adopted by Mohammad Hatta, who had also distanced himself from Sukarno's comments. On 29 November, the Indonesian motion aimed at obliging the Netherlands to enter into negotiations did not obtain the necessary two-thirds majority in the General Assembly. This failure heightened nationalist sentiments within the organisations supporting the president. On 3 December, the unions close to the PNI and the PKI took hold of most of the major plantations and companies belonging to the Dutch. On 5 December, the minister for justice ordered the deportation of some 46,000 Dutch living in Indonesia. It seemed at this point that Prime Minister Djuanda was overtaken by events; it was the president who appeared to have his hand on the tiller of the state. Djuanda warned his fellow Indonesians about the "ruinous" consequences of these abuses, and had to resign himself to letting the army regain control over the situation.[93] Having ordered them to leave the premises, the army promptly took control of the companies the union members had taken hold of.[94]

---

[91] Baladas, *Indonesian Politics 1955–1959*, p. 131.

[92] See Mohammad Natsir's declarations in this regard. *Abadi*, 9 November 1957.

[93] Lev, *The Transition to Guided Democracy*, p. 34.

[94] As it was out of the question to hand these assets back to their former owners, the military controlled these companies until their nationalisation one year later. This contributed to fostering military officers' economic ambitions, which subsequently flourished under the New Order.

This national hysteria contrasted keenly with the economic pragmatism which Masyumi had been advocating for many years. The party
was now facing the rising tide of an extremely popular movement
which, by cutting the "Gordian knot" of Dutch capitalism, put an end
to years of uncertainty and hesitation.[95] A speech given by Sjafruddin
Prawiranegara on 14 October 1957, during the widespread campaign
against Dutch interests, illustrated how out of touch the party's policy
was with the political mood in the country. The main architect of the
party's economic policy called on his fellow countrymen "not to be
afraid of the return of colonialism if we allow the entry of foreign
capital."[96]

A strictly economic analysis of subsequent events confirms Masyumi's prognosis. The confiscation of Dutch businesses led to chaos,
as the banking system and parts of the trading sector were completely
disrupted. The captains of ships owned by the KPM were given the
order to leave Indonesian territorial waters, leading to the loss over-
night of nearly 80% of the country's tonnage.[97] The events also led
to a diplomatic fiasco which was cruelly summarised by Mohammad
Natsir in Palembang: "the result of these actions … is that Indonesia
is more isolated on the international stage. It has fewer friends, more
enemies, and Irian Barat is still in Dutch hands."[98] For Masyumi's
president, however, this was not the most worrying aspect of the whole
affair. He maintained that the question of Western Irian had "become
the instrument of a wider project" aimed at "breaking our existing
links with Western democracies" in order to "move Indonesia closer to
the Russian bloc". As proof of this devious scheme, Natsir cited the
recent trip to Yugoslavia and Czechoslovakia by a government delegation charged with negotiating the purchase of arms which the United
States had just refused to give to Indonesia. According to him, evidence could also be found in the fact that the Indonesian Communist

---

[95] Feith, *The Decline of Constitutional Democracy in Indonesia*, p. 584.
[96] "Kita haruslah menghilangkan kechawatiran terhadap modal asing".
"Situasi internasional telah berobah sedjak kolonialisme mentjapai puntjak ke-
suburannja. Kita tidak usah takut akan kembalinja kolonialisme apabila kita
mengizinkan masuknja modal2 asing." *Abadi*, 15 October 1957.
[97] Feith, *The Decline of Constitutional Democracy in Indonesia*, p. 585.
[98] An article by Natsir originally published in the newspaper *Batanghari Sembilan*
in Palembang on 29 January 1958, and reproduced by *Abadi* on 1 February 1958.

Party saw "its position within the government guaranteed and ensured", while other organisations were "the victims of all sorts of stratagems designed to eliminate them."[99]

According to Natsir, then, the famous "salami tactic" described ten years earlier by the Hungarian Mathias Rakosia was at work in the corridors of power. This very bleak outlook on the future of the Republic of Indonesia, which presented Sukarno as an instrument being more or less exploited by the Communist Party in its march towards power, could, in many people's eyes, be put down to the personal situation of the party's president when he wrote these lines. It is true to say that by the end of January 1958, Natsir had become a pariah, a rebel trying to justify his cause. The Irian Barat crisis had definitively marginalised the political system which had come into existence in November 1945. The traditional political parties now had the choice between rebelling against the government or adopting a sterile "wait-and-see" policy, the path chosen by the PSII and NU who adhered, like the PNI and the PKI, to the nationalist jingoism whipped up by the president. Although a part of Masyumi's leadership chose the former option, it was not, as such, a political choice. Despite the profound upheaval which had affected Indonesian politics, the party had not changed its stance since 1955 and remained stubbornly attached to its pro-democracy policy. In a way, the party's rebellion was less against the government in Jakarta than it was against the old system of governance embodied by the party.

The PRRI: An Incongruous and Ill-Fated Rebellion

The seizure of Dutch companies and the attendant nationalist agitation gave the regionalist movement a new lease of life. The breakdown of most of the transportation links between the country's islands led the rebel authorities to develop more trade links abroad. In Jakarta, the Masyumi leadership, which had publicly spoken out against the confiscation of Dutch property, was now targeted as part of a campaign of intimidation led by youth organisations close to the PNI and the PKI. As the number of rumours and false accusations targeting the party continued to grow, Mohammad Natsir decided, in April 1957, to go

---

[99] Ibid.

to the state prosecutor in order to inform him of "the totalitarian propaganda methods which are beginning to spread."[100] Over the course of that year, the government brought a significant number of cases against the press: 125 proceedings were taken against journalists, 13 of whom ended up in prison.[101]

The Hijra of the Masyumi Leadership to Sumatra[102]

By the beginning of 1958, the attacks against Masyumi were no longer merely of a political nature. Attempts were made to intimidate Mohammad Natsir, Sjafruddin Prawiranegara and Boerhanoeddin Harahap, all of whom received threats. Rumours concerning their deaths or arrest swept the country; at one stage, Boerhanoeddin, for example, discovered that a part of his family living in Sumatra had come to Jakarta upon hearing of his death.[103] It is difficult to gauge, however, to what extent the Masyumi leaders were really in danger. Neither the contemporary press accounts nor their biographies have revealed any accurate details which could lead one to believe that their lives were in real danger. The violence seems to have been, above all, psychological in nature, but it was especially oppressive to the party leaders given how it contrasted with the atmosphere at the time in Sumatra, a region to which, as we have already seen, they had increasingly organised visits.

In mid-January 1958, several party leaders happened, for various reasons, to find themselves in Padang. Mohammad Natsir came there from Medan where he had attended a ceremony at the Islamic University of North Sumatra in the company of Mohamad Roem,[104] while Boerhanoeddin Harahap accompanied his wife there to visit an old

---

[100] "Teknik propaganda totaliter sudah mulai dilantjarkan sekarang ini." Masyumi's president in this instance was criticising a report in the communist newspaper, *Bintang Timur*, which claimed that Masyumi had 35 million rupiahs in the Bang Dagang Nasional Indonesia. Natsir deplored the fact that despite the party's formal and detailed denials of such rumours, they had spread throughout the capital.

[101] Edward C. Smith, "A History of Newspaper Suppression in Indonesia, 1945–1965", PhD diss., University of Iowa, 1969, quoted in Busjairi, *Boerhanoeddin Harahap Pilar Demokrasi*, p. 141.

[102] The expression used by Masyumi members at the beginning of the New Order.

[103] Busjairi, *Boerhanoeddin Harahap Pilar Demokrasi*, p. 142.

[104] Roem was the rector of the university.

friend.[105] While these explanations for their presence in Padang should perhaps not be taken at face value, it does not seem that there was an organised plan to convene the Masyumi leadership with a view to organising some form of collective action from Sumatra. Their main motivation was to get away from the pernicious atmosphere that reigned in the capital. Sjafruddin Prawiranegara was the only one who openly admitted to having fled the capital; in an open letter to the president, the governor of the Bank of Indonesia explained his actions, saying that "he was not ready to die stupidly, to become the prey of wild beasts in human clothing."[106]

On 9 and 10 January, the Masyumi leadership met in Sungai Dareh, a small locality in Central Sumatra, at the invitation of Lieutenant Colonel Husein, one of the military figures who was already in confrontation with the authorities in Jakarta. It was the party's visceral anti-communism which led its leaders to join sides with the army rebels,[107] a move which was helped, perhaps even prepared for, by the participation of local party branches in the protest movement which had started a few months earlier. In October 1957, regional party figures had participated, in Bukittinggi, in the creation of a Unitary Anticommunist Movement (Gerakan Bersama Anti-Komunisme) led by Colonel Djambek, one of the officers at loggerheads with Jakarta. The organisation was founded in the aftermath of the degradation of the "Rachmat" mosque in Surabaya, allegedly committed by communists, and it was principally designed to give a religious dimension to the struggle against the influence of the PKI. The head of the movement was Muhammad Djamil Djambek, one of the main figures of modernism in the region. Its declared goal was to fight against the growing influence in Indonesia, and particularly within the government, of the "ungodly" (anti-*Tuhan*) ideology.[108]

---

[105] Busjairi, *Boerhanoeddin Harahap Pilar Demokrasi*, pp. 143–4.

[106] "Saja tidak bersedia mati konjol mendjadi mangsa binatang2 buas dalam tubuh manusia". *Abadi*, 23 January 1958.

[107] In his letter to the president, Sjafruddin wrote that from his point of view, there were only two solutions available to restore order in Indonesia: either the immediate formation of a national government provided for by the Constitution or a request for help to Russia and other communist countries, much like the one made by Janos Kadar's government in Hungary. Ibid.

[108] *Abadi*, 8 and 10 October 1957.

In Sungai Dareh, Mohammad Natsir, Sjafruddin Prawiranegara and Boerhanoeddin Harahap met with another figure of civil society, Sumitro Djojohadikusumo, a member of the PSII and former minister for economic affairs, who had left the capital several months previously following accusations of corruption. Also attending the meeting were most of the officers hostile to General Nasution: Djambek, Simbolon, Lubis and Sumual. After a lively debate between the military and non-military participants at the meeting concerning what path the movement should take, the insurgents finally settled on a demand which was already quite old.[109] They considered the procedure used by the president to appoint the Djuanda cabinet to be unconstitutional, and so they called for the immediate resignation of the government and the nomination of Hatta and the Sultan of Yogyakarta as *formateurs*. They announced the formation of a Resistance Council (Dewan Perdjuangan), led by Lieutenant Colonel Husein which would have authority over all the country's insurgent regional councils, in particular Dewan Banteng and Permesta. After this meeting, the Masyumi leaders travelled to Bukittinggi where they met with Mohamad Roem, who had intentionally kept his distance in order to be able to act as a go-between. Natsir sent him back to Jakarta so that he could keep the party leaders there informed of the latest developments.

---

[109] According to accounts of this meeting written later by Masyumi figures or supporters, the non-military participants are said to have vigorously opposed a project to proclaim Sumatra's independence elaborated by the military officers. See, in particular, Busjairi, *Boerhanoeddin Harahap Pilar Demokrasi*, p. 145; Ajip Rosidi, *Syafruddin Prawiranegara Lebih Takut Kepada Allah SWT* (Jakarta: Inti Idayu Pers, 1986), p. 203; Yusril Ihza, "Prolog PRRI dan keterlibatan Natsir", in *Pak Natsir 80 Tahun, buku pertama, Pandangan dan Penilaian Generasi Muda*, ed. Anshary H. Endang Saifuddin and Rais M. Amien (Jakarta: Media Da'wah, 1988), p. 140 ff.

Sjafruddin Prawiranegara's son, Farid, explained that his father and the other Masyumi figures who went to Sungai Dareh had three objectives: to prevent the regionalist movements from becoming separatist movements; to refuse the participation of the PKI in cabinet; and to pursue dialogue with the government. See Anwar Harjono, ed., *Pemikiran dan perjuangan Mohammad Natsir* (Jakarta: Pustaka Firdaus, 1996), p. 144 ff. This interpretation of the meeting in Sungai Dareh was shared by Audrey and George Kahin in *Subversion as Foreign Policy: The Secret Eisenhower and Dulles Debacle in Indonesia* (New York: The New Press, 1995).

During the three weeks following the meeting in Sungai Dareh, there seemed no way out of the deadlock it had created. President Sukarno left Indonesia on 6 January on an official visit which lasted until 16 February. Greatly weakened by the crisis, the Djuanda government held a series of formal and informal meetings in the capital, including with the Masyumi leaders who had remained in Jakarta, in an unsuccessful attempt to find a peaceful solution to the problem. In the meantime, General Nasution began preparations for a military confrontation. On a trip to Sulawesi and Sumatra, he ensured the backing of those officers who had not yet joined the rebellion. The military officers belonging to the rebellion were also convinced that it was now necessary to see the confrontation with Java through to the end. The power they wielded in the regions gave them a taste for more. A profitable trade route was now in place with Singapore and Hong Kong, generating considerable amounts of revenue, both for the military officers and the local population, and the increasing number of declarations made by the United States denouncing the collaboration between President Sukarno and the PKI brought them hope that some foreign assistance might be forthcoming.[110]

On 10 February, Lieutenant Colonel Ahmad Husein sent an ultimatum to the government on behalf of the Dewan Perjuangan. In it, the rebels demanded the resignation of the Djuanda cabinet within five days, the appointment of Hatta and the Sultan of Yogyakarta as *formateurs* and a guarantee that both Parliament and the president— whose role was henceforth to remain strictly within the limits defined by the Constitution—would allow the new government to remain in office until the next elections. The following day, the government rejected these demands, and Nasution ordered the immediate arrest of all the rebel military officers on charges of attempting to assassinate the president and undermining the integrity of the state.[111]

When the ultimatum expired on 15 February, the rebels announced the formation of a Revolutionary Government of the Republic of Indonesia (Pemerintah Revolusioner Republik Indonesia, PRRI). Sjafruddin Prawiranegara was prime minister of this new government, with Boerhanoeddin Harahap as minister for defence and for justice and Soemitro Djojohadikusumo appointed business minister. Three

---

[110] Lev, *The Transition to Guided Democracy*, p. 38.
[111] *Abadi*, 13 February 1958.

rebel military officers, Colonels Simbolon and Warouw and Lieutenant Saleh Lahade, were also given portfolios, and Mohammad Natsir was appointed as the government's spokesman.

If one were to believe the accounts given by the Masyumi leaders who took part in this enterprise, their participation in the revolutionary government happened through a combination of circumstances over which they had very little control. It is true that the document establishing the formation of the PRRI was signed by only one person, Lieutenant Colonel Husein, the head of the Dewan Perdjuangan. Sjafruddin later claimed that Husein had asked him to add his signature to the declaration. The new prime minister refused to do so in order to make it clear who the responsibility for this initiative fell mainly upon.[112] A similar impression is given by the recollections of Boerhanoeddin Harahap, who claimed that a lot of what happened was improvised and that the Masyumi members' half-hearted participation in a symbolic government was dictated mainly by circumstances.[113]

These surprising remarks could be explained by the desire to whitewash an awkward past. However, there does seem to be proof that the Masyumi ministers' reservations towards the enterprise they found themselves involved in were not simply the figment of Boerhanoeddin Harahap's imagination. There is first of all the document proclaiming the existence of the PRRI, which only contains Husein's signature, but more importantly, there is the modest position occupied by Mohammad Natsir in the government. If the Masyumi leaders in Sumatra had wanted their participation in the government to be a meaningful one and if they had wished to carry as much influence as possible within it, they would have given the position of prime minister to the party president: he, much more than they, enjoyed a real stature both in Indonesia and abroad.

The ultimatum issued on 10 February was, then, an attempt at calling the government's bluff, and one whose failure the rebels had

---

[112] Rosidi, *Syafruddin Prawiranegara Lebih Takut Kepada Allah SWT*, p. 212.

[113] "When the PRRI government was formed, I was invited to participate in it. Initially, I was to be minister of home affairs. I was not wholeheartedly in favour as I did not want to become a minister, but in short what mattered most was the existence of a cabinet, which would be the basis for a rival government. Whether this cabinet had any real power or not was not the question. Before its inauguration, the military officers decided to change its composition, without explaining their decision to us." Busjairi, *Boerhanoeddin Harahap Pilar Demokrasi*, p. 153.

not envisaged. Forced into action by the political crisis, they chose, in a manner of speaking, to rekindle the flame of the PDRI which was still smouldering in the region.[114] In 1948, Sjafruddin Prawiranegara had not really contested Sukarno and Hatta's legitimacy; he had simply posed as the guardian of legitimacy, with the intention of ensuring that the procedures provided for by the country's provisional constitution were respected. Some ten years later, the PRRI also considered itself to be the symbol of resistance against the enemy, this time an internal one however, and above all the steadfast defender of constitutional rule. The similarity of the names given to the two provisional governments was not lost either on the country's political class for whom acronyms played an important role. However, unlike the PDRI whose authority was uncontested, the PRRI enjoyed no such legitimacy when its existence was proclaimed, and their only chance of acquiring it would have been through a widespread rebellion in the outer provinces and international recognition of its existence. Fearing that this might materialise, the government in Jakarta reacted rapidly to the challenge to their authority posed by the rebels.

A Military, Political and Diplomatic Defeat

When Sukarno returned to Indonesia on 16 February, intense discussions took place in the corridors of power in order to decide upon the attitude to adopt towards the PRRI. Hatta became the mouthpiece for those who wished, at all costs, to avoid a military intervention; these included Masyumi, the PSI but also the Christian parties. During a meeting he had with the president, Hatta proposed an overall solution to the crisis which involved the transformation of the National Council into a sort of Senate, whose members would be elected directly by the regions, the immediate breaking up of the PRRI accompanied by an amnesty for its members, and finally the formation of a presidential cabinet which he would head.[115] After the rejection of these proposals

---

[114] The Provisional Government of the Republic of Indonesia (Pemerintah Darurat Republik Indonesia) led by Sjafruddin Prawiranegara took on the role of the Indonesian state between December 1948 and July 1949. The president and the republican government were being detained at the time by the Dutch as part of their "second police action". See supra Chapter 2.

[115] Kahin and Kahin, *Subversion as Foreign Policy*, p. 143.

and the collective decision made by Sukarno, Djuanda and Nasution to opt for a military solution to the crisis, Mohammad Hatta refused to participate in any new discussions. From that point, his only role in the ensuing national drama was that of a spectator.

On 21 February, the Indonesian air force launched a large-scale bombardment of Padang and Bukittinggi, the two towns in Sumatra where the rebels had set up their headquarters, and also Manado, the capital of North Sulawesi. On 12 March, the ground offensive began, with Nasution's troops first of all seizing control of Pekanbaru, a strategic locality due to its proximity to the oilfields belonging to the American company, Caltex.[116] On 16 May, Medan fell to government troops, and in mid-April they took over Padang. The theatre of military operations then moved to Sulawesi where, in mid-May, the Indonesian army took control of Gorontalo. Finally, at the end of June, Manado, the last bastion of the PRRI-Permesta rebellion, fell.

The rebels' military defeat was complete after scarcely four months. The speed of this rout revealed not only the rebel troops' lack of preparation, but also the failure of the insurgents' attempts to form alliances both within the country and internationally. In reality, most of the rebel officers, both in Sumatra and in Sulawesi, had not believed that the authorities in Jakarta would be capable of initiating a military confrontation. The proclamation of the PRRI was above all a political act which the insurrectionists were not ready to defend by force. For various reasons, the general uprising in the country's regions which they had counted upon did not materialise. In Sulawesi, the core of the insurrection was made up of members of the Minahasa ethnic group who were Christian and, by and large, well-educated. Since colonial times, the Minahasa constituted a sort of elite, both in public administration and in the service sector, which made it very difficult for them to attract the support of those who were a lot less well-off and somewhat jealous of the Minahas's influence.[117] In Sumatra, the PRRI suffered from the defection of the commander of South Sumatra, Colonel

---

[116] The Indonesian government at the time feared a military intervention by the US marines in Pekanbaru on the pretext of protecting Americans living there. According to Sjafruddin Prawiranegara's son, it was the rebels themselves who refused the American proposal to invade the town. Harjono, ed., *Pemikiran dan perjuangan Mohammad Natsir*, p. 145.

[117] Ibid., p. 152.

Barlian. Though initially supportive of the protest movement, he refused to approve the creation of the revolutionary government, and decided to remain neutral during the conflict. His decision to maintain the region's oilfields under his control deprived the PRRI of an important lever against Jakarta as well as considerable financial resources.

The rebels' cause was also affected by defections from outside Indonesia, notably by the United States. Their decision to act had been, in part, predicated on the significant amount of American support they had received since the autumn of 1957. Concerned by the progress of communism, President Eisenhower, his Secretary of State, John Forest Dulles, and Dulles's brother Allen, director of the CIA, decided at that time to launch what Audrey and George Kahin described as "the most significant American operation since the Second World War".[118] By November 1957, the insurgents had benefitted from a significant delivery of arms. Boats and submarines collected rebel troops in order to bring them to training camps in the American military bases in Okinawa, Saipan and Guam. In December, after the seizure of Dutch assets by the government in Jakarta, the American policy of supporting the insurgents was carried out more openly. Parts of the Third Marine Division were posted off the coast of Sumatra, and this situation naturally encouraged the rebels' military intransigence. On 11 February, the day after the Dewan Perdjuangan had issued its ultimatum to Jakarta, Secretary of State Dulles publicly criticised President Sukarno and tacitly approved of the formation of a rebel government. Moreover, the CIA was convinced that the movement would obtain the support of all those who were at loggerheads with the government, whether they were Moluccan separatists, Darul Islam or even certain sections of the prestigious Siliwangi Division. The fact that most of Indonesia's neighbours did not hide their sympathy towards the rebellion was further evidence for the Americans that it would succeed; indeed some, such as Taiwan, the Philippines, Thailand and Malaysia, were already providing the rebels with assistance. After the proclamation of the PRRI, the United States reinforced their supply of military assistance, notably providing Sulawesi with considerable aerial support.[119] However, they never granted the Sumatran government's more political

---

[118] Kahin and Kahin, *Subversion as Foreign Policy*, p. 8.
[119] Harjono, ed., *Pemikiran dan perjuangan Mohammad Natsir*, p. 167.

requests, namely the recognition of the PRRI as a legitimate authority in Indonesia but also the freezing of the Jakartan government's assets held in American banks.

There were two reasons for the American authorities' about-turn in this affair. Firstly, the rebellion did not live up to the hopes of an emergent movement which would succeed in mobilising support amongst Indonesians living outside of Java who were disillusioned with the government in Jakarta. The insurrection never went beyond three regions in Sumatra—South Sumatra, South Tapanuli and Jambi—and the provinces of Central Sulawesi and North Sulawesi. Secondly, the speed and efficiency of the Jakartan authorities' reaction took the Americans by surprise, and they were disappointed by the feeble resistance offered by the rebels—they abandoned Medan and Padang having scarcely put up a fight. By the end of April 1958, the Americans had appointed a new ambassador in Jakarta, Howard Jones. His mission was to erase the disastrous impression left in the Indonesian capital by the American intervention, and to attempt to preserve some form of influence there for the United States.[120] His endeavours were greeted favourably by Djuanda, Sukarno and Nasution, who were eager to avoid the risk of the Americans landing in Sumatra (a part of the Seventh Fleet was still sailing near its coast). On 20 May, Secretary of State Dulles confirmed his new policy in a declaration condemning any intervention in favour of the rebels, and shortly afterwards a contract for the sale of arms was drawn up with the Indonesian government.[121]

An Incongruous Leap in the Dark

After the uprising's military failure and the loss of American support, the nature of the Masyumi leaders' participation in the PRRI changed. As we have already seen, the course of events over the first half of 1958 could support the theory that party figures played a secondary role in operations, but from mid-1958, it was clearly they who took hold of the movement's reins. They were now considered to be traitors to the

---

[120] The capture in May of an American pilot, A.L. Pope, jeopardised the secrecy of the operation, which had been kept secret from the American public, and thus made it urgent for the American government to repair relations with Jakarta.

[121] Harjono, ed., *Pemikiran dan perjuangan Mohammad Natsir*, p. 183.

nation by the Jakartan authorities, and they engaged upon a hardline policy, demonstrated by their entering into negotiations with movements which identified with Darul Islam in Aceh and Sulawesi. This new strategy gave rise to considerable tension within the rebel government, as the two main regions under its control—North Sumatra and North Sulawesi—contained Christian populations, and a certain number of PRRI officers, including Simbolon, Kawrilarang and Sumual, were Christians.

These army officers, who were supported by Sumitro Djojohadikusumo and Colonel Zulkifli Lubis—both Muslims—tried to oppose this attempt to create new alliances.[122] Despite their misgivings, a de facto collaboration began between what remained of the PRRI's troops and Daud Beureu'eh's men in Aceh as well as Kazar Muzakkar's forces in Sulawesi. The reinforcements provided by Darul Islam had little real effect, however. By the time these alliances were concluded, the authorities in Jakarta had already managed to considerably weaken the Islamic movements by forcing the surrender of a considerable number of their members in Sulawesi and Aceh.[123] By mid-1958, the members of the PRRI had been forced by the offensives carried out by government troops to lead an itinerant existence, more often than not in the jungle, and so no longer represented a real danger to the government in Jakarta.[124]

At the beginning of 1960, in a pathetic display of hubris, the Masyumi leadership tried to re-launch the rebellion through a political act. They managed to convince the members of the Dewan Perdjuangan, as well as a few representatives of the Aceh and Sulawesi movements, of the necessity of transforming the revolutionary government into a new state, and on 8 February 1960, the United Republic of Indonesia (Republik Persatuan Indonesia, RPI) was officially founded. For Natsir and his supporters, this move violated two of their long-held principles.

---

[122] Ibid., p. 202.

[123] In both cases, the government managed to foment dissident movements. In Aceh, it promised to create a "special region" (*Daerah Istimewa*) enjoying a considerable degree of autonomy.

[124] For an account of the roving lifestyle which Mohammad Natsir and his followers led at the time in the jungle, see Audrey R. Kahin, *Islam Nationalism and Democracy: A Political Biography of Mohammad Natsir* (Singapore: NUS Press, 2012), pp. 114–39.

Firstly, it was in flagrant contradiction with the initial aim stated by the movement of avoiding the creation of a separatist state; it also created, contrary to what its official name might lead one to think, a federation of states free to choose their own form of government in accordance with their own specific cultural values.

The United Republic of Indonesia was never more than an illusion. The state's future constitution which was announced at its proclamation was never drafted, and apart from the position of president, which was occupied by Sjafruddin Prawiranegara, no institution was established. There was no indication as to the founders' intentions, apart from the five principles proclaimed on 8 February:

> Faith in a unique God as link
> The preservation of and deference towards fundamental human rights
> A government founded on concertation and democracy
> The federal organisation of society
> Solidarity with all the world's nations[125]

The *Pancasila* as a source of inspiration is obvious here; one could even say it was plagiarised. Three of the five principles—the first, the third and the fifth—are virtually identical to those that appear in the preamble to the 1950 Constitution, and the changes made to the two other principles are not what one could call radical—"social rights" is replaced by "human rights" and "federal" takes the place of "national". On reading the RPI's only institutional credo, its project seems to be a decidedly modest one. The state's religious sources were formulated in a very classical style inspired by the Sanskrit tradition, far from what was openly feared by the Christian military officers at the time of the alliance with Darul Islam. Even though they were no longer, in theory, constrained by Sukarno and the PNI, they could not—or would not—allow the recognition of the primacy of Islam for which they had fought. It was their participation in a rebellion, then, which finally obliged the legalists within the party to recognise the truth which they had long refused to admit, namely that it was impossible to establish an Islamic state in Indonesia without seriously compromising the unity of the country. Although the party members who took part in the rebellion were politically marginalised, they reasserted the hierarchy of

---

[125] Quoted in Badruzzaman, *Boerhanoeddin Harahap Pilar Demokrasi*, pp. 154–5.

values which had always guided their action: democracy, religion and the unity of the nation. The creation of a federal state with the possibility for each of the individual states to freely choose its own mode of government settled once and for all the question of Islam's place in the country's institutions. As Natsir subsequently suggested, this institutional framework opened the possibility for certain regions to recognise Islam as a source of law, while preserving the right for all to choose other sources. It is one of history's ironies that the solution to the deadlock created by the Constituent Assembly debates was formulated far from the country's centres of power, somewhere in the Central Sumatran jungle in front of a scattering of troops.

In the early months of 1961, the rebellion's divisions worsened further. Sumitro Djojohadikusumo had already split from his comrades in Sumatra and now busied himself mainly with sending arms to Sulawesi from Singapore. In an attempt to negotiate the terms of their surrender, Simbolon and Husein founded a "Military Emergency Government" which disavowed the United Republic of Indonesia. Sulawesi was the scene of the movement's first capitulations, with Colonel Kawilarang coming to an agreement at the end of March with the army chiefs of staff on the conditions of a ceasefire. A few days later, he surrendered along with 36,000 men—the bulk of the Permesta forces. In Sumatra, Husein and Simbolon capitulated in July, while Zulkifli Lubis laid down his arms on 18 August, the day after a speech given by Sukarno in which he promised to award an amnesty to all those who returned to the fold of the motherland before 5 October.

At the end of August, deprived of any military support and under threat from the pro-PKI militia who were pursuing them, Sjafruddin Prawiranegara and Boerhanoeddin Harahap gave themselves up to government troops near Padang, having sent a pathetic letter to Nasution in which they announced that "the RPI was ceasing all hostilities". Meanwhile, Natsir remained in hiding for a few more weeks in the company of Colonel Djambek and a handful of loyal followers. For them, the question was no longer to know whether they should give up the game, but how to find a way of surrendering without getting killed. Dahlan Djambek had previously failed in his attempt to do the same: a communist militia, the Organisation of Popular Youth (Organisasi Pemuda Rakjat, OPR), having got wind of where he was supposed to surrender, waited in ambush for him and shot him down. Natsir was luckier, however: he managed to surrender without injury on 25 September and was imprisoned in Padang.[126] In 1962, he was transferred to Jakarta along with the other PRRI leaders.

The PRRI-Permesta movement not only failed, it collapsed. As Barbara S. Harvey very accurately remarked, the rebellion ended up favouring the development of a regime which it had set out to combat as "central authority was enhanced at the expense of local autonomy; radical nationalism supplanted pragmatic moderation, and the influence of Sukarno and the PKI were augmented at the expense of Hatta and the Masjumi."[127] The failure of the enterprise can be put down, in large part, to the rebels' lack of military preparation. This was not just a question of the rebel troops' motivation and military equipment; above all, it was because of their leaders' failure to convince the Indonesian military staff of the legitimacy of their struggle against communism. Most of the country's senior military officers were concerned about the influence of the PKI, but, like Nasution, they deemed it preferable to give their support to Sukarno. It seemed to them more effective to fight communism within the confines of Guided Democracy rather than to defy the president openly, and the rebel military officers adopted the same point of view after the failure of their operation. Their return to the fold of the army took place seamlessly: no charges were pressed against them and most of them maintained their rank. Quite a different fate awaited the civilian members of Masyumi. Their party was now unable to protect them from the wrath of the president, who seized this opportunity to get rid of this troublesome opposition party definitively.

The End of Masyumi

During the early months of 1958, the Masyumi leadership found itself on the horns of a dilemma. The man who had turned the revolutionary movement into a party of government, and who had converted the party to a legalist position which espoused moderation, had just flouted the law and jeopardised the country's unity. Its president's exodus from the capital, along with two of its most important figures, left Masyumi in a quandary. The strategy for opposing Sukarno's plans, to which the

---

[126] Kahin and Kahin, *Subversion as Foreign Policy*, p. 216.
[127] Harvey, *Permesta*, p. 150.

party had remained faithful up until that point, was based on a strict interpretation of the Republic's founding documents. If it did not now firmly condemn the party leaders who were involved in the PRRI, it would lose all credibility.

A Party Reprieved: The Ambivalent Condemnation of the PRRI

In January 1958, the party figures who remained in Jakarta organised a series of meetings in an attempt to find a way out of the crisis. On 1 February, three of Natsir's closest collaborators—Prawoto Mangkusasmito, Faqih Usman and Mohamad Roem—were dispatched to Sumatra to open discussions with the rebels. They informed the insurgents that they had received assurances from the army, via the Sultan of Yogyakarta, that no military operation would be undertaken as long as no dissident state was created.[128]

The ultimatum launched by the Dewan Perjuangan on 10 February was as much the result of the failure of these attempted negotiations as it was a consequence of the inability of the Masyumi leaders involved in the rebellion to keep a hold on the course of events. In response to the ultimatum, the party's vice president Soekiman and its general secretary Yunan Nasution issued a relatively nebulous declaration on behalf of the leadership, stating that: "the current difficulties will not be overcome by encouraging a confrontation between the centre and the regions; on the contrary, equality for both sides must be deepened as much as possible."[129] At this stage of the rebellion, it seems that the attitude adopted by Natsir and his two close supporters had not yet given rise to any wrangling between the Javanese branches and the non-Javanese branches of the party. The Masyumi branch in Yogyakarta, for example, voted a motion on 13 February which was virtually identical to the one published a few days earlier by the South Sumatran branch. The aim of these declarations was to denounce the rumours suggesting a possible proclamation of independence in Sumatra as the work of the PKI and its henchmen who wanted to exacerbate the crisis.[130]

---

[128] Lukman Hakiem, *Perjalanan mencari keadilan dan persatuan: Biografi Dr Anwar Harjono, S.H.* (Jakarta: Media Da'wah, 1993), p. 205.

[129] *Abadi*, 14 February 1958.

[130] *Abadi*, 4 and 13 February 1958.

The reaction by the leadership in Jakarta to the proclamation of the PRRI on 15 February was one of consternation. They eventually decided to maintain the legalist line which they had always stuck to, and the following day, voted a declaration proclaiming the Working Cabinet, the National Council and the Revolutionary Government to be "all three unconstitutional".[131]

The debates which preceded the adoption of this motion brought to light a significant amount of friction within the party. A few days earlier, Mohammad Natsir made it known that he did not wish his name to be associated with Masyumi in order to avoid the party being seen to be involved in the rebellion. Did this mean that he should be removed as president of the party? Most of the party leaders were against this solution, and some even called for an official declaration of support for Natsir's actions; however, others supported by Jusuf Wibisono and Soekiman demanded a firm condemnation of the PRRI. They explained that the revolutionary government had been created without any prior consultation with the Masyumi leadership and, in addition, that it supported an armed uprising, which the party had always denounced.[132] The solution which was agreed upon consisted of a compromise between these two positions: Natsir was neither officially supported nor directly denounced and he remained, in theory, the president of Masyumi and one of its main lieutenants. Prawoto Mangkusasmito, considered to be his spiritual son, was appointed interim president. The party's unity was thus preserved and Soekiman and Jusuf Wibisono abstained from making any public comment on the question.

However, one of the party's secondary figures, A.N. Firdaus, a representative of Persis and a member of the party's governing body, began a vigorous campaign denouncing the suicidal strategy of his colleagues. In March, he unsuccessfully appealed to the party to call an extraordinary sitting of the party congress in order to announce Natsir's deposition. In September, he published an article in *Pos Indonesia*—the successor to *Keng Po*, which had been banned in February—severely criticising the attitude of Kasman Singodimedjo. One of the artisans of the pro-Natsir branch's victory, Singodimedjo, had just been arrested

---

[131] "Kabinet Karya, Dewan Nasional, Pemerintah Revolutionner sama-sama inkonstitutionel." *Abadi*, 17 February 1958.
[132] Soebagijo I.N., *Jusuf Wibisono. Karang di Tengah Gelombang*, p. 233.

for having stated that the responsibility for the regional rebellion lay above all with the government.[133]

All of the party's leaders agreed with the rebels on two points: their call for a new government founded on a collaboration between Sukarno and Hatta; and their denunciation of the communist threat. By focussing all of its propaganda on these two issues, Masyumi succeeded in masking divisions over the following months. It did not manage, however, to shift the balance of power, which was very much weighted against it. The fears nourished by the army, the PNI and NU in relation to the communists' growing influence could have, a few weeks earlier, helped to form a formidable alliance and thus limited considerably the PKI's room for manoeuvre, but the participation of Masyumi leaders in the PRRI rendered such a prospect impossible. Masyumi was now isolated and this was confirmed by the PNI's attempt to create ties with the PKI.[134] The party leaders who had remained in Jakarta did find themselves, however, in complete opposition with their Sumatran colleagues on one point: they denounced any foreign intervention in the ongoing conflict. The rebels, on the other hand, on top of the assistance they received from abroad, called on a number of occasions for international mediation.[135]

Between February 1958 and January 1960, Masyumi adopted a much more low-key role on the political scene. The tone of its leaders' speeches became gradually less aggressive towards the government, and was sometimes even conciliatory, far from the enflamed rhetoric of Natsir's final months as president. The party was still very much part

---

[133] Firdaus described Kasman's speech as a "death trumpet" and accused those who refused to unequivocally condemn the rebels of sacrificing the interests of the *umma*. Lev, *The Transition to Guided Democracy*, p. 137. Firdaus's remarks were quoted by the prosecutor during Kasman's trial a few months later.

[134] In the days following the proclamation of the PRRI, Soekiman's only public intervention was an appeal launched on 23 February to the inhabitants of Java. Masyumi's vice president told them that their island was now at the forefront of the struggle against communism (*Djawa front terdepan dalam hadapi Komunis*). He deplored the fact that in several parts of Java, the local PNI leaders had concluded agreements with the PKI, explaining that the events taking place in the country's outer islands should not distract them from their struggle. *Abadi*, 24 February 1948.

[135] See the radio appeal launched by Sjafruddin Prawiranega. *Abadi*, 26 February 1958.

of the opposition, though: in December 1958, they voted against the government's budget[136] and on several occasions E.Z. Muttaquien, the highly dynamic leader of the party's parliamentary group, took the government to task about its economic policy.[137] But these criticisms were measured rather than systematic, and more importantly, the party's press sometimes took a much more benevolent view of the executive.[138] This restrained and moderate tone also characterised, though to a lesser extent, the party's reaction to the new advances made by President Sukarno.

Between July and November 1958, the National Council issued a series of proposals designed to reduce the role of political parties in favour of the functional groups. In September, it appointed a committee chaired by a trade unionist close to the PNI, Ahem, who took up an idea put forward by General Nasution a few months earlier, namely the revival of the 1945 constitution.[139] Sukarno then tried to get the parties to approve these proposals; the PNI, NU and the PKI, fearing the president would take further, more radical measures, accepted the idea of a "simplification of the political system" and proposed the abolition of small parties, much to the outrage of those concerned.

With Sukarno's ideas receiving an undeniably favourable echo amongst Indonesia's political class, there was once again a debate within Masyumi over what position to adopt. Those leaders who were close to Soekiman proposed a complete overhaul of the party's political strategy. Based on the supposition that a major shift in the balance of power between secular nationalists and the supporters of Islam was not in the offing, Jusuf Wibisono called on the Muslim parties to form a

---

[136] *Abadi*, 20 December 1958.

[137] *Abadi*, 3 November 1958 and 19 March 1959. In August 1958, the Djuanda government undertook wide-ranging monetary reform in an attempt to halt the country's spiralling inflation: the money supply was drastically reduced and the rupiah was devalued by 300%. The hopes raised by these draconian measures were soon dashed, however, as inflation continued and most of the production sectors of the economy which fuelled the country's exports, and thus were the principal source of foreign currency—sugar cane, rubber, tea and coffee—fell by almost 20% between 1957 and 1961.

[138] See, for example, the support provided by one of the leaders of the Yogyakarta branch, Ahmad Basuni, for the government's nationalist economic policies. *Abadi*, 3 December 1959.

[139] Lev, *The Transition to Guided Democracy*, pp. 201–11.

vast anti-communist front with the nationalists. Some concessions had to be made to achieve this, namely accepting the revival of the 1945 Constitution and recognising *Pancasila* as the only state ideology.[140]

The policy advocated by Prawoto and his supporters, and the one which was finally implemented, was essentially a classic Masyumi strategy. They held a series of meetings with leaders of the other Muslim parties, and endeavoured to recreate a united Islamic front which they thought would be capable of having a bearing on events. In January 1959, their efforts seemed to be making progress: a meeting with the representatives of the Muslim League, including NU, the PSII and Perti, produced an alliance based on their common desire to call on the Constituent Assembly for an Islamic foundation for the state.[141] Over the following days, thanks to carefully orchestrated negotiations, this initiative received the support of various Muslim organisations.[142]

It was, finally, left up to Masyumi's ninth congress—which turned out to be the last one—held at the end of April 1959, to decide which of the two strategies to adopt. For the members of the Prawoto branch, this congress was to be, as Yunan Nasution explained, "a simple routine affair";[143] for Soekiman's supporters, it represented their last opportunity for Masyumi to return to the political arena. The confrontation between the two wings took place first of all over the party leadership. Prawoto and his allies won a resounding victory: he was elected president of the party and his closest supporters retained their positions within the party's governing body—these included Fakig Usman, Mohamad Roem, Yunan Nasution, Kasman Singodimedjo and Anwar Harjono. Prawoto's followers were the uncontested winners, then, but they showed themselves to be magnanimous in victory towards their rivals and during the election for vice president, they withdrew their candidates in order to allow Soekiman to be elected to the position.[144]

---

[140] Soekiman's supporters rarely had the opportunity to publish articles in the Masyumi press organs, and so he communicated his proposals through *Pos Indonesia*, 27 September and 5 October 1958. Quoted in Lev, *The Transition to Guided Democracy*, p. 229.

[141] *Abadi*, 5 January 1959.

[142] GPII on 5 January, and Peladjar Islam Indonesia on 7 January. *Abadi*, 6 and 8 January 1959.

[143] *Abadi*, 20 April 1959.

[144] *Abadi*, 28 and 30 April 1959. The newspaper did not give the details of the vote but Jusuf later declared that the election was won by a very small majority.

Jusuf Wibisono, the staunchest opponent to Prawoto's wing, was not even present at the congress, having already relinquished his position within the party's governing body in December 1958.[145]

The Masyumi press only gave a very low-key account of the confrontation during the congress between the two wings. The daily newspapers close to the PKI and the PNI had a field day, however. According to them, the dividing line in the debates was between, on the one hand, the branches from Central Java and East Java who favoured Soekiman's ideas and, on the other, the representatives of West Java and the outer islands who supported the continuation of a policy of opposition.[146] It is impossible to confirm this hypothesis given that there are no precise records of the votes cast. It does seem a little simplistic, however, given that some of Soekiman's supporters, such as Firdaus, were Sumatran, and two of his opponents, Prawato and Kasman, were Javanese.

The Prawato wing's victory was confirmed when the congress came to consider the most recent proposal made by Sukarno, namely the abandonment of the 1950 Provisional Constitution and a return to the 1945 document which conferred far greater powers upon the head of state. This possibility was first touched upon by the government in February 1959, and it was officially presented by the president during an important address pronounced before the Constituent Assembly on 22 April 1959. The speech, entitled "*Res Publica, sekagli lagi* [once more] *Res Publica*" was in essence a virulent attack against the sluggishness of the proceedings in the Assembly. It contained an ultimatum implicitly addressed to the assembly members: if they did not manage to conclude their proceedings before the president's return—Sukarno was due to fly out the following day for a two-month international trip—the 1945 document would be brought into force by decree.[147]

The response of the Masyumi congress to this declaration was conciliatory in tone, but in substance it was very firm. In its resolution, voted on 29 April, the party refers enthusiastically to the return to "the spirit of the 1945 Constitution, founded on peace and national

---

[145] Soebagijo I.N., *Jusuf Wibisono. Karang di Tengah Gelombang*, p. 240.

[146] Lev, *The Transition to Guided Democracy*, p. 252.

[147] As J.D. Legge has highlighted, this tactic consisting in provoking a debate before departing on an official trip was a well-oiled strategy used by the president. Legge, *Sukarno*, p. 302.

unity as well as on the Dwitunggal Sukarno-Hatta." It accordingly called for the immediate formation of a presidential cabinet based on a cooperation between the two men, and aided by excellent and sincere men (*terbaik dan djujur*). Masyumi issued a very firm refusal concerning a return to the Constitution itself, however, and argued for the continuation of the proceedings at the Constituent Assembly which

> Up until now [had] shown nothing to suggest that it [was] unable to find points of agreement between the different groups and movements which exist within society and are the outcome of the elections.[148]

The party was convinced that a united *umma* "constituted a potential capable of stabilising the situation in all areas", and it asked the other Muslim parties to reject the government's programme designed to reinstate the 1945 Constitution, calling for a collaboration with the other democratic parties in order to organise a common struggle for the preservation of democracy in Indonesia.[149]

The confrontation between the Prawoto and Soekiman wings of the party also concerned another internal party problem, namely the status to be accorded to the extraordinary members and the constituent organisations—mainly unions—within Masyumi. Shortly before the congress, Jusuf Wibisono, president of the Union of Muslim Workers of Indonesia (Sarekat Buruh Islam Indonesia, SBII), had informed the party leadership of his desire to break the ties linking the two organisations. This was part of a project aimed at allowing the merger of the country's various Muslim unions, which had previously been suggested by his predecessor, Daljono. When the idea was initially proposed, Jusuf was against it and indeed had harnessed the grassroots support generated by his opposition to seize control of the leadership of the union.[150] However, the political context which the SBII operated in was completely different in 1959. Jusuf Wibisono, faced with an increasingly efficient communist union apparatus, and above all, being aware of the rumours circulating about a possible ban on Masyumi, wished to preserve his organisation's room for manoeuvre.

---

[148] *Abadi*, 30 April 1959.
[149] Ibid.
[150] Soebagijo I.N., *Jusuf Wibisono. Karang di Tengah Gelombang*, p. 131.

There was no doubt an ulterior motive behind this move. Jusuf Wibisono was one of the rare Masyumi leaders to have openly declared himself in favour of an active cooperation with the nationalists within Guided Democracy. He was hostile to the confrontational strategy adopted by his party in the Constituent Assembly, and since 1957 he had consistently expressed his point of view on this issue.[151] In April 1957, he was placed in custody on charges of corruption, but he was released again in March 1958 at the same time as other Masyumi members were entering prison.[152] The official reason given for his release was the prosecution's lack of evidence, but given the circumstances at that time—the state of war meant that the justice system was heavily reliant on the army—it is easy to surmise that he was shown a certain degree of clemency. Finally, let us not forget that he was the only Masyumi member to agree to join the DPR-GR in 1960, as a representative of SBII, which had since been rechristened Gasbindo.[153] Soekiman, who had been given the same opportunity, turned down Sukarno's offer.

The question of SBII's status obliged the congress, once again, to come to a decision on the attitude to be adopted in relation to Guided Democracy. The decision arrived at was consistent with the line set out by Prawoto: the party refused to break its links with the union.[154] However, the party was aware of the threat posed to the "Masyumi family" by the possibility of a ban on the party, and the congress thus declared that it was ready to envisage a change in the extraordinary members' status.

The 1959 congress marked the refusal of the majority of the party delegates to choose between loyalty to its former leaders, on the one hand, and the legalist line which the party had always defended, on the other. Although it was not what you could call a "routine congress", its refusal to reorient the party's strategy did mean that it was not a congress which broke with the past. In his closing speech, Prawoto paid generous homage to his predecessor:

---

[151] Ibid., pp. 205–6.
[152] Ibid., pp. 208–17.
[153] He used the words of the Philippines president, Manuel Quezon, to justify his decision: "my loyalty to my party ends where my loyalty to my country begins." Soebagijo I.N., *Jusuf Wibisono. Karang di Tengah Gelombang*, p. 239.
[154] *Abadi*, 12 May 1959.

You Natsir, wherever you are, will always remain for me a 'spiritual elder' and you can be sure that there will always be a place in your pupil's heart for you.[155]

The congress did, however, reveal a change in the party's tone. Both the speeches given and the resolutions adopted, were devoid of any mention of a Sukarno dictatorship. By the time the congress had opened, it was clear that the PRRI's rebellion was a complete failure which had undermined the party. Its leaders were now under close surveillance by the authorities, and any publicly expressed position which was too virulent could result in immediate arrest. Kasman Singodimedjo had been imprisoned since 5 September 1958 for having pronounced a speech a few days earlier in Magelang considered by the courts to be in support of the rebels.[156] Shortly afterwards, other members of the party's national leadership, such as Udin Sjamsuddin and Mardardi Noor, suffered the same fate, and in October 1958, five party figures from the Masyumi branch in West Java were sent to jail for having published one of their resolutions criticising the presidential "conception". Finally, in several parts of Sumatra and Sulawesi, the party was banned outright by the military authorities.

In this oppressive atmosphere, the Masyumi leadership's opposition became more moderate, though their policies remained substantially the same. They did not rule out a return to the 1945 Constitution, and indeed the party had on a number of occasions, over the previous years posed as an advocate of a strong executive branch. For the party leadership, however, institutional change could only be brought about by a vote in the Constituent Assembly. In fact, they hoped that such a vote would provide them with a chance to reap the rewards of their efforts to restore the unity of Muslim parties, and the Masyumi deputies

---

[155] "Buat aku sendiri kau Natsir, ditempat manapun kau berada, akan tetap mendjadi 'abang-rohaniku' dan pertjajalah, bahwa di-sudut hati adikmu tetap bersedia tempat untukmu." A speech made on 27 April 1959, quoted in S.U. Bajasut, *Alam Fikiran dan Djedjak Perdjuangan Prawoto Mangkusasmito* (Surabaya: Documenta, 1972), p. 76.

[156] Kasman accused a journalist working for the Antara news agency, whom he suspected of having communist sympathies, of having twisted his words. Panitia Peringatan 75 Tahun Kasman, *Kasman Singodimedjo 75 tahun, Hidup itu berjuang* (Jakarta: Bulan Bintang, 1982), p. 221.

began a campaign in the Assembly in an attempt to have the famous Jakarta Charter included in the 1945 document as a preamble. This symbolised for them the prospect of a certain political revival, but once more their hope to control events was an illusory one. Although the unity of political Islam's supporters held firm during the series of votes organised in the Constituent Assembly in early June 1959—almost 200 deputies supported the document which included the Jakarta Charter —at the same time, the nationalist camp, supported by the PKI, also remained solid in their support of the president's programme—260 votes in total—which only mentioned *Pancasila*. As neither side was able to obtain the two-thirds majority required by the Constitution, the Assembly remained in complete deadlock.[157]

In the president's absence—he was still abroad on an official visit —the army once again took the initiative. On 3 June 1959, Nasution outlawed all political activity, ostensibly in order to prevent any risk of confrontations.[158] The parties themselves were not banned, but it was now impossible for them to organise any political gatherings. The press, meanwhile, was invited to censor itself and was to report neither the discussions on the return to the 1945 Constitution, nor the debates in the Assembly opposing the supporters of Islam and Marxism. The army then launched an intense propaganda campaign designed to convince the president to bring the 1945 Constitution into force by decree, and all the parties, except for Masyumi and the PSI, eventually accepted this solution. Wahab Hasbullah, the *rais am* of NU, who had up until that point remained loyal to the "Muslim bloc" in the Constituent Assembly, declared that it was now the only possible alternative to the establishment of a military junta.[159] Sukarno, who was kept up to date regularly on events, had thus attained his objective once again. He held the key to an inextricable deadlock which he had himself

---

[157] See infra, Chapter 5.

[158] According to Daniel Lev, there was a real danger of this happening in Bandung where members of communist youth groups and GPII were spoiling for a fight. Lev, *The Transition to Guided Democracy*, p. 270.

[159] Ibid., p. 273. NU's leadership made no official declaration on the subject, but it had clearly made a choice to favour its political survival over either the defence of democracy or the demand for an Islamic state. Fealy, "Ulama and Politics in Indonesia", Chapter 6, "The Politics of Accommodation, 1957–1962".

partially brought about, although he was genuinely concerned about the increasingly important role played by Nasution during his absence. On 5 July 1959, less than a week after his return, he announced the dissolution of the Constituent Assembly and the return to the 1945 institutions. The Jakarta Charter, instead of being included as a preamble, was simply considered a source of inspiration for the Constitution.

The disappearance of the Constituent Assembly saw Masyumi lose the last forum in which it could still believe that it existed politically. It was absent from cabinet and marginalised in the DPR—whose replacement was expected before long. Its role seemed to be confined to the writing of its own eulogy for various commemorative ceremonies. The speeches made by the party leadership were now resolutely turned towards the past and contained no proposal for the future, which seemed to hold no place for them. On 17 August 1959, on the occasion of the 14th anniversary of independence, Masyumi's Religious Council (Madjelis Sjuro) recalled the sacrifices made for the nation's independence by the heroes of Islam and the attempt by the representatives of the *umma* "on all occasions" to communicate "the divine message".[160] A few days later, at the last meeting of the party's representatives in the Constituent Assembly, Prawoto Mangkusasmito relinquished the duties which he had been entrusted with by the Ninth Congress. He explained that the efforts deployed by the representatives of Muslim parties to see the adoption of a "new Constitution in conformity with the teachings of Islam" had failed because of the president's decision on 5 July, and that consequently the party's representatives were "discharged of the responsibilities which had been conferred upon them by the resolutions passed by the aforementioned congress."[161]

This interpretation, which excludes any consideration of Masyumi's responsibility for the failure of the debates to reach a consensus, was widely advanced in the subsequent writings of the party's leaders. Those accounts drew particular attention to the fact that when the Constituent Assembly was about to be dissolved, Prawoto and Sardjan,

---

[160] "Seruan Madjelis Sjuro Masjumi dalam menghadapi situasi baru dan ulang tahun kemerdekaan ke XIV", in Bajasut, *Alam Fikiran dan Djedjak Perdjuangan Prawoto Mangkusasmito*, p. 452.

[161] Ibid., pp. 92–3.

the leaders of the Masyumi group in the DPR, were on the verge of reaching a compromise with the president of the PNI, Soewirjo, and Prime Minister Djuanda.[162] Worried by the progress being made in the assembly, President Sukarno allegedly decided to act swiftly in order to be able to impose Guided Democracy.

Masyumi appeared to fall into a state of lethargic depression for the remainder of 1959. Its leaders hardly ever ventured outside the capital, and what rare events that were organised, such as the celebration of the 14th anniversary of the party's foundation, invariably harped on about past grandeur.[163] As the weeks went by, the party began to fall apart. Faced with the fast-growing threat of being outlawed, the leadership decided on 8 September to abolish the party's extraordinary member status in order to safeguard the futures of the organisations associated with it. With the party crumbling, SBII decided to leave the umbrella organisation and seize the independence which it had been refused a few months earlier. The particular role which its president, Jusuf Wibisono, played in the political scene gave it reason to hope that a place for it in the country's new political dispensation was possible.[164]

At the end of July 1959, Prawoto informed the president that his party had finally decided to accept the 1945 Constitution. He added that he reserved the right to demand from the executive, both the president and the government, the same respect for the country's institutions.[165] In July, the new government was formed, headed by Sukarno, along with a Supreme Consultative Council (Dewan Pertimbangan Agung), which took the place of the National Council and the National Project Council. The establishment of these new institutions provoked hardly a single reaction from the party. Likewise, the proliferation

---

[162] Anwar Harjono, "Mengenang Pak Sardjan (Alm.) dan beberapa pejuang lainnya", *Media Dakwah*, no. 216, June 1992. A former Muhammadiyah official, Lukman Harun, also informed me that Mohammad Natsir had told him of the existence of such a compromise. Interview, September 1996.

[163] See *Abadi*, 8 November 1959.

[164] This is what SBII's leaders explained during a meeting of the union's sections in Central Java at the beginning of November 1959. SBII announced that it was ready to take part in Indonesian-style socialism and to take advantage of the central role which the government claimed it wished to give workers' movements. *Abadi*, 3 November 1959.

[165] Hakiem, *Perjalanan mencari keadilan dan persatuan*, p. 193.

of pro-Sukarno slogans by the state propaganda machine—Manipol-USDEK and NASAKOM—sparked no debate within the party.[166]

It was only at the end of 1959, when Sukarno began to do away with the remaining vestiges of parliamentary democracy—the parties and Parliament—that Masyumi seemed to rediscover some semblance of life as it undertook to prepare its departure from the political scene with "its flag flying high".[167]

A Ban or a Sabotage? Masyumi, the New Regime's Expiatory Victim

In December 1959, Presidential Decree no. 7 (Penetapan Presiden, Penpres 7/1959) set out a certain number of conditions for the existence of political parties. Henceforth, they had to clearly state their adherence both to the principles of *Pancasila* and to the principles of the political manifesto outlined by the president earlier in the year on 17 August. Moreover, the president reserved the right to abolish any political organisation in opposition to the foundations of the state. In a break with the moderate attitude he had adopted towards the president in the previous months, Prawoto Mangkusasmito's reaction to the decree was a vigorous one. He questioned whether it was in conformity with the 1945 Constitution and explained that it should be considered a "political directive" (*penggarisan kebidjaksanaan*) rather than an "act of law" (*pembinaan hokum*). He went on to remind his readers that his party's ideology was founded on Islam and wondered, disingenuously, if this meant that it was in opposition to the foundations of the state. In a very sarcastic conclusion to his speech, he explained the intransigent attitude of his party through its respect for Sukarno's recommendation,

---

[166] "Manipol" referred to President Sukarno's political manifesto; "USDEK" referred to its foundations (Undang-Undang 45, Sosialisme à la Indonesia, Demokrasi Terpimpin, Ekonomi Terpimpin, Kepribadian Nasional: the 1945 Constitution, Indonesian-style socialism, Guided Democracy, a guided economy and national identity). The acronym NASAKOM (Nasional, Agama, Komunis) signified the alliance between nationalism, religion and communism.

[167] The expression was used by the American ambassador in Jakarta, Howard P. Jones, in his *The Possible Dream* (New York: Hartcourt Brace Jovanovitch, 1971), p. 155.

declared everywhere relentlessly, by inviting us, the Indonesian nation, to adopt the spirit of the royal eagle, the spirit of the buffalo, to 'break through the undergrowth and overturn the obstacle' [the Physical Revolution's slogan], and prevent us from becoming sheep-like men, capable only of bleating.[168]

The change of tone in this declaration was clear. Over the previous two years, Prawoto had conducted a policy focussed on limiting the damage to the party, but now he was rekindling the "Natsirian" spirit to condemn Sukarno's manoeuvre. This speech marked the beginning of a new offensive—the party's final stand—against Guided Democracy. Certain decisions by Sukarno, which heretofore had not provoked any reaction, were now lambasted by the Masyumi deputies in Parliament.[169]

In March 1960, Presidential Decree no. 3/1960 inflicted the final, mortal blow to parliamentary democracy in Indonesia. The Assembly elected in 1955 was dissolved and the president announced its replacement with a new Parliament *"Gotong Royong"*, whose members would be chosen by the president and where representatives of political parties would only hold a minority of seats—129 in total as opposed to 154 for the functional groups. The political class was this time unanimous in its condemnation of the new decree. On 7 March 1960, the day of the last parliamentary session, the Assembly Speaker, Sartono—a member of the PNI—announced that he would refuse to apply the presidential edict. In a moving show of unity, the entire Assembly rose to sing the national anthem, *Indonesia Raya*, and then organised a press conference. The deputies and the press had hardly left the Assembly building, however, before they were subjected to what was known at the time as the "telephone culture" (*kebudajaan tilpon*). This consisted of the military authorities rapidly making it known to the political leaders and the newspaper editors that they had better not take things any further.[170] On 12 March 1960, *Abadi*, ignoring this warning, published Prawoto Mangkusasmito's disillusioned reaction, offering a final illustrated lesson in parliamentary democracy:

---

[168] *Abadi*, 16 January 1960.

[169] The presidential decree no. 2/1959, for example, which had been issued several months previously, was castigated by one of Masyumi's representatives in the Assembly, Blaja Umar. The decree forbade senior civil servants (those who were "group F" civil servants) from joining a political party. *Abadi*, 22 January 1960.

[170] Soebagijo I.N., *Riwayat hidup dan perjuangan H. Zainal Abidin Ahmad* (Jakarta: Pustaka Antara, 1985), p. 101.

In relation to this question of the Assembly, I am no longer an actor in it, neither am I a candidate for such a role.... Concerning the Assembly, I have known up until now, two sorts: parliaments with an opposition and parliaments without an opposition. A parliament without an opposition that I have been able to observe is the People's National Congress in Bejing. When were able to attend a few sessions of this assembly, which counts almost 1,200 members, our experience of it was a rather curious one. As head of the Constituent Assembly's delegation, Mr Wilopo, had the honour of addressing the Congress. The applause during the speech did not seem to indicate that it had received a very warm reception, and we soon understood the reason why. Once he had finished giving his address, the chairman of the session whispered something to Wilopo which amounted to 'You should have applauded, so that they would do the same.'

What we also found rather curious was how voting was carried out. The motion to be voted on was read by the chairman of the session who then asked 'who is in agreement?' The chairman himself had already raised his hand and soon all the members of the assembly followed suit, indicating in this way their agreement. This is how a parliament without opposition functions in the People's Republic of China.... It is of course too early to claim that a similar conception will prevail when the 'DPR—Gotong-Royong' is formed. What we know today are a few signs which can help us to have an idea of how things will turn out.[171]

For Masyumi's president, the main sign he had of what was to come was the fate that his party, a symbol of the opposition to Sukarno's plans, was suffering. The party had already been both removed from cabinet and absent from the various institutions that had been created, and the same was likely to happen to them in the new assembly. Prawoto rebuffed Sukarno's promise to maintain an opposition force, citing the logic of Guided Democracy. It was now impossible to place any trust in the head of state who, a few months earlier, had guaranteed that the dissolution of Parliament was impossible within the framework of the 1945 Constitution. More attached than ever to a conception of democracy inherited from the Enlightenment, Prawoto

---

[171] *Abadi*, 12 March 1960.

concluded with a quotation by Voltaire, addressing one of his political enemies in these terms:

> Sir, I disagree with your opinions and I will combat them everywhere and always, but it happens to be your right to express these opinions and I will also defend it with all my force.[172]

The political class was ready to make one last defiant stand and Masyumi leaders seized this opportunity to set up the Democratic League a few days later. On 25 March, this provisional coalition published a manifesto denouncing as unconstitutional the formation of a new assembly through the nomination of deputies and demanding that the government suspend the measure.[173]

The identities of the 15 representatives who signed this document reflected the motley nature of this new alliance. The party with the most number of signatures was the IPKI, a party largely composed of members of the army. This may have seemed surprising given that, as we have already seen, the military had played a crucial role in the germination of Guided Democracy. It can be explained partially by the divisions which reigned within the military staff, but above all by the desire of numerous officers to put pressure on the president in an attempt to prevent the communists from enjoying too important a role in the new regime. The next most important party was Masyumi with three representatives: Fakih Usman, Anwar Harjono and Mohamad Roem; Prawoto did not sign the manifesto but a few days later he lent his support to it. Two NU leaders were also present—K.H.M. Dachlan and Imron Rosjadi—who both broke with their party's support for the president's line, and there were also two members of the PSI, two from Parkindo and finally, Kasimo, the leader of the Catholic party.

The first real effect created by the Democratic League's manifesto was to attract the wrath of the president. In a declaration made in Tokyo, where he was on visit, Sukarno accused its signatories of ignoring the suffering of the people, supporting the rebels and receiving funds from a foreign power.[174] What worried the president about this initiative was, of course, the participation of the IPKI. Sukarno was

---

[172] Ibid.

[173] *Abadi*, 25 March 1960.

[174] Hakiem, *Perjalanan mencari keadilan dan persatuan*, p. 201.

well aware of a part of the army's open hostility to his desire to include the PKI in his political game plan. In December 1959, military
officers had tried to ban the PKI's congress, and it was only on the
express order of the head of state that it had been able to go ahead.[175]
At that particular point in time, Masyumi and the PSI were no doubt
ready to back a temporary seizure of power by the army, as long as
it was carried out in order to enforce the 1945 Constitution and fight
against the influence of communism. Such a scenario would have
allowed the rehabilitation of their leaders who were involved in the
rebellion led by the PRRI-Permesta, and at the same time would have
provided a solution to the regional crisis. For the army to commit
itself further, however, it needed the assurance that it would have a
united Muslim bloc behind it. The PSII joined the enterprise late in
the day,[176] but once again, though, NU remained loyal to Sukarno; a
few days after the proclamation of the Democratic League, its general
secretary denounced the party members who had signed the famous
declaration.[177] The defection of NU consolidated the support Sukarno
enjoyed from the army chief of staff, General Nasution, who had
already condemned the new organisation. Deprived of the army's protection, the Democratic League spent the next few months involved in
verbal posturing. In March 1961, it was abolished by Sukarno for its
opposition to his Manipol.

By the end of March 1960, consultations had begun on the formation of the new Gotong-Royong Parliament. A preliminary list was
circulated containing the names of those whom the president had
intended to sit in the new assembly. Soekiman's name appeared on
the list as a representative of intellectuals (*cendekiawan*). A few days
later, Soekiman informed the *Antara* news agency of his refusal to take
his seat. He recalled the emotion he felt when singing the national
anthem along with his fellow deputies during the last session of the
elected Parliament, and he even appeared offended that "an attitude

---

[175] Lev, *The Transition to Guided Democracy*, p. 284.

[176] *Abadi*, 6 May 1959.

[177] Certain party leaders within NU, such as the head of the party in North
Sumatra, approved the initiative taken by the Democratic League. *Abadi*, 2 May
1960. The leadership of Anshor, NU's youth organisation, also supported the
league and tried to convince NU to forbid its members from participating in the
DPR-GR. *Abadi*, 2 June 1960.

demonstrating a certain cowardice or even feebleness of spirit" was expected of him.[178] Soekiman's decision, and more importantly the way in which he let it be known publicly, soured definitively his relations with Sukarno, who refused to meet with him thereafter.[179] The unity of Masyumi, then, was more or less preserved up until the end. Jusuf Wibisono was the only party figure to accept a seat in the new assembly: he was appointed as president of the SBII, which had broken all ties with Masyumi during its congress in Semarang in January 1960.[180] He had been removed from the party's governing body in December 1958 and after his appointment he broke off all relations with Masyumi. Within his own union, a number of voices spoke out against the support he had given to Guided Democracy.[181] The other main union within Masyumi, the STII, had also been approached to send a representative to the DPR-GR, but it had refused to do so.[182]

Despite the fact that Masyumi was now isolated on the political landscape, its stubborn refusal to collaborate with the new regime was in danger of ruining the new path of political consensus. At the beginning of July 1960, Sukarno decided to resort to the techniques he had honed the previous year. On 22 June 1960, he had the government issue a commencement order for Presidential Decree 7/59, authorising certain political parties to be banned. On 22 July, he summoned leaders representing the PSI and Masyumi to the presidential palace and gave them a week to prepare their defence. They were to explain whether or not their party came within the provisions of Article 9 of the decree.[183] This strange procedure was designed to give a vague semblance of legality to an authoritarian decision. The article in question had obviously been formulated with the intention of outlawing Masyumi. It provided for the dissolution of a party for two reasons: first for having a programme which violated the principles and goals of the state; and second for taking part in the support for a rebellion

---

[178] *Abadi*, 8 April 1960. Quoted in Dr. H Amir Hamzah, eds., *Wawasan Politik seorang muslim patriot: Dr. Soekiman Wirjosandjojo, 1898–1974* (Malang: YP2LM, Malang, 1984), pp. 301–3.
[179] Soebagijo I.N., *Jusuf Wibisono. Karang di Tengah Gelombang*, p. 238.
[180] Ibid., p. 240.
[181] See infra, Chapter 6.
[182] *Abadi*, 28 April 1960.
[183] *Abadi*, 22 July 1960.

either through direct participation or assistance provided by its leaders or through the party's refusal to denounce its members' actions.[184]

On 28 July, Prawoto Mangkusasmito and Yunan Nasution on behalf of Masyumi, and Sutan Sjahrir, Subadio Sastrosatomo and Murad for the PSI returned to the palace to deliver their written reply to the question they had been asked a week previously. The meeting only lasted seven minutes; no debate took place, although the exchanges were cordial and courteous. Sukarno enquired about each man's family, and then explained that their arguments would be examined during a meeting scheduled for this purpose on 30 July.[185] The documents which the Masyumi leaders handed over to the president gave a negative answer to the question asked. For them, Masyumi did not fall within the category of parties targeted by Article 9 of Presidential Decree 7/59. The party's fundamental orientation was not "in contradiction with the principles and goals of the state, as those principles and goals, which were defined by the preamble to the 1945 Constitution, were part of the teachings of Islam."[186] Consequently, "a programme which violates the principles and objectives of the state would be in contradiction with the principles and objectives of the party itself."[187] Concerning the accusations of Masyumi's involvement in a rebellion, the party leaders considered that they could not stand. When the presidential decree was published, the party leadership had been elected by the congress held in April 1959, and contained no member who had participated in an uprising or provided assistance to the rebels. Moreover, Masyumi had been banned since September 1958 in the country's troubled regions— Tapanuli, West Sumatra, Riau, North Sulawesi and Central Sulawesi— and these branches had sent no delegates to the party's ninth congress. Finally, in a declaration made on 17 February 1958, the party had clearly condemned the ongoing rebellions.

The party leadership had, then, submitted itself in good grace to the president's demands. It must have been aware, however, that by avoiding the central question concerning its refusal to denounce the party leaders who were implicated in the rebellion, it had failed to

---

[184] Quoted in Hakiem, *Perjalanan mencari keadilan dan persatuan*, p. 208.

[185] *Abadi*, 29 July 1960.

[186] Hakiem, *Perjalanan mencari keadilan dan persatuan*, p. 208. In his biography of Yunan Nasution (pp. 259–60), Badruzzaman Busyairi provides a version very close to the answer given to the president.

[187] Ibid.

exonerate the party from its responsibility under the terms of the new legal provision. Rather than contesting outright the legitimacy of the enquiry that Masyumi was subject to, which would after all have been in accordance with the party's stance over the previous two years, its leaders seemed to hope that they could convince the judicial authorities of their innocence. This legalist attitude had already led Prawoto to criticise the commencement order for Penpres 7/59 on the basis that it did not mention the consultation by the Supreme Court which had been initially intended.[188] For this same reason, he welcomed with satisfaction, on 30 July, the decision made by the Presidential Council (Badan Pembantu) to transfer the investigation files on Masyumi and the PSI to the Supreme Court, and declared himself to be confident that the court would be willing to examine the legality of the decree in question.[189] By respecting the measures taken against them, they endeavoured to maintain their ability to contest the legality of these measures before a court. The Masyumi leadership continued to stick with this line of defence despite the fact that it was clearly not working.

The reason for this failure was that Sukarno's attack on Masyumi was primarily a political act. This was demonstrated by the timing of his announcement outlawing the two parties. The speech which he pronounced every year on 17 August, on the event of the anniversary of independence, had provided in previous years the perfect occasion on which to define the ideology of Guided Democracy, and as expected, the address he gave in 1960 followed the same pattern. In a marathon speech overflowing with Anglicisms, the president announced the renewal of a "revolutionary logic" (*logika revolusioner*). According to him, Indonesia had gone through three phases since its emancipation from the colonial yoke: firstly, a period between 1945 and 1950 of "Physical Revolution"; then from 1950 to 1955, a "periode survival [*sic*]"; and finally from 1955 to the present day, a "periode investment [*sic*]". By this final period, he meant material investment, intellectual investment and investment in terms of "human skills", which together were supposed to contribute to a "socialist construction". This "construction" was to be pursued in a favourable political atmosphere "*suasana-politik-favourable*". Liberal democracy, however, clearly did not lend itself to creating such an atmosphere, and so it had to be "entirely destroyed"

---

[188] *Abadi*, 14 July 1960.
[189] *Abadi*, 1 August 1960.

(*bongkar sama sekali*). The construction of a "building of Indonesian socialism" (*gedung sosialisme Indonesia*) gave rise to "squawking by the inhabitants of the old house—the PRRI-Permesta, the RPI, a league here, a league there, a newspaper here, a newspaper there, an essay here, an essay there."[190]

For Sukarno, there were two attitudes to the Revolution which were equally blameworthy. One of them consisted in saying, like Kartosuwirjo had at the foundation of his Islamic state, that it had failed, while the other maintained that it was over. The head of state explained that the Revolution, which had in fact by then been going on at that point for 15 years, could very well last for another 25, 35 or even 45 years before reaching its end. It was because of this that the reorganisation of the party system, initiated by the December 1959 decree, was necessary. The aim of the new regulation was to clarify the political situation, as it was supposed to eliminate "counter-revolutionary parties". It did not, however, create a dictatorship; rather, it was "the application of a universal principle, a principle common to all countries according to which those in authority cannot be expected to authorise the existence of forces who want to destroy the state" and put "in danger the safeguard and the pursuit of the Revolution". It was on this basis "that after having consulted with the Supreme Court", Sukarno announced a measure which was more striking in its form than in its substance, namely that he had given Masyumi and the PSI a month to wind down their organisations. If the two parties had not complied with the demand within this time, they would be outlawed.[191]

The Masyumi leadership had already learnt the news of the president's decision to ban the party before he pronounced his speech. Very early the same day, at twenty past five in the morning, a letter had arrived in the party's headquarters from Sukarno's chief of staff, containing "Presidential Decision no. 200 of the year 1960" (Keputusan Presiden Republik Indonesia N° 200 Tahun 1960) that ordered the dissolution of Masyumi

> ...on the basis that this organisation (this party) has organised a revolt, because its leaders participated in a rebellion christened 'Revolutionary Government of the Republic of Indonesia' or 'United

---

[190] *Abadi*, 18 August 1960.
[191] Ibid.

Republic of Indonesia' or, at the very least, have given their assistance to a rebellion and that this organisation (this party) has not
officially denounced the actions of the members of its leadership
concerned.[192]

The Masyumi leadership's communiqué which accompanied the publication of the presidential document in *Abadi* merely indicated, in a
slightly ambiguous manner, that within the one-month deadline, the
measures "deemed necessary" (*jang dianggap perlu*) would be taken,
without specifying by whom. As soon as he received the president's
decision, Prawoto Mangkusasmito entered into a series of consultations
in order to determine the best attitude to adopt. He charged two law
firms with examining what legal recourse was open to it and took
soundings from within but also from outside the Masyumi leadership.[193]

A consensus quickly emerged that it would be better to comply
with the presidential order and avoid the party being officially outlawed. There was a fear within the party, it must be said, that a ban
would lead to the confiscation of the party's assets and the arrest of its
leaders. In addition, Prawoto and other senior party leaders seemed to
be hopeful that, despite all the evidence to the contrary, a court case
could succeed. On 13 September 1960, four days before the ultimatum
expired, the Masyumi leadership sent a letter to the president in which
they informed him of the dissolution of the party, "including its
Madjelis Sjuro and the Muslimat sections".[194] This short missive was accompanied by a memorandum from Prawoto Mangkusasmito, affirming
that his party's decision was in line with the party's steadfast tradition
of respect for the law, and he warned the president that he intended to
file a legal action before the courts in Jakarta as a "simple citizen".[195]

On 11 October 1960, the court's presiding judge, in his ruling on
Prawoto's petition, declared that the question was not within his juris-
diction to decide, and Masyumi subsequently disappeared definitively
from the political scene.[196] It would scarcely be an exaggeration to say
that the dissolution of the party was the one issue on which President
Sukarno and the Masyumi leadership had agreed on for several years.

---

[192] Ibid.
[193] Busjairi, *Catatan Perjuangan H.M. Yunan Nasution*, p. 262.
[194] Bajasut, *Alam Fikiran dan Djedjak Perdjuangan Prawoto Mangkusasmito*, p. 160.
[195] Ibid., pp. 161–3.
[196] Busjairi, *Catatan Perjuangan H.M. Yunan Nasution*, p. 263.

Strangely enough, the Masyumi leaders insisted on a number of occasions that their party's disappearance was a voluntary one. They spoke out vigorously against PKI allegations in the early 1960s claiming that they had been outlawed.[197] This insistence could be explained, in the aftermath of the party's dissolution, by the desire to protect its former members from repressive government measures. Why, though, 30 years later, was there still a stubborn insistency to establish a subtle distinction between being banned and disbanding under the threat of an impending ban?

My interpretation of this attitude is that it is indicative of the extent to which the party was traumatised by the participation of Natsir and his close supporters in the PRRI rebellion. This act constituted a violation of the law and was in defiance of the authority of the state. The fact that it had been committed in defence of a genuine form of democracy did not take anything away from its shamefulness, especially in a country where, until recently, the official conception of the exercise of power was closer to Guided Democracy than to the 1950s parliamentary regime. For Sukarno, on the other hand, it is easy to understand his interest in seeing the modernist party dismantle itself. By doing this, Masyumi was implicitly recognising its errors, and as it was one of the symbols of a parliamentary democracy incapable of functioning, it was also carrying with it the burden of the sins of this regime. By voluntarily abandoning the political scene, it was finally adhering to the consensus sought by the president, which was to be the foundation of a new Indonesia.

---

[197] See, in particular, Hakiem, *Perjalanan mencari keadilan dan persatuan*, p. 212; Bajasut, *Alam Fikiran dan Djedjak Perdjuangan Prawoto Mangkusasmito*, p. 159, Busjairi, *Catatan Perjuangan H.M. Yunan Nasution*, p. 264.

CHAPTER FIVE

Governing in the Name of Islam

The Pitfalls of a Self-Evident Notion

Today the issue of an Islamic state is a protean notion which cannot be readily systemised, and this is true for the entire Muslim world. The plan to found a state on the principles of Islam has too often been considered both by its opponents and proponents as a blueprint whose details are self-evident. This consensus surrounding what form an Islamic state should take has for many years constituted a rallying point in much the same way that Marxism did for a long time, dividing opinion on the question into two distinct groups which remain resolutely closed to all discussion.

In the case of Masyumi, the notion of an Islamic state was by turns, and sometimes simultaneously, a slogan, a myth, a programme and a reality. The debate surrounding *Negara Islam* in Indonesia has long been a problematic one littered with pitfalls. This was already the case in the 1950s when Masyumi attempted to mark itself out from both the secularist ideals of the nationalists and the destructive fundamentalism of Darul Islam; it remains the case today due to the radicalisation of Islamists' demands as well as the disparate nature of Islam in Indonesia, where religious divides often overlap with ethnic and economic divisions. It is an issue in which Western researchers can also easily become ensnared, as their cultural background can often lead them to believe that an Islamic state is the only alternative that exists to a democratic state. Finally, it should be remembered that the Indonesian term "Negara" is another possible source of confusion as it can be understood to refer to a state, a country or, in certain cases, a nation. The meaning of this word is ambiguous in Indonesian, unlike in English where the term "Islamic state" does not mean the same as "Islamic nation" or "Islamic country".

There are two major advantages to presenting an Islamic state as a self-evident notion. It allows one to suggest the sacred nature of such an entity and also to do away with the delicate task of providing a clear definition of such an entity. It is no doubt for this reason that Masyumi when elaborating its ideology never clearly defined in a founding document what constituted an Islamic state; this notion was gradually outlined at its party conferences and in the writings of its leaders. It also evolved over time in response to different events which often shaped the party's leaders' ideas. Given this mutability of Masyumi's concept of an Islamic state, it is difficult to comprehend this ideology without looking at its source and the context in which it was articulated. A speech made by Isa Anshary during the insurrection against the Dutch colonial power and a contribution by Zainal Abidin to a debate in the Constituent Assembly could be considered just as representative of Masyumi as an address by Jusuf Wibisono during the election campaign of 1955, despite the fact that the tone of the speeches, the chosen topics and the examples used to illustrate their points were very different and, in some cases, contradictory.

It is hardly surprising, then, that researchers looking to summarise Masyumi's policy in a few sentences should have so often come up with inconsistent conclusions which were often not mutually compatible. Some such as George McTurnan Kahin focussed on the moderate nature of Masyumi's aspirations, while others, such as Baladas Ghosal, considered Masyumi to be radical and intransigent.[1] It would, therefore, be illusory, perhaps even disingenuous, to claim to be able to provide a precise and coherent vision of Masyumi's ideal of an Islamic state. On the contrary, what this chapter proposes to acquaint the reader with is the chaotic and sometimes contradictory evolution of Masyumi's political ideology, starting with the first articles by its future leaders in the 1930s, and taking us up to the failed attempt by the Constituent Assembly in the late 1950s to establish a new constitution.

---

[1] Baladas Ghoshal, *Indonesian Politics, 1955–1959: The Emergence of Guided Democracy* (Calcutta: K.P. Bagchi & Company, 1982), pp. 46–7; George McTurnan Kahin, *Nationalism and Revolution in Indonesia* (Ithaca, NY: Cornell University Press, 1952), p. 305.

The Nationalist Perspective on an Islamic State

In order to understand the debate surrounding the notion of an Islamic state, which dominated the Indonesian political landscape from the proclamation of independence in 1945 until the banning of Masyumi in 1960, it is necessary to situate it in the context of the country's nationalist movement. The future leaders of Masyumi at this time were influenced by two different forces which shaped their political theory. They took part, alongside other representatives of the reformist movement, in a heated debate with secular nationalists concerning the foundation upon which to build an Indonesian national identity. The notion of a *Negara Islam*, which they presented as a natural and even necessary framework for a Muslim nation, placed them in opposition to secularists. At this stage, the debate was not concerned with which form of government to choose, nor was it about the nature of the country's institutions; it was rather about whether Islam should be recognised as a constitutive element of Indonesian society. The question, then, was not if Islam could constitute the cornerstone of an independent state, but instead to know if the future state of Indonesia could be built upon an ideological foundation which did not include Islam.

The main arguments put forward by Islamists were of a religious nature, tending to establish an organic link between a Muslim nation and an Islamic state. Islam being "a complete way of life", a good Muslim could only look to Islam as the source of his political inspiration. Naturally, this sense of a sacred duty left no room for compromise; it endured throughout Masyumi's history, though the political intransigence which it gave rise to was surmounted momentarily by a more pragmatic attitude, linked no doubt to the necessity to look for democratic approval and the compromises attendant upon the exercise of power. However, it came back to the fore again at the end of the 1950s during the debates in the Constituent Assembly.

Towards the end of the 1930s, however, the future leaders of the party went beyond the strictly religious aspect of the debate about the future Indonesian state. In response to the proposals made by secular nationalists, they eventually became convinced of the danger of their own intransigence. By refusing to envisage any other alternative to the recognition of the primacy of Islam in the future state, certain Muslim leaders could see that they were excluding themselves from any involvement in the building of that state. Breaking away from the isolationism of their mentors, Mohammed Natsir and his peers, both in their roles as political representatives and in their writings, contributed to a broad exchange of ideas aimed at defining the conditions under which a democracy would be established in Indonesia, and by doing so paved the way for the participation of Islamists in parliament.

Independence through Islam and for Islam

The future leaders of Masyumi arrived on the political scene at the beginning of the 1930s at a time when the leaders of the Muslim community were growing worried about their loss of influence in Indonesian society. Their initial cause was not the fight against the Dutch colonial power but rather the opposition towards those who were fighting for an independent Indonesia in which Islam would only have a secondary role. For Islamists, then, the main concern was not political independence, which was in danger of leading to a secularised state. Their desire was, first and foremost, to establish a society with the requisite conditions for the flourishing of Islam, and also to remind members of the Indonesian Muslim community of their duty towards the Almighty.

Continuing the work carried out by Sarekat Islam and Muhammadiyah for the defence of the Muslim community in the Dutch East Indies, the writings and speeches of the future Masyumi leaders had three aims which were intimately linked: to convince their fellow countrymen of the greatness of Muslim civilisation, to bring about a renewal of the teaching of Islam and to underline the unifying role of Mohammad's religion in the establishment of the Indonesian nation.

As we have already seen, the reformist movement in general was characterised by a harkening back to a golden age of Islam.[2] At the beginning of the 1930s, Mohammad Natsir, under various pen-names (Mu'azzin, IS., Spectator, A. Moechlis), devoted a considerable amount of his writings to this topic. In a series of articles which appeared between June 1936 and March 1937 in *Pedoman Majarakat* and *Pandji Islam*, he endeavoured to show the importance of Islam in the development of modern science. In "Islam and Culture", he set out to describe the main features of Muslim culture, insisting on the scientific projects carried out during the high-point of the Caliphate, its role in the transmission of knowledge from the Ancient Greek and Roman worlds

---

[2] See supra, Chapter 1.

to Renaissance Europe through its contributions in a variety of areas ranging from astronomy to medicine.[3] A few months later, Natsir paid homage to the early 19th-century Muslim philosopher, Ibnu Makawaih, whose introspective method may have influenced Schopenhauer.[4] In *Pedoman Masjarakat*, he also mentioned Abu Nasar Al-Farabi from the 10th century, who was one of the forefathers of political economics, according to Natsir. Finally, in an attempt to refute some of Islam's critics who claimed that it had invented nothing, Natsir, in *Pandji Islam*, cited, amongst others, the 11th-century polymath Ibn al-Haytham, the inventor of the camera obscura and, by extension, the precursor of modern photography.[5] These examples which Natsir used to illustrate the wealth of Islamic civilisation had another purpose, however, which was to show Muslims that there was a pressing need for them to develop the same critical frame of mind (*ruh intiqad*) which enabled illustrious Muslim scientists to question and surpass the accepted knowledge of their day.

Convincing fellow Muslims of the greatness of Muslim civilisation and making Islam the cornerstone of a new national consciousness, however, would only make sense if the population was educated in the Muslim faith. Yet despite the best efforts of the Muhammadiyah movement over the previous 20 years, there was still a long way to go before this would be the case. Islam was taught in *pesantren* in a way which prevented it from opening up to modern society. The vast majority of the future Indonesian elite attended schools which were based on the Dutch model where everything was designed to keep Islam at bay, as the development of a secularist nationalist movement later showed. Mohammed Natsir was so taken aback by the lack of religious knowledge of his secondary school classmates that he actually dedicated his first books to them. *Komt tot het gebed* (*Come and Pray*) (1930) was taken from classes he gave at Jalan Jawa School in Bandburg; *Guden Regels uit den Qu'ran* (*The Golden Rules of the Koran*) (1932) provided a selection of Koranic verses translated into Dutch; and finally, *Het Vasten* (*Fasting*) spoke of the main religious practices of Islam, in particular the practice of fasting. At the same time as he was writing these

---

[3] *Pedoman Masjarakat*, June 1936, in *Capita Selecta*, vol. 1 (Bandung: I.W. Van Hoeve, n.d.), pp. 3–9.

[4] "Ibnu Maskawah", *Pedoman Masjarakat*, February 1937, ibid., pp. 10–2.

[5] "Ibnu Sina", *Pedoman Masyarakat*, February 1937, "Djedjak Islam dalam kebudajaan", *Pandji Islam*, 1937, ibid., pp. 13–8, 24–9.

books, Natsir began his teaching career. He began modestly, teaching a few classes in 1930 while still at secondary school, and after completing a training programme organised by the government, he became the head of the Islamic Educational Committee (Komite Pendidikan Islam) and the Islamic Educational Institute which had been founded by Persatuan Islam.[6] In 1934, he published a short pamphlet entitled "The Ideology of Islamic Education", which contained a summary of his convictions concerning the teaching of Islam.

In this work advocating Muslim education, Natsir wished most of all to persuade his fellow Muslims of the necessity of a way of teaching Islam which was open to the modern world. Following a classical rhetorical formula used by Muslim reformists and frequently adopted by Masyumi, his pamphlet makes use of two types of arguments. The first takes its inspiration from secular examples by contrasting, for example, the model used by Japan, which managed to achieve quick and sustained development by providing access to education to as many people as possible, with the model used by Spain which was overtaken by most of its rivals because of its lack of investment in the educational field. The second argument made reference to a religious obligation based on verse 104 of the Al Imran surah.[7] For Natsir, the Holy Book advocated a form of teaching which was open to the modern world in general and to the latest developments from the West in particular. A significant part of the future Masyumi leader's work in the 1930s was devoted to this struggle for the development of education which he considered to be a necessary precondition for Islamic nationalism to exist.[8] His decision to become a teacher and by so doing to refuse a

---

[6] This institution offered classes for preschool up to secondary school. Ajip Rosidi, *M. Natsir, sebuah biografi*, vol. 1 (Jakarta: Girimukti Pasaka, 1990), pp. 169–70.

[7] "And let there be [arising] from you a nation inviting to [all that is] good, enjoining what is right and forbidding what is wrong, for those will be the successful." *Koran* (III, 104). Natsir concluded from this verse that the Indonesia *umma* had to recruit a group entrusted with the education of children so that this task "would not be delegated to those who do not have the same ideas, the same education, the same faith or the same religion as us." Mohammad Natsir, "Ideologi didikan Islam", in *Capita Selecta*, vol. 1, pp. 53–61.

[8] In "Sekolah Tinggi Islam" ("Islamic Higher School"), published in 1938 (*Capita Selecta*, vol. 1, pp. 66–79), Natsir deplored the absence of an Islamic university in Indonesia. This, he argued, encouraged the creation of an elite who were more interested in the West.

scholarship which would have enabled him to pursue his studies in the Netherlands typifies the third of the future Majumists' aims: to enable Islam to unify the disparate elements of Indonesian nationalism.

Natsir, who was very worried about the loss of the influence of Islam amongst Indonesia's elite, became convinced very early on that the religious neutrality encouraged by a section of the nationalist movement was merely the first step in a de-Islamification programme endorsed by the colonial government for the benefit of the Christian community. This conviction led him to become involved in the ongoing debate between progressive Muslims and nationalists since the end of the 1920s.[9] This wide-ranging debate had begun with a confrontation between Sukarno and Haji Agus Salim, who was soon to be joined by Ahmad Hassan and his followers from Persatuan Islam (Persis), Fachroeddin, Moenawar Chalil and Mohammad Natsir.

Secular nationalists refused to accept Islam as the principle inspiration for their struggle for three main reasons. They considered first of all that their religion was unable to respond to the problems of the modern world, and as such they even deemed it to be partly responsible for the 300-year-long colonisation of Indonesia. According to them, a strong independent nation could only be constituted by using the Western model of government which had managed to confine religion to the private sphere and to the field of religious worship. This point of view was confirmed by what were, in their eyes, positive examples of dynamic countries with secular governments, such as Turkey, Persia and Egypt. The second argument put forward was a little more particular to Indonesia and was based on the idea that it would be impossible for Islam to claim to have a unifying role in the Dutch East Indies, given that the country was home to minority groups of other religious faiths, namely Christianity, Buddhism and Animism. The final argument advanced was that the history of the Indonesian people's struggle for independence had shown that religious organisations had

---

[9] Several works have looked at the major stages of this debate: in 1936, Persatuan Islam published under the title *Soerat-soerat Islam dari Ende* letters sent by Sukarno, who was in exile at the time, to Achman Hassan; in 1968, the Association of Islamic Education in Padang (Jajasan pendidikan Islam, Padang) published a collection entitled *M. Natsir versus Soekarno: The Unity of Religion and State* (*Persatuan agama dengan negara*), containing around 10 texts written by the future president of Masyumi, most of which can be found in *Capita Selecta*.

failed to obtain any significant concessions from the Dutch colonial power despite their best attempts over two decades.[10]

The leaders of Persatuan Islam countered the arguments of secularist nationalists with their own line of reasoning, which appeared in numerous articles published mainly in *Pembela Islam, Pandji Islam* and *Al-Lisan*. In 1941, the figurehead of Persatuan Islam, Ahmad Hassan, gave a brief summary of the party's arguments in a book entitled *Islam and Nationalism* (*Islam dan Kebangsaan*). The premise posited by the advocates of Islamic nationalism was that independence did not constitute an end in itself, but rather that it could only be envisaged as a means towards another goal, namely the recognition of Islamic norms. The freedom of the nation could only flourish if it was exercised as part of a struggle for Islam, and so to venerate a secularist form of nationalism would be akin to polytheism (*shirk*).[11]

Mohammad Natsir, in his opposition to Sukarno, used the same type of reasoning when listing the religious entitlements one could enjoy in a "neutral" state: freedom of religion, the possibility of paying the *zakat*, legislation on marriage and divorce which was adapted to people's religions. His argument was that the same guarantees would be available under any form of government, including colonial government.[12] This argument was no doubt intended to provoke secularists, but the message was clear: the nationalists could count on the support of the Muslim community's leaders only if they recognised Islam's primordial role. The theorists belonging to Persis refuted the nationalists' argument that an Islamic state was impossible because of the presence of other religions in the country, insisting that they would refuse to give in to the "law of the minority".[13] The nationalists

---

[10] Dr. Muh. Ridwan Lubis, *Pemikiran Sukarno tentang Islam* (Jakarta: C.V. Haji Masagung, 1992), pp. 136–48.

[11] See the declarations made to this effect by Fachroeddin al-Kahiri, in *Pembela Islam*, no. 59, March 1933, quoted by Howard Federspiel, *Persatuan Islam: Islamic Reform in Twentieth Century Indonesia* (Ithaca, NY: Cornell University, 1970), p. 87.

[12] *Pandji Islam*, 20 February 1939. Quoted in Deliar Noer, *The Modernist Muslim Movement in Indonesia, 1900–1942* (Kuala Lumpur: Oxford University Press, 1973 [2nd edition, 1978]), p. 278.

[13] Ahmad Hassan asked the question: "Is it appropriate for us to dismiss the importance of a majority of 90% because of a minority of 10%? Would such an agreement be fair?" *Islam dan Kebangsaan*, p. 41. Quoted in Federspiel, *Persatuan Islam*, p. 88.

were given to understand that they were bad Muslims and were in-different to the danger that some of their fellow Muslims "could re-nounce their faith and abandon Islam for Christianity, Buddhism or Theosophy."[14] The political representatives who defended an Islamic state reminded those Muslims who had forgotten their religious duty —those who, according to Natsir, were guilty of "dishonesty towards Islam"[15]—of the role played by Muslim organisations in the first steps of the struggle for national independence; Natsir referred to the "willing sacrifices" whose debt needed to be repaid. When Sukarno and his sup-porters pointed out that Sarekat Islam had failed in its attempt to bring together the Indonesian people, Natsir maintained that this was the fault of those who had founded rival groups. Those groups, by trying to replace a commonly held set of values, Islam, with a purportedly original culture which harkened back to the great empires that once dominated the archipelago, had succeeded in distancing the people from their leaders.

Mohammad Natsir was not the only future prominent Masyumi member to use such arguments. A speech given by Kasman Singodi-medjo in 1925, shortly after he became a member of the leadership of the Jong Islamieten Bond used one of those arguments among its cen-tral themes. He heavily criticised the lack of communication between the members of the "intellectual group" (*golonga intelektuil*) and the people. He blamed this failing on linguistic problems (most of the organisations' members communicated in Dutch), and on a difference in lifestyles (most intellectuals had adopted a European lifestyle), but also on the lack of a set of common cultural references. The references used by "some" came from a classical Javanese culture, glorifying the era of the great Hindu kingdoms like Majapahit. He went on to ex-plain that these references made sense "for people like us who have the time to study these legends and wonderful stories" but they did not serve any purpose if you wanted to "recreate a bond with the people." Islam, on the other hand, constituted the natural bedrock for a "senti-ment of fraternity" amongst the people and should therefore become

---

[14] *Pandji Islam*, 30 January 1939. Quoted in Noer, *The Modernist Muslim Move-ment in Indonesia, 1900–1942*, p. 276.
[15] Ibid.

the cornerstone on which to build national unity.[16] The desire of the secular nationalists to rebuild a national culture without referring directly to Islam also influenced the choice of Soekiman Wirjosandjojo, future president of the Masyumi party, to leave the nationalist movement and join the ranks of Sarekat Islam. As he explained in an article published in 1930, he had been particularly shocked by a tendency amongst some of his friends in the nationalist movement to liken the exile of nationalists in Digul (one of the main internment camps set up by the Dutch) to the pilgrimage to Mecca.[17]

Initially, the involvement of the future members of the Masyumi party in the debate concerning the construction of the new Indonesian nation was essentially based on defending the place of Islam. Their disagreement with the leaders of the nationalist movement on the issue of Indonesia's Muslim identity, which they considered to be under threat, succeeded in acquiring them a certain prominence in the small circle of progressive Islamist activists, however. Their involvement was not merely based on a simple reminder of the religious obligations behoving their fellow Muslims; by carrying on the work of their illustrious predecessors, H.O.S. Tjokroaminoto and Agus Salim, they also wished to create the conditions which would allow their fellow countrymen to adhere to their political ideal.

Political Activism and the Beginnings of a Muslim Democracy

The debate within the Muslim community about how an Islamic state should be established in Indonesia was dominated by the central question of whether it should be an obligation or a choice. For a part of the community, the debate remained an academic one insofar as they never considered an alternative to demanding an Islamic state. Ahmad Hassan, for example, adamantly maintained his posture as the voice of truth and never attempted to go beyond it in order to adopt the

---

[16] A speech given by Kasman to the JIB, Panitia Peringatan 75 Tahun Kasman, *Kasman Singodimedjo 75 tahun, Hidup itu berjuang* (Jakarta: Bulan Bintang), pp. 434–48.

[17] "Tentangan tehadap agama Islam", *Pembela Islam*, October 1930, in Sukiman Wiryosanjoyo, *Wawasan politik seorang muslim patriot, Dr. Soekiman Wirjosandjojo, 1898–1974*, ed. Amir Hamzah (Jakarta: YP2LPM, 1984), pp. 15–22.

more difficult role of proposing compromise solutions. Others, however, wanted to engage in a more concrete debate on the question, and as a result, became politically active.

From its foundation in 1945, Masyumi welcomed both camps within its ranks, but there quickly appeared a distinction between party members who confined themselves to a strictly religious role within the religious council of the party (the *Madjelis Sjuro*, literally the consultative council) on the one hand, and those who by taking on an executive role in the party found themselves having to make political decisions on a regular basis, on the other. This distribution of roles no doubt reflected the aptitudes and preferences of the various members within the party, but more importantly, it was also evidence of a fundamental difference between how each group regarded their religion. For one group, it was an inherent truth which must remain immutable, and for the other it was a set of general principles whose application could be adapted to the present day.

The beginnings of this separation between the strictly religious roles and the political roles within the party were apparent well before independence. It could be seen in the involvement of certain members (Soekiman, Natsir, Sjafruddin and Prawiranegara) in political parties (the PSII, Permi and PII) and not merely in associations like Persis.[18] It could also be seen in their writings; unlike Ahmad Hassan, Fachroeddin or Moenawar Chalil, the future members of the Masyumi executive did not limit themselves to participating in the debate on nationalism and its religious nature. Soekiman and Natsir in particular devoted a significant part of their writings to more political and more pragmatic questions concerning how to emancipate their nation. This led them to reflect upon democracy, its manifestations and its evolution in the West, and on its compatibility with the substrata of Indonesian society, in particular with Islam. These reflections, which were not carried out exclusively with reference to religion, allowed Masyumi to sketch out what would become, a few years later, the main objective of its project, namely the construction of a Muslim democracy.

Of the four theorists within Persis involved in the debate with nationalists, Mohammad Natsir was the only one to pursue a political career. In a series of articles which appeared between December 1938

---

[18] See supra Chapter 1.

and December 1939, he analysed the fate of indirect rule, a policy which a section of the nationalist movement in the Volksraad had called for. This People's Council created by the Dutch in 1917 saw both its powers and in its number of representatives increase in 1927. From then on, it was no longer simply a consultative body; a series of texts in specific areas had to obtain its express approval in order to become law. In addition, the number of representatives in the Council rose from 38 to 60. However, though Indonesians still only made up half of the assembly members and the two separate electoral colleges (Indonesian and European) which elected the assembly's representatives totalled barely 2,000 members. This meant that the nationalists had no chance of obtaining a majority. Given this balance of power and the repressive policy carried out by the East Indies government since 1929, some parties decided to enter into a policy of cooperating with the colonial power.

The largest party to engage in this policy of cooperation with the Dutch East Indies government was Parindra (the Greater Indonesia Party). It was founded in 1935 through the merging of Budi Utomo with a few intellectual clubs and non-Javanese organisations favourable towards nationalism. In 1936, a section of the PSII, which up until then had been resolutely opposed to any cooperation, declared itself in favour of limited cooperation with the colonial power, which involved its participation in the Volksraad. In September of the same year, the "Sutardo petition" was presented by Parindra to the Volksraad, where it received a majority. The petition proposed a motion calling for the organisation of a conference to discuss the details of institutional change in the colony, which would eventually lead to an autonomous government that would remain part of the Kingdom of the Netherlands. The Sutardo petition was rapidly opposed by the government of the Dutch East Indies, and the Dutch government formally rejected it in November 1938.

In his analysis of this event, Natsir showed a clear capacity for political observation. Natsir the realist and man of action eclipsed Natsir the theorist of Islamic nationalism; he saw that the refusal to accept the Sutardjo petition by the Netherlands tolled the death knell for the hopes of those who favoured an egalitarian partnership between the Dutch metropolis and its colony. It was at the same time, however, a salutary event as it brought to an end the crisis within the nationalist movement which had begun with the attempt by some to collaborate with the colonial power in an attempt to gain influence and advance their aims. As Natsir said, what appeared to be a failure would turn out, on the contrary, to awaken a sense of unity in the national consciousness so long as one respected the maxim of the French sociologist Gustave Le Bon that "our opinion of things changes with the unfolding of events... [and] only a fool has unchanging opinions."[19]

The pragmatism Natsir showed in his choice of quotation is reflected in all his articles on the Sutardjo petition. It is evidence of his refusal to enclose himself in a struggle for an Islamic cause removed from political realities. The future president of Masyumi, much more so than his colleagues of Persatuan Islam, wished to be seen as a pragmatist. He pointed out that the absence of any prospect of evolution in the status of the Dutch East Indies put the survival of the colony in danger, as Snouck Hurgronje had predicted in the 19th century.[20] The Dutch government's opposition to change, the most recent example of which being their refusal to accept the Sutardjo petition, paved the way for the uniting of all nationalist currents within GAPI (Gabungan Politik Indonesia, Indonesian Political Union), the broad nationalist grouping of the late 1930s. In addition, nationalist aspirations were about to receive a boost with the outbreak of war in the West.[21] When German troops invaded the Netherlands a little over a year after the failure of the Sutardjo petition, Natsir urged the authorities to immediately recognise the inevitability of Indonesian independence, enjoining them not to "miss the bus" so as not to lose the support of a nation of 60 million inhabitants.[22] The question of Islam was for the moment not on the agenda; Natsir's demands were made in the name of a higher cause of freedom and in the name of modernity, which necessarily implied democracy. His vision for the future of his country—which involved obtaining first, independence and democracy, and then pursuing the recognition of Islamic values—naturally opened up numerous possibilities for cooperation with the defenders of secular nationalism.[23]

---

[19] Quoted in French in the article with a translation in Indonesian. "Diselitar Petisi Sutardjo", *Pandji Islam*, December 1938. In *Capita Selecta*, vol. 1, p. 237.

[20] "Aliran assosiasi Exit", *Pandji Islam*, January 1939, ibid., p. 244.

[21] "Parlemen Indonesia", *Pandji Islam*, October–December 1939, ibid., pp. 253–78.

[22] *Pandji Islam*, May 1941, ibid., pp. 356–60.

[23] He had already affirmed this in February 1939. *Pandji Islam*, 6 February 1939; Noer, *The Modernist Muslim Movement in Indonesia, 1900–1942*, p. 277.

At the same time, Soekiman, who started out in the nationalist movement, was also changing his ideas about Indonesian independence; contrary to Natsir, however, he was moving closer to Islam. Initially schooled in Western political culture, he also turned in the late 1930s to the founding texts of Islam as a source for his political ideas. In an article in 1939 denouncing the absence of a true parliament in Indonesia, for example, he reminded readers of the importance of this institution in the history of democracies such as England and the Netherlands, and also in the Koran. He quoted the Al-Imran Surah,[24] drawing from it the conclusion that the "form of government recommended by Islam was to be founded on consultation" and that an Islamic government was to speak and debate with the community about all things that concerned the fate of the community."[25]

Well before independence then, the foundations of what was to become the political ideology of Masyumi had already been laid by a few of its future members. What set these members apart was that they strove simultaneously to achieve the ideals both of Islam and of democratic independence. During the period of Japanese occupation which followed the outbreak of the Second World War, they were obliged to keep a low profile. The new occupiers of Indonesia adopted a strategy which intended to rely on the specific religious demands made by representatives of the Muslim community in order to counter the more political demands of the secular nationalists. When Masyumi was founded by the Japanese, it showed no interest in theorising about an Islamic state. Apart from a personal initiative which came very late in the day from a member of the Office of Religious Affairs (Shumbu), Haji Suzuki, to convince the Japanese military command to establish an Islamic state in Java, the Japanese did not have the slightest idea about the place Islam could occupy in an independent Indonesian state.[26]

---

[24] "So by mercy from Allah, [O Muhammad], you were lenient with them. And if you had been rude [in speech] and harsh in heart, they would have disbanded from about you. So pardon them and ask forgiveness for them and consult them in the matter. And when you have decided, then rely upon Allah. Indeed, Allah loves those who rely [upon Him]." *Koran* (III, 159).

[25] "Indonesia berparlement", *Adil*, 30 December 1939, 6 and 13 January 1940, in Wiryosanjoyo, *Wawasan politik seorang muslim patriot*, pp. 40–55.

[26] Harry J. Benda, *The Crescent and the Rising Sun: Indonesian Islam under the Japanese Occupation 1942–1945* (The Hague and Bandung: W. Van Hoeve Ltd, 1958), p. 286n67.

The influence of this period on the elaboration of the future Muslim party's political ideology was nonetheless important. By allowing the Islamic leaders to build a solid network throughout the entire archipelago, the Japanese created the necessary conditions to allow the establishment of a broad social movement, which the party was later to consider as the conditions for the construction of a *Negara Islam*.[27]

The Prospect of a Democratic Islamic State: Cautious Silence and Moderate Proposals

The party which was founded in November 1945 was very much at the crossroads of Indonesian Islam. Its mission was to represent on the political stage the disparate ambitions of a community composed of traditionalists, modernisers and neo-fundamentalists. As one of several political organisations in a parliamentary democracy, Masyumi had to go in search of as big a democratic mandate as possible, and these constraints were to weigh heavily on the party when it came to defining its political manifesto. Although it was a central topic, the question of the sources of Islamic law was a very sensitive one due to the difficulty in getting modernisers and traditionalists to agree. In addition, it became dangerous to even mention the possibility of an Islamic state because of the fear that the non-Muslim parts of the country would break away. From its foundation in 1945 until the announcement of the results of the Legislative and Constituent Assembly elections, Masyumi was aware that power was within its reach. It elaborated its political identity, then, with the constant idea of maintaining a consensus which was thought to guarantee victory in the elections. Over the years, in order to maintain public goodwill, Masyumi developed an institutional project which was both cautious and moderate in tone. The form of government that it called for was mainly inspired by Western democracies, and no reference was made to the place to be occupied in it by Islamic norms. This ideology for the main part originated in the influence held by a small group of moderate and progressive party leaders who followed Natsir's example and attempted to respond to the challenge posed by nationalists.

---

[27] See infra, Chapter 6.

Progressive Secularisation until 1956

Between 1945 and 1950, the prevailing party objective which over-shadowed any other was the preservation of Indonesian unity. It was a subject which was to dominate the resolutions adopted at the foundation of the party as well as during the first three party congresses, and it always appeared before considerations about the role of Islam. In the founding statutes of 1945, the first objective to be defined was "the consolidation of the Republic of Indonesia's sovereignty and of Islam" (*Menegakkan kedaulatan Repoeblik Indonesia dan Agama Islam*). In Solon in February 1946, emphasis was put on the principle of "100% independence" along with "the desire to remove Indonesian citizenship from any inhabitant who hindered the cause of independence." In Yogyakarta in 1947 and in Madiun in 1948, diplomatic questions linked to the struggle for independence made up the main part of the programmes adopted. The strictly religious aspect of the party's aspirations seemed at this time to take a backseat, and any mention of it was made with great caution.

The various documents which were adopted during the foundation of Masyumi and its successive party congresses (statutes, programmes and various motions) contained only one clear demand for an Islamic state (*Negara Islam*). This was contained in the domestic policy programme adopted in the Solo congress in February 1946. Instead of the term *Negara Islam*, however, which was used by party members themselves very often, vaguer terms were employed, thus opening up the possibility of compromise. The founding statutes in November 1946, for example, announced Masyumi's goal as "the achievement of the ideals of Islam within the state structure". The first party congress, held in February 1946 in Solo, adopted a formula which was often subsequently echoed: "a Republic of Indonesia founded on Islam". The programme published at the Solo congress spelled out the party's desire to "achieve the ideals of Islam within the state structure in order to build a state founded on popular sovereignty and a society based on the principles of justice found in the teachings of Islam."[28] The next four party congresses used virtually the exact same wording.

The party's priority, then, was the defence of the Republic of Indonesia, as it was defined in the Constitution of 1945. Masyumi

---

[28] Domestic policy programme adopted at the Solo congress, February 1946.

thus accepted not to challenge the compromise which had been hammered out on the subject of *Pancasila* during the debates in the Komite Nasional Indonesia Pusat (KNIP). The resolutions adopted by the party reflected the fact that it now adhered to this state ideology, even if the wording of the resolutions often had an Islamic flavour to them. The party's statutes of 1945 identified amongst its objectives the goal of "organising the life of the people on the principles of faith, devotion, humanistic social conscience, fraternity and equality before the law, in accordance with the teachings of Islam." This assimilation of the principles of *Pancasila* into the party objectives was not merely a temporary consequence of the revolutionary period, however. They were regularly adopted in successive programmes at party congresses, and they appeared again in the party statutes after their revision in 1952.[29] The new statutes this time had an additional section—an "exposition" (*Tafsir Azas*)—which was a good indication of how far the party members had come since the Jakarta Charter of June 1945 envisaging "the obligation for Muslims to apply Islamic law". Masyumi's ideal was now "a state imbued with divine grace...in which Muslims would have the possibility of organising the private as well as the social aspects of their lives in accordance with the teachings and the laws of Islam."[30] The replacement of the word "obligation" with the word "possibility" reflected the evolution of Masyumi's policy in the field of religion during the first years of the Revolution. The recognition of the role of Islam in public life could not be imposed from on high, but had to emerge as a conviction from a long and patient process of persuasion which would be carried out within a democratic state.[31]

After 1950, the Republic of Indonesia was no longer in danger of seeing its sovereignty hampered by its former colonial masters, but Masyumi's doctrine remained nonetheless consensual. This was due to

---

[29] The domestic policy programme approved by the 1946 congress proposed to "reinforce and enhance the cornerstones of the Republic of Indonesia's Constitution, namely faith in a unique God, a fair and civilised humanity, the unity of Indonesia, and a democratic system which operates wisely through consultation and representation so as to allow the creation of an Islamic society and an Islamic state." As we have already seen, this was the only official party document which made clear reference to an Islamic state, which appears here to be the consequence of the application of the principles of *Pancasila* rather than as a precondition for their acceptance.

[30] *Tafsir-Azas*, 1952.

[31] See supra Chapter 2.

another danger the party faced but which came, this time, from within. The proclamation by Kartosuwirjo in August 1949 of his "Negara Islam Indonesia" led to cautious responses by party leaders. Any demand in relation to an Islamic state formulated too heavy-handedly was in danger of leading to an association in people's minds between Masyumi and the rebellion in West Java. In 1952, during the sixth party congress, when new party statutes were drawn up, the "goals of the party" included the "application, in accordance with the divine scheme of things, of the teachings and the law of Islam in the life of every man, of society and of the Republic of Indonesia." However, wary of any tendentious interpretation of this aim, the party specified in the official commentary accompanying the new statutes that these goals would be pursued "in accordance with the rule of law and according to the normal procedures of a democratic country", and reminded the public that "unrest would only lead to the wasting of material and spiritual forces, and no responsibility could be taken for it [by Masyumi]."[32]

As the elections approached, the timidity of Masyumi's claims was even more obvious. The party's press made no bones about playing the Muslim card,[33] but the party itself seemed to want to hush up its Islamic identity as well as any demands which were of a religious nature. No reference to religion was made in the various documents (general resolutions, urgency programme and election manifesto) adopted during the conference of December 1954 in Surabaya. More surprising again was the fact that the only election manifesto published by the party entitled "Voting for Masyumi means..." ("Memilih Majumi Berarti") contained no reference to religion whatsoever. This was all the more unusual given that it was one of the most comprehensive manifestos to be published by the party: it set out 55 institutional, social and economic reforms which the party pledged itself to carry out if they were elected. There was only one single mention of the term "Islam" or allusion to the Muslim religion.[34] On the question of the form of government, the party's proposals stressed solely the democratic nature of the new state. It was a manifesto which could have been drawn up by a number of non-religious parties including the

---

[32] *Tafsir-Azas Angggaran Dasar*, 1952.

[33] We could cite the cover of *Hikmah* published on 24 September 1955, which reproduced the *fatwah* issued by the Congress of Medanese Ulamas making it obligatory to vote for the Muslim party.

[34] See Chapter 6.

Memilih Masjumi

BERARTI : . . . .

* Menegakkan Negara-hukum jang mendjamin keselamatan djiwa dan harta benda semua penduduk Indonesia, baik warga negara maupun asing.
* Mempertahankan azas2 musjawarat dan demokrasi sebagai dasar negara.
* Mendjamin kemerdekaan beragama serta menjuburkan keragaman hidup antara pemeluk agama.
* Mendjamin hak-hak asasi manusia.
* Mendjamin hak-hak kaum, wanita dalam lapangan politik, ekonomi dan sosial jang sederadjat-seimbang dengan kaum prija, sesuai dengan sifat, pembawaan dan kewadjiban masing2 djenis.
* Mengatur produksi dan distribusi barang2 menurut rentjana untuk kebahagiaan rakjat seluas-luasnja.
* Melarang adanja monopoli oleh perusahaan2 partikelir.
* Menjalurkan konkurensi jang terbatas dibawah pengawasan pemerintah kearah jang membangun (konstruktif).
* Menjesuaikan politik harga dan upah dengan keadaan perekonomian umum dalam negeri.
* Membangunkan berbagai matjam koperasi untuk memperkokoh ekonomi nasional.
* Menasionalisasi perusahaan2 vital menurut rentjana tertentu, dimana pelaksanaannja didjalankan mengingat keadaan dan keuangan negara.
* Mejelenggarakan industrialisasi setjepat-tjepatnja.
* Membuka kesempatan bekerdja jang luas bagi rakjat.
* Membebaskan Indonesia sebanjak2nja dari import hasil2 perindustrian dari luar negeri.
* Mengakui kaum tani sebagai faktor sosial dan politik jang menstabilisasi.
* Memperkuat kedudukan kaum tani dengan mempertinggi kesedjahteraannja.
* Memberikan perlindungan, bantuan moreel dan materieel kepada kaum tani.
* Membantras pemerasan kaum tani oleh golongan manapun djuga.
* Menghapuskan sistim tuan-tanah menurut hukum.
* Menghapuskan beban2 jang tidak adil atas kaum tani.
* Membagikan tanah kepada kaum tani.
* Membangun berbagai matjam koperasi dari oleh dan untuk kaum tani.
* Mendjamin upah jang lajak buat pekerdja2 tani dengan menentukan upah terendah.
* Mengakui pentingnja kaum nelajan dalam masjarakat Indonesia, jang negerinja terdiri atas kepulauan.
* Memperbaiki kedudukan kaum nelajan.
* Membantu dan melindungi koperasi2 kaum nelajan.
* Menjediakan pendidikan serta latihan2 untuk mempertinggi ketjakapan kaum nelajan.
* Memperluas modernisasi alat2 penangkapan ikan.
* Memperluas dan memodernisasikan pelabuhan2 perikanan laut.
* Mendjamin pendjualan ikan jang menguntungkan kaum nelajan dan masjarakat.
* Menjesuaikan undang2 agraria dari djaman kolonial dengan kepentingan masjarakat.
* Mengarahkan politik agraria kepada usaha2 untuk melipat-gandakan produksi pertanian, terutama bahan makanan.
* Mengakui pentingnja golongan middenstand Indonesia, dilihat dari sudut politik dan sosial.
* Membuka djalan2 bagi middenstand Indonesia, untuk berkembang dan memperkuat masjarakat kedudukannja.
* Mengadakan undang2 bank jang mengatur sjarat2 buat bank2, baik nasional maupun asing.
* Mengadakan undang2 pengawasan atas politik kredit bank2.
* Menjederhanakan sistim padjak jang ada.
* Mendjaga, agar pemungutan padjak tidak melampaui kekuatan masjarakat.
* Mengarahkan politik padjak kepada pembagian jang adil dari pendapatan dan kekajaan nasional dan kepada memadjukan perusahan2 nasional.
* Mengganti sedapat2nja padjak tidak langsung dengan padjak langsung.
* Membebaskan sebanjak mungkin barang2 keperluan rakjat banjak dari pemungutan padjak.
* Mendjamin ketentuan hidup jang lajak bagi kaum buruh.
* Mendjaga dan mempertahankan ditjapainja kegembiraan bekerdja dan perdamaian kerdja dalam proses produksi.
* Mengadakan atau menjempurnakan perundang-undangan pertanggungan nasional dan perundang-udangan perburuhan.
* Memberikan hak „Upah sosial" (social loon) kepada kaum buruh disamping upah kerdjanja (arbeidsloon).
* Memungkinkan kaum buruh hidup berkeluarga dan mengadakan simpanan buat hari tua mereka.
* Mendjamin upah jang tjukup buat hidup jang lajak, bagi siburuh, isterinja dan anak2nja.
* Mengakui adanja serikat2 buruh.

Plate 5.1 An example of the secularisation of campaign themes: The 1955 electoral programme.

PSI and even the PNI. Neither the press at the time nor the leaders of Masyumi, nor even the observers and historians of this period, ever commented upon or even pointed out this inconsistency, despite the fact that it was evidence of the complexity of the role of Islam in Masyumi's ideology. The party's project was certainly underpinned by religion—most of the measures proposed had been justified by virtue of their connection with the teachings of Islam—but with elections looming, it seemed neither prudent nor necessary to draw attention to that fact. In short, Masyumi's programme was as much a reflection of their fears as it was of the party's underlying beliefs. Its aim was to create a socially-minded democracy inspired by the West which would be in harmony with the party members' religious beliefs. This would allow religious convictions to flourish and as a result, they would no longer need to be represented politically.

The Party's Institutional Project: The Experience of Western Democracies

From its very first party congress, Masyumi busied itself in outlining the legal framework for the new state which it wished to see appear, and from the outset, parliamentary democracy was clearly affirmed as the favoured option. The requirement of a parliament elected directly by universal suffrage was amongst the resolutions adopted at the first congress in Solo (1946), and adopted again later at subsequent congresses. The religious justification for this choice was clearly outlined in the "struggle programme" (*Program perjuangan*) adopted in 1952, which stated that "the form of government which was most compatible with the democratic principles of Islam was the Republic."

In order to "protect the interests of the regions", the struggle programme provided for legislative power to be held jointly by the two houses of parliament. There was to be an assembly composed of members whose number for each region depended on the size of its population, and a senate in which every region was represented by the same number of members.[35] Concerning the executive branch, the party made an unusual proposal: it suggested that there should be "a presidential regime in which the president, as head of the executive, should be accountable before the People's Representatives' Assembly".[36]

---

[35] "Struggle Programme", 1952.
[36] Ibid.

This choice was a move away from the American form of government which had obviously inspired their choice of a legislative model. However, it can be explained by the vicissitudes of Indonesian politics, namely the ambiguous status of President Sukarno since the adoption of the 1950 Constitution, which needed to be clarified. The 1950 document allowed for no presidential accountability before Parliament and accorded Sukarno very limited powers in theory; yet it also permitted him to exercise considerable influence over political life. The party, then, intended to rebuild a new balance of powers by virtue of this rather unusual institutional innovation (a head of state can normally never be held accountable before the legislature except in cases of impeachment).

The type of election to be used for the head of state was never specified in the "struggle programme", nor did it appear in any other document published by Masyumi. It seems in any case unlikely, given his accountability before Parliament, that the president was to be elected by universal suffrage. Concerning the person of the president himself, the 1946 congress adopted a resolution stipulating that he had to be of Indonesian origin, without specifying if the fact of being born Indonesian was sufficient; this had the potential to be problematic, in particular for those with Chinese ancestry. The resolution also required the head of state to be "Muslim in religion and in spirit" (*beragama dan berdjiwa islam*). This second requirement was taken from the long-standing demand made by the representatives of Islam, which was regularly formulated during the debates in 1945. As it was in contradiction with the moderating tendency present in the subsequent official programmes, however, it fell out of favour after 1946.[37]

The second point mentioned in the proposals for the new constitution made by Masyumi concerned the guarantees to be made to the inhabitants of Indonesia. A rule of law founded on the teachings of Islam, which the party wished to see established, would allow them to ensure the "spiritual and material protection of the whole population of Indonesia, be they citizens or foreigners."[38] Human rights were to

---

[37] Moreover, the expression used seems to indicate that the mere fact of belonging to the Muslim religion (*beragama islam*) was not enough; the head of state also had to have the soul (*berdjiwa*) of a Muslim. This was a shot across the bows of the secular nationalists: the vast majority of them were Muslims but they may not have demonstrated the "spirit" implied by the resolution. However, no clarification was given about how to determine the requirements needed to be fulfilled.

[38] *Program perjuangan*, 1952.

be constitutionally guaranteed, and women were to have the same political, social and economic rights as men.[39] The election manifesto for the Constituent Assembly elections, which the party was later to adopt, stipulated, however, that this guarantee would apply "in conformity with the particular character, aptitudes and obligations of the sexes."[40] An essential human right for Masyumi was the freedom of religion. In November 1945, the defence of Islam had been the great unifying issue, but this preoccupation was soon extended to other religions also and in 1946, both issues—the defence of Islam and the defence of religious worship in general—were present. Masyumi gradually became a mouthpiece for the entire religious community without distinction of belief. Its 1955 manifesto stated that voting Masyumi signified "guaranteeing freedom of religion and promoting a harmonious coexistence between religions."[41]

It was imperative for Mohammad Natsir's party to banish the spectre of religious intolerance which the party's opponents regularly brandished. In order to lend weight to these commitments, the *Tafsir Azas* of 1952 referred to verse 256 of the *Al Baqarah Surah* in the hope of proving to the party's detractors that even a literal interpretation of the Holy Book protected religions other than Islam from any mistreatment.[42] The same document quoted another passage from the Koran in order to affirm the necessity to "fight for the protection of monasteries, churches and places of prayer as well as mosques, in short, wherever the name of Allah is invoked."[43]

---

[39] Ibid.

[40] Masyumi Electoral Programme, September 1955.

[41] "Mendjamin kemerdekaan beragama serta menjuburkan keragaman hidup antara agama".

[42] "There shall be no compulsion [in acceptance] of the religion. The right course has become clear from the wrong. So whoever disbelieves in Taghut and believes in Allah has grasped the most trustworthy handhold with no break in it. And Allah is Hearing and Knowing." *Koran* (II, 265).

[43] "Permission [to fight] has been given to those who are being fought, because they were wronged. And indeed, Allah is competent to give them victory. [They are] those who have been evicted from their homes without right—only because they say, 'Our Lord is Allah.' And were it not that Allah checks the people, some by means of others, there would have been demolished monasteries, churches, synagogues, and mosques in which the name of Allah is much mentioned. And Allah will surely support those who support Him. Indeed, Allah is Powerful and Exalted in Might." *Koran* (XXII, 39–40).

What few references to the Koran there were then in Masyumi's programmes only served to remove any suspicion that the party was guilty of religious intolerance. It was the accusations of its political opponents which had forced the party to airbrush out in this way any reference to the religious foundation of its programme. However, this circumspection presented a major drawback: it left the public in the dark concerning a central question, namely the role of Islamic norms in the construction of the new country's substantive law.

The Ambiguities of Sharia Law

During the debates leading up to the adoption of the 1945 Constitution, the demands made by the representatives of Islam concerning the application of Islamic norms seemed relatively clear. The Jakarta Charter, which seemed at the time to contain the essence of their demands, envisaged the application of Islamic law to all Indonesian citizens of the Muslim faith. As already mentioned, this demand was never clearly formulated by Masyumi before the debates in the Constituent Assembly between 1956 and 1957, and the official party line on that question never really appeared. The deliberate vagueness in party programmes surrounding which parts of Islamic law were to be included in the future laws of the land meant that it was very difficult to give a precise overview of this area. However, although it may not be possible to identify clearly what the party's intentions in this area were, one can at least understand their general philosophy.

Various motions voted by the party in congress called for the application of certain elements of Islamic law. The majority of these sought a minimalist application of Muslim penal law. The party congress in Solo, for instance, called for the banning of betting (*pendjudian*), liquor (*minuman keras*), opium (*madat*) and usury (*riba*). These demands appeared again in the urgency programme adopted in 1949, which added prostitution (*pembatasan*) to the list while at the same time calling for these social evils to no longer be banned but merely contained. Curiously enough, these measures appeared in the section of the programme devoted to the working class. Could this be seen as meaning that there was a desire to limit the devastation caused by these scourges in the poorer sections of society but to tolerate them elsewhere? It is hardly likely, but the way the poorest section of society was given priority in this regard is nonetheless striking. The outlawing of those particular social evils and the measured penal sanctions which were liable to be applied posed no real problem in a democratic state.

However, the banning of adultery, mentioned in 1946, was a much more sensitive topic, as *sharia* law specified a very heavy penalty for women—stoning. The Masyumi programme, however, did not set out any sanction, and subsequent comments by the party leadership indicated that if a punishment was to be chosen for this wrong, it would be done in accordance with the mores of the time. In any case, the question did not subsequently arise, since the issue was soon to disappear from the party programme.

Apart from a few measures directly inspired by the Koran, references to Islamic law remained very vague. One of the measures adopted in 1946 spoke of "applying the laws of Islam as widely and as completely as possible in society and in people's way of life."[44] Yet again, however, the part of the programme this demand appeared in meant that its significance was reduced: it figured in a section which concerned neither political measures nor social measures, but was devoted to religion. Is this yet again a sign of the desire to establish a de facto separation between social issues and religious issues, or does it merely reveal a certain amateurism in the party's drafting of official documents? The lack of structural organisation in the Masyumi party would lend us to think that the second hypothesis is more likely.[45]

Let us look finally at the question of which Islamic norms were to be referred to. There appeared to be no real debate on this question: the Koran and the *Sunnah* had always been presented as the unique sources of law.[46] In accordance with the reformist tradition, no later text was ever mentioned. Masyumi

> remained loyal to the principles of the Muslim religion, namely that our society must constitute a group of believers devoted to God, in other words one who obeys the laws and rules laid out by Allah in the Koran, and who are guided by the way the Prophet put into practice these commandments and these divine rules, that is to say by taking into consideration the situation and one's epoch.[47]

---

[44] "Melaksanakan hukum-hukum Islam seluas-luasnja dan sesempurnja-sempurnja dalam hidup dan kehidupan masjarakat." Urgency Programme, Solo Congress, 1946.

[45] See infra, Chapter 6.

[46] The 1952, *Tafsir Azas*, for example, referred to "the teachings of Islam as they are defined by the Koran and the Sunnah" ("adjaran dan hukum-hukum Islam sebagai jang terjantum didalam Qur'an dan Sunnah").

[47] *Tafsir Azas*, 1952.

The wording used here shows both the audacity of the Masyumi leaders in defining their doctrine and their caution in drafting it. Their audacity can be seen in the fact that their approach allows for some of the "sayings of the prophet" (*Hadiths*) not to be considered as literal sources of law. While Mohammad's ability to adapt to his time was emphasised and was to serve as a guiding light, one had to be careful not to automatically include in Indonesian substantive law the rules he had adopted as a head of government.[48] Caution needed to be exercised, however, as the wording was slightly ambiguous, and the subtle distinction just mentioned was perhaps not obvious to all the participants in the 1952 conference. Indeed, within the Muslim community, this point of view was not unanimously shared. The proposals for the new constitution elaborated by the Conference of the Preachers of Islam, held in April 1953, specified that the legal framework of the state was the Koran and the *Hadiths*. Because the wording of the *Tafir Azas* said nothing about the possibility of selecting from or interpreting "the Prophet's sayings", it left the door open for the Conference to adopt a literal application of the political rules of Islam. The resolutions of this eminent assembly, which was presided over by Daud Beureu'eh, the radical leader of Aceh, appeared in the preparatory documents for the seventh Masyumi party congress (1954), though they were not retained in the final resolutions.

The party's programme for Indonesia's institutions, as it was formulated in their official documents, appeared then to be the result of the conflicting influences mentioned earlier. The moderation and progressiveness of those who drafted the programme emerged from the text both in the very general, consensual tone of its proposals, as well as in the obvious references to the principles of government of Western democracies. However, this aspect of the party does not give us the full picture of its identity. Although the logic of Masyumi's proposals seemed to evince a complete overhauling of Muslim law and a system which would allow the elected parliament to exercise an almost total latitude of interpretation of Koranic principles, no document clearly set out the details of this new system. Faced with the vagueness of the party's official documents, it is useful to turn to the comments of the

---

[48] Certain Masyumi figures, notably Jusuf Wibisono and Rusjad Nurdin, echoed this interpretation in their writings, stating that the Prophet's state should not be considered as a model Islamic state.

various Masyumi leaders in order to find some useful insights into the party's political ideology and its developments.

The Project for a Muslim Democracy: Commentaries and Writings by Representatives of the Party's Progressive Wing

The resolutions and programmes adopted by Masyumi were often commented upon and elucidated by the party leaders. This was done on behalf of the party in front of various audiences (the Legislative Assembly, the Constituent Assembly and political rallies) or in the press, but also on their own behalf in various published works. Analysing these contributions to the debates with traditionalists, on the one hand, and with secular nationalists, on the other, allows one to better comprehend the ideological and political foundations of the party's official resolutions. It also enables one to understand how the different crises faced by the party influenced the formulation of its political programme.

Models and Counter-Models: The Thorny Question of the Sources of Law

The modernist branch of Islam held a considerable amount of influence within Masyumi's party executive. This was already the case before NU's split in 1952, and it became even more so subsequently. As we have already seen, this was never fully reflected in the institutional proposals made by the party. Even after 1952, the party's publications avoided the thorny question of the interpretation (*ijtihad*) of the holy texts, apart from a few carefully worded references to this fundamental notion. As they were wary of alienating the Muslim traditionalists, who made up a majority of the Muslim community, the party never officially rejected the legacy of the medieval schools of jurisprudence. In 1954, the party's religious council (the *Madjelis Sjuro*) even published a *fatwa* stating that the party "honoured the *madhhab*."[49]

When party leaders explained their programme, however, their opinions were bolder and often went beyond the official party line.

---

[49] "Muktamar Masjumi ke VII di Surabaja, 23–27 des 1954", in *Pemimpin, Madjallah Tengah berdasar islam*, no. 6 tahun II, December 1954.

Without putting it in so many words, most of them presented the institutional programme of their party with a view to distinguishing it from other programmes which were inspired by political Islam. They wished to distance themselves from two currents within Islam: on the one hand, traditionalists who conveyed an image of rural backwardness (*kolot*); and on the other hand, *wahhabite*-inspired fundamentalists who represented a refusal to accept any modernising of politics. Jusuf Wibisono, who was vice president of Masyumi on several occasions, became an expert in this type of rhetoric. He dreaded, as did the party leadership to a lesser extent, the confusion of the party's programme with the Islamic states of the Middle Ages and their contemporary descendants, notably Saudi Arabia.

In April 1945, he published two articles in *Hikmah* devoted to Masyumi's political ideology. These were meant to be a response to the criticisms that were so often levelled at the party. He took a particularly hard stance against the commonly held idea that "religion could not constitute the bedrock of a modern state".[50] He recognised, nonetheless, why many people held this point of view—European economic development had begun with the emergence of a separation between church and state. Moreover, the Muslim world had fallen behind the West economically, apart from Turkey which was the only country to have clearly separated Islam from the state. Although it was impossible to contest these facts, Wibisono maintained that the conclusions drawn from them were based on a complete misunderstanding, for it was not the Muslim religion which explained this lack of development; it was, "on the contrary, precisely because Muslims did not follow the teachings of Islam" that such stagnation existed. He explained that:

> According to the interpretation of progressive Muslims, for example, the form of government wished for by Islam is a republic and not an absolutist monarchy. If a state is established as an absolute monarchy, it runs contrary to the aspirations of Islam.[51]

A few months later, during a Masyumi rally in Yogyakarta, Wisibono repeated the same arguments more forcefully, saying that the Muslim community, according to him, had been living for several centuries contrary to the teachings of the Koran. To further this argument, he

---

[50] *Hikmah*, 3 and 10 April 1954.
[51] Ibid.

made reference to the writings of Schnouck Hurgronje, the illustrious Dutch Islamicist, who explained in one of his works that the *umma* had abandoned its principles. It was not that the Koran was not being read and recited, said Wibisono; the problem was rather that the sacred text was being referred to blindly "without any real reflection on its meaning."[52]

The causal connection made between the separation of religion and state on the one hand, and progressive politics and democracy, on the other, was an idea that Masyumi fought relentlessly against for several years. The first argument they used was of a religious nature, namely that Islam did not recognise such a separation, as it was a "complete way of life" (*nizam*).[53] However, as they were aware that this simple observation was of limited use, they developed the idea further, saying that Islam was indispensable as the moral cornerstone of political life and of the state. Some wily nationalists suggested that as it was something pure, religion should not mingle (*dicampur*) with politics which, by essence, was impure. Jusuf Wisibono turned this argument back on his opponents, however, saying that politics would be purified by contact with religious principles. He went on to say that the state had to be founded on a set of morals (*kesusilaan*) so as not to be in danger of becoming too authoritarian, and that the principle source of morality was religion "no matter which religion, Hinduism, Islam, Christianity or other religions". This well-meaning universalism, which was typical of Masyumi's attitude at a time when it was presenting itself as the defender of all religions, was nonetheless tempered by a reminder that "in Islam, religion and politics make up a whole and cannot be separated from one another."[54] Wibisono insinuated in his article that other religions which could make this distinction would be able to flourish without impediment in a state governed according to the principles of Islam, and he was joined in this point of view by other Masyumi leaders. It was then in the name of Islam that the Masyumi leadership consistently declared that the state it envisaged

---

[52] *Abadi*, 10 July 1954.

[53] Masyumi leaders often repeated this argument, a notable example being in a letter written by Mohammad Natsir to Prime Minister Wilopo protesting against the circular issued by the public prosecutor banning political discussions in places of worship. *Abadi*, 20 July 1953.

[54] Jusuf Wibisono, "Ideologi Politik Masjumi".

would be democratic and would respect fundamental human rights such as they were respected in the constitutions of modern states.[55] Sjafruddin Prawiranegara, for instance, explained during a meeting of senior party members in 1953 that the Muslim religion constituted "the surest of guarantees for democracy and for the rights and protection of recognised minority groups in society" because justice, which was the "source of that democracy", was "the keystone of the Muslim religion's principles (*soko-guru dari pokok2 agama islam*)."[56]

Masyumi's leaders recognised that the problem facing them was that the founding texts of Islam had often been misinterpreted by certain Muslims. This had provided nationalists with arguments in their campaign against the assimilation of Islamic laws into the substantive law of the country. In this respect, the party leaders were clearer in their comments than they had been when drafting their programmes. It became clear that the Koran and the *Hadiths* were indeed the only sources of Muslim law, but their instructions should be interpreted in such a way as to adapt them to one's time. Consequently, the *Fiqh* books, which had been subject to heavy criticism, could not constitute sources of law.[57] This refusal to recognise *Fiqh* as well as their rejection of *ijma* (here understood as the consensus of the *ulamas*) reveals the modernists' underlying conflict with traditionalists. Natsir highlighted the difficulty of determining with any precision what constituted *ijma*. Was it the consensus reached by all the members of the *ulama* or just by a majority? Was the *ulama* community to be considered as the national *ulama* or as the international *ulama*? Such uncertainty, concluded Natsir, meant that *ijma* could not be taken into consideration in the construction of the country's substantive law.[58] Anshary explained

---

[55] It being understood that these "modern states" were all "Western states", as Mohammad Natsir's speech in the 1952 Congress pointed out.

[56] *Abadi*, 10 March 1953.

[57] HAMKA described them as being "obsolete". Harun Nasution, "The Islamic State in Indonesia: The Rise of Ideology, the Movement for its Creation and the Theory of the Masjumi", MA thesis, McGill University, Montreal, p. 147. Isa Anshary explained that since the Muqallidieen period, which marked the end of direct reference to sources of Islam and the emergence of *fiqh*, the teachings of the *ulama* and the *kiyai* amounted to a blind repetition in front of people who in turn repeated what they heard without understanding it. See Isa Anshary, *Filsafah perdjuangan Islam* (Medan: Saiful, 1949 [2nd edition, 1951]), pp. 70–1.

[58] *Islam Sebagai Ideologie*, p. 14.

that in his opinion, only the consensus reached by the "companions of the prophet" (*Idjma shahabat*) could be followed (*jang boleh diturut*).[59] According to him, the only area which the *ulama* had authority over was the field of worship (*fard'ain ou ubudiyah*), an area in which there was no real room for interpretation. Muslims, for example, had to prostrate themselves towards Mecca three times (*raka'at*) for evening prayer (*sembahjang maghrib*) but only twice for morning prayer (*sembahjang subuh*) "without having to look for a reason why (*tidak boleh orang mentjari tahu*)."[60] The rules which dealt with the relations between men (*fard kifayah ou mu'amalah ma al-nas*), however, and which concerned the interpretation of divine norms (*ijtihad*), clearly came under the remit of a parliament elected by the people. Zainal Abidin Ahmad and Mohammad Natsir stressed the necessity of having parliamentary representatives who knew and understood the laws of Islam, but who were also versed in the modern sciences.[61] However, as the candidates were to be elected uniquely on the basis of universal suffrage, *ulamas*, including those who were progressive, would not benefit from any entitlement to sit in parliament.

Masyumi's most immediate political rivals were the Islamic traditionalists, but this did not mean there were no divisions within the party's reformist majority over which religious norms to refer to. These divisions were evidence of the ambivalent nature of Muslim reformism in Indonesia. Isa Anshary, for example, the virulent party head in West Java, was emblematic of the most intransigent tendency within the party. He was a product of the Persatuan Islam tradition and was a precursor of those tempted by neo-fundamentalism, who were later to grow into the organisation called Dewan Dakwah Islamiyah Indonesia.[62] With his inflamed rhetoric, he was well-versed in vilifying the impious (*kafirs*) and the unfaithful (*munafiks*) who, he said, claimed to love Islam but in fact acted contrary to its laws. In his eyes, the world and

---

[59] Anshary, *Falsafah perjuangan Islam*, p. 68.
[60] Ibid., p. 78.
[61] Zainal Abidin Ahmad, *Membentuk Negara Islam* (Jakarta: Widjaja, 1956), p. 231; Mohammad Natsir, *Islam sebagai Dasar Negara*, pp. 29 ff.
[62] For further reading on this matter, see Rémy Madinier and Andrée Feillard, *The End of Innocence? Indonesian Islam and the Temptations of Radicalism* (Singapore: NUS Press, 2011).

the human race would not be safe "as long as the laws of the Koran and the *Hadiths* are not applied throughout the world."[63] This political struggle to establish Islamic law was, for him, more about remaining strictly faithful to the holy text and less about interpreting the Koran through contemporary eyes. Jusuf Wisibono on the other hand, clearly followed the latter path, and he was fond of reminding his readers that

> The Masyumi group is composed of Muslim leaders who think that each generation is entitled to propose an exegesis of the Koran which is in tune with the situation of the day. If this were not the case, then Islam could not really serve as the bedrock of a developed country.[64]

Loyalty to the past was not an end in itself, and it was better, according to him, not to feel "bound too much by the lessons of the *ulama* who lived in a time far removed from our nuclear age", but on the contrary to "pursue *ijtihad* in order to look for explanations and teachings which, in my opinion, are purer."[65]

One of the stumbling blocks which constituted a barrier to agreement between the different sensibilities within the party was Islamic penal law (*hudid*). Some of its measures seemed to come from another age, and nationalists often brandished the spectre of those measures to win over voters. Given the progressive tendency of a majority of the party leaders, it could legitimately be expected that they did not intend to apply the sentences provided by such laws, but it was not always as simple as that. Certain sanctions written in the Koran and the *Hadiths* held a sacred value for a large part of the Muslim community, in particular those who were close to Persatuan Islam. This little radical organisation from Bandung, unlike Muhammadiyah, had always refused to envisage the possibility of adapting somewhat the sentences set out in the Koran and the *Hadiths*. Concerning the amputating of thieves' hands, for example, Ahmad Hassan explained that the severity of the sanction was intended to frighten those who might be tempted by such

---

[63] *Abadi*, 30 December 1953.

[64] "Ideologi politik Masjumi", *Hikmah*.

[65] The allusion to purity was, of course, not accidental. This issue was a real obsession for the most intransigent adherents of reformism, who wished to give it a new, modern interpretation.

a misdemeanour, and that if it were applied in Indonesia, it would
have the effect of dissuading thieves and thus promote the prosperity of
society, as it had already done in the Islamic states where it existed.[66]
For the most moderate members of Masyumi, there was a lot of unease
surrounding this topic. Yet again, one of the few members to mention
it openly was Jusf Wibisono. In his analysis of the political ideology of
Masyumi, he reminded his readers that this area of Muslim law was one
of the factors which discredited its application during colonial times:

> Within every state court sat a mosque official who acted as a
> 'religious counsellor'. The presiding judge was obliged to consult
> his opinion and ask 'what does your law provide for a thief?' The
> counsellor's reply was invariably 'the cutting off of his hand'. His
> hand had to be cut off, whatever he had stolen. Naturally, this
> consultation was merely a formality and the amputation was never
> carried out by the Dutch East Indies government. The presiding
> judge was [nonetheless] obliged to ask the question to the mosque
> representative acting as 'religious counsellor'.

Wisibono hoped that there was no danger of a similar situation arising
in an independent Indonesia, and he shot across the bows of traditionalists by writing that: "according to the current interpretation of
progressives, the sentence of 'cutting off hands' must not be applied to
a convicted thief."[67]

There remained, however, amongst most Masyumi leaders, a
certain amount of self-censorship which was distinctly visible in the
party's official documents. They clearly wanted to found a modern state
free from any reference to past Islamic states. Their inspiration for this
came incontestably from Western democracies, and, unlike successive
Islamic states in the Muslim world, it pushed them to reinterpret
thoroughly the sacred texts of Islam. In many cases, even the example
of the Prophet could not be followed. However, the presence within
the reformist leadership of a small but vocal minority who held up
the Prophet's era as an absolute model prevented any clear and cogent
formulation of a radical new ideological departure.

---

[66] Federspiel, *Persatuan Islam*, pp. 145–6. Federspiel points out, however, that
while Persatuan Islam maintained that the rules of Islamic criminal law were
divine commandments, it never really called for their application in Indonesia.
[67] Wibisono, "Ideologi politik Masjumi".

What to Do with Pancasila? The Pitfalls of Masyumi's Debate with the Nationalists

From the foundation of Masyumi in 1945 until the first session of the Constituent Assembly in 1956, its programmes regularly made reference to the principles of *Pancasila*, and the party's official positions on this doctrine were regularly commented upon by the party leadership. The question of the adoption of *Pancasila* as the definitive foundation upon which to build the Republic of Indonesia gave rise to a debate which opened up a new ideological front in the battle between Masyumi and the nationalists. The contributions to this debate by Masyumi leaders had a threefold aim. Firstly, they wished to persuade the Muslim community that retaining *Pancasila* in the Constitution was not contrary to the party's goals. Secondly, they wanted to convince the Indonesian people in general, and the non-Muslim section of the population in particular, of the sincerity of their stance by demonstrating that Masyumi's projects were not in contradiction with *Pancasila*. Finally, they endeavoured not to allow nationalists to have an exclusive claim over the national ideology but rather to use it as a propaganda weapon for the benefit of Islam.

Throughout the revolutionary period and up until the beginning of the 1950s, party officials busied themselves with justifying to their members the sacrifice which they had consented to when independence was declared, namely that the state would be founded on the five principles of *Pancasila* and not explicitly on Islam. One of the most prominent arguments put forward in favour of this decision was the necessity of achieving national unity in order to defend what were considered to be two intimately linked interests: independence and Islam. A number of arguments were also advanced concerning the nature of the Indonesian state founded in 1945. All the party's theorists agreed that the country's institutions were compatible with the principles of Islam. Some even pointed out that the Republic of Indonesia fulfilled one of the requirements laid out in the first programmes established by Masyumi, namely the obligation for the president to be Muslim. Since his exile on Sumatra at the beginning of the 1930s, Sukarno had often been considered close to the Muhammadiyah movement. He became a member of the movement at that time, and his third wife, Fatmawati, was the daughter of the local head of the reformist movement.[68] During

---

[68] For an account of this exile in Bengkulu and its influence on Sukarno's conception of religion, see Lubis, *Pemikiran Sukarno tentang Islam*, pp. 75–7.

the debates in 1945, the future president took the opportunity to draw attention to his Muslim identity, and also pointed to his desire to see Muslim ideals prosper in society. In addition, Mohammad Hatta, who was vice president and could thus be called upon to replace the head of state, was known for his piety and was close to most of the Masyumi leadership. Another source of satisfaction for the Masyumists was soon to appear with the creation in January 1946 of a Ministry of Religions. All religious questions, which had up until then come under the remit of various governmental departments, were now transferred to this ministry. It was the case, for example, of the appointment of *penghulus*, who had the responsibility of celebrating weddings, organising divorces and calculating the division of inheritances. The appointment of *imams*, which had previously been carried out by the regents, was also transferred to the new ministry, as were the supervision of religious education (for the public as well as for private schools) and the overseeing of religious courts.[69]

On a more general level, the enshrinement in the Preamble to the Constitution of *Pancasila*, whose principles included belief in a single God, the pursuit of solidarity and humanism as well as the democratic functioning of the state, was considered by Masyumi as a victory for the Islamic community. As Mohammad Natsir explained in 1954, "with *Pancasila*, the current foundations of the Republic of Indonesia are like extracts from thousands of *sila* which are to be found in Islam."[70] Certain Masyumi leaders pushed this idea of associating the existing institutions and their party's ideals very far. Z.A. Ahmad and Mohammad Natsir, in particular, went so far as to state that the Indonesian state already fulfilled all the conditions needed to be called an Islamic state. In one of his books, Zainal Abidin Ahmad set out eight requirements necessary for a state to be considered an Islamic state. It had to be sovereign; it had to have a constitution and a parliament; be a republic and be founded on Islam, law and consultation with the people; and finally, it had to pursue a policy of peace. He explained that Indonesia, unlike the majority of states who claimed to be Islamic,

---

[69] H. Aboebakar, *Sejarah hidup K.H.A. Wahid Hasjim dan karangan tersiar* (Djakarta: Panitya Buku Peringatan Alm. K.H.A. Wahid Hasjim, 1957), pp. 596, 600–1.

[70] A lecture given by Mohammad Natsir in Bukittinggi, *Antara*, 22 July 1954, reproduced in *Capita Selecta*, vol. 2, p. 293.

fulfilled almost all these conditions, the reference to Islam being the only one missing.[71] During a lecture given in Karachi in 1952, Mohammad Natsir declared that like Pakistan, Indonesia was "also an Islamic state...for Islam is obviously recognised as the Indonesian nation's religion and spiritual conviction, although it is not stated explicitly in the Constitution that it is the state religion."[72]

This insistence on the Islamic aspects of *Pancasila* had a dual purpose. It was intended both to persuade the most ardent supporters of a political role for Islam that they could be proud of their representatives' achievements, and to reassure the other wing of Masyumi concerning the party's plans. This latter objective came more and more to the forefront as the elections approached. Party officials were convinced that their victory would depend on their ability to attract not only confirmed Islamist activists, but also both Muslims and non-Muslims who seemed uneasy about the political role of Islam. The party's programmes and resolutions were thus cleansed of all egregious proposals which might wound the sensibilities of potential electors. Likewise, there was a reassuring character to the public statements made by party leaders, who had been forced by their opponents' brandishing of the spectre of an Islamic state to adopt a prudent tone. In August 1950, for example, the bi-monthly periodical, *Suara Partai Masjumi* (*The Voice of Masyumi*) tried to speak out against the systematic lumping together by nationalists of the notion of "*Darul Islam*" ("Abode of Islam") and the fundamentalist movement led by Kartosuwirjo.[73] This was already a lost cause, however, and the party officials had to abandon this expression, which had until then been used quite extensively in their speeches. The separatist insurrection which had been carried out under this name had definitively tarnished the vast majority of the population's understanding of it. The term "Darul Islam" belonged thereafter to Kartosuwirjo and his followers, and it now embodied the absolute

---

[71] Ahmad, *Membentuk Negara Islam*, pp. 114–5.

[72] To justify his argument, Natsir emphasised the fact that the belief in a unique God had moved from fifth to first place in the order of *Pancasila*'s principles. "Sumbangan Islam bagi perdamaian Dunia", *Capita selecta*, vol. 2, p. 61.

[73] "The expression 'Darul Islam' should not become a sort of were-wolf (*momok*) in the eyes of non-Muslims, but rather should constitute a call to unity under the protection of a single, generous and just God." *Suara Partai Masjumi*, August 1950.

antithesis of a *Pancasila* state, as Masyumi's political opponents endeavoured to show.[74]

Nationalist attacks against Masyumi's policies achieved a higher profile following a speech pronounced by the head of state in Amuntai (Kalimantan) on 27 January 1953. In this speech, Sukarno advocated a national state (*Negara nasional*) as opposed to a state founded on Islam (*Negara yang berdasar Islam*) which, according to him, would lead inevitably to the breakaway of the non-Muslim regions of the archipelago, and would irremediably compromise the reintegration of West Irian into the national territory. This was a direct and frontal attack on Masyumi, as the expression used by the president made explicit reference to the party's programme.

Several senior party members reacted strongly to this speech. Mohammed Saleh Suaidi, the mayor of Yogyakarta, upbraided the president for having inconsiderately "thrown himself into the cauldron of ideological struggle" (*menjeburkan dirinja dalam kantjah pertarugan ideology*). For him, the two concepts could not be juxtaposed, as only a "national state founded on Islam and its laws" (*Negara nasional jang berdasar dan berhukum Islam*) was acceptable. The use of the word "breaking away" by the head of state was a sign of prejudice against the Muslim community because nowhere in Indonesia did exclusively non-Muslim zones exist.[75] It was of course Isa Anshary, the radical troublemaker of the party who was to react the most virulently. In the weeks after Sukarno's speech, he penned a series of articles and speeches which denounced the head of state's understanding of Indonesian society, lamenting an attitude which was "far from the wisdom which one might expect from a head of state".[76]

---

[74] A good example of this is the speech given by Sukarno in March 1952 to the civil servants working in the Ministry of Information. The president explained that "the vocation of the five *sila* which make up the state ideology is to defend the unity of the different sections of the Indonesian people in order to turn it into a strong nation… The first *sila* is formulated as faith in a unique God, and not in Islam as Darul Islam would prefer." Quoted in Marcel Bonneff et al., *Pantsjasila, trente années de débats politiques en Indonésie* (Paris: Editions de la Maison des sciences de l'homme, 1980), p. 87.

[75] Mohammed Saleh Suaidi cited as an example the regional capital of the Maluku Islands, Ambon, where "according to an official report Muslims comprise 60% of the population, the remaining 40% being Catholics or Protestants." *Abadi*, 12 February 1953.

[76] *Abadi*, 11 February 1953.

It soon appeared to the senior members of the party, however, that the controversy was becoming a source of embarrassment for them. The outraged reactions to Sukarno's provocative speech and the series of demonstrations which it caused were in grave danger of tarnishing the reassuring image that the party had worked so hard to construct. As a result, the president and vice president of the party, Mohammad Natsir and Soekiman Wirjosandjojo, both attempted to calm passions. Speaking in early March in Medan, the day after a demonstration attended by 60 Muslim organisations protesting against the Amuntai speech, Natsir urged the public to solve this problem between Muslims in the spirit of Islam, so that "those outside Masyumi cannot take advantage of this unrest in order to turn Islamic organisations against the head of state, who is himself a Muslim."[77] Soekiman for his part carefully avoided any direct reference to the controversy. In the public statements he made following Sukarno's speech, he limited himself to adopting the official position of Masyumi on this question, which was to constantly remind the public of the guarantees made to other religions by Islam.[78] Beforehand, Soekiman and Natsir had succeeded in getting the party's executive to adopt the same stance. On 16 February, the Masyumi spokesman published a communiqué stating that the party was convinced that the president's speech did contain some wisdom, "whether we appreciate it or not".[79] For the party officials, rather than giving way to the cries of alarm which came from a community's sense of indignation, which would mean falling straight into the trap Sukarno had laid, Masyumi had to seize the opportunity to pursue and intensify the pedagogical approach which it had initiated several years previously.

This complex battle concerning the place of Islam in Indonesia's institutions continued over the following months. Sukarno, through

---

[77] *Abadi*, 5 March 1953.

[78] See, for example, his press conference in Solo. *Abadi*, 7 March 1953.

[79] *Abadi*, 17 February 1953. This declaration, which amounted to a stinging disavowal of Isa Anshary's comments, caused a certain amount of turmoil within the party. Two weeks later, the executive committee published a new document "in response to the accusations by certain newspapers which had declared that the Masyumi leadership considered that the Amuntai speech was a minor issue." This document explained that while the question it raised was certainly an essential one, it was necessary first of all "to eliminate the public's misunderstanding of Islam as an ideology for society and for a state, in particular concerning the freedom of religion." *Berita Masjumi*, 2 March 1953.

a series of speeches astutely designed to undermine Masyumi's fragile unity, endeavoured to appear both as the faithful disciple of a properly understood Islam as well as a defender of the non-Muslim population's interests, and hence of the cohesion of the Indonesian nation. On 13 April 1953, during the celebration of the *mi'raj* ceremony at the presidential palace, he explained that he had made his speech in Amuntai "as a Muslim", and that the question of whether his Islam was faultless or not, whether it was a "100% Islam" or not—an expression regularly employed by Masyumi members—"would be determined by God". As a member of the Islamic community, he invited his fellow Muslims to "steer clear of any exclusivist or isolationist attitudes" as they would be "in contradiction with the spirit of Islam". He made shrewd use of a speech given by Mohammad Natsir the previous year to illustrate his comments. The speech, said Sukarno, "contained a message which every Muslim should reflect upon", namely that a "genuine" Islam could not be reduced to the celebration of the birth of the Prophet (*mulud*) but also had to be faithful to the spirit and teachings of Islam.[80] Three weeks later, the head of state once again demonstrated his ability to incorporate his opponents' arguments. In a public lecture given at the University of Indonesia, he developed one of Mohammad Natsir's favourite themes: that "Islam is not only a religion, but also constitutes a way of life" (*Islam bukan hanja satu agama tapi juga satu way of life*). In his address, Sukarno explained that people often held the mistaken belief that religion should not get involved in a country's political affairs. This was an error because Islam was not only a "personal affair" (*suatu privaatzaak*), as it established no distinction between church and state.[81] He adopted one of Masyumi's classic arguments to explain that "contrary to what certain nationalists claim", if Muslims held power in the country, the state would not become a theocracy because such a form of government did not exist in Islam. The president considered that nationalists were spreading a number of misconceptions about the Muslim religion. He maintained, however, that Muslims, likewise, frequently misinterpreted what lay behind nationalists' aspirations. According to Sukarno, two different Islamic groups had, over the previous 30 years, held two opposing assessments of nationalism. The first,

---

[80] *Abadi*, 14 April 1953.
[81] Like many of Masyumi's thinkers, Sukarno made no distinction here between church and religion.

represented mainly by Permi (Persatuan Muslim Indonesia), considered that Islam recognised the legitimacy of nationalism as long as it was not interpreted narrowly. Persis (Persatuan Islam), on the other hand, refused any recognition of nationalism by Islam. Concluding his long speech, the president reminded his audience that in 1945, the unity of the nation had been threatened by the desire, albeit a legitimate desire, of each group to see their ideas prevail. It was only through the adoption of *Pancasila*, whose precepts, "as Mohammad Natsir himself agreed, did not contradict the principles of Islam", that this unity was preserved.[82]

President Sukarno in his speech demonstrated once again his political nous. By co-opting almost word for word the arguments of Masyumi's president, he made it impossible for the party to rebut his arguments without running the risk of amplifying the divisions to which he discretely drew his audience's attention. Masyumi was the main protagonist in this confrontation between political Islam and the head of state, and this clash exposed the party's internal contradictions, just as the debates over the 1945 Constitution had exposed the tensions within political Islam. In the eyes of a large section of the population, however, *Pancasila* remained an essential factor for the cohesion of the nation, and Sukarno was its protector, its incarnation almost, which did not seem to be inconsistent with his Muslim identity.

In May 1954, another presidential declaration put Masyumi's leaders in an awkward position. It took place during the inauguration of a church in the Maluku Islands, where the heated debate over the state's future form of government had led to an escalation in tensions between the Catholic and Muslim communities. Sukarno apologised to the audience for the acts committed by irresponsible Muslims, and exhorted young people to defend *Pancasila* as the constitutional cornerstone of Indonesia. This declaration was lambasted by one of the figures of the Indonesian Islamic Youth Front of the Maluku Islands (Front Pemuda Islam Indonesia Maluku), who criticised the head of state for his intervention in an ideological debate at a time when elections were about to be organised, and also asked him which Muslim community had instructed him to apologise to Christians. As the controversy grew, Masyumi intervened to take the defence of the president, with the

---

[82] *Abadi*, 8 May 1953.

local party leader, Mohammad Basir, indicating that he regretted the declarations of the Islamic Youth Front member.[83]

By this time, the party's leaders had accepted, albeit half-heartedly, the strategy of appeasement recommended by Natsir and Soekiman towards Sukarno. Isa Anshary continued to take the president to task, but he took care to point out that he was doing so in a personal capacity and not on behalf of the party.[84] On several occasions, he even tried to calm the debate. On 30 March 1953, he declared that the Muslim community "did not wish to create a new state".[85] This expression, which entailed a de facto recognition of *Pancasila* as the foundation for the country's institutions, was subsequently employed by other Masyumi figures.[86] With the elections looming, Masyumi came to the conclusion that the official ideology of the Republic of Indonesia appeared untouchable and that it would be wiser to swear loyalty to it; after all, its capacity to unite could allow the party to usurp some of its benefits.

This acceptance of *Pancasila* as a cornerstone for the foundation of the Indonesian state did not signify, however, that the party was aligning itself with the nationalist interpretation of this ideology. On the question of how to interpret *Pancasila*, President Sukarno had shown himself to be skilled at turning his opponents' own arguments against themselves, but the party leaders did not intend to be outdone by this. They adopted two types of attitude towards the question of *Pancasila*, the first of which consisted in posing as the guardians of the true *Pancasila* in order to better resist any attempt by their rivals to usurp the five principles.

Once the Masyumi leadership had committed itself to making an effort at presenting its political theories within the framework of *Pancasila*, despite the tension and debate this created within the party,

---

[83] *Abadi*, 14 May 1954.
[84] *Abadi*, 15 March 1953.
[85] *Abadi*, 31 March 1953.
[86] Mohamad Roem declared in April 1954, for example, that "the ideal of an Islamic state does not signify a break with our Republic. We do not want to build a new state. The notion of an Islamic state has been the victim of misrepresentations, owing in particular to the poor example shown by Kartosuwirjo, who strayed from the path when he decided to found a new state." *Abadi*, 21 April 1954.

they could no longer allow the nationalist camp to be the only ones to appropriate the state ideology. In an editorial that appeared in *Hikmah* on 29 September 1954, the magazine's chairman, Mohammad Natsir, and its editor, A.R. Baswedan, applauded the discernment shown by their political opponent. This was in reaction to a declaration made a short time before by Sukarno in which he stated that the national ideology could not belong to one party, and that the PNI could not present itself as founded upon *Pancasila*, as it would mean that "the others would not want any part in it".[87] Even Isa Anshary, who was reluctant to follow the party line set out by Natsir, was wont to criticise his opponents for their lack of respect for *Pancasila*. In a stinging diatribe against the Ali government, for example, he explained to Masyumi party activists that an analysis of *Pancasila*, article by article, led one to the conclusion that the members of the government "were not faithful to it, but, rather, were unprincipled (*tidak berpantjasila tapi nyataan bertanpasila*)."[88]

Emphasising the importance of *Pancasila* in Indonesia's heritage was not the only aspect of how Masyumi exploited the national ideology. The other attitude that the party's leaders adopted was aimed at offering a Muslim interpretation of *Pancasila* designed to explain to the electorate how it could serve as the cornerstone of a state which conformed to the teachings of Islam. For them, the ideology defined in 1945 was merely the outline of a theoretical framework which had to be interpreted in accordance with the teachings of Islam. The premise behind this conclusion was the fact that Sukarno, in a speech given on 1 June 1945, had moved the *sila* which exalted the faith in a unique God from fifth place to first place in the Preamble to the Constitution adopted on 18 August. This, they explained, was not done for practical reasons, but reflected instead a hierarchy of values.[89] For Masyumi, the Constituent Assembly, by doing this, wished to crown the first *sila* as the "foundation for the four others".[90] Masyumi's

---

[87] *Hikmah*, 25 September 1954.

[88] *Abadi*, 30 December 1953.

[89] Bonnef et al., *Pantsjasila, trente années de débats politiques en Indonésie*, pp. 22, 28.

[90] An expression often employed by Masyumi's leaders. See, for example, A.R. Daswedan's article entitled "Who Has Really Become the Enemy of Pancasila?". *Abadi*, 1 June 1956.

theorists used this idea as a starting point to develop a message presenting *Pancasila* as a "receptacle" (*wadah*) to be filled. This interpretation of the national ideology adopted one of President Sukarno's arguments that every political movement should take part in the definition of *Pancasila*. It allowed Mohammad Natsir, in May 1954, to assert his party's attachment to the five principles, but at the same time to suggest the limits of this attachment:

> In the eyes of a Muslim, the wording of *Pancasila* is not perceived in principle as a 'foreign thing' to which he must be opposed. He recognises in it the reflection of part of what he already sees around him. That does not mean, by the same token, that this *Pancasila* is the same thing as a hymn or that it embraces all the teachings of Islam. So long as *Pancasila* contains the goals of the Muslim religion, we, Muslims, in order to accomplish these virtues, will not, in all sincerity, want to see it abandoned. In a land steeped in Islam, *Pancasila* will flourish. Let us hope that this *Pancasila*, which was launched around nine years ago as a formulation of five aspirations but whose substance has yet to be fleshed out, will not materialise over time into something which is opposed to the Koranic principles.[91]

Islamic Democracy at an Impasse: The Debates at the Constituent Assembly (1957–59)

After the elections of 1955, the party's resolutions touched less often on the question of the country's institutions, which was now in the hands of the Constituent Assembly. The congress of 1956, however, reflected the hardening of Masyumi's position on this issue. After the Constituent Assembly elections, the party's message became noticeably more radical. While the party declared that it was now up to the Assembly to determine the foundations of the state, Masyumi's eighth congress, held in Bandung in 1956, also recalled the party's demands, namely that "Islam be decreed the absolute foundation of the Republic of Indonesia" and that "the Muslim religion be confirmed as a general source of law for the Republic of Indonesia."

---

[91] "Apakah Pantjasila bertentangan dengan Adjaran Al-Quran?", *Abadi*, 22 May 1954, *Hikmah*, 29 May 1954, *Capita Selecta*, vol. 2, pp. 144–50.

As for the last party congress held in Yogyakarta in April 1959, all that was left for it to do was note the Constituent Assembly's failure and to regret that the government had not given it the time to accomplish its task. The resolutions with respect to institutional questions were all devoted to the issue of the day: the return to the 1945 Constitution. The party's representatives were mainly concerned with showing that the Dwitunggal was indispensable in order for the new regime to function properly. The party put forward no other demand related to Islam and contented itself with pointing out that the Muslim community should play a stabilising role in the country.[92]

An "Island Lost in the Middle of Choppy Waters": The Political Conditions which Led to the Party's Intransigence

As a result of the party's decision to adopt more moderate positions, which ultimately led to it being punished at the polls, its leadership, as we have already seen, came under pressure from the party's rank and file. The balance of power thrown up by the election left Masyumi with little hope in the short term. The party's Islamic identity, which had rarely been highlighted during the campaign, became the rallying point for its new strategy. This new approach consisted in establishing itself as the clear leader of the Muslim parties in the Constituent Assembly and trying to obtain the recognition in the new constitution which it had failed to secure in the elections. This strategy of confronting the supporters of a state founded on *Pancasila* soon revealed itself to be fruitless; it did, however, allow the party's deputies to clarify their demands concerning the country's future institutions.

The Constituent Assembly was elected in December 1955 and inaugurated on 10 November 1956. During the two and a half years of its lifetime, it held seven plenary sessions, each lasting two to three weeks. It was convened for the last time on 2 June 1959, and on 7 July, the Assembly was officially dissolved by presidential decree. During its proceedings, the Constituent Assembly succeeded in adopting a certain number of resolutions concerning the nature of the state, its symbols and its protection of human rights. Apart from these provisions, which for the most part incorporated decisions already adopted in 1945 and reaffirmed by the country's two subsequent constitutions,

---

[92] See infra, Chapter 4.

the Assembly made no significant progress on the question of the country's institutions. It hit a stumbling block early on during the two sessions which took place in 1957 and which were devoted to the definition of the foundations—or philosophy—of the state (*Dasar Negara*).

The 514 members of the Constituent Assembly very rapidly split into three factions of varying size. The largest group was composed of supporters of *Pancasila*; it comprised the representatives of the PNI (116 deputies), its nationalist allies (the IPKI with 8 deputies and GPPS with 5), the Christian parties (16 deputies from Parkindo and 10 from the Catholic Party), the Communist Party (60 deputies) and its affiliated movements (such as Republik Proklamsi with 20 deputies), the PSI (10 deputies) and the Chinese party, Baperki (2 deputies) as well as a certain number of regional movements, making up a total of 274 seats. Islam's supporters were made up of the 112 Masyumi representatives, NU's 91 representatives, the 16 deputies belonging to the PSII and Perti's seven seats, as well as four regional movements such as the Gerakan Pilihan Sunda (Sudanese Election Movement) which held one seat each, giving a total of 230 seats. The 10 remaining members in the Assembly were from three small parties: Partai Buruh, Partai Murba and Acoma. They made up a small group claiming to be the guardians of the spirit of 17 August 1945 and they campaigned, in the name of a proletarian doctrine, for an "economic and social foundation" to the state. Its small number of supporters meant that this original ideology did not carry much weight in the Assembly debates; moreover, the other two factions each claimed that its essential principles were already contained in their programmes. They took on a more important role from 1958 onwards, however, as the official representatives of Sukarno. They defended the "presidential conception", campaigned for the adoption of "Guided Democracy", and were among the few deputies to support the government's proposals.[93]

The three groups did not change their positions one iota during the debates, and indeed the antagonism between them gradually worsened. At the close of the third session on 6 December 1957, the deputies merely adopted a preliminary report drawn up by an ad hoc

---

[93] For a complete treatment of the composition of the Constituent Assembly, see Adnan Buyung Nasution, *The Aspiration for Constitutional Government in Indonesia: A Socio-Legal Study of the Indonesia Konstituante 1956–1959* (Jakarta: Pustaka Sinar Harapan, 1992), pp. 32–4.

preparatory committee, chaired by Masyumi's Kasman Singodimedjo, and invited the committee to pursue its work.[94] From then on, no further significant progress was noted. The majority of the debates centred on the definition of the philosophy of the state (*Dasar Negara*), which the Assembly devoted three sessions to. The one matter that the various groups agreed on was that this question would effectively determine the entire institutional apparatus of the state. For want of being able to settle this essential question, however, the Assembly fell back on more consensual issues. In 1958, it defined the form of government, which was to be republican approved the provisions concerning the nation's symbols, such as the flag and the national anthem and confirmed that the country's language was to be Indonesian and its capital Jakarta. It also adopted 19 articles protecting human rights. The satisfaction expressed on behalf of the Assembly by its speaker, Jusuf Wibisono, masked an almost total failure, however. From the beginning of 1959, the Constituent Assembly lost any control it had over its own order of business, as it merely reacted to the various government initiatives motivated by Sukarno's desire to revive the 1945 Constitution. A large majority of deputies were opposed to this proposal, and the government responded by making a few concessions, notably the agreement to take into account the provisions already voted. However, the Assembly's opposition was confirmed in three consecutive votes, on 30 May, 1 and 2 June 1959, which effectively led to its dissolution.

Due to the balance of power which existed in the Assembly, the determining factor in its debates was whether the Muslim bloc and the *Pancasila* group could come to an agreement. The political configuration in the Assembly meant that the two groups were condemned to cooperate with each other, as in order to be adopted a proposal needed to receive a two-thirds majority. However, from the outset, the two sides were completely unable to come to an understanding, with both sides advancing similar arguments to justify their refusal to compromise. On the nationalist side, *Pancasila* was portrayed as a combination

---

[94] The report recommended that the state's philosophy should be established in accordance with the particularities of the Indonesian state; be inspired by the 1945 Revolution; guarantee the system of consultations (*musyawarah*) as the basis for resolving state affairs; guarantee the freedom of religion and worship; and guarantee the principles of humanity, of an open form of nationalism and of social justice. *Tentang dasar Negara Republik Indonesia dalam Konstituante*, 1958, vol. 1, p. 166.

of all of Indonesia's existing schools of thought, and it was argued that this original quality made it the only ideology liable to guarantee the unity of the nation. Given that they had won the most number of seats in the Assembly, the nationalists intended on maintaining the status quo adopted in 1945, which, they reminded their fellow deputies, had been rubberstamped by the Muslim representatives. The supporters of Islam, on the other hand, had quite another view of things. From an early stage, Masyumi's representatives, who were able to influence the debates considerably, demonstrated a rather peculiar state of mind. Breaking with the moderate line and the conciliatory tone which their party had adopted during the election campaign, they showed themselves from the outset to be hostile to any compromise.

There are several reasons which explain this new state of mind. The first of these is the euphoria created by the solidarity which the Muslim parties had rediscovered after years of in-fighting. This unity, which was often in stark contrast to the political manoeuvrings going on at that time, remained solid throughout the Assembly's lifetime. The Islamic parties constituted a genuine political bloc, and the Masyumi press took every opportunity to remind its readers of this. The second reason was linked to Masyumi's electoral misfortunes, which had been put down to the conciliatory strategy which Natsir had succeeded in imposing up until election day. The Masyumi president's policy was now being contested within the party, and he gave Isa Anshary and Kasman Singodimedjo, two advocates of a more radical approach, complete freedom to enter the fray against the nationalist camp. The desire to be seen to give no ground to the nationalist camp came from the need to give the party a new impetus. The Constituent Assembly was a setting tailor-made for this: its location in Bandung, four hours by train from the hectic atmosphere of the capital, gave it the feeling of being somewhat outside of time. It was, according to Natsir, "like an island lost in the middle of the choppy waters of politics... *tranquilis in undus*" a place conducive to endless debates which, it was hoped, would bring a comprehensive solution to the political problems which the inconclusive result of the elections had left unresolved.[95]

This intransigence was not exclusive to Masyumi, nor indeed to the leaders of political Islam in general. In fact, it was one of the common points shared by the entire Assembly. Amongst Masyumi's

---

[95] Ibid., p. 111.

representatives, however, this attitude was clearly a strategic choice. For the party, the Constituent Assembly's role was to make a clean sweep of the agreements which had been made since 1945; all of the country's institutional questions which had been settled were now to be put back on the table. The painfully wrought compromise reached in 1945 and which nationalists wished to use as a starting point for the Assembly's debates could no longer, in the eyes of Masyumi, be used as an undisputed model.

New Attitudes towards Pancasila

Contrary to the conciliatory tone adopted in previous years towards *Pancasila*, Masyumi's deputies, in their declarations, now engaged in a radical reassessment of the conditions under which they would be prepared to accept its inclusion in the Preamble. In their eyes, the Muslim community had conceded an immense sacrifice for the sake of national unity in 1945. Now that the country's independence was no longer in the balance, discussions should be reopened, and it was the nationalists' turn this time round to be prepared to make concessions. Although this attitude was new for the party, the underlying resentment had already been present. Some Islamists had never accepted the climb-down they had made on 18 August 1945. The intransigence of their position was due to their impression of having been duped by the nationalists, from whom they had received guarantees that the solution adopted—the withdrawal of the famous seven words from the Jakarta Charter—was a provisional one.

In their speeches in the Assembly dealing with that point in time, the Islamic representatives' appraisal of the 1945 compromise was clearly dominated by this sentiment of having been hoodwinked. Kasman Singodimedjo recalled that the urgency of the time, and the need to confront the Japanese and the Allies had been the reasons behind the Muslim representatives' decision to temporarily abandon their demands. Their three main requests had been the obligation for Muslims to put Islamic law into practice, the proclamation of Islam as a state religion, and finally, the requirement for the president to be a Muslim. He explained that these demands had been sacrificed in return for the nationalists' promise to start work on a new constitution within six months.[96] Isa Anshary took this idea much further and a part of

---

[96] A speech given by Kasman Singodimedjo, ibid., p. 187.

his marathon speech to the Assembly—the transcription is 70 pages long, without the appendices—was given over to a radical reassessment of the 1945 Constitution which was "the work of a few leaders and the choice not of a majority of the people, but of Jakarta."[97] Recalling the sacrifices conceded by Muslims for independence, he declared that the seven words of the Jakarta Charter:

> ...offered the Muslim community the opportunity and the freedom to put into practice the laws of Islam within the state which was about to be created. The way clearly seemed free, the Muslim community had the hope and the guarantee of seeing Sharia and the Muslim credo blossom in this world of freedom.[98]

For Isa Anshary, the Muslim community's participation in the struggle against the country's former colonial masters was inseparable from its hope of seeing its ideology triumph. The disappearance of the famous seven words had, therefore, "been perceived by the Muslim community as a 'disappearing trick' still covered in a mysterious pall...like an act of political fraud." Naturally, the nationalists were, for him, the driving force behind this manoeuvre, but for the first time, he also criticised the Muslim leaders who had accepted this compromise:

> The policy of tolerance, which was interpreted in a dogmatic fashion by Muslim parties and their politicians at that time, was felt by the Muslim community to have betrayed the hope and the future possibilities of Islam's struggle. This policy of tolerance only led to liquidation and capitulation, which meant giving in and submitting yet again, without attempting to fight and to resist. It is an account which illustrates and demonstrates the weakness of the ideological struggle led by the Muslim parties and their politicians.[99]

This was going beyond a condemnation of the nationalist camp's betrayal, and denouncing Masyumi's entire policy of conciliation which had been initiated by Soekiman in 1945 and continued by Natsir. A Pandora's box had now been opened and party members could openly express their refusal of *Pancasila*. Other party representatives plunged

---

[97] *Tentang dasar negara Republik Indonesia dalam Konstituante*, vol. 2, p. 182.
[98] Ibid., p. 185.
[99] Ibid.

into the breach, and in denial of the obvious, rejected the choices made by Masyumi over the previous ten years. Zainal Abdin Ahmad, for example, declared that *Pancasila* had in fact never been recognised by the previous constitutions as they had only enunciated five general principles common to numerous cultures.[100] For these Masyumi members, the real debate was about to start, and this time Islam's supporters would not back down.[101] Once the Masyumi deputies' objective was decided upon, they could only envisage one outcome, namely the unconditional surrender of the supporters of *Pancasila*. Was this a negotiating ploy on the part of Masyumi in particular—and the supporters of Islam in general—in order to put itself in a stronger negotiating position? The party's obstinacy in maintaining this position in the face of clear numerical evidence (not a single nationalist representative had rallied to their cause) and the changing political context (the Constituent Assembly's position was weakening daily as a result of Sukarno's programme) tend to lead one to the conclusion that this was not the case. It is possible, then, in light of these declarations, to conclude that Masyumi's entire political programme underwent significant change at this time. Although the discussions never dealt with the legitimacy of particular institutional provisions, the arguments used by the party figures to demand the inclusion of Islamic principles in the Preamble to the Constitution implicitly revealed a certain conception of democracy.

A Theist Democracy

Political Islam, which Masyumi represented, was in a minority in the Constituent Assembly. However, due to the requirement of a qualified majority—two-thirds of the votes—in order to adopt a new constitution, they enjoyed a blocking minority which they used liberally. In explaining their refusal of any compromise, the party's deputies could have merely invoked the logic underlying the Assembly's rules, which were the same as those used in most democracies, namely that as soon as the question of modifying the constitution arose, a qualified majority

---

[100] A speech given by Z.A. Ahmad, *Tentang dasar negara Republik Indonesia dalam Konstituante*, vol. 1, pp. 357–8.
[101] One such example of this intransigence can be found in a speech given by Kasman Singodimedjo, in which he replaces the expression "a unique God" (*Tuan yang Maha Esa*) with the word "Allah". Ibid., p. 168.

was required. It would not have been unreasonable for Masyumi's representative to oblige the nation's representatives to arrive at a consensus which would be sufficiently broad so as to give any constitutional reform indisputable political legitimacy. They only rarely ever availed of this argument though, preferring instead to use theoretical considerations to justify their refusal to compromise. By doing so, they allowed two important aspects concerning their programme for an Islamic state to be clarified.

The basic premise of their arguments was the need to establish a democracy within the framework of an immanent norm. Popular sovereignty was accepted, and even solicited, as long as it did not transgress the limits of divine law. It was in the name of this principle that the party's representatives objected to the nationalists' contention that the ideals of Islam were contained in *Pancasila*, a notion which all those who spoke on behalf of Masyumi argued vehemently against. The idea that there might exist a norm above their religion was unbearable to them because, as Kasman Singodimedjo explained, it was "impossible to consider *Pancasila* as a 'superfaith' (*supergeloof*)" and to see the "creation of Allah" subordinated to "the work of men".[102]

The question, then, was how to reconcile this superior Islamic norm and the laws which were passed by Parliament. Certain Masyumi deputies, such as Isa Anshary, did not bother to clarify this delicate issue further than by saying that "Islam as a principle and as law" held a solution "for all of humanity's problems, for all nations and in all eras."[103] Others, however, such as Mohammad Natsir, adopted a classic reformist distinction, pointing out that with relation to all matters concerning worship, namely "the relation between men and God", "everything which is not ordained is forbidden".[104] On the other hand, matters concerning "the world of men" were governed by the principle

---

[102] Ibid., p. 183.

[103] *Tentang dasar negara Republik Indonesia dalam Konstituante*, vol. 2, p. 201.

[104] According to Harun Nasution, Ibn Tamiyya was the first to establish this distinction between what concerned worship (*ibadat*) and what concerned the relations between men (*mu'amalat*). Mohammad 'Abduh adopted this distinction and introduced the idea that while the Koran and the Sunnah provided specific rules about *ibadat*, when it came to *mu'amalat* they only gave general principles which man would have to apply to the circumstances of his life. Nasution, "The Islamic State in Indonesia", pp. 127–8.

that "everything that is not forbidden is authorised". For the president of Masyumi, "beside these rules which have been fixed and those limits which must be taken into account for the safeguard of humanity", there existed "a vast area where man had to take initiatives, use his reason and his capacity for interpretation in all areas of life, in accordance with progress and the demands of one's time and place."[105] Natsir gave no details concerning the "limits" which were to circumscribe man's freedom to reason and interpret. Kasman Singodimedjo followed a similar line of reasoning. He presented the practice of free interpretation (*ijtihad*) not as a right but as an obligation written in the Koran (verse 27 of the Az-Zumar Surah),[106] which was to be carried out, however, under the guidance of "the leaders of the people, the state and the government...before the people and before God."[107]

For these Masyumi leaders, then, Islam contained a series of norms, some of which should become the object of interpretation with a view to adapting them to the circumstances of the day, but others which could not undergo any adjustment. At first sight, the existence of immutable rules in the area of worship did not seem to raise any insurmountable problems. In Indonesia, however, the question of which text to refer to was the source of much debate. This was attested to by the confrontation between traditionalists and modernists in their shared mosques during prayer time, when certain aspects of the ritual were considered by some to be obligatory and by others outlawed.[108] Concerning political questions, the problem seemed an even thornier one. The contributions made by Masyumi's deputies left two essential questions unanswered. Firstly, which were the norms considered to be absolute and to which the principle of democracy had to give way? Secondly, what body or authority could be charged with identifying these norms and ensuring they were respected, and where would it get its legitimacy from? Natsir refused to use the term "theocracy" to speak about a "state founded on Islam" (*Negara jang berdasarkan Islam*) due

---

[105] *Tentang dasar negara Republik Indonesia dalam Konstituante*, vol. 1, p. 130.

[106] "And we have certainly presented for the people in this Koran from every kind of example—that they might remember." Koran (XXXIX, 27).

[107] *Tentang dasar negara Republik Indonesia dalam Konstituante*, vol. 1, p. 174.

[108] One of the most important disputes over worship rituals is dealt with by N.J.G. Kaptein, "The *Berdiri Mawlid* Issue among Indonesian Muslims in the Period from circa 1875 to 1930", *BKI* 149, 1 (1993): 124–53.

to the absence in the Muslim faith of a hierarchical clergy who could act as God's representatives on Earth. This was a classic argument, and it led him to define the kind of state which he aspired to as a "democratic-Muslim state" (*Negara demokrasi Islam*) or, to "give it a generic name", a "theistic democracy".[109]

In the absence of an undisputed religious authority, the second of the two questions referred to above seemed to be left hanging in the air. In reality, although they never openly admitted it, the Masyumi members' attitude in the Constituent Assembly showed that they claimed for themselves a preponderant role in defining what constituted legal norms, thus sometimes violating the democratic principle which they otherwise defended. Given that the nationalist secularists held more than half the seats in the Assembly, a refusal to envisage the adoption of *Pancasila* as the foundation of the state obliged the theorists of an Islamic state to perform some verbal gymnastics on the link between democratic principles and majority rule. Kasman Singodimedjo declared himself to be in full agreement with Sukarno when the president denounced what he called *majokrasi*, the tyranny of the majority, a concept which, he claimed, Islam did not recognise. He added, however, that God did not authorise *minokrasi* either, "that is to say the pressure and threats of a small group on the majority!"[110] In the minds of Masyumi deputies, the majority held in the Assembly by the supporters of *Pancasila* did not reflect reality, namely the existence of an overwhelming majority of Muslims in Indonesia, which justified their demand for a state founded on Islam. Natsir denounced the paradox which consisted in the supporters of *Pancasila* wanting, in the name of democracy, to force the Indonesian people to accept an argument which flouted democratic values. Given that a democracy had to guarantee minorities the right to exist within society, there was opposition to Islam becoming the official philosophy of the state on the basis that non-Muslim groups also existed in the country. The president of Masyumi went on to ask "on what basis do we have to accept *Pancasila* as the philosophy of the state, when *Pancasila* also belongs only to one side which does not represent the other groups existing in Indonesia?"[111]

---

[109] *Tentang dasar negara Republik Indonesia dalam Konstituante*, vol. 1, p. 130.
[110] Ibid., p. 183.
[111] Ibid., p. 113.

By ceaselessly basing their legitimacy on the existence of a Muslim majority in Indonesia—and not on the number of votes received by the candidates who were campaigning for a state founded upon Islam— Masyumi effectively denied their fellow Muslims the right to complete political autonomy. Natsir was astute enough to base his criticism of a secularist vision of society, which he described as being "without religion" (*ladienyah*), on examples chosen from Western history. He explained, for example, that one could "clearly notice the consequences" in the constitutional domain, "through the emergence and the development of the Nazi ideology", which could be ascribed, according to him, not only "to a certain Adolph Hitler and the situation in Germany", but "also to the existence of several factors in Western culture". Natsir, as was his wont, quoted a European expert to support his argument—in this case it was Herman Rauschning—and pointed out that the most important of these factors had been "the carefree and irreverent attitude towards the rules of civilisation…and the setting aside of religion's teachings."[112] The decision to refer to a totalitarian ideology which had come to power through democratic elections was, naturally, not a fortuitous one. Natsir did not want to develop this point further, however, and it was once again Isa Anshary who voiced most clearly the problem posed by those Muslims with secularist aspirations.

Striking a much more religious note than Natsir, Isa Anshary expressed his surprise at having to "confront the Muslim community itself, that is to say the men who admit to being Muslim but who refuse Islamic law":

> Why, at a time when we are reading and remembering the divine revelation which commands us to…found our state and our society on the principles of Islamic law, why do a part of our brothers in the faith turn away from this call and from their conscience?[113]

This turbulent figure from West Java then went on to quote the Koran to denounce the true nature of those unworthy Muslims[114]

---

[112] Ibid., p. 122.

[113] *Tentang dasar negara Republik Indonesia dalam Konstituante*, vol. 2, pp. 196–7.

[114] "But the hypocrites say, 'We have believed in Allah and in the Messenger, and we obey'; then a party of them turns away after that. And those are not believers. And when they are called to [the words of] Allah and His Messenger to judge between them, at once a party of them turns aside [in refusal]." *Koran* (III, 47–48.)

before, a little later in his speech, warning them that God's wrath was imminent.[115] As for the consequences for Indonesia if the nation's deputies—the majority of whom were Muslim—refused definitively to fulfil their religious duties, Isa Anshary remained ambivalent. However, his espousal of *djihad fi sabililla*, which in this instance was clearly intended to mean an armed struggle, and the ambiguity of his declaration that "for the safeguard of the mother country, the only way to guarantee the security of the state and the nation's vigilance would be for the Republic of Indonesia to adopt Islam as its ideological foundation", seemed loaded with menace.[116] There was only one short step from the glorification of the defence of an Islamic state to the exaltation of an armed struggle to establish such a state. Although Isa Anshary refrained from taking this step, he nonetheless finished his address by stating "honestly and sincerely...that the seemingly endless problem of Darul Islam promoted by Kartosuwirjo, Daud Beureu'eh and Kahar Muzakkar could only be solved if the Constituent Assembly adopted Islam as the foundation stone of the state."[117] These comments allow one to appreciate the distance travelled by Masyumi since the party's firm condemnations of Darul Islam during the run-up to the election; Kartosuwirjo's movement, which had long been a millstone around the party's neck, now constituted an argument in favour of an Islamic state.

Another representative of the most intransigent wing of Masyumi who had now been given *carte blanche* to speak out on behalf of the entire party was Kasman Singodimedjo. He also referred to the Koran[118] to deny Muslims any latitude in their choice of institutions.

---

[115] "Indeed, those who disbelieve in Allah and His messengers and wish to discriminate between Allah and His messengers and say, "We believe in some and disbelieve in others", and wish to adopt a way in between—Those are the disbelievers, truly. And we have prepared for the disbelievers a humiliating punishment." *Koran* (III, 150–151).

[116] *Tentang dasar negara Republik Indonesia dalam Konstituante*, vol. 2, p. 205.

[117] Ibid.

[118] Not all of the rules laid down by Masyumi's leaders were inspired by the Holy Book. Some of them, although they were not based on any particular source, seemed to brook no discussion. This was the case with the rule decreed by Isa Anshary to disqualify any secular intepretation of nationalism: "Islam would not recognise a nationalist movement or a nationalist doctrine if it was to be used to fight against Allah's laws on the pretext of protecting the unity of the nation." Ibid., p. 211.

> O you who have believed, obey Allah [the Koran] and obey the
> Messenger [*Hadiths*] and those in authority among you. And if you
> disagree over anything, refer it to Allah and the Messenger, if you
> should believe in Allah and the Last Day. That is the best way and
> best result.[119]

For Kasman, the meaning of the verse was clear. The parallel drawn
between the terms "believers" and "those amongst you" indicated "with
certainty the obligation for believers to hold governmental power in
order to guarantee the realisation of the word of God (Koran) and
of the Prophet (*Hadiths*)."[120] Man's freedom to choose remained nonetheless at a much earlier stage. Man could "choose his religion, he does
so freely for it was what God wanted but if he becomes a Muslim,
then he must carry out what his faith commands." The Muslim community therefore, had to "put Islam into practice 100% in Indonesia".
It was an "order from God" whom "we fear even more than our fellow
man, whether he hold power or not, in Indonesia and/or throughout
the world."[121]

The Shura against Democracy

Given that no earthly authority, even one whose legitimacy had been
conferred by universal suffrage, could go against an obligation defined
by divine will, the Constituent Assembly's remit seemed markedly
restricted. One question remained, however: what gave Masyumi representatives the legitimacy to be able to declare themselves the sole inter-
preters of the divine will? Most of them did not provide any clarification on this point; they presented their interpretation of Koranic rules
as self-evident without feeling the need to justify their authority to
decree what constituted an immutable principle and what corresponded
to an adaptable norm.

The only ones to venture an attempt at such a justification were
the more hard-line supporters within the party. Isa Anshary and

---

[119] *Koran* (IV, 59). The references to the Koran and the *Hadiths* in square brackets
do not appear in the original verse, but correspond to Kasman's interpretations.
[120] *Tentang dasar negara Republik Indonesia dalam Konstituante*, vol. 1, p. 175.
[121] Ibid., p. 176. Kasman reminded his audience, shortly before, that if God had
wanted to convert all of humanity to Islam, he would have had no difficulty in
doing so, but that he had chosen to leave man free to convert or not.

Kasman Singomdimedjo both invoked the authority of organisations presented as being representative of the Indonesian Muslim community, although by doing so they unwittingly brought their conception of democracy closer to that held by their worst enemy. In order to justify the ban which, according to him, existed against Muslims joining organisations claiming to be communist, Isa Anshary referred to a long list of documents which he published along with his speech as an appendix.[122] Kasman Singodimedjo chose to refer in his speech to the programme published by the Joint Movement Against Communism (Gerakan Bersama Anti-komunisme) in Bukittinggi in October 1957.[123]

The fact that the two men used a variety of sources to illustrate their points was without doubt not a coincidence. It illustrated their desire to refer not to one single authority, such as an assembly of *ulamas* who were qualified to identify and interpret the divine norm, but to a consensus agreed upon by several bodies supposed to represent the Muslim community. This procedure, which was designed to circumvent a strict application of the democratic principle, was indicative of a shift in the interpretation of the meaning of the term *shura* (religious consensus). Previously, Masyumi's theorists' reading of this notion was consistent with the classic reformist approach, which used *shura* to prove the existence of a democratic ideal in Islam by likening it to universal suffrage, the foundation stone of popular sovereignty. The various declarations which we have just studied show that this notion now appeared to have been markedly diluted to a much narrower meaning. The right to participate in the emergence of this consensus was now

---

[122] A *fatwa* issued by the *ulamas* of Makasar in Sulawesi on 8 June 1954; a resolution voted by the Front Pembela Islam in Makasar which united all the Muslim parties and organisations in the region; two texts published in 1932 by the Al-Azhar University on "the cruelty of Russia towards the Muslim community" and on communism in general; testimony provided by a representative of the Turkestani people at the Asia-Afrika Conference in Bandung illustrating the "murderous terror of communism"; a declaration by Masyumi's West Java branch announcing the creation of its Anti-Communist Front in October 1954; a *fatwa* issued by Persatuan Islam's *ulamas* in 1954 on the role of Muslims in the establishment of an Islamic state; a *fatwa* issued by Masyumi's religious council on communism issued at the Sixth Congress in Surabaya in December 1954; and the resolution voted by the Indonesian Congress of Ulamas held in Palembang in September 1957 demanding the outlawing of the PKI. *Tentang dasar negara Republik Indonesia dalam Konstituante*, vol. 2, pp. 248–96.

[123] *Tentang dasar negara Republik Indonesia dalam Konstituante*, vol. 1, p. 187.

confined to those Muslims who were aware of their obligations towards God. Those faithful who had neglected the teachings of their religion—namely the supporters of *Pancasila*—had no choice but to comply with this, and the enemies of God—the communists—had to disappear. After more than two years of heated debate in the Assembly in Bandung, the proposition defining an Islamic state could be summed up in the form of a syllogism: the only Muslims who were capable of identifying the Islamic principles to be applied were those who respected those same principles.

The Constituent Assembly announced for Masyumi, then, the end of a period which had begun in 1945. In November of that year, the representatives of political Islam had accepted, in response to the challenge laid down by Sukarno the previous June, to form a party ready to take part in elections. The arguments which they developed in Bandung were for the most part the same as those used by their predecessors in the KNIP. When it had become clear that it would now be impossible to draw up a new constitution, the final debates in the Assembly began to sound like the echo of the discussions held 12 years previously. Masyumi's deputies, as well as the rest of Islam's representatives, declared themselves ready to accept a return to the 1945 Constitution, on condition that the Jakarta Charter would be included in the preamble, as was initially intended.[124] The term "Islamic democracy" once again took on the meaning it had in the first months of 1945, namely a regime in which the exercise of political freedom had to be oriented towards the accomplishment of an Islamic ideal.

A Collective Failure: Limited Democracy versus Guided Democracy

To only examine Masyumi's demands concerning the new constitution would run the risk of shouldering it with all the blame for the failings of the Constituent Assembly, when in fact the party does not bear full responsibility. In reality, the failure of the Assembly to reach a consensus and the resultant involuntary sabotaging of Indonesian democracy was caused collectively. As we have already seen, the head of state's denunciation of a Western-style parliamentary democracy, and the elaboration of his programme for Guided Democracy were not

---

[124] Nasution, *The Aspiration for Constitutional Government in Indonesia*, pp. 104–6.

the consequence of the Constituent Assembly's inability to draw up a constitution.[125] Sukarno's proposals were made officially on 21 February 1957, but they were merely the logical conclusion of what had already been alluded to in his speeches given on 28 and 30 October 1956, two weeks before proceedings in the Assembly began. From the outset, then, the Assembly's deputies were aware of the president's intentions.

What is fascinating about Sukarno's political programme was the parallels which could be drawn between it and Masyumi's. Just as their respective arguments in the run-up to the election on the necessity to give substance to *Pancasila* had far more points in common than either of them wished to admit, the doctrine behind the programmes they proposed from 1957 onwards was based on the same observations and the same logic. For both the president and Masyumi's theorists, the Indonesian people had shown, during the previous elections, their inability to adopt the *modus operandi* of a full-fledged democracy. The Indonesian nation, which was divided by movements with divergent aspirations and which was in danger of breaking up, had become incapable of providing itself with a coherent ideology and a collective structure capable of implementing it. What the president and Masyumi both proposed—each in their own different way—was to take on the difficult mission of imposing a narrow framework within which the ideals of the nation's various constituent groups could be voiced. In both cases, this was to be done in the name of values which were considered superior to democracy—Islam for Masyumi, national cohesion for Sukarno. What was most striking, however, in the final showdown between Masyumi and Sukarno was not the similarity between their proposals, but rather the incoherence of the Muslim party's overall strategy. Masyumi figures—foremost amongst them Natsir—were capable of simultaneously developing two contradictory lines of argument in order to rebut Sukarno's proposals. While within the Constituent Assembly they claimed to be ready to go along with Sukarno's programme to bury democracy, outside it on the other hand, and in particular in the Legislative Assembly where all of Masyumi's leading figures had a seat, they posed as the fiercest defenders of the very same concept. This Janus of Indonesian politics appeared, once again, as the conjunction of two conflicting traditions.

---

[125] See supra, Chapter 4.

The desire on the part of the Muslim parties to present a united front in Bandung was no doubt conducive to Masyumi's intransigence. The alliance of those supporting a state founded on the principles of Islam was established around a hard-line position, built upon a certain amount of one-upmanship between Muslim leaders, and consolidated by the opposition's cohesion. The attitude of Nahdlatul Ulama played an important role in this regard. The traditionalist party, thanks to its ideological flexibility but also the ties which it had established with nationalist leaders, seemed to be in the best position to attempt to bring the two movements together.[126] Moreover, one of its slogans during the election campaign was: "support for the ideals of a collaboration between Islam and Nationalism" (*Pendukung Cita-Cita kerjasama Islam-Nasional*).[127]

The political ideology of Nahdlatul Ulama was based upon the Islamic jurisprudence which had been developed over the space of five centuries by the great jurists of the Sunni school.[128] One of the essential elements of this doctrine was the very strong link established between order and piety. Only a stable regime, even if it was an unfair one, could guarantee the proper application of Islamic laws. This was summed up in the maxim, "a year of tyranny is better than a week of anarchy". This principle inspired the two ideas around which NU organised its participation in Indonesian political life. The first of these, known as *maslahat*, meaning useful or beneficial, was to guide *ulamas* in their political choices: any decision had to be the result of weighing up the benefit (*manfaat*) which one could calculate it to give and the wrong (*mafsadah*) which one feared it to bring. The second principle, called *Amar ma'ruf nahi mungkar*—meaning "the preservation of good and the hunting down of evil"—was taken from verse 104 of the Al-Imran *Surah*.[129] Following the tradition of their illustrious predecessors

---

[126] Andrée Feillard, *Islam et armée dans l'Indonésie contemporaine: Les pionniers de la tradition*, Cahier d'Archipel 28 (Paris: L'Harmattan, 1995), pp. 47–8.

[127] Gregory John Fealy, "Ulama and Politics in Indonesia: A Political History of Nahdlatul Ulama, 1952–1967", PhD diss., Monash University, 1998, Chapter 2, "Religio-Political Thought".

[128] Principally, al-Baqillani (950–1013), al Baghdadi (d. 1037), al-Mawardi (974–1058), al-Ghazali (1058–1111), Ibn Taimiyya (d. 1328); Ibn Jama'a (d. 1333) and Ibn Khaldun (d. 1406).

[129] "And let there be [arising] from you a nation inviting to [all that is] good, enjoining what is right and forbidding what is wrong, and those will be the successful." *Koran* (III, 104).

during the Abbasid Caliphate, the NU leaders drew from these precepts a form of political quietism which allowed them on several occasions to collaborate with nationalists.

According to Greg Fealy, NU had two objectives during its participation in the debates over the country's institutions. Firstly, to allow the broadest possible application of Islamic law in the country's substantive law—for matters such as marriages, inheritance and the payment and use of the *zakat*—and secondly, to guarantee Muslims the best possible conditions for the exercise of their religious obligations—employment law needed to be adapted to allow prayer and fasting during Ramadan, for example. The constitutional recognition of the Islamic character of the state, on the other hand, appeared secondary to NU, and unlike Masyumi, it would have been ready to find a compromise on that issue with the nationalists. However, the declarations of NU's representatives in the Assembly did not indicate any concessionary attitude. Rowing back from their previously conciliatory attitude towards *Pancasila*, the traditionalists refused its adoption as the foundation stone of the new Constitution. They feared in particular that the vague nature of the first principle—the belief in one supreme God—would turn out to be a thin edge of the wedge which the Javanese mystical movements (*kebatinan*) would drive home to demand their own official recognition.[130]

In some respects, the traditionalist party's institutional programme seemed far more comprehensive than its reformist rival's. As one of NU's representatives Ahmad Zaini pointed out in his speech, their legal corpus was significantly broader, integrating as well as the Koran and the *Hadiths* which were to serve as the foundations to the constitution and to the country's organic laws, all the Sunni jurisprudence (*ilmu fiqh*) containing most of what would constitute the country's substantive laws as well as their principles of application.[131] More importantly, Nahdlatul Ulama, unlike Masyumi, had solved without difficulty the thorny problem of arbitrating between the divine norm and the democratic norm. Its programme clearly envisaged the presence of *ulamas* within an upper chamber charged with verifying the laws voted by the lower chamber to ensure their conformity with what Islamic

---

[130] Feillard, *Islam et armée dans l'Indonésie contemporaine*, pp. 51–2.
[131] Nasution, *The Aspiration for Constitutional Government in Indonesia*, pp. 85–6.

law prescribed.[132] During the debate on Dasar Negara, one of the Nahdlatul Ulama deputies, Ahjak Sostrosugondo, pointed out the contradiction between divine sovereignty and popular sovereignty. For him, the belief in God which was written into *Pancasila* should lead to the recognition by all Indonesian citizens of divine sovereignty. He went on to explain that in actual fact, however, an atheistic ideology—communism—had developed in Indonesia by hiding behind the principle of popular sovereignty—a principle according to which anyone was entitled to express their opinion, and could freely deny the existence of God. From this, then, Ahjak Sostrosugondo drew the logical conclusion that popular sovereignty was incompatible with faith in God.[133] Far from playing the moderating role that one might have expected, the representatives of Nahdlatul Ulama exacerbated the intransigence of the "*blok Islam*" in the Constituent Assembly. While the limitation of democracy envisaged by Masyumi could be appreciated more in their attitude during the debates than in their speeches to the Assembly, Nadhlatul Ulama's members' view on this question was unambiguously clear.

If we look now at the positions adopted by the various Islamic organisations, Masyumi's stance appears to be a relatively moderate one. The sole representative of the Sudanese Election Movement (Gerakan Pilihan Sunda, Gerpis), a Muslim groupuscule from West Java, demanded in his speech the recognition of "mosques as centres of state power".[134] The Masyumi leadership was clearly also prone to such one-upmanship, especially seeing as it was sometimes carried out by organisations which were affiliated to it. One of the party hardliners, Isa Anshary, for example, who was a Masyumi deputy as well as a representative of Persatuan Islam within Masyumi, used this dual status adroitly. Quoting a manifesto which had been adopted shortly before by Persatuan Islam, he reminded his friends that "the representatives of the Muslim community in the Constituent Assembly...would not accept their responsibility before God and before the court of history"

---

[132] Fealy, "Ulama and Politics in Indonesia". It intended to establish a senate composed of regional representatives, although the exact nature of how they would uphold the Constitution was not specified.
[133] Nasution, *The Aspiration for Constitutional Government in Indonesia*, pp. 111–2.
[134] Ibid.

if they accepted "whether voluntarily or under duress" a constitution "which is not founded upon Islam (i.e. the Koran and the *Sunnah*)."[135] It should be pointed out, however, that not all of those who spoke on behalf of Masyumi succumbed to the temptations of such an unyielding position. Mohammad Sardjan, for example, reiterated the stance taken by the party throughout the election campaign, and refused to enter into a debate aimed at defining an Islamic democracy which was opposed to the nationalists' model or the Western version of popular sovereignty. For him, "democracy, like chemistry, knows no frontiers"; its principles were universal and foremost amongst these were the respect for the individual's fundamental freedoms and multi-partyism.[136]

On the whole, the Bandung Assembly was anything but the "island lost in the middle of choppy waters" which Mohammad Natsir had described. Here, as elsewhere, the formulation of Masyumi doctrine was subject to both the contingencies of the day and the rules imposed by an intractable two-sided confrontation. The speeches made by the party's leaders sometimes sketch the outline of the theistic democracy which embodied their cause, but more often than not, they leave us with more questions than answers. Masyumi's theorists never reached an agreement, for example, on the definition of an Islamic state; it was a question on which there were two often divergent points of view which converged only from time to time. The first theory was the most formalistic one; it followed the tradition of Masyumi's revolutionary heritage and one could define it using the words of H.M. Saleh Suaidy who, at the 1949 congress, described it as "a state in which the state itself implements the laws of Islam for all affairs and all problems."[137] This vision of an Islamic state was defended within the party's leadership by a minority group whose main spokesman was Isa Anshary. It offered Masyumi activists a clearly identified objective, which would be achieved "when [within the state] the guarantee of a religious way of life and the application of Islamic law [was] affirmed."[138] The second conception of an Islamic state was inspired by Mohammad Natsir, for whom this notion referred more to a process than a result. For him, a country like Indonesia, which already recognised the belief in a single

---

[135] *Tentang dasar negara Republik Indonesia dalam Konstituante*, vol. 2, p. 202.
[136] Nasution, *The Aspiration for Constitutional Government in Indonesia*, p. 114.
[137] *Kongres Muslimin Indonesia, 20–25 Desember 1949 di Jogjakarta.*
[138] Anshary, *Falsafah Perjuangan Islam*, pp. 207–8.

God, could automatically be considered as an Islamic state. Nonetheless, the Muslim community could not be satisfied with this label and had to strive, both in political life and in society, to put the teachings of Islam into practice.

Given these divergent definitions, it is easy to understand the unifying role of the notion of a "state founded on Islam" (*Negara yang berdasar Islam*) which was retained in the various official party documents. It avoided the party having to agree on a precise definition of their aspirations, and this ambivalence allowed it to be adaptable to the changes in the party's demands. A broad interpretation of this notion allowed it to serve as the basis of a very open electoral programme capable of appealing to the "statistical Muslims"; a narrow interpretation could justify the party's intransigence at the Constituent Assembly when it called vociferously for the formal recognition of Islam by the state. This second, more radical, attitude owed a lot to the political circumstances of the day. It turned out to be in contradiction with the Masyumi network's painstaking work, undertaken for more than ten years with the intention of bringing into existence the ideal of an Islamic society in Indonesia.

CHAPTER SIX

The Ideal of an Islamic Society

M asyumi was not a typical political party in the sense that its
aim was not solely to gain power in order to implement Islam's
values from above. It laid out a vision for society, but it also wanted
to realise this vision through the organisations which were affiliated to
it. In this sense, it was not so much the country's dominant party as
it was a social movement. The vagueness of its programmes and the
absence of a shadow cabinet contrasted with the scale of the activities
carried out by its social assistance network. This project for Islamisation
from below was a parallel activity which was not in competition with
the party's political objectives; both branches of the party suffered from
the same contradictions, however.

The Masyumi Network and How It Operated

Masyumi was a lot more than a simple political party; it was a vast
network whose ramifications were difficult to apprehend completely.
This was due partly to its organisational structure, which gathered
under one umbrella both individual members and numerous Muslim
associations. In addition, Masyumi exercised direct control over the
various organisations charged with providing social infrastructure to the
Muslim community, including militia groups and unions. Finally, the
party brought its influence to bear over most of the initiatives undertaken in the name of Islam.

A Family Portrait: The Three Circles of the Keluarga Masyumi

Founded by the representatives of the main Islamic organisations in
Indonesia who carried on the torch lit by the Japanese when they

founded the Muslim Consultative Council, Masyumi was originally more of a community-based organisation than a political party. Islam's representatives, as we have already noted, entered the political arena reluctantly, and the decision by the Provisional Assembly to authorise political parties had been severely criticised by the party. The Muslim leaders' political culture and the spirit of unity which had characterised the revolutionary period did not dispose the party to accepting a multi-partite system. It was not suited to debating ideas and taking part in verbal battles whose outcome was decided upon by a vote. However, as they could not just stand by and passively observe the reorganisation of public life, they were obliged to provide themselves with the political machinery which would allow them to make their voice heard. Until 1949, Masyumi's organisational structure was marked by the circumstances in which the party had originated when it was only one element in a vast network designed to provide social structures for the entire Muslim community.

A Federative Structure

The community-based nature of the party could best be seen in the party's two types of members. The party's statutes (*Anggaran Dasar*, AD) stipulated that there were to be ordinary members (*anggauta biasa*), composed of Indonesian citizens belonging to the Muslim faith; and extraordinary members (*anggauta istimewa*), comprising Islamic organisations (*perkoeempoelan2 Islam*). The party rules (*Anggaran Roemah Tangga*, ART) stated, however, that only ordinary members had the right to vote. The organisations could only voice an opinion (*timbangan*), though in order to allow this, the executive committee was supposed to organise consultative meetings "whenever necessary".[1]

The role of the constituent organisations was also recognised in the dual structure of the party leadership. "Next to" (*disamping*) the executive committee, the party statutes provided for a Consultative Council or Party Council (Madjelis Sjoero or Dewan Partai) which, as well as being composed of a chairman and three vice-chairmen, included "*ulamas* and Muslim figures representing the associations and

---

[1] *Anggaran Dasar*, Articles IVa and IVb. *Anggaran Roemah Tangga*, Articles Va, Vb, VIc, ibid., pp. 12–5.

movements which the Indonesian Muslim community is made up of."[2] This council was initially conceived as a sort of body which would lend credibility to the strictly political side of the organisation. It had a large remit: it was charged with "voicing opinions and *fatwas* for the intention of the leadership whenever it was deemed necessary."[3] The two main founding organisations, the Muhammadiyah and Nahdlatul Ulama, participated actively in this council, and between them they divided up the positions of chairman (K.H. Hasjim from NU) and the vice-chairman (K.H.A. Wahid from NU; and Ki Bagus Hadikusumo and Kasman Singodimedjo from Muhammadiyah). The two other Islamic associations which had joined Masyumi at its foundation, the Pekikatan Umat Islam and the Persatuan Umat Islam, were each simply given a seat as an extraordinary member. Most of the positions within the executive committee (*Pengurus Besar*), however, were reserved for those who had been active during the pre-war years in political parties, notably in the PII and the PSII. Amongst the 10 executive committee members endowed with specific roles, such as that of president, vice president, treasurer and spokesperson, Muhammadiyah only had two representatives and Nahdlatul Ulama only had one.[4]

Finally, Masyumis's extraordinary members were also able to use the party congress as another way of bringing their influence to bear on the party. The congress constituted the party's supreme authority: it had to be held every two years to determine the party's policy, and every four years it voted on the leadership of the party. The congress was composed of representatives from different party branches but also of delegates from the constituent organisations.[5]

The composition of the party's central leadership remained the same until 1952, at which point it was modified to ease the tensions which had arisen from the new balance of power between the members

---

[2] "…beberapa Alim-Oelama serta pemoeka-pemoeka islam jang meroepakan per-wakilan dari perkoempoelan-perkoempoelan dan aliran-aliran jang terdapat dalam kalangan Oemmat Islam Indonesia." *Anggaran Dasar*, IVb.

[3] "Memberi pertimbangan dan fatwa kepada Pimpinan setiap waktoe dianggap perloe." *Anggaran Dasar* V.B.

[4] These two groups were better represented, however, amongst the 10 members of the executive committee who did not have a specific role. Six of them belonged to Muhammadiyah or NU.

[5] *Anggaran Dasar*, 1945, Article V.

of the executive committee and the representatives of religious organisations. At this time, a new legislative body called the Party Council (Dewan Partai) was created to hold supreme authority within the party between congresses.[6] It was composed of members of the executive committee—now known as the *Pimpinan Partai*—three representatives elected by each regional branch, two delegates appointed by each constituent organisation, three Masyumi parliamentary deputies and two members of each special organisation (*badan chusus*).[7] The council had to assemble at least once a year, either at the invitation of the executive committee or at the request of a third of the party members.

From its outset, the party benefitted from its widespread presence throughout the country. This was initially thanks to Muhammadiyah, which was firmly established in the country's most populous regions, but also to Nahdlatul Ulama which was well-implanted across Java. As other Muslim organisations joined Masyumi, this network spread further to include Persatuan Islam of Western Java, Persatuan Ulama Seluruh Aceh, Al-Jamiyatul Wasliyah and Al-Ittihadiyah of Northern Sumatra, Mathla'ul Anwar of the Banten region (West Java), Nahdlatul Wathan of Lombok, and finally the Al-Irsyad movement, which had been revived by Indonesia's Arab community. The party, naturally enough, adopted a nationwide structure which mirrored the state's administrative divisions. Each region—known as *karesidenan*, following the terminology inherited from the Dutch—was given its own leadership (*pimpinan daerah*) which, because of its role as representative of the party's central leadership, was also called *Kommissariat Pengoeroes Besar*. This body was elected by different branches (*cabang*) within each region, with every district electing one representative. Every sub-district (*keasistenan*) formed a sub-branch (*anak-cabang*), and an office (*ranting*) was opened in every village.[8] In December 1949, when the new administrative divisions were drawn up, Masyumi revamped its party structure. The regions, which had been transformed into provinces, were now under the responsibility of a new authority called *wilajah*—

---

[6] It adopted the role previously played by the Religious Council (Madjelis Sjuro).
[7] *Anggaran Dasar*, 1952, Article X. As well as these members, the party statutes adopted in 1956 added the presidents of each regional branch (*ketua wilajah*), all of the party's parliamentary deputies and two representatives from the Central Religious Council (Madjelis Sjuro Pusat).
[8] *Anggaran Roemah Tangga*, 1945, Article I.

meaning zone or region—while the party's other subdivisions retained their original names.

Masyumi's Special Organisations (Badan Chusus)

Masyumi reflected a desire to provide structures for the entire Muslim community, and it presided over the birth of several organisations, sometimes termed "autonomous" (*badan otonoom*), whose role was to take charge of various sectors of society.

Muslim women of Masyumi

Muslimat—sometimes spelled Muslimaat—was founded at the same time as Masyumi on 7 November 1945. In accordance with the rules of Islam concerning the separation of the sexes, it constituted Masyumi's female counterpart. Its official name was "Muslim Women of Masyumi" (Masjumi Muslimat). The first role given to this organisation was to offer women the possibility of becoming party activists. The new Masyumi statutes adopted in 1952 mentioned explicitly, in Article 1, that it was open to the so-called weaker sex, but envisaged, in Article 13, that female members would dispose of their own organisation and leadership. Muslimat had identical goals (*azas dan tidjuan*) to its male counterpart, namely "ensuring the sovereignty of Islam as well as of the country and implementing the principles of Islam in the state."[9] On top of that, the organisation had set itself some specific goals to accomplish, such as "leading women from all social categories, including workers and peasants, to an awareness that they belong to the nation and to the state as well as to Islam"; "instilling [in them] a feeling of responsibility and an awareness of their own value (*rasa turut bertanggung djawab dan sadar atas harga diri pribadi*) as members of the nation (*bangsa*) and as members of womankind (*sexe-bewust*). Like the other special organisations within Masyumi, such as unions and youth movements, the Muslimat played an important role in providing the Muslim community with structures and in raising their awareness.

Muslimat had a dual mission, namely to help its members to think and act not just as women, but also as Muslim women. These

---

[9] "Menegakkan kedaulatan negara dan agama Islam; melaksanakan tjita-tjita Islam dalam kenegaraan." Muslimat's statutes can be found in H. Aboebakar, ed., *Sedjarah Hidup K.H.A. Wahid Hasjim dan karangan tersiar* (Jakarta, 1957), pp. 423–4.

two goals were not to be separated, but certain resolutions adopted during the foundation of the organisation emphasised the desire for emancipation—the resolution to encourage the election of women to Parliament and to regional assemblies, for example—while others insisted more on the need to be faithful to their religious identity, such as the resolution to campaign for legislation on marriage which would be in compliance with the teachings of Islam. The Muslimat organigram copied Masyumi's: it disposed of sections in villages and it was represented at the party congress by its own delegates sent by the local branches—one in ten delegates sent by the branches was to be a woman—and by the regional branches—a quarter of the regional delegates had to be female.[10] However, these representatives more often than not assembled in a "Muslimat Congress" held concomitantly with Masyumi's congress. From 1949 onwards, the president of Muslimat was entitled to sit on Masyumi's executive committee, and this right was extended in 1952 to the organisation's vice president.

The independence of the woman's organisation seemed reasonably significant. During its congress in December 1949, for example, it decided to found its own "women's party" (*partai wanita*), called the Muslimat Party. In order to give more substance to its election programme, Muslimat published, under its own name, a "struggle programme" (*program perjuangan*) as well as an urgency programme (*urgensi program*), whose content differed very little from Masyumi's versions and which revealed a desire to take into consideration all of the nation's problems, whether they be political, economic or social. This initiative, however, was not taken any further. There appears to be no evidence that the Partai Muslimat presented a list during the local elections, and for the elections to the Legislative Assembly and the Constituent Assembly in 1955, the Muslimat candidates were incorporated into Masyumi's list.

The Muslim youth movements

On 2 October 1945, at the Muslims' House in Jakarta (*Balai Muslimin Indonesia*), a students' hall of residence, a meeting was held between

---

[10] At the 1946 congress, for example, one in 10 of the representatives sent by local branches was a woman while the ratio was one in four for the regional branches. *Al-Djihad*, 4 February 1946. These proportions varied very little at subsequent party congresses.

Muslim leaders—K.H.A. Wahid Hasjim from Nahdlatul Ulama, Anwar Tjokroaminoto from the PSII and Mohammad Natsir—and young students from the Superior Institute for Islam (*Sekolah Tinggi Islam*) which had just opened its doors. It was during this meeting that the possibility of transforming the Japanese Masyumi into a new organisation was first raised—a possibility which one month later became a reality. The participants decided there and then to create an Indonesian Muslim Youth Movement (*Gerakan Pemuda Islam Indonesia*, GPII), whose leaders were chosen from amongst the students present.[11] The GPII embodied the youthful impetuosity which had played a significant role in the first months of the Indonesian Revolution, and in a certain sense, it paved the way for its elder counterparts in Masyumi. It was not until the Congress of Indonesian Muslims on 7 and 8 November, however, that the new organisation's statutes—quite a brief set of rules—were published. The aim of the Indonesian Muslim Youth Movement, like that of Masyumi and Muslimat, was to defend both Islam and the independence of Indonesia. Its missions (*oesaha*) was to "bring about the unity of Indonesia's young Muslims in order to trumpet the word of Allah" and to "improve their understanding of the mechanisms of the state."[12] The GPII wished to have as broad an appeal as possible and admitted to its ranks all those between the ages of 15 and 35. Although the organisation was open to both sexes, like Masyumi, the GPII quickly developed an organisation reserved for women: the GPII Puteri.

Contrary to the declarations made by its leaders, the GPII was in fact closely associated with Masyumi.[13] Its headquarters were located in the same premises as Masyumi, its statutes declared that it acted "under the authority of Masyumi,"[14] and like Muslimat, it sent its

---

[11] Aboebakar, ed., *Sedjarah Hidup K.H.A. Wahid Hasjim dan karangan tersiar*, pp. 449–50; Lukman Hakiem, *Perjalanan Mencari Keadilan dan Persatuan: Biografi Dr Anwar Harjono, S.H.* (Jakarta: Media Da'wah, 1993), pp. 70–7; I.N. Soebagijo, *Harsono Tjokroaminoto Mengikuti Sang Ayah* (Jakarta: PT. Gunung Agung, 1985), pp. 82–3.

[12] *Anggaran Dasar* GPII, Article 6.

[13] See, in particular, the remarks made by Anwar Harjono to the effect that the GPII was not affiliated to any party or any existing organisation. Hakiem, *Biografi Anwar Harjono*, p. 69. See also similar statements made by Ahmad Buchari during his trial. *Supra*, Chapter 3.

[14] *Anggaran Dasar*, Article 5.

own delegates to Masyumi's congresses. It should also be pointed out that Harsono Tjokroaminoto, elected president of the GPII in October 1945, was not re-elected to this position in November because he had just been appointed to the "youth section" (*bagian pemuda*) of Masyumi's executive committee along with Mh. Mawardi. They, however, both entered the GPII's new executive committee, chaired by R.A. Kasmat, as advisors. The dependant link between the youth movement and its elders in Masyumi was, then, clearly established in 1945, although it did fade somewhat subsequently. From the beginning of the 1950s, the GPII organised its own congresses at different dates to Masyumi's, and the speeches pronounced on those occasions often emphasised the independence of the movement. In October 1953, for example, Dhalan Lukman, a member of the movement's leadership, declared "the GPII is not a political party, it is an organisation which was founded autonomously and without interference."[15] This desire for independence seemed, on the whole, to have received the blessing of the party leaders. It should be said, however, that it was a relatively mild desire, as the youth movement adopted resolutions which, for the most part, echoed those voted by its elders.

When deciding upon the attitude to adopt towards its "autonomous organisations" in general, and the GPII in particular, the party command was torn between two different approaches. They appreciated the large political rallies at which the entire "Masyumi family" assembled, as they served the party's aim of bringing as much influence as possible to bear on Indonesian political life.[16] On the other hand, if the young activists in charge of the GPII appeared overly dependent on the political programme defined by their elders, they ran the risk of losing support. This was all the more likely given that there was stiff competition at the time between the various youth movements. The Marxist movements showed themselves to be very active, and organised numerous events which were open to all organisations.[17] There were also several other Muslim youth groups looking for support from the young Muslims targeted by the GPII: PSII and particularly

---

[15] *Abadi*, 12 October 1953.
[16] The congress in February 1946 in Surakata, for example.
[17] GPII systematically denounced these initiatives.

Nahdlatul Ulama had significant youth movements. Finally, there were two other organisations close to Masyumi—the Indonesian Muslim Pupil (*Peladjar Islam Indonesia*, PII) and the Association of Muslim Students (*Himpunan Mahasiswa Islam*, HMI)—who, in theory, both derived their membership from pupils and students but who, because they did not enforce their membership requirements strictly, also competed with the GPII for followers.[18]

Militia groups

The holy war against Dutch colonial power played, as we have already seen, a crucial role in creating the unity necessary for the formation of the party.[19] It also played an important role in the provision of social infrastructure by activist Islam. The Muslim party had inherited from the Japanese a powerful militia, the Hizboellah—meaning the Army of God—which was incorporated into the organisational structure of the "Masyumi family" at their congress in November 1945. The resolution passed at the time describing it as "the only place where young Muslims can take part in armed struggle" made Hizboellah the military wing of the GPII.[20]

The issue of whether this militia would be subordinated to the party was never properly settled, however. The militia had in its favour the prestige established by their participation in the armed struggle over the previous several months. The political and religious elite who had just taken over control of the group could, at most, provide it with moral support and material assistance. The desire to do so gave rise to the formation of the Barisan Sabilillah: "troops in the path of God" who in theory were the "special sections" (*barisan istimewa*) of the regular Indonesian army (*Tentara Kearman Rakjat*), but who in

---

[18] The PII was founded during the Indonesian Muslim Congress of 1949.The HMI was founded in 1949 and saw itself as the inheritor of the Jong Islamieten Bond. Several of its members subsequently joined Masyumi, though the organisation never had official links with the party. Victor Tanja, *Himpunan Mahasiswa Islam, sejarah dan kedudukannja di tengah gerakan-gerakan muslim pembaharu di Indonesia* (Jakarta: Pustaka Sinar Harapan, 1991), pp. 52–4.

[19] See supra Chapter 2.

[20] "Satoe-satoenja lapangan Pemoeda Islam oentoek berdjoeang dalam ketenteran (kemilitéran)." *Anggaran Dasar* GPII, Masjoemi, Partai Politik Oemmat Islam Indonesia, p. 23.

actual fact provided assistance to Hizboellah exclusively.[21] According to the group's statutes, membership of the Barisan Sabilillah was virtually automatic for any Muslim, and so all Masyumi members were considered to have joined this militia who, unlike Hizboellah, were clearly placed under the authority of the party.

The unions

Masyumi's leaders admired greatly the community support systems provided by the communists, and they adopted their practice of affiliating unions to their party. Four of Masyumi's constituent organisations became involved, in the name of Islam, in the field of labour relations.

Historically, the first union to rally behind Masyumi was Sarekat Dagang Islam Indonesia (SDII), the descendent of the prestigious organisation of the same name founded in 1912. Masyumi gradually took control of it over the course of 1946, and in January 1947, the party invited all the trade associations founded by party members to join SDII.[22] This "special organisation" subsequently contributed very little to spreading the party's social ideals. It never managed to rediscover its pre-war prestige, and Masyumi soon gave up its hopes of turning it into the main mouthpiece for the party's economic policy. Masyumi's press only very rarely reported on SDII's activities and in the preparatory documents for the party's seventh congress held in Bandung in 1956, the Union of Indonesian Islamic Traders no longer appeared on the list of the party's special organisations.[23]

This falling out took place despite the links between the small business community and the *santri*. According to Deliar Noer, it was due to that community's individualist mentality,[24] but two explanations could also be added, which are in fact interrelated. The first one is the historical links between the SDII and the Partai Sarekat Islam Indonesia, which split from Masyumi in 1947; the second is the Masyumi

---

[21] A decision made by the Kongres Oemmat Islam Indonesia which took place in Yogakarta on 7 and 8 November 1945, in *Masjumi, Partai Politik Islam Indonesia*, p. 19.

[22] *Al-Djihad*, 4 January 1947. A few months earlier, the Masyumi branch in Surakarta—the birthplace of the SDII—had announced the foundation of the Perikatan Dagang Muslimin Indonesia (PERDAMI). *Al-Djihad*, 18 October 1946.

[23] Pimpinan Partai Masjumi, *Muktamar Masjumi Ke VIII, 22–29 Desember 1956 Di Bandung*, p. 66.

[24] Deliar Noer, *Partai Islam di Pentas Nasional* (Jakarta: Pustaka Utama Grafiti, 1987), p. 56.

leaders' desire to counter the influence of communists in the workplace by appealing to the working classes a goal that an organisation comprising mostly of small businessmen would clearly find hard to achieve. The party could no longer maintain its pre-war elitist position; it now had to provide itself with mass movements which would be capable of appealing to the most modest social classes in society. Once the party was solidly established in the parts of the country controlled by the Republic, the leadership set about accomplishing this task.

In November 1946, the Union of Indonesian Muslim Peasants (Sarekat Islam Tani Indonesia, STII) was founded. Its aims were both political—"to ensure the sovereignty of Indonesia and help Masyumi to incorporate the teachings of Islam into the state"—and social—"to promote the status of peasants in Indonesian society".[25] The union intended to implement their policy by means of the creation of cooperatives, the organisation of training programmes on modern agricultural practices, tools and machinery as well as various measures designed to protect small landowners by combating problems such as loansharking, selling harvests at a loss and transferring land to foreigners.[26] The STII was officially charged with implementing Masyumi's economic policy in the countryside, and initially its demands were quite broad in nature, calling for measures such as the stabilising of prices and the improvement of the country's transport infrastructure.[27] It was only in the early 1950s that it focused on taking part in projects which specifically involved agricultural practices, such as the rice-harvesting programme, developed in conjunction with governmental bodies, and the creation of village cooperatives. However, it seems that the union's achievements on the whole, as we will see later, fell considerably below the goals it set for itself.

In November 1947, one year after the foundation of the STII, the Indonesian Muslim Workers Union (Sarekat Buruh Islam Indonesia, SBII) was created on the initiative of Soekiman. This organisation's main objective was to counter the growing influence of the All Indonesia Centre of Labour Organizations (Sentral Buruh Seluruh Indonesia, SOBSI), which was under the auspices of the Communist

---

[25] *Anggaran Dasar* STII, Articles I.b, I.a, II.1 and II.2. *Berita Partai Masjumi*, March 1950.
[26] Ibid., Articles IIIa, b, c, d.
[27] *Al-Djihad*, 6 November 1946.

Party.[28] The internal structure of the SBII was organised both according to the country's geographical divisions and to its members' sectors of activity. As with Masyumi, the union was divided into different branches which corresponded to the country's administrative divisions, but at the same time, within every local branch, members were divided up according to their sector of activity into a dozen different sections, including civil servants, employees of the Ministry of Religions, transportation industry, ports and the petrol industry.

The last Masyumi trade union was created much later in May 1945, when Mohammad Natsir inaugurated the Indonesian Islamic Fisherman's Union (Sarekat Nelajan Islam Indonesia, SNII). As with the other unions affiliated to Masyumi, its mission was twofold: "to accomplish/apply the teachings and the laws of Islam within the fishing sector" and "to increase fishermen's standard of living" by "raising their level of education, improving their knowledge of fishing techniques", but also by "strengthening fishermen's attachment to their trade through the removal of any inferiority complex in relation to the rest of society."[29]

The special organisations were part of the extended "Masyumi family". They were placed under the auspices of the party leadership and were supposed to pave the way for an ideal Islamic society which Muslim leaders wished to create. Their ability to garner political support was in theory considered to be incidental; their real role was to transform the sectors of society which they represented. They were invited to participate in discussions on national issues, but above all, they were charged with developing awareness amongst the country's Muslims of the values and rules of their religions. Their programmes and their achievements constituted a valuable indicator of the reality behind Masyumi's policies.

---

[28] I.N. Soebagijo, *Jusuf Wibisono, Karang du Tengah Gelombang* (Jakarta: Gunung Agung, 1980), p. 98. Iskandar Tedjasukmana, dates the creation of the SBII to 1948, on the basis of an article written by its vice president M. Dalyono, *The Political Character of the Indonesian Trade Union Movement* (Ithaca, NY: Cornell University Press, 1958), p. 45.

[29] Pengurus Besar SNII, bagian penerangan, *Anggaran-Dasar Serekat Nelajan Islam Indonesia*, Article 2, 1955.

The Muslim Network and Its Role

Masyumi's influence was not limited to the type of associations and organisations which were clearly defined in its statutes. As well as the official ties that it established with a large number of the *umma*'s support systems, more informal links were also made with different components of the country's Muslim network. To describe or even to give an exhaustive list of the associations which, at one stage or another, had ties with Masyumi either on a local or national level, would be both difficult and tedious. The Indonesian Muslim Congress (Kongres Muslimin Indonesia) held in Yogyakarta from 20 to 25 December 1949 does however give one an idea of the extent and great diversity of this network.[30] Masyumi clearly had a significant influence in the organisation of this vast gathering. Not only was it held directly after the party's fourth congress at the same venue, it was chaired by Wali al-Fatah, a member of the Masyumi leadership who was the party's communications officer, and its secretary general was H. Saleh Suaidy, a member of the Religious Council.

The undeclared intention of this vast gathering was to get the Muslim community to close ranks behind Masyumi, at a time when the country's independence had just been formally recognised. Political Islam's unity had been dented by the breakaway of the PSII two years previously, and at the recent Masyumi congress strong tensions had emerged between traditionalists and modernists. The Indonesian Muslim Congress was the first sign of a new political strategy which Masyumi subsequently employed enthusiastically, namely that of using as large as possible a federation—regardless of how big or representative its constituent organisations were—as an instrument for the key features of the party's policies. At the closure of the congress, its chairman, Wali al-Fatah was able to triumphantly announce the creation of a Committee of the Indonesian Muslim Congress (Badan Kongres Muslimin Indonesia, BKMI) which would be a "fortress of unity for the *umma*".[31] This liaison committee assembled 129 associations, including

---

[30] This was the eighth Indonesian Muslim Congress. The previous congress had been organised in November 1945 and had given rise to the formation of Masyumi.

[31] Badan Usaha dan Penerbitan Muslimin Indonesia, *Kongres Muslimin Indonesia, 20–29 Desember 1949 di Jogjakarta*, p. 18.

all of Masyumi's special organisations and extraordinary members, with the notable exception of Nahdlatul Ulama.[32] Alongside powerful organisations affiliated to Masyumi, the committee contained such obscure associations as the Purwokerto Muslim Committee, the Tegal Ulama (Alim-Ulama Tegal), the Amuntai Charity Committee (Badan Penjelenggara Amal Amuntai) and the Ambon Union of Muslim Workers (Persatuan Islam Buruh Ambon).[33] The BKMI was headed by a general secretariat composed of Abdul Gaffar Ismail, Anwar Harjono and Wali al-Fatah, all of whom were either current or future members of Masyumi.

The 1949 Muslim Congress also decided to create more specialised organisations, including a Women's Institute (Lembaga Kewanitaan) attached to the general secretariat and three youth organisations. The three youth organisations each had a different goal: one was geared towards attracting pupils (the Peladjar Islam Indonesia), one was aimed at students (Himpunan Mahasiswa Islam Indonesia), while the third (Dewan Pemuda Islam Indonesia) was supposed to federate all Muslim youth movements. A Union of Muslim Teachers (Persatuan Guru Islam Indonesia) was also created, as was an Association of Muslim Journalists of Indonesia (Wartawan Muslimin Indonesia). Finally, the congress set up a "committee of experts for the publication of Muslim magazines and books", responsible for organising the translation and publication of an unabridged Indonesian version of the Koran.[34]

In the years that followed, the Badan Kongres Muslimin Indonesia did not give the impression of being particularly active. It was considered, in the words of HAMKA, to be "only a creature of Masyumi" (*kuda-kuda Masjumi sadja*) and it never managed to attract the PSII back into the extended Muslim family.[35] This failure did not prevent the Masyumi leadership from founding other organisations designed to bring together Muslim associations. The party regularly tried to exploit the Muslim community's outrage provoked by various political spats. In 1953, in an attempt to make political capital out of the various

---

[32] NU's youth organisation, Anshor, was part of the committee, however.

[33] Badan Usaha dan Penerbitan Muslimin Indonesia, *Kongres Muslimin Indonesia, 20–29 Desember 1949 di Jogjakarta*, pp. 112–5.

[34] "Menjusun dan menerbitkan terdjamahan Quran jang lengkap dengan bahasa Indonesia." Ibid., pp. 89–92.

[35] *Hikmah*, 26 September 1953.

instances of "insults to Islam", Masyumi tried to re-establish the unity
that had been lost with the revival of Nahdlatul Ulama and the breakaway movement's participation in the Ali government by attempting
on several occasions to bring Muslim associations under one umbrella,
both at a local[36] and national level.[37]

The Lame Duck of Indonesian Politics:[38] *The Limits of Community-Based Politics*

Masyumi grew rapidly during the first years of the Revolution, a period
which lent itself to rather chaotic ways of functioning. For the party,
the end of 1945 and the early months of 1946 constituted a genuine
moment of euphoria. Taking advantage of the organisational structures
inherited from Japanese Masyumi, and also the very strong feeling
of unity which had emerged within the Islamic community after the
Muslim Congress of November 1945, the Masyumi leadership set up a
series of local party branches. The party's press often published triumphalist communiqués, such as the one published on 26 January
1946 in *Al-Djihad*, which proclaimed that in the region of Cirebon,
Masyumi was going to set up five branches, 64 sub-branches and 985
village sections, thus covering the entire region's localities. Two weeks
later, it was the turn of the regional leadership in Madiun to announce
grandiose projects for the party's development. This attempt by the
different regional leaderships to outdo one another by making eye-
catching declarations means that it is difficult to determine with any

---

[36] Amongst the organisations created were the Umma Action Union (Kesatuan
Aksi Ummat Islam) established in Yogyakarta also; and finally a Consultation
Council for the Muslim Community (Madjelis Permusjawaratan Ummat Islam)
in Bandung; and the Union of Muslim Troops (Kesatuan Barisan Islam) in Yogya-
karta between the HMI and the Association of Muslim War Veterans (Persatuan
Bekas Perjuang Islam), which never actually saw the light of day. Ibid.

[37] An example being the Coordination Committee for Islamic Organisations
(Badan Kontak Organisasi Islam) founded in Jakarta at the beginning of 1953.
It was run by Sjarif Usman, a senior figure within Muhammadiyah and Masyumi
who was elected to the Assembly in 1955, and it organised large demonstrations
in February and March 1954 to protest against various declarations made by
nationalist and communist figures which were judged to be disparaging towards
Islam. *Abadi*, 1 March 1954.

[38] To use an expression commonly employed in Indonesian politics at that time
when referring to Masyumi.

certainty the party's actual growth. What is certain, however, is that amongst both its rivals and the foreign observers present in Indonesia, Masyumi soon benefitted from the reputation of being the largest party in Indonesia, and continued to do so up until the 1955 elections.[39]

Calculating the number of party members remained a thorny problem even after the heady enthusiasm of its first years. This was a reflection of the grave crisis of identity which plagued the party right up to its dissolution, but also of its organisational disposition. The difficulty in calculating the number of party members lay in the uncertainty of what actually constituted a party member. Was one only to consider individual members or were extraordinary members to be included also? In other words, should a member of Nahdlatul Ulama—before the 1952 split—and a member of Muhammadiyah be automatically considered as a member of Masyumi? The question was complicated further in 1952 with the creation of a new category, known as core-members (*anggauta teras*).[40] This new group was to be composed of individual members who were particularly active within the party. They were selected from the party's ordinary members, and their role was "to undertake particular missions at the request and on behalf of the party leadership." This status allowed them to attend meetings of the party's executive committee and voice their opinions on the missions they had been entrusted with, though they were not entitled to vote there.[41] Finally, core-members were supposed to contribute more to the party's finances: their membership subscription cost 2.5 rupiahs per month, unlike ordinary members who only paid 0.5 rupiahs.[42] According to Deliar Noer, though, this arrangement, which was in violation of a custom of asking those who were most involved in the party to pay less, was not entirely respected.[43] We have no clear picture

---

[39] This was the conclusion arrived at by George McTurnan Kahin. "Indonesian Politics and Nationalism", in (*Asian Nationalism and the West*, ed. William L. Holland (New York: The Mac Millan Company, 1953), p. 74.

[40] According to Noer (*Partai Islam di Pentas Nasional*, p. 53), the existence of this category of core members had been decided at the party's inaugural congress in 1945. However, the decision only appears in the statutes adopted at the 1952 congress.

[41] "…diatas tanggung-djawab dan permintaan anggauta pengurus/pimpinan berkewadjiban aktip membantu sesuatu usaha partai." ART 1953, Article 8.4.

[42] ART, Articles 22 and 23.

[43] Noer, *Partai Islam di Pentas Nasional*, p. 53.

of what place this new category of members occupied within the party, as no accurate count was made of their number. It is my view that this supplementary, and ultimately futile, complication of the party's organisational structure was above all an illustration of an approach which consisted in identifying, often loosely, the entire Muslim community with their political cause, but which cloaked the party's difficulty in developing party activism to any real extent.

There were obvious reasons for Masyumi to regularly advance colossal figures when referring to its supporters. One of these was the need to justify its claim to be the unique representative of a Muslim community numbering in the tens of millions. Before the Round Table Conference Agreement in 1949, the party contended that it had more than two million members within the territory controlled by the Republic.[44] Two years later, after it had established itself across the country, it claimed to have founded 237 branches, 1,080 sub-branches and 4,982 village sections, making up a total of ten million members.[45] The first cracks in this veneer of self-importance appeared when Jusuf Wibisono, one of the party's vice presidents, explained in 1951 that although Masyumi membership was normally estimated to be around 13 million, the number of members registered with the party's executive office did not exceed 600,000, and those who possessed a valid membership card only numbered 400,000.[46] These harsh observations were accompanied by some very lucid considerations about the status of the party's constituent organisations, which we will come back to later on. Jusuf Wibisono's article had an undeniable impact on the party, and fanciful claims about its size subsequently became quite rare. The guide to political organisations published by the Ministry of Information, whose only source of information on membership numbers came from the parties themselves, did not provide any figures for Masyumi in its 1954 edition, unlike in previous years.[47] It was only in 1956—perhaps as a result of its poor performance in the elections— that the party leaders decided to carry out the very first exhaustive

---

[44] Statistics given by Soekiman in his presentation of the party in Kementerian Penerangan Republik Indonesia, *Kepartaian di Indonesia*, 1950, p. 9.

[45] Kementerian Penerangan, *Kepartaian di Indonesia*, 1951, p. 14.

[46] Jusuf Wibisono, "Masjumi di masa datang", *Suara Partai Masjumi*, February 1951.

[47] Kementerian Penerangan, *Kepartaiain dan Parlementaria Indonesia*, 1954.

inventory of the party's membership. The undertaking did not get very far however, as only six out of 13 regions and 63 out of 276 branches took part in the survey. Nonetheless, the 667,868 members that the survey listed allow one to have an idea of the party's magnitude.[48]

Masyumi's inability to calculate accurately how many members it had should not be seen simply as proof that the party's activists were not committed enough to its cause; quite the contrary in fact. During the revolutionary period, Masyumi gave the feeling of being, above all, a big family, and this lasted well beyond 1949. Paradoxically, however, the stronger people's feeling of attachment to this *"keluarga Masyumi"* was, the less they bothered with the party's administrative formalities. At all levels of the party, there was a significant number of keen activists who had never actually gone through the procedures required to register properly with the party. The most famous case concerning a national party figure was that of H. Rasjidi, who had been minister for religions in the first Sjahrir government formed in November 1945. Rasjdi was a member of Muhammadiyah, and so he had been given his place in cabinet as a member of Masyumi, despite the fact that he had never actually officially joined it. This type of embarrassing scenario still existed long after the Revolution had finished. At the 1956 party congress in Bandung, Deliar Noer met a university professor, Gadjah Mada, who was present as a representative of the Yogyakarta branch of Masyumi, but whose name appeared on no party membership list.[49] Another party figure in Yogyakarta, Achid Masduki, who headed the Masyumi group in the regional assembly during the 1950s, confided to me that he too had never obtained a membership card.[50]

The sense of community belonging amongst the party's closest supporters was forged during the period known as the "Physical Revolution". It was founded upon Masyumi's ability to provide support systems for diverse sectors of society and various activities. During the armed struggle with their former colonial masters, Masyumi not only formulated political and religious goals for their followers, but also helped to furnish the armed forces with supplies, to provision the local populations and to administer the parts of the country which had been

---

[48] Although one should not trust completely the sincerity of all of these declarations. Noer, *Partai Islam di Pentas Nasional*, p. 53.
[49] Interview in Jakarta, September 1996.
[50] Interview in Yogyakarta, September 1996.

devastated by the war.[51] It was perfectly natural, then, for the party to continue to expand in this way after the Revolution. Once Masyumi had established a new branch in a locality, it set about creating local sections of the Muslimat, the GPII, the STII and the SBII, sometimes even opening a branch of one of its constituent organisations if one did not already exist. In February 1951, for example, the Madjen branch of Masyumi announced the opening of an STII section as well as a local branch of Muhammadiyah.[52] This development of the party's offshoots favoured good relations between its different organisations, especially since the local heads more often than not came from the same small circle of people. A good example of this was H. Marcoesya, who founded the Masyumi branch in Banjarsari in Central Java in 1948, participated in the creation of the Muhammadiyah branch there in 1952, and as a landowner, also held a position within the local STII section. He and a small group of friends controlled the various Masyumi organisations jointly by rotating the key positions between themselves; although ordinarily, one person could not head two different organisations, nothing stopped him from chairing one while acting as treasurer in another.[53] In the case of Muslimat and the GPII —or the PII, depending on the locality—they were more often than not in the hands of the wives and children of Masyumi figures.

Relations between the different members of the *keluarga Masjumi* were also fostered by the holding of various local events, which provided an opportunity for the party's different organisations to come together. At village and district level, meetings were generally composed of Masyumi and its "autonomous organisations", such as Muslimat, the GPII and the party's unions. The visit of a senior party figure, who generally visited several localities per day and wished to meet as many people as possible in a short period of time, was another occasion for party gatherings. These visits gave the party an opportunity to organise strong shows of support in towns and villages by festooning the streets with flags bearing the star and crescent moon. When the election campaign started properly in 1954, a new custom appeared which consisted in organising a horn-honking motorcade throughout the locality being

---

[51] Throughout 1946, *Al-Djihad* reported on the wide range of activities being carried out by the party. See, in particular, 29 January, 4 March, 9 April and 7 May 1946.

[52] *Berita Masjumi*, 27 February 1951.

[53] Interview in Banjarsari, September 1996.

visited. The popularity of the visiting dignitary and the party's presence in the region was now no longer measured by the number of people attending a traditional rally, but rather by the size of the traffic jam created by their convoy. On 21 July 1954, during a visit to West Java, Isa Anshary was welcomed in Lumajang by "sixty cars and fifty motorbikes", which led the *Abadi* reporter to conclude that he had received a better welcome there than the previous day in Besuki.[54] On 27 March 1955, Mohammad Natsir attracted "eighty cars and numerous motorbikes sent by the GPII" in Mataram on the island of Lombok. A few weeks later in Massa, he improved his score with nearly 200 vehicles, "including jeeps and lorries",[55] though he never managed to surpass Isa Anshary and Jusuf Wibisono, who were welcomed on 3 July 1954 in Yogyakarta by "at least 125 cars and 200 motorbikes".[56]

Five years after the Physical Revolution, the preparation of the elections provided an opportunity for the cooperation between the different constituent organisations to be renewed, and the "Masyumi family" (*keluarga Masjumi*) was rechristened "the crescent moon and star family" (*keluarga bulan bintang*) in reference to the party's emblem. Between the Revolution and the elections, two crucial moments in Indonesian history, one area in which "family solidarity" was very strong was the communication of Masyumi's policies. When the party deemed it particularly important to air its position on a certain issue, the local sections of all the party's constituent organisations took care of matters. The party's press would subsequently be bombarded with messages and motions from the four corners of the country, generally using the same terms employed in the communiqué sent out from party headquarters.

Once Masyumi's network was firmly established throughout the country, its various components carried out their activities at a steady pace. Their diversity—they reached out to all areas of society and were represented at all political levels—and their number—there were several thousand local sections—means that it would be impossible here to paint a complete picture of them. I will restrict myself to examining a few examples which will give us an insight into the Masyumi family's *modus operandi*.

---

[54] *Abadi*, 23 July 1954.
[55] *Abadi*, 31 March and 6 June 1955.
[56] *Abadi*, 6 July 1954.

A Chaotic System

Masyumi appeared, on the surface, to possess a clear hierarchical structure, and also boasted an impressive catalogue of constantly updated party rules, but it suffered from three major flaws throughout its history. The first was linked to the internal hierarchy of the party, the second was connected to the party's finances and the third was related to the attribution of roles to Masyumi's different constituent organisations.

The relations between the sections, branches and leadership of the party and their respective roles and responsibilities never corresponded in practice to what the party's statutes had laid out. In theory, only the party bodies holding authority at the national level—the executive committee and the congress—were entitled to speak out, on behalf of all its members, on national or international issues. In reality, all local sections of the party did this. In most cases, this did not affect the running of the party, and was even part of a strategy, albeit an unspoken one. When the Sukabumi branch of Masyumi delivered a demand to the head of state, the government and the minister for defence, calling for the region's crime problems to be dealt with more efficiently, it stepped beyond its remit, but it nonetheless followed the party line on this issue.[57] However, when in December of the same year the West Java branch called for the resignation of the government and threatened to ask the president to name a new cabinet, or when the South Sumatra branch declared that it considered the second Ali government to no longer be in office since the announcement of the "Sukarno conception", they both went much further than Masyumi's "official" positions.[58] Likewise, although the party's statutes only allowed the congress to pass judgement on the policies pursued by the executive committee, local branches regularly voiced their opinions on this topic. In the vast majority of cases, this amounted to nothing more than a vote of confidence in favour of the party leadership, who did not pass any comment on it, but in at least one case, the opposite took place. In September 1956, the Masyumi branch in Sulawesi adopted a motion calling for the withdrawal of Masyumi ministers from cabinet. This declaration, which was reported by all of Indonesia's newspapers,

---

[57] *Abadi*, 4 February 1953.
[58] *Abadi*, 21 December 1953 and 6 March 1957.

was an embarrassment for the leadership. A few days later, Mohammad Natsir published a somewhat muddled explanation. He reminded the local party branches that they were entitled to speak out on regional issues, and not national ones. He also stated that the Sulawesi declaration had been adopted "because of the local situation" and that for this reason it was authorised by the party leadership.[59]

The second area which illustrates the party's malfunctioning was the management of its finances. The party's rules stated that every member had to pay a monthly contribution (*iuran*) to the party—this was fixed in 1953 at 0.5 rupiah for ordinary members. These funds were to be shared amongst the different components of the party according to a very strict division: 50% was to go to the sections, 10% to the sub-branches, 20% to the branches, 10% to the regional branches and 10% to the national leadership.[60] The treasury department regularly published announcements in the party's press reminding members of this rule, which would indicate that they did not apply these regulations strictly. The testimony which I managed to obtain from local party leaders confirmed this impression.[61] All of those with whom I spoke explained that the collection of members' contributions happened in a very piecemeal fashion—during a party rally, for example. At various party gatherings, people gave according to their means, and they did so with the feeling that they had fulfilled the duty in Islamic law to give alms (*zakat*). This way of raising money posed two problems for the party leadership. The first was how to calculate the amount of money which had been collected, and thus the sum which should be transferred to the party headquarters; the second was a question of principle which gave rise to several controversies: was it possible to use money raised as *zakat* for electoral purposes?[62]

---

[59] *Abadi*, 13 September 1956.

[60] Anggaran Rumah Tangga, Article 22.

[61] According to Mr Khamdan, who became a party member in Pamekasan in 1955, there was no subscription and membership cards were issued for free. Interview in Bandund, September 1996.

[62] In July 1954, for example, correspondent for the daily newspaper *Suluh Indonesia* accused the local Masyumi branch of having misappropriated 73,000 rupiah in 1950 and 1951 to fund its election campaign. The branch in question strenuously denied these accusations, citing testimony given by religious figures that the amount in question had indeed been transferred to the *zakat* committee, which contained representatives of all Muslim organisations. This scandal took on national significance and the minister for religions was asked to intervene.

Masyumi's inability to manage its financial affairs soundly and efficiently revealed the disparity between the wishes of the party leaders eager to build a modern political party and the country's sociological realities. The economist and senior party member, Sjafruddin Prawira-negara, who was charged with the difficult task of overseeing Masyumi's finances, bleakly noted this disparity in February 1951 in a long report on the party's financial situation. He pointed out the danger for the party's independence of its members' non-payment of subscription fees. The report was unequivocal: the budget for the previous year which had been managed by the party leadership amounted to 522,125.47 rupiahs, of which only 4% came from membership subscriptions; less than 5% of the party's members were actually fully paid up. Sjafruddin deeply regretted this state of affairs, and warned the party of the threat which this situation posed to its independence. If it was obliged to "apply for subsidies from the government", Masyumi "would no longer be in a position to exercise any oversight" over the government if ever it turned out to be corrupt.[63]

The third problem that the Masyumi network was confronted with was the distribution of roles between its different components. The party's desire to set up support structures for the Muslim community in Indonesia had led, as we have already seen, to the creation of a series of independent organisations—each charged, in theory, with a specific sector of society. In reality, however, things were not so simple. The national leaders and the local sections of the different movements did not always limit themselves to the activities provided for by their statutes; this sometimes owed to the fact that they possessed a certain set of skills or a marked interest in a particular area. The party itself did not appear to set strict boundaries to their projects, even if it meant that they encroached on the special organisations' domains. Apart from its purely political activities, it regularly initiated projects dealing with a wide variety of areas. On several occasions, for example, Masyumi took on the role normally occupied by its unions in order to intervene in labour disputes in various sectors of the economy. In January 1953,

---

The minister, however, refused to become involved in the affair, explaining that, in theory, only *imams* or an Islamic government were entitled to collect and distribute the *zakat*, but given that Indonesia did not recognise Islamic law, the state could not take on this task. It was thus up to the religious organisations to come to an arrangement on the question. *Abadi*, 2 December 1954.

[63] *Suara partai Masjumi*, February 1951.

one of the sections in Jakarta created a Mutual Assistance Association (Jajsan Usaha Bersama) which was a mutual savings cooperative designed to provide poor small farmers in the surrounding area with financial and technical assistance.[64] A few months later, the Masyumi regional branch in Jambi, without any particular regard for the Union of Muslim Peasants (STI), bought a part of the local suppliers' rubber production in order to maintain price levels, and then asked the government to buy it from them.[65] Likewise, the party regularly dealt with questions of education, which normally came within the remit of the GPII. It was, for example, behind the creation of several educational establishments, from an Islamic secondary school in Kediri in 1946 to an Islamic university in Medan a few years later.[66]

Two organisations with links to Masyumi—the Indonesian Muslim Youth Movement (GPII) and, to a lesser extent, Muslimat—took a very broad interpretation of their roles. The GPII's natural area of expertise covered all matters concerned with education in general, and in particular the place religion should occupy in schools. Some of the organisation's resolutions, which it had adopted both at local and national gatherings, dealt with this area. It campaigned, for instance, for government recognition of financial assistance to religious schools, and also for a change in the school curriculum in order to incorporate mandatory religion classes into public school timetables.[67] However, for reasons which we have touched on previously, the GPII endeavoured throughout the period concerned to establish itself as a political organisation in its own right, speaking out regularly on contemporary national and international issues. Among its forays into the political arena, were the organisation of a vast campaign on the problem of Irian, a demand made to France to stop its repression of the "Islamic Liberation Movement" in Morocco and its call for the Ali Sastro-amidjojo government to resign.[68] This wide-ranging activism enabled it to pose as a representative of the entire Muslim youth community and not just those young people who supported Masyumi. They thought, moreover, that the same attitude should apply to the organisation's

---

[64] *Hikmah*, 7 January 1953.

[65] *Abadi*, 22 October 1953.

[66] *Al-Djihad*, 21 November 1946.

[67] See, for example, the resolutions voted by the GPII's seventh congress. *Abadi*, 23 February 1955.

[68] *Berita Masjumi*, 5 January and 7 March 1951. *Abadi*, 7 January 1955.

elders, and called for Muslim unity, "regretting" the decision by Nahdlatul Ulama to leave Masyumi and later calling for the formation of a single Muslim group in the Constituent Assembly elected in 1955.

Masyumi's women's organisation focussed on three areas in particular: the fight against illiteracy, the establishment of marriage laws "in conformity with the teachings of Islam" and the defence of public morality. These objectives were closely linked insofar as they all aimed at protecting or improving women's condition: the difficulty women encountered acquiring a social status on a par with men's was due to their lower level of education; Muslim matrimonial law was considered to be the body of law which would best protect women's interests; finally, women were the greatest victims of the erosion of public morality. Muslimat initially set out to achieve these objectives through training programmes which they established both locally and nationally.[69] Over the years, however, initiatives taken regionally meant that the organisation extended its field of activity considerably. It became involved in the economic sector through its management of savings cooperatives designed to finance small-scale business projects, such as the door-to-door selling of goods. Its activities developed from simple courses on hygiene to managing hospitals, and its campaign against illiteracy brought it sometimes into the country's universities.[70] The Muslimat's extension of their sphere of activity led it, naturally enough, to broaden the scope of the resolutions it voted at its national congress. From 1949 onwards, various demands were made in the name of improving women's lot, which touched on areas as diverse as politics—a new constitution was called for—economics—a proposal was made to nationalise banks—and international affairs—a motion for Indonesian membership of the UN was passed.[71] These incursions into the political field

---

[69] In April 1954, for example, the organisation announced the creation of a centre designed to help women not only run their households but also understand the society in which they lived. The courses lasted six months, and on top of cooking lessons, they included classes on spirituality, politics and history. *Abadi*, 21 April 1954.

[70] The Muslimaat branch in Bandung was indicative of this evolution: during the 1950s, it ran several cooperative banks, two hospitals and also participated in the foundation of the Bandung Islamic University (UNISBA). Interview with Oya Somantri, September 1996.

[71] See the accounts of the Muslimat's congresses between 1946 and 1955 in Aboebakar, ed., *Sedjarah Hidup K.H.A. Wahid Hasjim dan karangan tersiar*, pp. 423–35.

for the most part echoed Masyumi's policies, and the women's organisation never provoked the party politically in the same way that its youth organisation did.

The unions were the only organisations within the Masyumi family who limited themselves to a specific field of activity. This was no doubt due to their limited resources: the Indonesian Muslim Workers Union (SBII) only had a membership of 250,000, while the Union of Indonesian Muslim Peasants (STII) had barely more than 100,000 members.[72] These organisations were both involved in providing their members with training programmes—their local sections regularly announced the holding of training sessions designed to improve workers' technical knowledge—but also to better their understanding of politics and religion. In SBII's case, the majority of its efforts were devoted to training programmes whose aim was to train union representatives capable of countering the influence of communist unions within factories and companies. Their knowledge of Islam enabled these officers to be appointed as *imams* in their workplace and to give advice both of a spiritual (*rohani*) nature and of a legal nature to the workers who were, "for the most part, Muslims".[73] The peasants union, on the other hand, focussed on acting as an intermediary in transactions between rice producers and the government, who bought their harvest. The outcome of this undertaking, which determined the influence held by the union, was ultimately dependent on whether Masyumi was in government. During Ali Sastroamidjo's first government in 1954, for example, the STII's calls for the sale of rice to be entrusted to the organisations that had already proved their ability to perform such tasks fell on deaf ears.[74]

Before finishing this brief description of the activities carried out by the Masyumi network, we should dwell a little on what turns out to be one of its main characteristics, namely the disparity between the programmes announced by the party and their implementation. Of the

---

[72] Masyumi's two other unions did not have a very significant role in labour relations. The Union of Indonesian Islamic Traders no longer appeared on the list of the party's "autonomous organisations" from the 1950s, while the activity of the Union of Muslim Fishermen was very limited and was rarely reported in the party's press.

[73] See the report on a training programme offered to workers, which lasted a month and included an exam at the end. *Abadi*, 18 July 1953.

[74] *Abadi*, 19 January 1954.

numerous reports in the party's press about the "Masyumi family's" activities, very few of them concerned projects which were actually completed—almost 70% of them announced upcoming initiatives.[75] It was obviously not in the interests of the party to hush up its own accomplishments, and as we have already seen, its leaders were wont to organise anniversary gatherings to celebrate its achievements. The only plausible explanation for this silence, then, is that most of these programmes either did not materialise or only lasted a couple of months.

This disparity between the enthusiasm with which projects were unveiled and the failure to follow through and accomplish them was prevalent at all levels of the Masyumi family. At the national level, we have already seen that the famous "core-members" (*anggauta teras*) set up by the Urgency Programme in December 1949 were only ever mentioned subsequently to note that they were not paying the requisite contributions. Likewise, the ambitious project for a political academy, which the party had announced with bells and whistles in September 1946, never in fact saw the light of day. This establishment, which was set to open in Yogyakarta, was supposed to become "one of the sources of Islam's renaissance". It was to offer courses given by experts in the fields of Islamic law, constitutional law, economics, sociology and history.[76] No further mention was made in the following years of this "political academy" and Achid Masduki, who in 1948 became a party representative in the regional assembly in Yogyakarta, has no recollection of such a programme.[77] As for the Study Committee on Decentralisation, whose creation was announced in April 1951, it never published a report on its activities, despite the fact that there was no shortage of matters to consider or opportunities to intervene in the debate.[78] At a local level, the party's achievements should, logically, have provided it with powerful leverage during the campaign leading up to the 1957–58 regional elections. However, the space devoted by *Abadi* to singing the party's praises at every regional election only mentioned its promises, and likewise the accounts of visits by national party leaders only rarely mentioned specific programmes which had actually been undertaken.

---

[75] This percentage was calculated based on the 310 dispatches which appeared in the 10 editions of *Berita Masjumi* published in March and April 1951.
[76] *Al-Djihad*, 25 September 1946.
[77] Interview, Yogyakarta, September 1996.
[78] *Berita Masjumi*, 3 April 1951.

The press's silence on party activities mentioned above did not always signify that those enterprises had met with failure, however. The party often co-opted activities which were already being carried out traditionally in villages, and so their success was not always dependent on Masyumi involvement. In Banjarsari, for example, the STII coordinated the custom of mutual help (*gotong royong*) in order to foster cooperation in certain activities, such as the upkeep of roads or the repairing of houses. This section of the union did not, however, found a cooperative.[79] In other villages, though, the ambition of a local party figure or a community's desire to broadcast its achievements could mean that these activities were given a more official air, and presented as being carried out in the name of the party. The link between these programmes and the party, which the press drew attention to, relied, then, on a small number of individuals. Masyumi's involvement in such projects was above all for publicity reasons. The organisational and financial capacity of the Masyumi family did not allow it to provide the kind of technical or financial assistance that would make it an indispensable part of such an operation.[80] It was enough, then, for a local Masyumi figure to lose interest in a project, or simply stop informing his superiors about it, and any links between it and the party would disappear; this, however, had very few real repercussions for what was actually happening on the ground.

Conflicts: The Battle for Power and the Confrontation between Traditionalists and Modernists

The dual nature of the party's membership, with both individual members and constituent organisations, meant that its internal disputes could originate from two different sources. They could come in part from the existence within the party of different wings which were led by rival party figures who disputed the party leadership and had different strategic visions for the party. They could also be caused by the difficulty in getting different organisations, who represented different trends within Islam and who had a long history of discord, to work together.

---

[79] Interview with H. Marcoesya, September 1996.
[80] There is no evidence of the larger branches sharing expertise with or lending material to the party's village sections. Moreover, money generally circulated, if at all, from the lower echelons of the party to its higher levels.

A bitter conflict occupied Masyumi's leaders for almost the entire lifespan of the party, opposing two men who represented two different wings within the organisation. The two men were Soekiman Wirjo-sandjojo, the party's first president, and Mohammad Natsir who suc-ceeded him as party leader in 1949. The two men's different political sensibilities could be traced back to 1945 and were often presented as being the result of a generational clash.[81] This clash should not merely be taken to indicate a difference in age between the two men, however —there was, after all, only 10 years between them. Nonetheless, Soekiman, who was born in 1898, had already attained some political experience before the war. By the time independence was proclaimed, he was already a noted leader and was recognised as such by Masyumi's inaugural congress where he was elected leader ahead of the chairman of the PSII Abikusno Tjokrosujoso. Like the other figures of this "generation of 45"—*angkatan 45* as it was custom to call them in Indonesia—Soekiman had been greatly affected by the internal wran-glings of the nationalist movement in the 1920s and 30s, including those caused by Muslims.[82]

Since that time, he was ready to make considerable concessions for the sake of the sacrosanct struggle for independence, and this made his relations both with the traditionalists of Nahdlatul Ulama and the secular nationalists of the PNI much easier.[83] Although Soekiman was a devout Muslim, his educational career meant that his knowledge of Islam was limited. He never contested the primacy of the *ulama* in religious matters, even if they were traditionalists, and always showed them profound respect. During his very active presidency from 1945 to 1949, religious officials within the party saw their role recognised within the Madjelis Sjuro, which entitled them to intervene in the elaboration of the party's central policies.[84] Although he belonged to the modernist movement within Islam, Soekiman always maintained good relations with the leaders of Nahdlatul Ulama. He wanted to turn Masyumi into the party of the entire *umma*, and as he was aware that the balance of power within Indonesian society was favourable towards the traditionalists, he always endeavoured to placate their sensibilities.

---

[81] See, for example, Noer, *Partai Islam di Pentas nasional*, p. 60.
[82] See, supra, Chapter 1.
[83] Amien Rais points this out in his preface to a collection of Soekiman's articles entitled *Wawasan Politik Seorang Muslim Patriot Jakarta* (Jakarta: YP2LPM, 1984).
[84] A right which the religious officials used very rarely in reality.

His relations with the nationalists were informed by the same mindset. Soekiman was part of the group of national leaders who had virtually never left Yogyakarta between 1946 and 1950. He had become instilled with the ultra-nationalist spirit which reigned at that time in the Republic's capital, and for two years he maintained a hard party line which consisted in demanding "100% independence" and refusing any official participation by Masyumi in Sjahrir's first two cabinets, which, at the time, were engaged in negotiations with the Dutch. This closeness of opinion between Soekiman and nationalists subsequently enabled him to maintain favourable relations with the head of state when Soekiman himself became prime minister from April 1951 to April 1952, and indeed he supported the president's intransigent position on Western New Guinea. When Masyumi, by this stage under Natsir's leadership, entered into open confrontation with the president over his institutional reforms, Soekiman attempted to avoid the deterioration of relations with Sukarno. When this finally became inevitable, his criticism of the head of state always remained moderate in tone, in contrast with the vitriolic attitude of other Masyumi leaders.

Soekiman had a vision of the party as a vast popular gathering, founded on a shared sense of belonging to a community which was both religious and national. This explains his insistence on the party's role in establishing social support structures, an objective he placed at the top of his party's agenda.[85] For him, the ideas defended by Masyumi had to progress from the bottom up through all levels of politics and society. From his point of view, discord was best avoided, and cooperation with other political forces, even if it was not perfect, was always preferable to getting involved in a power struggle. This consensual attitude was not extended towards the communists, however, and indeed the fight against communism was, for Soekiman, one of the main arguments in favour of a policy of harmonious cooperation between parties, based on a tireless search for the lowest common denominator.

Soekiman had arrived at religion through politics, and his political career reflected this order of priorities. Natsir, on the other hand,

---

[85] See, for example, a speech given by him on 6 May in Yogyakarta, reproduced in *Wawasan Politik Seorang Muslim Patriot*, pp. 277–300.

took the opposite path. He was first of all a teacher within Persatuan Islam before moving on to the Madjelis Islam Bandung during the Japanese occupation, and up until January 1946, his political role was a secondary one. In August 1945, he was appointed to the KNIP and at the same time he became head of youth affairs within the Masyumi leadership. Shortly afterwards, his organisational abilities as well as the excellent relationship he had with Sutan Sjahrir earned him a seat at cabinet in January 1946 as minister for information.[86] Natsir quickly emerged as the leader of the trio of Masyumi members composed of himself, Sjafruddin Prawinegara and Mohammad Roem, who had agreed to participate, initially in a personal capacity, in the government headed by the PSI leader.[87]

At the 1949 congress which saw Natsir take over the presidency of the party, he did not just represent the young generation against Soekiman. His experience within Persatuan Islam—an elitist organisation—and his collaboration with Sjahrir made him the representative of another vision of political action founded more on coherence than on consensus. The comprehensive religious education he had received and his conception of Islamic nationalism, which he had written about extensively, meant that he was not inclined to share a political platform with either traditionalists or nationalists. For him, Masyumi should not simply be a loosely defined expression of Muslim sensibilities exerting only a diffuse influence on Indonesian political society, but rather a body capable of exercising real political power. Soekiman had been the president of a vast movement which had established itself as an organisation. Natsir, on the other hand, was the president of a full-fledged party. By drawing the political consequences of Muslim reformism—through such measures as the significant curtailment of the *ulamas'* sphere of activity and the favouring of a pragmatic approach—he became the architect of a realignment of Masyumi towards the political centre-ground, focussed around a more coherent ideology. He refused on several occasions to accept nationalism as a principle of government; unlike Soekiman, he was convinced that Masyumi could lead the country without entering into an alliance with the PNI. According to

---

[86] A relationship which began in their Bandung secondary school at the end of the 1920s. Rudolf Mrazek, *Sjahrir: Politics and Exile in Indonesia* (Ithaca, NY: Cornell University, 1994), p. 47.
[87] See supra, Chapter 2.

him, popular support for the government should be founded on religious sentiment rather than on national sentiment. This was demonstrated by the alliances he made with Christian parties and the fact that he never tried to placate Sukarno.

Mohammad Natsir's rise through the party ranks was one source of the growing discord between modernists and traditionalists. The congress of December 1949, which saw him take over the presidency, was also the occasion of a modification in the party's statutes which reduced the power of the *ulama* within the religious council. In Natsir's opinion, a well-run party was one in which there was a clear hierarchy of its executive organs, and as the *Madjelis Sjuro*'s right to interfere in the efficient running of the party was deemed to be in contradiction with this, it was removed. By refusing to take into account the increasingly pressing concerns of the traditionalists, Natsir played an essential part in the 1952 split. Unlike Soekiman, however, he never recognised the underlying reasons for this schism, a schism which turned out to be extremely damaging for the party in the 1955 elections.[88]

The opposition between the two wings of the party was, then, a lot more than just a confrontation between two people. It led to a profound change not only in the party's strategy, but also in its very identity. For numerous reasons, this internal party quarrel and its consequences went largely unnoticed, however, outside a small circle of national leaders. A sort of tacit accord between the two protagonists meant that they never mentioned their differences publicly.[89] When

---

[88] In 1988, in an interview published in *Editor* and reproduced in Mochtar Rais and Lukman Fatahullah, eds., *Mohammad Natsir Pemandu Ummat* (Jakarta: Bulan Bintang, 1989), pp. 107–9. The former president of Masyumi maintained that NU's split from the party was solely due to its desire to be given the position of minister for religions.

[89] The only person to break this unwritten rule was Soekiman's close ally, Jusuf Wibisono. In an interview with the press agency *Aneta* in March 1951, he called for Mohammad Natsir to resign as prime minister so as to allow the party to reflect on the consequences of the failure of the conference on Irian. In May 1953, he also refused to give his support to the Wilopo government, which included several of Natsir's close supporters, such as Prawoto Mangkusasmito and Mohammad Roem. There was even talk in the press about Wibisono splitting from the party, a rumour which he quickly denied (*Abadi*, 27 May 1953). Later that year in September, the possibility was raised of Masyumi's Soekiman wing supporting the Ali government, which contained no Masyumi representatives, but Jusuf Wibisono eventually ruled it out (*Abadi*, 5 September 1953).

Mohammad Natsir succeeded Soekiman as head of the party in 1949, he endeavoured to allow his rival to step down gracefully as leader. The outgoing party chairman received the title of honorary president of the party, which had been created especially for the occasion, and was also named Head of the Congress and of the Party Council (Presiden Partai, ketua Muktamar dan Dewan Partai). Natsir succeeded him at the Head of the party's Executive Committee (ketua Dewan Pimpinan Partai) where all of the important decisions were taken.

The development of Masyumi between its birth and the mid-1950s was a paradoxical one, due in large part to its nature as a Muslim party. It was founded on an adherence to common values perceived as absolute and unchanging, and it grew very rapidly, brushing aside the political contingencies which could have hampered its emergence. Its dazzling expansion throughout the country was largely thanks to its dual membership procedure, with both individual members and Muslim organisations. Up until 1949, the country's pressing need for patriotism bolstered the sacred nature of the Muslim community's union and held the organisation steadfastly together; after that date, however, the party's foundations began to show signs of weakness. Masyumi was in fact built upon a somewhat illusory aspiration, namely that its constituent organisations would miraculously put their religious and social differences to one side once they entered the political arena. A few years after its creation, the party, in a way, paid the price for its initial effortless success. Sensitive issues, such as the status of *ulamas* or the recognition of *madhhabs* as a source of law, had been carefully avoided so as not to hinder the collaboration between modernists and traditionalists. The demands of a more coherent policy championed by Mohammad Natsir led to a painful reassessment of the party's unitary myth.

At Masyumi's foundation, as we have already seen, a distribution of roles between *ulamas* and political leaders naturally took place. The former had taken control of the party's religious council (Madjelis Sjuro), while the latter occupied the party's executive committee (Pengurus Besar). This allocation of roles led to an imbalance in the number of representatives between Muhammadiyah and Nahdlatul Ulama. Although the country's main traditionalist organisation had been given the chairmanship (K.H. Hasjim As'jari) as well as the position of first vice chairman (K.H.A. Wahid Hasjim, the chairman's son) on the religious council, it only possessed three seats within the executive committee. Muhammadiyah, on the other hand, not only enjoyed a strong representation on the *Madjelis Sjuro*, but also dominated the Pengurus Besar, with five of its members occupying seats there—K.H. Faqih Usman, R.A. Kasmat, H.M. Farid Ma'ruf, Junus Anies and M. Mawardi. In addition, the position of president was held by Soekiman, and two vice president positions were occupied by Wali al-Fatah and Prawoto Mangkusasmito, all three of whom were considered to be members of the modernist organisation. Nahdlatul Ulama was, to a certain extent, paying the price for its lack of political activity before the war. Unlike Muhammadiyah, its leaders had not got involved in any of the parties—the PSII, the PII or Permi—which might have allowed them to acquire the necessary experience in this field. This apparent imbalance had initially been accepted by NU's *ulamas* however, as their only power base, the religious council, was originally supposed to play a prominent role within the party. It appeared that the head of documents presenting the party's hierarchy could intervene when it so desired in the party's debates, had to be consulted by the executive committee on political issues which touched on religious matters, and its opinion prevailed within the party if it voted unanimously on an issue.[90] During the Physical Revolution, this distribution of roles worked relatively well. The *ulamas* gave Islam's seal of approval to the struggle against the colonial power and were therefore honoured at national and local meetings of the party.[91] The Madjelis Sjuro was regularly consulted for its opinion. In June 1946, for example, when the Masyumi leadership called on the Muslim community to respond favourably to the national loan which the government had just issued, it was careful to publish the decision by the Madjelis Sjuro to allow subscribers to receive a supplement (*tambahan*) to the amount lent.[92] The Indonesian people's "holy war" against the Dutch, which was perfectly conducive to bringing about unity and a heightened sense of religious sentiment within the Muslim community, represented, then, the golden age in the collaboration between political leaders and

---

[90] *Anggaran Dasar*, 1945.
[91] On 28 January 1946, for example, *Al-Djihad* reported on a series of meetings between Mayumi figures, *ulamas* and leaders of the Sabilillah and Hizboellah militias in order to "ensure the construction of a land of Islam or of an Islamic state (*Darul Islam atau Negara Islam*)."
[92] *Al-Djihad*, 21 June 1946.

ulamas. A few years later, Wahid Hajim himself drew attention to the fact that the two groups complemented each other. The political leaders allied solid theoretical knowledge with sound political sense, while the *ulamas* exerted a real influence over the Islamic community, though lack of coordination meant that it remained limited to a regional level.[93]

This admirable unity, which, with the passing years, was no doubt recast in an idyllic light, came to an end after 1949. With the conflict against the Dutch over, the *ulamas'* calls to holy war were no longer necessary and became embarrassing even. Kartosuwirjo's rebellion against the Republic was accompanied by the proclamation of an Islamic state in West Java, with the intention of extending such a state across the country. Within a party which now wished to join coalition governments, this uprising discredited the slogans which Masyumi had employed only a few years earlier.

This party's distancing of itself from the Darul Islam rebellion led to domination by its political wing, within which Muhammadiyah had always been better represented than Nahdlatul Ulama.[94] The first sign of this change was the modification at the 1949 congress of the *Madjelis Sjuro*'s status: it became a mere consultative organ with no real influence in defining the party's policy line as there was no longer an absolute obligation to refer issues to it. The leaders of Nahdlatul Ulama spoke out against what they considered to be a breach of their initial contract with the party. According to them, "all issues were now considered only from a political point of view without taking religious directives into account."[95] This crisis led to criticisms by each side becoming widespread, and old grievances between traditionalists and modernists resurfaced. The Nahdlatul Ulama leadership criticised Masyumi for having stepped outside a strictly political role and for organising religious and social activities, thus encroaching on the constituent

---

[93] Muhammad Asyari, "The Rise of Masjumi Party in Indonesia and the Role of the Ulama in Its Early Development, 1945–1952", MA thesis, McGill University, 1976, p. 124.

[94] Despite a drop in its numbers within the executive committee, which went from 45.83% in 1948 to 28.57% in 1949, according to Syaifullah's calculations. *Gerakan Politik Muhammadiyah dalam Masyumi* (Jakarta: Grafiti, 1997).

[95] "Riwajat singkat partai Nahdlatul-Ulama", in Kementerian Penerangan, *Kepartaian dan Parlementaria Indonesia* (Jakarta, 1954), p. 412.

member's prerogatives.[96] Having noted this loss of influence within Masyumi, they decided, shortly after the congress in Yogyakarta, to create their own political executive committee.[97]

In this emerging conflict, organisational issues were not the only bone of contention. The tone employed by a section of Masyumi's leadership towards religious dignitaries, which was often condescending, also contributed much to the worsening of this malaise. During the 1949 congress, for example, Mohammed Saleh, a member of Masyumi who was mayor of Yogyakarta, created an uproar by declaring that politics was too complex an area to be confided to the *ulamas*. The NU representatives protested in reaction to these comments, and when Saleh refused to withdraw them, some members left the room. A little later, during a meeting of the party leadership in Bogor, K.H. Wahid Hasjim's speech was disturbed by chatter and joking in the audience.[98] It was, however, precisely those within Masyumi who were the least respectful of the authority of traditionalist dignitaries who gained control of the party leadership in 1949, after the election of their champion, Mohammad Natsir, as president of the party's executive committee (*Dewan Pimpinan Partai*).[99]

Like the previous generation of leaders, the new leadership had mostly been educated in the Dutch system, and thus possessed clear management ability. It had also, on top of that, received a sound religious education which enabled it to claim a certain authority in that area. Mohammad Natsir had received his political education within

---

[96] In his opening speech at the Palembang Congress in 1952, K.H.A. Wahab Hasbullah explained that Masyumi organised celebrations for Islam's main feast days during which it collected the *zakat* and then distributed it to the needy. He then went on to say: "Given what I have just said, we can understand that most Muslims might not be able to see the dividing line between the role of a social and charitable organisation and that of a political party. That is the reason why many have become disenchanted with or even suspicious [of the party]." Quoted in Naim Mochtar, *Indonesia's Nahdlatul Ulama Movement: Factors that Led to Its Emergence as a Political Party* (New York, 1961), p. 9.

[97] *Madjelis pimpinian politik.* This committee was dissolved when NU became a party.

[98] Noer, *Partai Islam di Pentas Nasional*, p. 87.

[99] Soekiman retained the title of party president and in 1951 became president of the *Presidum* before being demoted, at the 1952 congress, to the rank of vice president, under Natsir's authority.

Persatuan Islam and was a confirmed reformist who had no problem criticising Islam's traditionalist movements. His relations with Nahdlatul Ulama were therefore strained. Soekiman, who was culturally, and no doubt spiritually, much closer to the NU's Javanese leaders, had managed during his leadership of the party to maintain a certain internal harmony;[100] in the leadership contest with Natsir, for example, he had enjoyed the support of traditionalists. Moreover, Natsir's conquest of the party leadership had coincided with the arrival of K.H. Wahab at the head of Nahdlatul Ulama. Wahab succeeded Hayim Asy'ari, who had died in 1947 and been one of the main architects of Nahdlatul Ulama's growth since 1926. The harmony between the two organisations under the leadership of Soekiman and Asy'ari was replaced, then, with a bitter rivalry between Wahab and Natsir, both equally convinced of their religious and political legitimacy to lead Muslims. Faced with the realisation that they were losing their influence within Masyumi and that their relations with the generation of young up-and-coming members in the party were deteriorating, the temptation for NU's *ulamas* to split from Masyumi was understandable. When the Wilopo government was formed in 1952, their "loss" of the Ministry of Religions— which was the last advantage resulting from their collaboration with the modernists—freed them of their last remaining ties with Masyumi.[101]

The traditionalist *ulamas'* discontent was not the only source of disagreement threatening the party's unity. Successive efforts by Masyumi's leadership to preserve a certain cohesion between its extraordinary members also came up against the problem of the reformist organisation's conflicting ambitions. As had been the case during the colonial period, Persis played, within Islam, a role which was incommensurate with its number of members—it had barely more than 10,000 members at the beginning of the 1960s. This small but vociferous organisation from West Java, which had been re-established in 1948, exerted considerable influence over Masyumi through four of its members. Mohammad Natsir remained in close contact with his former

---

[100] Unlike Natsir who had not hesitated to publicly criticise K.H. Wahid Hasjim, the minister for religions, concerning his policy on pilgrimages. Muhammad Asyari, "The Rise of Masjumi Party in Indonesia and the Role of the Ulama in Its Early Development, 1945–1952", p. 127.
[101] See supra Chapter 3.

fellow students, and although he took on no position within Persis when it was reformed, he helped in the reorganisation of its educational programme in Bangil.[102] There is no doubt that by the beginning of the 1950s, Natsir had emancipated himself from the influence of Ahmad Hassa; as a government figure who had been converted to moderate pragmatism, he could no longer be considered the spokesman of the fundamentalist position which the Bandung organisation was prone to adopt. However, the special relationship he maintained with its leaders, who now represented Masyumi's hard-line wing, no doubt contributed to the radicalisation of his stance after 1956.

Isa Anshary was, without doubt, one of the architects of this radicalisation. The man who Natsir had affectionately dubbed "Masyumi's McCarthy" had taken over the leadership of the party in West Java shortly before being elected head of Persatuan Islam in 1948. He entered the party's executive committee in 1954, and was one of the party's representatives in the Provisional Assembly, before being elected to both the Legislative and Constituent Assemblies in 1955. Ahmad Hassan, on the other hand, remained somewhat aloof from politics. Both within his own organisation and then within Masyumi from 1952 as a member of the Madjelis Sjuro, the spiritual leader of Persatuan Islam preferred to limit his activities strictly to the field of religion for health reasons and also because of his interest in that area. To complete this brief overview of Persis's figures who were involved with Masyumi, let us look quickly at the case of Moenwar Chalil, a respected *ulama* close to Natsir. Although he never occupied an official role in the party's national governing bodies, he enjoyed, thanks to Natsir, considerable influence within the *keluarga Masyumi* through the columns he wrote in the party's press.[103]

Persatuan Islam's influence over Masyumi was particularly strong in the area of relations between the constituent organisations. Its leaders considered that one of the party's main objectives was to provide a definitive resolution to contentious religious issues between the different movements within Indonesian Islam, be they questions of principle

---

[102] Howard M. Federspiel, *Muslim Intellectuals and National Development in Indonesia* (New York: Nova Science Commack, 1992), p. 118.

[103] Moenwar Chalil was for a long time in charge of the section in *Hikmah* entitled "Friday Reflections".

(*khilafiyah*) or subsidiary issues of less importance (*furu*).[104] This apparent desire to make concessions in actual fact led to the deterioration of relations between traditionalists and modernists within Masyumi, since for Isa Anshary, Moenwar Chalil and Ahmad Hassan, there was no room for compromise on these questions. Their proposal to put an end to the discord ruled out the possibility of the traditionalists continuing to use the *madhhab* as the basis for their religious interpretations. Naturally enough, when Nahdlatul Ulama decided to split with Masyumi, the harshest criticism of this move came from Persatuan Islam. Ahman Hassan accused the leaders of the traditionalist organisation of having betrayed the legacy of Hasjim As'jari, one of the architects of the unity of Islam in 1945. He rejected outright the arguments of a religious nature advanced by those who supported the split, and noted ironically that nearly six years had passed before NU had realised that a political party had to be founded on one of the Islamic schools of jurisprudence. For him, it was clear that the only reasons behind this schism were base political ones.[105] This denunciation by Persis's leaders was echoed by Masyumi's senior figures, thus jeopardising any possible future reconciliation with NU.

In a manifesto published by the Bandung organisation in 1956, it declared that it could not accept "the point of view which maintains that, in the name of unity, the questions of *furu* and *khilafiyah* should be evaded". It went on to say that it was impossible for it to accept "such a betrayal of religious principles". The document clearly accused the Masyumi leadership of "being completely aware of what constituted an innovation (*bid'ah*) and doing nothing to combat it."[106] Reading this document allows one to understand the pressure which Masyumi's leaders were under. Persis's influence had not only contributed to the sidelining of Soekiman but also hindered Natsir in his efforts to get

---

[104] The great dispute between *taqlid* and *ijtihad* belongs to the category of *khilafiyah*. The question of *talqin* (a sort of sermon pronounced by an *ulama* at the end of a funeral service) or that of the declaration made by believers before certain rituals (*ushalli* or *niyah*) belongs to the area of Islamic jurisprudence known as *furu*. Federspiel, *Muslim Intellectuals and National Development in Indonesia*, p. 158.

[105] Ibid., pp. 161–2.

[106] Quoted in Federspiel, *Muslim Intellectuals and National Development in Indonesia*, p. 159.

rid of this awkward issue by attempting to forge in the Constituent Assembly a new unity amongst Islam's representatives.

The problems which Masyumi encountered with Muhammadiyah were of a different nature. Masyumi never had disagreements with the modernist organisation over matters of religious ideology that it had with Nahdlatul Ulama, and to a lesser extent, Persatuan Islam. From the outset, Muhammadiyah held a position of considerable influence within the party's executive committee, and this was consolidated with the departure of Nahdlatul Ulama's representatives. Between 1952 and 1959, the percentage of Muhammadiyah members sitting on the executive committee varied between 54% and 68%.[107] It was the largest of Masyumi's extraordinary members, representing more than half of the party's members, and seemed satisfied about its status within the party, until the 1955 elections at least. The few modifications to the party's statutes it had requested had been granted,[108] and in return it regularly reminded its members of their duties towards Masyumi. In February 1953, it decided to reinforce its "ideological discipline" (*disiplin ideology*) by forbidding its members from becoming activists in non-Muslim parties. According to Kasman Singodimedjo, who was both a member of Muhammadiyah and part of Masyumi's leadership, some of the modernist organisation's members were also affiliated to the PNI, the PSI and even the PKI. This was considered to be harmful for the unity of the organisation,[109] and with the elections approaching it made regular announcements reminding the public that it belonged to Masyumi.[110]

The election results announced at the beginning of 1956 sparked off a grave crisis within the reformist movement, however, endangering its membership of Masyumi and thus the very existence of the party. Of the 57 Masyumi deputies elected to the Legislative Assembly, only 13 could claim to be members of Muhammadiyah, while at the Constituent Assembly, it held 21 of the party's 112 seats. If we look at the number of national representatives in 1956, we can see that

---

[107] Syaifullah, *Gerakan politik Muhammadiyah dalam Masyumi* (Jakarta: Grafiti, 1997), pp. 140–59.

[108] In particular the clarifications it had requested concerning the participation of constituent organisations in the party's governing bodies. Ibid., pp. 190–3.

[109] *Abadi*, 18 February 1953.

[110] See the declarations made by A.R. Sutan Mansur, the president of Muhammadiyah, in *Hikmah*, 27 February 1954, and in *Abadi*, 26 September 1955.

Muhammadiyah only represented 4% of the popular vote,[111] while Nahdlatul Ulama, whose candidates had stood for election independently of Masyumi, had won 45 seats in the Parliament and 91 in the Constituent Assembly, giving it 20% of the total number of deputies. The difference was considerable for two organisations of such a similar size—both possessed a few million members—and it was inevitable for the modernist organisation to feel some resentment towards Masyumi. According to HAMKA, who, at the height of this crisis, wrote a short book aimed at defending the organisation's membership of the Muslim party, several of Muhammadiyah's local branches had demanded that all ties with the party be severed. The Riau branch considered itself to have been particularly hard done-by: it represented the lion's share of Masyumi's local membership, and yet had not received a single seat at the elections, while the nearby Minangkabau branch, where the modernist organisation was less well-represented, had obtained five seats. Its leaders were the first to send a motion to Muhammadiyah's central leadership to demand the organisation's departure from Masyumi.[112] With more and more initiatives such as this being taken by local figures seizing advantage of the regionalist climate at the time to denounce their loss of political influence, Muhammadiyah's executive committee, the Madjilis Tanwir, decided to meet in early June 1956. Those who supported breaking away proposed several alternatives, including the establishment of a separate political party—with the possibility of establishing a federation with NU and the PSII—a similar request made by NU a few years previously had been rejected by Masyumi's leaders, including those belonging to Muhammadiyah. They also advocated a complete abandonment of politics and a concentration on the organisation's traditional activities, namely preaching and education. It was only after the organisation's main leaders threatened to resign that the "small calibre" (*kaliber ketjil*) leaders finally agreed to abandon their plans for a split and that the decision was made to maintain the organisation within Masyumi.[113]

---

[111] Syaifullah, *Gerakan politik Muhammadiyah dalam Masyumi*, p. 172. HAMKA, however, declared that half of the Masyumi parliamentary deputies were *orang Muhammadiyah*. This is further proof of the uncertainty surrounding who belonged to which organisation. *Muhammadijah-Masjumi* (Jakarta: Masjarakat Islam, 1956), p. 29.

[112] Ibid., p. 8.

[113] Ibid., pp. 27–30.

A Religious Party?

The religious aspect of the Masyumi party determined how it was organised, favoured its expansion and contributed to a party unity which, in the final analysis, turned out to be a fragile one. It also constituted for many activists and sympathisers an essential reason for their association with the party. The day-to-day running of the party revealed a certain increase in the influence of religion in political life—all Masyumi's meetings, including their congresses, opened with a reading from the Koran—but also a politicisation of religious life—all major Muslim feast days, such as *Isra dan Miraj* and *Idul Fitri*, gave rise, at all party levels, to very well-attended festive gatherings. On those occasions, political leaders were transformed into religious guides. When they spoke, they sounded more like preachers than politicians, and their speeches generally transcended the political concerns of the day. There was a much more solemn and consensual tone than usual to these speeches, which had a predicatory character, with constant evocations of the submission to God through the *takbir* and the *tahmid*.[114] Masyumi was never a religious organisation in the way that Muhammadiyah, Nahdlatul Ulama or Persatuan Islam were. It got involved neither in preaching programmes—the leadership had no section charged with *dakwah*—nor in the area of religious education, and *Hikmah* was the only one of its newspapers to have a section exclusively devoted to religion. Masyumi's ambition was somewhat different from that of its constituent members in that it wished to spread the values of Islam throughout society by non-religious means, such as economic, governmental, social and cultural programmes.

The Values of an Islamic Society

Establishing an Islamic society while at the same time building an Islamic state was the *raison d'être* for Masyumi's vast network. Despite the range of sensibilities represented within the party, its leaders never abandoned the idea of instilling the values which would form the framework of this society. They did so, however, in a piecemeal and

---

[114] The *takbir* corresponds to the recitation of *"Allahu akbar"*, while the *tahmid* concerns the expression *"Alhamdulillah"*. See, for example, Mohammad Natsir, "Sari Chotbah Idulfitri Dilapangan Ikada, Djakarta, July 1950", *Capita Selecta*, vol. 2, p. 81.

roundabout fashion, which sometimes led to open contradictions between the party's official message and the reality on the ground.

A Society Reconciling Islamic Morals and Modernity

The representatives of modernist Islam, who held a majority in the party's executive organs, were mainly concerned with not appearing as the defenders of an old-fashioned and outdated moral code. They were resolutely turned towards the future and denounced religious practices which they considered to be both intolerable innovations (*bida'h*) and vestiges of an outmoded (*kolot*) conservatism. They also endeavoured to embellish their programme for society with supposed Western values. In 1946, the party's daily newspaper *Al Djihad* spoke out against the "disparaging rumours being spread from village to village" by the enemies of Islam.

Darul Islam had not yet been associated with the incendiary air of rebellion, as it was later to be after Kartosuwirjo's call to arms. It did nonetheless conjure up the image of a rigid society which was anti-materialistic, against Indonesian culture and opposed to technical advances. It called for "no more automobiles, no more tanks and mortars, no more planes, but only camels; no more shows, no more Javanese percussion orchestras (*gamelan*), no more puppet theatres (*wayangan*); no more churches or temples or pagodas but only mosques"; a civil service "composed entirely of *hadjis*, from a village scribe to the highest position"; a society, in short, "which would turn its back on the modern world and become a society of Bedouins."[115]

However, Masyumi's programme for an Islamic society cannot be reduced to the blind assimilation of Western values and techniques. A civilisation which had given birth to the individualism of the Enlightenment, atheism, communism and Nazism could not claim to stand as a universal model. One needed to be circumspect when looking to modernity for inspiration, therefore, and seek a lucid adaptation of the teachings of Islam and the history of Indonesian society to the advances of the 20th century.

When one read Masyumi's theorists, this process seemed an easy one: they based it on Islam's sacred texts and presented their conclusions as indisputably self-evident. In reality, this way of proceeding made the

---

[115] *Al-Djihad*, 22 July 1946.

task of establishing norms extremely difficult, as the many contradictions inherent in the various compromises reached were often ignored, leading to an accumulation of approaches which were both inconsistent with each other and out of tune with what was happening on the ground. These difficulties should not lead us to give up on delineating Masyumi's social ideology. If one looks beyond the incoherence, the absence of comments and the vagueness which can be found in the party's programme, there was nonetheless a vision common to all the party's modernists. The details may well have been sketchy, but the overall philosophy had a sound basis.

If there was one area in which this desire to combine Muslim tradition with Western modernity was obvious, it was in the field of relations between men and women. Masyumi became aware from an early stage that their position on this issue would be a sort of litmus test in the eyes of many Indonesians. It was a particularly sensitive issue since it was not enough to simply announce general broad-ranging principles concerning relations between men and women. The principle of equality between the sexes, which had been a mainstay of the party's successive programmes, had to manifest itself through concrete measures both within the party and via legislative change. In 1938, in an article published in *Pedoman Majarakat*, Mohammad Natsir talked about his difficulty in reconciling the two legacies of the modernist movement, namely a faithfulness to Islam's teachings which established an unequal relationship in marriage between men and women, on the one hand, and the awareness that these same principles would inevitably be challenged by the developments inherent in a modern society, on the other.[116]

The fear of seeing their programme for society denounced by the proponents of social modernity because of its faithfulness to Islam's teachings concerning the status of women continued to haunt certain Masyumi leaders. Women's position in society and the question of marriage remained a thorny issue, and the difference of opinion between the party's various wings was such that it damaged the party's

---

[116] In the article, Natsir appeared far from convinced that he had succeeded in reconciling these two legacies. His tone seemed apologetic, and he explained how he was afraid of being called "anti-Western" or, worse again, of being compared with Mussolini or Hitler if he glorified the role of the housewife. "Disekitar soal Krisis Perkawinan", *Capita Selecta*, vol. 1, pp. 389–400.

unity. In a break with the party's tradition of not commenting on its internal divisions, Jusuf Wibisono, one of the most active members of its progressive wing wrote openly about it in the press in 1951:

> There exists a group of intellectuals who, although they are Muslim, are reluctant to join our party... Their opposition is partly directed at an outdated religious movement which influenced certain internal party rules such as the use of a curtain (*separating men and women*) during meetings. They have a good knowledge of Islamic history. They know that in the early centuries of that history, women could attain esteemed positions in society thanks to the considerable freedom of action they enjoyed. This was in accordance with the Koran and the *Hadiths*. If we study history, it shows us that one of the main reasons for the decline of the Muslim world was the control exerted in society by men over women's freedom of action. The use of a curtain in our meetings is seen by the intellectuals whom I referred to as an act which weakens (lessens) our women and which ends up hindering the development of our Muslim women. Because of that, they are loath to join a party using outdated rules which harm the community of Muslim women.[117]

Returning to these questions in 1954, Jusuf Wibisono advanced what could be considered as the Masyumi modernists' credo on the subject. He was still very concerned about the disastrous effect which a retrograde policy towards women would have on the party's support amongst the country's westernised middle classes, and he proposed that "the search for guarantees for women's position" be amongst the foremost objectives of an Islamic society. He understood that certain practices such as the "full body veil" could legitimately be perceived as having a regressive effect on women's status within Islam, and declared that such customs were contrary to the teachings of Islam. Without actually mentioning them, he based his arguments on the writings of "Western scholars", reminding his readers that polygamy could not be considered in Islam as a rule, but only as an exception. Where polygamy was "practiced like a sport", it was in complete contradiction with the principles of Islam. In response to the "so-called modern women who always cited the West as an example", he advanced the classic modernist argument that one could not attribute any value to Western

---

[117] *Suara Partai Masjumi*, February 1951.

monogamy which, although it was a legal obligation, often belied a covert form of polygamy which was much more regrettable than the "exception" narrowly prescribed by Islamic law.[118] The boundaries of the debate were clearly defined, then, even amongst the most Western-ised of the Masyumi leaders: certain practices of polygamy should be condemned but not its principle, since the Koran clearly referred to it. Party members jumped on any occasion to defend this party line from criticism, especially when it came from the Muslim camp. In November 1952, for example, the weekly magazine *Hikmah*, whose board of management was chaired by Natsir, took the Partai Sarekat Islam Indonesia branch in Semarang violently to task over comments made by one of its representatives who had claimed that "although we are an Islamic organisation, the PSII is a modern party, in harmony with its time and you cannot let it be said that the Muslim community, on the whole, agrees with polygamy." The magazine reminded readers that a Muslim party should "have as its foundation stone the Koran and the *Hadiths* which authorise, and sometimes oblige a person who really needs it, to have recourse to polygamy" and it called on the PSII's na-tional leadership to take firm measures against its Semarang branch.[119]

Masyumi's female members adopted a different approach to the question, however, starting a campaign against certain practices of polygamy which they considered to be abusive. Such cases of polygamy were considered to be on the increase, and they aimed their criticism in particular at the most illustrious Indonesian, President Sukarno. In 1954, the head of state, who was an incorrigible seducer, announced that he was going to take a second wife, Hartini.[120] His first wife, Fatmawati, handled the news very badly, and although she did not ac-tually go so far as to file for divorce, she took up residence in another house and refused to accompany her husband on the pilgrimage to Mecca despite gentle encouragement by two Muhammadiyah leaders, A.R. Sutan Mansur and HAMKA, to do so.[121] Muslimat's leaders took

---

[118] *Abadi*, 10 July 1954.

[119] *Hikmah*, 8 November 1952.

[120] Hartini was in fact Sukarno's fourth wife. His second wife Inggit had managed to get a divorce after her husband had married Fatmawati. J.D. Leddge, *Sukarno: A Political Biography*, 2nd edition (Sydney: Allen & Unwin, 1990), p. 277.

[121] *Abadi*, 5 February 1955.

up her cause and organised demonstrations protesting against the president's second marriage, whose consequence was to "transform women into household utensils" (*jang bikin wanita serupa perabot rumah*).[122]

There was an interesting epilogue to this whole affair when in June 1955, after her marriage to the head of state, Hartini Sukarno became a member of the Bogor branch of Muslimat in West Java. During the little welcoming ceremony organised for the occasion, she promised her new fellow members that she would work and pray hard for the organisation, and she accepted with joy the present which she had been offered: "a veil for her to wear" (*kudung untuk dipakainja*).[123] The whole controversy, which finally came to an end when Hartini joined the Masyumi family, had a definite political dimension to it. It also showed, however, that there was an extremely narrow line between the legitimate questioning of social practices which were deemed to belong to another age and a potentially unpardonable violation of the Holy Book; this greatly hindered Masyumi from adopting a clear policy line when the issue came before the legislature.

In the area of marriage law, Indonesia had inherited a very complex set of laws from its former colonial masters who had had the impossible task of establishing a single set of laws for all of the country's religious communities. Dutch marriage law had only been applied in Indonesia's Christian regions, and so the legal vacuum elsewhere allowed Islamic regions to maintain a custom which mitigated the inequality inherent in Islamic marriage. Instead of the traditional right held by the husband to unilaterally repudiate (*talak*) his wife, this custom entitled him to pronounce before the *penghulu* (the representative of the mosque charged with recording the exchange of vows between spouses) a conditional or "suspended" repudiation (*talik and talak*), which specified that his wife could make use of this repudiation order if he did not fulfil the commitments he had undertaken when he got married. This alternative form of marriage, which was in complete conformity with *fikh*, allowed a wife, by considering herself to be repudiated, to separate from her husband if, contrary to what he had initially promised, he wished to take a second wife. Aware of this possibility of conditional repudiation, Indonesian Muslim women were therefore able to avail of an efficient means of fighting against the

---

[122] Ibid.
[123] *Abadi*, 18 June 1955.

rise of polygamy which was condemned both by the country's first feminist movements and by the most advanced members of the *santri* community.[124]

In 1946, the republican government in Yogyakarta decided to deal with this thorny issue. In an attempt to placate the sensibilities of radical Muslims, the law, which was promulgated in 1946 and augmented the following year by a decree issued by the new minister for religions, did not adopt in its entirety the alternative form of marriage we have just described. The new law obliged marriages and revocations to be recorded by a *penghulu*, who was now a state official. In the event of a husband contracting a second marriage, the *penghulu* had to remind him of his obligations towards his first wife, and if a repudiation was being envisaged, he had a duty to summon the two spouses and attempt to discourage the husband from pronouncing the *talak*.

After the 1952 Constitution came into force, the issue of marriage legislation which would be applicable to the entire country came to the fore again.[125] Masyumi was wary of coming under attack from feminist associations or from secular nationalists, and so they wisely allowed their female representatives to lead the way in the matter, satisfied more often than not to refer to Muslimat's decisions on the matter. The feminist organisation did not baulk at the task and devoted a considerable amount of its work to the question. This is hardly surprising, given that its statutes, adopted in November 1945, already show that one of its main objectives was "to make women aware of their rights and obligations in terms of marriage."[126] In January 1951, during its fifth congress, it adopted a motion "to press the government to rapidly draw up a bill on marriage which would guarantee the rights of women in accordance with the rules of the Muslim religion." A few months later, the government, headed by Mohammad Natsir, set up a Committee for the Examination of new Regulations on Marriage, Repudiation and Revocation (Panitya Penjelidik Peraturan Hukum Perkawinan Talak dan Rujuk) chaired by two members of Masyumi: Teuku Mohammad

---

[124] Cora Vreede-de Stuers, "A propos du 'R.U.U.', histoire d'une législation matrimonial", *Archipel* 13 (1974): 21–30.

[125] For further reading on this issue, see Azyumardi Azra, *The Indonesian Marriage Law of 1974: An Institutionalization of the Shari'a for Social Changes*, in *Sharia and Politics in Modern Indonesia*, ed. Arskal Salim and Azyumardi Azra (Singapore: Institute of Southeast Asian Studies, 2003).

[126] Article 4 of its statutes.

Hassan and Zainal Abidin Ahmad. By the end of 1952, the Committee had put forward an initial proposal to codify marriage law for the entire country. Among the changes introduced by this new law were the recognition of equal rights between spouses in the case of a divorce and also, in cases where polygamy was permitted by one's religion, the obligation for a man's first wife to give her explicit consent before he could take a second wife.[127]

Curiously enough, Muslim organisations did not look upon these measures favourably, despite Zainal Abidin Ahmad's best efforts to explain them.[128] Muslimat in particular criticised them for being too general in scope, and called for specific rules for each religion. In accordance with Masyumi's position on the issue, Muslimat had voted, during its previous congress in August 1952, a report which firmly condemned certain forms of polygamy by men "who merely wanted to give free rein to their desires without any sense of responsibility towards divine law." However, the same report also recognised "that this misuse of polygamy does not only come from men, but also from women who wish to marry a man who is already married." Masyumi's women members set themselves two goals, then: "not to criticise polygamy as a part of divine law but to demand that the rules necessary for moral improvement be strictly implemented", and also "to pursue the education of women in order to make them aware of their own identity and their responsibility for their own lives." In the months that followed, Muslimat continued its work on the question, sending its proposals to Masyumi's religious council and then to the women's section of the Coordinating Committee for Muslim Organisations (BKOI Lembaga Wanita) which organised, in February 1953, a congress on the issue. The BKOI refused to adopt the programme drawn up by the government's committee and preferred instead Muslimat's proposals, namely that the 1946 law be extended throughout Indonesia, despite the fact that it was less favourable to women. This was the solution which Parliament finally adopted in 1954, in spite of opposition from several feminist organisations.

This was quite a tortuous route to take for a bill, which ended up with such a modest gain for women's condition. It was certainly not

---

[127] Vreede-de Stuers, "A propos du 'R.U.U.'".
[128] *Abadi*, 9 March 1953.

the result of a Machiavellian plot by Masyumi's male leadership; the solution agreed upon constituted an ideal scenario for the party, as it both strictly upheld Islamic law and allowed the party's leaders to preserve their image as modernists. By letting the party's female figures defend a law which was the result of a traditional application of Islamic law, the party protected itself from potential criticism. Furthermore, the question of men's responsibility for polygamy could be completely avoided as it was up to women to collectively give themselves the means, through education, to refuse any abuse of this practice.

Laying the responsibility for the safeguard of morality upon women was a classic technique within the Masyumi family. At the beginning of 1946, when the question of women participating in the armed conflict arose, Muslimat, although they approved of it, addressed two warnings to Islamic militia groups: that they should not give the impression that the Indonesian army was lacking in men; and also that they should ensure morality was upheld on the battlefield, notably by providing female militias with clothes which would "hide their charms".[129] Once peace had been restored, the issue of public decency was transposed to sporting activities, and one of the motions most frequently adopted during the meetings of local branches of Muslimat called for clothes to be worn during sporting activities which were in conformity with "public morality".[130] Another source of outrage for Masyumi's women's organisation was the growing number of beauty contests "which led women to expose themselves in front of men and to publish their measurements."[131]

However, the Masyumi family's moral stance was, in fact, not always so strict. The long articles which were published in the party's press on the question of physical appearance did indeed adopt a very strong moralising tone. In August 1958, for example, the journalist in charge of women's issues for the weekly magazine *Hikmah* warned its readers about beauty salons, "where they were likely to waste their time and their money". She also warned them about the easy option which consisted in "putting on make-up and shortening your clothes in

---

[129] *Al-Djihad*, 15 February 1946.
[130] See, for example, the resolution in this respect adopted by the Palembang branch of the Muslimat. *Abadi*, 4 May 1954.
[131] According to a communiqué issued by GPII Puteri in April 1956.

Plate 6.1   An advertisement for Lifebuoy soap made by Unilever which appeared regularly in *Suara Partai Masjumi, Hikmah* and *Abadi* in 1951 and 1952.

order to make yourself pretty", and invited them to pay attention, on the contrary, to the notion of inner beauty.[132] However, the Masyumi press also dealt with other questions which were no doubt more in tune with its readers. It published short articles, for example, reporting on fashion shows, particularly those in Paris, or giving accounts of the sophisticated and sometimes dissolute lives of Hollywood stars.[133]

---

[132] "Beauty: A Problem for Women", *Hikmah*, 2 August 1958.

[133] The demonstrations organised in 1995 by Dewan Dakwah Islam Indonesia against the Muslim daily newspaper *Republika*, which was accused, amongst other things, of conveying pernicious Western values through its reports on American stars, shows the transformation of those who claim to continue Masyumi's legacy. Robert W. Hefner, "Print Islam: Mass Media and Ideological Rivalries among Indonesian Muslims", *Indonesia* 64 (October 1997): 77–104.

Unlike in the Muslim press today, there was no particular censorship of advertisements, which were sometimes in stark contrast to the moral tone of the publication in question. While there were never any adverts for headscarf manufacturers presenting their latest models, a female figure in a sensual pose showing a partially revealed breast was often used to sing the praises of a skin-softening soap. The gap between principles and practice was to be found even more flagrantly in another area: the lottery. Masyumi had, naturally, made the outlawing of gambling one of the very concrete objectives of its social programme, and in July 1954, it joined with NU and the PSII to denounce a government project dealing with the regulation of a lottery. Despite this, *Abadi* nonetheless published a small section entitled "Who was Lucky" (*Siapa Beruntung*) which gave the winning numbers and the jackpot total—sometimes a considerable sum—of the very same lottery. Here again, the necessity for the party's press to satisfy its readership indicated the scale of the task facing Masyumi in order to establish the Islamic society which its leaders were calling for.

To conclude this examination of public morals, it may be interesting to look at how the party's leaders attempted to embody, at least partly, the ideal which they called on their supporters to aspire to. What such an inquiry reveals is that there was no clear disparity between the party's programme for society and the way of life of the Indonesian urban elite in the 1950s. The status and way of life enjoyed by women in the party was neither wholly consistent with their stated objective of total equality nor with the complete separation between the sexes called for by contemporary neo-fundamentalist groups. Naturally, many of Muslimat's members wore headscarves, but photos of their meetings also showed a sizeable number of them with their heads uncovered—often almost a quarter of the assembly—thus contradicting the notion that there was an obligation to wear one. The proportion of women sitting on the party's highest governing bodies did not differ from other political organisations; the party's executive committee counted two women for 12 men in 1954, while at the same time in Nahdlatul Ulama (Tanfizihah), the ratio was one woman for 16 men. The situation within left-wing parties was not better, despite their propensity for brandishing the banner of women's liberation from the constraints of Islam. There was only one woman on the PNI's 16-seat executive committee; the PSI had no woman either on its party council or on its executive committee; while the PKI's central committee and politburo were composed entirely of men.[134] Moreover, the Masyumi leaders of the 1950s were not austere religious types who imposed a strict way of life upon those around them. Unlike the leaders of Persatuan Islam, their lifestyles did not really distinguish them from the rest of the Westernised Jakartan bourgeoisie, something which Ahmad Hassan, a religious dignitary from the Persis movement, criticised Mohammad Natsir for. Disconnected from prevailing mentalities at the time, Hassan had adopted a very moralising stance on the issue of social mores. The notion of "reproachable" (*makruh*) behaviour which he regularly wielded tolerated no accommodation. He was, then, very shocked to see the Masyumi president's daughters dressed in Western clothes, going out with friends or serving refreshments to their father's guests.[135] Apart from Jusuf Wibisono, who had accumulated considerable wealth through his business activities, most party leaders enjoyed a comfortable, though non-ostentatious, lifestyle in the Menteng district of Jakarta. They endeavoured on occasion, however, to show their fellow countrymen the importance of a certain degree of humility. Mohammad Natsir, for example, immediately after having handed in his resignation as prime minister, refused to be accompanied to his house by his chauffeur and cycled home as a simple citizen.[136]

A Fair and Prosperous Society

The Masyumi leadership, following on directly from the ideas of Agus Salim and H.O.S. Tjokroaminoto, but also of Mohammad Hatta, portrayed Islam from an early stage as an alternative to the opposition between the imposed collectivism of the Marxist system and the un-fettered individualism of capitalism. In 1948, in a short book entitled *Politiek dan Revolusi Kita* (*Politics and Our Revolution*), the party's principle economic theorist, Sjafruddin Prawiranegara, reminded his readers that Islam condemned the excesses of these two doctrines

---

[134] Kementerian Penerangan, *Kepartaiain dan Parlementaria Indonesia* (Jakarta, 1954). Masyumi's situation in the Legislative Assembly elected in 1955 was comparable to that of other parties: it had four women representatives, as did the PNI, while the PKI had three women deputies and NU had two.

[135] Deliar Noer, *Aku bagian Ummat, aku bagian Bangsa, otobiografi* (Bandung: Mizan, 1996), p. 417.

[136] Anwar Harjono, ed., *Pemikiran dan perjuangan Mohammad Natsir* (Jakarta: Pustaka Firdaus, 1996), p. 6.

without repudiating their underlying principles, and that it also proposed a balanced combination of both systems, founded on encouraging individual initiative for the benefit of and under the control of the people.[137] This theory, which was christened "religious socialism", was adopted faithfully both by Sjafruddin in his numerous contributions to economic debates and by other party representatives.[138] Moreover, it held, in the eyes of the party, a practical importance which went far beyond economic questions. Within the context of the Cold War between the two blocs, whose transformation into a military conflict was seen as inevitable, this "third way" could offer Islam a historic opportunity to pose as the mediator of international affairs.[139] In tandem with their denunciation of the dangers of Marxist-Leninist theories in which, as we have already seen, they had become specialised, Masyumi's leaders also consistently condemned certain dangers inherent in capitalism. These regular reminders of capitalism's flaws were made by Masyumi out of political expediency in response to the PKI's portrayal of the party as the handmaid of capitalism and a leech on the working classes. In response to these accusations, Jusuf Wibisono, talking about Islam's founding principles, declared that anti-capitalism was second in order of priority, behind the improvement of women's status (another issue on which the party was often open to criticism). While recognising that some "good Muslims" could have "a capitalist mindset", the president of the SBII explained that Islam could be considered anti-capitalist "because its aim is to create equality"; he also enjoyed reminding his opponents, in an ironic tone, of the similarities between Islam's opposition to usury and the measures taken to combat it in the Soviet Union.

---

[137] Extensive extracts of this book can be found in George McTurnan Kahin, *Nationalism and Revolution in Indonesia* (Ithaca, NY: Cornell University Press, 1952), pp. 309–10.

[138] Sjafruddin called it *"sosialisme religious"*, while Z.A. Ahmad termed it *"religieus sosialisme"*.

[139] Sjafruddin Prawiranegara, *Islam dalam Pergolakan Dunia* (Bandung: Al-Ma'arif, 1950), Quoted in Noer, *Partai Islam di Pentas Nasional*, p. 136. The expression "third way" was not used by Masyumi figures, and those who claim the party's legacy today reject the legitimacy of this current within the party, which they consider to be a new form of capitalism. They prefer the term "fourth way" (*jalan keempat*) to refer to the religious socialism which has experienced a unique revival in Indonesia. See Muhidin M. Dahlan, ed., *Sosialisme Religius, suatu jalan keempat?* (Yogyakarta: Kreasi Wacana, 2000), a collective book published by supporters of HMI-MPO, a student organisation which identifies with Masyumi.

From a historical and theological point of view, Masyumi's theorists founded their condemnation of capitalism on the example set by
the Prophet. Z.A. Ahmad, in a book heavily imbued with revolutionary
socialism—particularly in its anti-semitic undertones—invited his
readers to "struggle against capitalism" (*berdjihad menentang kapitalisme*).
According to him, Mohammad had endeavoured, in Medina, to build
a society governed by principles of "loyalty and Muslim fraternity".[140]
The economic model that Ahmad referred to was based on an economy of solidarity, in which people's right to property could only be
exercised so long as it was done in the common good. For Ahmad,
this "collective and cooperative" conception of the production and exchange of goods stood in complete opposition to what was considered,
at that time, to be the germ (*bibit*) of contemporary capitalism, namely
the "Jews' selfish mentality". Capitalists were called the "source of all
destruction" and considered as the "enemies of all nations".[141]

Masyumi's theorists were undoubtedly much more comfortable
when explaining what could not be included in Islam's economic
model than when proposing a clear definition which could be applied
in concrete terms. In some cases, this tendency to stick to peremptory
maxims could be explained by their lack of expertise in the area of
economic policy. However, the example of Sjafruddin Prawiranegara,
who played a foremost role in the elaboration of Indonesia's economic
policy from 1950–58 when he served as minister for finance before
becoming governor of the Central Bank, shows that this explanation
is not entirely satisfactory. Even for one of Indonesia's rare experts in
this area, it was impossible to isolate economic questions from a programme incorporating all aspects of society, both material and spiritual.
He explained, for example, in a speech given to the Association of
Jakartan Catholic Students in May 1957, the meaning which his party
intended to give to the notion of social prosperity and the limits of
economic science in this area.[142] He opened his speech with a parable

---

[140] Zainal Abidin Ahmad, *Dasar-Dasar Ekonomi Islam* (Jakarta: Sinar Ilmu, 1950),
p. 40.
[141] Ibid., p. 42.
[142] "Peranan Agama dan Moral dalam Pembangunan Masyarakat dan Ekonomi
Indonesia", in *Sjafruddin Prawiranegara, Islam sebagai pedoman hidup, Kumpulan
karangan Terpilih*, vol. 1, ed. Ajip Rosidi (Jakarta: Inti Idayu Press, 1986), pp.
92–118.

of his own about "the poor man suddenly made rich by the discovery of a precious stone". Three possible destinies awaited this man, who, we discover later in the story, personifies the Indonesian people: he could go mad as a result of such riches, fall into an even worse state of poverty after having squandered all his wealth, or improve his lot by using his intelligence to capitalise on his discovery. In the eyes of economic science, only the latter scenario was worthy of interest, and thus allowed the man to be called "*homo economicus*". In other words, classic economic theory could only be useful in the case of a rational use of wealth; it was indifferent to the individual's psychological mechanisms, only enriched people in the material sense of the word and was of no help in the first and second scenarios. Islam, on the other hand, which looked at the question of wealth from a much broader perspective, could help the man at a much earlier stage as soon as he had found the precious stone, a discovery which symbolised Indonesian independence. Economic science, Sjafruddin continued, was based on a fear of the future and incited man to accumulate wealth upon wealth. Religion, however, allowed individuals to go beyond this fear by means of divine mercy. According to Sjafruddin, then, *homo economicus* had to also be a *homo religiosus*, "for only the individual aware of his duties towards God, and therefore devoted to his neighbour, would be able to enjoy these riches for the greater benefit of humanity."[143]

A large part of the young Republic's difficulties, according to him, came precisely from the excessive influence of classic economic thought cut off from any moral dimension. The move from a colonial economy to a national economy "had merely amounted to a replacement of men and capital from the Netherlands by men and capital from our own country, and no specific requirements had been formulated concerning what attitude these men should adopt and what use should be made of this capital."[144] For Sjafruddin, most Indonesian leaders were still enslaved in this insular, and thus illusory, way of thinking. President Sukarno, for example, was losing his way in an autocratic abuse of power and even Sutan Sjahrir, the leader of the Indonesian Socialist Party, "who was himself a confirmed democrat, was misguided to let himself be convinced that the evils of our society could be resolved by

---

[143] Ibid., p. 99.
[144] Ibid., p. 104.

economic tools and an economic method."[145] Sjafruddin concluded by saying that the implementation of an Islamic economy would come about by means of a "radical spiritual change", and was the only way for the country to free itself from the difficulties it was embroiled in.

The Masyumi leadership largely shared this economic vision. This no doubt informed the party's economic policy and justified, in particular, the apparent contradiction between its calls for prosperity and the economic stringency measures which it implemented in government. Masyumi's conception of wealth went beyond its material, and even its human, aspects; the party wanted to embody a social programme which would be able to ensure the salvation of its fellow countrymen. Although it was not glorified, poverty, or at least a certain frugality, did not constitute an obstacle to this programme.[146] As Natsir pointed out in February 1954, in a speech given before a gathering of *ulamas* in Padang, it was better "to resolutely consider the situation, even if it was a harsh one" and draw the necessary conclusions by implementing budgetary cuts and adopting a humble attitude towards foreign aid, rather than getting trapped in an illusory attitude of pride contrary to the principles of Islam.[147] This moral and even mystical approach to economic questions left the party open to several accusations. Was promising prosperity to people in the afterlife and emphasising the necessity of spiritual wealth over material riches not an ideal way to dampen the people's legitimate aspirations for material well-being while preserving the entitlements of the Muslim bourgeoisie which Masyumi was supposed to incarnate? The PKI used this argument liberally in its opposition to the modernist party, describing Masyumi as the representatives of "land-owners who exploited and oppressed peasants".[148]

Although the party's adherence to its religiously inspired economic doctrine was genuine, two additional elements could shed more light on Masyumi's economic policy. The first, mentioned earlier, was the pragmatism which typified the young generation that took over the

---

[145] Ibid., p. 113.

[146] See, for example, Soekiman's speech given at a Masyumi conference in Yogyakarta on Islam's desire to improve man's destiny on Earth, but also in the hereafter. *Hikmah*, 12 November 1953.

[147] *Abadi*, 27 February 1954.

[148] D.N. Aidit, *Indonesian Society and the Indonesian Revolution* (Jakarta: Jajasan Pembaruan, 1958), p. 57.

party leadership in the 1950s. These men were keenly aware of the vision which Western leaders had of their country. Sjafruddin Prawiranegara was well-known in international economic circles, and was certainly aware of the concerns of the world's financial elite with regard to Indonesia's future. The solutions he advanced were to a large extent influenced by the economic doctrines in favour at that time in Europe and in the United States. Moreover, Masyumi was not alone in displaying such receptiveness to the opinions of the capitalist world; the leaders of the PSI, and in particular the economist Sumitro Djojohadikusumo, also served as mouthpieces for such theories.[149] The second element is of a different nature: by emphasising the moral—and therefore universal—dimension of their economic programme, the Masyumi leaders camouflaged somewhat their lack of concrete achievements in the name of Islam. Since the foundation of the party, numerous manifestos had been published to remind its members of what constituted the cornerstones of an economy in conformity with the teachings of the Prophet. These had emphasised the importance of the cooperative sector, the necessity of society to be regulated, the role played by obligatory alms (*zakat*) in the redistribution of wealth, and the outlawing of loan-sharking (*riba*). Most of these documents, however, were more concerned with theological definitions and historical reminders than with proposals which could be applied to contemporary Indonesia, and so the party's accomplishments in this area remained limited.[150]

The term "Islamic economy" never appeared as such in the party's programme. The only principle which the party referred to was the notion of a "planned economy" (*ekonomi terpimpin*) first laid out in 1949 and returned to regularly in the following years. It was a programme which included planned production, limited and constructive competition between companies under state supervision, price and salary controls and incentives for the cooperative sector designed to

---

[149] On 1 and 4 March 1954, *Abadi* published a very long appeal made by Sumitro in favour of a contractionary monetary policy, entitled "Kenjataan sebenarja tentang keuangan kita".

[150] A good example of this is the contribution made by the theologian Z.A. Ahmad to the question of the *zakat*. He traced the evolution of this notion from the Prophet's State up to the writings of Muhammad Rasjid Ridha, distinguishing eight groups of beneficiaries and four types of donations. However, he showed no interest in establishing links between the *zakat* and modern economic realities. Ahmad, *Dasar-Dasar Ekonomi Islam*, pp. 47–50. The articles on Islamic economics published in *Hikmah* generally followed the same logic.

promote a national economy.[151] Most of the programme's aims were not the preserve of Masyumi; apart from the parties inspired by communism, all the country's political organisations shared the same ideal of cooperative-based socialism mingled with economic nationalism.

One of the few areas in which Masyumi strove to apply the principles drawn from its religious analysis of society was that of cooperatives. These economic entities, in the eyes of the entire population, embodied the concrete application of the middle way between capitalism and communism which the party claimed to represent, and they received incentives from both the Natsir and the Soekiman governments. The idea for their development was not exclusive to Masyumi, however. It had been launched in 1895 in the region of Purwokerto, and was developed by a small number of Dutch civil servants, before being adopted first in 1920 by Mohammad Hatta, the "founding father of the cooperative system", then by the PNI and finally by Dr. R. Sutomo, who used it as one of the cornerstones of his Parindra party in 1935.[152] After the Physical Revolution, the Hatta government put in place in 1949 a plan encouraging small producers to come together. This was continued and developed further by successive Masyumi-led governments. In accordance with the programme laid out in 1949 and continued in 1952, the Natsir government set up the "Sumitro Plan".[153] It was based around the Cooperative Service (Jawatan Kooperasi), an organisation created in October 1950 and charged with encouraging the creation of cooperatives in rural centres, as well as providing small-scale producers with both technical advice and financial assistance. This plan encountered a certain amount of success, thanks in no small part to the fact that it was renewed by successive governments.[154] Apart from these measures taken while Masyumi was in power, the party

---

[151] *Program Perjuangan Masjumi* (II.1), 1949. Masyumi never abandoned this principle. Although the party fought relentlessly against Sukarno's Guided Democracy, it continued to support the president's Guided Economy. *Abadi*, 26 February 1960.

[152] Denys Lombard, *Le carrefour Javanais*, vol. 2, p. 103.

[153] Named after the minister for trade and industry, Sumitro Djojohadikusumo. Sumitro was a member of the PSI who had formerly been a commercial attaché in Washington. He was close to Natsir and Sjafruddin Prawiranegara.

[154] Between 1952 and 1954, for example, the number of cooperative members increased from 1 million to 1.4 million. "L'évolution économique de l'Indonésie", *Notes et études documentaires*, nos. 2014 and 2015, May 1955 (Paris: La Documentation française).

leadership's policy for establishing a cooperative economy consisted more in rejoicing in the success of local initiatives than in making any real attempt to build such an economy. The media impact of such projects was much more important to the party than their actual long-term development.[155]

The party adopted a similar attitude to its role in the collection and distribution of the *zakat*, which should have constituted one of the cornerstones of an Islamic economy.[156] As we have already seen, the party and its organisations benefitted from the *zakat* as a source of funding since their supporters had the impression that they were paying the obligatory alms by contributing to the party's finances. However, any attempts Masyumi might have made to organise a system of re-distribution of wealth based on the payment of the *zakat* at a local or national level were unsuccessful. There was no system of coordination within the party, and its leaders merely cited initiatives which Masyumi had not launched as examples of the successful use of the *zakat*. In January 1952, for example, *Hikmah* devoted a long report to a visit by Mohammad Natsir to Pasarean in West Java where he had been impressed by the method of redistribution set up by the villagers, which he considered to be a model for an Islamic economy. Every Thursday evening, a Committee of Legal Alms-giving, comprising representatives from the 11 villages in the surrounding area—totalling 5,000 inhabitants—gathered at a meeting chaired by the mayor of Pasarean. Every three months, a collection was organised, with all landowners whose paddy fields produced more than 900 kg of rice at harvest-time—a quantity fixed by the *ulama* of the village—having to make a contribution. The *zakat* rice was then distributed amongst five types of beneficiaries: poor people (*fakirs* and *miskins*, "those who had real difficulty in surviving"); people participating in the spread of Islam, such as preachers (*muballigh*) and teachers (*guru*); vagabonds ("those who could not leave Pasarean for want of money" who were given the name

---

[155] Between 1946 and 1960, the Masyumi press (*Al-Djihad, Abadi, Hikmah* and *Suara Partai Masjumi*) regularly reported on the party's initiatives in this area. Generally, these efforts consisted in mutualising some money and tools under the aegis of a figure belonging to Masyumi or to Muslimat, and sometimes they merely consisted in officialising the traditional custom of mutual assistance (*gotong royong*).

[156] Ahmad, *Dasar-Dasar Ekonomi Islam*, p. 48.

ibnusabil, meaning "sons of saints"); the members of the *zakat* committee who were classified in the category of *amils* (religious officials); the *mualafs* (a term which was understood here to mean "those whose religious beliefs are not yet very strong and not new converts as there are none of those in the village"); and finally the *gharim,* "those towards whom society is indebted owing to their participation in the war of independence". In all, according to *Hikmah,* a total of 17 tons of rice (2,514 *gedeng*) were redistributed every year. This system was exemplary, according to Mohammad Natsir, because it was not only designed to relieve the misery of the poor, but was also supposed to allow them make a fresh start and participate once more in the village economy, as the beneficiaries were encouraged to sell a part of their rice, which would enable them to set up a small business and thus escape from the poverty trap.[157]

This method of organising the *zakat* in Pasarean clearly illustrates Masyumi's approach to the Islamic society which it advocated. The party's programme, far from being part of a radical break with the past, was in fact steadfastly anchored in the reality of 1950s Indonesia, adopting initiatives which had already been implemented, or simply citing them as examples. By doing so, it no doubt engendered a certain degree of emulation between various communities—both local and professional—and sometimes helped them to coordinate their activities. However, Masyumi never managed, either through its actions or its concrete proposals, to show how a modern state, using its laws, its budgetary policy and its administrative machinery, could harness the activity carried out by those communities and use it to bring about an Islamic society.

---

[157] *Hikmah,* 2 November 1952.

CHAPTER SEVEN

Conclusion

The task of summing up in a few short pages Masyumi's place in the history of the relation between Islam and politics soon runs up against what appears to be a contradiction between the party's two aspects. While it carried out an original experiment in Muslim democracy, founded on a sincere adherence to a Western-style parliamentary regime, it also incarnated an eminently classical form of integralist Islam, which occupied a moral position demanding respect for Islamic norms. The party's multi-faceted heritage is no doubt less incongruous than it initially appears to be, however, and can provide valuable insights into the characteristics of Indonesian Islam. It also invites us to rethink our conception of the link between Islam and politics, both by analysing Masyumi's ideology in relation to the doctrines of other Islamic movements and by comparing this Muslim-democratic party with other religions' ventures into politics, notably the Christian-democrats in Europe.

Laying Down Markers for a Muslim Democracy

Masyumi was without doubt one of the most comprehensive attempts in the history of the Muslim world to reconcile Islam and democracy. Nonetheless, this political experiment was never successfully completed, and for many Muslims, both in Indonesia and across the world, it is an area which remains as yet unexplored. The theories elaborated by the party's main leaders and, more importantly, the nature of their involvement in Indonesian politics in the 15 years following independence, place them firmly in the tradition of a "conciliatory apology"[1] of Islam, as advocated by the founding fathers of modernism, Djamalal-Din al-Afghani and Mohammad 'Abduh. However, unlike their illustrious predecessors who based "Islam's adaptation to the modern world on a compromise rather than on an intellectual conversion",[2] Masyumi's leaders clearly showed in their choices an almost total adherence to the political culture of modern Western society. In this respect, they were a lot closer to moderate Indian reformists such as Sayyid Ahmad Khan, Amr Ali and Muhammad Iqbal than to more radical thinkers like Mawdudi from Pakistan or al-Bannah and Sayyid Qutb from Egypt, to whom they are often compared in Indonesia.[3]

One can certainly find in the writings of Masyumi leaders some of the concepts which were defined by the forebears of modern fundamentalism. Like Hassan al-Bannah, Sayyid Qutb and Mawdudi, Natsir and his colleagues envisaged Islam as an all-encompassing ideology able to give contemporary meaning to both Indonesia's society and its new state. They also followed the example found in fundamentalist writings of interpreting politics and society through the prism of the Koran by reconsidering important Islamic notions such as *ijma*, *shura* or the *Amarma'ruf Nahi Mungkar* in the light of modern-day needs. The programmes for a Muslim democracy drawn up by al-Bannag and Mawdudi, however, had theological foundations and were radically opposed to the western model. Their reinterpretation of Koranic vocabulary formed the basis of a type of Islamic government which distinguished itself markedly from Western regimes. The consensus of the *ulama* and the use of deliberation as a remedy, for example, were presented as tools particular to Muslim political culture; they were not common points with Western democracy, but rather alternatives to it.[4]

---

[1] To use Olivier Roy's expression. Olivier Roy, *L'échec de l'Islam politique* (Paris: Seuil, 1992), p. 59.
[2] "L'affirmation musulmane au XXe siècle", *Encyclopaedia Universalis*.
[3] This is particularly the case with Harun Nasution, "The Islamic State in Indonesia: The Rise of Ideology, the Movement for its Creation and the Theory of the Masjumi", MA thesis, McGill University, Montreal, 1965, pp. 133–65, and with Yusril Ihza Mahendra, "Modenisme dan Fundamentalisme dalam Politik Islam: satu Kajian Perbandingan kes Parti Masyumi di Indonesia dan Jama'at-i-Islami di Pakistan (1940–1960)", PhD diss., Universitas Sains Malaysia, Pulau Pinang, Malaysia, 1993, published in 1999 in Jakarta by Paramadina.
[4] See, in particular, Ali Aouattah, "L'Etat islamique d'al-Banna à Sayyed Qutb", *Etudes*, February 1995.

For most of the Masyumi theorists, however, Islam did not have a problematic relation with Western political modernism. Their desire to assimilate the above-mentioned Islamic notions with European and American ideas led them to be seen as the champions of a programme of inclusiveness. "The state founded on the principles of Islam" which they aspired to did not present itself as a rival to parliamentary democracy but as a witness to the universality of democratic values. In this regard, they were much closer to the movement initiated by Muhammad Iqbal, sometimes known as "contemporary critical Islam".[5] The Muslim community's duty of *ijtihad*, which Masyumi's thinkers reminded them of, was first and foremost to be practised with this conciliatory aim in mind. It was not to be exercised so as to purify Islam like the "pious ancestors" had done, and even less so in order to bring about a return to the "original paradigm" of the Medina community and the early days of Islam, as advocated by Mawdudi.[6] This explains the significant room to manoeuvre that the Masyumi leadership possessed when drawing up its model of Islamic government. Not only were the self-proclaimed Islamic states in the Arabic peninsula with their undemocratic regimes not one of Masyumi's models for Indonesia's new institutions, but in addition, no other regime in the history of the Muslim world, including the one founded by Mohammad in Medina, could claim to embody the party's political ideal. The "return to the tradition of the Prophet was of course the basis of the reform (*islah*)"[7] called for by the founders of the modernist movement, but for Natsir and his partners, it was the spirit of this tradition and not its practices which mattered.

Numerous authors have demonstrated the limits of the ambitions nurtured by the founding fathers of Muslim reformism. Al-Afghani, Mohammad 'Abduh and Rachid Rida never undertook a scientific historical analysis of Islam's sacred texts and dogmas, for example.[8] It should be said that Masyumi's leaders never took on such a task either,

---

[5] See Rachid Benzine, *Les nouveaux penseurs de l'islam* (espaces libres) (Paris: Albin Michel, 2008 [1st edition, 2004]), pp. 52 ff.

[6] Marc Gaborieau, "Le néo-fondamentalisme au Pakistan: Maudûdî et la Jamâ'at-i Islâmî", in *Radicalismes islamiques*, vol. 2, ed. Olivier Carré and Paul Dumont (Paris: L'Harmattan, 1986), pp. 33–76.

[7] Roy, *L'échec de l'Islam politique*, p. 49.

[8] Olivier Carré, "Islam apolitique et christianisme politique? Clarification", *Revue tunisienne de sciences socials* 111 (1992).

at least not on a theoretical level. However, their refusal to be obliged to refer to Islam for their political positions when in opposition and more importantly for their policy decisions when in power, did constitute a challenge to what some considered to be the absolute superiority of the divine norm over the democratic norm. When it came to consolidating this freedom and transforming it into a coherent doctrine, the party was certainly found wanting; nevertheless, if we refuse to believe that Masyumi's policies were simply guided by a principle of inconsistency, we must consider its policies as the manifestation of an underlying theoretical reflection.

Maxime Rodinson noted in *Islam, politique et croyance* that the party's doctrines often gave way to the demands of reality, and that for want of taking this obvious factor into account, too many observers attributed the party's actions to its deference towards Islamic dogma.[9] He noted, for example, that the Catholic Church, despite the theological separation between the Kingdom of God and the Kingdom of Man suggested by the Bible ("Render unto Caesar what is Caesar's and unto God what is God's"), had often sought temporal as well as spiritual power. The fact that Islam, unlike Christianity, had emerged in a tribal society without any state structures and was thus forced by the circumstances of the day to allow the Islamist movement to sacralise this politico-religious structure which drew no distinction between a believer and a subject, and which obliged the divine norms to be transposed into the state's substantive laws. Like many other Muslims who became involved in politics, Masyumi's leaders did not wish to detach themselves formally from this theoretical framework. If we focus on the party's political record, however, there is no doubt that it adopted a minimalist and inconsistent approach to the link between religion and politics. The party's distancing of itself from this classical Islamist model was initially a question of omission, which can be explained by the circumstances of the moment, and in particular the predicaments of a turbulent period in Indonesian history.[10] What is much more

---

[9] Maxime Rodinson, *L'Islam: politique et croyance* (Paris: Fayard, 1993), p. 245.

[10] The term "classical" here is to be understood in its common 20th-century conception which considers religion and politics to be inextricably linked. For Olivier Carré, this vision of Islam constitutes a misrepresentation of its practices prior to the modern era. According to him, the true Muslim tradition advocates, on the contrary, a certain secularisation of institutions. Olivier Carré, *L'Islam laïque ou le retour à la grande Tradition* (Paris: Armand Colin, 1993).

unusual, however, is the progressive disappearance of any reference to Islam in the party's programmes, a phenomenon which reached its apogee in the government manifesto entitled "Choosing Masyumi means...", drawn up before the 1955 elections. This document was, in a certain sense, the most significant in the history of the party as it was supposed to lay the foundations for widespread popular support for the party. One could of course claim that this electoral programme merely cloaked the party's crypto-Islamism which it had been forced into adopting because of the suspicions of religious intolerance and hostility towards democracy which hung like a pall over activist Islam. This would not explain Masyumi's final stand against the abuses of President Sukarno's Guided Democracy, however. If one were to consider that the party advocated the primacy of religion over politics, it should logically have condemned Sukarno's programme in the name of Islam's values, or at the very least mentioned them alongside the universal Western democratic values which they invoked. This was not the case, however—no such mention was made of Islam.

Beyond these voluntary omissions of any reference to Islamic norms, two more concrete elements also reveal Masyumi's emancipation from the classical political culture of Islamism. The first of these was the party's acceptance, and even defence, of the Republic of Indonesia as a nation-state, despite the fact that most movements which claimed to belong to political Islam condemned such recognition, preferring to aspire to the emergence of a form of Pan-Islamism which would at least be regional in nature.[11] Masyumi, however, always considered the *umma* in a national context. Apart from a few rare trips overseas and occasional speeches, its party leaders never took any firm commitments in favour of Pan-Islamism. Their ideal of an Islamic state did not go beyond the borders which had been inherited from the Dutch and no claim was laid to any other Muslim territory in the region, such as the Malaysian peninsula, the south of the Filipino peninsula or Sabah and Sarawak. This attitude was all the more remarkable since certain thinkers within the nationalist movement at the time, notably Muhammad Yamin, mooted the idea of a Greater Indonesia. One of the consequences of Masyumi's relative lack of interest in Pan-Islamism was the total abandonment of any calls for the revival of the Caliphate. The party's stance on this issue was not a unique one within modernist

---

[11] Roy, *L'échec de l'Islam politique*, p. 27.

Islam. In 1938, the Algerian reformist Ibn Badis had already hailed the end of an institution which he deemed to be obsolete.[12] Although numerous Muslim reformists wished to see the re-emergence of an authority capable of governing the entire Islamic community—Rachid Ria, for example, had argued in 1923 for its transformation into a sort of elective papacy (*Imanat*)—Masyumi never took up this cause.[13] The party's criticism of Turkey and Mustapha Kemal was aimed at the brutal secularisation of Turkish society, particularly the ban on any religious education, and not at the removal of the Caliphate. This lack of interest in an institution which embodied the indissoluble link between politics and religion no doubt demonstrates a further step towards the emancipation mentioned earlier of the political sphere from religion.

The second element which shows the party's disengagement with the classical conception of Islamic political culture concerns the evolution of the party itself. As Pierre Rondo has already pointed out, generally speaking, "Islam's demand for unity makes it suspicious of the divisions which divide men into groups and factions, awakening in them particular allegiances and loyalties."[14] We saw this very phenomenon at work in 1945 in the months following the proclamation of independence when the representatives of the Islamic community tried to oppose the creation of a multi-partite system, arguing instead for the formation of a new single party, an alternative generally considered more in line with Islamic principles.[15] After the KNIP's decision to allow the creation of political parties, Masyumi continued to follow this unitary goal but limited it henceforth to the Muslim community. The desire to unify the political representation of Muslims was not just a tactical ploy on the part of Masyumi; it also echoed *tawhid*, the doctrine of divine oneness, and implied that there was only one type of political Islam possible. Over the years, however, this myth died away. This was in no small part due to Natsir's leadership of the party, which forced it to clarify its aspirations, abandon its insular foundations (leading to Nahdlatul Ulama's painful split from the party in 1952), and be one Muslim party among others. Yet again, however, this transformation was never actually formulated into a doctrine.

---

[12] Ali Merad, *L'Islam contemporain* (*Que sais-je?*) (Paris: PUF, 1984 [5th edition, 1995]), p. 79.
[13] Ibid.
[14] "Political Parties in the Muslim World", *Pouvoirs* 12 (1979): 71–91.
[15] Ibid.

All the above evidence clearly leads us to the conclusion that by refusing to systematically characterise their choices as choices made in the name of Islamic values, and by absolving themselves from obedience to a certain form of international Islamist culture, Masyumi contributed to a detachment from the religious norm in Indonesia. By doing so, it led to the development in Indonesian politics of a certain secularisation, which I take here to mean "de-sacralisation", a notion we shall come back to later. Such a stance is not without precedent in the recent history of the Muslim world. It recalls in particular the evolution which the Turkish party, the AKP, has undergone in recent years. A comparative study—between these two organisations focussing in particular on the similarities between the two countries' experiences of secularisation and on the influence which their relations with the West had on the evolution of Muslim parties—would indeed be a fruitful one.[16] It would no doubt confirm the hypothesis that the parties who occupied positions of power played a key role in bringing Islamic organisations to gradually elaborate a programme for Muslim democracy. Politicians who are confronted with the reality principle are much more capable of initiating such an evolution than learned groups of *ulama*.[17]

The path followed by Masyumi, then, was part of a transformation in Muslim reformism which did not only affect Indonesia. What is unique, however, is the precociousness of this detachment from Islam by a political organisation which claimed to belong to that very same religion. Two reasons, which are both linked to peculiarities within Indonesian Islam, can explain this. Both of these reasons are linked to the sociological groups which provided the party's breeding ground rather than to the political context of the day.

The first of these reasons lies in the peripheral nature of Indonesian Islam and its general composition which, in comparison with

---

[16] Turkish secularism, which was much more radical than its Indonesian counterpart, was not, however, founded on the necessity for different religions to live together, as other religions had already disappeared from the country. See Jenny White, "The End of Islamism? Turkey's Muslimhood Model", in *Remaking Muslim Politics: Pluralism, Contestation, Democratization*, ed. Robert W. Hefner (Princeton, NJ: Princeton University Press, 2005).

[17] Vali Nasir points this out in his article, with the help of several examples, including Turkey. Vali Nasir, "The Rise of 'Muslim Democracy'", *Journal of Democracy* 16, 2 (April 2005).

the Arab world, is rather disparate.[18] Because of its late development and the strong influence which syncretism had upon it, Indonesian Islam gave birth to a large range of religious attitudes, the political consequences of which we have already mentioned.[19] As Masyumi was, broadly speaking, an inheritor of the Islamic reformist movement, it stood as a rival to *abangan* Islam and, after 1952, to traditionalist Islam. Unlike an organisation such as Persatuan Islam which cultivated a very elitist approach to its mission (an approach which led it to adopt intransigent positions), Masyumi's leaders were concerned with the need to build a party with a broad appeal and were involved in the actual exercise of power. This lent them a much more acute sense of the necessity of taking events and circumstances into account when drawing up its policies. Their awareness of Indonesia's social, cultural and political peculiarities made it impossible for them to attempt a literal application of some politico-religious doctrine imported from abroad and encouraged them to look for original solutions. In its search for such solutions, the party, paradoxically, was often guided by Sukarno. It did not adhere to the president's ideals, of course, but on several occasions, he obliged it, in reaction to his proposals, to clarify its ideal and thus contributed to the elaboration of the model for Muslim democracy which it evoked.

Pancasila, which was the embodiment of Sukarno's political genius, played a vital role in this evolution. The national ideology, which Masyumi accepted, was chosen so as to forge Indonesia's identity from its pre-Muslim past—etymologically, both the term "*Pancasila*" and the expression used to describe the principle of a unique God (*Tuan yang Maha Esa*) come from Sanskrit—and was opposed to the idea that the natural form of government for the country should be Islamic. The absence of a direct reference to any Arabo-Muslim concept situated it outside the narrow field of Islamic references and thus, for Muslims, amounted to an involuntary step towards secularisation. Finally, and most importantly, it deprived Islamic parties of any exclusive right to interpret *Pancasila*'s religious values. The president made some skilful

---

[18] One should nonetheless be careful not to give too much credence to the notion that a pure form of Islam exists in the centre and a diluted form at the periphery. See Martin Van Bruinessen, "Global and Local in Indonesian Islam", *Southeast Asian Studies* 37, 2 (September 1999).

[19] See supra Chapter 1 and also M.C. Ricklefs, *Polarising Javanese Society: Islamic and other Visions (c. 1830–1930)* (Leiden: KITLV Press, 2007).

compromises on *Pancasila*, accepting changes of little consequence, such as the modification of the order of the five tenets which put the principle of a unique God in first place; however, Sukarno and his allies were also able to remain firm on what was essential. The appearance in the Jakarta Charter of a direct reference to *sharia* law established a link between a person's condition as a believer and his condition as a citizen and was thus unacceptable because it broke with the mindset of *Pancasila*; at the same time, none of what was contained in the five principles was in contradiction with Islamic belief. The universal character which allowed them to be interpreted as Islamic in spirit, if not in origin, meant that *Pancasila*'s principles could appear to be a step on the way towards Masyumi's ideal state. In his June 1945 speech, Sukarno showed Muslims the way to follow in order to put into practice this process of Islamisation. It required, according to him, their participation in a Western-style parliamentary democracy. On the whole, then, *Pancasila* seemed sufficiently indigenous to appeal to a party aware of the political expediency of promoting an Indonesian national identity—though Masyumi did also try to Islamise Indonesian history through its portrayal of the country's heroes—but also general enough in its terms to allow it to be adapted by the party to its Muslim ideals. Confrontation with democracy was the price to pay, but the hard core of Masyumi leaders who gravitated towards Soekiman and Natsir accepted this all the more easily as it resonated with their own personal convictions.

This compromise, which formed the ideological basis for the country's institutions and allowed the two main political forces— nationalism and Islam—to confront each other in parliament, constituted one of the main peculiarities of Indonesian political life. It lasted a little over 10 years, continuing to work as long as each side could entertain hopes of political success. The more open the democratic debate was, the further Masyumi distanced itself from a literalist Islamic conception of power.[20] In fact, in the run-up to the 1955 elections, the

---

[20] Thus prefiguring the "substantialist" movement within Indonesian Islam, which, in line with Bachtiar Effendy, considered that *Pancasila* was not secular as it does not reject *in toto* the normative aspects of Islam and allows laws to be made which are not in contradiction with the precepts of Islam. Bachtiar Effendy, *Islam and the State in Indonesia* (Singapore: Institute of Southeast Asian Studies, 2003), particularly Chapter 4.

"pancasilisation" of Islam within the party prevailed very much over the Islamisation of *Pancasila*. After 1956, however, the move towards Guided Democracy limited the party's prospects and led it to modify its political message radically. There is no doubt that one of the reasons for this was that any hopes they had for an Islamic interpretation of *Pancasila* were dashed by the new possibilities which the president was exploring, notably his desire to govern with the communists. This affront to Islamic orthodoxy was too brutal not to solicit a response from the Masyumi leadership within the Constituent Assembly: it was a radical one and led them towards a return to integralist Islam which we will again examine to below. The party's reaction was quite different outside the Assembly, however, where it attacked Sukarno's plans by invoking a conception of democracy inherited from the West.

The second factor which explains Masyumi's evolution towards Islamic democracy was its position towards the influence of the West, which differentiated itself from other Islamic movements of the day. There were no signs within the party of the sense of humiliation in relation to the West which Roland Palou noted in Mawdudi,[21] nor was there any indication of "the reconstruction of a sense of identity... by individuals conflicted by their sense of belonging to two different value systems", which Jacques Couland has rightly identified as one of the sources of radical Islam.[22] The schooling received by those who attended the education system set up by the Dutch at the turn of the century made them the children of the colonial government's ethical policy. This included the Masyumi party leaders of the 1950s who, like the secular nationalists, refused to put colonisation into the same basket as Western liberalism, which had been inspired by the Renaissance and the Enlightenment. They did, however, adhere to an interpretation, still prevalent amongst Islamists today, which considers that the former had been spawned by the latter; but for Masyumi's leaders, old Europe had sired other offspring also, in particular democracy, which the Muslim world not only could, but should, be inspired by.

---

[21] Roland Palou, "Abul A'la Mawdudi, penseur de l'islam politique", *Etudes* (July–August 1996).
[22] Jacques Couland, "Islam et politique au regard des formes historiques d'identification. Une esquisse", *La pensée* 299 (Summer 1994).

The Limits of Integralist Islam

The manner in which Masyumi laid down the markers for a Muslim democracy is analogous to the appearance of Christian democracy in Europe,[23] but the history of the party also shows the limits of its attempts to establish such a form of government. The party's liberal identity was linked to certain moments in its history and certain figures within its leadership. Leaders such as Natsir, Roem, Sjafruddin, Prawoto, and even Soekiman and Wibisono were the principal architects of its ideology before the 1955 elections, but others, such as Isa Anshary, Zainal Abidin Ahmad or Kasman Singodimedjo, also left their mark on the party, notably in the Constituent Assembly debates. During the Assembly's attempts to draw up a new constitution, the latter group tirelessly represented a current which was eventually to prevail within the party leadership, advocating a form of government inspired by intergalist Islam, which, naturally enough, was difficult to reconcile with the principles of democracy. One could put this metamorphosis down to a sea change within the party resulting from the victory of one branch over another, but it is not as simple as that. It was a transformation which should be considered more as a shift within the party caused by specific political contingencies which led it to favour one aspect of its political identity over another. It should be remembered that there was, after all, a general consensus within the party concerning the hardening of its stance in the Assembly, as is evidenced by the unconditional support of its deputies for this new position.

At its foundation in November 1945, Masyumi's numerous social benefit programmes gave it the appearance of a party which reflected an integralist conception of Islam. It seemed, then, to invite a parallel with an aspect of intransigent Catholicism in the late 19th century which aspired to solve all political and social problems through religion.[24]

---

[23] The description of Konrad Adenauer and his colleagues ("His political activity was carried out in a Christian manner, but he never claimed that this meant his policy was a Christian policy, and even less so that it was *the* Christian policy") can in my view apply *mutatis mutandis* to Mohammad Natsir and his principal supporters within the party. Joseph Rovan, *Konrad Adenauer* (Paris, 1987), p. 13, quoted in Jean Dominique Durand, *L'Europe de la Démocratie chrétienne* (Paris: Ed. Complexes), p. 95.

[24] Emile Poulat, *Le catholicisme sous observation, du modernisme à aujourd'hui, Entretiens avec Guy Lafon* (Paris: Le Centurion, 1983), pp. 100–1.

Catholic and Islamic integralism were both animated by a rejection of secularisation and they vigorously combated any doctrine which either attempted to limit religion strictly to the private sphere or tried to separate religion from politics. For Masyumi, this characteristic was exemplified by their desire to see the famous Jakarta Charter included in the preamble to the Constitution. The charter had been drawn up on 22 June 1945 and was subsequently forgotten until 1957, when it re-emerged during the debates in the Constituent Assembly. Its demands revealed the limits of the party's evolution towards a Muslim democracy: the words establishing an almost automatic link between one's status as a believer in Islam and the obligation to be subject to its laws made a complete separation of religion and politics impossible. By demanding the inclusion of the Jakarta Charter in the Constitution, Masyumi was returning to a much more classical conception of Islam's relation to politics, a relation based on the notion of divine oneness (*tawhid*) which was "extended to the individual, whose practices are to be considered holistically and are not to be classified according to the domain in which they operate."[25] By opposing President Sukarno's projects through a defence of parliamentary democracy, which could only be legitimised by universal suffrage, while at the same time demanding in the Constituent Assembly the recognition of an immanent norm which would apply to all, even the people's representatives, Masyumi revealed the tensions and contradictions which it had been riddled with for years and which contributed to the radicalisation of some of its former leaders in the years after it was outlawed.

What, then, were the shortcomings in Masyumi's programme for democracy which led it to fall prey to the party's integralist current? There are two possible answers. The first of these is linked to the political events of the day, namely the party's failure to secure a popular mandate. The programme for a Muslim democracy in Indonesia never actually received the democratic approval of its people. As we have already seen, Masyumi's poor performance in the 1955 elections announced the end of Indonesia's liberal period, leading to the party's decline and to its adoption of a classically Islamist position. The voters' refusal to back Masyumi did not, however, signify a rejection of its

---

[25] Roy, *L'échec de l'Islam politique*, p. 26.

programme for democracy. Much of its potential electorate voted instead for Nahdlatul Ulama, whose programme, though a little unclear, also called for a system of parliamentary democracy. Democracy, then, did not appear as a central issue in the election. The electorate made their choice along much older divisions partly pertaining to religious identity but even more so along fault-lines separating Java and the other regions in the archipelago. The second reason for the instability of Masyumi's programme can be attributed to the institutional structures within Islam. A comparison with European Christian democracy offers a few interesting analytical perspectives on this question.

The development of a Christian movement in politics only took place once Christians had emancipated themselves from Catholic integralism under the permission granted by a series of papal concessions. Under pressure from Catholic liberal opinion, Rome gradually abandoned its opposition to the republican system of government along with its claim that the Church should dictate the political activism of its flock. In 1901, Pope Leo XIII issued the encyclical, *Graves de Communi Re*, which marked his desire to limit Christian democracy to works of social benefit, thus preventing the movement from extending its activities to the field of politics, while at the same time reminding the Catholic faithful that their political activity could only be exercised in accordance with the wishes of the Church's hierarchy. In 1905, Pius X in his encyclical, *Il Fermo Proposito*, confirmed the principles laid down by his predecessor, but at the same time opened the way for derogations to the general rule, which would allow Catholics to present themselves for election.

Despite several setbacks, Christian parties gradually managed to emancipate themselves from the authority of the Catholic hierarchy, opening the doors for the emergence, after the Second World War, of the leading Christian democrat parties. The seeds for this difficult compromise had been sown several decades previously during the first debates dealing with the crisis of modernism, which provided the intellectual and rhetorical framework for such a development. A good example of this was the rhetorical process which would allow the Catholic hierarchy to loosen the reins on its flock's political activities without losing face—this involved condemning as "utterly reprehensible" the freedom espoused by modernity as a *thesis*, while recognising as "legitimate" the same freedoms when they were *hypotheses*, that is to say "the appropriate dispensation for the specific conditions in a particular country".[26] Using this possibility to contextualise Christian principles as his theoretical basis, the philosopher Jacques Maritain established his famous distinction between acting on a spiritual level "as a Christian", and acting "in a Christian-minded way" on a temporal level. This affirmation of a separate temporal order was soon adopted by the Christian democrats.[27] It did not mean that religion was to be completely evacuated from the political sphere, however, and so distinguished itself from secular parties. As the philosopher Etienne Borne later wrote: "Christian democrats refuse to allow politics to be a separate and self-sufficient universe, and they maintain that politics can only have substance and meaning through a realm beyond politics."[28]

Through its programmes and political activity, Masyumi managed to elaborate a doctrine which, on the whole, was quite comparable to that of Christian democracy. However, unlike its Christian counterparts, the party did not avail of an uncontested religious hierarchy which could validate its theoretical developments. Natsir and his party colleagues could establish de facto a category which distinguished "acting in a Muslim-minded way" on a temporal level from "acting as a Muslim" on a spiritual level, but such theoretical developments remained fragile. There was no requisite religious authority which would allow them to enshrine such a distinction in black and white in their party's official doctrine. In the case of Catholicism, the dialogue between the clergy and their faithful enabled the former to continue holding the Truth (the "thesis") while allowing the latter the task of dealing with the contingencies of the day and working out compromises (the "hypotheses"). Such a scenario was impossible for Masyumi, as some of its leaders, such as Natsir, were both religious dignitaries and politicians. Thus, when the party's poor results in the elections and the changes in Indonesia's political situation seemed to punish the failure of its decision to distance itself from Islam's political culture, it soon reverted to *sharia* law, that "mainstay of Islamic culture... the only incarnation for

---

[26] *Civilita Cattolica*, 2 October 1863.

[27] Durand, *L'Europe de la Démocratie chrétienne*, p. 120.

[28] A lecture by Etienne Borne at the conference entitled *La Démocratie chrétienne, force internationale*, organised by H. Portelli and T. Jansen, Nanterre, 1986. Quoted in Durand, *L'Europe de la Démocratie chrétienne*, p. 94.

Muslims of what would otherwise be a community of worshipers on a purely formal level."[29]

In hindsight, then, one can see the perspicacity of Nurcholish Madjid's analysis in 1971 of the party to which he was the putative heir. He called on the Muslim community to elaborate a theoretical framework and a reform programme around three intimately linked principles, namely secularisation, intellectual freedom and openness towards modernity—the tenets which, according to him, had effectively guided Masyumi's policies. Nurcholish's former mentors were shocked by his harsh judgement of their political failings and rejected his analysis out of hand. They focussed their attacks in particular on the term "secularisation" (*sekularisasi*), which was unacceptable to them, despite the fact that Madjid had himself contrasted it with the word *sekularisme* which signified an atheistic system of thought.[30] Moreover, he went on to define the effort required by the Muslim community as one of de-sacralisation (*desakralisasi*), that is to say avoiding the sacralisation of human institutions which some Muslims inferred from the divine message. Madjid's reasoning was part of an approach aimed at ridding politics of the shackles of religious norms, which was very much in line with the stance adopted by Masyumi throughout the period of parliamentary democracy. His falling out with the party's former leaders could no doubt have been avoided if he had confined himself to using the term "de-sacralisation", but referring to "secularisation" evoked the sensitive issue of internal tensions and contradictions within Masyumi during the 1950s.

Although they never managed to gain theological approval for it, this theme of secularisation was one of the focal points around which Natsir and his supporters elaborated Masyumi's policies. However, their

---

[29] H.A.R. Gibb, *La structure de la pensée religieuse de l'Islam* (Paris: Larose, 1950), p. 35.

[30] "Therefore secularization is not intended to apply secularism and change Muslims to be secularists. It is intended to profanize everything profane, and free Muslims from the tendency of sacralising the profane. The willingness to always re-evaluate a truth-value before material, moral or historical conditions, should be the very attitude of Muslims." Quoted in Greg Barton, "Neo-modernism: A Vital Synthesis of Traditionalist and Modernist Islamic Thought in Indonesia", *Studia Islamika* 2, 3 (1995).

approach was challenged by the more radical theorists within the party, such as Z.A. Ahmad and Isa Anshary, who criticised their 1955 election campaign for being based almost exclusively on references to Western democratic values without any explicit mention of Islam's teachings. Following the party's electoral defeat, they imposed a return to classic Islamist political demands, thus paralysing the proceedings in the Constituent Assembly.

At first sight, then, the Indonesian experience of political Islam appears to confirm the observations made by H.A.R. Gibb, a specialist on Islam who claims that the absence of a religious hierarchy in Sunni Islam often ends up pushing "Islamic theology into adopting extreme positions".[31] On closer examination, however, the desire expressed by Masyumi during the debates in the Assembly to break with its pre-election positions was not an overarching one. Although it would not be unreasonable to conclude from Mohammad Natsir's political writings and actions that he recognised the principle of Islam's sovereignty over Indonesia, he did not envisage any important political decision being taken without a democratic debate. Moreover, the majority of Indonesia's citizens, non-Muslims included, would probably have agreed that there existed within Islam a certain number of universal principles which were capable of providing the cornerstone for the Republic's legal framework and of inspiring its laws.[32] The identification and application of such principles would, naturally, have required an ambitious project of interpretation taking into account the country's cultural

---

[31] Gibb, *La structure de la pensée religieuse de l'Islam*, p. 41. As we have already seen, Gibb was an author whom Masyumi figures liked to quote, but for other reasons.

[32] It is worth pointing out in this regard that beyond any questions of religion, general, non-written rules can sometimes prevail in a democratic state, insofar as they are founded on a general consensus. In France, for instance, since a landmark decision in 1971 concerning the freedom of association, the Constitutional Council has awarded itself the right to examine the conformity of acts passed by the legislature with "the fundamental principles recognized under the laws of the Republic." This notion was invented by the Council, which reviews the constitutionality of laws and is thus the only institution capable of defining these very "fundamental principles" which cannot be found in any legal document. The decision appears to be a serious violation of democratic principles, but it is now a universally accepted procedure, as it is based on a widespread consensus in French society.

distinctiveness. This could only have come about through a search for consensus (*mufakat*), which was so important in Indonesian politics but was clearly lacking at that time in the Constituent Assembly. If the Assembly had not been dissolved, would Masyumi have managed to achieve within its ranks the cohesion necessary to win significant cross-party support for such a project? An anecdote heard on the streets of Jakarta at the end of the 1990s holds a possible answer: during the debates in the Assembly, one of the Christian leaders was said to have gone in search of Mohammad Natsir in order to inform him that he, personally, was prepared to back the establishment of an Islamic state.[33] The one condition to his support, however, was a guarantee that Natsir, and Natsir alone, would be its president.

---

[33] This story was recounted to me in September 2000 by Hoedaifah Koeddah, a figure belonging to the Pemuda Pancasila organisation, whose role during the New Order was rather murky.

Archetypal Contradictions within Muslim Reformism in Indonesia: Masyumi as Inheritors and Perpetuators

The Chains of Guided Democracy[1]

Masyumi's leaders were the main opponents to President Sukarno's slide towards authoritarianism, and they were to pay a heavy price for this when Guided Democracy emerged. An amnesty was promised to the rebels and promptly given to those who played a military role, but the party figures who had participated in the PRRI uprising found themselves in jail as soon as they returned from Java. Mohammad Natsir was placed under house arrest in Malang in 1960 before being transferred in 1962 to the military prison on Keagungan Street in Jakarta,[2] while Sjafruddin Prawiranegara and Boerhanoeddin Harahap were both arrested in 1961. The government's crackdown was not confined to the rebels; those who supported them, even if they only did so verbally, were also imprisoned. In 1960, for example,

---

[1] For more detailed analysis of the questions raised here and of the transformations within Indonesian Islam since the New Order, see Andrée Feillard and Rémy Madinier, *The End of Innocence: Indonesian Islam and the Temptations of Radicalism* (Singapore: NUS Press, 2006).

[2] Moch. Lukman Fatahullah Rais, ed., *Mohammad Natsir Pemandu Ummat* (Jakarta: Bulan Bintang, 1989), p. 107.

Kasman Singodimedjo, who had been detained since 1958 for having given a speech in Magelang in which he "willingly provided help to enemies during a state of war",[3] was sentenced to three years in prison.[4] The Masyumi leaders who had not participated in the Hijrah—to use the expression employed within the party to refer to the PRRI rebellion —continued to meet regularly after their party was banned. Before they were arrested in 1962, Prawoto Mangkusasmito and Mohamad Roem were the unofficial leaders of this "Masyumi family", a role which was subsequently adopted by Faqih Usman, the president of Muhammadiyah.[5]

Between 1960 and 1962, numerous members of the Minang diaspora, who "had just come out of the jungle" after their participation in the PRRI uprising, began to gather in certain mosques in Jakarta.[6] An informal network soon sprang up around the Al-Azhar Mosque in the new district of Kebayoran, where activities such as preaching were developed, and themes were elaborated which were to become central to the party's policies for many years, in particular the denunciation of Christianity.

The main force behind the party's fragile revival was the former Masyumi deputy, HAMKA. Of Minang origin, he had become a member of Muhammadiyah's leadership and taken up the position of *imam* in the Al-Azhar mosque. His virulent opposition to Guided Democracy, which he branded as *Totaliterisme* in his speeches and in *Pandhi Masjarakat*—a monthly magazine which HAMKA founded in July 1959 and whose title signified "Society's Banner"—in which he published an article entitled "*Demokrasi Kita*" written by the former vice president, Mohammad Hatta, led in August 1960 to the banning of the magazine. He enjoyed very cordial relations with the army's top ranks, and this no doubt protected him from the first wave of government arrests. According to his son, he regularly received visits from both Lieutenant-

---

[3] The terms used in the indictment. *Abadi*, 24 August 1960.
[4] Panitia Peringatan 75 Tahun Kasman, *Kasman Singodimedjo 75 tahun, Hidup itu berjuang* (Jakarta: Bulan Bintang, 1982), p. 224.
[5] Deliar Noer, *Partai Islam di Pentas Nasional* (Jakarta: Pustaka Utama Grafiti, 1987), p. 411.
[6] H. Rusydi Hamka, "Mengiringi Safari Da'wah warga Bulan Bintang", in *Pak Natsir 80 Tahun, buku pertama, Pandangan dan Penilaian Generasi Muda*, ed. H. Endang Saifuddin Anshary and Amien Rais (Jakarta: Media Da'wah, 1988), pp. 15–25.

General Sudirman, who was the commandant of the Army Staff and Command School, and Colonel Muchlas Rowi, head of the Army's Muslim Spiritual Centre (PUSROH Islam angkatan Darat).[7] In April 1961, these two military figures, acting on behalf of General Nasution, the Army Chief of Staff, encouraged HAMKA to launch a new Islamic magazine, and in April 1962, with the help of money provided by Nasution, the first edition of *Gema Isalm* ("the Echo of Islam") was published. In theory, Lieutenant-General Sudirman was the newspaper's publisher and Colonel Rowi its editor-in-chief, but in actual fact, it, was run by HAMKA.

The Al-Azhar mosque became a refuge point for those concerned at the growing influence of the Communist Party over the government. As Indonesia at that time was being ruled under a state of emergency, no political meetings were authorised, but despite this ban, every Friday after prayer, numerous figures gathered at meetings presided by HAMKA in order to discuss the country's future.[8] At these gatherings, the beginnings of an alliance emerged between the army and the Muslim leaders who had not taken part in the Guided Democracy programme. In 1961, General Nasution and his military staff took the symbolic decision to celebrate *idul fitri* at the Al-Azhar mosque, while Sukarno and his ministers gathered at the Palace mosque.[9] In addition, the system used to organise *da'wah* at Al-Azhar inspired others to imitate this model: General Sudirman, along with several officers, founded the Higher Institute of Islamic Preaching (Perguruan Tinggi Dakwah Islam, PDTI) and in several regions, local *da'wah* organisations were created, often run by former Masyumi activists.[10] This burgeoning opposition force made HAMKA one of the favourite targets for the LEKRA and the Lembaga Kebudayaan Nasional (LKR), both of which were cultural organisations close to the Communist Party and the PNI. The magazine *Bintang Timur* ("the Star of the East"), for example, launched a virulent campaign against him in October 1962, claiming that three of his novels were plagiarised from the Egyptian writer

---

[7] H. Rusydi Hamka, *Pribadi dan Martabat, Buya Prof. DR. Hamka* (Jakarta: Pustaka Panjimas, 1983), p. 165.

[8] HAMKA, "Mengiringi Safari Da'wah warga Bulan Bintang".

[9] HAMKA, *Pribadi dan Martabat, Buya Prof. DR. HAMKA*, p. 166.

[10] Ibid.

[11] *Di bawah Lindungan Ka'bah* (1938), *Tenggelamnya Kapal van der Wijk* (1938) and *Di dalam lembah Kehidupan* (1940).

Mustafa Lutfi al-Manfaluti (1876–1924),[11] while the daily newspaper *Merdeka* denounced the activities of "new-Masyumi" in the Al-Azhar Mosque.

Shortly afterwards, in a second wave of arrests, almost all of the remaining former leaders of Masyumi who had not yet been brought into custody were locked up. Along with Prawoto Mangkusasmito, who had recently called for Sukarno to be tried for violating the Constitution, Mohamad Roem, Yunan Nasution, E.Z. Muttaqien and Isa Anshary were all imprisoned in Madiun.[12] The following year in 1963, government repression hit the outer circle of the Masyumi family, starting in November with the detention of, Anwar Harjono, the leader of GPII, who was held for two months at the army's headquarters before being placed under house arrest.[13] In late December and early January, HAMKA, Ghazali Sjahlan and Jusuf Wibisono were all arrested: they were accused of having taken part in a secret meeting held a few months previously in Tanggerang at the house of a former Masyumi member, Arif Suhaemi, during which a secret plot was hatched to overthrow the government. The former minister for finance, Jusuf Wibisono, had been one of the few party leaders to clearly condemn the participation of his party colleagues in the PRRI and so his arrest clearly indicated that the regime was hardening its attitude towards all who had occupied a position within Masyumi's leadership. After the failure of the Constituent Assembly to carry out its mission, he had called for a rapprochement with Sukarno, and he was subsequently appointed to the leadership of the National Front by the president. Wibisono had cut off ties with all his former party colleagues, apart from Soekiman who had withdrawn from public life and as such did not represent a threat for Sukarno's regime; he was nonetheless held in detention without trial for almost three years.[14]

Disenchantment with the New Order

In the wake of the crisis which shook the country between 1965 and 1966, the advent of a new Indonesian order asserting its opposition to

---

[12] Noer, *Partai Islam di Pentas Nasional*, p. 415.

[13] Lukman Hakiem, *Perjalan Mencari keadilan dan persatuan: Biografi Dr Anwar Harjono* (Jakarta: Media Dakwah, 1993), p. 13.

[14] I.N. Soebagijo, *Jusuf Wibisono. Karang di Tengah Gelombang* (Jakarta: Gunung Agung), pp. 247 ff.

Sukarno's abuse of power raised great hopes amongst the leaders of the now-defunct Masyumi. They hoped that the moribund regime's treatment of the organisation and its members would enable them to claim a prominent role in the new political dispensation. This hope was short-lived, however, as the new government's strategy towards the two branches of political Islam—traditionalism and modernism—soon turned out to be very similar in nature to the approach adopted by the Guided Democracy system.

In December 1965, while most of Masyumi's leaders were still in prison, a Coordination Committee for Islamic Activities was created, designed to bring together all the Islamic organisations campaigning for Masyumi's reinstatement. It received the support of several army officers who wished to see Nahdlatul Ulama's influence diminished and who were of the belief that the modernist branch within Islam could not remain unrepresented any longer.[15] As the Masyumi leaders were progressively released from prison—the last in early 1967—they began, from May 1966, to hold meetings at 58 Menteng Raya Street in an attempt to adopt a common strategy.[16] These gatherings of Islamic modernists soon gave birth to two competing projects. The first one proposed purely and simply to revive Masyumi, banking on the good relations which existed between its former leaders and certain high-ranking military officers—General Sudirman, in particular. The second proposal was put forward by the former vice president, Mohammad Hatta, and his supporters, who, deeming Masyumi to have been a failure, intended to found a new organisation. This second group was composed of former leaders of Himpunan Mahasiswa Islam, notably Mohammad Daud Ali, Ismail Metareum and Nurcholish Madjid (though Madjid later distanced himself from the group), but also received support from figures who formerly belonged to the Masyumi family. Hanwar Harjono, for example, took part for a while in the meetings before rallying behind Natsir,[17] while Jusuf Wibisono, who had always been critical of his former party colleagues' choice of strategy, also threw his support behind Hatta.[18]

---

[15] Allan A. Samson, "Islam in Indonesian Politics", *Asian Survey* (December 1968).

[16] Deliar Noer, *Aku bagian Ummat, aku bagian Bangsa, otobiografi* (Bandung: Mizan, 1996), p. 590. Most of Masyumi's leaders were released in May and June 1966.

[17] Ibid., p. 592.

[18] Soebagijo, *Jusuf Wibisono. Karang di Tengah Gelombang*, p. 331.

It was the army who finally settled the debate between these two groups. In the second half of 1966, the president of the Committee for the Revival of Masyumi, Sjarif Usman, held several meetings with influential military officers, such as Generals Amir Machmud, Kemal Idris, Sutjipto and Alamsjah as well as Colonel Murtopo. A spirit of optimism reigned at that time: during the second army seminar organised at Bandung, a resolution was taken to allow the former leaders of outlawed parties to once again take an active part in public life.[19] However, on 21 December 1966, the army's regional commandants published a report, whose main aim was to prevent any political coups or manoeuvring by Sukarno, stressing that the army would take resolute action against any group that contravened *Pancasila* or the 1945 Constitution, as Gesapu, Darul Islam, Masyumi, the Socialist Party and the PKI (during the Madiun Rebellion) had all done.[20] This strategy of recalling the party's rebellious past soon became the New Order's official policy. On 26 January 1967, General Suharto announced that the armed forces and the soldiers' families who had suffered during the campaigns against Darul Islam and then against the PRRI were not ready to accept Masyumi's reinstatement.[21] The government's decision was an irrevocable one and when Prawoto Mangkusasmito protested strenuously against it, Colonel Ali Murtopo reminded him that "the prison door was still wide open".[22] In response to this impasse, Deliar Noer, who was able to observe these negotiations at close range, tried to convince Natsir and Prawoto to lend their support to Mohammad Hatta. The two men, however, despite their sympathy for the former vice president's programme, felt imbued with a sense of moral duty towards their supporters, and so refused to abandon their campaign for the revival of Masyumi.[23] In any case, the question soon became a moot one, as in May 1967, Suharto indicated to Mohammad Hatta that the government would not authorise him to establish his Indonesian Islamic Democratic Party (Partai Demokrasi Islam Indonesia, PDII).[24]

---

[19] K.E. Ward, *The Foundation of the Partai Muslimin Indonesia* (Ithaca, NY: Cornell University Press, 1970), pp. 24–5.

[20] B.J. Boland, *The Struggle of Islam in Modern Indonesia* (The Hague: Martinus Nijhoff, 1982), p. 190.

[21] Ward, *The Foundation of the Partai Muslimin Indonesia*, p. 25.

[22] Noer, *Aku bagian Ummat, aku bagian Bangsa*, p. 593.

[23] Ibid. At the time, Deliar Noer was part of Suharto's committee of political advisors.

[24] Deliar Noer, *Mohammad Hatta, biografi politik* (Jakarta: LP3ES, 1990), p. 648.

By mid-1967, the efforts of those who supported a return of Islamic modernism to the political scene had come to naught. At this point, they resolved to begin the foundation of a new political party, the Partai Muslimin Indonesia (Parmusi). The government authorised its creation on the express condition that none of the former Masyumi leaders would be able to sit on the party's governing bodies. When Parmusi's inaugural congress was held in Malang in December 1968, the participants were firmly reminded of this requirement, which Suharto had promised to remove after the general elections.[25] Initially, the leadership that the party members elected was dominated by former members of the modernist party: Mohamad Roem was the president, and beside him on the executive committee were, amongst others, Anwar Harjono and Hasan Basri. Figures deemed to be too close to the government, such as Agus Sudono, Naro and Sanusi, were overlooked.[26] Although the most troublesome former Masyumi leaders withdrew voluntarily from the election, the government nonetheless let it be known on the last day of the congress that they would refuse to recognise the new party's leaders. The former Masyumi leaders therefore had to stand down and leave their positions to the provisional leadership which had already received the authorities' approval in February 1968. The provisional leadership was composed mainly of Muhammadiyah leaders, such as Djarnawi Hadikusuma and Lukman Harun, who had never played any role in Masyumi.[27] The only individual close to Natsir and Prawoto, who served for a while on Parmusi's leadership, was the former GPII figure, Hanwar Harjono.

Following Parmusi's congress, the government proceeded to exclude the modernist branch once and for all from the political landscape in two stages. In 1969, the government fomented serious disputes within Parmusi and placed one of its allies, John Naro, at the head of the party. Its credibility with Masyumi's former electorate had completely disappeared by the 1971 elections, during which the party only received 5.4% of the vote. Two years later, the Suharto administration began a "rationalisation" of political life which consisted in obliging parties to gather under one of three umbrella organisations which were supposed to represent the main currents in society. Parmusi, the

---

[25] Ibid., p. 57.
[26] Ibid., pp. 52–3. Natsir was not even present at the congress.
[27] For the composition of this provisional leadership, see ibid., p. 38.

PSII, Perti and NU were all to be part of the United Development Party (Partai Persatuan Pembangunan, PPP) representing political Islam. Having already succeeded in sabotaging the political rebirth of Islamic modernism, the government was now attempting to neutralise Nahdlatul Ulama which had almost unwittingly become the symbol of Islamic opposition to the regime. Although the traditionalist party had received the support of almost 70% of Muslims and 18.7% of the total electorate in 1971, it only received 44% of the seats allotted to the PPP representatives in the new assembly.[28] This was scarcely more than the percentage received by Parmusi (with 5.4% of the popular vote), and from that point on, Masyumi's abortive successor was firmly established as the New Order's fifth column within the Muslim community.

More than five years after their release from prison, the former leaders of Masyumi remained pariahs on the Indonesian political landscape. Their struggle for the revival of their former party and their attempt to maintain its legacy had both ended in complete failure due to three major obstacles.

They were first of all the victims of the new regime's fears. President Suharto's refusal to allow the modernist movement to re-emerge reflected, above all, his concern that those who had appeared as the most ardent defenders of Western-style parliamentary democracy between 1957 and 1960, were to be excluded from political life. Following the example of the Sukarno regime during the 1960s, the New Order reorganised the political landscape by means of a clever manipulation of special interests, and it could not condone the revival of a political movement inspired by Masyumi and Mohammad Hatta which, a few years earlier, had opposed the very same abuse of power. In addition, with its resolutely Western form of modernism and its culture of democracy, Masyumi may have appeared, in the eyes of the New Order generals, as a dangerous rival in their quest for American approval.

The second obstacle which attempts to reinstate the modernist party concerned the interests of its traditionalist rival. With the re-emergence of a modernist party whose legitimacy was reinforced by its long-standing opposition to the PKI, Nahdlatul Ulama was in danger of being subjected to fresh criticism over their support for the Old Order, as well as running the risk of losing its dominant position within

---

[28] Andrée Feillard, *Islam et armée dans l'Indonésie contemporaine: Les pionniers de la tradition*, Cahier d'Archipel 28 (Paris: L'Harmattan, 1995), p. 143.

Indonesian Islam and its monopoly over the Ministry of Religious Affairs. Under the leadership of Kiyayi Wahab, NU had adopted a strategy which was radically different to Masyumi's. The traditionalist party had considered that the struggle against communism would be better served from inside the government, and so took the risk of giving its unconditional support to Sukarno, while simultaneously leading a vigorous campaign to counter the spread of the PKI in the countryside.[29] This struggle culminated during the 1966–67 massacres in which Anshor, the NU youth movement, played an important role. NU's participation in this dramatic episode which marked the birth of the New Order, did not, however, signify the creation of an alliance between the founders of the new regime and the traditionalists against their modernist rivals. It remains difficult to determine the extent of the former's participation in the manoeuvres aimed at thwarting the modernists, and what's more, Nahdlatul Ulama also ended up being a victim of the New Order's policy of "political rationalisation". None-theless, certain former Masyumi members did not hesitate to make specific accusations. Husni Thamri, for example, declared that two NU leaders, Idham Chalid and Subchan ZE, had approached Ali Murtopo and other New Order leaders in order to convince them to annul the election of former Masyumi figures at the congress in Malang.[30]

Finally, Masyumi's former leaders were also faced with a significant generation gap between themselves and the young Muslim activists who had played a primordial role in establishing the New Order but who did not support the modernist party's cause. From 1964, harsh criti-cism of large Muslim organisations began to circulate in the Koranic schools in Java. The young *santris* criticised equally Nahdlatul Ulama, whom they accused of being opportunistic, and Masyumi for being too Westernised.[31] In addition to that, the main leaders of the the GPII—

---

[29] Ward, *The Foundation of the Partai Muslimin Indonesia*, p. 62n21. Like its pre-dicament in 1959 over how to react to Guided Democracy, NU was divided over the question of which attitude to adopt towards Sukarno, who continued to support the PKI. The young generation who was active in Anshor criticised on numerous occasions the "opportunistic" attitude of the traditionalist leaders, and eventually it was the most anti-communist leaders, such as Subchan Z.E., who prevailed within the movement after September 1965.

[30] Ibid., p. 62.

[31] Lance Castles "Notes on the Islamic School at Gontor", *Indonesia*, 1, April 1966.

E.Z. Muttaqien, Soemarsono, Achmad Buchari and Anwar Haryono—
had been imprisoned along with the older counterparts in Masyumi.
There was no advantage to be gained for them in participating in the
events of 1965–66, and so this left the way clear for the Association
of Muslim Students (Himpunan Mahasiswa Islam, HMI). Although
HMI was very close to the modernist movement, it always insisted
on maintaining its independence vis-à-vis Natsir's party. Following the
advent of the New Order, some of its leading figures let it be known
that they viewed the Masyumi more as "wrecks" of the old regime
than as heroes who deserved a place in the new dispensation.[32] In this
strained atmosphere of the late 1960s, a new generation of Muslim
intellectuals emerged. In 1967 in Yogyakarta, a small discussion group
known as the "Limited Group" began to meet regularly at the house
of Professor H.A. Mukti Ali, whose main admirers included Ahmad
Wahib, Djohan Effendi, Dawam Rahardjo and Nurcholish Madjid.
The latter, who had been president of HMI since 1966, was one of
the great bright hopes of the modernist party. He was often called "the
young Natsir" (Natsir Muda) and enjoyed an excellent relationship with
Masyumi's former president who saw in him the embodiment of a possible resurgence of the party. Madjid himself, however, soon deflated
the hopes which the party had invested in him when, on 3 February
1970, he gave a lecture before a gathering of student organisations
entitled "The Necessity for a Renewal of Muslim Thought and the
Integration of the *Umma*" (Keharusan Pembaruan Pemikran Islam dan
Maslah Intergrasi Umat). His thesis was founded on a very harsh
appraisal of the endeavours of Muslim parties. For Nurcholish, their
leaders had lost all credibility in the eyes of public opinion and had
discredited the political ideal which they wished to bring about. The
prevailing mood within the Islamic community at that time was "Islam,
yes! Islamic Party, no!"[33]

Nurcholish Madjid's lecture was seen as a betrayal by the former
Masyumi leaders, especially given that the address was not published
in the Muslim press but in the socialist-oriented *Indonesia Raya*. Natsir

---

[32] Ward, *The Foundation of the Partai Muslimin Indonesia*, p. 31.
[33] Greg Barton, "Neo-Modernism: A Vital Synthesis of Traditionalist and Modernist Islamic Thought in Indonesia", *Studia Islamika* 2, 3 (1995). The transcript
of Nurcholish Madjid's lecture was published in *Islam Kemodernan dan Keindonesiaan* (Bandung: Mizan, 1987).

and those close to him castigated the secularisation (*sekularisasi*) which Nurcholish was promoting.[34] This dispute, which we will revisit later, no doubt contributed to the embitterment of Masyumi's former leaders and thus to the radicalisation of their message.

The Besieged Citadel and the Sanctuary Afforded by the Da'wah

In 1967, Mohammad Natsir and his closest supporters—Mohamad Roem, Anwar Harjono and Yunan Nasution—founded the Indonesian Islamic Propagation Council (Denwan Dakwah Islam Indonesia, DDII). DDII emerged from the Indonesian Islamic community's recognition that they needed a renewal, and it provided them temporarily with an organisation to rally around. As the prospect of their former party's rehabilitation grew increasingly less likely, it became the sanctuary in which Masyumi's values could be safeguarded but also one in which they would be transformed.[35]

Some of the former Masyumi leaders did not join the DDII, including Jusuf Wibisono and Soekiman who had considered for a period of time the idea of establishing their own party. They envisaged a party which would be founded on Islam but which "mustn't be too religious" (*tidak terlalu agamis*). However, having consulted with figures within the new regime, they were soon persuaded to renounce these plans.[36] Jusuf Wibisono decided to join the ranks of the PSII (he claims to have done so in mid-1970), but the party's poor results, which he attributed to unfair competition from Golkar, led him to retire from politics definitively.[37]

---

[34] Further reading on this issue can be found in Marcel Bonneff, "Les intellectuels musulmans, le renouveau religieux et les transformations socio-culturelles de l'Indonésie", in *Renouveaux religieux en Asie*, ed. Catherine Clémentin-Ojha (Paris: École française d'Extrême-Orient, 1997).

[35] On the popularity within Masyumi of the term *dakwah* (proselytization), which replaced the term *tabligh* (transmission) and gave a broader dimension to its mission, see Yudi Latif, *Indonesian Muslim, Intelligentsia and Power* (Singapore: Institute of Southeast Asian Studies, 2008), pp. 350–1.

[36] Soebagijo, *Jusuf Wibisono. Karang di Tengah Gelombang*, p. 311.

[37] K.E. Ward claims that Jusuf Wibisono and Soekiman became members of the PSII shortly after Masyumi was banned in 1960, but Wibisono vehemently contests this claim. Ibid., p. 312.

Dewan Dakwah's headquarters were located in Masyumi's former central office at number 45 Jalan Kramat Raya and remained the only stable landmark for a generation of modernists who had grown disenchanted with Indonesia's social and political transformations. The organisation launched into an energetic publishing programme, with the monthly journal *Serial Media Dakwah*—initially aimed at an educated readership and later to become *Media Dakwah*—becoming its flagship publication. Other publications produced by the organisation included: *Suara Masjid*, geared towards a more modest audience and containing commentaries of sacred texts in very accessible language; *Serial Khutbah Ju'mat*, which proposed sermons to be used by those who preached on Fridays; *Sahabat* aimed at children; and *Buletin Dakwah*, which was a simple leaflet distributed outside mosques after Friday prayer.[38]

It was these publications which diffused the modernist movement's radicalised new message. During the 1950s, the Masyumi leaders were moderate, confident and imbued with a remarkable spirit of tolerance, but like the vast majority of the Islamic movement worldwide, they gradually succumbed to a siege mentality. The West, which up until that point had been seen as an ally against communism, was now considered a threat. There was a marked change in tone towards the Christian community from the early years of the New Order. By 1966, rumours began to circulate within the Muslim community describing mass conversions by Muslims to Christianity, and the triumphalist declarations by Protestant missionaries claiming that they had won over two million converts added further fuel to such talk.[39] Although such assertions were not completely baseless, they were nonetheless blown out of proportion. According to Robert Hefner, nearly 500,000 people were concerned by this wave of conversions; in certain towns in West Java, the Christian population rose from one or two per cent of the population in the 1950s to more than 10 per cent in the 1970s.

---

[38] H.M. Yunan Nasution, "Pak Natsir, pemandu ummat", in *Mohammad Natsir Pemandu Ummat*, ed. Moch. Lukman Fatahullah Rais (Jakarta: Bulan Bintang, 1989), p. 15.

[39] Further reading on these declarations can be found in Avery T. Willis, *The Indonesian Revival: Why Two Million Came to Christ* (South Pasadena, CA: William Carey Library, 1977).

438 Islam and Politics in Indonesia

These converts came for the most part from former bastions of communism where the population had been traumatised by the massacres of 1966–67 and the role played in them by certain Islamic organisations.[40]

Masyumi's former leaders soon became concerned about this phenomenon, and in 1967, HAMKA published his first anti-Christian diatribes in *Pandji Majarakat*.[41] His tone had changed radically from the 1950s: his tolerant attitude towards the anti-Christian violence perpetrated in Jakarta and Makassar reveals the insularity which had taken hold of his supporters and their feeling that Christians were taking advantage of their economic superiority to compete unfairly with Islam.[42] In response to these early incidents, the government organised on 30 Nov 1967 a consultation meeting between the dignitaries of the country's different religious communities at which the Muslim community was represented by Natsir, Rajidi, Fakih Usman, Prawoto Mangkusasmito and HAMKA. Their call for a *modus vivendi* to be established by the government which would outlaw any proselytising amongst the members of other religions was rejected by representatives of the Christian community on grounds that it would violate human rights.[43]

Dewan Dakwah, which saw itself as a sanctuary able to preserve Islam's threatened identity, sent an increasing number of preachers to the regions it deemed to be the most vulnerable to Christian conversion.[44] Through the organisation's publications, former Masyumi leaders showed their adoption of the new Islamist message being spread across the world, which considered the West as a corrupt oppressor to be combated. In the 1950s, the modernist party had focussed its attention on national problems, but now its former leaders were opening up to the causes pursued by the international Islamic community. The Six-Day War in 1967 and especially the Yom Kippur War of 1973

---

[40] Robert W. Hefner, "Print Islam: Mass Media and Ideological Rivalries among Indonesian Muslims", *Indonesia* 64 (October 1997): 77–103.

[41] HAMKA, *Pribadi dan Martabat, Buya Prof. DR. Hamka*, p. 173.

[42] "All of these conflicts arose because of Christians who had apparently taken advantage of the transition period between the Old Order and the New Order to spread their religion within the Muslim community which, at the time, was both politically and economically weakened." Ibid., p. 174.

[43] Mujiburrahman, "Feeling Threatened: Muslim-Christian Relations in Indonesia's New Order", ISIM dissertations, Amsterdam University Press, 2006, p. 41.

[44] Hefner, "Print Islam".

reinforced their involvement in the Arab-Israeli conflict, at least at a verbal level. They established an increasing number of contacts throughout the Muslim world and made more and more trips to Malaysia. Mohammad Natsir occupied important positions within international Muslim institutions: during the 1970s, he was vice president of the World Islamic Congress (Muktamar Alam Islami) in Karachi and a member of the World Organisation of Mosques (Organisasi Masjid Sedunia) in Mecca.[45] The foreign ties which Dewan Da'wah's leaders established allowed the organisation to become part of international Islamic financial networks. It was able to benefit, for example, from the generous donations which came from Saudi Arabia, Kuwait, Egypt and Pakistan.[46]

The ideology transmitted by the DDII since the 1960s turned out to be based on the same ambivalence as Masyumi's had been, albeit of a different nature. In the 1950s, the modernist party emphasised a broad-minded approach towards the interpretation of the Koran at the expense of the literalist interpretation defended by Persis; 20 years later, the requirements related to the application of *sharia* law dominated the question. Moreover, Dewan Dakwah was more efficient in its campaign for the Islamisation of the country's institutions than Masyumi had been when in government. It was behind vast campaigns which mobilised the Muslim community and forced the government to make significant concessions: a law on marriage in 1974; obligatory religious education in 1988; and most importantly, the 1989 law allowing a large degree of autonomy to *sharia* courts.[47] The organisation's main publication, *Media Da'wah*, became the mouthpiece for a branch of Islam which the political scientist R. William Liddle called "scripturalist" and "fundamentalist".[48] The magazine reacted violently to the use of these terms. Their response to Liddle's article was published

---

[45] Nasution, "Pak Natsir, pemandu ummat", p. 19.

[46] Hefner, "Print Islam".

[47] On these advances made by Islamic law, see Arskal Salim and Azyumardi Azra, eds., *Sharia and Politics in Modern Indonesia* (Singapore: Institute of Southeast Asian Studies, 2003).

[48] R. William Liddle, "Media Dakwah Scripturalism: One Form of Islamic Political Thought and Action in New Order Indonesia", in *Toward a New Paradigm: Recent Developments in Indonesian Islamic Thought*, ed. Mark R. Woodward (Tempe, AZ: Arizona State University, 1996).

below a caricature of the illustrious professor depicted with a Star of David in the background, thus illustrating his very remarks.[49]

The former Masyumi members who belonged to DDII nonetheless retained an almost atavistic attachment to the principles of democracy and for this reason refused to bargain with the New Order. Very few of them accepted to sit on any of the new regime's institutions. Although HAMKA accepted the leadership of the newly created Indonesian Council of Ulama, he was severely criticised for this decision by his former party colleagues and resigned in 1981 after a dispute with the minister for religions.[50]

Relations between former Masyumi members and the government remained tainted with mutual suspicion. The army had long suspected the party's former leaders of their involvement in the violent demonstrations which punctuated the Japanese prime minister's visit in January 1974.[51] Mohammad Natsir showed himself to be very critical towards the regime, and was accustomed to saying that "Sukarno was a gentleman in comparison with Suharto."[52] In May 1980, along with Anwar Haryono, he signed the "petition of the fifty" (Petisi 50) criticising the government's use of *Pancasila* to muffle opposition to it. Like most of the petition signatories, Natsir was subsequently no longer allowed to leave the country, though he did not feel especially intimidated by this measure. In 1990, three years before he died, he co-authored with General A.H. Nasution and the former PNI leader Sanusi Hardjninata, a book entitled *Indonesia at a Crossroads* (*Indonesia di persimpangan jalan*) in which the Suharto regime was criticised for betraying the social ideals of the Revolution and for concentrating power in a small number of hands.

Inheritors and Perpetuators

The creation of the Association of Indonesian Muslim Intellectuals (Ikatan Cendekawan Muslimin Indonesia, ICMI) in 1990 under the

---

[49] Hefner, "Print Islam".

[50] HAMKA, *Pribadi dan Martabat, Buya Prof. DR. Hamka*, p. 217.

[51] *Abadi* was once again banned. François Raillon, *Les étudiants indonésiens et l'Ordre Nouveau. Politique et idéologie du Mahasiswa Indonesia (1966–1974)* (Paris: Editions de la Maisons des sciences de l'homme, 1984), p. 102.

[52] George McTurnan Kahin, "In Memoriam: Mohammad Natsir", *Indonesia* (February 1994).

leadership of Jusuf Habibie, who was at the time minister for research and technology, was the culmination of the subtly elaborated strategy implemented by the Suharto regime which consisted in manipulating Muslim organisations for its own benefit.[53] It also showed the regime's gradual transformation from one which was initially founded exclusively on the support of the army, but was now looking for a new legitimacy by turning to Islam. The initiative considerably boosted the hopes of modernist Muslims, who represented a significant majority within ICMI, convinced that they had at last found the means for their social and political recognition. The new organisation, however, soon came to embody the profound divisions which affected Muslim organisations.

Three different groups vied for the moral leadership of ICMI. The first was composed of the technocrats within the regime who were close to either Jusuf Habibie or senior figures in Golkar, the official party. The second consisted of Muslim figures, such as the intellectual Nurcholish Madjid or the former minister Emil Salim, representing a moderate branch which was concerned above all with gaining recognition for the social aspect of Islam's values. Finally, the third group comprised Muslim leaders, such as Amien Rais, Adi Sasono and Lukman Harun, who, unlike the other two groups, wanted to turn ICMI into a vehicle for their political ambitions. They wanted to be seen as the mouthpiece for a Muslim community which had long been oppressed by the government and was a victim of the growing influence of the Christian minorities in the country.[54] Amongst this third group, the rhetoric used by certain radical preachers such as Imaduddin Abdulrahim became increasingly tinged with fundamentalism. They put pressure on ICMI to find ways of eroding the ascendancy held by the Christian community over public opinion. They launched their own daily newspaper, *Republika*, and set up a think-tank, the Centre for Information and Development Studies (CIDS) designed to counter the

---

[53] Further reading on the aims and organisation of ICMI can be found in Donald J. Porter, *Managing Politics and Islam in Indonesia* (London and New York: Routledge Curzon, 2002), pp. 89–94.

[54] Robert W. Hefner, "Islam, State, and Civil Society: ICMI and the Struggle for the Indonesian Middle Class", *Indonesia* 56 (October 1996). Adam Schwarz, *A Nation in Waiting: Indonesia's Search for Stability* (St. Leonards, NSW: Allen & Unwin, 1999), pp. 176–7.

analysis developed by the Centre for Strategic and International Studies (CSIS) which was considered to be both pro-Christian and too close to Javanese mysticism (*kejawan*).

Suharto's fall from power in May 1998 and the subsequent election campaign which took place in June 1999 led to the different branches of Islam within ICMI reasserting their autonomy. This new-found freedom brought about a profound reconfiguration of Indonesian Islam in its entirety and was a contributing factor in the disintegration of Masyumi's political legacy.[55] When studying this period, one is inevitably led to the fundamental issue of the participation by party figures (or at least by those who claimed to defend its legacy) in the radicalisation which a section of the Islamic community underwent at the time.[56] When attempting to convey the diversity of the various intellectual and political paths taken by the members of the Masyumi family, a useful distinction can be established between two currents which former party members typically belonged to. Although these two types of attitude are fairly representative of the complexity of Masyumi's evolution, one should bear in mind the danger of such a categorisation being too rigid.

The most visible and vociferous of these two currents developed in the same vein as the transformation which had already begun within the DDII. It was one of the main protagonists of the neo-fundamentalist revival which permeated Indonesian Islam from the beginning of the 1980s. The message and the actions of this movement were part of a mutation which saw it evolve from intransigent religious insularity to open interreligious violence.

This radicalisation was facilitated by several factors. The first of these was a combination of the former Masyumi leaders' disenchantment and the provision of financial assistance by the Wahabi propaganda machine at the beginning of the 1970s. Masyumi's leaders had been openly critical of Saudi Arabia during the 1950s, but having been

---

[55] Several parties and organisations have claimed to be the bearers of Masyumi's legacy: the Crescent Moon and Star Party (Partai Bulan Bintang, PBB); the New Masyumi (Masyumi Baru); and the Islamic Fraternity Forum (Forum Ukhuwah Islamiyyah, FUI). None, however, have managed to be convincing successors to Masyumi. See Bernhard Platzdasch, *Islamism in Indonesia: Politics in the Emerging Democracy* (Singapore: Institute of Southeast Asian Studies, 2009), pp. 30 ff.
[56] See Feillard and Madinier, *The End of Innocence*.

marginalised and left penniless by the dominant New Order regime, they began in the 1960s to accept the money provided by the international proselytising networks put in place by the Saudi monarchy. In 1969, for example, Mohammad Natsir became a member of the Muslim World League (Rabithah al-Alam al-Islami) based in Jeddah in Saudi Arabia. The oil crisis of 1973 bestowed considerable financial means on the League, and in the same year, the DDII was made its official representative in Indonesia, thus becoming one of the principal vehicles for the spread of Wahhabism in the country. The organisation was charged with attributing scholarships to Indonesian students to enable them to pursue their studies in the Middle East, and in the early 1970s, it opened an office in Riyadh.[57] Later in 1980, the DDII helped in the creation of the Institute of Arabic and Islamic Studies (Lembaga Ilmu Pengetahuan Islam dan Arab, LIPIA) which, thanks to the financial assistance of the Saudi kingdom, allowed thousands of Indonesians to obtain degrees at the Imam Muhammad bin Saud Islamic University in Ryad, where the brightest students were sent to pursue their studies. The network established by the DDII and the LIPIA also played a key role in the distribution of the financial assistance which came from the large Salafi foundations based in the Gulf countries and allowed the construction of hundreds of mosques on the Indonesian archipelago.

The participation of these Indonesian Muslims in networks which had long been steeped in a neo-fundamentalist ideology contributed, naturally enough, to their radicalisation. The translations they read of books and brochures written in Egypt or in the Gulf countries resonated with their feeling of resentment towards the government, the Christian minorities and the West; this encouraged them to adopt a very black-and-white vision of their struggle as part of an age-old battle of global proportions opposing the forces of good and evil.[58] Their sense of being part of a final confrontation in which the existence of the entire *umma* was at stake justified the violence used in the Moluccas, Poso and elsewhere. It was the experience of the Afghan

---

[57] Details on the links between the DDII and Saudi Arabia can be found in the extremely well-documented report published on 11 December 2004 by the International Crisis Group.

[58] During the 1980s, the DDII also published around 20 translations of books written by the most radical members of the Muslim Brotherhood.

jihad, however, which was to play a much more decisive role in the radicalisation of Indonesian Islamist activists than any ideological indoctrination. Several hundred of these activists, foremost amongst them the future leaders of both the terrorist group Jemaah Islamiyah and the militia group Laskar Jihad, did more than just spend time studying in Mecca or Riyad. They followed the well-trodden route taken by international militant Islamists during the 1980s, who, on their way home, were invited to spend time in Pakistani training camps close to the border. Very few of them, however, took an active part in the fight against the Soviets; most of them simply received military and ideological training aimed at allowing them to open new fronts in the future global struggle against the enemies of Islam, a struggle which was already beginning to take shape beyond the realms of the Afghan war.[59]

The influence of these militant networks was particularly strong in Indonesia because of their association with figures who were keen to revive the group which had formerly constituted the Darul Islam movement. Two figures who played a key role in this respect were Abu Bakar Ba'asyir and Abdullah Sungkar, whose biographies are indicative of the complexity and disparity of the motivating forces behind this militant Islamist movement. They founded the Ngruki Koranic School near Surakarta in Central Java, and had been imprisoned initially in 1978 for their association with members of the Darul Islam movement which had organised an Islamist rebellion in the 1950s. They had in fact been victims of an intricate operation carried out by the Indonesian secret service aimed at reviving this group, under the pretext of combating communism, with the ultimate aim of muzzling it completely. Their trial turned them into martyrs for the Muslim cause. They were released on appeal in 1983 and two years later, having learnt that the Supreme Court had just overturned the appeal court's decision, thus obliging them to return to prison, they decided to flee the country for Malaysia. There they took advantage of the very favourable atmosphere for Islamist organisations which reigned in the country. Amongst other activities, they were involved in the recruitment of several dozen

---

[59] Further reading on this involvement in the Afghan war can be found in an article entitled "Jemaah Islamiyah in South East Asia Damaged but Still Dangerous", published in the International Crisis Group's *Asia Report*, no. 63, 26 August 2003. See also Zachary Abuza, *Militant Islam in Southeast Asia: Crucible of Terror* (London: Lynne Rienner Publishers, 2003).

Southeast Asian youths who were sent to fight in Afghanistan. When the war against the USSR ended, these recruits were to become the backbone of Jemaah Islamiyah and participated in the propagation of the Afghani *jihad* across Southeast Asia. After 1995, for example, with a Muslim rebellion brewing in the south of the Philippines, the organisation moved its training camps there; later in 1999, the group's militants set up operations in the Moluccas and central Sulawesi to exploit the bloody conflict which had taken hold there. The networks which Jemaah Islamiyah developed at that time played a key role in the descent of a part of Indonesia's radicals into a blind and nihilistic form of violence. The two attacks in Bali in October of 2002 and 2005 and those which took place in Jakarta (August 2003, September 2004 and July 2009) were proof, as it were, that the use of political and even military means to bring about an Islamic state in Indonesia had failed. For want of being able to mobilise sufficient support to bring about a balance of power which would allow its political claims to be expressed, this disreputable organisation, composed of Indonesians, Malaysians and Filipinos, turned to a sort of primal chaos, whose advent was to be accelerated by large-scale massacres and on which the hope of a Southeast Asian caliphate could be founded. The leaders of the Jemaah Islamiyah took comfort in a phantasmagorical universe made up of a programme—the battle of good against evil—which was as grandiose as it was vague. They ended up not only isolating themselves from other radical movements with more concrete goals but, more importantly, discrediting the use of physical violence in the eyes of the Indonesian Muslim community, who had long been rather tolerant towards the use of such means.[60]

Other movements were better able to take advantage of the widespread disarray which accompanied the chaotic final phase of Suharto's regime. Between 1998 and 2002, a number of militias dominated the Indonesian political scene, proposing, in the name of defending Islam's values, to take the place of a state which was considered to be inadequate. The removal of General Suharto, Jusuf Habibie's presidency, the elections of June 1999 and finally Abdurrahman Wahid's short-lived

---

[60] Rémy Madinier, "L'Asie du Sud-Est musulmane produit d'un imaginaire afghan? Le Daulah Islamiyah Nusantara à l'épreuve des sciences sociales", in *Figures d'Islam après le 11 septembre: disciples, martyrs, réfugiés et migrants*, ed. Aminah Mohammad-Arif and Jean Schmitz (Paris: Khartala, 2006), pp. 123–49.

term in office provided these groups with ample opportunity to attract significant media attention. These organisations capitalised on the resonance which their simple message undoubtedly held for a population disoriented by the scale of the political, social and economic crisis the country was enduring; they recruited a fairly considerable number of new members, and by doing so extended Islamic radicalism beyond the small groups to which it had heretofore been confined. This desire to impose Islamic norms concerned two areas of public life in particular. The first of these was public morals, an issue taken up by a number of groups for its usefulness in mobilising popular support. Across the country, hundreds of militias had sprung up, roaming the disreputable quarters of cities armed with bamboo canes in order to attack brothels, clandestine gambling houses and other dens of iniquity. Although on the surface these punitive expeditions appeared to be spontaneous, the mobilisation of reasonable men who were incensed with the inaction of the police, they often gave rise to a sort of religiously based racketeering. During the largest punitive expeditions, "popular anger" was often quite selective and depended on the sums of money paid by those who ran the dens of iniquity, who were also strongly advised to employ thugs, linked to these self-same organisations, in order to "guarantee their protection".

Since 2003, the operations carried out by the "moral militia" have become scarcer. The leader of the Islamic Defenders Front (Front Pembela Islam, FPI), Habieb Rizieq, who has received a lot of media attention, has been arrested twice and has already agreed on several occasions to rein in his organisation's activities. Although the actions of these militias today are less spectacular than before, their influence remains nonetheless real. They are still dreaded by local authorities looking for legitimacy from Islam as well as by small traders who fear for their stalls; they continue to strive to denounce the "Christianisation of Indonesia", and they have contributed considerably over the past number of years to the religious one-upmanship prevalent in Indonesia which incites people to prove their purity as Muslims.

The second area in which these organisations endeavoured to replace the mechanisms of a democratic state with religiously based violence was that of inter-religious conflicts. The collapse of the state's authority which accompanied the deposition of Suharto led in the east of the country to the poisoning of relations between Muslims and Christians, which traditionally had been rather good. In the Moluccas between 1999 and 2001, more than 5,000 people died during the war that waged between Christian and Islamic militias. The latter received decisive support from different organisations throughout Indonesia. In May 2000, for example, Laskar Jihad, led by Ja'far Umar Thalib, another scion of the Arab network which had fought in Afghanistan, managed to leave Java and go to fight in the Moluccas. Having called on the government to do a better job of defending Muslims—the conflict at that stage was relatively balanced between the two sides— Ja'far managed to land his militia group on the island despite President Abdurahman Wahid's orders to the contrary. Laskar Jihad undoubtedly benefitted from complicity at the highest military level, as they were welcomed and even partially equipped by the army on their arrival in Ambon. Along with other militias such as Mujahidin Kompak and linked to the Jemaah Islamiyah network, they contributed largely to the wave of violence which shook the east of the country. Having helped to swing the conflict in favour of the Muslim militias, some of these militant groups moved on to the neighbouring island of Sulawesi in an attempt to spread *jihad* there, and subsequently in the region of Poso, a veritable purge took place against the Christian community.

As a result of the agreements which became known as Malino 1 and Malino 2, signed respectively in December 2001 and February 2002 by representatives of the different religious communities, direct confrontations between the two sides eventually ended. In the following years, however, attacks aimed at Christians were carried out regularly in the Central Sulawesi region, maintaining a climate of fear amongst the Christian population there. Elsewhere in Indonesia, it remains difficult today for religious minorities to open new places of worship, and militias such as the FPI often intervene to demand the closure of churches which have not received the necessary authorisations. Moreover, in recent years, a shift in the nature of religious violence has been observed within the country. While Christian minorities were the main target of attacks during the chaotic period surrounding Suharto's fall from power, since 2010 these attacks have mainly been directed against Islamic minorities considered to be deviant, particularly Shias and the Ahmadiyya community. Up until now, these minorities have not been granted protection by the authorities, who remain paralysed by an interpretation of *Pancasila*'s first principle which is extremely timorous.[61]

---

[61] Jeremy Menchik, "Productive Intolerance: Godly Islam in Indonesia", *Comparative Studies in Screen and History* 56, 3 (2014): 591–621.

This may change, however, with the new president, Joko Widodo, elected to office in July 2014. Widodo is one of the few members of the country's political class to affirm the Javanese nature of his Islamic belief; this may lead the government to modify its approach in dealing with Indonesia's multi-confessional society and thus move away from the frustrating attitude adopted by Bambang Yudhoyono during his two terms in office, which was essentially to refuse to deal with such questions.

Although Masyumi's "perpetuators" were far from being at the root of Indonesian Islam's violent excesses, they nonetheless, through the alarmist propaganda disseminated by DDII, fuelled feelings of urgency and hatred which pushed some Muslims onto the path of intolerance and violence. Masyumi's legacy amounts to more than just this attitude of aggressive and fearful insularity, however. The liberal legacy of the party, although it is less spectacular and has received less media attention, continues to have a voice in the debate concerning Islam's place in Indonesian society. The main figure of this liberal legacy is, of course, Nurcholish Madjid, mentioned earlier. His foundation, Paramadina, has given birth to a university of the same name, which includes several thousand students. Other figures who formerly belonged to the "Masyumi family" have also played influential roles in Indonesian Islam. Amongst these, special mention should be made of Harun Nasution, a graduate of McGill University in Canada and the founder of the State Islamic Institutes (IAIN), which were recently transformed into State Islamic Universities.[62] The high standard of scholarship at these third-level institutions, and more importantly, the possibility of being able to hold reasoned and civilised debates there made it home to an open and tolerant form of Islam.[63] Moreover, radical organisations, whether they were linked to the Muslim Brotherhood or to the Salafi-inspired groups, were much likelier to recruit their members in the mainstream universities—particularly amongst students of science, medicine and computing—than in the institutions devoted to the study of Islam. In keeping with the legacy of Harun Nasution, the State Islamic Universities often have prominent figures

---

[62] Harun Nasution was close to Masyumi and wrote his MA dissertation on the party.
[63] This has been confirmed by the violent campaigns carried out recently by radical groups against these establishments.

from the liberal branch of Islam at their head. Two notable examples are Azyumardi Azran, an eminent expert in Indonesian Islam and the rector of the Syarif Hidayatullah State Islamic University in Jakarta between 1998 and 2006, and Amin Abdullah, the rector of the Sunan Kalijaga State Islamic University in Yogyakarta, who was for a long time the leader of the liberal wing of Muhammadiyah. Abdullah had hoped to succeed Syafii Maarif, another moderate, at the head of the reformist organisation during its elections in 2005, but the victory of Din Syamsuddin, a member of the movement's conservative wing and much closer to the DDII, shows the current balance of power between the "inheritors" and "perpetuators" within what was the most important of Masyumi's constituent organisations.

Despite this defeat, the branch of Islam which claims to be an inheritor of the 1950s liberal legacy retained within Indonesian Islam a significant degree of power, and one which is without doubt unparalleled elsewhere in the Muslim world. Under the leadership of Aburahman Wahid, Nahdlatul Ulama provided a constant and sometimes efficient opposition to the excesses of a version of Islam, backed by the regime in place, which prevailed at the end of Suharto's reign. Its interventions to appease the interreligious tensions which have been rife in Java since the turn of the century were often successful. More importantly, it is an organisation which emerged from the traditionalist movement which now spearheads an open and confident form of Islam. The genesis of the Liberal Islam Network (Jaringan Islam Liberal, JIL), founded in 2001, stems from the acknowledgement by a handful of young intellectuals close to NU that the voice of Islam had been hijacked by radicals. Led by Ulil Abshar-Abdallah, these activists used lectures, radio programmes and a particularly active internet site to disseminate ideas which follow directly in the tradition of the reformist movement inherited from the beginning of the 20th century. They denounced in particular any literal interpretation of the Koran or the Sunnah and called for a revival of *ijtihad*.[64]

The confrontation within Masyumi between reformists and traditionalists, which deprived the party of a lasting place at the cabinet table after the 1955 elections, weakened the party's liberal legacy for a

---

[64] See, for example, the editorial which Ulil Abshar-Abdallah wrote on the issue in July 2007. "The Aftemath of the Opening of the Door of Ijtihad" ("Setelah Pintu Ijtihad Terbuka", http://islamlib.com).

long time. However, this legacy is no doubt more widespread today in Indonesia, in a society where the debate on the role of Islam remains very lively. Although the advent of a democratic system in 1998 may have allowed an intolerant and conservative form of Islamic populism to make a spectacular breakthrough both in public opinion and in the country's institutions, Indonesia has none of the problems which have paralysed numerous Muslim countries where authoritarian regimes claim to defend an open form of Islam at the expense of democracy. This opens up the prospect of some interesting future developments, as the history of the PKS has demonstrated.

Founded in July 1998, the Justice Party (Partai Keadilan) obtained 1.3% of the vote in the 1999 elections. It subsequently changed its name to the Prosperous Justice Party (Partai Keadilan Sejaterah, PKS) and made a remarkable breakthrough in 2004, winning 7.3% of the electorate's support. Despite the drop in support for Islamic parties, the PKS managed to maintain its share of the vote in 2009 with a score of 7.9%, and became the foremost Islamic party in Indonesia. The political deftness it showed in striking an alliance with the party of the future president, Susilo Bamban Yudhoyono, allowed it in 2004 to obtain the speakership of the People's Consultative Assembly for its president Hidayat Nur Wahid, and later in 2009 to secure several ministerial portfolios. Its unambiguous electoral success was just reward for a party whose activists were both conscientious and efficient and whose image was that of being much less corrupt than other political organisations. It can also be explained, however, by the adoption of a far more moderate line by the party. As it moved closer to joining government, the PKS appears to have undergone a similar transformation to that which Masyumi experienced. The questions of *sharia* law and an Islamic state, favoured by purists, were to a large extent eclipsed by a political message which emphasised the need to see the values of Islam permeate public life and the workings of the state. *Pancasila*, which had not been mentioned in 1999, was in 2004 and 2009 considered the natural foundation upon which all political programmes in the Indonesian Republic should be built.[65] In 2002, much to the anger

---

[65] Masdar Hilmy, "Partai Keadilan Sejahtera", *Studia Islamika* 14, 1 (2007); Ahmad-Norma Permata, "Prosperous Justice Party and the Decline of Political Islam in 2009 Election in Indonesia", in *Islam and the 2009 Indonesian Elections, Political and Cultural Issues: The Case of the Prosperous Justice Party (PKS)*, ed. Rémy Madinier (Bangkok: IRASEC, 2009).

of other Islamic organisations represented in Parliament, namely the United Development Party (PPP) and the Crescent Star Party (PBB), the party also proposed to replace the Jakarta Charter with another concept called the Charter of Medina (Piagam Madinah) which would allow all religions to be treated equally and to apply their own religious laws, including *sharia* law for Muslims.

These changes in stance by the PKS have raised questions about its sincerity. The participation of the party's local representatives in the shift towards a stricter form of Islam which has taken a grip over some of the country's counties and towns in the past few years has also left it open to accusations of extremism. The widespread decentralisation which the country has undergone since the beginning of this century has increasingly allowed local authorities to announce and sometimes implement coercive measures aimed at enforcing respect for a certain form of Islamic morality. Among these measures figure a ban on women being out in public alone after a certain hour, the closing of certain main roads on Fridays during prayer, and fines for Muslims caught drinking alcohol or breaking their fast before nightfall during Ramadan. The power to issue such ordinances did not generally come within the remit of local government and thus they could be, though rarely were, revoked by the Home Affairs Ministry; they are part of a tendency within Indonesian Islam to constantly look for the moral high ground which, in recent years, has profoundly transformed the face of the country. Islam has become the only paradigm able to offer an alternative to globalisation, which has become a byword for Westernisation, and so referring to Islam allows Indonesians to, as it were, bite the hand that feeds it.[66] In addition, it offers an anchor to communities whose identities have been shaken by profound changes in society and has also benefitted from the competition which exists between local party elites concerned about the political fallout of not participating in the construction of a society in accordance with Islamic law.

However, the radicalisation of those who either out of conviction or convenience have followed these somewhat irrational inclinations has, in the past few years, given rise to a backlash which may announce a decline in its fortunes. In June 2006, a section of the political elite,

---

[66] Along the lines of the phenomenon of Mekka-Cola expertly analysed by Gabriel Martinez-Gros and Lucette Valensi in their *L'Islam en dissidence: genèse d'un affrontement* (Paris: Seuil, 2004), p. 11.

bolstered by the support of nationalist military officers, launched a vast movement calling for a revival of *Pancasila*, the only way, in their eyes, to guarantee peaceful coexistence between religions. Moreover, recent opinion polls have shown a clear shift in public opinion: in 2001 and 2002, a sizeable majority (67%) declared themselves in favour of recognising *sharia* law for Muslims (which would have implied the implementation of the Jakarta Charter), whereas almost 83% of the population declared themselves in favour of *Pancasila* in 2006, and in 2007, 85% affirmed their attachment to a unitary Indonesian Republic founded on *Pancasila* rather than on Islam.[67]

The parliamentary elections of 2014 seem to have confirmed this underlying trend. Political Islam's share of the vote has stagnated: it received 31% in 2014, better than its score of 29% in 2009, but down from its performances in the previous two elections (37.5% in 2004 and 36.5% in 1999). Within this disparate political family, the most successful parties have been the most moderate ones, more inclined to promote "Islamic values" rather than an "Islamic project". The PBB, the PPP and in particular the PKS, who represent a more intransigent form of Islam, have on the whole seen their political fortunes decline. Despite the PKS's move towards a more tolerant political message, its share of the vote dropped slightly in 2014, and, more significantly, remains much lower than its Middle Eastern counterparts who, like the PKS, emerged from the Muslim Brotherhood movement.[68]

It would no doubt be premature to speak of a sea change within Indonesian Islam. However, both the transformations within the PKS and changes in public opinion show the very real confrontation today between the partisans of an intransigent and literalist form of Islam—the perpetuators of an insular tradition which influenced the Masyumi movement from the 1960s onwards—and those who advocate an open and tolerant form of Islam—the torchbearers of the great liberal tradition of the 1950s.

---

[67] Surveys carried out by the Centre for the Study of Islam and Society (Pusat Penelitian Islam dan Masyarakat, PPIM) in 2001, 2002 and 2007 and by the Lembaga Survey Institute in 2006.

[68] Detailed analysis of recent transformations in political Islam can be found in Kikue Hamayotsu, "The End of Political Islam? A Comparative Analysis of Religious Parties in the Muslim Democracy of Indonesia", *Journal of Current Southeast Asian Affairs* 3 (2011): 133–59 and in Vedi R. Hadiz, "No Turkish Delight: The Impasse of Islamic Party Politics in Indonesia", *Indonesia* 92 (October 2011): 1–18.

Glossary[1]

abangan (J) [red]   Usually designates[1] in Indonesia Javanese inclined towards mysticism or *kejawen*, that is less inclined towards Islamic orthodoxy than the *santri*.

adat (A)   By extension custom. As a source of law, *adat* or custom is different from *hukm* (pl. *ahkam*), rules revealed in the Koran or the Traditions.

Al-Irsyad   Reformist movement founded at the beginning of the 20th century by Ahmad bin Soorkati, a Sudanese specialising in education for the Hadrami community.

AMS   Algemene Middlebar School. Dutch upper secondary school for Indonesians during the colonial period.

BFO   Bijeenkomstvoor Federaal Overleg (Consultative Federal Assembly of the United States of Indonesia).

BKMI   Badan Kongres Muslimin Indonesia (Committee of the Islamic Indonesian Congress). Mainly controlled by Masyumi.

BKOI   Badan Koordinasi Organisasi Islam (Coordination Committee of Islamic Organisations). Founded in the run-up to the 1955 elections and close to Masyumi.

---

[1] The etymology of the terms cited in this glossary is indicated in parentheses: J = Javanese; A = Arabic; S = Sankrit.

BKPRI   Badan Kongres Pemuda Republik Indonesia
                             (Committee of the Congress of Indonesian
                             Youth Organisations). Founded in November
                             1945 to organise the country's youth
                             movements.

BPUKI   Badan Panjelidik Usaha-Usaha Kemerdekaan
                             Indonesia (Review Committee for the
                             Preparation of Independence). Created in March
                             1945 by the Japanese.

CIDS   Centre for Information and Development
                             Studies.
                             A think-tank founded by the ICMI at the
                             beginning of the 1990s to counter the
                             interpretations given by the CSIS.

CSIS   Centre for Strategic and International Studies.
                             A think-tank founded at the beginning of
                             the New Order era to support the regime's
                             developmentalist policies.

dakwah (A)   In Arabic, *da'wa*. Invitation to accept the word
                             of God, Islam. In the 20th century, the term
                             is used in the sense of proselytisation and
                             preaching activities.

Daulah Islamiyah   Nusantarian Islamic State. This term was used
Nusantara   by Jemaah Islamiyah and is distinguished from
                             Kartosuwirjo's Negara Islam which recognises
                             the existence of national frontiers in Southeast
                             Asia.

DDII   Dewan Dakwah Islamiyah Indonesia
                             (Indonesian Islamic Propagation Council).
                             Large predication movement founded in 1967
                             by the reformist Muslims of Masyumi. It is
                             a conservative Islamist movement, and its
                             press organ, *Media Dakwah*, emphasises the
                             superiority of Islam and the threats surrounding
                             it in a world dominated by undercover anti-
                             Islamic forces. Headed by Mohammad Natsir
                             until his death in 1993.

DI (A)
Darul Islam (House of Islam). Name given to the Muslim movement led by Kartosoewiryo in West Java that declared an Indonesian Islamic State (Negara Islam Indonesia) on 7 August 1949, and by extension, name given to the ensuing rebellion in Aceh, South Sulawesi and Kalimantan.

dwitunggal
A coined term of Sanskrit origin, meaning "inseparable". It was used to refer to the duumvirate constituted by Sukarno and Hatta (president and vice president) at the head of Indonesia.

fatwa (A)
In Arabic, *fatwā*. A jurist's pronouncement on a point of Muslim law (see *mufti*). In Indonesia, *fatwas* are pronounced by various religious organisations but have no legal authority.

FDR
Front Demokrasi Rakjat (The People's Democratic Front). Left-wing coalition founded in 1948.

fiqh (A)
Jurisprudence in Islam. Legal prescriptions pertaining to civil law and the family, inheritance, property, criminal and constitutional law.

FKASWJ
Forum Komunikasi Ahlu Sunnahwal-Jama'ah (Communication Forum for the Followers of the Sunna and the Community of the Prophet). Religious group founded by Ja'far Umar Thalib in Yogyakarta which was behind the creation of the Laskar Jihad militia.

FPI
Front Pembela Islam (Islamic Defenders Front). Militia (vigilante group) founded in 1998 by Habib Rizieq Shihab, its president.

GAPI
Gabungan Politik Indonesia (Indonesian Political Federation). It brought together a significant number of nationalist organisations during the 1930s.

Gerakan Pemuda Ansor/Ansor
Traditionalist Islamic youth movement linked to the Nahdlatul Ulama (NU).

Golkar

Golongan Karya (Functional Groups). Governmental party formed under the New Order.

GPII

Gerakan Pemuda Islam Indonesia (Movement of Masyumi Youth). Former youth organisation of Masyumi whose legacy DDII circles try to maintain. After the ban on Masyumi, it survived under the name of Gerakan Pemuda Indonesia (GPI).

hadith (A)

In Arabic, *ḥadīth*. Traditions recounting the actions or words of the Prophet or his tacit approval of words or acts effected in his presence.

Haji (A)

Title of one who has made the pilgrimage to Mecca.

HIS

Holland Inlander School. Dutch primary schools for Indonesians during the colonial period.

Hizbullah (A)

Muslim militia formed during the Japanese Occupation of Indonesia. Armed wing of the Masyumi party during the fight for independence.

HMI

Himpunan Mahasiswa Indonesia (Association of Muslim Students). Influential modernist Muslim student association.

HMI-MPO

Himpunan Mahasiswa Indonesia-Majelis Penyelamat Organisasi (Association of Muslim Students-Council to Save the Organisation). Scission of HMI as MPO refused Suharto's 1985 policy of ideological uniformisation.

hudud (A)

In Arabic, *ḥudūd*. Punishment laid out by Islamic law for specific crimes considered as offences against Allah, such as fornication (flagellation) or theft (chopping off of the hand).

IAIN

Institut Agama Islam Negeri (State Institute of Islamic Studies). Third-level institution of higher Islamic learning dependent on the Ministry of Religions and whose teachers are civil servants. The first IAIN was created in 1952. The four largest IAINs have been transformed into State Islamic Universities (Universitas Islam Negeri, UIN).

ICMI	Ikatan Cendekiawan Muslim se-Indonesia (Association of Indonesian Muslim Intellectuals). Founded in 1990 by B.J. Habibie, President of the Republic of Indonesia from May 1998–October 1999.
ijma (A)	In Arabic, *ijmā'*. Third source of Muslim law after the Koran and the Sunna. Consists traditionally of the consensus of the *ulamas*.
ijtihad (A)	In Arabic, *ijtihād*. In Islamic law, the use of individual reasoning and the method of reasoning by analogy. The scholar qualified to do so is the *mudjtahid*.
IPKI	Ikatan Pendukung Kemerdekaan Indonesia (Association for the Defence of Indonesian Independence). This political organisation was founded in 1954 in military circles.
JI (A)	Jemaah Islamiyah. Terrorist organisation responsible for several bombings in Bali and Jakarta between 2002 and 2005. The bombings in 2009 of the JW Marriott and Ritz-Carlton hotels in Jakarta were organised by a JI splinter group.
JIB	Jong Islamieten Bond (Organisation of Young Muslims). Founded in 1925 under the joint initiative of Sarekat Islam and Muhammadiyah.
KAMI	Kesatuan Aksi Mahasiswa Indonesia (Indonesian Student Action Front). Anti-communist organisation active after 1965, which supported the army during the change in power.
kaum muda	Modernists, in contrast to the *kaum tua*, traditionalists.
kauman	Appointed quarter for religious officials.
kenduri	Ceremonial meals to honour and petition the supernatural spirits. See also *slametan*.
keramat	Sacred places, saints' tombs.

Kiai (J)

Title given to Muslim scholars or Sufi sheikhs in Java, or to respected personalities with religious charisma. Use of the term was recently expanded to include charismatic Muslim persons not necessarily erudite about Islam.

KNIP

Komite Nasional Indonesia Pusat (Central Indonesian National Committee). Independent Indonesia's first assembly.

Laskar Jihad

FKAWJ militia led by Ja'far Umar Thalib, especially active in the Moluccas conflict from 2000–02.

LIPIA

Lembaga Ilmu Pengetahuan Islam dan Arab (Jakarta Institute of and Arabic Studies). Islamic institute of learning linked to the al-Irsyad Indonesian reformist movement and to Saudi Arabia.

madhhab (A)

Also known as *mazhab*. School of Islamic law. There are four schools in Sunni Islam: Shafi'i, Hanafi, Maliki and Hanbali.

Manipol-USDEK

Manifestopolitik/Undang-Undang Dasar 1945, Sosialisme Indonesia, Demokrasi Terpimpin, Ekonomi Terpimpin dan Kepribadian Indonesia (Political Manifesto, 1945 Constitution, Guided Democracy, Guided Economy, Indonesian Identity). One of the pillars of Sukarno's ideology during Guided Democracy.

Marhaenism

Political doctrine developed by Sukarno which adapted Marxism to the conditions of an agrarian society. It was embodied by a fictional figure known as Marhaen.

Masyumi

Madjlis Sjuro Muslimin Indonesia (Consultative Council of Indonesian Muslims). Founded by the Japanese in 1943; its acronym was adopted by the party founded in 1945.

MIAI

Majelis Islam A'laa Indonesia (Supreme Islamic Council of Indonesia). Federation of Muslim organisations formed in 1937 which subsequently became Masyumi.

Muhammadiyah Reformist Muslim organisation founded in 1912.

MULO Meer Uitgebreid Lageer Onderwijs. Dutch lower secondary school for Indonesians during the colonial period.

mushrik (A) Polytheist.

NASAKOM Concept forged by Sukarno at the end of the 1950s, gathering the main ideological movements within Indonesia, namely nationalism (*nasionalisme*), religion (*agama*) and communism (*komunisme*).

NII Negara Islam Indonesia (Islamic State of Indonesia). Declared by Kartosuwirjo in 1949. After the execution of its founder in 1962, this Darul Islam movement re-formed covertly under the New Order.

NU Nahdlatul Ulama. Association of *ulamas* formed in 1926 in East Java to defend traditionalist Islam practices.

Parkindo Partai Kristen Indonesia. Indonesian Christian (Protestant) party founded in 1945.

Parmusi Partai Muslimin Indonesia (Muslim Party). Indonesian modernist Islamic party founded in 1968 after the government refused to rehabilitate Masyumi, which was banned by Sukarno in 1960.

Partai Katolik Catholic Party. Founded in 1949, it came about from the fusion of several regional Catholic parties and was the inheritor of the Javanese Catholic Political Association (Pakempalan Politiek-Katholiek Djawi, PPKD) created in 1927.

Partai Murba Proletarian party, founded in 1948 by Tan Malaka.

PARTII Indonesia Islamic Partai (Indonesian Party of Islam). Emerged in 1933, following a split within the PSII.

PBB Partai Bulan Bintang (Crescent Star Party). Close to DDII, it calls for the implementation of the *sharia*. A small minority party.

peranakan	See *totok*.
PKS	Partai Keadilan Sejahtera (Prosperous Justice Party). Sejahtera is the new name of Partai Keadilan (PK, Justice Emerged from the *usroh/tarbiyah* Party) movement. Its share of votes (then PK) went from 1.3 per cent in 1999 to more than 7 per cent in 2004 and 2009.
PRRI	Pemerintah Revolusioner Republik Indonesia (Revolutionary Government of Republic of Indonesia). Opposition government that arose against Sukarno and the rising Communist Party in 1958 in West Sumatra. It was suppressed within a few months.
PERMESTA	Regionalist movement from south Sulawesi which developed at the end of the 1950s and whose name is an acronym of the expression *"perjuangan semesta"*, meaning total struggle.
PERMI	Persatuan Muslimin Indonesia (Indonesian Muslim Union). This modernist organisation was founded in Sumatra in 1930 and was dismantled by the colonial authorities in 1937.
PERSIS	Persatuan Islam (Islamic Union). An intransigent reformist movement founded in 1923 in Bandung.
PESINDO	Pemuda Sosialis Indonesia (Indonesian Socialist Youth Movement).
PETA	Soekarela Tentara Pembela Tanah Air (Volunteer Army of Defenders of the Homeland). Militia group close to PUTERA.
Piagam Jakarta	Jakarta Charter. Controversial accord of the 1945 Constitution between representatives of secularist nationalism and leaders of political Islam. Suppressed at the last minute on 18 August 1945, it carried mention of the obligation for Indonesian Muslims to obey the *sharia*, with no other specification other than "in accordance with the principles of a just and civilised humanity".

PII	Peladjar Islam Indonesia (Association of Indonesian Islamic Pupils). Close to Masyumi.
PKI	Partai Kommunis Indonesia (Indonesian Communist Party). Founded in 1920 under the name Communist Union of the Indies.
PNI	Partai Nasional Indonesia (Indonesian National Party). Founded in Bandung in 1927 and under the leadership of Sukarno, was one of the main actors in the post-war nationalist movement. After independence, it remained a major political party.
PPP	Partai Persatuan Pembangunan (Party of Unity and Development). Founded by the New Order in 1973 as part of the "rationalisation of political life" and it included all the country's Muslim parties until the beginning of the 1980s.
pribumi (J)	"Son of the soil" or native Indonesian. Used in particular to discriminate against Chinese Indonesians.
PSI	Partai Sosialis Indonesia (Indonesian Socialist Party). Founded in 1945 from the merging of Sutan Sjahrir's People's Socialist Party (Partai Rakjat Sosialis) and Amir Sjarifuddin's Socialist Party. The latter withdrew from the party in 1948.
PUTERA	Pusat Tenaga Rakjat (Centre of People's Power). Created in 1943 by the Japanese. A federation of all of the political and social organisations in Java and Madura which were charged with preparing Indonesia for independence.
raissam	The *rais aam* or *rois aam* is the highest position within Nahdlatul Ulama.
Reformasi	Name given to the "reform" movement that arose in 1998 in Indonesia, encompassing not only a change in government but also a long-term reform of institutions, moving towards greater democracy.

Sajap Kiri   Left Wing. Founded in 1946 and composed of the Socialist Party, the PKI, the Pesindo, the Partai Buruh and the Christian parties.

SAKTI   Sarekat Tani Indonesia (Union of Indonesian Peasants). Close to the PKI.

santri (J)   Student of *pesantren*, Islamic boarding schools in Java; praticising Muslims (as opposed to *abangan*).

SBII   Sarekat Buruh Islam Indonesian (Union of Indonesian Muslim Workers). Affiliated to Masyumi.

SDII   Sarekat Dagang Islam Indonesia (Union of Muslim Traders). Affiliated to Masyumi.

sharia (A)   In Arabic, *shar'iyya*. Islamic law, that is, the rules revealed in the Koran and the Traditions forming the basis of Islamic law, thus a general term to designate divine law in its entirety. Islamists sometimes use it in the narrow sense of "punishments" (*hudud*).

shirk (A)   Associationism or association of God with other divinities or with Man. Condemned by Islam as being contrary to the principle of monotheism (*tauhid*).

Shumubu   Office of Religious Affairs during the Japanese occupation.

slametan   See *kenduri*.

SNII   Sarekat Nejalan Islam Indonesia (Union of Muslim Fishermen). Affiliated to Masyumi.

SOBSI   Sentral Organisasi Buruh Seluruh Indonesia (Central Organisation of Indonesian Workers). Close to the PKI.

STII   Sarekat Islam Tani Indonesia (Union of Indonesian Muslim Peasants). Affiliated to Masyumi.

sunna (A)   Normative custom or precedent based on the example of the Prophet Mohammad, consigned by the traditionalists after the death of the Prophet.

tafsir (A)	In Arabic, *tafsīr*. Commentary of the Koran.
taqlid (A)	In Arabic, *taqlīd*. Blind obedience to *ulamas*.
tawhid (A)	In Arabic, *tauḥid*. Uniqueness of God, monotheism.
TNI	Tentara Nasional Indonesia (Indonesian National Army).
totok	"Indigenous". Refers to foreigners born in their home country who have recently emigrated, in contrast to *peranakan*, a term which refers to the descendants of *totok*.
UIN	Universitas Islam Negeri (State Islamic University). Name given after 1998 to major institutes of higher Islamic learning, previously called IAIN.
umma	Entire Muslim community (in Indonesian, *umat islam*).
wakaf (A)	In Arabic, *waqf*. Property donated for religious purposes, which cannot be sold or transferred.
wali (A)	In Arabic, *waliyy*. Designates a saint in Islam. One who is "close to God".
zakat (A)	In Arabic, *zakāh*. Religious tax due annually at a rate of 2.5 per cent of one's disposable income.
ziarah (A)	In Arabic, *ziyāra*. (Non-canonical) pilgrimage, generally to the tomb of a saint.

Bibliography

ABAZA, Mona. *Indonesian Students in Cairo: Islamic Education, Perceptions and Exchanges*. Cahier d'Archipel 23. Paris: Association Archipel, 1994.

ABDULGANI, Ruslan. *Nationalism, Revolution and Guided Democracy in Indonesia*. Clayton: Monash University, 1973.

ABDULLAH, Taufik. *Islam dan Masyarakat, pantulan sejarah Indonesia [Islam and Society: Echoes of Indonesian History]*. Jakarta: LP3ES, 1987.

ADNAN BUYUNG NASUTION. *The Aspiration for Constitutional Government in Indonesia. A Socio-Legal Study of the Indonesian Konstituante (1956–1959)*. Jakarta: Pustaka Sinar Harapan, 1992.

AHMAD S. MOUSSALLI. *Moderate and Radical Islamic Fundamentalism: The Quest for Modernity, Legitimacy, and the Islamic State*. Gainesville, FL: University Press of Florida, 1999.

AHMAD SUMARGONO. *Saya Seorang Fundamentalis [I am a Fundamentalist]*. Bogor: Global Cita Press, 1999.

AHMAD WAHIB. *Catatan Harian, Pergolakan pemikiran Islam [Diary: The Turbulence of Islamic Thought]*. Jakarta: LP3ES, 1981.

ALFIAN. *Muhammadiyah: The Political Behavior of a Muslim Modernist Organization under Dutch Colonialism*. Jogyakarta: Gadjah Mada University Press, 1989.

ALGADRI, Hamid. *Politik Belanda Terhadap Islam dan Keturunan Arab di Indonesia [Dutch Policies towards Islam and the Arabic Community in Indonesia]*. Jakarta: Haji Masagung, 1988.

_____. *Suka duka masa revolusi [Joy and Sadness of the Revolutionary Period]*. Jakarta: Universitas Indonesia Press, 1991.

ALI, Mohammad Daud, and Habidah Daud ALI. *Lembaga-lembaga Islam di Indonesia [Islamic Institutions in Indonesia]*. Jakarta: P.T. RjajaGrafindo Persada, 1995.

ALI SAID DAMANIK. *Fenomena Partai Keadilan, Transformasi 20 tahun Gerakan Tarbiyah di Indonesia [The Phenomenon of the Justice Party: Twenty Years of Transformations in the Tarbiyah Party in Indonesia]*. Jakarta: Teraju, 2002.

AMIN DJAMALUDDIN. *Capita Selekta Aliran-Aliran Sempalan di Indonesia* [*Capita Selecta: Dissident Islamic Movements in Indonesia*], 1st edition. Lembaga Penelitian dan Pengkajian Islam (LPPI). South Jakarta, August 2002.

ANDERSON, Benedict R. O'G. *Java in a Time of Revolution: Occupation and Resistance, 1944–1946.* Ithaca, NY: Cornell University Press, 1961a.

————. *Some Aspects of Indonesian Politics under the Japanese Occupation: 1944–1945.* Interim Reports Series. Ithaca, NY: Cornell University Press, 1961b.

————, ed. *Interpreting Indonesian Politics.* Ithaca, NY: Cornell University Press, 1982.

————, ed. *Violence and the State in Suharto's Indonesia.* Ithaca, NY: Cornell University, 2001.

ANSHARY, H. Endang Saifuddin. *Piagam Jakarta 22 juni 1945 dan sejarah konsensus nasional antara nasionalis islami dan nasionalis "sekular" tentang dasar negara republik Indonesia, 1945–1959* [*The Jakarta Charter of 22 June 1945 and the History of the National Consensus between the Islamic Nationalists and Secular Nationalists on the Constitution of the Indonesian Republic, 1945–1959*]. Bandung: Pustaka, 1983.

ANSHARY, Isa. *Falsafah Perdjuangan Islam* (Medan: Saiful, 1949 [2nd edition, 1951]).

ASSYAUKANIE, Luthfi. *Islam and the Secular State in Indonesia.* Singapore: Institute of Southeast Asian Studies, 2009.

ASYARI, Muhammad. "The Rise of Masjumi Party in Indonesia and the Role of the Ulama in its Early Development, 1945–1952". MA thesis, McGill University, 1976.

AZIZ, Muhammad Abdul. *Japan's Colonialism and Indonesia.* The Hague: Martinus Nijhoff, 1955.

AZRA, Azyumardi and Arska SALIM, eds. *Shari'a and Politics in Modern Indonesia.* Singapore: Institute of Southeast Asian Studies, 2003.

AZRA, Azyumardi. *The Origins of Islamic Reformism in Southeast Asia: Networks of Malay-Indonesian and Middle Eastern 'Ulama' in the Seventeenth and Eighteenth Century.* Sydney and Honolulu, HI: Allen & Unwin, University of Hawai'i Press, 2004.

————. *Indonesia, Islam and Democracy: Dynamics in a Global Context.* Jakarta and Singapore: The Asia Foundation, Soltice, ICIP, 2006.

Baladas, Goshal. *Indonesian Politics 1955–1959: The Emergence of Guided Democracy.* Calcutta: K.P. Bagchi, 1982.

BARREAU, Jean-Claude. *De l'islam en général et de la modernité en particulier.* Paris: Le Pré aux Clercs, 1991.

BARTON, Greg. "Neo-modernism: A Vital Synthesis of Traditionalist and Modernist Islamic Thought in Indonesia". *Studia Islamika* 2, 3 (1995).

BECK Herman L. *Les Musulmans d'Indonésie. Les fils d'Abraham.* Turnhout: Éditions Brepols, 2003.

BENDA, Harry J. *The Crescent and the Rising Sun: Indonesian Islam under the Japanese Occupation 1942–1945.* The Hague and Bandung: W. Van Hoeve Ltd, 1958.

BENZINE, Rachid. *Les nouveaux penseurs de l'islam* (espaces libres). Paris: Albin Michel, 2008.

BERTRAND, Romain. *Indonésie: la démocratie invisible.* Paris: Karthala, 2002.

————. *État colonial, noblesse et nationalisme à Java.* Paris: Karthala, 2005.

BEY ARIFIN. *Dialog Islam dan Kristen* [*The Dialogue between Islam and Christianity*]. Surabaya: Pustaka Progressif, 1983.

BOLAND, B.J. *The Struggle of Islam in Modern Indonesia.* The Hague: Martinus Nijhoff, 1982.

BOLAND, B.J. and I. FARJON. *Islam in Indonesia: A Bibliographical Survey, 1600–1942, with post-1945 Addenda.* Dordrecht: Foris Publications, 1983.

BONNEFF, Marcel. "Le *kauman* de Yogyakarta. Des fonctionnaires religieux convertis au réformisme et à l'esprit d'entreprise". *Archipel* 30 (1985).

————, ed. *L'Indonésie contemporaine: un choix d'articles de la revue Prisma.* Paris: L'Harmattan, 1994.

————. "Centini, servante du Javanisme". *Archipel* 56 (1998).

————. "Les Intellectuels musulmans, le renouveau religieux et les transformations socio-culturelles de l'Indonésie". In *Renouveaux religieux en Asie*, ed. Catherine Clémentin-Ohja. Paris: École française d'Extrême-Orient, 1997, pp. 195–210.

BONNEFF, Marcel et al. *Pantjasila, trente années de débats politiques en Indonésie.* Paris: Édition de la maison des sciences de l'homme, 1980.

BOURCHIER, David and John LEGGE, eds. *Democracy in Indonesia, 1950s and 1990s.* Clayton: Centre of Southeast Asian Studies, Monash University.

BUSJAIRI BADRUZZAMAN. *Boerhanoeddin Harahap Pilar Demokrasi Boerhanoeddin* [*Harahap: The Pillar of Democracy*]. Jakarta: Bulan Bintang, 1982.

CARRÉ, Olivier, éd. *L'Islam et l'Etat dans le monde d'aujourd'hui.* Paris: PUF, 1982.

————. "Islam apolitique et christianisme politique? Clarification". *Revue tunisienne de sciences socials* 111 (1992).

————. *L'Islam laïque ou le retour à la grande Tradition.* Paris: Armand Colin, 1993.

CAYRAC, Françoise. *L'Indonésie. L'état des travaux. FNSP. Revue Française de Science Politique* (October 1967).

CAYRAC-BLANCHARD, Françoise. *Le parti communiste indonésien.* Paris: Armand Colin, 1973.

————. *L'armée et le pouvoir en Indonésie, de la révolution au développement.* Paris: L'Harmattan, 1992.

CAYRAC-BLANCHARD, Françoise, Stéphane DOVERT and Frédéric DURAND, eds. *Indonésie, un demi-siècle de construction nationale*. Paris: L'Harmattan, 2000.

CAYRAC-BLANCHARD, Françoise and Philippe DEVILLERS. *L'Asie du Sud-Est*, vol. 1, coll L'Histoire du XXe Siècle. Paris: Sirey, 1970.

CHARFI, Mohamed. *Islam et liberté, le malentendu historique*. Paris: Albin Michel, 1998.

CROUCH, Harold. *The Army and Politics in Indonesia*. Ithaca, NY: Cornell University Press, 1978.

DAYA Burhanuddin. *Gerakan Pembaharuan Pemikiran Islam. Kasus Sumatera Thawalib* [*The Renaissance of Islamic Thought: The Case of Thawalib in Sumatra*]. Yogyakarta: PT. Tiara Wacana, 1990.

DE JONGE, Huub and Nico KAPTEIN, eds. *Transcending Borders: Arabs, Politics, Trade and Islam in Southeast Asia*. Leiden: KITLV Press, 2002.

DEPARTEMEN AGAMA. "Data Umat Kristen Protestan Menurut Propinsi dari Tahun 1980 sd 1987" [Data on the Protestant Community by Province from 1980–87]. In *Data Keagamaan Kristen Protestan Tahun 1987* [*The Data of the Protestant Religion 1987*]. Jakarta: Direktorat Jenderal Bimbingan Masyarakat (Kristen) Protestan Departemen Agama, 1987.

DOBBIN, Christine. *Islamic Revivalism in a Changing Peasant Economy: Central Sumatra, 1784–1847*. London and Malmö: Curzon Press, 1983.

DOVERT, Stéphane and Rémy MADINIER, eds. *Les Musulmans d'Asie du Sud-Est face au vertige de la radicalisation*. Bangkok and Paris: IRASEC, Les Indes Savantes, 2003.

DREWES, W.J. "New Lights on the Coming of Islam to Indonesia?". In *Readings on Islam in Southeast Asia*, ed. Ahmad Ibrahim et al. Singapore: Institute of Southeast Asian Studies, 1985.

DUBUS, Arnaud and Nicolas REVISE. *Armée du peuple, Armée du roi, les militaires face à la société en Indonésie et en Thaïlande*. Bangkok and Paris: IRASEC, L'Harmattan, 2002.

DWI PURWOKO. *Pemuda Islam di Pentas Nasional* [*The Islamic Youth Movements on the Indonesian Political Stage*]. Jakarta: Bonaciptama, 1993.

ECHOLS, John M. *Preliminary Checklist of Indonesian Imprints (1945–1949)*. Ithaca, NY: Modern Indonesia Project, Southeast Asia Program, Department of Asian Studies, Cornell University, 1965.

EMMERSON, Donald. "The Bureaucracy in Political Context". In *Political Power and Communications in Indonesia*, ed. Karl D. Jackson and Lucian W. Puye. Berkeley, CA: University of California Press, 1978.

ESPOSITO, John L. and John O. VOLL. *Islam and Democracy*. New York: Oxford University Press, 1996.

FAISAL BAKTI, Andi. "Paramadina and its Approach to Culture and Communication: An Engagement in Civil Society". *Archipel* 68 (2004): 315–41.

FEALY, Greg. "Islamic Politics: A Rising or Declining Force". In *Indonesia: The Uncertain Transition*, ed. Damien Kingsbury and Arief Budiman. Adelaide: Crawford House Publishing, 2001, pp. 119–36.

————. "Divided Majority: The Limits of Indonesian Political Islam". In *Islam and Political Legitimacy*, ed. Shahram Akbarzadeh and Abdullah Saeed. London and New York: RoutledgeCurzon, 2003, pp. 150–68

FEALY, Gregory John. "Ulama and Politics in Indonesia: A Political History of Nahdlatul Ulama, 1952–1967". PhD diss., Monash University, 1998.

FEALY, Greg and Virginia HOOKER. *Voices of Islam in Southeast Asia: A Contemporary Sourcebook*. Singapore: Institute of Southeast Asian Studies, 2006.

FEALY, Greg and Sally WHITE, eds. *Expressing Islam: Religious Life and Politics in Indonesia*. Singapore: Institute of Southeast Asian Studies, 2008.

FEDERSPIEL, Howard M. *Persatuan Islam: Islamic Reform in Twentieth Century Indonesia*. Ithaca, NY: Cornell University, 1970.

————. *Muslim Intellectuals and National Development in Indonesia*. New York: Nova Science Commack, 1992.

FEILLARD, Andrée. *Islam et armée dans l'Indonésie contemporaine: Les pionniers de la tradition*. Cahier d'Archipel 28. Paris: L'Harmattan, 1995.

————, ed. *L'Islam en Asie: du Caucase à la Chine*. La Documentation française, coll. International. Paris, December 2001.

FEILLARD, Andrée and Rémy MADINIER. "Entre traditionalisme et modernisme, l'expression politique de l'islam en Indonésie". In *Indonésie, un demi-siècle de construction nationale*, ed. Françoise Cayrac-Blanchard, Stéphane Dovert and Frédéric Durand. Paris: L'Harmattan, 2000, pp. 217–68.

————. *La fin de l'innocence? L'Islam indonésien face à la tentation radicale, de 1967 à nos jours*. Bangkok and Paris: IRASEC, Les Indes Savantes, 2006.

————. *The End of Innocence? Indonesian Islam and the Temptations of Radicalism*. Singapore: NUS Press, 2011.

FEITH, Herbert. *The Indonesian Elections of 1955*. Ithaca, NY: Cornell University, 1957.

————. *The Wilopo Cabinet, 1952–1953: A Turning Point in Post-Revolutionary Indonesia*. Ithaca, NY: Cornell University Press, Ithaca, 1958.

————. *The Decline of the Constitutional Democracy in Indonesia*. Ithaca, NY: Cornell University Press, 1962.

————. "Dynamics of Guided Democracy". In *Indonesia*, ed. Ruth T. McVey. New Haven, CT: Yale University, 1963.

FEITH, Herbert and Lance CASTLES. *Indonesian Political Thinking, 1945–1965*. Ithaca, NY: Cornell University Press, 1970.

FINCH, Susan and Daniel LEV. *Republic of Indonesia Cabinets, 1945–1965*. Ithaca, NY: Cornell University Press, 1965.

FORMICHI, Chiara. *Islam and the Making of the Nation: Kartosuwiryo and Political Islam in 20th Century Indonesia*. Leiden: KITLV Press, 2012.

FREDERICK, William H. *Vision and Heat: The Making of the Indonesian Revolution*. Athens, OH: Ohio University Press, 1989.

FURKON, Aay Muhammad. *Partai Keadilan Sejahtera, Ideologi dan Praksis Politik Kaum Muda Muslim Indonesia Kontemporer* [*The Prosperous Justice Party: Ideology and Political Practice of Islamic Modernists in Contemporary Indonesia*]. Jakarta: Teraju, 2004.

GABORIEAU, Marc, éd. *Islam et société en Asie du Sud*. Paris: Éditions de L'EHESS, 1986.

————. *Un autre islam. Inde, Pakistan, Bangladesh*. Paris: Albin Michel, 2007.

GEERTZ, Clifford. *The Religion of Java*. Glencoe, IL: Free Press, 1960.

GHALIOUN, Burhan. *Islam et politique, la modernité trahie*. Paris: La découverte, 1997.

GHOSHAL, Baladas. *Indonesian Politics, 1955–1959: The Emergence of Guided Democracy*. Calcutta: K.P. Bagchi & Company, 1982.

GIBB, H.A.R. *Modern Trends in Islam*. Chicago, IL: University of Chicago Press, 1947.

GORDON, Alijah, ed. *The Propagation of Islam in the Malay Archipelago*. Kuala Lumpur: Malaysian Sociological Institute, 2001.

HADIZ, Vedi R. "No Turkish Delight: The Impasse of Islamic Party Politics in Indonesia". *Indonesia* 92 (October 2011): 1–18.

HAMAYOTSU, Kikue. "The End of Political Islam? A Comparative Analysis of Religious Parties in the Muslim Democracy of Indonesia". *Journal of Current Southest Asian Affairs* 3 (2011): 133–59.

HARTONO AHMAD JAIZ. *Di Bawah Bayang-Bayang Soekarno-Soeharto: Tragedi Politik Islam Indonesia dari Orde Lama hingga Orde Baru* [*In the Shadow of Sukarno-Suharto: The Political Tragedy of Indonesian Islam from the Old Order to the New Order*]. Jakarta: Darul Falah, 2001.

HARVEY, Barbara S. "Tradition, Islam and Rebellion: South Sulawesi 1905–1965". PhD diss., Cornell University, 1974.

————. *Permesta: Half A Rebellion*. Ithaca, NY: Modern Indonesia Project, Cornell University, 1977.

————. *Pemberontakan kahar Muzakkar Dari Tradisi ke DI/TII* [*The Rebellion of Kahar Muzakkar: From Tradition to DI/TII*]. Jakarta: Grafiti, 1989.

HASAN, Noorhaidi. *Laskar Jihad, Islam Militansi dan Pencarian Identitas di Indonesia Pasca-Orde Baru* [*Laskar Jihad: Islamic Militancy and the Search for Identity in Indonesia after the New Order*]. Jakarta and Leiden: LP3ES, KITLV, 2008.

HEADLEY, Stephen C. *Durga's Mosque: Cosmology, Conversion and Community in Central Javanese Islam*. Singapore: Institute of Southeast Asian Studies, 2004.

HEFNER, Robert W. "Islamizing Java? Religion and Politics in Rural East-Java". *Journal of Asian Studies* 46, 3 (1987): 533–54.

————. "Islam, State, and Civil Society: ICMI and the Struggle for the Indonesian Middle Class". *Indonesia* 56 (October 1993): 1–35.

————. "Print Islam: Mass Media and Ideological Rivalries among Indonesian Muslims". *Indonesia* 64 (October 1997): 77–103.

————. *Civil Islam: Muslims and Democratization in Indonesia*. Princeton, NJ: Princeton University Press, 2000.

HEFNER, Robert W. and Patricia HORVATICH. *Islam in an Era of Nation-States: Politics and Religious Renewal in Muslim Southeast Asia*. Honolulu: HI: University of Hawaii Press, 1997.

HILMY, Masdar. *Islamism and Democracy in Indonesia: Piety and Pragmatism*. Singapore: Institute of Southeast Asian Studies, 2010.

HOOKER, M.B., ed. *Islam in South-East Asia*. Leiden: E.J. Brill, 1983.

————. *Indonesian Islam: Social Change through Contemporary Fatawa*. Crows Nest, NSW: Asian Studies Association of Australia in association with Allen & Unwin, 2003.

HUNTINGTON, Samuel. *The Clash of Civilizations and the Remaking of World Order*. New York: Simon and Schuster, 1996.

HUSAINI, Adian. *Yusril Versus Masyumi*. Jakarta: DEA Press, 2000.

ILETO, Reynaldo. "Religion and Anti-Colonial Movements". In *The Cambridge History of Southeast Asia (From c. 1800 to the 1930's)*, vol. 3. Cambridge: Cambridge University Press, 1994, pp. 193–253.

INGLESON, John. *Road to Exile: The Indonesian Nationalist Movement, 1927–1934*. Singapore: Heinemann for the Asian Studies Association of Australia, 1979.

INTERNATIONAL COUNCIL ON ARCHIVES. *Guide to the Sources of Asian History, vol. 4, Indonesia*. Jakarta: National Archives of Indonesia, 1989.

ISMATU ROPI. "Depicting the Other Faith: A Bibliographical Survey of Indonesian Muslim Polemics in Christianity". *Studia Islamika* 6, 1 (1999): 77–111.

JACKSON, Karl D. *Traditional Authority, Islam and Rebellion: A Study of Indonesian Political Behaviour*. Berkeley, CA: University of California Press, 1981.

JONES, Howard Palfrey. *The Possible Dream*. New York: Hartcourt Brace Jovanovitch, 1971.

KAHIN, Audrey R., ed. *Regional Dynamics of the Indonesian Revolution: Unity from Diversity*. Honolulu, HI: University of Hawaii Press, 1985.

————. *Islam Nationalism and Democracy: A Political Biography of Mohammad Natsir*. Singapore: NUS Press, 2012.

KAHIN, Audrey and George McTurnan Kahin. *Subversion as Foreign Policy: The Secret Eisenhower and Dulles Debacle in Indonesia*. New York: The New Press, 1995.

KAHIN, George McTurnan. *Nationalism and Revolution in Indonesia*. Ithaca, NY: Cornell University Press, 1952.

————. "Indonesian Politics and Nationalism". In *Asian Nationalism and the West*, ed. William L. Holland. New York: The Macmillan Company, 1953.

KALUS, Ludvik and Claude GUILLOT. "Réinterprétation des plus anciennes stèles funéraires islamiques nousantariennes: II. La stèle de Leran (Java) datée de 475/1082 et les stèles associées". *Archipel* 67 (2004).

KEPEL, Gilles. *Jihad: The Trail of Political Islam*. Cambridge, MA: Harvard University Press, 2002.

————. *The War for Muslim Minds: Islam and the West*. Cambridge, MA: Harvard University Press, 2004.

KOENTJARANINGRAT. *Javanese Culture*. Singapore: Oxford University Press, 1985.

LATIF, Yudi. *Indonesian Muslim Intelligentsia and Power*. Singapore: Institute of Southeast Asian Studies, 2008.

LEGGE, J.D. *Central Authority and Regional Autonomy in Indonesia: A Study in Local Administration 1950–1960*. Ithaca, NY: Cornell University Press, 1961.

————. *Problems of Regional Autonomy in Contemporary Indonesia*. Ithaca, NY: Cornell University Southeast Asia Program, 1967.

————. *Sukarno: A Political Biography*. Sydney: Allen & Unwin, 1990 [1st edition, 1972].

LEIRISSA, R.Z. *PRRI-PERMESTA, Strategi Membangun Indonesia Tanpa Komunis* [*Strategy for Developing Indonesia without Communism*]. Jakarta: Grafiti, 1991.

LEV, Daniel S. *The Transition to Guided Democracy: Indonesian Politics, 1957–1959*. Ithaca, NY: Cornell University Press, 1966.

LEWIS, Bernard. *L'islam d'hier à aujourd'hui*. Paris: Payot, 1994 [1st edition, 1976].

————. *Le langage politique de l'Islam*. Paris: Gallimard, 1988.

LIDDLE, William. "*Media Dakwah* Scripturalism: One Form of Islamic Political Thought and Action in New Order Indonesia". In *Toward a New Paradigm: Recent Developments in Indonesian Islamic Thought*, ed. Mark R. Woodward. Tempe, AZ: Arizona State University, 1996, pp. 323–56.

LOMBARD, Denys. *Le Carrefour javanais*. Paris: Éditions de L'EHESS, 1990.

LUBIS, Muhammad Ridwan. *Pemikiran Sukarno Tentang Islam* [*Sukarno's Reflections on Islam*]. Jakarta: C.V. Masagung, 1992.

LUCAS, Anton. *One Soul, One Struggle: Region and Revolution in Indonesia*. Sydney: Asian Studies Association of Australia, Allen & Unwin, 1991.

MAARIF, Ahmad Syafii. *Studi tentang Percaturan dalam Konstituante, Islam dan masalah kenegaraan* [*A Study of the Constituent Assembly: Islam and the Problem of Creating a State*]. Jakarta: LP3ES, 1985.

————. *Islam dan Politik di Indonesia pada Demokrasi Terpimpin (1959–1965)* [*Islam and Politics in Indonesia during Guided Democracy (1959–1965)*]. Yogyakarta: IAIN Suana Kalijaga Press, 1988.

MADINIER, Rémy. "Que conseillait la 'Sagesse' lors des élections législatives de 1955 en Indonésie? Une analyse de la campagne du Masyumi à travers la revue *Hikmah*". *Archipel* 52 (1996).

──────. "Le Masjumi, parti des milieux d'affaires musulmans?". *Archipel* 57 (1999): 177–89.

──────. "Du temps des chameaux à celui du béton radioactif, les nouveaux usages islamistes du passé". *Archipel* 64 (October 2002): 145–63.

──────. "L'Indonésie entre démocratie musulmane et islam integral". In *Religion et politique en Asie. Histoire et actualité*, ed. John Lagerwey. Paris: Les Indes Savantes, 2005, pp. 109–18.

──────. "L'Asie du Sud-Est musulmane produit d'un imaginaire afghan? Le Daulah Islamiyah Nusantara à l'épreuve des sciences sociales". In *Figures d'Islam après le 11 septembre: disciples, martyrs, réfugiés et migrants*, ed. Aminah Mohammad-Arif and Jean Schmitz. Paris: Khartala, 2006, pp. 123–49.

──────, ed. *Islam and the 2009 Indonesian Elections, Political and Cultural Issues: The Case of the Prosperous Justice Party (PKS)*. Occasional Paper No. 12. Bangkok: IRASEC, 2009.

MADJID, Nurcholish. *Islam Kemodernan dan Keindonesiaan* [*Modernity and Indonesian Identity in Islam*]. Bandung: Mizan, 1987 [8th edition, 1995].

──────. *Indonesia Kita* [*Our Indonesia*]. Jakarta: Paramadina, 2003.

MAHENDRA, Yusril Ihza. "Modenisme dan Fundamentalisme dalam Politik Islam: satu Kajian Perbandingan kes Parti Masyumi di Indonesia dan Jama'at-i-Islami di Pakistan (1940–1960)" [Modernism and Fundamentalism in Political Islam: A Comparison of the Masyumi Party in Indonesian and of Jama'at-i-Islami in Pakistan], PhD diss., University of Kuala Lumpur, 1993.

MARTINEZ-GROS, Gabriel and Lucette VALENSI. *L'Islam en dissidence: genèse d'un affrontement*. Paris: Seuil, 2004.

MARYANOV, Gerald S. *Decentralization in Indonesia as a Political Problem*. Ithaca, NY: Cornell University Press, 1958.

MATRINGE, Denis. *Un islam non arabe, Horizons indiens et pakistanais*. Paris: Téraèdre, 2005.

MENCHIK, Jeremy. "Productive Intolerance: Godly Nationalism in Indonesia". *Comparative Studies in Society and History* 56, 3 (2014): 591–621.

MERAD, Ali. *L'Islam contemporain* (*Que sais-je?*). Paris: PUF, 1984 [5th edition, 1995].

MERVIN, Sabrina Mervin. *Histoire de l'Islam. Fondements et doctrines*. Paris: Flammarion editions, Champs Université, 2000.

MIETZNER, Marcus. *Military Politics, Islam, and the State in Indonesia: From Turbulent Transition to Democratic Consolidation*. Singapore: Institute of Southeast Asian Studies, 2009.

MOBINI-KESHEH, Natalie. *The Hadrami Awakening: Community and Identity in the Netherlands East Indies, 1900–1942.* Ithaca, NY: Southeast Asia Program, Cornell University, 1999.

MRAZEK, Rudolph. *Sjahrir Politics and Exile in Indonesia.* Ithaca, NY: Studies on Southeast Asia, Cornell University, 1994.

Mujiburrahman. "Feeling Threatened: Muslim-Christian Relations in Indonesia's New Order". ISIM dissertations. Amsterdam University Press, 2006, p. 41.

NAIM, Mochtar. *Indonesia's Nahdlatul Ulama Movement: Factors that Led to Its Emergence as a Political Party.* New York, 1961.

NASHIR, Haedar. *Dinamika Politik Muhammadiyah* [*The Political Dynamic of Muhammadiyah*]. Yogyakarta: Bigraf, 2000.

NASUTION, Adnan Buyung. *The Aspiration for Constitutional Government in Indonesia: A Socio-Legal Study of the Indonesian Konstituante (1956–1959).* Jakarta: Pustaka Sinar Harapan, 1992.

NASUTION, Harun. "The Islamic State in Indonesia: The Rise of Ideology, the Movement for Its Creation and the Theory of the Masjumi". MA thesis, McGill University, Montreal, 1965.

NEIL, Wilfried T. *Twentieth-Century Indonesia.* New York and London: Columbia University Press, 1973.

NOER, Deliar. "Masjumi: Its Organization, Ideology, and Political Role in Indonesia". MA thesis, Cornell University, 1960.

_____. *The Modernist Muslim Movement in Indonesia, 1900–1942.* Kuala Lumpur: Oxford University Press, 1973 [2nd edition, 1978].

_____. *Administration of Islam in Indonesia.* Ithaca, NY: Cornell Modern Indonesia Project, 1978.

_____. *Partai Islam di Pentas Nasional.* Jakarta: Pustaka Utama Grafiti, 1987.

_____. *Mohammad Hatta, biografi politik.* Jakarta: LP3ES, 1990.

_____. *Aku bagian Ummat, aku bagian Bangsa, otobiografi.* Bandung: Mizan, 1996.

PEACOCK, James L. *Indonesia: An Anthropological Perspective.* Pacific Palisades, CA: Goodyear, 1973.

PENDERS, C.L.M., ed. *Mohammad Hatta, Indonesian Patriot: Memoirs.* Singapore: Gunung Agung, 1991.

PLATZDASCH, Bernhard. *Islamism in Indonesia: Politics in the Emerging Democracy.* Singapore: Institute of Southeast Asian Studies, 2009.

PORTER, Donald J. *Managing Politics and Islam in Indonesia.* London and New York: RoutledgeCurzon, 2005 [1st edition, 2002].

PRINGLE, Robert. *Understanding Islam in Indonesia: Politics and Diversity.* Singapore: Editions Didier Millet, 2010.

PUSAT INFORMASI ISLAM YAYASAN MASAGUNG [The Masagung Association's Centre for Information on Islam]. *Buku Islam sejak tahun 1945*

[*The Book of Islam since 1945*], 3rd edition. Jakarta: CV Hajji Masagung, 1990.

RAILLON, François. *Les étudiants indonésiens et l'Ordre Nouveau. Politique et idéologie du Mahasiswa Indonesia (1966–1974)*. Paris: Éditions de la Maisons des sciences de l'homme, 1984.

—————. *Indonésie: la réinvention d'un Archipel*. Paris: La Documentation française, 1999.

RAMAGE, Douglas E. *Politics in Indonesia: Democracy, Islam and the Ideology of Tolerance*. London and New York: Routledge, 1995.

RICKLEFS, M.C., ed. *Islam in the Indonesian Social Context*. Clayton: Monash University, 1991.

—————. *Mystic Synthesis in Java: A History of Islamization from the Fourteenth to the Early Nineteenth Centuries*. Norwalk: EastBridge, 2006.

—————. *Polarising Javanese Society. Islamic and Other Visions (c. 1830–1930)*. Leiden: KITLV Press, 2007.

—————. "The Middle East Connection and Reform and Revival Movement among the *Putihan* in 19th-Century Java". In *Southeast Asia and the Middle East: Islam, Movement and the Longue Durée*, ed. Eric Tagliacozzo. Singapore: NUS Press, 2009, pp. 111–35.

—————. *Islamisation and Its Opponents in Java, c. 1930 to the Present*. Singapore: NUS Press, 2012.

RODINSON, Maxime. *L'Islam: politique et croyance*. Paris: Fayard, 1993.

ROFF, W. *The Origins of Malay Nationalism*. Kuala Lumpur: Oxford University Press, 1994 [1st edition, 1967].

ROSE, Mavis. *Indonesia Free: A Political Biography of Mohammad Hatta*. Ithaca, NY: Cornell University Press, 1987.

ROSIDI, Ajip. *Beberapa Masalah Umat Islam Di Indonesia* [*Some Issues concerning the Indonesian Islamic Community*]. Bandung: Bulan Sabit, 1970.

—————. *Kebangkitan Islam Era Orde Baru* [*Islamic Revival under the New Order*]. Jakarta: LSIP, 1993.

ROY, Olivier. *L'Échec de l'islam politique*. Paris: Seuil, 1992.

—————. *L'Islam mondialisé*, coll. La couleur des idées. Paris: Seuil, 2002.

SAIDI, Ridwan. *Pemuda Islam dalam Dinamika Politik Bangsa* [*Islamic Youth Movements in National Politics, 1925–1984*]. Jakarta: C.V. Rajawal, 1984.

—————. *Islam dan Nasionalisme Indonesia* [*Islam and Nationalism in Indonesia*]. Jakarta: LSIP, 1995.

SALEH, Fauzan. *Modern Trends in Islamic Theological Discourses in 20th Century Indonesia: A Critical Survey*. Leiden: Brill, 2001.

SALIM, Arskal and Azyumardi AZRA, eds. *Sharia and Politics in Modern Indonesia*. Singapore: Institute of Southeast Asian Studies, 2003, pp. 1–16.

SAMSON, Allan A. "Islam in Indonesian Politics". *Asian Survey* 8, 12 (December 1968): 1001–17.

—————. "Islam and Politics in Indonesia". PhD diss., Department of Political Science, University of California, Berkeley, 1972.

SANTOSO, Agus Edi, ed. *Tidak ada negara Islam: surat-surat politik Nurcholish Madjid-Mohamad Roem* [*There is No Islamic State: Political Correspondence between Nurcholish Madjid and Mohamad Roem*]. Jakarta: Djambatan, 1997.

SARTONO KARTODIRDJO. *Protest Movements in Rural Java: A Study of Agrarian Unrest in the 19th and Early 20th Century.* Singapore and New York: Oxford University Press, 1973.

SCHWARZ, Adam. *A Nation in Waiting: Indonesia's Search for Stability.* St. Leonards, NSW: Allen & Unwin, 1999, pp. 176–7.

SHIRAISHI, Takashi. *An Age in Motion: Popular Radicalism in Java, 1912–1926.* Ithaca, NY: Cornell University Press, 1990.

SJAMSUDDIN, Nazaruddin. *Pemberontakan kaum republik: kasus Darul Islam Aceh* [*The Republicans' Uprising: Darul Islam in Aceh*]. Jakarta: Grafiti, 1990.

SMAIL, John R.W. *Bandung in the Early Revolution, 1945–1946: A Study in Social History of the Indonesian Revolution.* Ithaca, NY: Cornell University Press, 1964.

SMITH, Edward C. "A History of Newspaper Suppression in Indonesia, 1945–1965". PhD diss., University of Iowa, 1969.

STEENBRINK, Karel. *Dutch Colonialism and Indonesian Islam: Contacts and Conflicts 1596–1950, Currents of Encounter, Studies on the Contact between Christianity and Other Religions, Beliefs and Cultures.* Atlanta, GA: Rodopi, 1993.

SYAFIQ A. MUGHINI. *Hassan Bandung, Pemikir Islam Radikal* [*Hassan Bandung: Radical Islamic Thinker*]. Surabaya: Pt. Bina Ilmu, 1980.

TAGLIACOZZO, Eric, ed. *Southeast Asia and the Middle East: Islam, Movement and the Longue Durée.* Singapore: NUS Press, 2009.

TANJA, Victor Immanuel. *Himpunan Mahasiswa Islam* [*The Association of Islamic Students*]. Jakarta: Pustaka Sinar Harapan, Jakarta, 1991 [1st edition, 1982].

TARLING, N. *The Cambridge History of Southeast Asia*, vol. 3. Cambridge: Cambridge University Press, 1992.

TEDJASUKMANA, Iskandar. *The Political Character of the Indonesian Trade Union Movement.* Ithaca, NY: Cornell University, 1958.

THUNG, Yvonne and John M. ECHOLS. *A Guide of Indonesian Serials (1945–1965) in the Cornell University Library.* Ithaca, NY: Modern Indonesia Project, Southeast Asia Program, Cornell University, 1966.

TICKELL, Paul, ed. *The Indonesian Press: Its Past, Its People, Its Problems.* Annual Indonesian Lecture series, n° 12. Monash University, 1987.

VAN BRUINESSEN, Martin. "L'Asie du Sud-Est". In *Les Voies d'Allah. Les Ordres mystiques dans l'islam des origines à aujourd'hui,* ed. Alexandre Popovic and Gilles Veinstein. Paris: Fayard, 1986, pp. 274–84.

_____. "Genealogies of Islamic Radicalism in post-Suharto Indonesia". *South East Asia Research* 10, 2 (2002): 117–54.

————. "Global and Local in Indonesian Islam". *Southeast Asian Studies* 37, 2 (1999): 46–63.

VAN DEN END, Theodore. *Ragi Carita, Sejarah Gereja di Indonesia, th. 1500–1860* [*The Ferment of History: The Church in Indonesia from 1500–1860*]. Jakarta: Badan penerbit Kristen Gunung Mulia, 1980.

VAN DEN GERG, L.W.C. *Le Hadhramout et les colonies arabes dans l'archipel indien.* Imprimerie du gouvernement. Batavia, 1886.

VAN DIJK, Cees. *Rebellion under the Banner of Islam: The Darul Islam in Indonesia.* The Hague: Martinus Nijhoff, 1981.

————. "Survey of Political Developments in Indonesia in the Second Half of 1984: The National Congress of the PPP and the *Pancasila* Principle". *Review of Indonesian and Malaysian Affairs* 19, 1 (1985): 177–202.

————. *A Country in Despair: Indonesia between 1997 and 2000.* Leiden: KITLV Press, 2001.

VAN NIEL, R. *The Emergence of the Modern Indonesian Elite.* The Hague and Bandung: W. Van Hoeve Ltd, 1960.

WARD, K.E. *The Foundation of the Partai Muslimin Indonesia.* Ithaca, NY: Cornell University Press, 1970.

WILD, Colin and Peter CAREY. *Born in Fire: The Indonesian Struggle for Independence.* Athens, OH: BBC publications, Ohio University Press, 1988.

WILLIS, Avery T. *The Indonesian Revival: Why Two Million Came to Christ.* South Pasadena, CA: William Carey Library, 1977.

YAMIN, Muhammad. *Naskah Persiapan Undang-Undang Dasar 1945* [*Preparatory Documents for the 1945 Constitution*], 3 vols. Jakarta, 1959–1960.

YUSRON ASROFIE. *Kiai Ahmad Dahlan: Pemikiran dan Kepemimpinannya* [*Kiai Ahmad Dahlan: His Thought and His Leadership*]. Yogyakarta: Yogyakarta offset, 1983.

ZEGHAL, Malika. "Le gouvernement de la cité: un islam sous tension". *Pouvoirs* 104 (2003): 55–69.

Index